P9-CFI-090

HISTORICAL TRADITION IN
THE FOURTH GOSPEL

. MARY'S COLLEGE OF MARYLAND
ST. MARY'S CITY, MARYLAND

47524

HISTORICAL TRADITION
IN THE
FOURTH GOSPEL

BY

C. H. DODD

C.H., HON. D.D., F.B.A.

Professor Emeritus in the University of Cambridge

CAMBRIDGE
AT THE UNIVERSITY PRESS
1965

PUBLISHED BY
THE SYNDICS OF THE CAMBRIDGE UNIVERSITY PRESS

Bentley House, 200 Euston Road, London, N.W. 1
American Branch: 32 East 57th Street, New York, N.Y. 10022
West African Office: P.O. Box 33, Ibadan, Nigeria

©

CAMBRIDGE UNIVERSITY PRESS
1963

First printed 1963
Reprinted 1965

Printed in Great Britain at the University Printing House, Cambridge
(Brooke Crutchley, University Printer)

STVDIORVM PARTICIPIBVS

VIVIS ADHVC ET IN MEMORIAM DEFVNCTORVM
QVI CANTABRIGIAE
IN SCHOLA SACRAE THEOLOGIAE
AB ANNO SALVTIS MCMXXXVII
VSQVE AD MCMXLIX
HVIVSMODI QVAESTIONIBVS
COMMVNITER VACABANT

GRATVS AC MEMOR
D. D.
AVCTOR

PREFACE

This book embodies the first course of Sarum Lectures in the University of Oxford, delivered in 1954–5. The actual contents of the lectures are represented by the Introduction and Part I, A and B, though the version here given is substantially fuller than the lectures as delivered. The whole work may be regarded as a sequel to my earlier book, *The Interpretation of the Fourth Gospel* (Cambridge, 1953), or as an expansion of the Appendix to that book, entitled 'Some considerations upon the historical aspect of the Fourth Gospel'.

In the course of fifty years I have learnt much about this gospel from books, much also in conference and discussion with fellow-students of the New Testament—more, certainly, than I could now trace to its sources. But here I have tried to take a fresh look at the gospel itself as it lies before us, with the historical question in mind. Where I have consciously borrowed information or suggestions, I have made my acknowledgements. If through ignorance or forgetfulness I have omitted to do so, I offer my apologies. It cannot but be that many of my observations have been anticipated; *vivant qui ante nos nostra dixerunt!* But such as they are, they are the fruit of an individual approach along one particular line, and I hope they may prove some contribution to the collective effort by which our understanding of the Gospel story must be enlarged.

C. H. D.

OXFORD
15 August 1961

My thanks are due to the Rev. C. F. D. Moule, Lady Margaret's Professor of Divinity in the University of Cambridge, who did me the great kindness of reading the book in proof. I am indebted to him for many valuable corrections and suggestions.

C. H. D.

22 April 1963

CONTENTS

CONTENTS

PART II

THE SAYINGS

AUTHOR'S NOTE

In quoting from books of the New Testament it is my practice to give either the original Greek or my own translation. If the latter should occasionally appear to follow the rendering of the New English Bible, this must be regarded as a coincidence.

C. H. D.

INTRODUCTION

'Historical tradition in the Fourth Gospel.' But is there such a thing as an historical tradition in the gospels at all? The revolt against 'historicism' which declared itself in Germany during the second decade of this century was comparatively slow in making its full impact upon theological thought in this country; but in recent years its influence has been wide and deep. The climate of our studies is transformed. The 'quest of the historical Jesus', which stimulated the critical study of the New Testament in the nineteenth century, is by some of the most influential theologians of our time no longer believed to be a profitable, or indeed a feasible, enterprise. A study of the theological symbolism and typology embodied in the gospels will (it is urged) bring us further in understanding them than any attempt to establish a residuum of factual record. In any case they were written (in the current cliché) 'from faith to faith'. To seek in them sources of historical information is to misunderstand their character and the intention of their authors.

It is of course possible, without proceeding to the extreme position here adumbrated, to believe (as I do myself) that the revolt against 'historicism' was a salutary reaction, justified by the increasing sterility of 'liberal' criticism in its latest phase, and to welcome the awakened interest in the witness of the gospels to Christian faith and worship as expressed in the liturgy and theology of the early Church. But the general effect of the movement certainly has been to discourage any serious attempt to learn from the gospels an answer to questions of historical fact.

Yet even if the theologian disinterest himself in the quest for 'mere' facts, the historian, who must take account of the Christian movement in the Roman Empire, will still wish to discover whether the meagre information about its origins offered by Tacitus and the Talmud can be supplemented from Christian sources. If we tell him that the gospels, because they are religious, not historical, documents, are not available for his purpose, he may feel obliged to take our word for it. But if we go into detail, and explain that these documents contain an element of myth or legend, typology or symbolism, that most of their contents were transmitted through the dubious channels of popular tradition, and that the whole has been moulded by the masterful influence of a body of strongly held beliefs (which we may regard as divinely inspired truth, but he can only treat as a particular 'ideology'), he might be surprised that we should consider such characteristics as these—even stating them in the most extreme terms—sufficient grounds for excluding the gospels from serious consideration as sources for history. For he is familiar with documents of equally unpromising character, which nevertheless can be made, by suitable critical treatment, to yield results of solid historical value. The Homeric poems were once regarded (much as some moderns would have us regard the biblical narratives) as a corpus of sacred allegory, to be interpreted by experts in such matters. In my schooldays their main contents were confidently classed as myth. Nowadays they are accepted as valuable sources, when critically treated, for the history of the dark age lying between the fall of Knossos and the Dorian invasions. That is already an old story. More recently, and indeed at this very time, historians are having a surprising measure of success in distilling trustworthy historical information from the popular traditions of various societies, full as they are of legend and myth. It is largely a matter of employing suitable methods of criticism for the study of material of this kind. In view of contemporary achievements in this field, the historian might be pardoned for thinking that we throw up the sponge too readily, and for overhearing, when we sing the praises of the new approach to the gospels, a half-smothered sigh of relief at escaping from a peculiarly difficult and embarrassing problem.

That the historical problem in the gospels *is* one of peculiar difficulty is certainly true. A survey of the long series of failures, or dubious successes, in the effort to solve it, as they lie embalmed in the mortuary chambers of Schweitzer's *Geschichte der Leben-Jesu-Forschung*, is not encouraging. Yet there are weighty theological reasons to be urged against a one-sidedly non-historical approach to the gospels. It was not for nothing that the early Church repudiated gnosticism, with all its speculative breadth and subtlety and its imaginative mythology. It may be true (though it is by no means so self-evident to me as it is to some of my fellow-workers in this field) that the evangelists had no biographical interest, but it is possible that even in writing 'from faith to faith' they may, perhaps unintentionally, have let out facts that may prove to have biographical interest for us. At any rate, whatever theologians may say, it is the plain duty of the historian to make use of every possible source of information in the effort to learn the facts about an historical episode which on any showing was a significant and influential one.

2

Such is my apologia for returning to so well worn a theme as the existence and extent of historical elements in the Fourth Gospel. In spite of all that has already been said and written in the course of a prolonged debate, it may be that an approach from a somewhat different angle will usefully carry the discussion a step forward.

The changed theological climate to which reference has been made has proved of positive advantage to Johannine studies, and that in several ways.

(i) In the first place, these studies have benefited from the mere fact that the problem of 'historicity' receded for a time into the background. The debate over 'the historicity of the Fourth Gospel' had pretty well reached a position of deadlock by the opening decade of the twentieth century. All the important arguments had been canvassed; only minor points could be added. The debate became repetitive. Each side remained convinced of its own position without being able to carry conviction to its opponents. Not only so; a disproportionate preoccupation with a perpetually inconclusive discussion upon this single aspect of the Johannine problem prejudiced the consideration of other aspects of it. It gave a bias to criticism. The discussion of the (perhaps unanswerable) question of authorship acquired an exaggerated importance from the belief, shared in the main by both sides, that upon its settlement depended the assessment, positive or negative, of the value of the gospel as an historical source. Again, the spate of partition-hypotheses and schemes of source-analysis which appeared in the early years of this century can be seen in retrospect to have been largely inspired by the wish to recover some kind of *Grundschrift* to which the critic might feel justified in assigning the historical credibility which he could no longer attribute to the work as a whole. Most serious of all, the dominant historicism hindered an adequate appreciation of the Fourth Gospel as it lies before us. It led some to undervalue it, and others to esteem it on precarious grounds.[1] In the new

---

[1] It would not, I think, be unfair to say (as a generalization requiring various qualifications) that the conservative or traditionalist school tended to value the Fourth Gospel as the most authoritative record of the teaching of Jesus, being the work of his most intimate disciple, while the liberal school, having decided against the 'historicity' of the work, could make little of the teaching in it beyond a hotch-potch of borrowings from popular Hellenism with a 'deutero-Pauline' setting. As for the narrative, the factual accuracy of the miracle stories was vital to the one school, while the other, for which miracles as such were a scandal, rejoiced to be free to get rid of them. In the current semi-popular presentations, at least, of the liberal position the Fourth Gospel appeared as a second-rate work, while the high conservative estimate of it stood or fell by the criterion of 'historicity'.

climate of our time, in which the religious and theological character of the gospels commands attention, it is easier to see this gospel for what it really is in its full scope and intention.

Some such reassessment of the character of the work, of the author's turn of mind, the direction of his thinking, and his attitude to his subject matter, was in fact called for as a preliminary to any further advance in the discussion of the historical question. Thanks to work that has been done on these lines we are in a position to open up that question afresh. For the more clearly the theological position of the Fourth Gospel is examined, the more clearly is it seen to involve a reference to history. This has been implicit in much of the recent movement of thought, at least in this country. A landmark in that movement is the great, though incomplete, commentary by Hoskyns and Davey. It is avowedly, and consistently, a 'theological' commentary. Its author and its editor deprecate the preoccupation of critics with the problem of 'historicity'; they regard with suspicion any attempt to distinguish between the facts themselves and their interpretation; and they discourage any expectation of finding an answer to the question whether the Fourth Evangelist had command of trustworthy information upon the facts beyond that which is accessible to us in the Synoptic Gospels. Yet they recognize, and state with all possible emphasis, that the Johannine theology has its centre in the historical person and the historical action of Jesus Christ. 'The historical tension of the Fourth Gospel' (they say) is not to be lightly resolved by any theory which would lay the evangelist under 'the charge of inventing history, or of using it merely as symbolism'.[1] But if this is so, it appears to bring us back by a different approach to the problem of historicity.

(ii) Secondly, the comparison between the Fourth Gospel and the Synoptics has been placed in a fresh light. That there is a real difference between them is a fact which has been manifest to clear-sighted readers of the gospels ever since the time when Clement wrote that 'John, observing that the bodily facts had been made clear in the [earlier] gospels...composed a spiritual gospel'.[2] But the difference was exaggerated by nineteenth-century criticism, as if the Synoptic Gospels were entirely

---

[1] *Op. cit.* Introduction, p. xxxiv. With much of what they say, and with the general trend of the argument, I find myself in cordial agreement, but I cannot see that it makes the historian's question, *wie es eigentlich geschehen ist*, either illegitimate or unimportant, or, in principle, unanswerable.

[2] Euseb. *H.E.* VI. 14. 7.

4

'somatic' and John nothing but 'pneumatic'; as if, in other words, the Synoptics gave us nothing but plain, brute facts of history and John nothing but abstract theology in symbolic guise. The newer school of criticism recognizes the presence of 'History and Interpretation in the Gospels' (to quote the title of R. H. Lightfoot's influential book)—in the Synoptics as well as in John—and it believes that the factor of interpretation is not one which can conveniently be taken out and set aside as *Gemeindetheologie*, leaving the residue pure matter of fact, but is organic to the whole structure of the gospels. Where the Fourth Gospel differs from the others is that its interpretation is not only in different thought-forms, but is also deliberate, coherent, and in the full sense theological, as theirs is not. And if there is more of the 'spiritual' element of interpretation in the Synoptics, it may be that there is more of the 'bodily' element of fact in John, than earlier criticism allowed. In any case, each version demands consideration on its merits, allowance being always made for the different intentions of the evangelists and the different 'setting in life' to which their renderings of the story belong.

(iii) Thirdly, the new attitude to our documents has been accompanied by the development of the method of *Formgeschichte*, or form-criticism,[1] and this has altered the conditions of our investigation in various ways, but most particularly in that it has directed our attention to the pre-literary, or at least non-literary, tradition, which lies behind our written gospels and their hypothetical documentary sources. The old 'oral hypothesis' which used to be offered as the solution of the Synoptic problem was already antiquated by the beginning of this century. The improved methods of documentary criticism developed during the late nineteenth century commended themselves by their greater precision, and the possibility they offered of presenting a case through actual statistics of agreements and differences. They seemed to open up a more 'objective'

---

[1] Most of those who have written on biblical *Formgeschichte* in this country refer to German and Scandinavian authorities. But it should not be forgotten that we have in English *Formgeschichte* on the grand scale in the three massive volumes of H. M. and N. K. Chadwick on *The Growth of Literature* (Cambridge). Mrs Chadwick's short book, *The Beginnings of Russian History*, is a brilliant example of the application of the method to the elucidation of a singularly dark period. The volume *Studies in Early British History*, by the Chadwicks and others, applies the same method to the study of early Welsh and Irish traditions, with, it appears, a considerable measure of success. Even the Arthurian legends find a place. Other writers seem to be doing much the same thing for the history of the Maori of New Zealand, which rests entirely upon oral tradition, and there is evidently a large body of similar work being done on other dark ages.

way of accounting for the phenomena. And in fact I still believe that the 'two-document hypothesis' did, within its limits, offer a solution which is basically capable of standing against attack, although various adjustments may be called for. This solution, however, covered only those parts of the Synoptic Gospels which were sufficiently closely parallel to allow of the agreements and differences being precisely measured. When the method of search for documentary sources extended itself to those parts of Matthew and Luke which had no parallels, or only remote ones, it lost its claim to precision and objectivity. Still less fruitful (in my judgement) has it proved in attacking the Johannine problem, because here the area over which parallelism can be traced on anything like the Synoptic scale is extremely narrow; consequently any analysis into documentary sources must allow greater play to conjecture, or even speculation, and become less convincing as it becomes more detailed.

But while documentary criticism was working itself to a standstill, the application of form-criticism opened up new lines of approach. It began by studying the various *literary* forms to which the several writings of the New Testament belong,[1] but soon developed a special interest in the long neglected oral tradition lying behind the gospels. It did so under the influence of writers who had applied this method to various kinds of folk-tradition, such as the Germanic sagas and the stories of the Pentateuch. It was observed that much of the material of the Synoptic Gospels could be analysed into units showing features which these writers had discovered to be characteristic of popular oral tradition. It may fairly be objected to the work of some of the form-critics in the field of the New Testament that they have not always sufficiently allowed for the disparity in the span of time to be taken into consideration. A tradition with several centuries of oral transmission behind its first appearance in written form cannot be expected to exhibit canons or 'laws' directly applicable to one with a pre-literary history of less than a normal human lifetime. It is necessary to bear this in mind, and, while making use of the valuable experience of form-critics in other fields, to refrain from insisting that the New Testament material must rigorously conform to the same canons. But when all allowance is made for an enthusiasm which has sometimes claimed too much for the method, it is certainly true that the form-critics have done great service in leading us to recognize afresh the importance of oral tradition in the New Testament period.

[1] E.g. P. Wendland, *Die neutestamentlichen Literaturformen* (1912).

Attention was given to this tradition in the first place in the hope of penetrating into the obscure period between the death of Jesus Christ and the writing of the earliest extant gospel. But it is important to realize that we are not dealing with a primitive period of oral tradition superseded at a given date by a second period of literary authorship, but that oral tradition continued to be an important factor right through the New Testament period and beyond. Papias, in the first half of the second century, still preferred oral tradition, where it was available, and Irenaeus, towards the close of that century, could cite with great respect that which he had 'heard from a certain presbyter who had heard it from those who had seen the apostles'.[1] We have to think of the life of the Church as being nourished, and its faith and fellowship maintained, by a living tradition. This tradition served (among other purposes) to guard and hand on what was remembered or believed concerning that which Jesus had done, said and suffered—in other words, the raw material of gospel composition; and it was still very much alive at the time when the Fourth Gospel was written and in the region where (in all probability) it was written. This we know from contemporary evidence.[2]

The recognition of the continuity of oral tradition has been accompanied by the recognition that, just because it was so vitally related to the whole life of an active community, it has been shaped and coloured by the conditions, interests and needs of various groups within the community, at different times. Among its other contents, statements about the life and teaching of Jesus Christ bear the stamp of the varying *Sitz im Leben*, or 'setting in life', within which the tradition was formed and had currency. The primary task of the historical criticism of the gospels is the recovery of this tradition in its unity and variety, as a function of the continuing life of the Church, unbroken from its earliest days. From the nature and content of the tradition thus recovered and described we may in turn hope to work back to the events themselves which started it on its course. For unquestionably the tradition, in all its forms, *intends* to refer to an historical episode, closely dated *sub Pontio Pilato*, apart from which (this is the uniform implication) there would have been no church to shape or hand

---

[1] *Sancti Irenaei adversus Haereses*, ed. W. W. Harvey, IV. xlii. 2. Cf. IV. xlvii *et passim*.

[2] And note that this Asian tradition is associated with the names, not only of two persons of the name of John, both of whom have been put forward as candidates for the post of author of the Fourth Gospel, but also of Andrew, Philip and Thomas, who figure importantly in it, though they play little or no part in the Synoptic Gospels (see below, pp. 304–5, 308–10).

down such a tradition.[1] It is in this sense an historical tradition, whatever degree of absolute historical or factual value may attach to various parts of it.

In the ensuing investigation we are not asking, in the first place, whether this or that statement in the Fourth Gospel is likely to be historically correct, or more or less correct than such another statement in Mark or Luke; nor, in the first place, whether the Johannine picture as a whole is more or less probable than that of the Synoptics. No doubt we must, in the long run, take responsibility for our judgements of historical probability, a responsibility which no serious historian can avoid, with all its risks of 'subjectivity'; but there is much useful investigation of a more 'objective' kind that can be done before we come to that. The first question we are asking is this: Can we in any measure recover and describe a strain of tradition lying behind the Fourth Gospel, distinctive of it, and independent of other strains of tradition known to us? This will inevitably raise afresh the much debated question of the relation of the Fourth Gospel to the Synoptics.

For some time it has been almost a dogma of criticism that John depends on the Synoptics, much as Matthew is held to depend on Mark, Matthew and Luke on the hypothetical 'Q'; that the author employed these works as sources, or, if not all three, then two of them, or at least Mark. Recently there has been a certain trend away from this position.[2] Yet the most outstanding recent English commentary, that of C. K. Barrett, still maintains the older view. The matter is perhaps ripe for a more thorough reconsideration. The presuppositions of the discussion have been modified by recent developments in the method and outlook of criticism more, perhaps, than is commonly allowed for. The early Church was not such a bookish community as it has been represented. It did its business in the world primarily through the medium of the living voice, in worship, teaching and missionary preaching, and out of these three forms of activity—liturgy, *didache*, *kerygma*—a tradition was built up, and this tradition lies behind all literary production of the early period, including our written gospels. The presumption, therefore, which lay behind much of the earlier criticism—that similarity of form and content between two documents

[1] For some reasons for regarding the tradition behind the gospels (with all the theological or liturgical elements that they contain) as essentially an historical tradition, see my book, *History and the Gospel* (Nisbet, 1938).

[2] The turn of the tide might be marked, for this country, by the publication of P. Gardner-Smith's *St John and the Synoptic Gospels* (1938), a book which crystallized the doubts of many, and has exerted an influence out of proportion to its size.

points to the dependence of the later of these documents on the earlier—
no longer holds good, since there is an alternative explanation of many
such similarities, and one which corresponds to the conditions under
which gospel writing began, so far as we can learn them: namely, the
influence of a common tradition. To establish literary dependence something more is needed—some striking similarity in the use of words
(especially if the words are somewhat unusual) extending over more than
a phrase or two, or an unexpected and unexplained identity of sequence,
or the like. It is evidence of this kind that has convinced most critics that
the Synoptic evangelists made use of written sources in certain parts of
their works, and it is the lack of such evidence in other parts, in spite of a
general parallelism, that has led many rightly to limit the use of such
sources more narrowly than was at one time customary. In comparing,
therefore, a given passage in the Fourth Gospel with a parallel passage in
the other gospels, we have to inquire whether there are coincidences of
language or content going beyond what might be reasonably expected in
works having behind them the general tradition of the early Church, and
next whether any marked differences might be accounted for (supposing
he were copying the Synoptics) by known mannerisms of the evangelist,
or his known doctrinal tendencies. If not, then there is a *prima facie* case
for treating the passage as independent of the Synoptics, and we have to
ask whether it has characteristics, in form or substance, or possible
indications of a *Sitz im Leben*, which would associate it with traditional
material so far as this is known to us.

This approach to the critical problem throws into the background two
questions which have bulked largely in discussions of it in the past: the
questions of Johannine and Synoptic chronology, and of the authorship of
the Fourth Gospel. Neither is irrelevant, yet neither now appears to have
the overwhelming importance attached to it by many critics, on both sides
of the controversy. It will be well to indicate briefly at the outset the light
in which I should view these questions.

(i) First, the question of the chronology of the ministry of Jesus Christ.
In appearance, at least, John offers a narrative neatly arranged according
to a calendar of Jewish festivals, and covering, it is thought, about three
years. Mark, on the other hand, has been supposed to bring the whole
ministry within a period of less than a year. The problem thus posed
has caused the shedding of much ink and the display of endless ingenuity.
In the main, the 'conservative' critics tended to take the Johannine

framework as normative, and to fit the Synoptic material into it, while 'liberal' critics tended to use Mark to discredit John. But the arrangement of the narrative in the Fourth Gospel is now widely regarded as dictated by the order of thought much more than by the order of events.[1] Johannine chronology, in fact, in the sense in which it has been the critic's bugbear, melts in our hands. This does not, however, mean that the Marcan chronology is left in possession of the field. Recent criticism has shown that it would be possible to account for Mark's order on grounds other than chronological, for example by a system of typology, or by a liturgical sequence. None of these theories can be said to have yet won general assent, but at least they have shown that it is precarious to regard the Marcan order as a strictly chronological sequence of events, offering a fixed standard by which other arrangements of the narrative may be tested. But apart from any particular theory of the determining motive of Mark's arrangement of his material, the form-critics have shown that relatively complete units of narrative, without any necessary connection before or after, are the part of the material which can, on grounds of form, with greatest confidence be traced to an earlier oral tradition, while it is in the arrangement and connection of these units that we are to recognize the individual work of the evangelist as editor.[2] If this is true of Mark, then we may reasonably expect (though the expectation must of course be tested by examination of the material) that any pre-canonical tradition to be found in John must also be sought primarily in the units of narrative and discourse rather than in the chronological arrangement. Form-criticism has in fact reduced to manageable proportions, if it has not removed, one of the most intractable elements in the problem as it was formerly handled.

(ii) Secondly, the question of authorship. The long debate has so far been inconclusive, and is perhaps likely to remain so, unless some happy accident should bring us altogether fresh evidence. A brief summary of the position may be useful.

The external evidence for the apostle John son of Zebedee as author of

---

[1] This subject is treated at length in my book *The Interpretation of the Fourth Gospel* (1938), to which I shall have frequent occasion to refer. That the 'festival' framework may reflect in one way or another liturgical usage is a theory, advocated in various quarters, for which there is much to be said.

[2] I believe that this editorial work of Mark was less arbitrary and uncontrolled than some critics suppose, and that he was guided in part by some sort of outline which was also traditional (see my book *New Testament Studies*, Manchester University Press, 1953; also below, pp. 233–4).

the Fourth Gospel is relatively strong. From the closing decades of the second century the tradition is firm. Apparently the first writer to cite a passage from the work expressly as from 'John' is Theophilus of Antioch, if the *ad Autolycum* is rightly dated to A.D. 181. The virtually contemporary Irenaeus ascribes the gospel to 'John the disciple of the Lord' ('Ἰωάννης ὁ τοῦ κυρίου μαθητής), whom he expressly identifies with the 'beloved disciple' (ὁ καὶ ἐπὶ τὸ στῆθος αὐτοῦ ἀναπεσών *Adv. Haer.* III. i. 2), and by implication includes among the apostles (*ibid.* II. xxxiii. 3, *non solum Johannem sed et alios apostolos*). Although there is perhaps no passage in his writings which is completely unambiguous, there can be no reasonable doubt that Irenaeus believed the Fourth Gospel to have been the work of John son of Zebedee. The same is probably true of the author (? Hippolytus) of the Muratorian Canon, though here again John is described as *ex discipulis*, oddly in contrast to Andrew, who is *ex apostolis*. Clement of Alexandria, again, must be assumed to have identified the John who wrote the 'spiritual gospel' with the apostle John about whom he has a tale to tell which is not a mere tale but sober fact (μῦθον οὐ μῦθον ἀλλὰ ὄντα λόγον).[1] From that time on the tradition of authorship is unvarying,[2] but it does not appear that subsequent writers, though they embroider the tradition with details about the circumstances and methods of composition, had any independent knowledge of the facts. The sheet anchor of the tradition is the evidence of Irenaeus, and it is of special strength because Irenaeus had in his boyhood (παῖς ἔτι ὤν, Euseb. *H.E.* v. 20. 5, ἐν τῇ πρώτῃ ἡμῶν ἡλικίᾳ, *Adv. Haer.* III. iii. 4) listened to Polycarp and heard him speak of his intercourse with 'John the disciple of the Lord'. On this point it is impossible to doubt Irenaeus's veracity. The link is an important one. It appears to be the only link between the first known formulation of the tradition of the authorship of the gospel at the close of the second century and the time, perhaps a century earlier, to which its composition may with probability be assigned—unless indeed we should count among 'external' evidence the statement which occurs at the end of

[1] Euseb. *H.E.* III. 23. 6.

[2] This statement perhaps needs some slight qualification. In the John Rylands Library, Manchester, there is a Syriac MS. (Mingana Syriac 540) in which the Fourth Gospel is headed, 'The holy Gospel of our Lord Jesus Christ (according to) the preaching of John the younger'. The MS. is dated 1749, but is believed to be a copy of an eighth-century archetype. Its discoverer, Alphonse Mingana, proposed to identify 'John the younger' with the 'presbyter' John, as a disciple of the apostle John, and in that sense 'younger', and to claim the MS. as supporting evidence for the presbyter as author of the Fourth Gospel. (*Bulletin of the John Rylands Library*, vol. XIV, no. 1, pp. 333–9.)

the gospel itself, xxi. 24: οὗτός ἐστιν ὁ μαθητὴς ὁ μαρτυρῶν περὶ τούτων καὶ ὁ γράψας ταῦτα. This is commonly taken to be a colophon indicating the authorship of the gospel, a colophon which must have been attached at an early date, since it forms an integral part of the MS. text. Even so, however, it only claims authorship for the 'beloved disciple', without necessarily identifying him with John son of Zebedee. I have however suggested elsewhere[1] that it would be more natural to understand ταῦτα as referring to the *pericopé* immediately preceding (at most, the appendix as a whole), and designed to claim the authority of the 'beloved disciple' for the correct version of the Lord's saying about him, as against the incorrect version which had obtained currency in the Church (xxi. 23). If that is so, then the 'colophon' ceases to represent an early affirmation of authorship for the Fourth Gospel as a whole. In fact, try as we will, it does not seem possible to go behind Irenaeus. His evidence is formidable, even if it is not conclusive. Anyone who should take the view that in the absence of any cogent evidence to the contrary it is reasonable to accept Irenaeus's testimony is on strong ground.

Of any external evidence to the contrary that could be called cogent I am not aware. The theory recently popular, that John son of Zebedee was martyred at an early date, and so could not have lived, as Irenaeus supposed the author of the Fourth Gospel to have lived, at Ephesus to the time of Trajan, rests upon the flimsiest evidence—that of George the Sinner (ninth century), of Philip of Side (*c.* 450), or rather of his Epitomator (seventh or eighth century), and of a Syrian martyrology of about 411 and some hardly relevant odds and ends—supported by an argument from the prediction of the fate of the sons of Zebedee in Mark x. 39, which rests upon an unproven major premiss.[2]

---

[1] *Journal of Theological Studies* (new series), vol. IV, part 2 (October 1953), pp. 212–13.

[2] The evidence is summarized in C. K. Barrett's commentary (S.P.C.K. 1955), though Barrett does not accept the conclusion. The argument is never stated explicitly. It would run somewhat as follows:

(i) All alleged predictions are necessarily *ex eventu*.

(ii) Therefore the sons of Zebedee must have been dead when the prediction of Mark x. 39 was put forth.

(iii) Therefore John cannot have lived long enough to have written the Fourth Gospel, which is later than Mark.

On the strength of this, the statements of all authorities earlier than Philip of Side are set aside. But if proposition (i) is denied, the argument will not stand. On the contrary, if the tradition that John was long-lived and died a natural death be true (and I see no reason why its falsity should be assumed), then the prediction in its

Yet there are weaknesses in the external evidence. The earlier the composition of the gospel is placed, the more surprising it becomes that, if it were indeed known to be the work of an apostle, Justin (who almost certainly quotes from it) should not have included it in the 'Memoirs of the Apostles', the title under which he cites the Synoptic Gospels, and that as late as the close of the second century there should have been controversy over its apostolic authority, which was denied by those whom Epiphanius facetiously calls ἄλογοι,[1] perhaps even by the respectable and ultra-orthodox Gaius of Rome.[2] And after all, Irenaeus does not actually say that Polycarp told him that his old master, 'John the disciple of the Lord', wrote the gospel, and it is odd that Polycarp, who shows acquaintance with almost every other book of the New Testament, has no clear reminiscence of the Fourth Gospel.[3] That may not argue that he did not know of its existence (which would be hard to believe, since he cites the First Epistle of John, which is in all probability later than the Fourth Gospel), but if he knew it, and knew it to be the work of his old master, could he have failed to bring it in? Such considerations may not necessarily invalidate the testimony of Irenaeus, but they leave it, and therefore leave the external evidence as a whole, something short of full certainty.

Turning to internal evidence, we have Westcott's classical statement of the case for the traditional authorship,[4] proceeding in concentric circles from circumference to centre: the evangelist was (a) a Jew, (b) a Jew of Palestine, (c) an eyewitness, (d) an apostle, and, finally, (e) the apostle John. Many of the points he makes remain significant and merit serious consideration in any discussion of the Johannine problem (though we might not draw from them precisely his inferences), but his accumulation of evidence is subject to discount, especially in the crucial inner circles.

plain and natural meaning was not fulfilled, and is all the more likely to be genuine. It is to be noted that though the evidence (such as it is) is often cited as from Papias, our earliest actual evidence is what the eighth-century epitomator said that Philip said that Papias said. On the other hand Eusebius, who had Papias's work before him, and gave much attention to the matter, knows nothing of any such statement of Papias. Eusebius may not be an unimpeachable authority, but he is to be preferred to George the Sinner.

[1] *Panarium sive Adversus Haereses*, bk. II, vol. I, Haer. 50 (iii) (Migne, p. 423): οὓς δικαίως ἀλόγους καλέσομαι ἐπειδὴ τὸν λόγον τοῦ θεοῦ ἀποβάλλονται. There never was a sect named Alogi.

[2] See, for example, the discussion in B. W. Bacon, *The Fourth Gospel in Research and Debate* (1910), ch. IX.

[3] See P. N. Harrison, *Polycarp's Two Epistles to the Philippians* (1936), pp. 285–335.

[4] *The Gospel according to St John* (1889), Introduction, pp. v–xxi.

If the evangelist can be shown to have been well-informed on various matters, it may follow *either* that he had personal acquaintance with these matters, *or* that he made judicious use of good sources of information. Some of the details, such as the naming of persons and the specification of numbers, which for Westcott were evidence of intimate personal knowledge, are of a kind which can often be shown elsewhere to be legendary accretions upon a traditional story. If the form-critics are wrong (as I believe they are) in regarding such details as *invariably* a sign of legendary development, it would be naïve in us at this date to take them at their face value. The vivid dramatic traits which are distinctive of Johannine narrative and dialogue, the characterization, the apparent insight into the inner emotional content of a situation, which Westcott took to be overwhelming proof that the evangelist had been there at the time, may be due rather to his literary skill. At any rate two episodes where dramatic characterization is at its highest, the interview with the Samaritan woman at Jacob's Well, and the examination of Jesus *in camera* by Pilate, are expressly indicated as taking place in the absence of anyone belonging to the *entourage* of Jesus. Of the passages which Westcott counts as direct appeal to eye-witness[1] one only seems significant, xix. 35. Here I cannot think that the plain statement, ὁ ἑωρακὼς μεμαρτύρηκεν, with the solemn asseveration of its truth, can reasonably be treated as a plain falsehood, occurring as it does at the very climax of a work to which the Aristotelian epithet σπουδαῖος is eminently applicable.[2] But the form of statement is most naturally understood as the writer's appeal to the evidence of someone other than himself, on whose authority he ventures to relate so remarkable a fact. Such at least is the *prima facie* impression. It may no doubt be true that the author has chosen this odd way of introducing himself as eye-witness, but we cannot safely base an argument for apostolic authorship on the assumption that he did so.

Yet when all deductions have been made, the case stated by Westcott remains impressive, though far from conclusive. But there is other internal evidence which seems to point in a different direction. We need not, indeed, take very seriously the argument that the Fourth Gospel represents too advanced a stage in the 'evolution' of Christianity to be the work of

[1] The first person plural in i. 14 (cf. i. 16) cannot be used as evidence that the writer in his own person was an eyewitness of the incarnate life of Christ; see my note on 1 John i. 4 (*Moffatt Commentary, The Johannine Epistles*, 1946, pp. 9–15).

[2] The possibility remains that the verse is an addition by a late editor, who believed, *bona fide*, that the statement in the text was made by an eyewitness, and he may have been right or wrong in his belief (see further below, pp. 133–4).

a personal disciple of the Founder. That is to assume knowledge which we do not possess, or which we can learn only from the documents themselves, and which consequently cannot afford standards for criticizing the documents. But the Fourth Gospel (as I have shown elsewhere) is penetrated by two diverse strains of thought, combined in a highly complex unity, the one closely related to rabbinic Judaism, the other equally closely related to the religious philosophy of Hellenism. The Jewish strain is far from being the simple acquaintance with the Old Testament and with the contemporary practice of Judaism which any devout Jew might possess. It implies some degree of rabbinic learning. The author's thought can be shown to be moving among themes which were the subject of rabbinic debate between the fall of the temple and the catastrophe of Bar Cochba, or thereabouts. It appears that our evangelist would have been in a position to take an intelligent part in the discussions of such scholars as Gamaliel II, Eliezer ben Hyrcanus, Eliezer ben Azariah, Joshua ben Chananiah, and Aqiba.[1] The debate may indeed have started earlier—probably did—but the earlier we date it, the less likely was it to stray beyond the circle of the 'disciples of the Wise'. Similarly, the Hellenistic strain is no matter of picking up a few clichés from current talk or street-corner propaganda. The mind of the evangelist moves familiarly among the conceptions of 'Hellenistic mysticism' and constrains them to his purpose with easy mastery.[2]

Now so far as our evidence goes the apostle John was a Galilaean fisherman. Earning a living by a laborious craft, he must have had little leisure for the study of Torah, and in fact he was, in the year of the crucifixion, ἀγράμματος καὶ ἰδιώτης (Acts iv. 13; ?=בּוּר וְחֶדְיוֹט) in the eyes of the professional exponents of Judaism. After that time he could have found little opportunity for making up the deficiencies in his knowledge.[3] His acquaintance with Hellenistic ways of thinking might perhaps

---

[1] See *Interpretation*, pp. 74–85, 320, 336.

[2] See *Interpretation*, pp. 20–73, *et passim*.

[3] Some recent writers have put forward the theory that our evangelist was under the influence of the Qumran sect. I must confess that I am unable to discern the close and striking affinity between the Fourth Gospel and the literature of Qumran which has been found by some of those whose acquaintance with that literature is more extensive and profound than my own. So far as my knowledge goes, I should endorse F. C. Grant's judgement (*The Gospels, their Origin and Growth*, 1959, p. 175–6), from which I quote two sentences: 'Included in the vast array of parallels found in Hellenistic religious literature, especially Greek, Egyptian, and near Eastern...the few which are found in the Dead Sea Scrolls are really minor and only "more of the same". They simply testify to the widespread religious syncretism

be more easily accounted for. 'Galilee of the Gentiles' was in any case open to Hellenistic influences.[1] Moreover, the tradition which names the apostle John as author also avers that he spent many years at Ephesus, where he lived to a ripe old age. He may have absorbed much that was 'in the air', whether through converted Hellenistic Jews of the synagogue or more directly. We cannot say what a residence of more than half a lifetime in that stimulating intellectual atmosphere may have done for a man of active and open mind. It is the *combination* of rabbinic and Hellenistic motives, their combination at a deep level, that should give us pause. It is not impossible to imagine that a Galilaean fisherman may have grown into the accomplished theologian whom we meet in the Fourth Gospel, but I find it difficult.[2]

This brief survey is intended to justify the view which I have taken, that the question of authorship is, on the basis of data at present available, incapable of decision, and that in consequence no particular theory about it can be assumed as a premiss for argument upon the historical value of the gospel. It should be observed that if once the traditional authorship is abandoned, nothing is gained, for our present purpose, by substituting a conjectured author. It is no doubt possible that Irenaeus really meant John the presbyter, and since we know little about the presbyter or his antecedents he is not exposed to the objections we felt bound to raise to

---

which existed in that period and influenced the most diverse types of religious life and thought, even Jewish, even Essene—or "sectarian Judaism"—especially in their religious imagery.' In any case, I see no evidence that our evangelist could have learned at Qumran the kind of rabbinic thought with which he shows acquaintance. Nor indeed could he have improved in that circle his acquaintance with Hellenistic thought and literary method. The application of the term 'Hellenistic' to the Qumran literature appears to me unilluminating.

[1] A student in the rabbinical schools at Jerusalem need not have been without some quite substantial acquaintance with Greek learning. See, for example, D. Daube, *The New Testament and Rabbinic Judaism* (Athlone Press, 1956), pp. 86–9, 151–7; and W. L. Knox, *Pharisaism and Hellenism* in *Judaism and Christianity*, ed. Oesterley, Loewe and Rosenthal (1937), vol. II.

[2] A minor argument, which nevertheless carries some weight in my own mind, is the surprising fact that a work proceeding directly from the hand of one of the Galilaean disciples should show such indifference to the Galilaean ministry, should minimize its importance, and should betray all through what can only be called a metropolitan outlook (see below, pp. 245–7). However much we allow for theological motives in the selection of incidents, it remains odd that one whose mind must have been stored with Galilaean memories should have given us so little from Galilee. It remains odd even if we recall that John son of Zebedee was for some years a 'pillar' of the church in Jerusalem. It was not those years, but the time when he was in the company of Jesus, that was, surely, the formative period.

the candidature of the apostle John. Yet the theory which substitutes the presbyter for the apostle (popular as it has been in this country) is conjectural and no more. And if the presbyter John is in some shadowy way an historical personality (as I believe him to be), a composite author produced by identifying the unnamed disciple who left the Baptist to follow Jesus (John i. 35–40), the disciple who was γνωστὸς τῷ ἀρχιερεῖ (xviii. 15), and the 'beloved disciple' (assumed *not* to be the son of Zebedee) remains a mere hypothesis, and for the purpose of our investigation an unfruitful one.[1]

But in fact the question of authorship is not so important for the problem of historicity as has been supposed. Even if it were certain that the work was by a personal disciple, we could not proceed directly to the inference that his account is a transcript of the facts, or that he intended it to be such. No one, I suppose, doubts that Plato, the author of the *Republic* and the *Symposium*, was a personal disciple of Socrates, yet few would hold that the stories of the meeting with Polemarchus and Adeimantus, and of Agathon's dinner party, necessarily describe in accurate detail historical incidents in the life of Socrates, and still fewer that the speeches, whether of Thrasymachus and Glaucon, of Aristophanes and Diotima, or of Socrates himself, verbally reproduce what these persons said upon these occasions. No more could we safely draw similar conclusions if we knew the Fourth Gospel to be the work of an apostle. If, on the other hand, our author was not John son of Zebedee, it is far less important (for our historical investigation) to try to give him a name than to attempt to trace and assess the kind of material of which he availed himself.

And in fact (to come back to what was said above) the development of form-criticism has tended to turn our attention away from what was one of the most lively interests of nineteenth-century criticism: the attempt to

---

[1] If the balance of probability should appear to be on the side of authorship by John son of Zebedee, much of what is written in the following pages would require some modification, but I do not think it would all fall to the ground. The material ascribed here to tradition would turn out to be the apostle's own reminiscences; but even so, it would be obvious that they had been cast at one stage into the mould of the corporate tradition of the Church—as why should they not be, if the apostle was actively immersed in just that ministry of preaching, teaching and liturgy which *ex hypothesi* gave form to the substance of the Church's memories of its Founder? However, for reasons given, I cannot think this a probable solution of the problem of authorship, though no one can say it is impossible. In what follows I have used the name John for the author, without prejudice, and I have not thought it necessary to place it in inverted commas.

connect the gospels, or the sources behind them, with outstanding personalities of the apostolic age—Mark with Peter, the conjectured document 'Q' with the apostle Matthew, the special source of Luke, perhaps, with Philip and his prophesying daughters, and the Fourth Gospel with the son of Zebedee, or failing him, the presbyter John. Emphasis is now rather upon the corporate nature of the tradition, as a function of the life and thought of the Christian community as such, whatever the individual channel of transmission may have been. Possibly the recent tendency was to go too far in that direction and it is beginning to be corrected. In greater or less degree the idiosyncrasy, and the special situation, of the individual author, and in particular the extent of his opportunities for acquiring first-hand information, must have counted; and certainly the Fourth Evangelist shows a marked individuality. His work is, to a degree unequalled by the other gospels, an original literary composition. Yet since we do not know who this individual was, the more promising way, it seems, is to attempt, for a start, to discover the particular strain of the common tradition upon which he worked.

PART I

THE NARRATIVE

A. THE PASSION NARRATIVE

1. INTRODUCTORY

In all four gospels the closing chapters stand apart from the rest in form and character as well as in contents. These chapters contain a long continuous narrative—the only such narrative found anywhere in the gospels—moving from stage to stage in orderly sequence and forming a unity. By contrast, the earlier parts of each of the four, giving an account of the Ministry of Jesus in word and deed, lack any such unity or continuity. Form-critics who have studied the structure of the Synoptic Gospels regard the units of narrative and teaching as the primary constituents of the gospels, preserving even as literary products much of the character of the oral tradition in which they had originally been current. The arrangement of *pericopae* is regarded as due to the editorial work of the evangelists. There is no sign that they felt themselves strictly bound by any fixed scheme.

In the Passion narrative, by contrast, the three Synoptic Gospels scarcely differ in the order of incidents. Attempts to show that the Passion narrative, like the account of the Ministry, grew up out of separate units have not, in my judgement, succeeded. It may be that some two or three of the incidents which now appear in the course of that narrative were handed down separately, but for the most part each incident is intelligible only in its place within the continuous sequence, depending on what has gone before and preparing for what comes after. The fact is that the attempt to explain the Passion narrative as an aggregation of originally independent units is fundamentally misguided. Form-criticism depends largely upon comparison between the forms embodied in the gospels and those of other traditional literatures, and such comparison does indeed reveal some analogies. But in so far as the Passion narrative has analogues in other comparable literature (and no such analogy goes very far), they are to be found in the legends or sagas of the hero's last fight and death;[1] and in such stories the sequence of incidents, like successive strokes of doom, is intrinsic to the story. So it is in the Passion narrative.

In all this the Fourth Gospel conforms to the same general scheme as

---

[1] Arthur's battle with Mordred, Roland at Roncesvalles, the death of Hector in the *Iliad*, etc.

the Synoptics. Here too we find the distinction between the earlier part—the account of the Ministry of Jesus in word and deed—and the narrative of the Passion. Here too the latter preserves the same broad sequence, with no more variation from the common order than is to be observed among the Synoptics themselves. Here too the earlier part consists of separable units of narrative, or of teaching, or of a combination of the two. Some of them, it is true, are much longer and more elaborate than those of the Synoptics, but others are similar in form and character. And here the Fourth Evangelist, like the others, has used much liberty in the arrangement of the several units. It seems clear that in spite of the wide difference in many respects between this gospel and the others, all are designed on the same general idea of a γραφὴ εὐαγγελίου (as Irenaeus has it, *Adv. Haer.* III. i. 2), whether this is due to the influence of Mark, the oldest extant composition of the kind, or to the constraint of an older tradition followed by all gospel writers. The distinction between the narrative of the Passion, where all follow a common scheme, and the account of the Ministry, where the arrangement is much more fluid, seems to be inherent in the idea of a written gospel. I have elsewhere[1] tried to show that in this respect the written gospels betray their descent from the spoken Gospel, or κήρυγμα, in which, it appears, the story of the Passion was communicated with emphasis and some particularity, and the Ministry passed over lightly.

The Passion narrative, then, as the one portion of the gospels where they all run parallel over a considerable length and contain a wealth of comparable material, affords the best starting point for our investigation. It will be useful first to try to determine the point at which the common Passion narrative properly begins, from a study of the way in which each evangelist has marked the transition.

Mark (xiv. 1–11), having wound up his account of the Ministry in a discourse ending with the solemn injunction, ὃ ὑμῖν λέγω πᾶσιν λέγω · γρηγορεῖτε, indicates a fresh departure by inserting a date—the first precise date in his gospel: ἦν δὲ τὸ πάσχα καὶ τὰ ἄζυμα μετὰ δύο ἡμέρας. He proceeds to describe the situation as it then was: the Jewish authorities were seeking an opportunity to put Jesus under arrest. The verbs in the imperfect tense, ἐζήτουν, ἔλεγον, show that he is not reporting a single decision, but sketching the position of affairs at the moment when his narrative begins. At this point he has inserted the story of the anointing of Jesus by a woman at Bethany, after which he records a fresh development in the situation

---

[1] *The Apostolic Preaching and its Developments* (1936), pp. 77–129, 164–73.

sketched above, when Judas made his traitorous offer and the authorities accepted it. This is recorded in sentences where the verbs are in the aorist: ἀπῆλθεν, ἐχάρησαν, ἀπηγγείλαντο. The resultant situation is once again described in the imperfect: ἐζήτει πῶς αὐτὸν εὐκαίρως παραδοῖ. All this has the appearance of being preliminary to the main story. The Anointing at Bethany, which does not appear in Luke, and has been given at an earlier point by John, seems to be introduced here by Mark's favourite device of 'sandwiched' narratives.[1] It is obviously the kind of *pericopé* which may well have circulated independently, and is probably no original part of the Passion narrative. But now at last the story gets really under way. Once again we have a date: τῇ πρώτῃ ἡμέρᾳ τῶν ἀζύμων ὅτε τὸ πάσχα ἔθυον, and with that we are told how preparations were made for the Last Supper. From this point the narrative flows continuously on.

Matthew (xxvi. 1–16) seems to be following Mark fairly closely, even to the extent of including the story of the Anointing. Yet he introduces a number of significant changes. After his favourite formula of transition, καὶ ἐγένετο ὅτε ἐτέλεσεν ὁ Ἰησοῦς πάντας τοὺς λόγους τούτους, he turns Mark's simple indication of date into a solemn pronouncement of Jesus himself: 'You know that Passover comes in two days' time, and the Son of Man is to be handed over for crucifixion.' Again, Mark's concise setting of the scene— the authorities on the watch for an opportunity of effecting an arrest—is replaced by an ostensible report of a session of the Sanhedrin, with the verbs in the aorist, συνήχθησαν, συνεβουλεύσαντο. There is an unmistakable echo of the language of Ps. xxx. 14: ἐν τῷ συναχθῆναι αὐτοὺς ἅμα ἐπ' ἐμὲ τοῦ λαβεῖν τὴν ψυχήν μου ἐβουλεύσαντο. This psalm has elsewhere yielded *testimonia*,[2] and there can be little doubt that we should reckon the present passage among those in which the Passion narrative has been moulded upon testimonies. If so, then there is some ground for suspecting

---

[1] Cf. Mark v. 25–34, the Haemorrhousa sandwiched into the story of Jairus's daughter; vi. 14–29, the death of the Baptist, inserted between the dispatch of the Twelve and their return; and in the Passion narrative, xiv. 66–72, Peter's denial, inserted between the conclusion of the examination before the High Priest and the further proceedings. The use of this device seems to be intended either to mark a lapse of time or to indicate simultaneity between two incidents which have to be related separately. The Anointing may be conceived either as taking place at Bethany while Judas was making his nefarious plans in Jerusalem (in which case Mark would not agree with John, who represents the traitor as being present at Bethany), or as falling in the interval between the hatching of the plot and Judas's offer to lend himself to it.

[2] See below, pp. 33–4.

that Matthew is here following a form of tradition independent of Mark; and this suspicion is confirmed when we observe that he gives the place of meeting as the palace of the High Priest Caiaphas. The name Caiaphas is unknown to Mark, and it does not figure in the Passion narrative of Luke. But it does occur in two passages of the Fourth Gospel: in the narrative of the trial, xviii. 13–14, 28 (see pp. 93–5), and, outside the Passion narrative, in the account of a meeting of the Sanhedrin in xi. 47–50.

It is an obvious conjecture that John xi. 47–53, a detached *pericopé* complete in itself, represents a piece of oral tradition in typical form, and that this might underlie Matthew's brief summary statement. But such a conjecture would be precarious. The *pericopé* has indeed a general resemblance in form to some of those in the Synoptic Gospels, where a scene is briefly introduced, and a dialogue leads up to a pregnant utterance. But if it be compared with such *pericopae* it is at once seen to be exceptional: the pregnant utterance is not attributed to Jesus but, surprisingly, to one of his enemies; indeed Jesus does not appear on the scene at all. This is so unlike anything else in any of the gospels that it is difficult to believe that it formed part of the general body of the common tradition, as it is known to us. Yet it is unlikely that it is a composition of the evangelist. The proposition indeed in which it culminates—that Jesus was to die to gather together the scattered children of God—is thoroughly and characteristically Johannine;[1] but it is given as a gloss on a 'prophecy' which in itself suggests nothing of the kind. The 'prophecy' therefore must have reached John from some source or other. It must surely have been some source in very close contact with Jewish ways of thought and practice, for it implies a singular respect for the high priesthood, even when held by an unworthy occupant, and associates with it the gift of prophecy—for which there is good Jewish authority.[2] While therefore I should not care to make use of this passage in an attempt to envisage the tradition lying behind this gospel, it does perhaps provide a clue to the kind of *milieu* within which the evangelist sought for information.[3] But that it represents a

[1] Cf. John xii. 32, where the Crucified is to draw all men to him; x. 14–18, where by clear implication, though not in so many words, he is to die to bring in the sheep of another fold.

[2] See Strack–Billerbeck, *Kommentar zum neuen Testament aus Talmud und Midrasch, ad loc.*

[3] The presuppositions of the above argument should become clearer after my discussion of other *pericopae* in part 1, A 2, B 1, 2, and part II. I have discussed this *pericopé* more fully in my article, 'The Prophecy of Caiaphas', in *Neotestamentica et Patristica in honorem sexagenarii O. Cullmann*, ed. W. C. van Unnik and B. Reicke (Brill, 1962).

tradition accessible to Matthew, and the basis of his statement in xxvi. 3, 4, seems unlikely.

To return to Matthew: in spite of the non-Marcan features we have noted, the opening section of his narrative, ending like Mark's with the statement that Judas was on the watch for a suitable occasion (ἐζήτει εὐκαιρίαν, xxvi. 16), still has the character of a summary of the situation preparatory to the narrative proper, which begins, as in Mark, with the date, τῇ πρώτῃ τῶν ἀζύμων.

Luke, having wound up his account of the Ministry with a summary of the activity of Jesus in Jerusalem (xxi. 37–8)—the verbs being all in the imperfect (ἦν διδάσκων, ηὐλίζετο, ὤρθριζεν)—marks the new departure, like the others, with a date, though a vaguer one: ἤγγιζεν ἡ ἑορτὴ τῶν ἀζύμων ἡ λεγομένη πάσχα (xxii. 1). He then describes the situation much as Mark does (with imperfects), but even more briefly, and recounts the treachery of Judas in impressive terms: Satan entered into the traitor, who thereupon made his infamous compact with the authorities; after which, as in the others, ἐζήτει εὐκαιρίαν τοῦ παραδοῦναι αὐτόν (xxii. 2–6). Then we have, once again, the date, ἦλθεν ἡ ἡμέρα τῶν ἀζύμων, ᾗ ἔδει θύεσθαι τὸ πάσχα, and from that point the narrative becomes continuous.

It would seem, then, that the common plan of the Synoptic Gospels conceived the Passion narrative proper as beginning with the incidents of the Last Supper (including the preparation for it), and that the dating (at Passover-tide), the hostility of the authorities, and the plot of Judas are briefly related to form an exordium to the narrative proper, placing the reader in possession of the minimum he must know in order to follow it intelligently. It is possible to hold that the versions given by Matthew and Luke are no more than reproductions of Mark, somewhat 'edited', and indeed there is little doubt that both used Mark here as a source. Yet there are slight indications that they may have drawn also upon traditional matter. It would be a tenable hypothesis that a primitive exordium to the Passion narrative, in oral tradition, underlying all three, was extremely concise, containing simply the date, and the statements that the authorities were seeking an arrest and that Judas had lent himself to their schemes. To this Mark (followed by Matthew but not by Luke) added the story of the Anointing, and Matthew (alone) added an account of a session of the Sanhedrin, and elaborated the account of Judas's compact with the priests, while Luke may have borrowed from some other form of tradition the peculiar language in which he relates the treachery of Judas. Such an hypothesis may at this point seem purely speculative, but if it should become probable as we go on that more than one pre-canonical form of Passion tradition has left its traces at various points, then our hypothesis about the exordium would appear not wholly in the air.

We now turn to the Fourth Gospel. John has marked the end of his account of the Ministry with a formal conclusion, containing a comment on the upshot of Jesus's appeal to his countrymen and a general summary of his teaching (xii. 37–50). He then marks a fresh departure (xiii. 1–4) with two sentences into which he has packed most of what the Synoptics give as preliminaries to the Passion narrative, namely:

(a) the date, as vague as Luke's: πρὸ τῆς ἑορτῆς τοῦ πάσχα.

(b) Jesus's foreknowledge of his fate, as in Matthew: εἰδὼς ὅτι ἦλθεν ἡ ὥρα κ.τ.λ.[1]

(c) the diabolical inspiration of Judas to his act of treachery, as in Luke: τοῦ διαβόλου ἤδη βεβληκότος εἰς τὴν καρδίαν ἵνα παραδοῖ αὐτὸν 'Ιουδᾶς Σίμωνος 'Ισκαριώτης.

To this he has added interpretative comments which are full of the distinctive language and ideas of Johannine theology. The first specific statement of a concrete and overt action comes at last, after much parenthetic matter (which for the evangelist is the pith of the whole), in the words, ἐγείρεται ἐκ τοῦ δείπνου, and so, with the incidents of the Supper, the Passion narrative has begun. The Supper itself, indeed, is reported only in a circumstantial clause in the genitive absolute, δείπνου γινομένου (v.l. γενομένου), as in Mark, who has ἀνακειμένων αὐτῶν καὶ ἐσθιόντων. It is not the Supper itself, as a meal, but significant words and actions associated with it, that both evangelists wish to bring into prominence.

Thus the core of John's exordium, underlying the theological elaboration, is closely similar to that which we have hypothetically postulated as the common basis upon which the Synoptic evangelists may have worked.

There are two notable features of the Synoptic exordium which are absent from the Johannine: the reference to the hostility of the authorities,

[1] The clause affirming Jesus's foreknowledge of his fate (εἰδὼς ὅτι ἦλθεν αὐτοῦ ἡ ὥρα κ.τ.λ.) is thoroughly Johannine in language and style, but its motive is similar to that which lies behind Matt. xxvi. 2, where Jesus foretells to the disciples his arrest during the approaching Passover-tide. There is nothing of the kind in Mark or Luke. We may take it that the tradition of the Passion in its simplest, and probably its earliest, formulation did not contain any such explicit affirmation. Yet it was natural enough that the theme of Christ's foreknowledge of his Passion, which crops up in various forms and at various points in all gospels, should be brought into prominence at the outset of the story of the Passion. There is no question of anything like literary dependence between Matthew and John, but they are both obeying a common impulse in amplifying a common tradition.

and Judas's compact with them. The former John perhaps felt no need to introduce at this point, since he has given earlier, not merely a stylized report of the conspiracy against Jesus, such as we find in Matthew, but a vivid account of a debate in the Sanhedrin, with a speech by Caiaphas, in a *pericopé* (xi. 47–53) which ends with a phrase not unlike that of Matthew:

Matt. xxvi. 4	John xi. 53
συνεβουλεύσαντο ἵνα τὸν ᾽Ιησοῦν	ἐβουλεύσαντο ἵνα
. . . ἀποκτείνωσιν	ἀποκτείνωσιν αὐτόν

We have already seen some reason to suppose that Matthew here supplemented what he took from Mark out of a separate tradition. It would seem that the account given by John had some contact with this tradition, though literary derivation is most unlikely.

The other omission is more interesting. John does not mention Judas's approach to the authorities and their offer of a bribe. What he does say is that Satan prompted him to his act of treachery. Luke says much the same: εἰσῆλθεν σατανᾶς εἰς ᾽Ιουδᾶν τὸν καλούμενον ᾽Ισκαριώτην.[1] At a later point John has an almost identical phrase: at the giving of the ψωμίον (xiii. 27), εἰσῆλθεν εἰς ἐκεῖνον ὁ σατανᾶς. In Luke the phrase is introductory to the account of Judas's overtures to the priests, which to all appearance is derived from Mark, but it looks like a reminiscence of a tradition more fully represented in John. The latter shows no knowledge of the story that Judas was paid for his treachery. This story appears in Mark in the form that Judas approached the priests ἵνα αὐτὸν παραδοῖ αὐτοῖς, and that they, delighted at the suggestion, promised him a reward. That is all. In Matthew it takes the form that Judas bargained with the priests—Τί θέλετέ μοι δοῦναι, κἀγὼ ὑμῖν παραδώσω αὐτόν;—and they agreed upon the sum of τριάκοντα ἀργύρια, a sum which, as the evangelist points out later, was guaranteed by prophecy (xxvii. 9). It is clear that the theme of the venality of the traitor was greatly elaborated in the development of the story. Is it not possible that the earliest tradition of all knew nothing about the motive of Judas's treachery? It was a horrible, incredible

[1] The construction and meaning of the sentence, τοῦ διαβόλου ἤδη βεβληκότος εἰς τὴν καρδίαν ἵνα παραδοῖ αὐτὸν ᾽Ιουδᾶς Σίμωνος ᾽Ισκαριώτης, is a notorious *crux interpretum*, nor is the text certain. Βάλλειν εἰς τὴν καρδίαν might mean either to make up one's mind, or to suggest to another. Here there is no pronoun to help out. The meaning may be that Satan had already decided that Judas was to be the instrument, and that later (xiii. 27) he carried out his decision, or that before Passover Satan had insinuated the suggestion into the mind of Judas, and at the giving of the ψωμίον entered in and took possession of his tool. In either case the intention is to trace the traitor's action to diabolical inspiration.

manifestation of sheer evil, for which no normal human motive could be assigned; in other words, it was the work of the devil, and that is all that could be said about it. Later, as an attempt to rationalize an act which really lay beyond the confines of reason, it was said that Judas was actuated by a truly human motive, albeit one of the baser human motives, avarice. Out of this grew the whole dramatic story as we have it in Matthew. John, I suggest, preserves the simpler tradition, as it was framed by those who were still stunned by the sheer horror of the act, not wishing, or daring, to explain it. Luke has combined the diabolical with the human motivation.

It would appear, then, that in the common plan underlying all the gospels the Passion narrative was conceived as beginning with the incidents of the Last Supper (including, in the Synoptics, the preparation for it), and that a certain amount of preliminary matter was set down briefly to place the reader in possession of the minimum he must know in order to follow it intelligently. This preliminary matter included, at least, the date and the defection of Judas. The presence, and the character, of this exordium tell strongly in favour of the view that the Passion narrative was framed in tradition as an independent whole, which could be recited by itself. Even in our finished gospels it stands out from all that precedes. So far as the Synoptic Gospels are concerned, it seems probable that Mark has provided the framework for the others, though in both there are features which may betray acquaintance with other forms of tradition, and, as it happens, some of these features are represented also in the Fourth Gospel, which at this point shows no clear sign of any particular relationship with Mark. At this stage it is open to anyone to argue that John arrived at the bare summary which underlies xiii. 1–4 by distillation out of one or more of the other gospels,[1] but it is at least as tenable an hypothesis

---

[1] But any attempt to carry through at this point a rigorous theory of the dependence of John on the Synoptics leads to an incredibly complicated account of the process of composition. John must be supposed to have followed Matthew, since he includes (a) Jesus's foreknowledge of his fate, and (b) the session of the Sanhedrin, which he must be supposed to have transferred to an earlier position in the narrative (xi. 47–53), as well as the incident common to Matthew and Mark, the Anointing, which he must be supposed similarly to have transposed to xii. 1–8. But the Johannine story of the Anointing has traits also which connect it with Luke (vii. 36–50). A rigorous theory of dependence would therefore oblige us to postulate that John used Luke, and this would also follow from his inclusion of the idea of the diabolical inspiration of the traitor. All this is too cumbrous to be plausible. Perhaps no one has wished to carry through the theory of dependence of John on the Synoptics quite

that a slightly different version of the common exordium reached him by an independent channel.

Assuming that we have now established the point at which, and the manner in which, the Passion narrative is, by all our evangelists, conceived to begin, we may take a general survey of its character and contents. In all four gospels the narrative (after the brief exordium) falls naturally into five stages, which may be presented as acts in a drama.

Act I. The Leave-taking
 Incidents of the Last Supper (including, in the Synoptics, the preparation for it, and in John the Farewell Discourses).
Act II. The Arrest
 Retirement to a place on or near the Mount of Olives.
 Betrayal and arrest.
Act III. The Trial
 Scene 1. Examination before the High Priest.
 Scene 2. Trial before the Roman Governor.
    The question, Σὺ εἶ ὁ βασιλεὺς τῶν Ἰουδαίων; and the answer.
    Declaration of innocence.
    The choice of Barabbas.
    Sentence of crucifixion.
Act IV. The Execution
 Crucifixion at Golgotha, with two others.
 The division of the garments.
 The offer of ὄξος.
 Death of Jesus.
Act V. The Reunion
 Scene 1. The burial.
 Scene 2. The discovery of the empty tomb.
 Scene 3. The appearance of the risen Christ.

The incidents indicated by brief headings in this list are reported in all gospels in identical order, except that in Mark the final scene of Act v is wanting. Yet even here an appearance of the risen Christ is twice over forecast (Mark xiv. 28, xvi. 7). Contrary to the present trend of opinion, I continue to believe, in view of these forecasts, that Mark either intended to report such an appearance, but for some reason failed to do so, or else did in fact write such a report, which was lost through mutilation of the archetype. It is not, however, important for our present purpose to

so rigorously, but this is where the logic of it leads. For a different view of the relation of John and the Synoptics in respect of the Anointing, see below, pp. 162–73.

decide this much disputed question. It is enough that Mark quite clearly points to the completion of the story by an appearance of the risen Christ, and therefore necessarily implies that the tradition he followed knew of such appearances. He agrees therein, not only with his fellow-evangelists, but also with practically every form of the primitive apostolic *kerygma* found in the New Testament. Since we are at present engaged in an attempt to trace forms of tradition lying behind the gospels, Mark's attestation of the tradition suffices, whether we suppose that in writing he deliberately suppressed it, or that his purpose to include it was frustrated, or that what he had written was lost through sheer mischance.

In addition to these incidents related in identical order, all our gospels contain the following incidents, with only slight variation in their setting within the general course of the narrative:

(*a*) Forecasts of the treachery of Judas, of Peter's denial, and of the desertion of the disciples, introduced either during the Supper or between the Supper and the Betrayal.

(*b*) The story of Peter's denial, always placed in close relation with the examination before the High Priest, but with minor differences of arrangement.

(*c*) Scenes of mockery, variously placed.

There are other incidents introduced in one or more gospels, though not in all four, but never in such a way as to disturb the common scheme.

This survey in itself justifies the inference that so striking a measure of agreement among the four gospels permits only two alternative ways of explaining the facts: either there is literary interdependence among the four—a theory which almost invariably takes the form of dependence of John on one or more of the Synoptics; or all four evangelists felt themselves to be bound by a pre-canonical tradition in which the broad lines of the story were already fixed. In detail, of course, it is always possible that one evangelist (John, for example) may have followed in part a common oral tradition and in part one of the other gospels. But for the fundamental explanation of the situation as we have surveyed it, only the two alternatives seem open. It is these alternative explanations that we shall have in view in the detailed examination which follows.

2. TESTIMONIES

Before coming to the detailed examination of the successive stages of the Passion narrative, we must notice a significant feature which is common to all its forms, namely the introduction from time to time of references to passages in the Old Testament, sometimes quoted expressly, sometimes recalled to the reader by verbal echoes. These references cannot be regarded as mere literary embroidery. The reason for their introduction is patent in the passage of the apostolic *kerygma* in Acts ii. 23, where the death and resurrection of Christ are said to have happened τῇ ὡρισμένῃ βουλῇ καὶ προγνώσει τοῦ θεοῦ. The 'testimonies' from the Old Testament supply the key to this 'settled plan and purpose of God'. They thus give to the narrative its specific religious and theological character, and they must have done much to determine the forms which the narrative assumed, even, as we must suppose, in the earliest oral tradition.[1] So far from being embroidery, they must be regarded as the firm scaffolding supporting the structure. A study, therefore, of the *testimonia*, as they appear in the several gospels, should throw light upon the history of their differing forms. The accompanying tables set forth the testimonies cited by the four evangelists.[2]

Table 1. 'Testimonies' in the Passion Narrative

(i) Mark

1	xiv. 18	ὁ ἐσθίων μετ' ἐμοῦ	Ps. xl. 10
2	xiv. 21	[καθὼς γέγραπται]	—
3	xiv. 24	τὸ αἷμα τῆς διαθήκης	Zech. ix. 11, cf. Exod. xxiv. 8
4	xiv. 24	ὑπὲρ πολλῶν (?)	Cf. Isa. liii. 11, 12
5	xiv. 27	σκανδαλισθήσεσθε (?)	Cf. Dan. xi. 41 LXX, Mal. ii. 8 Theod.
6	xiv. 27	πατάξω τὸν ποιμένα καὶ τὰ πρόβατα διασκορπισθήσονται	Zech. xiii. 7
7	xiv. 34	περίλυπός ἐστιν ἡ ψυχή μου	Ps. xli. 6, 12, xlii. 5
8	xiv. 49	[ἵνα πληρωθῶσιν αἱ γραφαί]	—
9	xiv. 57	ἀναστάντες ἐψευδομαρτύρουν	Ps. xxxiv. 11, xxvi. 12
10	xiv. 62	τὸν υἱὸν τοῦ ἀνθρώπου...ἐρχόμενον μετὰ τῶν νεφελῶν τοῦ οὐρανοῦ	Dan. vii. 13

[1] On all this, see my book *According to the Scriptures* (Nisbet, 1952), in which I have argued for positions which are here taken for granted.

[2] Here and elsewhere references are to the LXX (ed. Swete, Cambridge) in which the numeration sometimes differs from that of the Massoretic Hebrew.

(i) Mark (*continued*)

11	xiv. 62	ἐκ δεξιῶν καθήμενον τῆς δυνάμεως	Ps. cix. 1
12	xiv. 65	ἤρξαντό τινες ἐμπτύειν αὐτῷ...καί... ῥαπίσμασιν αὐτὸν ἔλαβον	Isa. l. 6
13	xv. 24	διαμερίζονται τὰ ἱμάτια αὐτοῦ βάλλοντες κλῆρον ἐπ᾽ αὐτά	Ps. xxi. 19
14	xv. 29	κινοῦντες τὰς κεφαλάς	Ps. xxi. 8
15	xv. 34	ἠλί, ἠλί, λαμὰ σαβαχθάνι	Ps. xxi. 2
16	xv. 36	ὄξους...ἐπότιζεν αὐτόν	Ps. lxviii. 22
17	xv. 40	ἦσαν...ἀπὸ μακρόθεν θεωροῦσαι	Ps. xxxvii. 12

Mark has seventeen certain or probable references to *testimonia* from the O.T. Two of these, nos. 2 and 8, are general or unidentified. Of the rest, one only, no. 6, has a formula of quotation (γέγραπται).

(ii) Matthew

1	xxvi. 24	[καθὼς γέγραπται]	—
2	xxvi. 28	τὸ αἷμα τῆς διαθήκης	Zech. ix. 11, cf. Exod. xxiv. 8
3	xxvi. 28	ὑπὲρ πολλῶν (?)	Cf. Isa. liii. 11, 12
4	xxvi. 28	...διαθήκης εἰς ἄφεσιν ἁμαρτιῶν (?)	Cf. Jerem. xxxviii. 34
5	xxvi. 31	σκανδαλισθήσεσθε (?)	Cf. Dan. xi. 41 LXX, Mal. ii. 8 Theod.
6	xxvi. 31	πατάξω τὸν ποιμένα κ.τ.λ.	Zech. xiii. 7
7	xxvi. 38	περίλυπός ἐστιν ἡ ψυχή μου	Ps. xli. 6, 12; xlii. 5
8	xxvi. 54	[...πληρωθῶσιν αἱ γραφαί]	—
9	xxvi. 62	τὸν υἱὸν τοῦ ἀνθρώπου ἐρχόμενον μετὰ τῶν νεφελῶν τοῦ οὐρανοῦ	Dan. vii. 13
10	xxvi. 62	καθήμενον ἐκ δεξιῶν τῆς δυνάμεως	Ps. cix. 1
11	xxvi. 67	ἐνέπτυσαν...ἐράπισαν	Isa. l. 6
12	xxvii. 9–10	ἔλαβον τὰ τριάκοντα ἀργύρια κ.τ.λ.	Zech. xi. 12–13
13	xxvii. 34	ἔδωκαν αὐτῷ πιεῖν οἶνον μετὰ χολῆς μεμιγμένον	Ps. lxviii. 22
14	xxvii. 35	διεμερίσαντο τὰ ἱμάτια κ.τ.λ.	Ps. xxi. 19
15	xxvii. 39	κινοῦντες τὰς κεφαλάς	Ps. xxi. 8
16	xxvii. 43	πέποιθεν ἐπὶ τὸν θεόν κ.τ.λ.	Ps. xxi. 9
17	xxvii. 46	ἠλί, ἠλί, λεμὰ σαβαχθάνι	Ps. xxi. 2
18	xxvii. 48	ὄξους...ἐπότιζεν αὐτόν	Ps. lxviii. 22
19	xxvii. 52–3	πολλὰ σώματα τῶν κεκοιμημένων... ἠγέρθησαν κ.τ.λ. (?)	Cf. Dan. xii. 2 Theod.
20	xxvii. 55	ἦσαν...ἀπὸ μακρόθεν θεωροῦσαι	Ps. xxxvii. 12

Matthew has all Mark's *testimonia* except no. 1 ὁ ἐσθίων μετ᾽ ἐμοῦ, and no. 9, ἀναστάντες ἐψευδομαρτύρουν. He has added nos. 4, 12, 13, 16, 19. To these should probably be reckoned his rephrasing (xxvi. 3–4) of Mark's introductory statement (xiv. 1–2), where Matthew's language recalls that of Ps. xxx. 14. Two of Matthew's references, nos. 1 and 8, are general or unidentified, as in Mark. Of the others, two, nos. 6 (from Mark) and 12, have a formula of quotation.

TESTIMONIES

(iii) Luke

1	xxii. 20	καινὴ διαθήκη (lect. dub.)	Jer. xxxviii. 31
2	xxii. 37	μετὰ ἀνόμων ἐλογίσθη	Isa. liii. 12
3	xxii. 69	καθήμενος ἐκ δεξιῶν τῆς δυνάμεως τοῦ θεοῦ	Ps. cix. 1
4	xxiii. 30	λέγειν τοῖς ὄρεσιν, Πέσατε ἐφ᾽ ἡμᾶς κ.τ.λ.	Hos. x. 8
5	xxiii. 34	διαμεριζόμενοι τὰ ἱμάτια αὐτοῦ ἔβαλον κλήρους	Ps. xxi. 19
6	xxiii. 34–5	...θεωρῶν· ἐξεμυκτήριζον δὲ καὶ...	Ps. xxi. 8
7	xxiii. 36	ὄξος προσφέροντες	Ps. lxviii. 22
8	xxiii. 46	εἰς χεῖράς σου παρατίθεμαι τὸ πνεῦμά μου	Ps. xxx. 6
9	xxiii. 49	εἱστήκεισαν...ἀπὸ μακρόθεν	Ps. xxxvii. 12
10	xxiii. 49	οἱ γνωστοί...ἀπὸ μακρόθεν	Ps. lxxxvii. 9

Of Mark's seventeen *testimonia* Luke has four: nos. 3, 5, 7, 9. He has six non-Marcan: nos. 1, 2, 4, 6, 8, 10. Of the ten, one only, no. 2, has a formula of quotation.

(iv) John

1	xiii. 18	ὁ τρώγων μου τὸν ἄρτον ἐπῆρεν ἐπ᾽ ἐμὲ τὴν πτέρναν αὐτοῦ	Ps. xl. 10
2	xiii. 21	ἐταράχθη τῷ πνεύματι (cf. xii. 27)	Ps. xli. 7
3	xv. 25	ἐμίσησάν με δωρεάν	Ps. xxxiv. 19, lxviii. 5
4	xix. 1, 3	...ἐμαστίγωσαν...ἐδίδοσαν αὐτῷ ῥαπίσματα (cf. xviii. 22)	Isa. l. 6
5	xix. 24	διεμερίσαντο τὰ ἱμάτια κ.τ.λ.	Ps. xxi. 19
6a	xix. 28	Διψῶ	
6b	xix. 29	σπόγγον μεστὸν τοῦ ὄξους...προσήνεγκαν αὐτῷ	} Ps. lxviii. 22
7	xix. 36	ὀστοῦν οὐ συντριβήσεται αὐτῷ	Ps. xxxiii. 21, cf. Exod. xii. 46
8	xix. 36	ὄψονται εἰς ὃν ἐξεκέντησαν	Zech. xii. 10

Of Mark's seventeen *testimonia* John has four: nos. 1, 4, 5, 6b; he has five non-Marcan: nos. 2, 3, 6a, 7, 8. None of his non-Marcan testimonies coincides with the non-Marcan testimonies in Matthew or Luke. Of the eight (nine) references, six have a formula of quotation: nos. 1 (contrast Mark), 3, 5 (contrast Mark), 6b, 7, 8.

(v) Conspectus

Psalms

		Matthew	Mark	Luke	John
xxi.	2	Matthew	Mark		
	8a			Luke	
	8b	Matthew	Mark		
	9	Matthew			
	19	Matthew	Mark	Luke	John
xxvi.	12		Mark		
xxx.	6			Luke	
xxxiii.	21				John
xxxiv.	11		Mark		
	19				John
xxxvii.	12	Matthew	Mark	Luke	
xl.	10		Mark		John
xli.	6 (= 12 = xlii. 5)	Matthew	Mark		
	7				John
lxviii.	5				John
	22a	Matthew			
	22b	Matthew	Mark	Luke	John
lxxxvii.	9			Luke	
cix.	1	Matthew	Mark	Luke	

Isaiah

		Matthew	Mark	Luke	John
l.	6	Matthew	Mark		John
liii.	11, 12 (? πολλοί)	Matthew	Mark		
	12			Luke	

Jeremiah

		Matthew	Mark	Luke	John
xxxviii.	31			Luke	
	34 (?)	Matthew			

Daniel

		Matthew	Mark	Luke	John
vii.	13	Matthew	Mark		
xi.	41 (?)	Matthew	Mark		
xii.	2 (?)	Matthew			

Hosea

		Matthew	Mark	Luke	John
x.	8			Luke	

Zechariah

		Matthew	Mark	Luke	John
ix.	11	Matthew	Mark		
xi.	12–13	Matthew			
xii.	10				John
xiii.	7	Matthew	Mark		

Malachi

		Matthew	Mark	Luke	John
ii.	8 (?)		Mark		

Mark has seventeen certain or probable references to the Old Testament. The large majority of these, where their sources can be identified, come from the Psalms, and in particular from that group of them which may be defined as Psalms of the Righteous Sufferer. These psalms recite, either in the first or the third person, the trials of a person (who may be an individual or a representative figure) who is devoted to the service of God and sustained by faith in Him, and his ultimate deliverance by divine grace. Apart from these, one testimony is taken from the prophecy of the deutero-Isaiah about the Suffering Servant of the Lord, who may be taken to be the Righteous Sufferer in another guise, two from the latter part of Zechariah, and one from the prophecy of the Son of Man in Daniel. Two or three (unimportant) references remain unidentified. The intention is clearly to present the sufferings of Jesus as those of the Son of Man (standing for the 'people of the saints of the Most High' in humiliation and in triumph), of the martyred Shepherd of Israel in Zechariah, and of the Suffering Servant who made his life an offering for sin, shed his blood to inaugurate a new covenant, and was vindicated in glory after death. That is how Mark understood the article of the primitive *kerygma* which declared that Christ died and rose again 'according to the Scriptures'. It is in this sense that the Marcan Passion narrative is designed to be read.

In Matthew, fifteen of Mark's seventeen testimonies reappear, with five others in addition. Of these, two come from the same quarry as Mark's (Zechariah and the Psalms of the Righteous Sufferer), one, perhaps, from Daniel, and one, apparently, from Jeremiah's prophecy of the New Covenant. All in all, the Matthaean Passion narrative may be said to be supported by the same scaffolding as Mark's, and it implies the same understanding of the sufferings and death of Christ. The phenomena would be entirely consistent with the usual view that the First Gospel, and in particular its Passion narrative, is a revised and expanded version of Mark.

With Luke and John the case is different. To take Luke first, of Mark's seventeen testimonies he has only four, but he adds six non-Marcan ones. Of these, one (from the Jeremianic prophecy of the New Covenant) is absent from many MSS. Of the other five, one is from Hosea, and this differs from other references to the Old Testament in that it is not regarded as fulfilled in the passion and death of Jesus, but remains a forecast for the future. It has therefore no direct significance for the interpretation of the story. The remaining four are taken from the same parts of the Old Testament as most of Mark's—the Psalms of the Righteous

Sufferer and the deutero-Isaianic prophecies of the Suffering Servant. How are these phenomena to be accounted for? Upon the assumption that Luke is dependent on Mark, it might be possible to explain his omission of some of the Marcan testimonies on the ground that he is somewhat less addicted to quotation from the Old Testament than are Mark and Matthew;[1] but why, having cut down Mark's list, has he then added fresh testimonies which do not occur in Mark? And why, if he did not wish to reproduce Mark's list, did he, while rejecting some of his testimonies, substitute others drawn from the *same* parts of scripture, and carrying the *same* implications for the understanding of the passion and death of Jesus? The answer is not obvious, if we suppose Luke to be doing no more than 'edit' Mark. But considering the importance which the *testimonia*, as evidence of the 'settled plan and purpose of God', and its fulfilment in the sufferings of Christ, manifestly had for the shaping of the Passion narrative from the first, we should not be rash in concluding that Luke was probably acquainted with an account formed independently of Mark, supported by a different set of testimonies, and representing another variant of the common tradition.

I now turn to the Fourth Gospel. Of Mark's seventeen testimonies John has only four. To these he has added four (which might be reckoned as five) non-Marcan ones. As with Luke, we could readily understand that this evangelist, who is certainly less addicted to Old Testament quotation than the others,[2] may have preferred to reduce the number, but it is less easy to see why, in that case, he should have added fresh testimonies— unless, indeed, they are such as to give a different theological turn to the narrative; but, as we shall see, they do nothing of the kind. But it will be well to examine his whole list of eight (or nine) *testimonia*, one by one.

(1) xiii. 18: ὁ τρώγων μου τὸν ἄρτον ἐπῆρεν ἐπ᾽ ἐμὲ τὴν πτέρναν αὐτοῦ

This is a non-septuagintal version of Ps. xl (xli). 10, where the M.T. reads, אוֹכֵל לַחְמִי הִגְדִּיל עָלַי עָקֵב. Mark xiv. 18 refers to the same passage, citing only the words, ὁ ἐσθίων μετ᾽ ἐμοῦ. These words are woven by Mark into the fabric of his narrative, without express formula of quotation, but the natural presumption is that he knew the passage in a version

---

[1] In the Bible Society's text (1958) 53 passages are printed as quotations in the 64 pages of Mark (excluding xvi. 9–20), 58 in the 111 pages of Luke (excluding chs. i–ii, parts of which are a virtual cento of O.T. material).

[2] In the Bible Society's text (1958) twenty passages are printed as quotations, in strong contrast with the other gospels. It is all the more remarkable that in the Passion narrative there are four (or five) quotations found in no other gospel.

similar to, or identical with, the LXX: ὁ ἐσθίων ἄρτους μου ἐμεγάλυνεν ἐπ' ἐμὲ πτερνισμόν. John, on the other hand, introduces his citation with the formula, ἵνα ἡ γραφὴ πληρωθῇ, and while Mark has cited only just enough to suggest the passage to the mind of his reader, John has quoted the whole sentence. Where Mark, with the LXX, uses the verb ἐσθίειν, John uses the more 'vulgar' τρώγειν. This may be due to a certain pre-dilection for this verb, which occurs five times in the Fourth Gospel, as against a single occurrence in the Synoptics (Matt. xxiv. 38, for Luke's ἐσθίειν, xvii. 27). John never uses ἐσθίειν,[1] which the others use freely. The other variations from the LXX cannot be explained simply as matters of individual style. John uses the singular ἄρτον, with the M.T., where the LXX gives the plural ἄρτους (legitimately enough: לֶחֶם has no plural, the singular being used collectively). Further, his rendering of הִגְדִּיל עָקֵב, ἐπῆρεν τὴν πτέρναν, is at any rate clear in sense, as well as reasonably close to the Hebrew, even though a Greek reader might find the phrase a little odd; whereas the LXX rendering ἐμεγάλυνεν πτερνισμόν is crude 'translation Greek' and barely intelligible. Either the evangelist has gone to the original and translated for himself, or he has had recourse to a non-septuagintal version.[2] If John is here dependent on Mark, we must suppose that having recognized the words ὁ ἐσθίων μετ' ἐμοῦ as a loose citation of Ps. xl (xli). 10, he looked up the passage, either in the original, trans-lating for himself, or in a non-septuagintal version, in order to give the citation in a complete form. Possible, no doubt, but not very likely. The simpler explanation would be that he received the *testimonium* already embedded in a tradition independent of Mark's.

(2) xiii. 21: ἐταράχθη τῷ πνεύματι

This is not given expressly as a quotation, but it seems to echo the language of Ps. xli (xlii). 7, ἡ ψυχή μου ἐταράχθη, with πνεῦμα for נֶפֶשׁ where the LXX has ψυχή. That the evangelist regarded the passage as a *testimonium* becomes highly probable when we observe that it is echoed again in xii. 27, νῦν ἡ ψυχή μου τετάρακται.[3] Mark does not cite, or refer

---

[1] He uses φαγεῖν, but although in grammars this is conventionally given as the aorist of ἐσθίειν they are of course different verbs. In John φαγεῖν serves rather as the aorist of τρώγειν, as βεβρωκέναι serves as perfect (vi. 14).

[2] Possibly akin to Aquila or Theodotion, both of which have πτέρναν, not πτερνισμόν.

[3] John seems prepared to use ψυχή or πνεῦμα indifferently as an equivalent for נֶפֶשׁ. In xiv. 1, καρδία is used with ταράσσειν, without difference of sense (cf. Ps. xxxvii. 11, ἡ καρδία μου ἐταράχθη).

to, this passage, but in xiv. 34, at a point in the narrative almost corresponding to John xiii. 21, he has περίλυπός ἐστιν ἡ ψυχή μου, which follows fairly closely the LXX of Ps. xli (xlii). 6, ἵνα τί περίλυπος εἶ ἡ ψυχή; (repeated in xli. 12, xlii. 5). If John is borrowing from Mark, why did he reject Mark's quotation from Ps. xli. 6, only to substitute a quotation from the verse immediately following, with no great difference of meaning? It would be an odd way of composing. If however Ps. xli was understood from an early period as depicting the sufferings of Christ and his confidence in the Father,[1] then it would be in no way surprising if one branch of the tradition cited one verse, and one another, as a pointer to the whole.

(3) xv. 25: ἐμίσησάν με δωρεάν

This is expressly introduced as a quotation, in the words, ἵνα πληρωθῇ ὁ λόγος ὁ ἐν τῷ νόμῳ αὐτῶν γεγραμμένος, the term νόμος being used in its extended sense, meaning the Old Testament as a whole,[2] for the quotation clearly comes either from Ps. xxxiv. 19 or from Ps. lxviii. 5, both of which have the identical phrase, οἱ μισοῦντές με δωρεάν. No other evangelist has cited this particular phrase, but both psalms are of the type laid under contribution for testimonies. Ps. lxviii. 10a, ὁ ζῆλος τοῦ οἴκου σου καταφάγεταί με, is cited in John ii. 17 (under the rubric γέγραπται). Ps. lxviii. 10b, οἱ ὀνειδισμοὶ τῶν ὀνειδιζόντων σε ἐπέπεσαν ἐπ᾽ ἐμέ, is cited in Rom. xv. 3. Ps. lxviii. 22a, ἔδωκαν εἰς τὸ βρῶμά μου χολήν, is echoed in Matt. xxvii. 34; and 22b, ἐπότισάν με ὄξος, in Mark xv. 36 and John xix. 29. Ps. lxviii. 26 is quoted at length, under the rubric, γέγραπται ἐν βίβλῳ ψαλμῶν, in Acts i. 20. This psalm therefore is firmly established as a source of testimonies.[3] The other psalm, xxxiv, has not been exploited to the same extent, but the language of verse 11, ἀναστάντες μάρτυρες ἄδικοι, and of verse 16, ἐξεμυκτήρισάν με μυκτηρισμόν, is echoed in the course of the Passion narrative: Mark xiv. 57, ἀναστάντες ἐψευδομαρτύρουν κατ᾽ αὐτοῦ, and Luke xxiii. 35, ἐξεμυκτήριζον οἱ ἄρχοντες (though this comes more directly from Ps. xxi. 7). The psalm is certainly in the vein of the 'Passion' psalms, and it was probably in the minds of those who shaped the tradition,[4] but John's quotation is more likely to be drawn from Ps. lxviii. In any case we note that where he cannot be suspected of any

[1] For a further notice of this psalm, see below, pp. 42, 53, 69–71.
[2] Cf. Rom. iii. 10–18, and see my book *The Bible and the Greeks*, pp. 35–6.
[3] See also *According to the Scriptures*, pp. 57–9.
[4] Upon this psalm see further below, p. 76.

possible dependence on the other gospels he still draws testimonies from their traditional sources.

(4) xix. 1, 3: τότε ἔλαβεν ὁ Πειλᾶτος τὸν Ἰησοῦν καὶ ἐμαστίγωσεν, καὶ οἱ στρατιῶται...ἐδίδοσαν αὐτῷ ῥαπίσματα (cf. also xviii. 22, ἔδωκεν ῥάπισμα τῷ Ἰησοῦ)

There is here no express quotation, but the language is coloured by reminiscences of Isa. l. 6, understood as referring to the Servant of the Lord.[1] The significance of these reminiscences will appear if we have before us the whole verse in Isaiah, and observe how it is echoed in various passages of all four gospels referring to the Passion. The prophet, speaking in the person of the Servant, writes: τὸν νῶτόν μου ἔδωκα εἰς μάστιγας τὰς δὲ σιαγόνας μου εἰς ῥαπίσματα,[2] τὸ δὲ πρόσωπόν μου οὐκ ἀπέστρεψα ἀπὸ αἰσχύνης ἐμπτυσμάτων. There are here three forms of torture or degradation which the Servant must suffer. All appear in one form or another in the Passion narrative:

μάστιγες: John xix. 1; Mark x. 34 (in forecast of the Passion); Matt. xx. 19 (in forecast); Luke xviii. 33 (in forecast).

ῥαπίσματα:[3] John xviii. 22, xix. 3; Mark xiv. 65 (cf. Matt. xxvi. 67 (ῥαπίζειν)).

ἐμπτύσματα (ἐμπτύειν): Mark xiv. 65, xv. 19, x. 34 (in forecast); Matt. xxvi. 67; Luke xviii. 32 (in forecast).

In view of the importance of the prophecies of the Suffering Servant in relation to the sufferings of Christ all through the New Testament,[4] we

---

[1] Isa. l. 4–9 is identified by modern critics as the third of the 'Servant Songs' (though we are not to suppose that early Christian readers distinguished these 'songs' from their context). It has not been so freely exploited for *testimonia* as other Servant passages; but l. 7, ἔθηκα τὸ πρόσωπόν μου ὡς στερεὰν πέτραν, may be echoed in Luke ix. 51, τὸ πρόσωπον ἐστήρισεν τοῦ πορεύεσθαι εἰς Ἱερουσαλήμ, since this is for Luke the first step towards the Passion. Again, the language of John xi. 10, xii. 35–6 may well be coloured by reminiscences of Isa. l. 10, οἱ πορευόμενοι ἐν σκότει καὶ οὐκ ἔστιν αὐτοῖς φῶς, and even John v. 25, ἀκούσουσιν τῆς φωνῆς τοῦ υἱοῦ τοῦ θεοῦ (cf. x. 16, xviii. 37) reminds us of Isa. l. 10, ὑπακουσάτω τῆς φωνῆς τοῦ παιδὸς αὐτοῦ. The passage probably entered deeply into Christian thought at a very early stage.

[2] ῥαπίσματα is not a true translation of M.T. מֹרְטִים. The word is not found elsewhere in the LXX. The Isaiah scroll has מטלים, which means 'beaters'.

[3] ῥάπισμα does not occur in the N.T. outside these Passion contexts—which supports the view that the evangelists owe it to the traditional use of Isa. l. 6 as a testimony. Matt. v. 39 has the verb: ὅστις σε ῥαπίζει εἰς τὴν δεξιὰν σιαγόνα σου, στρέψον αὐτῷ καὶ τὴν ἄλλην. In view of the threefold echo—ῥαπίζει, σιαγόνα, στρέψον—does not this mean, 'Follow the example of the Servant', i.e. of Christ? Cf. Mark x. 45, where the argument is: Jesus fulfils in his own action what the prophet said of the Servant; his disciples must do likewise.

[4] See *According to the Scriptures*, pp. 88–96.

need not hesitate to conclude that all the evangelists found Isa. l. 6 associated with the tradition of the Passion which came down to them. Of the three significant terms Mark and Matthew have all three, Luke has μάστιγες and ἐμπτύσματα, John has μάστιγες and ῥαπίσματα. Moreover, they are introduced at different points. There is therefore no strong reason to suppose that their occurrence in John is due to borrowing from the other gospels. They may be supposed to have entered into variant forms of the common tradition in different ways.

(5) xix. 24: διεμερίσαντο τὰ ἱμάτιά μου ἑαυτοῖς καὶ ἐπὶ τὸν ἱματισμόν μου ἔβαλον κλῆρον

This is a word-for-word quotation of the LXX of Ps. xxi. 19. In the Synoptic Gospels the language of the psalm is woven into the fabric of the narrative, naturally in less exact correspondence with the LXX, but without any reason to suspect the use of any other version. In John the incident itself is described in terms which do not echo the language of the psalm, and the *testimonium* is appended under the rubric, ἵνα ἡ γραφὴ πληρωθῇ. It is possible that John (if he was using Mark as a source) recognized the language of the Old Testament and looked up the passage in the LXX in order to give it in a complete form. But I do not think this procedure very probable. There is every reason to think that this psalm (which has yielded perhaps more testimonies than any other comparable scripture except Isa. lii. 13–liii. 13) was from the earliest days the great stand-by of Christian thinkers and teachers seeking an understanding of the sufferings and death of Christ,[1] and such portions of it as seemed particularly apposite entered deeply into the traditional account of the Passion. There were two ways in which it could thus enter. The language of the Old Testament might be absorbed into the narrative, or the story might be told without any Old Testament colouring, and the passage associated with it in Christian teaching might then be adduced as a *testimonium*. Mark (xiv. 18), as we have seen, has adopted the former method with Ps. xl. 10, while John (xiii. 18) has adopted the latter.[2] Since he was there working on a different Greek version, it is improbable that he was indebted to Mark. In our present passage there is no reason to suppose that they were using different versions, but it seems nevertheless probable that the difference of treatment goes back to different forms of tradition. In any case, the story, although its language is quite free from Old

---

[1] See *According to the Scriptures*, pp. 97–8.
[2] See above, pp. 36–7.

Testament influence, is told in obvious dependence on the passage quoted; for the two clauses of Ps. xxi. 19, which are in fact parallel, are here taken as referring to two separate stages in the division of the garments, and the story is told accordingly.[1] Whether this is to be attributed to the evangelist himself, or whether it is a feature in the development of the traditional use of testimonies, it is impossible to say. It does not serve the purposes of Johannine theology, but it is very much in the evangelist's vein of dramatic narrative.

(6) xix. 28–9: ἵνα τελειωθῇ γραφὴ λέγει, Διψῶ. σκεῦος ἔκειτο ὄξους μεστόν· σπόγγον οὖν μεστὸν τοῦ ὄξους ὑσσ[ωπ]ῷ περιθέντες προσήνεγκαν αὐτοῦ τῷ στόματι. ὅτε οὖν ἔλαβεν τὸ ὄξος ὁ Ἰησοῦς εἶπεν, Τετέλεσται, καὶ κλίνας τὴν κεφαλὴν παρέδωκεν τὸ πνεῦμα

The formula, ἵνα τελειωθῇ ἡ γραφή, makes it clear that John is referring to the Old Testament, and the following mention of ὄξος pins down the reference to Ps. lxviii. 22, εἰς τὴν δίψαν μου ἐπότισάν με ὄξος. In Mark xv. 36 the language of this psalm is woven into the narrative (after Mark's custom) without express citation: γεμίσας σπόγγον ὄξους περιθεὶς καλάμῳ ἐπότιζεν αὐτόν. Mark however says nothing of thirst. The offer of ὄξος is a response to the cry of derelicition, misunderstood as an appeal to Elijah. John, it appears, has found a double fulfilment of prophecy: not only the offer of ὄξος, but the thirst which it was designed to assuage, is a trait proper to the picture of Jesus as the Righteous Sufferer.[2]

Here a plausible case could be made out for the dependence of John on Mark. The coincidence in the use of the words σπόγγος and περιθεῖναι, neither of which comes out of the Old Testament passage, cannot be said to be inevitable if the story was to be told at all. There are signs of the influence of Johannine theology in the context. If John was acquainted with the cry of derelicition he may well have wished to avoid it for

---

[1] Similarly Matthew (xxi. 5–7) has taken the ὄνος and the πῶλος in (his version of) Zech. ix. 9 to be two separate animals, instead of parallel descriptions of the same beast. John (xii. 14–15) takes no account of the parallelism, and has only one beast, which he describes (in his own language uninfluenced by the O.T.) as ὀνάριον. It looks as if this exploitation of the verbal form of Old Testament passages belonged to a secondary stage of the study of testimonies rather than to the idiosyncrasy of one writer or another. See below, pp. 122–3. For an illuminating study of secondary stages in the exploitation of *testimonia* see B. Lindars, *New Testament Apologetic* (S.C.M. Press, 1961).
[2] On this passage see further below, p. 123.

dogmatic reasons.[1] The cry which he has substituted, τετέλεσται, contains an idea essential to his theology. The emphasis laid upon actual thirst and the actual drinking of the ὄξος[2] would fit in with the evangelist's obvious intention to admit no questioning of the real humanity of Christ.[3] John may therefore be thought to have worked upon Mark as a basis, looking up in the Old Testament the passage to which Mark referred, and completing it. On the other hand, we may note that there was no *necessity* for John to learn from Mark the use of this passage as a testimony. Ps. lxviii was clearly one of the recognized quarries for testimonies. John himself has cited two passages from it (verses 5 and 10a) which are not cited by any other New Testament writer. If it be considered probable (as I have argued) that these two testimonies had entered into the tradition which our evangelist followed, that tradition may well have transmitted also verse 22, and transmitted it primarily as a testimony to the thirst and only secondarily to the ὄξος. Here we find strong ground for believing that John has not copied from Mark. The two writers do indeed quote from the same verse of scripture, but they quote in such a way as to lay the stress differently, showing that their interest in the passage is by no means the same. 'Thirst' plays no essential part in Mark's conception of the sufferings of God's Servant; in John's conception it is vital. The difference reaches back to the stage at which the Passion tradition was being shaped by motives drawn from scripture.

(7) xix. 36: ὀστοῦν οὐ συντριβήσεται αὐτοῦ

This is introduced with the formula, ἵνα ἡ γραφὴ πληρωθῇ. It is however not entirely clear what passage of the Old Testament is intended.

[1] That he was unacquainted with it is unlikely, since Ps. xxi, from which it is drawn, is a classical source of testimonies, and John has used it as such, whether directly or after Mark. It is perhaps worth noting that there is another psalm, beside lxviii, which speaks of the 'thirst' of the Righteous Sufferer, and a psalm which was certainly drawn upon by John or by the tradition which he followed: Ps. xli. 3, ἐδίψησεν ἡ ψυχή μου πρὸς τὸν θεὸν τὸν ζῶντα. In this psalm there is the same sense of the absence of God as in xxi. 2, though it is expressed with less intensity. Is the 'thirst' of the Crucified in some sort an equivalent (symbolically) of the cry of dereliction?

[2] The LXX ἐπότισαν (aorist) certainly implies that the Sufferer drank the ὄξος. Mark's ἐπότιζεν (imperfect) does not. It might mean 'tried to get him to drink'. Nor is it clear that Mark intends the reader to understand that Jesus did in fact drink it. It is clear that John does.

[3] As in iv. 6, xi. 35. The evangelist would in any case not be unconscious of the tragic irony of the cry διψῶ from one who had offered to men the drink that satisfies all thirst for ever (iv. 14). But that is not to say that he would have introduced this

The following are the two possible passages:

(a) Exod. xii. 46: ὀστοῦν οὐ συντρίψετε ἀπ' αὐτοῦ (or its parallel, Num. ix. 12: ὀστοῦν οὐ συντρίψουσιν ἀπ' αὐτοῦ).

(b) Ps. xxxiii (xxxiv). 21: Κύριος φυλάσσει πάντα τὰ ὀστᾶ αὐτῶν, ἓν ἐξ αὐτῶν οὐ συντριβήσεται.

Neither passage is exactly reproduced. John is nearer to Ps. xxxiii. 21 than to either of the pentateuchal passages in that the passive of the verb is used, and that the sentence is a prediction or promise, whereas in Exodus and Numbers it is an injunction. On the other hand the pronoun is singular in Exodus and Numbers, as in John, plural in the psalm. Further, Ps. xxxiii. 21 contains poetical parallelism, which is absent both from John and from the pentateuchal passages. John, however, is quite capable of ignoring parallelism in quoting from the Old Testament.

The usual view is that John intends an allusion to the paschal ritual, pointing to Christ as the true Paschal Lamb, as he is supposed to do also in i. 29, 36. In that case we must suppose him to mean that the executioners (unconsciously) observed the liturgical order for Passover. The death of Christ is thus to be understood as that of the Paschal Victim. I have argued elsewhere[1] that it is doubtful whether the ἀμνὸς τοῦ θεοῦ of i. 29, 36 is, in the evangelist's intention, the Paschal Lamb, and doubtful whether paschal symbolism played any part, or any but a minor one, in his thought. His distinctive interpretation of the death of Christ moves on quite other lines. No doubt paschal ideas may have been present in the tradition he received, and it may have embodied this *testimonium* in that sense, though he has not developed such ideas. But if this quotation be supposed to come from the Pentateuch it falls outside the series of Passion-testimonies cited in this gospel, all the rest of which are drawn either from the psalms of the Righteous Sufferer, or from the Isaianic prophecy of the Suffering Servant (who is almost a *Doppelgänger* of the Righteous Sufferer of the psalms), or from the part of Zechariah which can be shown to belong to the primitive group of testimony-scriptures. It is an erratic block, unique of its kind.

Ps. xxxiii, on the other hand, is closely akin to the psalms of the Righteous Sufferer. It is a hymn of praise to God for delivering the 'righteous' (plural) or his 'servants' out of all their troubles. Yet, although the plural is used, the psalmist speaks in the first person singular,

---

trait into the story without authority. For him the thirst is guaranteed by prophecy, as incorporated in the tradition he had received.

[1] *Interpretation*, pp. 230–8.

or as οὗτος ὁ πτωχός. Among God's righteous servants, he is *the* Righteous Servant (or so it might be read). The psalm is frequently quoted, or referred to, in the New Testament. Verses 9, 13–17b are quoted at length in 1 Pet. ii. 3, iii. 10–12; verse 11, πλούσιοι ἐπτώχευσαν καὶ ἐπείνασαν, would seem to underlie the 'woes' of Luke vi. 24–5; the κύριος ἐγγύς of verse 19 finds an echo in Phil. iv. 5; the promise of 'redemption' in the concluding verse links up readily with early Christian ideas. It does not, however, appear that any passage from this psalm (unless the one now under discussion) is actually employed as a testimony to the Passion. Yet, in view of the rabbinic interpretation which found in the verse we are now discussing a promise of the resurrection of the body,[1] it might well suggest to a Christian reader familiar with rabbinic exegesis a promise of the resurrection of Christ, as the Righteous Sufferer. So understood, it would readily fit into the series of testimonies which John has adduced. It seems on the whole more probable that the quotation is taken from Ps. xxxiii. 21 than that in this one place the evangelist has had recourse to a part of the Old Testament in which he has given no certain evidence of interest, and which is not otherwise employed as a source for testimonies to the Passion of Christ.

In either case, this quotation is certainly not drawn from any of the other gospels. If the view be taken that the Fourth Evangelist himself was interested in paschal symbolism, then this alone among the testimonies he adduces may be his own contribution. If, as I hold more probable, it falls into the series of testimonies drawn from the psalms of the Righteous Sufferer, then we may take it to have been a feature of the tradition he followed.

(8) xix. 36: ὄψονται εἰς ὃν ἐξεκέντησαν

This is introduced as ἑτέρα γραφή. It is clearly a quotation of Zech. xii. 10 in a translation differing from the LXX, which reads, ἐπιβλέψονται πρός με ἀνθ' ὧν κατωρχήσαντο.[2] The M.T. reads, הִבִּיטוּ אֵלַי אֵת אֲשֶׁר־דָּקָרוּ. The LXX has rightly preserved the first personal pronoun, and ἐπιβλέψονται is perhaps a more forcible rendering of הִבִּיטוּ; but otherwise it represents an inferior reading of the Hebrew text, with רקדו for דקרו by metathesis. Either the evangelist is translating for himself, from

---

[1] See p. 132 n. 2.
[2] The LXX rendering is presumably intended to mean 'they shall gaze upon me because they had performed a dance of triumph', but as Greek it is intolerably harsh, and perilously near nonsense.

a better text than that which underlies the LXX, or he is using a non-septuagintal version. The same rendering is presupposed in the text of Rev. i. 7: ἰδοὺ ἔρχεται μετὰ τῶν νεφελῶν καὶ ὄψεται αὐτὸν πᾶς ὀφθαλμὸς καὶ οἵτινες αὐτὸν ἐξεκέντησαν, καὶ κόψονται ἐπ' αὐτὸν πᾶσαι αἱ φυλαὶ τῆς γῆς. Those who find themselves able to believe that the evangelist wrote the Apocalypse will find it natural that he should use his own translation. Those for whom this is a feat of credulity beyond their powers will see here presumptive evidence of an alternative version of the prophecy of Zechariah,[1] akin to the later versions of Theodotion and Aquila, both of whom give ἐξεκέντησαν for דקרו.

That John does not owe this testimony to any of the other gospels is manifest. It might be suggested that the citation is due to the influence of Johannine theological conceptions, in view of the evident intention to exploit the symbolism of 'blood and water'. But it is to be observed that the piercing of the side has in itself no theological significance for the evangelist; it is the issue of blood and water that is symbolical, and for this the evangelist does not cite any scriptural testimony.[2] The possibility cannot be excluded, at this stage, that the incident of the piercing of the side came into the narrative out of the prophecy, but if so, the motive would not be one arising out of the distinctive theology of the evangelist, but one common to all evangelists—the desire to interpret the sufferings and death of Jesus out of the mysterious 'messianic' prophecies of Zechariah.[3] There is consequently no adequate ground for excluding this *testimonium* from the series which appears to be derived from pre-canonical tradition, and in this case a tradition independent of that which lies behind the Synoptic Gospels.

From this study of the Johannine *testimonia* I should draw the following conclusions:

(i) The phenomena of Old Testament citation and allusion, so far as they go, lend no support to the view that John used Mark as the basis for his Passion narrative. There are only two cases (those numbered (5) and (6b)) where it is in any degree plausible to suppose that John found an allusion to the Old Testament in Mark and went on to complete the

---

[1] If the works are by different authors, the widely different treatment of the passage makes it unlikely that one borrowed it from the other. A common use of a non-septuagintal version is more probable.

[2] See further below, pp. 132–3.

[3] For the importance of Zech. ix–xiv as a source of *testimonia*, see *According to the Scriptures*, pp. 64–7.

quotation out of the same context, and in (6b) at any rate the degree of plausibility is very low. In (1), where the two evangelists make use of the same passage in the Old Testament, John's treatment of it is difficult to understand on the assumption that he was working with Mark as a basis. In at least four cases there is no Marcan parallel at all. If it be true that *testimonia* were an influential factor in giving form to the tradition of the Passion, the fact that Mark and John have so few testimonies in common, and that where they have such their treatment is in most cases so different, suggests that each was following a tradition formed independently, though based upon the same group of scriptures.

(ii) There is no evidence to suggest that the selection or application of testimonies was dictated by distinctively Johannine theological considerations (with one possible exception which I do not admit); and consequently no evidence that this was the work of the evangelist himself, although of course there is (so far) no positive evidence that it was not.

(iii) As compared with Mark, John shows a tendency to adduce *testimonia* with a formula of quotation, instead of weaving them into the text of his narrative. Occasionally also he shows a probable tendency to elaborate the narrative in order to emphasize the exactness of fulfilment. Unlike Mark he tends to prefer a non-septuagintal version.[1] There is only one case where he follows the LXX with any conspicuous exactness, and there are two cases where he has a markedly different, and on the whole a better, rendering, one of them being a case where Mark appears to have followed the LXX.

(iv) The Johannine testimonies are all, with one possible exception (which I do not myself admit), drawn from the same portions of the Old Testament as those employed by the other evangelists. Since the use of testimonies was designed from the first to provide a key out of scripture (which reveals the 'settled plan and purpose of God') to the meaning and purpose of the sufferings and death of Christ, we must say that the Johannine body of testimonies provides the *same* key as the other forms

---

[1] In the Fourth Gospel outside the Passion narrative the only citations common to John and the Synoptics are those in i. 23, xii. 13, 15, 40. Of these, xii. 13 is similar to Mark, and probably represents a liturgical adaptation of the LXX (see below, p. 154) where Matthew and Luke diverge more widely; i. 23 may be from a non-septuagintal version or may be freely after the LXX, and in any case is different from the other gospels (see below, p. 252); xii. 15, 40, are widely different both from the LXX and from the other gospels. John's other quotations, where there is no Synoptic parallel, ii. 17, x. 34, xii. 38, follow the LXX closely, vi. 31 somewhat less closely, but without any ground for assuming a different version.

of Passion narrative. They do not reflect the interpretation which is peculiar to the Fourth Gospel. For this interpretation he has provided no testimonies out of scripture. That is to say, there is embodded in the Passion narrative of the Fourth Gospel an understanding of the Passion in terms of the Righteous Sufferer of the Psalms, the Suffering Servant of deutero-Isaiah, and the martyred leader of Zechariah, which we have every reason to believe primitive, and which John may fairly be supposed to owe to pre-canonical tradition.

At this point a question arises upon which something should be said here. What is the bearing of the use of 'testimonies' from the Old Testament upon the historical value of the gospel narratives? Since it appears that references to prophecy have had an important influence on the shaping of those narratives, and in particular of the Passion narrative, are we to say that any given story may represent nothing more than the conviction of the evangelist (or of those who formed and handed on the traditions upon which he worked), that so it *must* have happened *because* there was a prophecy requiring fulfilment? It seems pretty clear that in some cases a datum of the narrative has been elaborated, perhaps without justification, in order to dot the i's and cross the t's of the fulfilment. For example, we have noted that John appears to have separated the division of the garments into two stages to fit the duplicate form of expression in Ps. xxi. 19, although this duplication is no more than an instance of Hebrew parallelism; and similarly Matthew has taken the parallelism in Zech. ix. 9 as implying two beasts, an ass and a colt, and has shaped his narrative accordingly. There are other places where critics have suspected, not unreasonably, that an entire incident may have been produced out of a postulated fulfilment of prophecy. Most critics, I suppose, have taken this view of Matthew's report of the flight into Egypt, attested by a citation of Hos. xi. 1.[1]

There are, however, reasons for thinking that the scale on which this motive has acted upon the tradition is strictly limited. If we survey the body of Old Testament scriptures which have afforded testimonies it is clear that a selective process has been at work. By no means *all* prophecy that was, or could be, regarded as 'messianic' is exploited by writers of the New Testament. On the contrary, the range of scripture which can be proved to have been so used in the earliest period is practically limited to certain well-defined groups of passages.[2] As I have pointed out elsewhere,[3]

[1] But see *According to the Scriptures*, p. 103.
[2] See *According to the Scriptures*, ch. III.   [3] *History and the Gospel*, pp. 59–63.

47

large sections of 'messianic' prediction—including not only those which belong to the so-called 'apocalyptic' conception of messiahship, but also all those passages which present the Messiah as earthly ruler, warrior and judge—are absent from the picture of Jesus in the gospels. These traits are either ignored or relegated to prophecies of the future.

Not only so, even within those passages which are used as sources for testimonies not *every* detail is alleged to have been fulfilled. Thus, in Ps. xxi the Church found depicted in anticipation the rejection of Jesus as ἐξουδένημα λαοῦ (verse 7), the division of his garments among his enemies (verse 19), the mockery of those who beheld his sufferings, their bitter sarcasms as they 'wagged their heads' (verses 8–9), and his last cry of dereliction (verse 2). But the same psalm speaks of the Sufferer as beset by bulls, lions and dogs (verses 13, 17, 22). Yet we have in the gospels no 'ideal scene' in which Jesus is exposed to wild beasts, like his followers Ignatius and Perpetua. It speaks of his being threatened by the sword (verse 21); but the only sword drawn in the Passion narrative is drawn in defence of Jesus. Again, in Ps. lxviii the Church recognized a description of the causeless hatred with which Jesus was pursued (verse 5), of the fatal consequences of his zeal for the temple (verse 10), and of his thirst on the cross and the drink that was offered to assuage it (verse 22). But in the same psalm the Sufferer is in danger of drowning (verse 3); yet although the gospels give us two scenes of storms at sea, neither of these has for motive the peril in which Jesus stood.[1] To take another example (not from testimonies to the Passion), in the prophecy of Isa. xi. 1–9 the Church welcomed the description of the Messiah as born from the root of Jesse (Rom. xv. 12; Rev. v. 5, xxii. 16), which they found fulfilled in the claim of the family of Jesus to Davidic descent; and the prediction, 'the Spirit of the Lord shall rest upon him', in its context, seemed to them to indicate the true significance of the experience ascribed to Jesus at his baptism. Yet the supposed mythopoeic genius of primitive Christianity missed the opportunity to construct an 'ideal scene' in which Jesus should fulfil another part of the same prophecy—'with the breath of his lips shall he slay the wicked'[2]—although stories of the deadly effect of the

---

[1] In Mark iv. 37–41, vi. 47–51, and the parallel passages the motive is suggested by such scriptures as Ps. cvi. 29, lxxvi. 17–20, etc., and not by prophecies of the Righteous Sufferer. It is not Jesus but his disciples who are in peril or fear (cf. Matt. xiv. 30, (Πέτρος) ἀρξάμενος καταποντίζεσθαι ἔκραξεν, with Ps. lxviii. 3–4, καταιγὶς κατεπόντιζέν με, ἐκοπίασα κράζων).

[2] It has been suggested that some such idea lies behind John xviii. 6, but on this see pp. 76–7.

words of Peter (Acts v. 1–11) and Paul (Acts xiii. 9–11) suggest the lines on which such a construction might have proceeded. Instead, the fulfilment of this scripture is postponed until the final advent of Christ in the future (2 Thess. ii. 8). Here, as elsewhere, the development of a Christian 'futurist' eschatology has provided a repository for elements in prophecy which could not be incorporated in the account of the historical ministry of Jesus, and yet could find a place (at least as symbolically interpreted) in the total theological picture.

Without further multiplication of examples it is surely clear that the selection of passages of scripture for use as testimonies has been controlled by some canon. Shall we say it is a theological canon? Are those prophecies alone cited which conform to the theological conceptions of the early Church, so that the incidents in which fulfilment of prophecy is alleged lie under suspicion of having been created out of the prophecies? Certainly there is a close relation between the testimonies and the earliest formulation of Christian theology; but the theology depended on the testimonies and not *vice versa*. It was not to provide documentation for a previously formulated theology that the early Church searched the scriptures; it was to find an explanation for attested facts, many of which appeared to run counter to their inherited beliefs and even counter to the scriptures as they were currently understood. The facts themselves exerted pressure upon their understanding of prophecy and fulfilment, and dictated the selection of testimonies. Thus the extent to which the element of fulfilled prophecy has stimulated a legend-making tendency in primitive Christianity is strictly limited. Fundamentally, the framers of the tradition were in bondage to facts, although here and there they strained at their bonds. The important thing for our present purpose is this: where the narrative is intimately related to testimonies from the Old Testament— at any rate where these are drawn from portions of scripture which can be proved to have been objects of especial interest at an early date—there we may be fairly sure that we are in touch with the common tradition of the Church, and not with the theological construction of some individual. The exceptions are few and scarcely weaken the general rule. The interest which certain facts acquired from their association with specific prophecies fixed these facts in the corporate memory of the Church, and determined their place in the tradition.

3. THE LEAVE-TAKING

The opening scenes of the drama are set forth in Mark as follows:

(1) The preparation for the Supper (Mark xiv. 12–16).

(2) The Supper: prediction of the treachery of Judas (xiv. 18–21).

(3) The Supper (continued): the sacramental words and actions (xiv. 22–5).

(4) Departure for Olivet: prediction of the desertion of the Twelve and of Peter's denial (xiv. 26–31).

This scheme is followed by Matthew, whose language, in spite of occasional abbreviation and occasional expansion, is so close to Mark's as to leave no reasonable doubt that the one depends on the other as a source.

Not so with Luke. In his account of the preparation for the Supper he keeps even closer to Mark than does Matthew. There can be little doubt that Mark is the common source, and there is therefore nothing to suggest that the preparation figured in any other form of tradition. After that, he diverges widely. The sacramental words and actions (Mark's no. 3) follow immediately on the notice of the beginning of the Supper (xxii. 15–20). The situation is here complicated by the existence of variant texts; but whether we adopt the shorter or the longer text, the agreement with Mark is not very close. The liturgical formulae are in part similar to Mark's, in part (if the longer text be read) to those of 1 Cor. xi. 23–5; but agreement in liturgical formulae would in any case be poor evidence of literary dependence. Apart from any verbal agreements or disgreements, Luke's general conception of the sequence of words and actions, and indeed of the scene as a whole, and its significance, seems so different from that which controls the Marcan account that his dependence on Mark as a source at this point is more than doubtful.

After the sacramental words and actions, Luke goes back to the prediction of the treachery of Judas (Mark's no. 2), which he gives in a form widely different from Mark's. After this he inserts a report of dissensions among the Twelve (xxii. 24), leading to a sequence of sayings, in two groups, the first about humility and service (xxii. 25–7), and the second about the association of the Twelve with Christ in his sufferings and his triumph (xxii. 28–30). The first group is parallel with Mark x. 42–5, the second, in part, with Matt. xix. 28; but in each case the differences are so striking that it is hazardous to assume that Luke is directly indebted to

Mark for the first, or to another documentary source, supposed to have been used also by Matthew, for the second.

After this interpolation into the common scheme he returns to the sequence as we have it in Mark, and gives an equivalent for the Marcan predictions of the desertion of the Twelve and Peter's denial (Mark's no. 4). These are introduced at the supper-table instead of on the way to Olivet (xxii. 31–4). The whole conception, however, of these predictions differs from Mark's. For Luke it is a matter of the 'sifting'[1] of the Twelve, in which Peter is involved as one of the company, and Jesus prays that in the course of this 'sifting' his faith may not be 'eclipsed', so that he may later recover himself and support the others. Peter in response (much as in Mark but in different words) declares himself ready to die with his Master, and the forecast of his denial follows, in terms similar to Mark's. It is noteworthy that in the part of the prediction which is nearest to Mark (xxii. 34) the name used is Peter, whereas in the part which has no parallel with Mark it is Simon (xxii. 31).

Here, finally, Luke deserts the Marcan scheme altogether, and inserts a passage (xxii. 35–8) without parallel in the gospels: the dialogue about the 'two swords', introducing a *testimonium* from Isa. liii. 12: μετὰ ἀνόμων ἐλογίσθη. This clearly comes from some non-Marcan source, and one in close relation with the primitive body of testimonies.

Thus we have a long passage, beginning with the words 'When the time came he sat down and the apostles with him' (xxii. 14) and covering the whole of the incidents of the Supper, in which, though it runs roughly

---

[1] The figure of 'sifting' (σινιάζειν, apparently a late form for σήθειν) is not elsewhere found in this connection. The process of sifting is directed towards separating out the valuable parts from a mixed mass. Here, therefore, the meaning would seem to be that Satan is permitted to put the disciples through a test which will separate the faithful from the unfaithful. A similar process, that of winnowing with a πτύον, is employed to separate grain from the chaff, and this is used as a metaphor by John the Baptist in describing the work of the Coming One (Matt. iii. 12; Luke iii. 17). In Amos ix. 9 Israel is to be 'sifted' (the verb used is λικμᾶν, but the Hebrew נוע seems to refer rather to sifting than to winnowing). As this is almost immediately followed by the prophecy ἀναστήσω τὴν σκηνὴν Δαυείδ κ.τ.λ., which is cited as a testimony in Acts xv. 15–16, it is possible that the ordeal of the disciples was understood as the sifting or purging of Israel, in preparation for the restoration of the people of God in the form of the Church. Similarly in Zech. xiii. 8–9 the smiting of the shepherd and the scattering of the sheep are followed immediately by a purge of the people, the metaphor here being the commoner one of the firing of metallic ore. When the purge is complete, ἐρῶ, Λαός μου οὗτός ἐστιν. I cannot help suspecting that an interpretation of scriptures of this kind lies in the background of Luke's special tradition at this point. They have no echo in Mark.

4-2

parallel with Mark, verbal agreements are at a minimum, the order different, and parts of the material without Marcan parallel, and in which there seems to be a recognizable difference of standpoint. All this contrasts strongly with xxii. 7–13, where the agreement with Mark is unusually close. The widely held view that the whole was produced by a process of 'editing' Mark has no plausibility, if once the presumption is abandoned that the Synoptic problem is to be solved completely on the basis of dependence on documentary sources. The probability is that Luke, having followed Mark down to xxii. 13, now turns to another strain of tradition, in which the Passion narrative, while conforming in a general way to the common scheme, was developed on lines distinguishable from Mark's. That this may have been combined with material drawn from Mark remains possible, but the verbal agreements on which such a theory might be founded are scanty, and perhaps no more than might naturally occur even in divergent forms of a common tradition referring to the same events. The question now before us is whether a similar hypothesis might plausibly be held to account for the phenomena of this part of the Johannine narrative.

In the Fourth Gospel this stage of the story is dominated by the great sequence of dialogue and monologue which we call the Farewell Discourses, and which is among the most characteristic, the most original, and the most highly wrought of all the passages in which this evangelist has presented the religious and theological core of his message. Nevertheless, we can discern behind it distinct traces of the scheme we have studied in the Synoptic Gospels. The preparation for the Supper, which, as we have seen, is probably a Marcan feature copied by the others, is absent. Further, there is one striking omission, the sacramental words and actions, and one unparalleled incident, the washing of the feet. But we shall do well to consider first those features which have Synoptic parallels, recognizing that their incorporation into an elaborate structure of dialogue and discourse would in any case impose some inevitable alteration.

The first parallel we note is with Mark's no. 2, the prediction of the treachery of Judas (xiii. 18). This is first announced, in the course of a sequence of sayings which have Synoptic parallels, in the form of a quotation from Ps. xl. 10. This is, so far, deliberately cryptic in the evangelist's manner. The prediction is then made explicit in the course of a short dramatic dialogue, which now follows (21–30), and it is at this point that comparison with the Synoptics becomes worth while.

The passage opens impressively with an allusion to the words of the Righteous Sufferer in Ps. xli. 7: Ἰησοῦς ἐταράχθη τῷ πνεύματι.[1] Then abruptly Jesus turns to the disciples with the words, Ἀμὴν ἀμὴν λέγω ὑμῖν ὅτι εἷς ἐξ ὑμῶν παραδώσει με. Apart from the repetition of the ἀμήν, which is a mannerism, this is identical with the Marcan form of the prediction. Mark proceeds, ὁ ἐσθίων μετ' ἐμοῦ, in allusion to the same verse of Ps. xl which John has quoted above, but in a different translation.[2] Luke's form is quite different, and contains no allusion to the Old Testament: ἰδοὺ ἡ χεὶρ τοῦ παραδιδόντος με μετ' ἐμοῦ ἐπὶ τῆς τραπέζης. So far, therefore, John might well be following Mark, though it must be said that while the Lucan form is oracular and semi-poetical, the form of the saying in Mark and John is the simplest and most matter-of-fact way of conveying the warning, and might well occur in any form of the narrative. John then records the anxious questioning of the disciples: ἔβλεπον εἰς ἀλλήλους οἱ μαθηταὶ ἀπορούμενοι περὶ τίνος λέγει. Similarly (but less dramatically) Luke says, ἤρξαντο συνζητεῖν πρὸς ἑαυτοὺς τὸ τίς ἄρα εἴη ἐξ αὐτῶν ὁ τοῦτο μέλλων πράσσειν. The sense is the same, the wording entirely different. In Mark the question is a different one: ἤρξαντο λυπεῖσθαι καὶ λέγειν αὐτῷ εἷς κατὰ εἷς, Μήτι ἐγώ; In Mark the first thought of each is that he may himself be the traitor. In Luke and John they simply ask who it is to be. In Mark the answer to the question is, εἷς τῶν δώδεκα ὁ ἐμβαπτόμενος μετ' ἐμοῦ εἰς τὸ τρύβλιον. It is however not clear whether this is intended to point to an individual, or whether ὁ ἐμβαπτόμενος μετ' ἐμοῦ is as generic as ὁ ἐσθίων μετ' ἐμοῦ, or as Luke's μετ' ἐμοῦ ἐπὶ τῆς τραπέζης. In John the matter is not left in doubt. The question, περὶ τίνος λέγει (cf. Luke's τίς ἄρα εἴη), is passed by Peter to the beloved disciple, εἰπὲ τίς ἐστιν περὶ οὗ λέγει, and Jesus replies, ἐκεῖνός ἐστιν ᾧ ἐγὼ βάψω τὸ ψωμίον καὶ δώσω αὐτῷ, and then, by giving the ψωμίον to Judas, he identifies him as the traitor. It is not, however, alto-gether clear whether this identification is intended for the whole company, or whether it is a sign given privately to the beloved disciple, who is in the secret. It might well be argued that John, having before him Mark's ἐμβαπτόμενος, has given it a sharper point. Yet the actual verbal echo is slight. The immediate sequel is the possession of the traitor by the power of evil, which is expressed in terms virtually identical with the phrase in Luke's form of the exordium: εἰσῆλθεν εἰς ἐκεῖνον ὁ σατανᾶς.[3]

Mark ends the scene with the solemn 'woe' pronounced on the traitor: οὐαὶ τῷ ἀνθρώπῳ ἐκείνῳ δι' οὗ ὁ υἱὸς τοῦ ἀνθρώπου παραδίδοται · καλὸν

---

[1] See above, pp. 37–8.   [2] See above, pp. 36–7.   [3] See above, pp. 27–8.

αὐτῷ εἰ οὐκ ἐγεννήθη ὁ ἄνθρωπος ἐκεῖνος (words which are echoed almost identically in Matthew and Luke). This is missing in John, scarcely because of any tenderness towards Judas. Indeed, the fearful finality of the concluding words of the *pericopé*, ἐκεῖνος ἐξῆλθεν εὐθύς· ἦν δὲ νύξ, almost amounts to a Johannine equivalent for the doom of Judas in the Synoptics. For νύξ is the absence of light (John xi. 10), and to lack the 'light of life' (viii. 12) is to relapse into the primeval darkness of death and not-being (i. 4). This sombre conclusion is authentically Johannine. How much of the rest—the intervention of the beloved disciple at Peter's instance, the deliberate identification of the traitor by a sign between Jesus and the disciple, as well as the impressive exit of Judas—is to be put down to the evangelist's literary and dramatic skill, it is impossible to say. The question is, whether a narrative which plays so closely about themes common to John and the Synoptics, echoing at one point Mark, at another Luke, sometimes in almost identical words, is to be regarded as a secondary composition based upon a conflation of these two written sources, or whether a third form of oral tradition is the more likely explanation. On the showing of this passage alone the answer to this question is equivocal, but if it appears probable that there was an independent form of tradition which John has sometimes followed, the simpler solution would be that this tradition underlies the present passage, however much the evangelist may have written it up.

After the departure of Judas into the night the conversation at the supper-table takes, from xiii. 31 on, the form of an elaborate sequence of dialogue and monologue in the manner of this evangelist. Whatever he has taken up out of tradition or other sources has been re-minted. We may fairly see here a further stage—an immensely more advanced stage—of the process by which the Passion narrative attracted to itself material not originally part of it, because such material was found, when associated with the remembrance of the death of Christ, both to illuminate the mystery of his Passion and itself to acquire deeper meaning. Such is the material which Luke has grouped together in the setting of the Last Supper. And indeed some of the contents of the Farewell Discourses in the Fourth Gospel recall the themes of the Lucan table-talk, though without echoes of language (cf. John xiv. 3, xv. 18, xvi. 22, with Luke xxii. 28–30a). This does not mean, as I take it, anything like literary dependence; it means that both gospels reflect in greater or less degree a growing customary practice in the Church—a practice in a wide sense liturgical—of grouping certain articles of teaching under the proclamation of Christ's passion and death.

Nevertheless, there are two places in these discourses from which it appears that the evangelist still had before his mind the common scheme of the Passion narrative, one of them near the beginning of the long sequence and the other at the end, namely, xiii. 36–8, the prediction of Peter's denial, and xvi. 32, the prediction of the desertion of the Twelve. As compared with Mark they come in reverse order.

The prediction of Peter's denial is set in a short dialogue which develops naturally enough out of the main discourse. Jesus has announced his approaching departure. Peter asks, 'Where are you going?' Jesus replies, 'Where I am going you cannot follow me at present, though you will follow hereafter'. Peter protests his readiness to follow now, even if it means risking his life; to which Jesus replies with the solemn warning to which the whole passage is leading up. The actual prediction is expressed in similar terms in all Gospels, but most concisely in John.

Mark xiv. 30	Luke xxii. 34	John xiii. 38
ἀμὴν λέγω σοι	λέγω σοι Πέτρε	ἀμὴν ἀμὴν λέγω σοι
ὅτι σὺ σήμερον	οὐ φωνήσει σήμερον	
ταύτῃ τῇ νυκτὶ		
πρὶν ἢ δὶς ἀλέκτορα	ἀλέκτωρ	οὐ μὴ ἀλέκτωρ
φωνῆσαι		φωνήσῃ
τρίς με ἀπαρνήσῃ	ἕως τρίς με ἀπαρνήσῃ	ἕως οὗ ἀρνήσῃ με τρίς
	μὴ εἰδέναι	

The structure is closely similar in John and Luke, different in Mark, while Mark and Luke agree against John in the word σήμερον, and Mark and John against Luke in the words ἀμὴν (ἀμὴν) λέγω σοι. Matthew is virtually identical with Mark except that he omits σήμερον and δίς, agreeing with John in the former omission and with both Luke and John in the latter; for it is Mark alone who has two cockcrows. All this looks less like conflation of sources than the kind of variation which arises without deliberation within an oral tradition.

If we now examine the immediate setting of the prediction, we note that in John and Luke alike it is given in reply to a declaration by Peter of his readiness to die for his Lord, but the wording of his declaration differs totally in the two versions: in Luke xxii. 33 it runs, μετά σου ἕτοιμός εἰμι καὶ εἰς φυλακὴν καὶ εἰς θάνατον πορεύεσθαι, in John xiii. 37, τὴν ψυχήν μου ὑπέρ σου θήσω. In Mark the dialogue takes a different course. It is only *after* the forecast of his denial that Peter declares himself willing to die rather than deny, and in this he is followed by all the rest. His words are, ἐὰν δέῃ με συναποθανεῖν σοι, οὐ μή σε ἀπαρνήσωμαι. Looking to the substance rather than to the wording, we note that in Mark and Luke Peter protests his willingness to share the fate of his Master, in John, his readiness to 'lay down his life' on his Master's behalf, which would naturally imply risking his life to save Jesus from death; and this is, in fact, what John represents him as doing when he draws his sword upon the posse sent to effect the arrest (xviii. 10).

Further, in Mark Peter makes his bold protestation in a spirit of rivalry or competition with the other disciples: εἰ καὶ πάντες σκανδαλισθήσονται ἀλλ' οὐκ ἐγώ. He will prove himself *more* trustworthy than the rest. Jesus warns him that, on the contrary, while all will desert, he will expressly deny. In Luke it is Jesus who singles Peter out: all will be 'sifted', but Peter is to recover and prove a strength to his colleagues. His protestation of unshakable loyalty is thus in some measure prepared for, and carries no flavour of rivalry or egotism. In John the process of the dialogue is more subtle. Jesus has addressed the Twelve in a body, warning them of his approaching departure on a journey where they cannot accompany him. Peter asks (on behalf of all, it may be) the harmless question, 'Where are you going?' It is then that Jesus, changing from the second person plural to the second person singular, repeats ὅπου ὑπάγω οὐ δύνασαί μοι νῦν ἀκολουθῆσαι. Naturally enough, and without any thought of rivalry or even comparison with the others, Peter asks, 'Why not? I would gladly risk my life for you'. The warning comes equally naturally in reply. How much of this is another example of this evangelist's sense of drama, or which of the three accounts is most likely to be true to historical fact, I do not ask. I only draw attention to the fact that the structure of the *pericopé* depends in each gospel on a somewhat different conception of the situation, and no one of them, it seems, could readily be derived from another (except Matthew from Mark). The one sentence which is most nearly invariable is the word of the Lord predicting denial before cockcrow, which is what we should expect, however traditions might diverge, and even here the structure of the sentence is different in Mark and in Luke–John.

Between the prediction of Peter's denial and the prediction of the desertion of the Twelve comes almost the whole of the Farewell Discourses. After a long monologue by Jesus, the disciples respond with a confession of faith: πιστεύομεν ὅτι ἀπὸ θεοῦ ἐξῆλθες. To this Jesus replies, in the same spirit in which he damped down Peter's over confident profession of devotion, Ἄρτι πιστεύετε; ἰδοὺ ἔρχεται ὥρα καὶ ἐλήλυθεν ἵνα σκορπισθῆτε ἕκαστος εἰς τὰ ἴδια κἀμὲ μόνον ἀφῆτε (xvi. 30–2). There is no corresponding prediction in Luke. In Mark (followed, with trifling variations, by Matthew) it takes the form, πάντες σκανδαλισθήσεσθε, supported by a *testimonium* from Zech. xiii. 7: πατάξω τὸν ποιμένα καὶ τὰ πρόβατα διασκορπισθήσονται. The two gospels agree in the use of the verb (δια)σκορπίζειν, which in John has been lifted out of the Old Testament quotation and applied directly to the disciples. This verb, however, though it appears (in various forms, διασκορπισθήσονται, -θητω, -θητωσαν) in A and some other MSS. of the LXX, is not present in the אB text, and probably does not represent the true LXX reading. It is a better rendering of the Massoretic text, תְּפוּצֶיןָ, than the ἐκ(σ)πάσατε of אB. The *prima facie* suggestion is that John is here dependent on Mark, and this might find support in the fact that the other verb in Mark, σκανδαλίζεσθαι, is found in a neighbouring context in John, namely xvi. 1, where Jesus says that he is preparing his disciples in order that they may *not* be 'scandalized'. We note, moreover, that although John has here represented the dispersal of the Twelve as a desertion in face of the enemy, even more emphatically than the other evangelists (ἐμὲ μόνον ἀφῆτε), his account of the arrest in xviii. 4–9 does not put the affair quite in that light: there Jesus gives himself up on condition that his disciples shall be allowed to go free, and the evangelist lays stress upon this as a fulfilment of the words of Jesus, οὓς ἔδωκάς μοι, οὐκ ἀπώλεσα ἐξ αὐτῶν οὐδένα. This is one of the few places where (as we shall presently see) a distinctively theological motive intrudes into the Johannine Passion narrative. The explanation that suggests itself is that in xvi. 32 John has preserved a traditional trait of the Passion narrative, while in xviii. 8 he has given a somewhat different aspect to the incident, in the service of his theological interpretation of the story.[1] Then are we to say that in xvi. 32 (with xvi. 1) he is directly dependent on Mark? Not necessarily, for the verb σκανδαλίζεσθαι, of the apostasy of Israel, and derivatively of similar apostasy or unfaithfulness on the part of the followers of Christ, appears to be deeply rooted in the vocabulary of primitive Christianity, perhaps under the influence of Daniel xi. 41 LXX (πολλαὶ σκανδαλισθήσονται, cf. Matt. xxiv. 10), helped by the oft-quoted passage of Isa. viii. 14, πέτρα σκανδάλου. It is to be noted that this rendering of the Isaianic *testimonium*, which is adopted in Rom. ix. 33 and 1 Pet. ii. 8, is not septuagintal; yet

---

[1] This does not necessarily mean that the account in John xviii is entirely unhistorical. Even though Jesus may have made an opportunity for his disciples to escape, yet their willingness to use such an opportunity showed a failure at least of nerve, if not of fundamental loyalty, and it did in fact mean that he was 'left alone'.

it does not appear that 1 Pet. ii. 8 is borrowed from Rom. ix. 33, or *vice versa*. There are many signs which suggest that in the early Church *testimonia* were quoted from a translation (or translations) differing from the LXX (whatever its origin). This may be the explanation of the agreement of Mark and John in quoting Zech. xiii. 7.[1]

There is no further parallel in this part of the Passion narrative between the Fourth Gospel and the corresponding portions of the other three. We now turn to the most remarkable of the passages which, present in the Synoptics, are absent from John: the sacramental words and actions of Jesus at the Last Supper. The reasons for the omission (on the supposition that John was in general following the Synoptics) have been much discussed. Certainly there could be no theological motive for it, since (as is very generally recognized) the sacramental idea expressed in the Synoptic account of the Supper finds ample expression in the discourse on Bread of Life in John vi. 22–58. But it is possible to go a little further than this recognition of a general affinity of idea between John and the Synoptics at this point. In the Synoptic (and Pauline) versions of the 'words of institution' there are many textual variants. These are not to be regarded as due to simple manuscript corruption in the ordinary sense. They probably reflect differing liturgical usage in the churches where the archetypes of our MSS. were produced. Now the crucial *hoc est corpus* appears in the text of Luke xxii. 19, according to the great Uncials, with much support from minuscules and versions, in the form, τοῦτό ἐστιν τὸ σῶμά μου τὸ ὑπὲρ ὑμῶν διδόμενον (a form of text which is given by some versions also in 1 Cor. xi. 24). In the Sinaitic Syriac it takes the form, ‎ܗܢܘ ܦܓܪܝ ܕܐܢܐ ܝܗܒ ܐܢܐ ܚܠܦܝܟܘܢ‎ that is, 'This is my body which I will give[2] for you'. The underlying Greek might be, τοῦτό ἐστιν τὸ σῶμά μου ὃ ἐγὼ δώσω ὑπὲρ ὑμῶν. If we now confront this with John vi. 51, ὁ ἄρτος ὃν ἐγὼ δώσω ἡ σάρξ μού ἐστιν ὑπὲρ τῆς τοῦ κόσμου ζωῆς, the affinity of

---

[1] Isa. vi. 9–10 is cited in a version differing from the LXX (which is quoted by Matt. xiii. 14–15) in John xii. 40, and this version appears to have been known also to Paul, and perhaps to Mark, though John certainly did not draw it directly from Mark. Isa. xl. 3 is quoted in John i. 23 in a version differing from the LXX and from Mark. Zech. ix. 9 is quoted by Matthew (xxi. 5) in a version approximating to the LXX, and by John (xii. 15) in a widely different version. Mark does not cite this prophecy (see *According to the Scriptures*, pp. 31–54). When the evidence is put together it seems to me to point convincingly to the existence of non-septuagintal versions of the 'testimony' passages, which Christian writers might quote without any suspicion of borrowing from one another.

[2] The Syriac participle with the personal pronoun is constantly used for the future. ‎ܝܗܒ ܐܢܐ‎ translates δώσω in John xiii. 26, Luke iv. 6.

the two is evident, the characteristically Johannine expression ὑπὲρ τῆς τοῦ κόσμου ζωῆς being substituted for the simpler ὑπὲρ ὑμῶν. But where the Lucan form of the saying speaks of the 'body', the Johannine speaks of the 'flesh'. In the LXX σῶμα and σάρξ are alternative renderings of בָּשָׂר. Jeremias, in his careful study of the 'words of institution',[1] comes to the conclusion that we must assume an Aramaic בִּשְׂרָא behind the σῶμα of Paul and the Synoptics. If so, the same Aramaic word would underlie the Johannine σάρξ. We may therefore with great probability take John vi. 51 to be derived, not from any reminiscence of the Synoptic Passion narrative, but from a liturgical tradition going back independently to the Aramaic of the Church's earliest days.

The question whether John knew the 'words of institution' solely from liturgical sources, or whether they also entered into his tradition of the Passion narrative, is not easily answered. On the one hand, 1 Cor. xi. 23–6 is sufficient evidence that the account of the institution of the Eucharist could be, and was, recited as an independent unit (for the way in which it is introduced proves that we have not here an extract from a longer narrative). On the other hand, since Paul tells us that the celebration of the Eucharist (as ἀνάμνησις of Christ) was invariably (ὁσάκις ἄν κ.τ.λ.) accompanied by a recital of his Passion (καταγγέλλετε τὸν θάνατον τοῦ κυρίου), it is a probable conjecture (though no more than a conjecture) that the fundamental Passion tradition took shape in this context. If so, it is on general grounds likely that the 'words of institution', which provide the most direct clue to the meaning of the whole, would have been included. If the sacramental words and actions were included in the form of Passion narrative known to the Fourth Evangelist, it would not be difficult to assign probable motives for their omission, but it remains possible that they had a different setting in the tradition on which he depended.

In Mark, and Matthew after him, the Last Supper itself is referred to only in a circumstantial clause, which serves to introduce the incidents in which these evangelists are particularly interested. In Mark xiv. 18 we have καὶ ἀνακειμένων αὐτῶν καὶ ἐσθιόντων, leading up to the prediction of the treachery of Judas, and again in xiv. 22 καὶ ἐσθιόντων αὐτῶν, leading up to the sacramental words and actions. Similarly in John, after the introductory clauses, we read καὶ δείπνου γινομένου (v.l. γενομένου), and this, after a longish parenthesis, leads up to a narrative which finds no place in the

[1] J. Jeremias, *Die Abendmahlsworte Jesu* (1949), pp. 103–4.

Synoptics, that of the washing of the feet of the disciples. It is embedded in a long and complex *pericopé* (xiii. 4–15, or, including associated sayings, xiii. 4–20). Much of this is of the nature of theological comment or interpretation. The evangelist has in fact packed into this passage a wealth of symbolism which renders it a fitting 'frontispiece' to the whole Passion narrative.[1] Yet the incident which forms the centre of the whole is told simply enough: 'He rose from supper, and, laying aside his outer garments, took a towel and tied it about him. He then poured water into a basin and began to wash the feet of his disciples. . . .Having washed their feet and resumed his garments, he said. . .."I have set you an example; you are to do as I have done to you".' Stripped of the theological commentary, which we may fairly attribute to the evangelist himself, it is a simple story about Jesus, enforcing by his example a lesson of humility and service.[2]

It has often been noted that a precept for which this story provides an effective illustration is to be found in the Lucan Passion narrative, not indeed in precisely the same sequence as the story in John, but with comparatively slight transposition: Τίς γὰρ μείзων, ὁ ἀνακείμενος ἢ ὁ διακονῶν; οὐχὶ ὁ ἀνακείμενος; ἐγὼ δὲ ἐν μέσῳ ὑμῶν εἰμὶ ὡς ὁ διακονῶν (Luke xxii. 27). The situation here pictured is exactly reproduced in the Johannine story: the disciples are οἱ ἀνακείμενοι, Jesus ὁ διακονῶν.[3] So close is the correspondence that it is often held that the Johannine story is directly derived from the Lucan saying. But it is premature to draw this conclusion before placing the comparison on a wider basis.

The saying I have quoted from Luke is part of a sequence which begins with the statement that a quarrel about precedence arose among the disciples. Jesus interposed with a saying in which the behaviour of kings and persons in authority among the Gentiles is contrasted with that which is to be expected of his own disciples: ὑμεῖς δὲ οὐχ οὕτως, ἀλλ᾽ ὁ μείзων

---

[1] See *Interpretation*, pp. 401–12.

[2] Somewhat similarly, Bultmann *ad loc.* describes xiii. 4–5, 12–20 as a *Quellenstück*, with 6–11 as Johannine comment.

[3] In Luke xvii. 8 there is a typical description of ὁ διακονῶν. He is the slave to whom his master says, Ἑτοίμασον τί δειπνήσω καὶ περιзωσάμενος διακόνει μοι ἕως φάγω καὶ πίω. When the master–servant relation is reversed, it is the master who περιзώσεται καὶ. . .διακονήσει αὐτοῖς (Luke xii. 37). So here John emphasizes by the repetition of the verb (4–5) that Jesus was διεзωσμένος for his act of service. Note, however, that in the Lucan passages, as in Luke x. 40, John ii. 5–9, xii. 2, the typical διακονία is waiting at table. If the present passage had been an 'ideal scene' illustrating the idea of Christ as διάκονος, we should have had a story about Jesus waiting upon his disciples as they sat at table for the δεῖπνον.

ἐν ὑμῖν γινέσθω ὡς ὁ νεώτερος καὶ ὁ ἡγούμενος ὡς ὁ διακονῶν. This in turn leads up to the saying for which John supplies so apt an illustration. The whole of this passage has a parallel in Mark x. 42–5, but with so little verbal resemblance that it would be rash to conclude that Luke is here copying from Mark. But that is not all. In Luke ix. 48 we have a repetition of what is obviously the same saying as xxii. 26, but again in such different language that it almost certainly comes from a different source (written or oral): ὁ μικρότερος ἐν πᾶσιν ὑμῖν ὑπάρχων οὗτός ἐστιν μέγας. Again, we find variant forms of the same saying in Mark ix. 35, Matt. xx. 26–7, xxiii. 11. In all, the saying in various forms appears six times in the Synoptic Gospels. Whatever may be the truth about the tangled literary interrelations of these several passages, it seems clear that a maxim to this effect held a position of peculiar importance in the tradition of the sayings of the Lord, and entered into several different formulations of his teaching. In Mark x. 43–5 the Lord's example of διακονία is specifically connected with his sacrificial death, and so in Matt. xx. 26–8, which follows Mark. In Mark ix. 35 there is no such connection, nor in the other Matthaean and Lucan parallels. But in xxii. 26–7 Luke has in effect made the connection through the setting in which the saying is placed, at the table of the Last Supper, immediately before the Passion.

But we are not yet at the end of this series of comparable passages. The Christological passage in Phil. ii. 6–11, with its emphatic appeal to the Passion of the Lord as an example to Christians, develops directly out of an exhortation to humility and care for the interests of others. This passage is now thought by many critics to be a kind of credal hymn, pre-Pauline in origin. When we reflect on the importance which precepts of humility and mutual subjection and service hold in various forms of catechesis,[1] and the various ways in which such precepts are often related to the thought of Christ's self-sacrifice,[2] we shall be disposed to find in

---

[1] Mutual subjection and mutual service, Eph. v. 21, ὑποτασσόμενοι ἀλλήλοις ἐν φόβῳ Χριστοῦ, Gal. v. 14, δουλεύετε ἀλλήλοις, 1 Pet. v. 5, πάντες ἀλλήλοις τὴν ταπεινοφροσύνην ἐγκομβώσασθε, Rom. xii. 10, τῇ τιμῇ ἀλλήλους προηγούμενοι.

[2] Rom. xv. 2–3, ἕκαστος ἡμῶν τῷ πλησίον ἀρεσκέτω . . . καὶ γὰρ ὁ Χριστὸς οὐχ ἑαυτῷ ἤρεσεν, with a quotation from Ps. lxviii. 10 (a psalm of the Righteous Sufferer, which has yielded several testimonia). Ἀρέσκειν generally carries with it (especially in Paul) a suggestion of subordinating one's own desire, choice, or even freedom to another. In Col. iii. 12–13 (καθὼς καὶ ὁ κύριος), taken with the parallel passage Eph. iv. 32–v. 2 (καθὼς καὶ ὁ Χριστός . . . παρέδωκεν ἑαυτόν), it is clear that the thought of Christ's sacrifice is very near the surface when χρηστότης and ταπεινοφροσύνη are in question. Similarly in Eph. v. 21 sqq. the general idea of mutual subjection soon leads to ὁ Χριστὸς ἠγάπησεν τὴν ἐκκλησίαν καὶ ἑαυτὸν παρέδωκεν

Phil. ii. 1–11 not (in substance at least) a Pauline creation, but one form of a very fundamental article of Christian *didaché*, deeply rooted in the primitive tradition of the words, deeds and sufferings of Jesus Christ. We find it variously formulated, in aphorism, in dialogue, in extended passages of combined narrative and dialogue where the whole setting gives point to the particular saying, in catechetical maxims, and, finally, in the kind of credal hymn (if such it be) which we have in Phil. ii. To these manifold forms under which this fundamental *Lehrstück* might be presented we must now add what we may call the 'exemplary story', as we have it in John xiii. 4–17.

There is therefore no sound reason to suppose that the Fourth Evangelist found the saying about humility and service in the Lucan Passion narrative and made a story out of it. It is far more likely that he drew it independently out of tradition, and then handled it after his fashion, to suggest, through symbolism, the profoundly theological ideas which he wished to be in the mind of his readers in embarking on the story of Christ's sufferings and death. It is all the more likely, because the story in itself is not particularly well adapted to the purpose for which the evangelist has employed it, except in so far as the use of water for washing opens up the whole range of water-symbolism which plays so large a part in this gospel. The primary meaning of the story is to be found in the idea of *imitatio Christi*, expressed quite simply in xiii. 15. There are several subsidiary meanings, connected with the ideas of washing–bathing–cleansing, of the unity of Christ's disciples with him through being 'washed' (baptized) by him, and of the possibility that even one (Judas) who has been 'washed' by Christ may not be 'clean'. But the way in which these are linked with the story is patently artificial. John, we conclude, did not make it up; he found and used it.

If, then, we set aside the evangelist's comments, the *pericopé* appears as a narrative comparable with some of those to be found in the Synoptic Gospels. Its pattern is similar to that of some *pericopae* classed as 'pronouncement stories', but here the action of Jesus, treated as an example to his followers, carries the weight of emphasis, rather than the words in which the example is applied. Exemplary stories as such are not common among the traditional units recognized in the gospels, although an appeal to the example of Jesus is probably a formative motive more frequently

ὑπὲρ αὐτῆς (v. 25). All this shows how natural is the transition in Phil. ii from the idea τῇ ταπεινοφροσύνῃ ἀλλήλους ἡγούμενοι ὑπερέχοντας ἑαυτῶν to the thought of Christ's self-sacrifice.

than is usually recognized. But at any rate the story about Jesus and the child in Mark ix. 36–7 is expressly an example to his disciples, who are similarly to 'receive any such little child'. Indeed, if we reflect on such maxims as προσλαμβάνεσθε ἀλλήλους καθὼς καὶ ὁ Χριστὸς προσελάβετο ἡμᾶς (Rom. xv. 7), τὸν ἀσθενοῦντα...προσλαμβάνεσθε...ὁ θεὸς γὰρ αὐτὸν προσελάβετο (Rom. xiv. 1–3), we may be disposed to think that not only the *pericopé* just referred to, but also gospel narratives about Jesus and the 'publicans and sinners' (οὗτος ἁμαρτωλοὺς προσδέχεται, Luke xv. 2), may have been framed in part as exemplary stories. It is more than likely that some at least of the stories about healing were preserved as examples to Christian healers; and surely stories depicting the attitude of Jesus to the Sabbath were intended to guide the Christian conscience in such matters of controversy as are alluded to in Rom. xiv. 5.

There are therefore strong reasons for believing that the *pericopé* of the *pedilavium* was drawn from the same general reservoir of tradition as many of the units of narrative in the Synoptics. Whether it was handed down, like some of them, as an independent unit, or as an integral part of the special form of Passion narrative known to the Fourth Evangelist, is another question. As we have seen, its introduction, with the circumstantial clause, δείπνου γινομένου, is analogous to the way in which the Synoptic evangelists have used a genitive absolute to introduce incidents of the Supper. Yet the genitive absolute is a not unusual opening for a *pericopé*, with no necessary connection with what has preceded,[1] and δείπνου γινομένου, meaning in effect 'one day at supper', would be a perfectly natural opening for such a story as this. If on the other hand we are to regard it as an integral part of the Johannine Passion tradition, then δεῖπνον would bear its technical meaning: it is the κυριακὸν δεῖπνον of 1 Cor. xi. 20. In that case we should have an additional piece of evidence that John is not following the Synoptics, for they never describe the eucharistic meal as δεῖπνον, though the longer text of Luke, which appears to reflect liturgical usage in a Pauline church, has the verb δειπνεῖν (xxii. 20). But I should not lay much stress on this.

To sum up: in our investigation of this first stage, or act, of the Passion narrative we have discovered two points at which there is a very strong

---

[1] As in Mark v. 21 διαπεράσαντος τοῦ Ἰησοῦ εἰς τὸ πέραν means 'once when Jesus had crossed the sea', in Luke ix. 57 πορευομένων αὐτῶν ἐν τῇ ὁδῷ means 'once when they were on a journey', Luke xvii. 12 εἰσερχομένου αὐτοῦ εἴς τινα κώμην 'once as he was entering a village' (cf. Luke xi. 29; Matt. xvii. 24, etc.).

probability that the Fourth Gospel depends on a form of tradition entirely independent of the Synoptics: its rendering of the 'words of institution', which seems to presuppose a translation of the original Aramaic different from that which underlies the Synoptic rendering; and the *pedilavium*, an exemplary story similar in pattern and ethos to certain units of the Synoptic Gospels, but neither derived from them nor freely composed by the evangelist for symbolic purposes. Of neither of these, however, can we be sure that they formed part of the Passion tradition as it reached John. For the rest, the three predictions—of the treachery of Judas, Peter's denial, and the desertion of the Twelve—are firmly embedded in the Johannine Passion narrative, as in the others. They have certainly been worked over by the evangelist in composing his highly individual account, but there is not enough evidence to say with confidence whether he derived them from the Synoptics or not. But granted that a reasonable probability has been established that an independent tradition did exist, the phenomena are entirely consistent with the view that, just as Luke reported these predictions after a tradition apparently different from that of Mark, so did John.

4. THE ARREST

In Mark, the predictions of the desertion of the Twelve and of Peter's denial (already discussed) are conceived as being uttered in conversation on the way from Jerusalem to the Mount of Olives. The next act of the drama begins with the arrival at χωρίον οὗ τὸ ὄνομα Γεθσημανεί (xiv. 32). This is the scene of the events now to be portrayed. They fall into two main groups:

(1) The prayer of Jesus and the sleep of the disciples.
(2) (a) Betrayal and arrest;
    (b) the attack on the High Priest's slave;
    (c) protest of Jesus and flight of the disciples;
    (d) escape of a young man.

The last episode is peculiar to Mark and has left no trace elsewhere. For the rest, Matthew follows Mark closely, as a rule with far-reaching verbal agreement, inserting a few significant additions without disturbing the Marcan scheme. Literary dependence is certain.

Not so with Luke. His divergences from Mark are considerable and raise acutely once again the question of a second source. In this respect, however, there is a marked difference between parts (1) and (2). In Luke xxii. 40–6, which covers the same ground as Mark xiv. 32–42, though much more briefly, verbal agreements are few.[1] The expression προσεύχεσθε ἵνα μὴ (εἰσ)έλθητε εἰς πειρασμόν is common to both. In Luke it closes the whole scene, but it also occurs in a slightly different form at the beginning: προσεύχεσθε μὴ εἰσελθεῖν εἰς πειρασμόν. This at once gives a somewhat different emphasis: the scene is from the first a πειρασμός for the disciples; in fact it is the 'sifting' of which they have been warned a few verses back, in Luke xxii. 31. As there Jesus prayed for Peter under trial, so now he urges them all to pray, and himself sets the example. The

---

[1] Comparison is complicated by the presence of variant texts in Luke. Verses 43–4, though attested by ℵDΘ and others, are absent from many authorities, while others insert them in the parallel passage of Matthew. If these verses are included in the text, the divergence from Mark is emphasized. But even if they are omitted, the proportion of words common to both is not great. Out of 171 significant words in Mark xiv. 32–42, Luke has only 18 (as compared with 123 in Matthew). The 18 may be increased to 23 if we count the repeated προσεύχεσθε μὴ εἰσελθεῖν εἰς πειρασμόν. Even so they do not amount to more than 32 per cent of Luke's shorter text, 23·5 per cent of his longer text; while of Matthew's 195 words 63 per cent are Marcan.

logical development is plainer in Luke. The wording of the prayer agrees with Mark in the words, παρένεγκε τοῦτο τὸ ποτήριον ἀπ᾽ ἐμοῦ, but its second clause is not very close to Mark, rather closer to Matthew. Beyond this there is no verbal agreement apart from indispensable words like προσεύχεσθαι and καθεύδειν. Mark's keyword γρηγορεῖτε is missing. Altogether Luke is far briefer, and yet he finds room for such a phrase as ἀπεσπάσθη ἀπ᾽ αὐτῶν ὡσεὶ λίθου βολήν—which does not look as if he were deliberately abbreviating an account which lay before him. Still less is it like an abbreviator if verses 43–4 are to be accepted as part of the genuine text. They portray the distress of Jesus, in terms differing entirely from Mark's corresponding description (xiv. 33–4), and an answer to the prayer, of which Mark knows nothing. In short, there is no sufficient reason to believe that Luke used Mark at all in this section (for the two clauses common to both are such as would be likely to occur even in independent forms of tradition), and there is good reason to believe that the second source which we recognized in the preceding section is still the basis of the Lucan narrative. The question may be raised, whether Luke does not represent a more primitive state of the tradition. Mark is here very elaborate. His presentation lends itself to the enforcement of one of the most constant themes of Christian *paraenesis*: the theme of 'sleeping' and 'waking'.[1] The threefold return of Jesus to find his disciples asleep, while he is praying in deep distress of soul, is well calculated to impress upon the reader the enormity of the sin of which they are guilty, and of which Christians may be similarly guilty if they do not obey the call to 'awake out of sleep'. The gnomic phrase, τὸ μὲν πνεῦμα πρόθυμον ἡ δὲ σὰρξ ἀσθενής, fits well this paraenetic character of the *pericopé*.[2]

In the second part of this section the relations of Mark and Luke are different. The verbal agreements are more substantial,[3] and the general conception of the scene is the same. There are good grounds for holding that here Luke had Mark before him, though it remains possible that some of his minor peculiarities (in xxii. 48, 52, 53b) may betray the continued use of an alternative form of tradition alongside of Mark. Such a second

[1] See *Parables of the Kingdom* (Nisbet, 1961), pp. 122–5 ((Collins, 1961), pp. 115–18).

[2] 'A fine piece of rhetorical prose, drawn perhaps from a Christian sermon' (W. L. Knox, *Sources of the Synoptic Gospels*, vol. I, p. 126).

[3] The common expressions are by no means all such as are inevitable in recording the same matters: note αὐτοῦ λαλοῦντος, the unnecessary εἰς τῶν δώδεκα, εἷς τις (which occurs again in Mark xiv. 51, but nowhere else in the Lucan writings), and the curious expression for removing an ear, ἀφεῖλεν.

source might account for the striking additions which Luke, in his highly abbreviated version, has nevertheless made to the material which he has in common with Mark, namely (*a*) the question, Κύριε εἰ πατάξομεν ἐν μαχαίρῃ; (*b*) the stroke on the *right* ear, the rebuke, ἐᾶτε ἕως τούτου, and the healing of the wound; (*c*) the pregnant saying, αὕτη ἐστὶν ὑμῶν ἡ ὥρα καὶ ἡ ἐξουσία τοῦ σκότους.

We now turn to the Fourth Gospel. The transitional sentence (xviii. 1) which brings Jesus and his disciples to the scene of the arrest differs from Mark significantly. Mark (having earlier recorded that after supper they made for the Mount of Olives) now records their arrival at 'a plot of ground called Gethsemane'. John says nothing about the Mount of Olives and does not mention the name Gethsemane. Instead, he says that Jesus went with his disciples πέραν τοῦ χειμάρρου τῶν Κέδρων[1] ὅπου ἦν κῆπος, which they entered; adding that it was a place to which he often resorted with his disciples (cf. Luke's κατὰ τὸ ἔθος, of the retirement to the Mount of Olives—which however perhaps does not mean exactly the same).[2] There is no contradiction between the two statements: a party on the way from Jerusalem to the Mount of Olives would certainly cross the Kidron. But equally certainly John could not have learnt this from Mark. If he had before him the name Γεθσημανεί, there seems no good reason why (with his penchant for local names) he should not have copied it,[3] even if he felt obliged to add that the plot so named was in fact not an oliveyard (as the name might seem to suggest, if it represents גַּת־שְׁמֶן, 'oil-press'), but a garden![4] If we regard the description as the result of

---

[1] Ὁ χείμαρρος τῶν Κέδρων, 'Wady of Cedars', is obviously a popular attempt (based on the sound) to give an intelligible meaning in Greek to the name נַחַל קִדְרוֹן (much as the Welsh mountain Yr Eifl has been given the English name The Rivals, suggested by the sound of the name in Welsh). It occurs sometimes in MSS. of the LXX, which elsewhere have χείμαρρος Κεδρών. Josephus has χείμαρρος Κεδρῶνος (*Ant.* VIII. 17). The name occurs nowhere else in the New Testament.

[2] Luke xxii. 39 probably refers back to xxi. 37 where the proceedings of the period immediately preceding the fatal Passover are summarized: ἦν δὲ τὰς ἡμέρας ἐν τῷ ἱερῷ διδάσκων τὰς δὲ νύκτας ἐξερχόμενος ηὐλίζετο εἰς τὸ ὄρος τὸ καλούμενον Ἐλαιών. John xviii. 2, πολλάκις συνήχθη Ἰησοῦς ἐκεῖ μετὰ τῶν μαθητῶν αὐτοῦ, would suggest that the garden was used as a rendezvous.

[3] Luke also has omitted the name Gethsemane. Luke had no liking for these uncouth Semitic names; he has omitted Γολγοθᾶ also; but John is fond of using them.

[4] Whether κῆπος could be used in a broad sense to cover an oliveyard I do not know. Normally it seems to mean a plot where herbs, vegetables and flowers are grown, as distinct from a shrubbery or plantation (παράδεισος), as well as from the specialized ἀμπελών, συκών, ἐλαιών (cf. Amos iv. 9). Yet the παράδεισος in which

'editing' or 'correcting' Mark, it would seem a singularly pointless proceeding, with no possible interest for readers at Ephesus in the late first century. The whole matter is trivial, and for that reason it appears to me one of the strongest pieces of evidence we have yet found that John was here writing in independence of Mark, and yet on the basis of good information, probably handed down in a separate strain of tradition.

The opening scene of this act of the drama according to Mark is missing from the Johannine Passion narrative, which contains neither the prayer of Jesus nor the sleep of the disciples. There is an apparent echo of the Marcan phrase ἐγείρεσθε ἄγωμεν, with which the scene terminates as the actors move on to a fresh scene, at an altogether different point in the narrative (John xiv. 31). To this I shall return presently. There is also what might well be a reminiscence of Synoptic language in the words in which Jesus repudiates the attempt to resist his arrest: τὸ ποτήριον ὃ δέδωκέν μοι ὁ πατὴρ οὐ μὴ πίω αὐτό; (xviii. 11). This recalls the wording of the prayer, which in all three Synoptics has the keyword ποτήριον, though Matthew alone has the verb πίνειν. John, it might be said, has drawn a veil over the scene from motives of reverence,[1] and, omitting the inward struggle, has turned the final acceptance into an overt declaration. There is force in this; but the idea of the Passion as a 'cup' to be drunk is not confined to this context. It occurs also in Mark x. 38-9 (τὸ ποτήριον ὃ ἐγὼ πίνω). The background of the expression is to be found in such prophetic passages as Isa. li. 17-23, Jer. xxxii. 1-17 (xxv. 15-31), where the ποτήριον is a symbol for the terrible judgements of God.[2] Such passages are echoed in Rev. xiv. 10, xvi. 19, etc. The sacramental use of the word (Mark xiv. 23, 1 Cor. xi. 25) kept the idea of the 'cup' as symbol of the sufferings of Christ always in mind. It is therefore not

---

Susanna was falsely said to have misbehaved (36), and which contained trees (including a σχῖνος (51) and a πρῖνος (58)), is also called κῆπος, and you could grow ῥάμνοι in a κῆπος (Ep. Jer. 71). To 'correct' χωρίον οὗ τὸ ὄνομα Γεθσημανεί into κῆπος would in any case be mere pedantry.

[1] Not theological motives; John is no docetist; see pp. 123-4, 325-6.

[2] In Jer. xxxii. 1 *sqq.* (xxv. 15 *sqq.*) the word of the Lord comes to the prophet: λάβε τὸ ποτήριον τοῦ οἴνου τοῦ ἀκράτου τούτου ἐκ χειρός μου, καὶ ποτιεῖς πάντα τὰ ἔθνη...καὶ ἐρεῖς, Οὕτως εἶπεν Κύριος, Πιόντες πίεσθε. It seems impossible not to suspect that such expressions lie behind the liturgical language of Matt. xxvi. 27: λαβὼν ποτήριον...ἔδωκεν αὐτοῖς λέγων, Πίετε ἐξ αὐτοῦ πάντες. The 'cup' of suffering is accepted by Christ, and given by him (the κοινωνία τῶν παθημάτων αὐτοῦ) to his disciples. Because Christ has drunk it, it is the 'cup of salvation' (cf. Ps. cxv. 4: ποτήριον σωτηρίου λήψομαι καὶ τὸ ὄνομα Κυρίου ἐπικαλέσομαι). We ought not to be surprised to find the symbolism of 'drinking the cup' at any point, in any branch of the tradition, where the Passion of Christ is in view.

necessary to trace the idea of 'drinking the cup' in John xviii. 11 to any particular passage in the other gospels; it is intrinsic to the total tradition.

These considerations go far to qualify the *prima facie* case for the dependence of John on the Synoptics at this point. They gain weight when we observe that there is evidence that John was not ignorant of the tradition of the prayer of Jesus, but knew it in a non-synoptic form.

The passage in question is xii. 27–8, which has been widely recognized as in some sort an equivalent for the Gethsemane *pericopé* in the Synoptics.[1] The core of it is a prayer which passes through two stages closely parallel to the two stages of the prayer in Gethsemane. The Lucan form lends itself best to comparison:

Luke xxii. 42	John xii. 27–8
Πάτερ...παρένεγκε τοῦτο τὸ ποτή-ριον ἀπ' ἐμοῦ	Πάτερ σῶσόν με ἐκ τῆς ὥρας ταύτης (cf. Mark xiv. 35 : προσεύχετο ἵνα... παρέλθῃ ἀπ' αὐτοῦ ἡ ὥρα)
μὴ τὸ θέλημά μου ἀλλὰ τὸ σὸν γινέσθω	Πάτερ δόξασόν σου τὸ ὄνομα

The language has a Johannine stamp; ὥρα, δοξάζειν, ὄνομα, though none of them is peculiar to this gospel, are favourite expressions. But the underlying conception is the same as in the Synoptics.[2] So far, the phenomena might be explained by a Johannine re-writing of the Synoptic account. But there are further facts to be taken into account.

In John xii the passage opens with an allusion to Ps. xli. 7, ἡ ψυχή μου ἐταράχθη (in John, νῦν ἡ ψυχή μου τετάρακται, cf. xiii. 21, Ἰησοῦς ἐταράχθη τῷ πνεύματι). In Mark it opens with an allusion to the preceding verse of the same psalm: ἵνα τί περίλυπος εἶ, ἡ ψυχή (in Mark, περίλυπός ἐστιν ἡ ψυχή μου (xiv. 34)).[3] The coincidence proves that in both gospels Jesus is conceived as speaking in the character of the Righteous Sufferer of the psalm. Both therefore give expression to the same conception of the

---

[1] Some critics, strangely, have treated it as a parallel to the Transfiguration. The only point in common is the *bath qol*, which however has a different content in each case. Otherwise in form and content there is no resemblance, except in so far as the concept of the δόξα of Christ comes into both. But see next note.

[2] Christ glorifies the Father by completing His work (xvii. 4), and the work is completed in his passion and death (xix. 30), for the ἐντολή of the Father, which the Son obeys, is to 'lay down his life' (x. 17–18). This is the θέλημα of the Father which the Son seeks (v. 30), which he came to do (vi. 38), and which, while he is on earth, is his βρῶμα (iv. 34). It is thus that the sacrificial death of Christ (his self-dedication, xvii. 19) is his glory, because in it (in his full acceptance of the Father's θέλημα) the Father is glorified. Thus, in the context of Johannine thought, there is no substantial difference between θέλημα τὸ σὸν γινέσθω and δόξασόν σου τὸ ὄνομα..

[3] See pp. 38, 42–3.

Passion. Yet dependence of John on Mark here seems to be out of the question.

Further, in Mark there is no answer to the prayer. In Luke (longer text) there is an answer: ὤφθη αὐτῷ ἄγγελος ἀπ' οὐρανοῦ ἐνισχύων αὐτόν. Similarly in John there is an answer: ἦλθεν οὖν φωνὴ ἐκ τοῦ οὐρανοῦ, on which bystanders comment, ἄγγελος αὐτῷ λελάληκεν. That this could have been modelled on Luke is not to be supposed, yet there is surely some common background. We have already seen reason to believe that Luke and Mark are following independently separate forms of tradition. Here we discern a third form of tradition behind John, a tradition having some more or less remote affinity with Luke's.

But that is not the end of the story. There is a passage in Heb. v. 7-8 which describes the prayer of Jesus 'in the days of his flesh'. Most commentators have rightly seen in it an allusion to the prayer before the Passion as we have it in the Synoptics. The passage is written in the rhetorical style characteristic of this author, and we cannot expect any marked verbal resemblances to our other accounts, but the movement of thought is similar: there are three stages: (*a*) prayer accompanied with great mental stress, (*b*) an answer to prayer, (*c*) the achievement of the perfection of obedience. In substance, the first and third stages correspond with all our other accounts, the second with Luke and John. Echoes of language are slight. In Hebrews Christ offers supplications πρὸς τὸν δυνάμενον σώζειν αὐτὸν ἐκ θανάτου. For δυνάμενον compare Mark xiv. 36 πάντα δυνατά σοι (contrasted with the hypothetical εἰ δυνατόν ἐστιν, Matt. xxvi. 39; εἰ οὐ δύναται τοῦτο παρελθεῖν, Matt. xxvi. 42; Luke has nothing of the kind); and for σώζειν compare John xii. 27, σῶσόν με ἐκ τῆς ὥρας ταύτης: the verb σώζειν does not occur in the Synoptic context. The mental distress accompanying the prayer is described by both Mark and Luke, in widely different terms (Mark, ἀδημονεῖν, ἐκθαμβεῖσθαι, in Luke ἀγωνία). Neither is echoed in Hebrews, which speaks of κραυγή and δάκρυα, both unknown to the gospels. But here as in the gospels we catch unmistakable echoes of the psalms of the Righteous Sufferer. In Ps. xli. 4 (the same psalm echoed in Mark and John) the Sufferer complains, ἐγενήθη τὰ δάκρυά μου ἄρτος ἡμέρας καὶ νυκτός, and declares, σωτήριον τοῦ προσώπου μου ὁ θεός μου...παρ' ἐμοὶ προσευχὴ τῷ θεῷ τῆς ζωῆς μου, and similarly in Hebrews Christ offers prayers and supplications πρὸς τὸν δυνάμενον σώζειν αὐτὸν ἐκ θανάτου.[1] In a still more

---

[1] The echo is of thought rather than of language; yet if we put together all the expressions which seem to be more or less clearly echoed, within only six verses of

important Passion psalm (xxi. 25) the Sufferer proclaims, ἐν τῷ κεκραγέναι με πρὸς αὐτὸν εἰσήκουσέν μου, and similarly in Heb. v. 7 Christ offers prayers μετὰ κραυγῆς, and is heard—εἰσακούσθεις. These psalms, we recall, were accepted in the primitive Church as a prophetic picture of the sufferings of Christ. Their language entered into the story of his Passion, probably at the earliest stage of oral tradition, and it can still be recognized in the gospels. Ps. xli, in particular, underlies the three accounts of the prayer of Jesus which we are examining, in Mark, John and the epistle to the Hebrews, although no two of these have the same phrases.

There are thus strong grounds for believing that an account of the prayer of Jesus before his Passion formed part of the central and primitive tradition, and was preserved in as many as four variant forms, which have entered into the canonical writings of the New Testament. It is therefore one of the most strongly attested elements in the gospel story. Each writer has in greater or less measure remoulded the tradition as it reached him, in accordance with his own style and aim: Mark has developed it in the direction of *paraenesis*; Luke (or a supplementer of Luke) has heightened the emotional colouring; the author to the Hebrews has adorned it in his own rhetorical manner; and John has clothed it in the language of his distinctive theology.

Whether this incident formed part of the general scheme of Passion narrative from the first is another question. The use made of it in Hebrews shows how readily it might have been handed down as an independent unit, and the strongly didactic element in the Marcan version suggests that it had a history in Christian *didaché* apart from its connection with the Passion story. Conceivably therefore John may have taken over a form of Passion tradition which lacked this feature. Yet its connection with the Passion is so intimate that even where it was repeated in isolation the hearers must have been aware that it took its place in the sequence of incidents leading to the cross. It would be in no way surprising if John deliberately moved it from its original setting, preferring to give it a place in a passage where he is preparing his readers for the Passion narrative by exhibiting its meaning in various aspects.[1]

this psalm, it becomes difficult to resist the conclusion that the psalm as a whole has played a part in the shaping of the tradition: verse 4, δάκρυα, Heb.; verse 6, περίλυπος ἡ ψυχή, Mark; verse 6, σωτήριον ὁ θεός μου, John, Hebrews; verse 7, ἡ ψυχὴ ἐταράχθη, John; verse 9, προσευχὴ τῷ θεῷ τῆς ζωῆς μου, the general idea common to all, the verb in the Synoptics.

[1] See *Interpretation*, pp. 373–9.

But we have still to consider the other phrase which suggests *prima facie* that John was acquainted with Mark. The words in which Mark has made the transition from the first to the second scene of this act in the drama, ἐγείρεσθε ἄγωμεν, reappear in a different context in John xiv. 31.[1] In Mark, Jesus puts an end to the conversation with his disciples with the words, 'Bestir yourselves; let us advance; look, the traitor is at hand!' In John it is not the human adversary who approaches, but the power of evil whose instrument he is: ἔρχεται ὁ τοῦ κόσμου ἄρχων, to which Jesus adds, ἐγείρεσθε ἄγωμεν ἐντεῦθεν. There is no consequent movement in space; the advance upon the enemy is Christ's own resolve to do the Father's will: καθὼς ἐνετείλατό μοι ὁ πατὴρ οὕτως ποιῶ (John xiv. 31). Here therefore, as in Mark though in a different way, there is an inner connection between the acceptance of the will of God and the advance on the enemy. The natural setting of the words ἐγείρεσθε ἄγωμεν would seem to be that which Mark has given them. The motives which may have led John to give them a different setting, supposing him to have been acquainted with something like Mark's narrative, are not altogether difficult to discern, in view of his known tendencies.

If we now review the whole problem presented by the comparison of John and the Synoptics at this point, we seem led to the conclusion that the Passion tradition which John followed probably did contain something corresponding to the Marcan scene of the prayer of Jesus and the sleep of the disciples, but he has preferred to transfer its essential elements to other contexts, leaving the scene of the arrest to be presented in terms of a highly dramatic confrontation between Jesus, now completely isolated, and his adversaries; a confrontation conceived wholly in the spirit of that acceptance of the will of God which is the motive both of the prayer of John xii. 27–8 and of the moment of resolve in xiv. 30–1. That John had a source other than the Synoptics for the prayer of Jesus we have seen to be highly probable, and it is likely enough that the watchword ἐγείρεσθε ἄγωμεν was not confined to any one form of tradition.[2]

With the appearance of Judas and the posse John falls into line with the Synoptics, and xviii. 3–13 corresponds with Mark xiv. 43–50 and the Synoptic parallels, but there are substantial differences in the way the story

[1] See *Interpretation*, pp. 406–9.

[2] It is perhaps worth observing that the use of the verb ἐγείρεσθαι does not necessarily imply that the Johannine tradition contained a scene in which the disciples were asleep, for although it is frequently used of waking from sleep it is also used of bestirring oneself from a state of inactivity. In Mark the disciples are already awake when the words ἐγείρεσθε ἄγωμεν are used.

is told. The common nucleus tells how Judas arrived with a body of armed men to make the arrest, how Jesus confronted them, how one blow was struck in his defence, and how he was taken into custody. The order of events differs slightly, Luke and John agreeing in placing the actual arrest at the end, while in Mark (followed by Matthew) Jesus is already in custody before the blow is struck and before he makes his protest. This is a minor difference; in the main the story is the same. Verbally, the closest resemblances are in the episode of the attack on the High Priest's slave: I will discuss this presently.[1] There is partial agreement between John and Mark also in the description of the party sent to make the arrest. According to Mark it was an ὄχλος[2] παρὰ τῶν ἀρχιερέων καὶ τῶν γραμματέων καὶ τῶν πρεσβυτέρων (scil. the Sanhedrin, consisting of these three 'estates'). According to John it contained ἐκ τῶν ἀρχιερέων καὶ ἐκ τῶν φαρισαίων ὑπηρέτας. Allowing for John's (apparently mistaken) view that the Pharisees were a constitutional body parallel with the priesthood, this does not differ from Mark. Luke, on the other hand, brings the ἀρχιερεῖς on the scene in person, accompanied by the στρατηγοὶ τοῦ ἱεροῦ, whom we might regard as officers commanding John's ὑπηρέται, if these are to be understood as the temple police. According to Mark (and Luke) the party was armed with swords and truncheons (μετὰ μαχαιρῶν καὶ ξύλων), according to John, more vaguely, with weapons (ὅπλα). He adds that they bore lights (μετὰ φανῶν καὶ λαμπάδων). This feature might equally well be a piece of independent information or an intelligent inference. That it corresponds with the facts need not be doubted.[3]

There is, however, one really significant difference. John says that the party included a σπεῖρα under the command of a χιλίαρχος. Normally this should mean a cohort (at this time usually 600 men) under a *tribunus militum*. Σπεῖρα, however, is also used for the maniple, a subdivision of the cohort. If a whole battalion under its commanding officer was turned out to effect the arrest, the authorities must have gravely overestimated the

[1] See pp. 77–80.
[2] In Mark ὄχλος does not appear to convey the meaning of a disorderly mob, which it often (though by no means always) bears in classical Greek. He seems to mean by it no more than a considerable, but indefinite, number of people gathered together. There is therefore no necessary contrast between a disorderly mob in Mark and a disciplined cohort in John.
[3] The objection that lights would be unnecessary on a night of full moon (which is urged against the credit of the Johannine version of the story) is captious. We do not know that it was not a cloudy night, and in any case, if you are searching for a person supposed to be hiding in a garden it would be a wise precaution to be provided with lights.

strength of the adherents of Jesus, and expected more formidable resistance. Even a maniple, say 200 men, would seem a very ample provision.
Perhaps the evangelist had no very accurate acquaintance with Roman
military terminology.[1] But in any case he would certainly have us believe
that Roman troops were among the party which came upon Jesus and his
disciples in the garden, and (xviii. 12) that they co-operated with the
temple police in making the arrest. There is no hint of this in any of our
other sources. It raises difficulties when we try to relate it to the subsequent proceedings in court. But the question we are asking here is
whether there is reason to suppose that the evangelist had authority for his
account of the arrest in non-Synoptic tradition, and so far as the presence
of Roman troops is concerned, there seems to be no material for answering
that question. All we can say is that there does not appear to be any
recognizable theological or apologetic motive for the introduction of the
Romans at this point. That in general this evangelist is much more aware
than the others of the imperial authorities as a factor in the situation is
certainly true, but at this stage we have no means of knowing whether
this represents a tendency of his own, or had its roots in the tradition he
was following. This matter had better be left for discussion at a later
point.[2]

After the introduction of Judas and the posse the Johannine narrative
temporarily loses contact with the Synoptic. There is no betrayal with a
kiss, and no word is spoken either by Judas to Jesus, as in Mark, or by
Jesus to Judas, as in Matthew and Luke. Judas does not in any way
identify Jesus as the person to be arrested (as he does pointedly in Mark).
His function is, to all appearance, solely to direct the party to the place
where he knew Jesus was to be found (xviii. 2). Similarly in Acts i. 16 he
is described as ὁδηγὸς τοῖς συλλαβοῦσιν Ἰησοῦν. The context in Acts is
deeply penetrated with 'testimony' material,[3] and seems to belong to the

---

[1] Mark brings on the σπεῖρα at a later stage. After Pilate had pronounced
sentence the soldiers (scil.: the small detachment which had been engaged in guarding
the Prisoner during the trial) called together ὅλην τὴν σπεῖραν into the Praetorium.
Did Mark seriously mean that the entire battalion of 600 men was assembled for this
scene of brutal buffoonery? Or did he think only of a considerable body of troops?
How large a force did the author of Judith (xiv. 11) envisage when the men of Israel
ἐξήλθοσαν κατὰ σπείρας?

[2] See pp. 112–15, 118–20.

[3] Acts i. 20 cites Ps. lxviii. 26, cviii. 8. The latter psalm is not a source of testimonies,
unless verse 25, ἐσάλευσαν κεφαλὰς αὐτῶν, be supposed to be echoed in Mark xv. 29,
κινοῦντες τὰς κεφαλάς, which however is closer to Ps. xxi. 8. But Ps. lxviii has
yielded several Passion testimonies: verse 4 is cited in John xv. 25, verse 10 a is cited in

same general climate of thought as that in which the Passion narrative took shape. That John should have wished in any way to spare the traitor, or to minimize his treachery, is not to be supposed. It looks as if he had followed a tradition which, as it knew nothing of the bribery of Judas by the priests, so also knew nothing of the crowning enormity of the traitor's kiss.

In any case there is, in the Johannine rendering of the story, no need for Judas to identify Jesus, who himself steps forward and discloses his identity. The scene is intensely dramatic, in our author's manner. The few details are carefully selected and vividly depicted: the armed men with torches and lanterns entering the garden, their sudden recoil as Jesus confronts them, his noble gesture in giving himself up to secure the escape of his followers. All this might well be the product of that sense for character and drama which we recognize all through this gospel. Whether or not we suppose it to be strictly historical, it certainly brings the whole scene to life. But we have further to note certain characteristic motives underlying the narrative.

(i) The evangelist has been at pains to observe that Jesus was in no way taken by surprise, because he foreknew all that was to befall him (εἰδὼς πάντα τὰ ἐρχόμενα ἐπ' αὐτόν, xviii. 4). This is in fact presupposed in all forms of the Passion narrative, but it is like our author to make it explicit.

(ii) Jesus gives himself up to death of his own sovereign will. Again, it is implicit in all gospels that Jesus freely accepted his fate as the will of God, declared in the Scriptures;[1] but here the voluntary character of his action is brought into strong relief, in accordance with the doctrine of John x. 17–18. A theological motive, we may say, has selected this element in the common tradition, and isolated it for special emphasis.

(iii) The repeated ἐγώ εἰμι (xviii. 5, 6, 7), with which Jesus makes himself known to his opponents, can hardly have failed to carry, for the evangelist, mysterious overtones, even although in itself it means no more than 'I am the man you are looking for—Jesus of Nazareth'.[2]

John ii. 17 and verse 10b in Rom. xv. 3, verse 21a is echoed in Matt. xxvii. 34, verse 22b recalled in Mark xv. 36 and expressly cited in John xix. 28 (see also *According to the Scriptures*, pp. 57–9).

[1] This is the implication of Mark xiv. 49, where Jesus, after protesting against the use of violence to arrest him, adds, ἀλλ' ἵνα πληρωθῶσιν αἱ γραφαί—'Let the Scriptures be fulfilled'.

[2] The threefold repetition of the significant phrase may be compared with the threefold repetition of ὁ υἱός σου ζῇ in iv. 50, 51, 53. In each place an expression entirely natural in the circumstances is given a special importance by a repetition which is sufficiently unnatural to draw the reader's attention.

(iv) Jesus gives himself up to save his disciples: the Good Shepherd, seeing the wolf coming, lays down his life for the sheep (x. 15). Here John has expressly called attention to the fulfilment of Christ's own words, οὓς δέδωκάς μοι οὐκ ἀπώλεσα ἐξ αὐτῶν οὐδένα (xviii. 9). I have elsewhere[1] shown that this note is not open to the suspicion of having been added by a redactor who misunderstood the meaning of xvii. 12. It is entirely in this evangelist's manner to see, in apparently matter-of-fact incidents, 'signs' of deeper realities. The self-surrender of Christ to save his disciples from the police is, *sub specie aeternitatis*, no other than the sacrifice by which he saves mankind from darkness and death. Both are the expression of the love with which God loved the world.

It seems clear, therefore, that motives arising out of the Johannine theology have influenced this part of the Passion narrative. This, however, does not foreclose the question, whether or not the evangelist was working upon material derived from tradition. If so, it must have been independent of the Synoptic tradition.

I have already noted, as regards points (i) and (ii), that all forms of tradition are unanimous in representing Jesus as aware of his approaching fate, and as meeting it voluntarily in a spirit of self-sacrifice. So far, the theological colouring amounts to no more than added emphasis. The use of the expression, ἐγώ εἰμι, although it is patient of a profound theological purport, is not necessarily a product of the evangelist's theology, any more than it is in vi. 20, where it occurs also in the Marcan parallel. John delights in such double meanings. The test-passage is that which describes the recoil of the assailants before the presence of Jesus. But it is just here that apparent reminiscences of passages in the Old Testament suggest that the evangelist is working on traditional material. When Jesus made himself known, we are told, ἀπῆλθαν εἰς τὰ ὀπίσω καὶ ἔπεσαν χαμαί (xviii. 6). Now in Psalm xxxiv. 4—a psalm which has yielded several *testimonia*,[2] including one cited by John in xv. 25—the Righteous Sufferer prays, ἀποστραφείησαν εἰς τὰ ὀπίσω καὶ καταισχυνθείησαν οἱ λογιζόμενοί μοι κακά.[3] Again, in Ps. xxvi. 2, another 'Passion'

---

[1] See *Interpretation*, pp. 423–33.

[2] Ps. xxxiv. 11, ἀναστάντες μάρτυρες ἄδικοι, cf. Mark xiv. 57, καί τινες ἀναστάντες ἐψευδομαρτύρουν κατ' αὐτοῦ; Ps. xxxiv. 16, ἐξεμυκτήρισάν με μυκτηρισμόν, cf. Luke xxiii. 35, ἐξεμυκτήριζον οἱ ἄρχοντες.

[3] Cf. also Ps. xxxix. 15, ἀποστραφείησαν εἰς τὰ ὀπίσω καὶ ἐντραπείησαν οἱ θέλοντές μοι κακά. This Psalm has yielded the important *testimonium* cited in Heb. x. 5–9.

psalm,[1] the Sufferer declares, according to the LXX, οἱ ἐχθροί μου αὐτοὶ ἠσθένησαν καὶ ἔπεσαν. The Hebrew runs, כָּשְׁלוּ וְנָפָלוּ, 'they stumbled and fell', which is somewhat closer to the Fourth Gospel.[2] It seems, therefore, that the Johannine description has behind it those psalms which played so large a part in the formation of the Passion tradition, and whose language colours so much of that of the Passion narrative in this and other gospels. That is to say, behind the Johannine theology of this passage we can discern once again the more primitive conception of Christ as the Righteous Sufferer of prophecy. If so, then there is strong ground for believing that John is drawing upon tradition, as he is in other places where the primitive stock of 'testimony' scriptures is laid under contribution. In that case, we are justified in concluding that the picture of the assailants recoiling before their intended victim, though it is here made to serve a theological purpose, was an integral part of one form of tradition.

In all our gospels the account of the arrest includes an attack on the posse, in which a slave of the High Priest is injured. The setting of the episode varies. In Mark, followed by Matthew, it follows the apprehension of the Prisoner, and has the aspect of an attempted rescue.[3] In Luke and John it precedes the arrest, and looks like an attempt to prevent it. In the description of the blow, and there alone, there is some measure of verbal agreement among the four. For the purpose of comparison we may place Mark and John side by side.

Mark xiv. 47	John xviii. 10
εἷς τῶν παρεστηκότων	Σίμων Πέτρος
σπασάμενος τὴν μάχαιραν	ἔχων μάχαιραν εἵλκυσεν αὐτὴν
ἔπαισεν τὸν δοῦλον	καὶ ἔπαισεν τὸν τοῦ
τοῦ ἀρχιερέως	ἀρχιερέως δοῦλον
καὶ ἀφεῖλεν αὐτοῦ	καὶ ἀπέκοψεν αὐτοῦ
τὸ ὠτάριον (v.l. ὠτίον)	τὸ ὠτάριον (v.l. ὠτίον)[4]

---

[1] Ps. xxvi. 12, ἐπανέστησάν μοι μάρτυρες ἄδικοι, cf. Mark xiv. 57. For John, the repeated use of the verb ὑψοῦν with reference to the vindication of the Sufferer (verses 5, 6) would be significant.

[2] If the attractive, though poorly attested, reading ἀπῆλθεν...ἔπεσεν should be adopted, the allusion to the psalms would still be pertinent; the whole body of the Sufferer's adversaries (οἱ λογιζόμενοί, θέλοντές, μοι κακά) would then be incorporate in the person of the traitor.

[3] But perhaps it was an act of defiance rather than defence. An injury is inflicted upon the servant, as surrogate for his master, which would have disqualified the latter from performing his sacred office (D. Daube, in *Journal of Theological Studies*, vol. XI, part 1 (1960), pp. 59–61).

[4] It is not certain whether Mark and John agree in the word for 'ear', or whether ὠτάριον is to be read in the one and ὠτίον in the other. It is possible that in both

Matthew and Luke differ from Mark and John in using the verb πατάσσειν instead of παίειν. Matthew agrees with Mark in using the verb (ἀπο)σπᾶν where John has ἑλκύειν, and Luke says nothing about the 'drawing' of the weapon. Where all three Synoptics use the somewhat odd expression ἀφεῖλεν for the removal of the ear, John has the more natural ἀπέκοψεν. But John agrees with Luke against the others that it was the *right* ear that suffered. Further, whereas the Synoptics do not name the assailant but describe him merely as one present, or one of the adherents of Jesus,[1] John knows that it was Simon Peter, as he also knows the name of the injured man, Μάλχος.

After the 'removal' of the ear, Mark has nothing further to say of the episode. According to Luke, Jesus used the somewhat enigmatic words, ἐᾶτε ἕως τούτου—meaning, probably, 'Let them have their way as far as this', and in any case implying disapproval of the attack—and he then healed the injured ear. Of the healing the others know nothing, but the expression of disapproval is more clear and emphatic in Matthew and John. Both report an order to sheathe the weapon, but in different terms:

Matt. xxvi. 52	John xviii. 11
ἀπόστρεψον τὴν μάχαιράν σου	βάλε τὴν μάχαιραν
εἰς τὸν τόπον αὐτῆς	εἰς τὴν θήκην

Matthew then gives an aphorism, πάντες γὰρ οἱ λαβόντες μάχαιραν ἐν μαχαίρῃ ἀπολοῦνται, which betrays the use of the story for purposes of ethical instruction.[2] He adds a saying about legions of angels without parallel elsewhere, and concludes with a dogmatic statement about the fulfilment of prophecy.[3] Of all this John has nothing. After the command

---

ὠτίον is due to assimilation to Matthew, where all MSS. give this reading. Luke has οὖς.

[1] Mark's εἷς τῶν παρεστηκότων is indeterminate; it might mean 'a bystander'; that Mark conceived others to have been present beside the Twelve and the posse, is clear from the episode of the νεανίσκος. Matthew has interpreted it as meaning one of those who accompanied Jesus, εἷς τῶν μετὰ 'Ιησοῦ. Luke similarly speaks of οἱ περὶ αὐτόν, one of whom uses his sword.

[2] The epigrammatic generalization is comparable in form with the aphorism which Mark has introduced into the Gethsemane *pericopé*, τὸ μὲν πνεῦμα πρόθυμον ἡ δὲ σὰρξ ἀσθενής (Mark xiv. 38). Both are probable evidence that the form of tradition lying behind each of these gospels had had a prior history in the context of Christian *didaché*. The didactic motive persists in what follows in Matthew.

[3] The difference between Mark and Matthew here should not be overlooked. Mark's ἵνα πληρωθῶσιν αἱ γραφαί, 'Let the scriptures be fulfilled', is the direct expression of a personal and ethical resolve. Matthew's πῶς οὖν πληρωθῶσιν αἱ γραφαί, ὅτι οὕτως δεῖ γενέσθαι (xxvi. 54), followed by τοῦτο δὲ ὅλον γέγονεν ἵνα

to sheathe the sword, Jesus expresses his acceptance of the Father's will, in terms which (as we have seen)[1] recall the Marcan, and still more the Matthaean, rendering of the prayer in Gethsemane, while in substance they are the equivalent of the concluding words in Mark: ἵνα πληρωθῶσιν αἱ γραφαί.

Briefly, then, John agrees with all the Synoptics in the use of the expressions μάχαιρα, and τὸν δοῦλον τοῦ ἀρχιερέως, with Mark against Matthew and Luke in the verb παίειν, with Matthew and Mark against Luke in avoiding the term οὖς, and with Luke against Matthew and Mark in the words τὸ δεξιόν. That is the extent of verbal agreement. In substance, though not in words, the Johannine account agrees with the Lucan in representing the attack as an attempt at defence, not rescue, and with the Matthaean in giving a direct order to sheathe the weapon. In the final expression of acceptance of the will of God (as declared in the Scriptures) John goes with Mark (rather than Matthew), in spirit though not in words, while Luke has nothing to correspond.

There is here no sufficient ground for inferring that the story of the assault on the slave was derived from the Synoptic Gospels, in spite of the striking verbal resemblance in the clause describing the actual blow. It is impossible to treat any one of the Synoptics as the primary source of the Johannine version of the narrative, since he is sometimes closer to one and sometimes to another of the three. Once again, the hypothesis of literary conflation of documentary sources seems less probable than that of variation within an oral tradition. It does not appear that theological motives have been at work. The one original contribution which John makes to the narrative is the naming of the assailant and his victim. It is customary at the present time to regard the insertion of names into a narrative in which the persons are elsewhere anonymous as a symptom of 'legendary development'. That story-tellers do delight in individualizing their characters by supplying them with names is certainly true; but it is not true that the line of development is always in that direction, nor are the names supplied always fictitious. In the Gospels, Mark's Jairus has lost his name in Matthew, his Bartimaeus in Matthew and Luke, and his Alexander and Rufus have vanished from both. On the other hand, in introducing Caiaphas for Mark's vague ὁ ἀρχιερεύς Matthew has certainly not invented a fictitious name. It is therefore not legitimate to assume

πληρωθῶσιν αἱ γραφαὶ τῶν προφητῶν (xxvi. 56), is conceived in the form of dogmatic instruction. John is more akin to Mark than to Matthew here.
[1] See above, pp. 68–9.

from the outset that the identification of the assailant as Simon Peter and of the slave as Malchus is fictitious. If we are to take account of the general probabilities of the situation, we should reflect that if there were two swords among the Twelve, as Luke says there were (xxii. 38), it is more than likely that Peter had one of them, and if he had, he was (so far as we know him) not the man to let it rest in its sheath.[1] This is an inference, and an inference which the Fourth Evangelist might have made as readily as we do. If, on the other hand, there was a tradition to this effect, it is not difficult to see why it might have been covered over at a time when Peter was a marked man (cf. Acts xii. 3, 17) and it was not politic to let him be represented as a man of violence—above all, as one who deliberately affronted the High Priest in the person of his servant (if that be the true significance of the injured ear). As for Malchus, the name may well be fictitious, and the introduction of his kinsman in the group round the fire in the High Priest's courtyard (xviii. 26) may be no more than a dramatic touch of verisimilitude. On the other hand, if there was present at the palace (xviii. 15) a μαθητής who was γνωστὸς τῷ ἀρχιερεῖ (and I see no a priori reason for rejecting the statement),[2] then we have a channel through which knowledge of the man's name might have passed into Christian tradition. So far as I can see we have no sufficient evidence for either accepting or rejecting the names of Peter and Malchus as traditional.

To sum up:

1. The second act of the Passion drama in John begins with a topographical note which would be pointless as a correction of Mark, and indicates with fair certainty the use of a different strain of tradition.

2. Although there is here no account of the prayer of Jesus, a comparison of John xii. 27–9 with relevant passages in other New Testament writings makes it probable in the highest degree that John had a distinct form of tradition about the prayer, and reasonably probable that it was part of the Passion tradition as it reached him. Its displacement could be understood on the basis of his known practice.

[1] As we noted above, Peter's action in the Garden is consistent with his offer to die *for* his Master (as in John xiii. 37), rather than to die *with* him (as in Mark xiv. 31; Matt. xxvi. 35; Luke xxii. 33). This evidence might be interpreted in more than one direction. If John chose (for some reason not obvious to us) to make Peter the champion of his Master when he was in danger, he would naturally make the necessary adjustment in the form of Peter's profession of loyalty. But it is equally plausible, at least, to suppose that the tradition which John followed was itself consistent in this respect, and different from that followed by the Synoptics.   [2] See below, pp. 86–8.

3. The introduction of Roman troops into the scene of the arrest has no obvious theological or apologetic motive, and may or may not be derived from a special strain of tradition.

4. The account of the assault on the High Priest's servant resembles Mark so closely that we could well believe it to be derived from Mark, but that the immediate context contains features resembling at one point Matthew and at another Luke, as well as other passages in Mark. These phenomena seem to point to the kind of variation that arises within an oral tradition, rather than conflation of documentary sources.

5. THE TRIAL

The account of the judicial proceedings follows the same general scheme in all four gospels. They are reported in two stages, the first in a Jewish court, the second in a Roman. So far all agree. They differ in the ways in which they have interwoven with the main narrative two subordinate themes, those of Peter's denial and of the maltreatment and mockery to which Jesus is subjected during the proceedings. In all this Matthew follows Mark closely, with a large amount of verbal agreement, interpolating certain episodes without any dislocation of the Marcan sequence. Luke also has interpolated an episode, that of the interview with Herod, but apart from that he diverges substantially from the Marcan order. While Mark places Peter's threefold denial after the examination in the Jewish court, Luke places it before this examination, in the interval of waiting for the Sanhedrin to assemble at daybreak. Again, Mark recounts two scenes of mockery, the first by the hangers-on of the Jewish court, immediately after the conclusion of the hearing, the second by Roman soldiers after Pilate has passed sentence. In the former Jesus is mocked as a would-be prophet, in the latter as a would-be king. Luke has a scene in which he tells (very briefly as compared with the others) how the guards who held Jesus in custody for the Sanhedrin mocked his prophetic claims, and he places this immediately after Peter's denial and before the examination by the Jewish court; and he has a second scene in which Jesus is mocked by soldiers, but the soldiers of Herod, not of Pilate, during an interlude in the course of the Roman trial. The characteristic features of the Marcan scene—the crown and purple of mock-royalty—are here missing, nor is there anything of the kind at the point where Mark has placed the mockery by Roman soldiers.

In the Fourth Gospel the interweaving of Peter's denial with the proceedings before the Jewish court is more subtly contrived. His first denial precedes, his second and third follow, the examination. John has thus carried through more effectively what was no doubt Mark's intention, to represent the scenes within the palace and outside in the courtyard as taking place during the same period of time.[1] The scene of maltreatment

---

[1] Critical objections which have been urged against the order of the text are unfounded, and attempts to improve it misguided. In particular, the suggestion that the repetition of the words ἦν δὲ Πέτρος ἑστὼς καὶ θερμαινόμενος (with slight

and mockery by the hangers-on of the High Priest's entourage, as we have it in Mark, has here shrunk to a single blow from one of the apparitors of the court, during, not after, the examination. The mockery by Roman soldiers is given with all the detail of crown and purple, as in Mark, but, once again, during and not after the trial, at a point where it leads up to the great central scene of *Ecce Homo*, which is peculiar to this gospel. This measure of rearrangement, which is not very radical, might well be due to conscious design on the part of a writer who has exhibited in this part of his work, more brilliantly than anywhere else, his power of dramatic narrative.

In what follows I shall deal first with the account of Peter's denial, in order to go through the two stages of judicial proceedings without interruption.

(a) Peter's Denial (xviii. 15–18, 25–7)

In the account of Peter's threefold denial of his Master the four gospels are closely parallel, and introduce identical or nearly identical words and phrases more often than in any other part of the Passion narrative. We might easily believe that John was here doing no more than edit Mark, improving the *mise-en-scène* in the process, and adding some details. Yet the position is perhaps not quite so simple. The three versions of the story (for Matthew follows Mark so faithfully that his account cannot be regarded as a distinct version)[1] differ in a number of points in such a way (apart from those places where John stands alone) that sometimes Mark and Luke agree against John, sometimes Mark and John against Luke, and sometimes Luke and John against Mark.[2] These points are mostly trivial,

variation), in xviii. 18 and 25, indicates a seam where the text has been dislocated and joined up clumsily, appears to me singularly uncalled for. Surely, on the contrary, the repetition serves both neatly and effectively to suggest the continuity of the narrative of events in the αὐλή in spite of the fact that it has been necessary to interrupt them to report the simultaneous occurrences inside the palace.

[1] The changes which Matthew has made are such that they might easily have been made (if one may put it so) by the use of a blue pencil on a written sheet, without rewriting the whole, as Luke and John would have had to do if they had used Mark as a source.

[2] See Table 2, p. 85. This table compares the four accounts only in respect of the essential or nuclear features of the story, neglecting special individual traits, such as Mark's ἀναθεματίζειν καὶ ὀμνύναι (copied by Matthew), Luke's statements that 'about an hour' elapsed between the second denial and the third, and that when the cock crew στραφεὶς ὁ κύριος ἐνέβλεψεν τῷ Πέτρῳ, and the special Johannine features to be considered. These might well be contributions of the evangelists as authors, yet if there is a case for the view that the core of the story came down with minor variations through different channels of oral tradition, then the existence of these further variants strengthens the case.

and if we conceive them as the result of deliberate alteration of a documentary source the changes seem motiveless. The only difference in substance is the reduction of Mark's two cockcrows to one in Luke and John (as also in Matthew). That John was conflating Mark and Luke is improbable; that he was copying Mark, and in altering his source happened from time to time to hit on the same changes as Luke, is no doubt possible. But even here (where the theory of dependence on the Synoptics could more easily be defended than elsewhere) the simplest explanation of the facts would seem to be undesigned variation within an oral tradition.[1]

There is thus some ground for thinking that we are here once again in touch with a separate strain of tradition lying behind the Fourth Gospel. If so, then the features of the story which are peculiar to this gospel deserve examination. It must in any case be conceded that John's account is in some ways more perspicuous, and indeed answers some questions which the Synoptics leave unanswered in the minds of readers. How did Peter come to be there at all? Luke says merely that when Jesus was led to the High Priest's palace Peter was following at a distance (ἠκολούθει μακρόθεν—following the crowd, that is). In the next breath he adds that when a fire had been lit in the middle of the courtyard Peter sat down among them.[2] How he got there we are not told. Mark is a little clearer.

---

[1] The question has been raised by various critics, whether the episode of Peter's denial is to be regarded as an original or integral part of the Passion narrative. It is clear that, unlike most other episodes, it *could* have existed as an independent unit of narrative; and it might well have had a place in Christian *didaché* to enforce the constantly recurring theme of 'confessing' and 'denying' Christ (Matt. x. 33, Luke xii. 9; cf. 1 John ii. 22–3 and see my note *ad loc.*). If it originally circulated separately, this might help to account for the insertion of this episode at different points of the narrative in the several gospels. It is even suggested that the tradition followed by Luke (before it was conflated with Mark) had no prediction of a denial, but only in general terms of an 'eclipse' of faith (Luke xxii. 31–3)—and therefore no denial. But without verse 33 the dialogue has no climax. In fact, the story derives much of its force from its setting in the Passion narrative, and the variation in position may be readily accounted for by the difficulty of representing in a convincing way two simultaneous sequences of events in different places. But I should hold it very probable that the story was often told for didactic purposes, even apart from its present setting, and that its form may have been affected by such use (as I have suggested is the case with the Marcan account of Gethsemane and the Matthaean account of the attack on the High Priest's slave and its sequel (p. 78)). It may indeed have been largely in the course of frequent use in oral teaching that the story acquired its peculiar blend of general uniformity with variation in detail. But I believe it to be an integral element in the common Passion tradition.

[2] The subject of the verbs in participial form (περιαψάντων . . . συγκαθισάντων) is the indefinite third plural, for the reference cannot be to the last-mentioned

Table 2. *Peter's threefold denial*

Differences in respect of		Matthew	Mark	Luke	John
I. Challenger	1	maid	maid	maid	maid
	2	another (maid)	(the same) maid	another (ἕτερος)	'they'
	3	bystanders	bystanders	another (ἄλλος)	slave
II. Mode of statement	1	2nd person	2nd person	3rd person	2nd person
	2	3rd person	3rd person	2nd person	2nd person
	3	2nd person	2nd person	3rd person	2nd person
III. Substance of allegation	1	'with Jesus' (μετά)	'with Jesus' (μετά)	'with him' (σύν)	'one of his disciples'
	2	'with Jesus' (μετά)	'one of them'	'one of them'	'one of his disciples'
	3	'one of them' (ἡ λαλιά δῆλον ποιεῖ)	'one of them' (a Galilaean)	'with him' (μετά) (a Galilaean)	'with him' (μετα)
IV. Use of verb	1	ἠρνήσατο	ἠρνήσατο	ἠρνήσατο	—
	2	ἠρνήσατο	ἠρνεῖτο	—	ἠρνήσατο
	3	—	—	—	ἠρνήσατο
V. Form of reply	1	'I do not know' (τί λέγεις)	'I do not know' (τί λέγεις)	'I do not know' (αὐτόν)	'I am not'
	2	'I do not know' (τὸν ἄνθρωπον)	—	'I am not'	'I am not'
	3	'I do not know' (τὸν ἄνθρωπον)	'I do not know' (τὸν ἄνθρωπον)	'I do not know' (ὃ λέγεις)	—

In I, all four agree on (1); John differs from all in (2) and (3); in substance his (2) = Matthew and Mark (3) against Luke.

In II, John agrees with Matthew and Mark against Luke on (1), with Luke against Matthew and Mark on (2), and with Matthew and Mark against Luke on (3).

In III, John differs from all on (1), agrees partially with Mark and Luke against Matthew on (2), and agrees with Luke against Matthew and Mark on (3).

In IV, John differs from all on (1), agrees with Matthew against Mark and Luke on (2), and differs from all on (3).

In V, John differs from all on (1), agrees with Luke against Matthew and Mark on (2), and differs from all on (3).

Out of fifteen points listed above, there are seven in which John differs from all other gospels.

He says that when Jesus was led away to the High Priest's house (πρὸς τὸν ἀρχιερέα) Peter followed him at a distance as far as the interior of the courtyard (ἀπὸ μακρόθεν ἠκολούθησεν αὐτῷ [he followed Jesus, not the crowd] ἕως ἔσω εἰς τὴν αὐλὴν τοῦ ἀρχιερέως). There 'he was sitting (ἦν συνκαθήμενος) with the attendants warming himself at the fire' while the events next related were taking place inside the palace. John is more circumstantial. When Jesus was taken to the house of Annas, Peter was following Jesus (ἠκολούθει Ἰησοῦ—the expression is surely chosen with design: Peter was still a follower of his Master). But he got no further than the gate of the courtyard. There was, however, with him another μαθητής, who belonged to the circle of the High Priest. While Peter stood at the gate outside, this person went straight in along with Jesus (συνεισ-ῆλθεν τῷ Ἰησοῦ εἰς τὴν αὐλὴν τοῦ ἀρχιερέως). He then turned back and went out again, and, after a word to the portress, brought Peter with him into the courtyard.[1] She half-recognized Peter, and asked, 'Are you another of his disciples?'[2] And so we come to Peter's first denial. Then we learn that the slaves and attendants had lit a charcoal fire because it was a cold night, and that Peter 'was standing with them (ἦν μετ' αὐτῶν ἑστώς) and warming himself' when the events next related happened within the palace.

This vivid narrative, every step of which is clear and convincing, is either the product of a remarkable dramatic *flair*, or it rests on superior information. The choice between these alternatives will go along with the view taken of the disciple who was γνωστὸς τῷ ἀρχιερεῖ (xviii. 15), or was a γνωστὸς τοῦ ἀρχιερέως (xviii. 16).[3] Is he merely a *dramatis persona* created to provide a plausible means of getting Peter inside? It is now generally recognized that γνωστός implies something more than mere

---

persons, ἀρχιερεῖς καὶ στρατηγοὶ τοῦ ἱεροῦ καὶ πρεσβύτεροι: the reference of αὐτῶν therefore is equally indefinite. Mark names ὑπηρέται (xiv. 54); so does Matthew, but he has no fire. John names δοῦλοι and ὑπηρέται.

[1] Or, possibly, spoke to the portress who then brought Peter in.

[2] Καὶ σύ perhaps implies that the maid knew Peter's sponsor to be a μαθητής of Jesus, and surmised that Peter was another of them. Similarly John has supplied a reason for the third challenge to Peter (xviii. 26): the questioner had seen him in the garden. In the Synoptics the third challenger recognizes Peter as a Galilaean—by his accent, according to Matthew.

[3] It is possible that the substantival construction with the genitive makes γνωστός somewhat more of a formal description than the adjectival construction with the dative, as *amicus Caesari* has a slightly different shade of meaning from *amicus Caesaris*, which suggests membership of the *cohors amicorum*.

acquaintance.[1] It means that the person so described was a member of the High Priest's circle, possibly a kinsman and himself of priestly birth, or at any rate one who stood in intimate relations with the governing high priestly family. To a reader approaching the Fourth Gospel from the Synoptics it is certainly surprising to find such a person among the 'disciples' of Jesus, even if μαθητής be given a somewhat extended connotation.[2] But to assume that the Synoptic picture is exhaustive or exclusive would be to beg the very question we are discussing. There are after all hints even in the Synoptics[3] that among ruling circles the attitude to Jesus was not at all times so uniformly hostile as they usually represent it. They probably do not give a complete picture. Moreover, the Synoptic neglect of Judaea, before the period of the final clash, is notorious, and few critics would now be prepared to rule out the possibility that Jesus worked in the south a good deal more than Mark, or even Luke, allows; or the possibility (therefore) that he had adherents there who do not appear in the Synoptic narrative. If John shows frequent interest in μαθηταί

---

[1] Γνωστός of persons is not very common. It is a by-form of γνωτός, which from Homer can be used in the sense of 'kinsman'. In 2 Esdras xv. 10 (Neh. v. 10) we have οἱ ἀδελφοί μου καὶ οἱ γνωστοί μου, where γνωστοί is a mistranslation of נְעָרַי (or represents a variant text). Yet the translator probably felt that ἀδελφοί and γνωστοί went naturally together. In Luke ii. 44 συγγενεῖς καὶ γνωστοί form a group, and in Luke xxiii. 49 οἱ γνωστοί are certainly not mere acquaintances. This passage echoes the language of Ps. lxxxvii. 9, ἐμάκρυνας τοὺς γνωστούς μου ἀπ' ἐμοῦ. In the same Psalm (19) γνωστοί occurs in parallelism with φίλος.

[2] To find a person of priestly family among the disciples of Jesus would not in itself be very surprising. According to Acts vi. 7 the primitive Church included in its membership πολὺς ὄχλος τῶν ἱερέων. John the Baptist was himself of priestly family, according to Luke i, and it now appears that his mission was in some way related to the priestly community of Qumran. On any showing there was interchange between the circle of Jesus and the circle of John the Baptist, and according to the Fourth Gospel the first disciples of Jesus came from the Baptist circle. But to belong to a priestly family, or to be under the influence of a priestly community, is one thing; to belong to the circle of the aristocratic Annas and Caiaphas is another thing. The surprising thing is to find a member of the governing class described as a μαθητής of Jesus. But John similarly describes Joseph of Arimathaea. It may well be that he uses μαθητής in a somewhat wide sense.

[3] E.g. Mark xii. 28–34 (might John have described this γραμματεύς, who accepted the teaching of Jesus about the two chief commandments with enthusiastic assent, and who was pronounced οὐ μακρὰν ἀπὸ τῆς βασιλείας τοῦ θεοῦ, as a μαθητής in his sense of the term?), Mark x. 17 (the man of great possessions was at least a potential disciple, since he received the call, ἀκολούθει μοι). And Joseph of Arimathaea was at any rate friendly, according to the Synoptics, as well as the Fourth Gospel, and the former say he was προσδεχόμενος τὴν βασιλείαν τοῦ θεοῦ, which perhaps, again, points to a potential μαθητής.

resident to the south, we are not obliged to reject all this out of hand because the Synoptics say nothing about them.[1] The question of the μαθητής who was γνωστός τῷ ἀρχιερεῖ cannot be decided apart from a general consideration of these alleged Judaean disciples. I shall attempt some such consideration later.[2] But at present I would observe that if this evangelist did have information about otherwise unknown southern disciples, we should naturally be prepared to learn from him new facts which we might never have inferred from a reading of the Synoptic gospels alone, such as that Jesus had at least one adherent in high-priestly circles. That we hear no more about this μαθητής does not count against the acceptability of John's statement. Quite the contrary. Legend-makers always like to identify anonymous characters in a story with other, better known, figures.[3] Here, however, the disciple is characterized only by the one feature necessary to explain his role in the particular incident—his relation to the High Priest. This is quite in the manner of traditional units of narrative.[4] While therefore it remains possible that the evangelist is merely elaborating the details of the scene out of an imaginative appreciation of the situation, there is nothing inherently suspicious in the appearance of this otherwise unknown disciple, whose intervention makes intelligible and natural an enigmatic feature of the Synoptic narrative.

(b) The Examination before the High Priest (xviii. 12–14, 19–24)

According to Mark the purpose of the examination was to discover evidence on which Jesus might be sentenced to death. His account of proceedings is full and circumstantial. There are four main items:

---

[1] I see no reason to reject the *prima facie* implication of the Synoptic Gospels that Jesus had at least three friends or adherents in Judaea, namely: the owner of the donkey borrowed for the entry into Jerusalem, the landlord of the house in which the Last Supper was eaten, and 'Simon the leper' of Bethany.

[2] See pp. 244–7.

[3] John has not resisted the temptation when he identifies the woman who anointed Jesus with Mary the sister of Lazarus (unless we choose to make a redactor responsible for the note in xi. 2). The legend-makers early got to work to identify the γνωστός τοῦ ἀρχιερέως. He has been identified with the unnamed disciple of John i. 40, and with the Beloved Disciple of xiii. 23, etc., without the slightest support in the text, and even with John son of Zebedee; and in order to maintain this third identification the expression γνωστός τῷ ἀρχιερεῖ is taken to mean that the Galilaean fisherman was Purveyor of Fish to his Holiness the High Priest; which scarcely carries conviction.

[4] Cf. the disciples who were fishermen, the man who had great possessions, the woman who was a Syrophoenician, the leper who was a Samaritan, etc.

(*a*) the charge of threatening to destroy the temple, dropped because the witnesses did not agree;

(*b*) the High Priest's question, Σὺ εἶ ὁ χριστός; and an affirmative reply from Jesus;

(*c*) his prediction of the enthronement of the Son of Man;

(*d*) his condemnation on the capital charge of blasphemy.

Matthew has the same four items, but his account differs in detail. Luke says nothing of (*a*) the charge of threatening to destroy the temple, or of (*d*) the condemnation on a charge of blasphemy. The other two items he has, but with only occasional verbal agreement with Mark and (or) Matthew.

There is no reference to any of these four points in the Johannine account. Yet it is not a case of simple omission. As with the sacramental words and acts at the Last Supper, and the prayer of Jesus before his arrest, there are Johannine parallels to three of them, (*a*), (*b*) and (*d*), in other contexts.[1]

The saying about the destruction of the temple (*a*), which according to Matthew and Mark was cited against Jesus in evidence, is given by John in a variant form, in the context of his account of the cleansing of the temple (ii. 14–22). It will be useful to place the three reports of the saying side by side for comparison.

Mark xiv. 58	Matt. xxvi. 61	John ii. 19
ἐγὼ καταλύσω τὸν ναὸν	δύναμαι καταλῦσαι τὸν ναὸν	λύσατε τὸν ναὸν
τοῦτον τὸν χειροποίητον	τοῦ θεοῦ	τοῦτον
καὶ διὰ τριῶν ἡμερῶν	καὶ διὰ τριῶν ἡμερῶν	καὶ ἐν τρισὶν ἡμέραις
ἄλλον ἀχειροποίητον	αὐτὸν	
οἰκοδομήσω	οἰκοδομῆσαι	ἐγερῶ αὐτόν

[1] There is a theological equivalent for item (*c*), though not a parallel. The citation of Dan. vii. 13 and Ps. cix (cx). 1 in combination in Mark xiv. 62 gives a highly condensed picture based on the two passages. Dan. vii. 9–14 describes a scene in which the symbolic figure of the Son of Man comes with clouds to the Eternal, to be invested with universal sovereignty. This symbolical figure is here fused with that of the victorious priest-king of Ps. cix, who is enthroned at the right hand of Jehovah. This enthronement of the Son of Man (i.e. the reality which the combined imagery of Dan. vii and Ps. cix signifies) is to be manifested to those who are about to put Jesus to death (ὄψεσθε). In John the Son of Man is to be 'exalted', the verb ὑψοῦν being appropriate to the elevation of a person to royal status (it is in fact found in Ps. cix. 7, διὰ τοῦτο ὑψώσει κεφαλήν, which might easily be understood as meaning 'The Lord shall exalt him', as the climax of the whole paean of victory). Thus John viii. 28, ὅταν ὑψώσετε τὸν υἱὸν τοῦ ἀνθρώπου τότε γνώσεσθε ὅτι ἐγὼ εἰμί, is in a deep sense a theological equivalent for Mark xiv. 62. For John, the crucifixion of Christ is itself his ὕψωσις, the enthronement of the Son of Man. That the profound treatment of the theme in the Fourth Gospel is in any way dependent on Mark is entirely improbable. It represents a process of independent and original reflection upon traditional data.

That it is the same saying can hardly be doubted, though both the wording and the form of the sentence differ and the purport of the saying itself is not the same in all three. In Mark it is the declaration of an intention to destroy the temple and to build another temple, which, unlike the existing one, will be of more than human workmanship (ἀχειροποίητος). According to Matthew it is a claim to have the power to destroy the temple (without any expressed intention of doing so), and to rebuild the *same* temple (αὐτόν). In John we are probably to understand the clause λύσατε τὸν ναὸν τοῦτον as the protasis of a conditional sentence, with the imperative replacing the indicative,[1] the meaning being, 'If you destroy this temple, I will raise it up' (or 'If this temple be destroyed I will raise it up'). Here therefore the saying is neither a threat to destroy the temple nor a claim to have power to do so, but a promise to restore it after its (hypothetical) destruction. As in Matthew, against Mark, it is the *same* temple (αὐτόν) that is to be destroyed and restored, though the annexed interpretation makes it clear that neither as destroyed nor as restored is it χειροποίητος. The question of the relation between Matthew and Mark need not here be discussed. It is doubtful whether it could be answered in terms of the simple formula that Matthew 'edited' Mark. That John's version is derived from either is in no way probable. His sentence is of a different mint. His form is simpler than either of the others, and his ἐν τρισὶν ἡμέραις is certainly inferior grammatically to Mark's διὰ τριῶν ἡμερῶν as an expression for lapse of time. The substitution of ἐγείρειν for οἰκοδομεῖν might perhaps be credited to the evangelist's desire to find a verb which would fit his interpretation of the saying; yet ἐγείρειν was a current, and perfectly proper, word for erecting a building.[2]

The most probable account of the matter is that a saying about the destruction of the temple was current in oral tradition, and was something of an embarrassment to the Church. Stephen, we are told, was accused of

[1] We have the same idiom in English—'Spare the rod and spoil the child'. It is well established in Hebrew (see Davidson, *Hebrew Syntax*[3], p. 191), and it is by no means rare in Greek, its basis being perhaps the classical 'concessive' use of the imperative (see Goodwin, *Moods and Tenses of the Greek Verb*, 1889, §254). Here indeed the concessive use might be intended: 'though the temple be destroyed I will erect it in 3 days'.

[2] Cf. Lucian, *Alexander* 10: ἐκεῖνοι γὰρ καὶ νεὼν αὐτίκα ἐψηφίσαντο ἐγεῖραι καὶ τοὺς θεμελίους ἤδη ἔσκαπτον, *O.G.I.* 5. 677 (ii A.D.), οἱ ἐγείραντες τὴν οἰκοδομὴν τοῦ πυλῶνος (similarly in modern Greek). It is not a septuagintal term, its only occurrence being 1 Esdras v. 43 (44), εὔξαντο ἐγεῖραι τὸν οἶκον ἐπὶ τοῦ τόπου αὐτοῦ (with no Hebrew original), but קום, which is frequently rendered by ἐγείρειν, is used of the erection of altar, tabernacle, heap of stones, etc.

THE TRIAL

saying ὅτι Ἰησοῦς ὁ Ναζωραῖος οὗτος καταλύσει τὸν τόπον τοῦτον (*scil.* the temple; Acts vi. 14). The statement, says the author, was false; yet it is echoed in three of the gospels. Each evangelist tries to guard against misconstruction of it in his own way. Mark, like the author of Acts, says that the evidence that Jesus threatened to destroy the temple was false and was in fact not accepted by the Sanhedrin. Matthew says that Jesus was not even alleged to have threatened to destroy the temple but only to have said that he could do so if he wished; and even so, he adds, the witnesses were not to be believed. Luke simply drops the embarrassing saying (and the reference to it later on, Mark xv. 29). John gives it in a form in which Jesus is not the destroyer but the restorer of the temple,[1] and at the same time offers an interpretation which removes any reference to the actual temple at Jerusalem. This interpretation we may safely attribute to the evangelist, but his rendering of the saying itself almost certainly depends on a tradition different from that which lies behind the Synoptic Gospels (and Acts).

The crucial part of the Marcan *pericopé* consists of the question and answer about messiahship (*b*) and the verdict of guilty on a charge of blasphemy (*d*). A Johannine parallel is to be found embedded in the dialogue of John x. 22–38, which is staged at the Encaenia. That passage is an elaborate composition entirely in the style and manner of the evangelist, expounding some of the central ideas of his theology. Yet the basic elements of the dialogue are those of the Marcan account of the Sanhedrin proceedings, indicated by the key phrases, σὺ εἶ ὁ χριστός (x. 24), υἱὸς τοῦ θεοῦ[2] εἰμί (36), βλασφημία, βλασφημεῖς (33–6). The nucleus, in fact, of the Encaenia dialogue appears to be an alternative formulation of material which we possess also in the Marcan *pericopé*.

Further, the opening of this dialogue shows a striking resemblance to the opening of the Sanhedrin proceedings according to Luke (who differs widely from Mark at this point).

Luke xxii. 67–8	John x. 24–5
εἰ σὺ εἶ ὁ χριστός,	εἰ σὺ εἶ ὁ χριστός,
εἰπὸν ἡμῖν.	εἰπὸν ἡμῖν παρρησίᾳ.
εἶπεν δὲ αὐτοῖς	ἀπεκρίθη αὐτοῖς ὁ Ἰησοῦς
ἐὰν ὑμῖν εἴπω	εἶπον ὑμῖν
οὐ μὴ πιστεύσητε	καὶ οὐ πιστεύετε

[1] It is perhaps not too rash a conjecture that the form of tradition which spoke of restoration of the destroyed temple came down through Jewish Christian channels, where the *mystique* of the temple at Jerusalem was still alive.
[2] So also Matthew and Luke; Mark has τοῦ εὐλογητοῦ.

The resemblance is hardly accidental. It seems clear that we have before us a Johannine rehandling of material closely akin, at any rate, to that which has been incorporated, in part by Mark, in part by Luke, in their several renderings of the Passion narrative. If we are to adopt the hypothesis of literary dependence of John on the Synoptics, we shall be obliged to suppose that he conflated the two accounts, since, while the opening resembles Luke, it is Mark, and not Luke, who speaks of the charge of blasphemy. The more probable hypothesis, surely, is that John has worked on an independent form of tradition. There seem to be two possibilities: (a) John may have found this material already incorporated in a form of Passion narrative different from that followed by the Synoptics though akin to it in certain respects, and may have chosen to transfer it to a different part of his gospel, with the freedom which we have noted as being characteristic of his method; or (b) the material may have been handed down without any direct connection with the Passion narrative—the dialogue about messianic claims separately from the saying about the temple—and while Mark and Luke have used it for their account of the examination before the High Priest, John has found another setting for it. It is in any case clear that our evangelist had no theological motive for excluding from his Passion narrative material so closely germane to his own thought.

The Johannine account of the proceedings before the High Priest is entirely different from that of Mark and of the other Synoptic gospels. The High Priest questions Jesus περὶ τῶν μαθητῶν αὐτοῦ καὶ περὶ τῆς διδαχῆς αὐτοῦ. Jesus replies that his teaching has been given in public, and asks for witnesses to be produced and interrogated. He is thereupon struck by one of the apparitors, who asks, 'Is that how you answer the High Priest?' Jesus protests: If there is anything wrong about his reply, evidence should be given to that effect (instead of violence being used). Thereupon the hearing is closed, and Jesus is sent on to Caiaphas. The contrast with Mark is striking. Where the Marcan scene has profound theological significance, John, the most theological of the evangelists, has given a version which has no theological content, but moves altogether on a matter-of-fact level.

At two points only the Johannine account shows some contact with the Synoptic Gospels.

(i) The reply of Jesus to the High Priest's question about his teaching, ἐγὼ πάντοτε ἐδίδαξα ἐν συναγωγῇ καὶ ἐν τῷ ἱερῷ, recalls his protest in

Gethsemane against the use of violence to effect his arrest, as given by Mark (xiv. 49) and, with some variation, by the others: καθ' ἡμέραν ἤμην πρὸς ὑμᾶς ἐν τῷ ἱερῷ διδάσκων, καὶ οὐκ ἐκρατήσατέ με. The ethos of both passages is the same, and in both the stress falls upon the public character of the ministry of Jesus (as against any suggestion of furtive conspiracy). This was probably a constant element in the tradition, which could be introduced in various contexts.

(ii) The single ῥάπισμα delivered by one of the ὑπηρέται might well be a reduced reminiscence of Mark xiv. 65, where, at the conclusion of the hearing before the High Priest, οἱ ὑπηρέται ῥαπίσμασιν αὐτὸν ἔλαβον. Yet the whole situation is so different, and the ῥάπισμα fits so differently into its context, that it would be hazardous to argue for the dependence of John on Mark. The word ῥάπισμα itself is deeply embedded in the Passion tradition through its dependence on Isa. l. 6.[1]

These two points of resemblance, then, do not amount to evidence for the use of the Synoptic Gospels as sources, though they do indicate that a common tradition lies somewhere in the background. But the scene as a whole is so strongly in contrast with the Synoptic account that we must regard it as essentially independent. That it is the free composition of the evangelist is inherently improbable, since it lacks entirely any trace of theological interest. There are two special features which seem to point definitely to the use of a separate form of tradition.

(a) The mention of the *two* hierarchs, Annas and Caiaphas, both of whom are well known from non-Christian sources. Mark leaves his ἀρχιερεύς anonymous, and so does Luke. Matthew gives the name Caiaphas; certainly rightly, for we know that Caiaphas was appointed High Priest by Gratus and deposed under Vitellius.[2] Luke elsewhere names Annas and Caiaphas as ἀρχιερεῖς at the time when John the Baptist began his ministry, and he mentions them again together in Acts iv. 6, where, however, Annas alone is given the title ἀρχιερεύς, while Caiaphas is only one of those ἐκ γένους ἀρχιερατικοῦ.[3] It seems highly improbable that John should have dug out the names from remote passages of the Lucan writings to adorn his narrative. The fact that he appears somewhat

---

[1] See pp. 39–40, 102.

[2] Jos. *Antiq.* XVIII. 35, 95.

[3] Luke's language is very loose. The dating of a year by two ἀρχιερεῖς (like two consuls at Rome) is certainly anomalous. At the time represented by Acts iv. 6 Caiaphas was certainly in office, even though Annas may still have been called ἀρχιερεύς. See below.

confused about the parts played by the two hierarchs,[1] perhaps about the use of the title ἀρχιερεύς,[2] and about that official's tenure of office,[3] is in no way inconsistent with the view that he was drawing upon a good source of information. Indeed, it is rather in favour of that view, for an author composing freely would not be so likely to allow himself to fall into this kind of confusion as one who was incorporating material which, at a distance of place and time, he did not fully understand. It is probable

[1] In John xviii. 13 Jesus is taken before Annas, the father-in-law of the ἀρχιερεύς Caiaphas. In xviii. 24 he is sent by Annas to the ἀρχιερεύς, here unnamed. Meanwhile, in xviii. 19 ὁ ἀρχιερεύς (unnamed) interrogates Jesus: as he has not yet been sent to Caiaphas, the ἀρχιερεύς intended can hardly be other than Annas. The confusion may perhaps be due to some primitive corruption of the text; the variants in the MSS. do not seem to be anything more than ex post facto attempts to remove a difficulty. Nor do the speculative attempts of modern critics to mend matters by rearrangement carry conviction. The confusion is, however, perhaps not so inexcusable as it seems. See next note.

[2] The term ἀρχιερεύς (almost unknown in the Greek translation of O.T. books extant in Hebrew; only in Lev. iv. 3, Josh. xxii. 13, and a few other places as v.l.) has two uses: (a) ὁ ἀρχιερεύς properly means the single head of the priestly order, called הַכֹּהֵן absolutely, הַכֹּהֵן הַמָּשִׁיחַ, הַכֹּהֵן הַגָּדוֹל, הַכֹּהֵן הָרֹאשׁ; (b) ἀρχιερεῖς in the plural stands for a class of superior clergy, consisting of all ex-High Priests and of members of a particular group of families from which High Priests were chosen. A member of a group of ἀρχιερεῖς is necessarily an ἀρχιερεύς, and if he has already been mentioned in the context he is, by rule of Greek grammar, ὁ ἀρχιερεύς. Hence there is opening for some ambiguity of usage. Thus in Vit. 193–4 Josephus first speaks of τοὺς ἀρχιερεῖς Ἄνανον (our Annas) καὶ Ἰησοῦν τὸν τοῦ Γαμαλᾶ, and then, almost immediately, of ὁ ἀρχιερεὺς Ἄνανος. If in our present passage John had first introduced Annas as ὁ ἀρχιερεὺς καὶ πενθερὸς τοῦ Καιάφα ὃς ἦν ἀρχιερεὺς τοῦ ἐνιαυτοῦ ἐκείνου, his language would have been hardly more anomalous than that of Josephus. The meaning would have been, 'that member of the hierarchy whose name was Annas and who was father-in-law of the High Priest for the year'. At his second appearance in xviii. 19 the reference to him as ὁ ἀρχιερεύς, 'the said member of the hierarchy', would then have been natural enough. It is simply the twofold use of the term, in the singular for an individual functionary and in the plural for a class, that causes confusion—a confusion of which apparently Josephus was hardly conscious. But it is noteworthy that Annas in particular continues to be called ὁ ἀρχιερεύς long after his deposition (Jos. Antiq. xviii. 34).

[3] It is hardly possible to acquit the evangelist of a misconception of the High Priest's tenure of office. Attempts to do so fail to convince. He must have thought of it as an annual tenure, like that of priesthoods in the Greek cities. There was, however, much excuse for such a misconception, to anyone who was writing on the basis of information received and not from direct personal knowledge, in the very rapid succession of High Priests under the Roman provincial administration. The immediate predecessor of Caiaphas, and his predecessor, held office for no more than a year each (Jos. Ant. XVIII. 34). See also W. L. Knox, Some Hellenistic Elements in Primitive Christianity, p. 74; St Paul and the Church of Jerusalem, p. 61.

therefore that the introduction of the two names points to the independent use of a tradition different from that of the Synoptics, a tradition which, though the evangelist has not clearly appreciated it, accurately fits conditions in the Jewish hierarchy about this time, as depicted by Josephus: the aging Annas, formally deposed from the office of High Priest some fifteen years ago, continuing to hold the reins of power behind the scenes, while members of his family in succession received the titular dignity. As he contrived to put no fewer than five sons into office, it is likely enough that he had a son-in-law who also conveniently occupied the pontifical throne, although this is stated nowhere but in John xviii. 13; he was, says Josephus, the luckiest of men![1]

(b) The statement that Jesus was interrogated περὶ τῶν μαθητῶν αὐτοῦ καὶ περὶ τῆς διδαχῆς αὐτοῦ gives an aspect to the proceedings different from that which we gather from the Synoptic accounts; but it agrees well with the statement of a baraita in Bab. Sanh. 43b, that Jesus of Nazareth was condemned to death because he practised sorcery and 'incited and impelled' Israel (הסית והדיח את ישראל). The reference is clearly to the legislation of Deut. xiii, where these verbs are used of persons who try to pervert Israel to apostasy and idolatry. It is there laid down that if a prophet or visionary should seek to 'impel' Israel away from the way which the Lord commanded (לְהַדִּיחֲךָ מִן־הַדֶּרֶךְ אֲשֶׁר צִוְּךָ יהוה) he is to be put to death (xiii. 6). If a friend or near relation should 'incite' one to serve other gods (יְסִיתְךָ...לֵאמֹר נֵלְכָה וְנַעַבְדָה אֱלֹהִים אֲחֵרִים) he shall suffer the same penalty (xiii. 7). The implication therefore of the baraita clearly is that Jesus was arraigned as a false prophet or heretical teacher who was leading people into apostasy, and who therefore merited the death penalty under the deuteronomic legislation. If this was the view taken by the Jewish authorities, then it was entirely in order for Jesus to be questioned about the nature and content of his teaching and about the adherents he had won, as John says he was.

We are led to the conclusions (a) that for the hearing before the High Priest John is entirely independent of the Synoptic form of Passion narrative, although (b) at two points we recognize traits which belong to the common tradition underlying all our accounts; and (c) his account of the interrogation is drawn from some source, almost certainly oral, which

---

[1] Jos. Antiq. xx. 198, τοῦτόν φασι τὸν πρεσβύτατον Ἄνανον εὐτυχέστατον γενέσθαι· πέντε γὰρ ἔσχε παῖδας καὶ τούτους πάντας συνέβη ἀρχιερατεῦσαι τῷ θεῷ. The House of Annas was, according to rabbinic tradition, guilty of worse misdemeanours than nepotism.

was well informed about the situation at the time, and had contact with the Jewish tradition about the trial and condemnation of Jesus.

(c) The Trial before the Roman Governor[1] (xviii. 28–xix. 16)

The proceedings in the Roman court are depicted on a large canvas, with an elaboration of detail, and a dramatic power and psychological subtlety, far beyond anything in the other gospels. The portrait of Pilate is vivid and convincing, and, not less so, the picture of the wily pertinacity of the priests, willing to exploit their status of political subjection to throw responsibility upon the foreigner, and yet knowing well how to play upon his weakness to get their own way. How much of this is to be attributed to the creative skill of the writer it would be hard to say.

There are certain indications that the scene has in some respects been written up. In the first place, we observe that in reporting two hearings *in camera* the author ostensibly gives the actual words of judge and Prisoner in circumstances where, on his own showing, it is difficult to see how any possible informant could have been present. It appears therefore that he has felt himself at liberty, following a well established convention of ancient historiography, to compose speeches and dialogues which shall display the character of the situation as he conceives it, without professing to report *verbatim* what was actually said on the occasion.

Further, there is a certain kind of dramatic technique which we can trace in other parts of this gospel, and which is here used with marked effect. The author employs the device of two stages upon which the action is exhibited, a front stage and a back. As I have pointed out elsewhere,[2] the great sequence of controversial dialogues at the Feast of Tabernacles, which forms the central panel of the Book of Signs (vii–viii), is constructed

---

[1] Tacitus (*Ann.* xv. 44) calls him *procurator*, but this appears to be an anachronism. Provincial governors of equestrian status bore the title *procurator Augusti* from the time of Claudius. Earlier the usual style was *praefectus* or *pro legato*. See A. H. M. Jones, *Studies in Roman Law and Administration*, pp. 117 *sqq*. The question of Pilate's proper style appears now to be settled by the discovery, in 1961, of an inscription at Caesarea which contains the words PON]TIVS PILATVS [PRAE]FECTVS IVDA[EAE (see *Journal of Biblical Studies*, vol. LXXXI, part 1, March 1962, p. 70). After this chapter was written, I had the opportunity of hearing Mr A. N. Sherwin-White's lecture on the legal and administrative aspects of the trial before Pilate, in his course of Sarum Lectures. I would refer the reader to the lectures, to be published under the title *Roman Law and Roman Society in the New Testament* (Oxford University Press, 1963), for a clear, well documented and authoritative account of the background of the gospel reports of the trial. The account given in P. Winter, *On the Trial of Jesus* (De Gruyter, Berlin, 1961), differs in some points.

[2] See *Interpretation*, pp. 315, 347–8.

on this plan. Similarly here scenes of growing tension and tumult in public alternate with dialogues conducted in private within the praetorium. Again, in the same sequence at the Feast of Tabernacles I have pointed out how repeated references to attempted violence against the person of Jesus (vii. 30, 32, 44; viii. 59) are designed to keep alive in the mind of the reader a sense of the atmosphere of intense hostility in which the dialogues are conducted, and need not be understood as a record of separate and successive outbreaks. Similarly here, the repeated interventions of 'the Jews' (xviii. 30–1, 39–40; xix. 6–7, 12, 15) do not necessarily represent successive stages of the proceedings, but serve most effectively to keep the reader aware of the unrelenting pressure which the priests exert, while the governor turns and doubles like a hunted hare.

There is, on the other hand, little trace of directly theological motives. In xviii. 32 a formula similar to that which we met with in xviii. 9 calls attention to the fulfilment of the saying of Jesus in which he had spoken of his death as an 'elevation' (ὑψωθῆναι). The proposed remission of the case to the Jewish court, the evangelist means, would have ruled out death by crucifixion; a Roman trial would inevitably lead to such a death; and crucifixion lent itself to the macabre *double entente* conveyed by the verb ὑψοῦν, which for the evangelist held profound theological meaning. But there is no possible suspicion here that the theological idea has created the reported fact, for nothing in the whole story is more certain than that Jesus died by crucifixion, and if so, he died by sentence of a Roman court. The only other point where a theological conception is directly introduced is in the discussion on the nature of the kingship claimed by Jesus, where the definition of true kingship as the sovereignty of the truth bears the stamp of Johannine thought. This interpretation of kingship, however, is superimposed upon a discussion of the claim of Jesus to be a king which proceeds on entirely non-theological lines. Accused of being a pretender to the throne of Judaea, he defends himself by the plea that a political pretender would not have allowed himself to be arrested, as he himself had done, without a resort to arms. We may perhaps overhear in this the defence of Christians in the evangelist's own time accused of rebellion against the emperor; yet in the presumed situation it is a perfectly natural and valid plea, without any theological implications. That is to say, in composing the dialogue the evangelist has preserved the character of the tradition as it reached him, while adding a pointer to the theological interpretation. Similarly in the other hearing *in camera* Jesus acknowledges the authority exerted by the Roman governor as conferred on him by God, and in this again we may perhaps hear echoes of early Christian apologetic; but it is not the product of Johannine theology.

In the great central scene which has imprinted itself most deeply on the Christian imagination of all periods—the scene of *Ecce Homo*—it is permissible to suspect that the evangelist intended a *double entente*, and that the words which are ostensibly an expression of contempt for the exposed Pretender convey to the instructed reader the theological meaning, 'Here is the Man—the heavenly Man, the Son of Man'. But this is in any case below the surface, and it may well be that the evangelist's primary intention in the scene is truly dramatic rather than theological.

It appears therefore that the author's imagination has been at work in the production of this intensely dramatic narrative; yet where we have tested it, the impression we form is that he is not creating, but working upon given material. We have next to ask whether, if that is so, there is reason to think that this given material was derived from the Synoptic Gospels, or whether we can recognize traces of a separate tradition.

First, we may briefly review the Synoptic versions. In Mark the account of the trial falls into two parts: (i) the abortive interrogation of the Prisoner (xv. 2–5); (ii) the choice of Barabbas and sentence of death on Jesus (xv. 6–15). The trial being over, Mark adds a scene of mockery by the troops (xv. 16–20). Matthew follows Mark closely all through, but interpolates two additional episodes, without disturbing the general structure: (i) the dream of Pilate's wife (xxvii. 19), and (ii) the washing of Pilate's hands (xxvii. 24–5). Both of these have obvious apologetic interest. Luke diverges considerably. The passage which corresponds to Mark's account of the interrogation of the Prisoner (xxiii. 2–5) takes quite a different course, and verbal agreement with Mark is at a minimum. Out of 78 words (compared with Mark's 47), only 18 are common to both, and of these the question and answer, Σὺ εἶ ὁ βασιλεὺς τῶν Ἰουδαίων; Σὺ λέγεις, account for 8.[1] Luke interpolates at this point a hearing before Herod, unknown to the other gospels, and then comes to the episode of Barabbas (xxiii. 18–23), which again is differently conceived. The only significant words which are common to both are the name Barabbas, the terms στάσις and φόνος for his crimes, the repeated verb σταυροῦν (but in different grammatical forms), Pilate's question, Τί γὰρ κακὸν ἐποίησεν; and finally the antithetic ἀπέλυσεν—παρέδωκεν. In all, out of 162 words (where Mark has 125) no more than 30 are common to both. That is to say, in

---

[1] Matthew, in the same section, has 60 words, of which 32 are Marcan.

the whole of the account of the proceedings in the Roman court there is scarcely more than the indispensable minimum of verbal agreement between Luke and Mark, and there is little ground for regarding Mark as more than a contributory source, while there are features which strongly suggest that an alternative form of tradition lies behind parts of the Lucan account.

With this preface we turn to the Fourth Gospel. That it is describing the same proceedings is clear; there is no such radical divergence as we have noted in the examination before the High Priest. Yet places where contact with the Synoptics is close are rare—surprisingly rare where all are dealing with the same sequence of events. The following list exhausts such places.

(i) Pilate's question, Σὺ εἶ ὁ βασιλεὺς τῶν Ἰουδαίων; and the reply, Σὺ λέγεις. This is the core of the trial in all gospels. John alone has expanded the enigmatic reply[1] so as to make clear the sense in which he understood it: σὺ λέγεις ὅτι βασιλεύς εἰμι, i.e. '"King" is your word, not mine'. It may be that he borrowed the phrase itself from Mark, but it is hardly necessary to assume such direct dependence. The pregnant expression, σὺ λέγεις, may well have so taken hold of the imagination of early Christians that the story could not be told without it.

(ii) The verdict of not guilty. There is no such verdict in Mark, for the question, τί γὰρ ἐποίησεν κακόν; (Mark xv. 14, copied by Matthew and Luke), is not a verdict, but an expostulation. Luke, however, has the explicit οὐδὲν εὑρίσκω αἴτιον ἐν τῷ ἀνθρώπῳ τούτῳ (xxiii. 4), and again, οὐθὲν εὗρον ἐν τῷ ἀνθρώπῳ τούτῳ αἴτιον ὧν κατηγορεῖτε κατ' αὐτοῦ (xxiii. 14), and finally, οὐδὲν αἴτιον θανάτου εὗρον ἐν αὐτῷ (xxiii. 22).

---

[1] That 'You say' is either in Greek or in Aramaic a recognized form of expression for an affirmative reply to a question is a theory for which I have been able to find no sufficient support in actual examples. Matthew's σὺ εἶπας (xxvi. 25, 64, but *not* xxvii. 11) might be a translation of אָמַרְתָּ, of which S.–B. are able to produce one single instance with the meaning 'You are right' (scarcely enough to establish a usage). Exod. x. 29, εἴρηκας = כֵּן דִּבַּרְתָּ, is no real parallel. The phrase seems to have been felt to have an appropriately enigmatic or even mysterious tone, and as such was preserved in tradition. Its intended meaning is well illustrated by the passage in *Old Mortality* where the fanatical Covenanter Ephraim Macbriar is being examined by Lauderdale. '"Were you at the battle of Bothwell Bridge?" "I was", answered the prisoner, in a bold and resolute tone. "Were you armed?" "I was not—I went in my calling as a preacher of God's word, to encourage them that drew the sword in His cause." "In other words, to aid and abet the rebels?" said the Duke. "Thou hast spoken it", replied the prisoner.' Macbriar will not deny that he was present, encouraging the Covenanters, but he would not describe this as aiding and abetting rebels; that is Lauderdale's way of putting it: '*thou* hast spoken it'. Sir Walter was no doubt imitating the language of the gospels, and he has rightly grasped its nuance, which John has made explicit.

Similarly, John has ἐγὼ οὐδεμίαν εὑρίσκω ἐν αὐτῷ αἰτίαν (xviii. 38), and again, οὐδεμίαν αἰτίαν εὑρίσκω ἐν αὐτῷ (xix. 4), and a third time, ἐγὼ γὰρ οὐχ εὑρίσκω ἐν αὐτῷ αἰτίαν (xix. 6). The similarity of language is striking, and so is the triple repetition. If it were supported by other significant resemblances, the agreement here between Luke and John might well be explained by literary dependence. Yet if (as is probable) both writers are imitating the current language of the law-courts, the verbal resemblance would be less significant, and if (as is certain) both wished to emphasize as strongly as possible the innocence of Jesus, a common motive, rather than literary indebtedness, may account for the repetition.

(iii) The episode of Barabbas. John gives, in a much briefer manner, essentially the same account of the affair as Mark and Matthew, while he has nothing in common with Luke except the name and the verb ἀπολύειν. He puts into the mouth of Pilate the statement which Matthew makes as an introduction to the episode—that the governor was accustomed to concede an amnesty of one prisoner at the feast:

Matthew	John
κατὰ δὲ ἑορτὴν εἰώθει ὁ ἡγεμὼν	ἐστὶν δὲ συνήθεια ὑμῖν
ἀπολύειν ἕνα τῷ ὄχλῳ δέσμιον	ἵνα ἕνα ἀπολύσω ὑμῖν ἐν τῷ πάσχα

Pilate then proceeds, in words which closely resemble those of Mark, departing somewhat widely from Matthew, to propose the release of Jesus:

Mark	John
θέλετε ἀπολύσω ὑμῖν	βούλεσθε οὖν ἀπολύσω ὑμῖν
τὸν βασιλέα τῶν Ἰουδαίων;	τὸν βασιλέα τῶν Ἰουδαίων;

The reply is given more dramatically in John than in any of the others, and shows no sign of being derived from any of them: μὴ τοῦτον ἀλλὰ τὸν Βαραββᾶν. He then adds the explanation, ἦν δὲ ὁ Βαραββᾶς λῃστής. Matthew says no more than that he was δέσμιος ἐπίσημος. Mark is more explicit: Barabbas had taken part in a στάσις, in the course of which (he and the other) στασιασταί had committed murder. Luke also knows that he was in prison for στάσις καὶ φόνος. John's term λῃστής is hardly a mere paraphrase of Mark or Luke. It is the term regularly used by Josephus for the malcontents who took to the hills during times of troubles in Judaea, in protest against the existing administration, whether of Herod the Great or of Roman governors.[1] From one point of view they were

[1] Hezekiah ὁ ἀρχιλῃστής (*Antiq.* XIV. 159, *B.J.* I. 204) is thought to be the person referred to in the cryptic saying attributed to Hillel (who may be the famous rabbi) that there is no Messiah for the Israelites because they devoured him in the days of Hezekiah (*Bab. Sanh.* 98 b). His son Judas is presumably the same person as

'bandits', from another 'heroes of the national resistance movement'. The type has become familiar enough during the first half of the twentieth century. The use of the term ληστής therefore puts Barabbas in a recognizable historical setting.

Thus the close resemblance to Mark extends only to one sentence. There is in another sentence a slight resemblance to Matthew, and the description of Barabbas as a ληστής is not derived from either, but fits contemporary usage as reflected in Josephus.

(iv) The scourging and mockery (xix. 1–3). Mark (followed by Matthew) says that Jesus was scourged before being handed over for crucifixion.[1] Thereupon the troops made sport of his claim to kingship by a caricature of royal state, with crown and purple robe and a mock acclamation. Luke, on the other hand, says that Pilate *proposed* scourging (disguised under the euphemism παιδεύειν) as a milder penalty, preparatory not to execution but to release; and he has no scene of mockery at this point. John agrees with Mark in recording a scourging followed immediately by the scene of mockery. In describing this scene his language in the essential phrases is closely similar to Mark's, though his order is somewhat different.

Mark	John
οἱ στρατιῶται...	οἱ στρατιῶται
πλέξαντες[2] ἀκάνθινον στέφανον[3]	πλέξαντες στέφανον ἐξ ἀκανθῶν (but below, ἀκάνθινον στέφανον)
ἐνδιδύσκουσιν αὐτὸν πορφύραν...	ἱμάτιον πορφυροῦν περιέβαλον αὐτόν...
χαῖρε βασιλεῦ τῶν Ἰουδαίων	χαῖρε ὁ βασιλεὺς τῶν Ἰουδαίων

Judas the Galilaean or Gaulonite, the zealot leader (*Antiq.* XVII. 271, *B.J.* II. 56, *Antiq.* XVIII. 4–23), and Μανάϊμος υἱὸς Ἰουδᾶ τοῦ καλουμένου Γαλιλαίου (*B.J.* II. 433 *sqq.*), who was one of οἱ πρῶτοι τοῦ ληστρικοῦ στίφους (*Vit.* 21), is perhaps the מנחם בן־חזקיה whom some took to be the Messiah, according to *Bab. Sanh.* 99 a. The λησταί who with their wives and families established themselves in caves, and were there killed or captured by Herod the Great (*Antiq.* XIV. 415, 421 *sqq.*), were hardly ordinary brigands. The language Josephus uses of one of them who, although offered quarter, flung his wife and children down the precipice and followed them to his death, is significant: θάνατον πρὸ δουλείας ὑπομένων. For Josephus the extremists who barricaded themselves in the temple for a last stand against Titus in A.D. 70 are λησταί (*B.J.* VI. 123–9, etc.).

[1] This was normal procedure; cf. [Lucian], *Piscator* 2, ποικίλον τινὰ ἐπινοῶμεν θάνατον κατ' αὐτοῦ...ἐμοὶ μὲν ἀνασκολοπισθῆναι δοκεῖ αὐτὸν μαστιγωθέντα γε πρότερον, and passages cited by commentators.

[2] This word is omitted by D, with some support from Old Latin MSS. In the Matthaean parallel (xxvii. 29) it is read by all authorities. As assimilation of Mark to Matthew is very common, there is ground for suspecting that πλέξαντες is no part of the genuine Marcan text.

[3] Θ and some minuscules read στέφανον ἐξ ἀκανθῶν, with all MSS. in the Matthaean parallel, probably by assimilation.

On the other hand, where Mark says ἔτυπτον αὐτοῦ τὴν κεφαλήν, John gives ἐδίδοσαν αὐτῷ ῥαπίσματα, as he gives in place of Mark's vulgar Latinism φραγελλοῦν the more correct μαστιγοῦν. These changes might be without any great significance, but for the fact that they introduce into the passage the vocabulary of Isa. l. 6, where among the torments of the Servant of the Lord are μάστιγες and ῥαπίσματα. This suggests that John is here drawing upon a form of tradition coloured by the language of *testimonia* from the Old Testament.

If so, the question would remain, whether in writing up this tradition the evangelist was also influenced by Mark. In favour of this view we have both the close resemblance of language in the key phrases, and the coincidence in order. It is, however, by no means impossible that more than one strain of tradition preserved the details of robe and crown in almost (though not quite) identical language. The one word which gives one pause is πλέξαντες, a natural, but not inevitable, word in the context. This word, however, is absent from some of our authorities. Where assimilation is such a constant factor in MS. transmission, we may doubt whether the participle was in fact an original part of the Marcan text. In Matthew it stands firm, as does also the phrase στέφανον ἐξ ἀκανθῶν, which in Marcan MSS. varies with ἀκάνθινον στέφανον. Did John, then, follow Matthew here, and not Mark? Yet Matthew goes his own way. Instead of the purple robe he gives a scarlet mantle (χλαμὺς κοκκίνη), which is a different thing, without the strong suggestion of royalty inherent in ἱμάτιον πορφυροῦν. The case is not quite so clear as it seemed. If John is indeed dependent on the Synoptics, we might have to postulate conflation of Mark and Matthew.

The argument from order is formidable. In Mark the scourging is the normal preliminary to crucifixion. The trial is now over, and nothing remains but the infliction of the extreme penalty. The troops (we may suppose) occupy themselves with this rough horseplay while the necessary preparations are being made. In John the mockery becomes, surprisingly, the prelude to the great scene of *Ecce Homo*, which is associated with Pilate's continued attempts to manipulate the trial towards an acquittal of the Prisoner. The scourging is clearly not the customary preliminary to crucifixion, for there has been so far no question of a death sentence. In the dramatic situation depicted by John it may be either the milder penalty proposed but not carried out in Luke as a prelude to release, or it may represent the use of torture to elicit evidence, which was a recognized feature of judicial procedure under the

Roman Empire.[1] But while the relation of the scourging and mockery to the development of the plot differs widely from that which they bear in Mark, the Marcan order is reproduced, in so far that they follow directly upon the episode of Barabbas. Either, therefore, John is here influenced by Mark, or we must suppose that more than one strain of tradition preserved this sequence of events.

These four passages, then, suggest *prima facie* dependence of John on the Synoptics—chiefly on Mark, but also on Luke, and perhaps also on Matthew where he differs from Mark. Where a theory of conflation is indicated, the cogency of the evidence in favour of dependence is *pro tanto* weakened. It remains, however, that so far as they go these four passages tell in favour of the view that John employed the Synoptic Gospels as sources. It must, however, be admitted that they do not provide a very wide basis for inference, relatively to the considerable extent of the narrative in the Synoptics and still more in John.

There are two further points where contact with the Synoptic record is somewhat more remote, and these we must now examine.

(*a*) The silence of Jesus. In Mark this feature is emphasized. In the Jewish court, when Jesus does not answer the charges brought by the false witnesses, the High Priest asks, 'Have you no answer to the statements of these witnesses?' But Jesus, we read, 'kept silence and made no reply' (ἐσιώπα καὶ οὐκ ἀπεκρίνατο οὐδέν). It is only when the High Priest asks point-blank, 'Are you the Messiah?' that he gives a categorical answer, elaborating it with an enigmatic allusion to the enthronement of the Son of Man (Mark xiv. 60–2). Again, during the hearing before Pilate (xv. 2–5) Jesus is asked, 'Are you the king of the Jews?' and replies, ambiguously, σὺ λέγεις. The priests press their charges, and Pilate asks, 'Have you no answer? (οὐκ ἀποκρίνῃ οὐδέν;) You see how many charges are brought against you.' But Jesus, we read, 'no longer made any answer at all' (οὐκέτι οὐδὲν ἀπεκρίθη). Matthew follows Mark, though without complete identity of language. Luke says nothing of the silence of Jesus before the High Priest, or before Pilate; but when he was brought before Herod, we are told, the tetrarch 'questioned him at great length (ἐπηρώτα αὐτὸν ἐν λόγοις ἱκανοῖς), but Jesus gave him no reply (οὐδὲν ἀπεκρίνατο αὐτῷ)'.

---

[1] Cf. Acts xxii. 24, where Paul is threatened with this treatment: ἐκέλευσεν ὁ χιλίαρχος εἰσάγεσθαι αὐτὸν εἰς τὴν παρεμβολὴν εἴπας μάστιξιν ἀνετάζεσθαι αὐτόν. How essential a part of Roman judicial practice evidence under torture was considered to be is strikingly illustrated by Augustine, *De Civitate Dei*, XIX. 6.

The passage we have to consider in the Fourth Gospel has obvious affinity with these, though the wording is not particularly close. When the accusers (at a late stage in the trial) informed Pilate that Jesus claimed to be υἱὸς θεοῦ, Pilate asked, πόθεν εἶ σύ; but Jesus gave him no reply (ἀπόκρισιν οὐκ ἔδωκεν αὐτῷ). When, however, Pilate pressed the matter (ἐμοὶ οὐ λαλεῖς; do you refuse to speak to *me*, Caesar's representative?) Jesus replied at length, but not to the original question. Upon that, his silence remained unbroken.

The quick and easy explanation of these phenomena is that Mark is the source upon which the other gospels depend. This would indeed be a plausible account if we were obliged to look for literary sources. Yet the hypothesis that both Luke and John took note of this feature of the Marcan narrative, and while passing over it in the Marcan context worked it in at different points, is not without difficulty. On the other side it must be observed that the prophecy of Isa. liii. 7–8, ὡς ἀμνὸς ἐναντίον τοῦ κείροντος ἄφωνος οὕτως οὐκ ἀνοίγει τὸ στόμα αὐτοῦ, is cited as a *testimonium* in Acts viii. 32, and unmistakably alluded to in the passage about the sufferings of Christ in 1 Pet. ii. 22–4. In view of the importance of *testimonia* in shaping the evangelical tradition, it seems probable that the silence of Jesus was a primitive datum, present in various forms of the tradition of the Passion, though not necessarily at a fixed point,[1] and that as such it persisted even where (as in Mark xiv. 60–2 and John xix. 9–11) the silence is soon broken. If therefore there was, as we have found reason to suppose, a special form of tradition behind the Fourth Gospel, it would almost certainly include this feature in one way or another.

(*b*) Pilate's avoidance of responsibility. It is intrinsic to the Marcan account that Pilate in effect abdicated his judicial prerogative and allowed the fate of his Prisoner to be decided by popular clamour inspired by the priests. In Matthew this theme is dramatized in the scene where Pilate washes his hands of the whole affair, and the λαός accepts responsibility (Matt. xxvii. 24–5). The apologetic and polemical motive is manifest. There is no parallel to this scene in any other gospel. Nevertheless, in the Fourth Gospel also the theme of Pilate's avoidance of responsibility is emphasized; only whereas in Matthew he succeeds in transferring respon-

---

[1] This phenomenon of what we may call 'wandering details' is of not infrequent occurrence in the gospels (see pp. 169–73). Such details are, I believe, often of the highest historical value, but in the oral tradition they easily attached themselves to different parts of a story or to different stories—much more easily than in a composition resting upon written sources.

sibility to the Jews, in John he fails to do so. At the outset of the trial Pilate offers the Sanhedrin jurisdiction in the case. They refuse, on the ground of their incompetence to pass sentence of death.[1] It is true, as we have seen, that the evangelist associates this statement with the fulfilment of the words of Jesus according to which his death must be by 'lifting up'. Yet the fulfilment is in any case secured by the Roman sentence of crucifixion, no matter how that sentence came to be passed. In other words, the statement that the Jewish authorities refused jurisdiction and remitted the case to the governor is not one which we could well imagine to be the product of theological reflection upon the crucifixion of Jesus. It could not, on the other hand, have been derived from the Synoptics. Either therefore it is an intelligent (even though possibly mistaken) inference of the evangelist, or it rests upon independent information. Whether it does in fact correspond to the historical situation is a much-debated question. Precise information is lacking. One thing is certain: the prefect of Judaea had the power of life and death.[2] Any exercise of that power by the municipal government (unless it was a violent usurpation) must have been either by express privilege or by connivance (which, no doubt, was always a possibility, with weak or unscrupulous governors). Of the former we have no evidence, except, perhaps, in regard to one particular offence, that of a Gentile who should trespass beyond the barrier in the temple. If we are to take literally the words of Josephus in *B.J.* VI. 126, the right to inflict the death penalty in such cases was granted to the Jewish authorities. The emperor Titus is represented as addressing the Jewish extremists who had entrenched themselves in the temple: 'Did not you yourselves throw up this barrier to fence the sanctuary? Did not you place pillars at intervals in it, engraved in Greek and Latin characters, forbidding anyone to pass beyond it? And did not we give you permission to put to death (ὑμῖν ἀναίρειν ἐπετρέψαμεν) those who should trespass, including even Romans?' Rhetoric, however, is not to be interpreted as

---

[1] Somewhat strangely, the offer appears to be repeated at a late stage in the proceedings, xix. 6, where Pilate has appealed in vain to the priests to accept his verdict of not guilty, and they have responded with the demand (here made for the first time) that Jesus be crucified. Pilate then says, λάβετε αὐτὸν ὑμεῖς καὶ σταυρώσατε. The offer can hardly be intended to be taken seriously, for John knows (and assumes that his readers will know) that crucifixion was a Roman and not a Jewish form of execution; else the point of xviii. 31–2 would be missed. There must be some irony; Pilate may be supposed to mean, 'Crucify him yourselves, if you can! You cannot expect me to do it, for I believe him to be innocent.'

[2] Cf. Josephus, *B.J.* II. 117 (of the first Roman governor, Coponius), μέχρι τοῦ κτείνειν λαβὼν παρὰ τοῦ Καίσαρος ἐξουσίαν.

if it were the language of an Act of Parliament. It may be that even in this case the execution was subject to formal authorization by the governor. And the same may be true (for all we know) of the few cases cited of Jewish executions which seem to fall within the period between the deposition of Archelaus and the destruction of Jerusalem,[1] apart from those which were purely tumultuary actions, as was certainly the death of James and perhaps that of Stephen. There is, however, a statement in a *baraita* in *Sanh.* 1. 18 a. 37 that criminal jurisdiction was taken from the Sanhedrin forty years before the destruction of the temple,[2] i.e. in or about A.D. 30 (for we need not press meticulously what is probably a round number). The implication seems to be that some drastic restriction of rights previously enjoyed by the Jewish municipal government took place about that time, which was in any case, we may note, not far from the date of the death of Jesus. The interpretation of this statement is much disputed; but the position may fairly be stated thus: two completely independent documents, one Jewish, one Christian, state that in or about A.D. 30 the Sanhedrin was not in a position to inflict the death penalty. Their statements are made in entirely different contexts. Whatever problems these two passages may raise, their fortuitous agreement must carry weight. It is more probable than not that John is well informed when he represents the priests as bringing the case to the governor because they were bent on a capital sentence and their own powers did not extend so far. It does not, of course, necessarily follow that Pilate wished the Sanhedrin to decide the case. But his reluctance to take responsibility for the sentence is implicit in all the gospel accounts. In particular, Matthew and John emphasize his reluctance, and their agreement on this point, with no possibility of dependence of one on the other (so different are their ways of presenting the theme), is significant of the trend of the common tradition.

The sting, however, of the Matthaean account of the washing of Pilate's hands lies in the solemn acceptance of responsibility by the Jewish people: τὸ αἷμα αὐτοῦ ἐφ' ἡμᾶς καὶ ἐπὶ τὰ τέκνα ἡμῶν. There is nothing like this

---

[1] See Strack–Billerbeck *ad* Matt. xxvii. 2.

[2] The passage is cited in S.–B., *loc. cit.* They take the view that the statement is true, except that the date is wrong, the withdrawal of the power of life and death having been in force ever since A.D. 6, and suggest a reason why the year 30 should have been assigned (another reason is suggested, after Juster, in Barrett, *The Gospel according to St John, ad loc.*). But may it not be that some further restriction took place about A.D. 30? The review of the evidence as a whole in S.–B. appears to me quite fair, and I accept their conclusions in general.

in John. Yet there is a passage which assigns the major (though not the whole) responsibility to the Jewish authorities (not the λαός). In xix. 11, after Pilate has asserted his authority to pass sentence of life or death, Jesus admits that he has such authority, by divine ordinance,[1] but adds, ὁ παραδούς μέ σοι μείζονα ἁμαρτίαν ἔχει. It is disputed who is meant by ὁ παραδούς, Judas or Caiaphas. As it appears to me, it *must* refer to the representative of the Jewish court, namely the ἀρχιερεύς, who carried out the formal act of παράδοσις which placed Jesus within the jurisdiction of the governor. The act of Judas had placed him within the power of the Sanhedrin, but of that Pilate may have had no official cognizance. It would be difficult, on any construction of the events, to shake the judgement—a sober and moderate judgement—that as between Pilate and Caiaphas the *major* responsibility lay with the latter, although the sentence was actually pronounced (of necessity under the law) by the governor. The statement, which is often made, that the Johannine account is influenced by the motive of incriminating the Jews cannot be substantiated, when it is compared with the other gospels.

So far we have been considering places where the narrative of the Fourth Gospel has some degree of contact with the other gospels, though in the last two passages examined the contact is too remote to provide even a tenuous basis for a theory of dependence upon Synoptic sources. We now turn to features peculiar to the Fourth Gospel, and, in part, dissonant from the Synoptics.

First, there are notes of time and place, such as often give a clue to the use of independent information.

(i) The name of the place where Pilate set up his tribunal is given in Greek and in the vernacular: εἰς τόπον λεγόμενον Λιθόστρωτον, Ἑβραϊστὶ δὲ Γαββαθᾶ (xix. 13). There is no reason to suppose that the Greek term is a translation of the 'Hebrew' (Aramaic).[2] Neither name is otherwise attested. The word λιθόστρωτος is an adjective meaning 'laid with stones'; here it may be intended to be construed with τόπος. But, like other Greek adjectives, it may be used as a substantive, τὸ λιθόστρωτον, and this is probably the author's intention. The λίθοι, apparently, may be

[1] This is orthodox Jewish doctrine; see H. Loewe, *Render unto Caesar*, pp. 4–37. It is adopted by Paul, Rom. xiii. 1. There is not the slightest reason to suppose that John is dependent on Paul, though both intend to lay down a principle of general application for Christians.
[2] Any more than Holyhead is a translation of Caergybi or Sovietsk of Tilsit.

either large paving blocks, or the small tesserae used in a mosaic or tessellated pavement.[1] In recent years excavations in Jerusalem have brought to light an extensive pavement made of large blocks of stone (about three to six feet square) in front of the castle called Antonia, which stood at the north-west corner of the temple area.[2] It evidently served as a parade ground for the garrison which was kept in the castle. The discoverers proposed to identify this with the Λιθόστρωτον of John xix. 13. The appropriateness of the description is obvious. Moreover, if the name Γαββαθᾶ represents some derivative of the root גבע, having the sense of 'high', 'projecting', it would fit the locality, which is on high ground overlooking the whole temple area. Thus the Aramaic גִּבְעָתָא (=Hebrew גִּבְעָה), which seems the most probable of the derivations that have been proposed, would be an entirely appropriate name. This identification, however, is faced with the difficulty that the λιθόστρωτον must have been close to the praetorium, and that the Roman governors seem to have had their Jerusalem residence in the old palace of Herod the Great,[3] which was in the western part of the city, separated from the temple hill by the Tyropoeon valley. It is, however, suggested that Pilate may have chosen to fix his headquarters for the time being in Antonia, which was certainly amply suited to the purposes of an official residence, and where the governor would be in immediate and constant contact with the garrison, and in a position to keep an eye on all that went on in the temple area. Such a move might well have been made in the extremely disturbed conditions of these years. But could the term *praetorium* be applied to any building whatever which a governor might choose as temporary headquarters? It is upon the answer to this question that the possibility of identifying the pavement before Antonia with the λιθόστρωτον called Gabbatha seems to depend. And the answer seems uncertain.[4] In any case the new discovery probably points to the sense in which we are to under-

---

[1] Abundant examples are given in Wetstein *ad loc.*; and see Moulton and Milligan, *Vocabulary of the Greek N.T., s.v.*

[2] See *Revue Biblique* (1933), pp. 83–113; (1937), pp. 563–70.

[3] This is recorded of Gessius Florus, Jos. *B.J.* II. 301. It was there (presumably at his own headquarters) that Pilate displayed the shields which gave offence to the Jews, Philo, *Leg. ad Gaium* 299.

[4] Vincent, the discoverer (*Revue Bib. ll.cc.*), identified his discovery with the λιθόστρωτον of the Fourth Gospel. P. Benoit (*Rev. Bib.* 1952, pp. 531–50) discussed the question and came to an opposite conclusion. Vincent replied, *ibid.* (1954), pp. 87–107. The matter may be considered *sub judice*. The identification is accepted by W. F. Albright in *The Background of the N.T. and its Eschatology*, ed. Davies and Daube (Cambridge, 1956), pp. 158–9.

stand the term λιθόστρωτον: it is not a mosaic or tessellated pavement, but one constructed of large blocks. That there may have been another such (as yet undiscovered) before the true praetorium, Herod's palace, is likely enough.

Whether or not we conclude that the pavement called Gabbatha on which Pilate's tribunal was set up has now been discovered, it is in the highest degree unlikely that the Greek and Aramaic names were invented by the evangelist, or that, even if he might have intelligently conjectured that there would be a λιθόστρωτον at the praetorium, he would have been able to give the Aramaic name unless he had some source of information at his disposal. That this name is not otherwise attested is no serious objection; our acquaintance with the vernacular names of localities in and near Jerusalem is by no means exhaustive. It is reasonable to conclude that the name was handed down in a tradition which John has used, a tradition independent of the Synoptics.

(ii) The final stage of the judicial proceedings is precisely dated: ἦν δὲ παρασκευὴ τοῦ πάσχα, ὥρα ἦν ὡς ἕκτη (xix. 14). The term παρασκευὴ τοῦ πάσχα is the normal translation of עֶרֶב־הַפֶּסַח, and there is no ground for understanding it in any other sense here.[1] It is implied also in xviii. 28, where the priests refuse to enter the praetorium because they wish to preserve their ritual purity for the celebration of the paschal meal, which therefore is conceived as pending. The hour is given as the sixth, i.e. noon. This is in direct contradiction to Mark, according to whom the crucifixion took place at the third hour, that is, 9 a.m.[2] The date is also in contradiction to the apparent implications of the Marcan narrative, which treats the Last Supper as the paschal meal. The divergence has given rise to interminable and inconclusive debate, beginning in the patristic period. It is often held that the Fourth Evangelist has designedly altered both date and time in order to synchronize the death of Christ with the slaughter of the paschal victims. It may, however, fairly be urged that the early interpretation of the death of Christ as a paschal sacrifice (as early as 1 Cor. v. 7) would be more readily accounted for if it was known that he had died on the day, and about the hour, dedicated to that sacrifice. But John has not given the slightest indication that he attached this signi-

---

[1] See below, p. 111, n. 2.

[2] The reading τρίτη for ἕκτη in some MSS. is an obvious harmonizing correction, perhaps based on the ingenious patristic conjecture that the sign for 3, Γ, was misread as Ϝ (digamma), the sign for 6. Westcott's attempt to show that John, here and elsewhere, follows the modern western usage in reckoning the time of day involves gross improbabilities.

ficance to the day and hour, nor is it clear (as I have tried to show else-where) that the idea of the death of Christ as paschal sacrifice plays any part, or any regulative part, in Johannine theology.[1] Further, the date is corroborated in a source which is under no suspicion of a theological motive, namely the *baraita*, already cited, in *Bab. Sanh.* 43 b, which says that 'Jesus was hanged on the Eve of Passover' (בערב הפסח תלאוהו לישו). We have already noted that the account which John gives of the examina-tion before the High Priest readily fits in with the estimate of Jesus which the *baraita* attributes to the Jewish authorities. For a second time, there-fore, we are led to recognize behind the Johannine Passion narrative a tradition in contact with the Jewish account of these events.

Again, the quartodeciman practice of the Church in Asia was apparently associated with the belief that Jesus suffered on Nisan 14,[2] the date given by John. But it is noteworthy that the advocates of the Asian practice do not appeal to the authority of the Fourth Gospel, but to uninterrupted tradition derived from the fathers of their Church. The practice was therefore, in their belief, primitive in the Church of Asia; and their reasons for so believing seem to be strong. The first discussion on the subject (so far as we know) between Rome and Ephesus took place as early as A.D. 155, or thereabouts. The protagonist of the Asian position was Polycarp. He represented to Anicetus that the tradition which he and other Asians followed went back to 'John the disciple of the Lord'.[3] While there may be some uncertainty about the identity of this John, it is certain that he was one of the fathers of the Church in Asia. That Polycarp had personal contacts with him we know on the authority of Irenaeus, who had himself heard Polycarp speak of them.[4] At the time,

[1] See *Interpretation*, pp. 233–5. It is of course possible that John followed a source which was under the influence of this idea, but the nearer to the time of the events we come, the more likely is it that the idea of Christ as paschal sacrifice was shaped by the living memory that he had in fact suffered on Nisan 14.

[2] Apollinaris of Hierapolis, an advocate of quartodeciman practice, complains of the ignorance of those who say ὅτι τῇ ιδ' τὸ πρόβατον μετὰ τῶν μαθητῶν ἔφαγεν ὁ κύριος, τῇ δὲ μεγάλῃ ἡμέρᾳ τῶν ἀзύμων αὐτὸς ἔπαθεν...ἡ ιδ' [he adds] τὸ ἀληθινὸν τοῦ κυρίου πάσχα, ἡ θυσία ἡ μεγάλη (*Liber de Paschate*, fragments *ap.* Routh, *Reliquiae Sacrae*, vol. 1).

[3] Euseb. *H.E.* v. 24. 16.

[4] Euseb. *H.E.* v. 5–6. It seems to me impossible for anyone who has the ex-perience of recalling in advanced life the teachers of his school or undergraduate years to doubt that Irenaeus is recalling to Florinus authentic memories of the great teacher whose lectures they had attended together. Polycarp nowhere betrays know-ledge of the Fourth Gospel; it is the living tradition mediated by 'John the disciple of the Lord' that he relies on. Irenaeus himself says, 'Quid autem si neque apostoli

Anicetus admitted that Polycarp had as much right to maintain the tradition of the fathers of his Church as he himself had to maintain the tradition of his predecessors in the Roman see. Some forty years later, when the question was reopened, Polycrates again appealed to immemorial tradition (τὸ πάλαι πρότερον αὐτοῖς παραδοθέν), going back to Philip and John. He declares the observance of Nisan 14 to be κατὰ τὸ εὐαγγέλιον, and claims to have 'gone through every holy scripture' (πᾶσαν ἁγίαν γραφὴν διεληλυθώς); yet it is no proof from scripture that he offers, but evidence of immemorial tradition.[1] That evidence appears to me to be convincing. There was therefore from earliest times a practice of celebrating the passion and resurrection of Christ on the Eve of Passover, and this practice almost certainly carried with it the belief that Christ had suffered on that day. This is attested for the Church of Asia, in which the Fourth Gospel was published. We seem therefore to have a firm attachment in history for the tradition, independent of the Synoptics, which we have been led to suspect from an examination of the texts themselves. Whether the Johannine tradition is in this respect superior or inferior to the Synoptic, or whether the two can be harmonized, I do not here propose to discuss. I would only observe that it is the only tradition of the date which can be confirmed by external testimony, namely that of the tractate *Sanhedrin*, and as such deserves respect.[2]

quidem scripturas reliquissent nobis, nonne oportebat ordinem sequi traditionis quam tradiderunt iis quibus committebant ecclesias?' (III. 4. 1). The belief of the Church of Asia, therefore, that Christ suffered on Nisan 14 was not derived from the statement in the Fourth Gospel, but from a tradition probably older than that gospel itself.

[1] Euscb. *H.E.* v. 24. 1–7.

[2] The arguments recently set forth by J. Jeremias (*Die Abendmahlsworte Jesu*, 1949), though they are not all of equal weight, make it very difficult, if not impossible, to regard the meal described by Mark as anything other than a paschal meal. On the other hand, attempts to show that John did not really mean Nisan 14 fall short of conviction. The suggestion that παρασκευὴ τοῦ πάσχα does not represent the current phrase ערב הפסח, but a hypothetical Aramaic עֲרוּבְתָּא דִי פַּסְחָא (of which no instance is produced), with the dubious meaning 'Friday in Passover', I cannot think felicitous, even though supported by the weighty authority of the late C. C. Torrey. Billerbeck's judgement stands: 'so konnte ein Mann, der an jüdische Vorstellungs- und Ausdrucksweise gewöhnt war,... nimmer den Ausdruck παρασκευὴ τοῦ πάσχα im Sinne von παρακευὴ τοῦ σαββάτου ἐν πάσχα verwenden' (S.–B. II, p. 836); as does his judgement that φαγεῖν τὸ πάσχα (John xviii. 28), although in some circumstances it *can* refer to the eating of the *chagiga* offerings of the week of unleavened bread, is most unlikely to have been used in that sense in a work addressed to a public uninitiated into the minutiae of Jewish observance, with nothing in the context to point to it (*ibid.* pp. 839–40). The

Beyond these two individual concrete data it seems hardly worth while to pursue in detail the divergences between John and the Synoptics; they are so numerous, and in themselves so little susceptible of any test but those of coherence and general probability. It may be more rewarding to consider certain broad general features which give a distinctive character to the whole.

First, no reader can fail to be arrested by the fact that all through the trial the issue is political. Everything turns upon the title βασιλεύς. The word itself occurs twelve times in John's Passion narrative, as compared with six times in Mark's and four times in each of the others. This is because the question of kingship is being taken seriously. At its first introduction there is a discussion of the sense in which the term is to be understood. It is only the concluding clause of this discussion that gives it a theological twist. For the rest the question is examined on the basis of the plain sense of the term βασιλεύς, as denoting a person who has followers able to fight for his throne. The fact that the followers of Jesus are not at that moment in arms[1] proves that he is not claiming to be a king in

contradiction, I think, is not to be eliminated along any such lines. The hypothesis that the Last Supper was indeed a paschal meal (as Mark says), but that it was held, for some reason, on a date other than the regular date (as John says), seems to be the only way in which the two accounts could be reconciled. The patristic theory that Jesus and his disciples deliberately celebrated the Passover on an evening different from that on which their Jewish co-religionists celebrated it, has in recent times not commanded much respect. The theory that different groups or parties among the Jews may, on one ground or another, have kept Passover on different days, advocated in various forms by Chwolsohn, Billerbeck and others, has recently attracted fresh attention through the observation that the Qumran community followed a separate calendar in fixing the date of Passover. According to this calendar, Passover fell always on a Wednesday. The Qumran community, therefore, must in many years have 'eaten the Passover' on a different date from the orthodox. J. Daniélou (*Les Manuscrits de la Mer Morte et les origines du Christianisme*, pp. 26–7) accepts the view put forward by Mlle Jaubert (*La Date de la Cène*) that Jesus and his disciples followed the use of Qumran and celebrated passover on Wednesday, Nisan 12; on that night he was arrested; the various stages of the judicial proceedings occupied Thursday, Nisan 13, and on Friday, Nisan 14, when orthodox Jews were keeping Passover, he was crucified. The theory should, I think, not be accepted without hesitation. We do now know, however, that there was no absolute uniformity among all parties and groups of Jewish worshippers in the first century in regard to the paschal calendar, and it remains possible that for one reason or another the paschal meal celebrated by Jesus and his disciples was not held on Nisan 14 but on the evening of the previous day. For the present, so far as I can see, we must be content to admit that our two outstanding authorities for the events are in apparent opposition, and, without either attempting to explain away the contradiction, or hastily devaluing the one account or the other, wait for further information.

[1] ῍Αν ἠγωνίζοντο (not ἠγωνίσαντο).

the only sense relevant in a Roman court. Pilate shows what he thinks about it (with calculated malice) by exhibiting Jesus to the priests in a parody of royal state as 'king of the Jews'. They repudiate him violently. The governor still attempts to contrive an acquittal, but the priests insist on the plain, straightforward implication of the title βασιλεύς. Within the *fines imperii* there is, and can be, only one βασιλεύς. For anyone else to claim the title is high treason—and 'we have no βασιλεύς but Caesar'. And on that ground the case is decided.

But that is not the end of the matter. When Jesus is crucified, as a pretender to royalty, he is proclaimed, with the utmost publicity, in three languages, 'the king of the Jews', and nothing will induce the governor to alter the inscription. The only thing that will justify the execution, and justify him, in his own eyes and those of others, in ordering it, is the assertion that he has put to death a political rival to the emperor. He does not himself believe it, but this is the legal ground for his action. The priests must swallow the affront.

The emphasis on the political issue is all the more striking when we consider the one point in the narrative where a theological issue threatens to come up. The Jewish accusers urge that Jesus has incurred penalties under Jewish law ὅτι υἱὸν θεοῦ[1] ἑαυτὸν ἐποίησεν. This is the first time that this claim has appeared in the Johannine Passion narrative. In Mark it figures in the examination before the High Priest, and there it is of decisive importance, both for the course of the proceedings and theologically for the Christian reader. In John it is not mentioned in the course of proceedings in the Jewish court, and at the point where it is introduced it has no important influence upon the progress of the case. Pilate, we are told, 'was more afraid than ever' (μᾶλλον ἐφοβήθη). What fear is this? Clearly it is not fear of the priests, for the effect of it is a renewed attempt to cheat them of their prey and secure an acquittal.[2] Then does the evangelist intend to represent Pilate as sharing the Christian faith in the Son of God,

[1] This is unquestionably the correct text, although some inferior authorities have υἱὸν τοῦ θεοῦ.

[2] In spite of his sinister reputation Pilate's bark was sometimes worse than his bite. When the Jews approached him at Caesarea to protest against the introduction of Roman standards into Jerusalem, he surrounded them with troops and ἠπείλει θάνατον ἐπιθήσειν ζημίαν ἐκ τοῦ ὀξέως εἰ μὴ παυσάμενοι τοῦ θορυβεῖν ἐπὶ τὰ οἰκεῖα ἀπίοιεν, yet when they persisted he gave way at length (Josephus, *Antiq.* XVIII. 57–9, *B.J.* II. 172–4). It would be perfectly in character if he used the threat of crucifixion in the hope that the threat would suffice and that he would not need to carry it out; he would really have preferred this result, as John indicates (xix. 10–12).

and showing a becoming reverence? Hardly; his invariable form of phrase, where the Christian confession of Christ is in view, is (ὁ) υἱὸς τοῦ θεοῦ.[1] Nowhere else does he omit the article before θεοῦ, according to the best texts. This is normal usage.[2] The question of the High Priest in Matthew is, Σὺ εἶ ὁ χριστὸς ὁ υἱὸς τοῦ θεοῦ; (making explicit Mark's paraphrastic τοῦ εὐλογητοῦ). That is in itself a reason against the (otherwise improbable) view that John xix. 7 is a faint echo of the Synoptic narrative.[3] The phrase υἱὸς θεοῦ is in Mark and Matthew put into the mouth of a pagan (Mark xv. 39, Matt. xxvii. 54). For such a person it would carry the sense 'son of a god'. John's readers in the Graeco-Roman world would understand that Pilate shared the superstitious regard entertained by many pagans for the θεῖος ἄνθρωπος, the adept or mage, credited with occult powers, who often claimed divine origin.[4] This is the 'fear' by which Pilate was moved, and his next question is a natural one in the circumstances: πόθεν εἶ σύ; do you indeed claim to be a θεῖος ἄνθρωπος? The whole episode therefore is entirely in character, and to all appearance it owes nothing to theological motives. Thus in the one place where the course of the narrative directly invites theological exploitation, it remains on a strictly matter-of-fact level. This is surely a very remarkable feature in a work so dominated by theological interests.

Little of all this could have been derived, by however free indulgence in imaginative expansion, from the Synoptic Gospels, in which the political aspect of the case is unimportant. Then is this politically coloured account the free composition of the evangelist? It is certain that the

---

[1] i. 34 (v.l. ὁ ἐκλεκτὸς τοῦ θεοῦ), 49, iii. 18, v. 25, ix. 35 (v.l. ἀνθρώπου), x. 36 (τοῦ omitted in some MSS.), xi. 27, xx. 31.

[2] The Synoptics are not quite consistent. Mark has τοῦ θεοῦ in iii. 11, v. 7, xiv. 61, and, quite properly, θεοῦ in xv. 39, in the mouth of the centurion, but θεοῦ, without article, in i. 1, if this is part of the original text. Matthew has the article in iv. 3, 6, viii. 29, xvi. 16, xxvi. 63, and θεοῦ without article in xxvii. 54, in agreement with Mark, but θεοῦ υἱός, exceptionally, in xiv. 33. Luke has (ὁ) υἱὸς τοῦ θεοῦ in iv. 3, 9, 41, viii. 28, xxii. 70, υἱὸς θεοῦ without article only in i. 35.

[3] The statement that Jesus has deserved death κατὰ τὸν νόμον because of his claim to be θεοῦ υἱός may perhaps imply that John was acquainted with a tradition (not necessarily the Marcan one) which represented this charge as having figured in the proceedings before the High Priest; but this is not necessarily so, since there was no Christian tradition which was not aware that this claim was made. In any case, John does not regard the charge ὅτι υἱὸν θεοῦ ἑαυτὸν ἐποίησεν as having carried any weight in the Roman court, or as having contributed to the decision of the governor.

[4] See *Interpretation*, pp. 250–1, and cf. references in Arndt–Gingrich, *s.v.* υἱός 2b. The emperor is in inscriptions θεοῦ υἱός (= *divi filius*), but it is unlikely that this usage is in mind here: Pilate does not treat the claim to be θεοῦ υἱός as another form of the claim to be βασιλεύς in rivalry to Caesar.

allegation that Christians were not loyal to the emperor, but acknowledged βασιλέα ἕτερον 'Ιησοῦν (Acts xvii. 7), was very dangerous to the Church in the Roman Empire. Yet the evangelist has boldly represented the issue on which Jesus was condemned as that of the kingship of Christ over against the kingship of Caesar. Not only so, he has represented his Jewish accusers as professing full allegiance to the emperor: οὐκ ἔχομεν βασιλέα εἰ μὴ Καίσαρα. This might very naturally be read as an admission that Jews were loyal subjects and Christians were not: a damaging admission, surely, in the situation in which Christians found themselves at the time when the gospel was published. If the evangelist set himself to reproduce with essential fidelity the ethos of the actual situation in which Christ was condemned, as it was handed down (however much he may have felt free to dramatize it), the preservation of these challenging traits could be understood; but I should find it difficult to imagine a Christian writer under Domitian (let us say), or even under Nerva or Trajan, going out of his way to introduce them into a relatively harmless account.

I could much more easily believe that the Synoptics have reduced the political element in the tradition that had come down to them. Mark wrote almost under the shadow of the imperial palace. Luke dedicated his work to a *vir egregius* of the Empire. Neither could be blamed for trying to avoid unnecessary misunderstanding. John has sought the same result by inserting the two dialogues in which it is explained (*a*) that the kingship of Christ is not a worldly monarchy resting on armed force, (*b*) that it is essentially the sovereignty of truth and so of him who reveals truth, and (*c*) that Christians fully recognize the authority of the imperial government as divinely sanctioned. With these safeguards he is free to give full weight to the title βασιλεύς in the development of proceedings before the governor.

But in order to appreciate more justly the distinctive character of the Johannine rendering of the trial it may be worth while to recall what we know of the earlier history of the tradition regarding the circumstances in which Jesus was put to death. Our earliest documents, the Pauline epistles, make two statements: (*a*) that he was killed by the Jews (1 Thess. ii. 15), and (*b*) that he was crucified (Gal. iii. 1 *et passim*). On the face of them they are contradictory, for crucifixion was not a punishment known to Jewish law or practice, but was commonly inflicted by the Romans upon condemned persons who did not possess the privileges of citizenship. Yet both are independently attested. Tacitus (*Ann.* xv. 44) admits (or claims) responsibility for the Romans, and the *baraita* in *Bab. Sanh.* 43 (with other Talmudic passages) claims it for the Jews. Any account therefore of the affair which is to do justice to historical facts must find a place for the actions of both these parties, and, if possible, show how they were related. The earliest Christian tradition divided the responsibility in a way which may be inferred from the phrase put into the mouth of Peter in Acts ii. 23: 'You [Jews] killed him through the agency of men without the law [i.e. Gentiles]' (διὰ χειρὸς ἀνόμων ἀνείλατε).

The account of the proceedings in Mark keeps closely to this formula, in the sense that the real authors of the judicial murder are Jews, and Pilate no more than their tool. The trial in the Jewish court is treated with relative fulness. There is a hearing and weighing of evidence, an interrogation of the Prisoner, a vote of the court, and a verdict of guilty on a capital charge. Mark does not explain how it came about after all this that the case came before a Roman court.[1] The account of the trial before Pilate is brief and uninformative:[2] no precise charge is formulated, there is no hearing of evidence, the interrogation of the Prisoner is perfunctory and elicits only an ambiguous reply, and there is no verdict. The governor's decision is dictated directly by the voice of the mob choosing Barabbas for amnesty in place of Jesus. This cannot be accepted as an account of a Roman provincial trial.

Matthew's account is not, in substance, different from Mark's. He too lays all the emphasis on the proceedings in the Jewish court, and his only substantial addition to the account of the hearing before the governor is the dramatic scene in which Pilate washes his hands, leaving the Jews fully and solely responsible for the outcome. More clearly than ever the Roman is a mere tool by which the Jewish authorities work their will.

In Luke the perspective is appreciably different. He has drastically curtailed the proceedings in the Jewish court, and there is no express verdict. The priests produce their Prisoner in the governor's court, and forthwith formulate their charges. Here, therefore, it is clear that they are not asking for confirmation of a sentence previously passed, but appearing as prosecutors. The proceedings in the Roman court are given

[1] Since there has already been a formal condemnation—κατέκριναν αὐτὸν ἔνοχον εἶναι θανάτου—we should suppose that this had to be submitted to the governor for confirmation. Yet in xv. 3 (*after* Pilate has interrogated the Prisoner) the priests appear in the guise of accusers (κατηγόρουν αὐτοῦ πολλά). The fact is that Mark has no clear conception of the legal position, and was not interested in it.
[2] Of the twenty-five lines (in Nestle) devoted to the proceedings before Pilate, eighteen are occupied with the episode of Barabbas, which is not a judicial affair at all.

enhanced importance. There is a formal indictment under three heads, in reasonable agreement with known Roman forms. The three charges are those of (a) subverting the people, (b) hindering the payment of tribute, and (c) claiming to be an anointed king. Only the third charge, however, is proceeded with,[1] and of the interrogation of the Prisoner Luke knows no more than Mark. The governor, however, returns a formal verdict: first a verdict of not guilty (xxiii. 4), and then a verdict of not guilty of a capital offence (verses 14–15), proposing, accordingly, a milder penalty. In the end, however, as in Mark, Pilate passes sentence of death to satisfy the popular demand. In Luke, as in Mark, the Jewish authorities are the prime movers, and ultimately get their way, but Luke gives, as Mark does not, something like an intelligible description (however abridged) of a possible Roman trial.

His account, however, is interrupted by the enigmatic episode of the remission of the case to Herod.[2] I will not here discuss the historical problem it raises, but only recall that in Acts iv. 25–6 the same author has cited a passage from Ps. ii, a scripture which is one of the most important

---

[1] Yet Pilate's summing-up seems to imply that charge (a) has been investigated with negative results: 'You brought this man before me as one who is subverting the people; and, as you see, I have examined him in your presence and found him not guilty of the offences with which you charge him' (xxiii. 14). The charge of subversion is here expressed by the verb ἀποστρέφειν (in the charge sheet it is διαστρέφειν, xxiii. 2): ἀποστρέφειν is in one LXX passage (2 Chron. xviii. 31) the translation of the hiphil of סוּת, which is one of the verbs used of the charges brought against Jesus in Sanh. 43 b. In several other passages of the LXX הסית is rendered by ἐπισείειν, and in Luke xxiii. 5 the charge runs, ἀνασείει τὸν λαόν. It looks as if some reminiscence of the actual language of the accusation lurks in the background of the Lucan account, and this encourages the belief that he is not simply 'editing' Mark (see also my article in J.T.S., October 1954, pp. 244–5).

[2] The appearance before Herod cannot be described as a trial in any intelligible sense, and it is quite inconclusive, though Pilate construes it as supporting his view that the Prisoner is not guilty of any capital offence. The attitude of Herod does not suggest that of a judge to his prisoner. He was, we are told, delighted to see Jesus, because he had heard much about him and had long wished to see him, and indeed was hoping to see him perform a miracle (xxiii. 8). Whether it was mere disappointment of his hope, or pique because the Prisoner refused to answer his questioning, that led to his change of attitude, we are not told, but he now joined with his own troops in vulgar mockery. It is all somewhat confusing, and does not suggest that Luke had much information beyond the mere fact that Herod had a part in the proceedings. That Antipas was interested in reports of the miracles of Jesus he might have gathered from a passage (ix. 7–9) which he has taken from Mark, and the tetrarch's ambivalent attitude is not unlike that which he is said by Mark to have had towards John the Baptist, whose conversation he enjoyed, and whom he nevertheless put to death (Mark vi. 20).

sources of *testimonia*.[1] The psalm speaks of an attack upon the Messiah by ἔθνη, λαοί, βασιλεῖς and ἄρχοντες. The author points to the fulfilment of this prophecy in the following terms: συνήχθησαν. . .ἐπὶ τὸν ἅγιον παῖδά σου ᾽Ιησοῦν ὃν ἔχρισας ῾Ηρώδης τε καὶ Πόντιος Πειλᾶτος σὺν ἔθνεσιν καὶ λαοῖς ᾽Ισραήλ. Here therefore the judicial murder is not so simply as in Mark a Jewish plot with Pilate as its tool, but rather a conspiracy of tetrarch and governor, with (unspecified) Jews and Romans as accomplices. This conception of the affair seems to underlie some of the peculiar features of the Lucan trial narrative, which may therefore, not improbably, be traced to a form of tradition shaped largely under the influence of the *testimonium* from Ps. ii, but by no means to be neglected in any attempt to reconstruct the actual situation; this has been conflated with a trial narrative of Marcan type.

We are now in a position to appreciate the Johannine trial narrative as a whole, taking account of both parts of the proceedings. Here the examination before the High Priest has shrunk in importance. It is strictly preliminary—almost one might say a 'fact-finding' investigation. The representatives of Jewry appear before Pilate, unmistakably, as prosecutors; for his first question is 'What is the charge?' (τίνα κατηγορίαν φέρετε;). Their answer is vague: the Prisoner is a mischievous character (κακὸν ποιῶν). Pilate, taking the charge at no more than its face value, offers them jurisdiction.[2] They refuse, on the ground that the Sanhedrin has no power to inflict the death sentence. The implication is that the prosecution seeks such a sentence. Pilate therefore proceeds to try the case himself. There is a lacuna here, for we are not told what led the governor to ask the question, Σὺ εἶ ὁ βασιλεὺς τῶν ᾽Ιουδαίων; We are, however, not left in doubt that the crucial charge brought by the priests

[1] See *According to the Scriptures*, pp. 104–5.
[2] The natural implication appears to be that Pilate is willing for the case to be treated as one of minor importance, suitably dealt with by the municipal authorities under their limited powers. If, however, this is accepted as historical, it becomes difficult to accept the presence of a large contingent (σπεῖρα) of Roman troops at the arrest. We do not know how far the Jewish authorities were entitled to call for assistance from the garrison in case the temple police were faced with trouble beyond their power to handle. It might be conjectured that the garrison had already been alerted as a result of the στάσις in which the 'resistance leader' (λῃστής) Barabbas had been arrested, and the tribune may have supposed that he was called upon to meet some further outbreak. All is conjecture. It is permissible to suspect that the evangelist, aware that the case was one handled by the Roman authorities, assumed without warrant that Roman troops participated in the arrest. But our information is too defective for any dogmatic decision.

was that of claiming to be a king. After hearing the Prisoner's defence on this charge (a perfectly valid defence), the governor returns a verdict of not guilty, reports it to the waiting priests, and asks their agreement to the release of the Prisoner. The episode of Barabbas is passed over lightly; we do not even hear that he was released. The declaration of the innocence of Jesus is expanded into the dramatic scene of *Ecce Homo*, which, instead of disposing the accusers to withdraw their proposal of the death sentence, leads to an express demand for crucifixion. Pilate reiterates his verdict. It is at this point that the priests, fearing that the case will collapse, for the first time bring up a religious charge. But it comes to nothing; and then they play their trump card: ἐὰν τοῦτον ἀπολύσῃς οὐκ εἶ φίλος τοῦ Καίσαρος. That settles the matter. Pilate, with all due formality,[1] passes sentence of crucifixion, revenging himself upon the priests for his humiliation by labelling their Victim 'King of the Jews', and refusing to alter it.

This account, it is clear, adheres to the fundamental formula: the Jewish authorities have done the deed διὰ χειρὸς ἀνόμων. Here John agrees with our other sources. But he makes it plausible, as they do not, that the governor could be used as a tool without quite abdicating his judicial character. The Pilate of the Synoptics is a poor stick; he is tricked into passing sentence by the simple device of substituting Barabbas for Jesus as the beneficiary of a proposed amnesty. In John, the episode of Barabbas has been reduced to its proper subordinate place, and Pilate has a real issue to try, and one which genuinely falls within his competence as a Roman magistrate. The question which emerges is, Can a prisoner who has been subjected to examination (perhaps accompanied by torture) and is proved not guilty of criminal action or intent, but who has by implication admitted that he regards himself as in some sense a king, be given the benefit of the doubt and acquitted? Pilate thinks he can. Yet the fact remains that he has refused, when given the opportunity, to repudiate the regal title, and has used the expression 'my kingdom', with whatever qualification. If the accusers insist on this point, it becomes difficult for the governor to acquit the prisoner. It is this that gives the priests their chance. They threaten Pilate himself, at the same time

[1] John xix. 13. Some exegetes wish to take καθίσας as transitive, meaning that Pilate placed Jesus (in mockery) on the tribunal—why, I cannot imagine: the phrase καθίσαι ἐπὶ βήματος is a perfectly normal way of describing the formal act of a magistrate about to give a decision, cf. Josephus, *B.J.* ii. 172, ὁ Πιλᾶτος καθίσας ἐπὶ τοῦ βήματος ἐν τῷ μεγάλῳ σταδίῳ καὶ προσκαλεσάμενος τὸ πλῆθος κ.τ.λ., which is closely parallel to John xix. 13–14, ὁ οὖν Πειλᾶτος...ἐκάθισεν ἐπὶ βήματος εἰς τόπον λεγόμενον Λιθόστρωτον...καὶ λέγει τοῖς Ἰουδαίοις κ.τ.λ.

protesting their own unbounded loyalty to his imperial master. No doubt if Pilate had been a stronger character, or if his record had been less equivocal, he might have risked his position and seen justice done. But his yielding to pressure is entirely intelligible.[1]

Here we have for the first time an account which, although it leaves some gaps, is coherent and consistent, with a high degree of verisimilitude. Verisimilitude, no doubt, is not the same thing as historical accuracy. But leaving aside for the moment the question of historical accuracy, let us ask, where could the evangelist have got this account? Matthew and Mark could give him no help. Luke might have given him a hint about the formulation of an indictment in a Roman court; but if he knew Luke he has ignored him. But I doubt very much whether a writer whose work we must place late in the first century and in a Hellenistic environment, could have invented such a persuasive account of a trial conducted under conditions which had long passed away. It is pervaded with a lively sense for the situation as it was in the last half-century before the extinction of Judaean local autonomy. It is aware of the delicate relations between the native and the imperial authorities. It reflects a time when the dream of an independent Judaea under its own king had not yet sunk to the level of a chimaera, and when the messianic idea was not a theologumenon but impinged on practical politics,[2] and the bare mention of a 'king of the Jews' stirred violent emotions; a time, moreover, when the constant preoccupation of the priestly holders of power under Rome was to damp down any first symptoms of such emotions. These conditions were present in Judaea before A.D. 70, and not later, and not elsewhere. This, I submit, is the true *Sitz im Leben* of the essential elements in the Johannine trial narrative. This narrative is far from being a second-hand *rechauffé* of the Synoptics. While there is evidence of some degree of elaboration by the author, the most probable conclusion is that in substance it represents an independent strain of tradition, which must have been formed in a period much nearer the events than the period when the Fourth Gospel was written, and in some respects seems to be better informed than the tradition behind the Synoptics, whose confused account it clarifies.

[1] The scene is entirely in character. Pilate's contempt for the subject people, and particularly for their religious chiefs, rings true; and we know that his standing was not too secure: it was not many years later that he was recalled by the emperor to answer charges brought by the Jews (Jos. *Antiq.* XVIII. 89).

[2] Political messianism of course revived under Hadrian, but in a totally different situation. There was no longer any priestly body exercising limited local autonomy at Jerusalem.

6. THE EXECUTION

In the account of the last scenes (xix. 17–37) there is a certain general similarity of structure between John and Mark (who is followed closely by Matthew), in so far as both concentrate principally on two moments, the actual crucifixion with its immediate accompaniments, and the death of the Crucified (filling the interval differently), and both append significant sequels. Beyond this there is little resemblance.

Verbal agreement does not go beyond the minimum without which the story could hardly be told at all, except where the words common to both, διαμερίζεσθαι, τὰ ἱμάτια αὐτοῦ, βάλλειν κλῆρον, ὄξος, come out of Old Testament passages employed as *testimonia*. Beside these there are Γολγοθᾶ, κρανίου τόπος, δύο (λῃσταί in Mark, κακοῦργοι in Luke, unqualified in John), σταυροῦν, (ἐπι)γράφειν (of the inscription on the cross), σπόγγος, περιθεῖναι—and no more. Even in the few verses where the two accounts run closely parallel the verbal form is different. Thus, where Mark has ἐπὶ τὸν Γολγοθᾶν τόπον ὅ ἐστιν μεθερμηνευόμενον κρανίου τόπος, John has εἰς τὸν λεγόμενον Κρανίου τόπον ὃ λέγεται Ἑβραϊστὶ Γολγοθᾶ. For Mark's ἐπιγραφή he gives τίτλος, representing the regular Latin *titulus*. Where Mark says of the two λῃσταί that they crucified ἕνα ἐκ δεξιῶν καὶ ἕνα ἐξ εὐωνύμων αὐτοῦ, John expresses exactly the same fact in the words, ἐντεῦθεν καὶ ἐντεῦθεν μέσον δὲ τὸν Ἰησοῦν.[1]

It will, however, be well to examine further those parts of the narrative which thus run parallel.

First, Mark and John alike record that an inscription was placed over the cross. In Mark xv. 26 we have no more than the bald statement ἦν ἡ ἐπιγραφὴ τῆς αἰτίας αὐτοῦ ἐπιγεγραμμένη· Ο ΒΑΣΙΛΕΥΣ ΤΩΝ ΙΟΥΔΑΙΩΝ. In John xix. 19 the *titulus* is given in an extended form, ΙΗΣΟΥΣ Ο ΝΑΖΩΡΑΙΟΣ Ο ΒΑΣΙΛΕΥΣ ΤΩΝ ΙΟΥΔΑΙΩΝ, and it is said to have been inscribed in three languages, so that all could read it. Not only so, the priests are made to protest at the implied affront to their national honour,[2] and Pilate

---

[1] Ἐντεῦθεν... ἐντεῦθεν appears to be a Semitism, representing Heb. מִזֶּה... מִזֶּה; Num. xxii. 24, φραγμὸς ἐντεῦθεν καὶ φραγμὸς ἐντεῦθεν, and so Josh. viii. 22, 2 Kms. ii. 13. Mark's is certainly the better Greek, and there seems no reason why a writer copying him should have altered it for the worse.

[2] Note the subtle difference here between the attitude of the priests in John and in Mark. In Mark they themselves apply to the Crucified the title ὁ βασιλεὺς Ἰσραήλ,

replies with an emphatic refusal to alter it. The effect of all this is to concentrate the reader's attention upon the idea of the kingship of Christ, and this carries on an emphasis which, as we have seen, is characteristic of the Johannine account of the trial. That it serves John's theological tendency is evident. He presents the crucifixion as the ὕψωσις, or enthronement, of Christ the King—'king' being understood in a sense which he has previously made clear—and Pilate is subpoenaed as a witness to the fact. But this treatment presupposes a form of tradition in which the claim to kingship was prominent, as it is not in the Synoptics. I have already argued that the condemnation of Jesus on an ostensibly political charge is an inherent element in the tradition, which the Synoptists have minimized, for quite intelligible reasons. How much of the peculiarly Johannine matter in xix. 19–21 can reasonably be assigned to a traditional source it would be hazardous to conjecture: the dialogue between Pilate and the priests might well be another example of the literary device exemplified in the two hearings *in camera*, xviii. 33–8, xix. 9–11, employed here once again to bring out the true implications of the whole situation. In all three dialogues we recognize the author's sense for drama; nothing could be more effective than Pilate's final 'curtain': ὃ γέγραφα γέγραφα. But if we recognize, as we no doubt should, a certain amount of dramatic elaboration here, as in other places, it remains probable that the tradition upon which this elaboration was based had a character and outlook different from Mark's, and it may well have been in some respects more fully informed.

Next, the incident of the division of the garments, John xix. 23–4, is again described more fully than in Mark xv. 24. In John it is related to a *testimonium* from Ps. xxi. 19. This passage is not expressly quoted in Mark, but the language of the psalm reappears in Mark's narrative. As I have already argued, it is unlikely that John worked back from the concealed allusion in Mark to the text of the LXX, and far more probable that he drew the *testimonium* from another form of tradition. The procedure of the soldiers is not described in John, as it is in Mark, in language borrowed from the Old Testament. On the contrary, the parallel clauses in the psalm are misunderstood as if they referred to distinct actions: διεμερίσαντο τὰ ἱμάτια: they divided the garments into four shares; ἐπὶ

in bitter mockery. In John their feeling for the honour of their nation revolts against any application of the title to a crucified criminal. The difference, I suggest, has nothing to do with our author's predilections, but reflects the tendencies of different channels of tradition. But they combine to set in strong relief the ambivalent reaction of official Judaism before the fall of Jerusalem to popular messianic claims, and this is genuinely historical.

τὸν ἱματισμόν μου ἔβαλον κλῆρον: they drew lots for the undivided tunic. This is a secondary stage in the treatment of *testimonia* (similar to Matthew's treatment of the testimony from Zech. ix. 9). Whether it is to be attributed to the evangelist himself or to the tradition he followed, it is impossible to say, but the result is a dramatic scene quite in our author's manner.

Thirdly, the offer of ὄξος is common to both accounts, but is very differently treated. In Mark xv. 34–6 the cry of dereliction, ἠλί, ἠλί,[1] is misunderstood as an invocation of Elijah, and in response to it ὄξος is offered on a sponge, with the words, ἄφετε ἴδωμεν εἰ ἔρχεται Ἡλείας καθελεῖν αὐτόν. The words are apparently meant in mockery; whether the offer of drink is also conceived as mockery is not clear; nor indeed is it clear what relation the words have to the action. In John, the cry of dereliction is absent. If our evangelist was acquainted with it, we could well understand his omission of it on theological grounds. The allusion to Elijah might well go with it, and in any case it is not of a kind to interest this evangelist. The offer of ὄξος remains. The Marcan form clearly echoes the language of Ps. lxviii. 22, ἐπότισάν με ὄξους, both verb and noun recurring. In John the verb does not occur, but the allusion to the *testimonium* is made certain by the use of the word διψῶ, echoing the δίψαν of the psalm. The incident thus acquires a simple and natural motive: the Crucified is suffering the torment of thirst which was one of the most distressing effects of that barbarous punishment, and in response to his cry some kindly person bethinks him of the jar of ὄξος (the soldier's ordinary drink) which stood at hand, and offers it to him on a sponge. The action is one of simple kindness, and needs no such far-fetched motive as Mark alleges. The difference between John and Mark lies in a different use of the *testimonium* which is common to both. I have argued that it is more likely that John derived the *testimonium* from an independent tradition than that he worked back from Mark to the LXX; and apart from what comes out of the *testimonium* itself there is no trait which is common to the two except the use of a sponge (unavoidable in the circumstances) and the verb περιθεῖναι.

The incident is embedded in a context deeply marked with Johannine theology.[2] The keynote is given in the recurrent τετέλεσται (xix. 28, 30).

---

[1] This, the reading of DΘ, supported by 565 and other minucules and by MSS. of the Old Latin, alone makes sense of Mark's statement that it was misunderstood as Ἡλεία (vocative), for the resemblance of ἐλωΐ to ἠλεία is remote.

[2] It is often held that the substitution of 'hyssop' for a 'reed' as a vehicle for the sponge is also due to a theological motive, in view of the employment of that herb in

The verb does not occur elsewhere in this gospel, but it is a virtual equivalent of the τελειοῦν which is used of the 'completion' of the work of Christ in iv. 34, v. 36 and xvii. 4. The form τελεῖν is perhaps chosen because of its use for the due completion of rites of sacrifice and initiation, since the death of Christ is conceived as both sacrifice and initiation.[1] In all this we see plainly the hand of the evangelist remoulding his material. But the nucleus of the passage is not due to any such theological motive, but rests upon a *testimonium* which interprets the death of Christ, in primitive fashion, as that of the Righteous Sufferer of the Psalms.

Beyond this the parallels between John and Mark do not extend. There are two further points at which there is some contact between the narratives, but where their accounts appear, at any rate at first sight, to be discrepant.

First, John knows nothing of the incident of Simon of Cyrene, who, according to Mark xv. 21, was conscripted ἵνα ἄρῃ τὸν σταυρὸν αὐτοῦ, thus becoming the first to fulfil, literally however involuntarily, the precept of Jesus, ἀράτω τὸν σταυρὸν αὐτοῦ (Mark viii. 34). John, on the contrary, says that Jesus left the Lithostroton 'bearing the cross for himself'. With Mark before us, we naturally think of this as a deliberate correction of Mark. But suppose we had no Mark: we should surely then be struck with the resemblance of John's language here to Luke xiv. 27, which is a different rendering of the same saying as Mark viii. 34.

the paschal rite as described in Exod. xii. 22. I have elsewhere questioned the view that John represents the death of Christ as a paschal sacrifice, but in any case it is difficult to parallel the use of hyssop to administer drink to the Victim with its use to sprinkle the blood of the victim as prescribed in Exodus. The symbolism has gone wrong. Nor, if general probability is to be consulted, is it easy to see how a bunch of 'hyssop', or marjoram, could serve any useful purpose, in the circumstances. Moreover, how could you 'put a sponge round' (περιθεῖναι) a bunch of marjoram? You could 'put it round' a reed (κάλαμος, as in Mark) or similar implement, such as a spear or javelin. For these reasons I am disposed to adopt the reading of one minuscule, ὑσσῷ for ὑσσώπῳ. Palaeographically it is a perfect example of corruption by dittography, υσσωπωπερι for υσσωπερι, and a copyist seeing the letters υσσωπ might easily suppose that he had before him the word 'hyssop' with its ritual associations. Ὑσσός is a word for a javelin, = Latin *pilum*, found in Polybius, Plutarch (an almost exact contemporary of our author), and other writers. It is not a common word, and all the more likely for that to elude a copyist. A javelin is an implement which might well lie to hand, and would admirably serve the purpose. This seems to be a place where there are strong grounds for postulating a primitive corruption (for the reading of 476 is more likely to be an accidental reversion to the true text than a genuine survival).

[1] See *Interpretation*, pp. 420–1.

Luke	John
ὅστις οὐ βαστάζει	βαστάζων
τὸν σταυρὸν ἑαυτοῦ	ἑαυτῷ τὸν σταυρὸν
καὶ ἔρχεται ὀπίσω μου	ἐξῆλθεν
(οὐ δύναται εἶναί μου μαθητής)	

Jesus, bearing his own cross, is an example to his followers, called to do likewise. As therefore Mark's language here refers the attentive reader to a much-quoted saying of Jesus in the form in which he has himself reported it, so John's language echoes another form of the same saying, known to us from Luke. The expression therefore, βαστάζων ἑαυτῷ τὸν σταυρόν, can be accounted for without assuming that John knew, or wished to correct, the statement of Mark. The little paragraph, Mark xv. 21, is peculiar in containing three names otherwise unknown to the gospel tradition, and in the quite unparalleled identification of Simon as 'the father of Alexander and Rufus'. This note would be of interest only to a community for which these two persons were well-known figures, that is, the particular local community—Rome, as generally supposed—for which the Gospel according to Mark was in the first instance designed.[1] Matthew and Luke, writing for a public which lacked this local interest in Alexander and Rufus, have omitted the names. It seems probable that this incident was introduced by Mark himself into his version of the common tradition, and passed from him to the other Synoptics, and that John had no knowledge of it because he followed a branch of the tradition into which it had not been introduced.[2]

[1] The introduction of the names, it should be observed, is not an instance of the identification of anonymous characters which is often (though by no means always) a mark of legendary development. Alexander and Rufus play no part in the story; it is only as witnesses that they can be introduced, and as such the names would be pointless unless they were those of persons known to the readers. Mark is saying, in effect, 'The cross was carried by Simon—and if you don't believe me, ask his sons, whom you know'. If there is any question of a 'correction' on one side or the other, it would seem to be Mark who is 'correcting' an earlier tradition which did not mention Simon of Cyrene, and who supports his version by appeal to living witness.

[2] The hypothesis upon which the statements of John and Mark have commonly been harmonized, that Jesus broke down under the weight of the cross, and was then relieved by Simon, deserves perhaps more respect than some other harmonizing hypotheses. Quite apart from the statement in John xix. 17, we should be justified in assuming that Jesus, like any other prisoner condemned to crucifixion, left the precincts of the court carrying his own cross. This was normal practice, and in default of information to the contrary we might be reasonably certain that it was followed in this case. Mark does not in fact contradict it. The conscription of Simon is clearly an emergency operation, and not part of the normal or planned procedure. That Jesus ἐξῆλθεν (scil. from the Lithostroton) carrying his own cross, but later had to be relieved of it, is a perfectly reasonable interpretation of the evidence.

Secondly, John and the Synoptics agree that certain women were witnesses of the crucifixion, but they differ in detail.

The list of names varies. Mark xv. 40 has Mary Magdalene, Mary mother of James the Little and Joses, and Salome (for which Matthew substitutes 'mother of the sons of Zebedee'). Luke at this point (xxiii. 49) gives no names, speaking only of 'the women who had followed him from Galilee', but subsequently (xxiv. 10) he identifies them as Mary Magdalene, Joanna and Mary ἡ ᾽Ιακώβου (which should mean either the wife or the daughter of James, but is probably intended to agree with Mark's ἡ ᾽Ιακώβου...μήτηρ). John has the mother of Jesus (unnamed here as elsewhere in this gospel), his mother's sister, Mary (wife or daughter) of Clopas, and Mary Magdalene.[1] With these lists should be compared the list in Luke viii. 2 of women αἵτινες διηκόνουν αὐτοῖς (cf. Mark xv. 40–1, αἳ...διηκόνουν αὐτῷ): these are Mary Magdalene, Joanna γυνὴ Χουӡᾶ ἐπιτρόπου Ἡρώδου, Susanna, and others. This comes at the close of a section where Luke has been writing in independence of Mark, and to derive this list from Mark xv. 40–1 would be entirely arbitrary. In all probability the list of viii. 2 represents a tradition peculiar to Luke, and this reappears in Luke xxiv. 10 contaminated with Mark's list. It would be equally arbitrary to derive John's list from either of the others. In all probability it represents a third traditional list.

Further, there is a marked divergence between John and the Synoptics in regard to the position occupied by the women in the scene. According to Mark xv. 40 they watched at a distance (ἦσαν ἀπὸ μακρόθεν θεωροῦσαι). The language recalls that of Ps. xxxvii. 12, οἱ ἔγγιστά μου μακρόθεν ἔστησαν. Luke seems to have in mind the language both of this passage and of Ps. lxxxvii. 9, ἐμάκρυνας τοὺς γνωστούς μου ἀπ᾽ ἐμοῦ, for he writes, εἱστήκεισαν πάντες οἱ γνωστοὶ αὐτῷ ἀπὸ μακρόθεν καὶ αἱ γυναῖκες κ.τ.λ. The picture, therefore, of the friends of the Crucified standing at a distance is a part of the traditional presentation of the Passion of Christ in terms of the Righteous Sufferer of the Psalms. Of this John shows no awareness. According to John xix. 25 the women stood by the Cross. The expression, εἱστήκεισαν παρὰ τῷ σταυρῷ, might well be read as a 'correction' of Luke's εἱστήκεισαν...ἀπὸ μακρόθεν (rather than of Mark), if it were otherwise thought likely that John was acquainted with Luke; but it

---

[1] There is no means of deciding whether John intends three or four women, for Μαρία ἡ τοῦ Κλωπᾶ might equally well be an appositional clause further defining ἡ ἀδελφὴ τῆς μητρὸς αὐτοῦ, or an additional name. Legend and conjecture have made play with cross-identifications, but positive evidence is lacking.

might equally have arisen from a different tradition without reference to Luke, inasmuch as we have already been led to infer the existence of such a tradition preserving the names of the women.

There is, however, a further point to be considered—the connection in which the several evangelists have introduced the reference to the women, and the motive which has determined this connection. In Mark it is introduced after the story of the Crucifixion is complete, and is clearly intended as a transition to the account of the entombment and of the subsequent discovery of the empty tomb. The women are introduced, then we are told how Joseph carried out the burial of Jesus, and then the narrative turns back to the women (xv. 47) (though now Salome is missing). From this point it moves on directly to the story of Easter morning, in which the women (all three being named once more) are the principal characters. In Luke all this is somewhat smoothed out, and repetitions are avoided, but it is no less clear that the women are introduced at xxiii. 49 for the sake of the part they are to play in the discovery of the empty tomb. The story of the discovery is completed, and then at last we learn the names of the hitherto anonymous women. That is to say, in the Synoptic version the women belong, not to the story of the Crucifixion, but to the sequel. In John, on the other hand, they are introduced at the beginning, immediately after the division of the garments. In this connection the statement that these women stood by the Cross serves to introduce the incident of the Mother and the Beloved Disciple, which is peculiar to this gospel. We are therefore left with a choice of alternatives: either the introduction of the women at this point was a feature of the special form of tradition which transmitted the Johannine list of names, or it is a piece of editorial work on the part of the evangelist himself. There is perhaps a hint of literary composition in the classical form of sentence, οἱ μὲν οὖν στρατιῶται ταῦτα ἐποίησαν· εἱστήκεισαν δὲ...κ.τ.λ.—a form of transition beloved of Greek narrative writers.

We cannot, however, leave this passage without taking note of the little *pericopé* which it serves to introduce, in which Jesus commends his Mother to the care of the Beloved Disciple. Obviously, if this episode was to be reported, it had to be made clear that the Mother and the Disciple were near enough to the Cross for such a conversation to take place. It is to be observed that this episode has two features which set it apart: it breaks the unities of time and place, since we are obliged for the moment to leave the scene of Golgotha on Good Friday afternoon and place ourselves at the home of the Beloved Disciple in the time following; and it shows an interest in the subsequent fortunes of subordinate characters. But this interest, and the breach of the unities, are features otherwise found only in the Matthaean supplements to the narrative: the story of the fate of Judas, interpolated between the transfer of the case to the Roman court and the trial itself (xxvii. 3–10), and the report of the appearance of departed saints in Jerusalem μετὰ τὴν ἔγερσιν αὐτοῦ, interpolated between the rending of the veil and the confession of the centurion (xxvii. 52–3). Apart from these, the Passion narrative in all its forms derives much of its weight and force from its severe concentration upon the one tremendous theme, with no subordinate interest to slacken the tension, and from the impression it conveys of an unbroken and ineluctable march of events to the destined catastrophe and περιπέτεια. Analogy therefore would suggest the conclusion that the *pericopé* we are now discussing did not form part of the form of Passion narrative which reached our evangelist through oral tradition. On the other hand, it serves no obvious theological interest, and the attempts to give it a profound symbolical purport are unconvincing.[1] If the Beloved Disciple (whoever he may have been historically) stands, as he probably does, for the principal guarantor of the Ephesian tradition, then this story may well have been an independent element in that tradition. But we have no means of controlling it.[2]

This discussion has wandered somewhat from the question from which it started, that of the relation of John to the Synoptics in this part of the Passion narrative, but the answer to that question has emerged: there is no cogent reason to suppose that John knew (without adopting) Mark's story of Simon of Cyrene, or that he knew (and 'corrected') either Mark's

---

[1] Such as the theory that the Mother represents the Church, committed to the care of the Beloved Disciple (the Ephesian apostle) rather than to Peter (the Roman); or that she stands for the Jewish 'church', the old Israel, the 'mother' of the Messiah and of the Christian Church, with the implication that Jewish Christians are to be received and honoured. All very far-fetched, and with no demonstrable relation to Johannine thought. It may, however, be that a certain rivalry between Rome and Ephesus led to the emphasis in the Ephesian tradition upon the special mark of confidence shown to its patron apostle.

[2] If the evangelist had (*a*) a form of Passion tradition which, like those of Mark and Luke, included a note of the presence of women, and their names, but was not, as were theirs, associated with the *testimonia* from Ps. xxxvii. 12, lxxxvii. 9, and (*b*) a separate tradition about the Mother and the Disciple, the obvious way of combining them would have been just what we have here: the Mother added to the traditional group, and the group placed near to the Cross. But such speculations are to little profit.

or Luke's account of the women at Golgotha; but beyond that we can say nothing with confidence.

There is thus very little of the Marcan narrative which in any form reappears in John. The omissions (if that is the proper word) are numerous and some of them remarkable. Beside Simon of Cyrene, we note the following.

(a) The offer and rejection of drugged wine (Mark xv. 23). This omission need have no special significance. The evangelist might well have thought the detail unimportant to the development of the main theme.

(b) The mockery and abuse of the Crucified (Mark xv. 29–32). It is suggested that this is due to the reverential motive of reluctance to depict the shameful treatment of Christ. Yet this motive has not deterred the Fourth Evangelist from describing the mockery by Roman troops, and even emphasizing it by making Pilate exhibit the King of the Jews crowned and robed in a caricature of royalty. Indeed the sarcasms of the priests in Mark at the expense of 'the Messiah the King of Israel' are so much in the vein of the Fourth Evangelist that it would be surprising if he had omitted this feature from any source which lay before him. Nor could he have any theological misgivings, for it is an essential part of Johannine theology that the moment in which the Son of Man is 'lifted up' is the very moment of his deepest humiliation. The absence therefore of this part of the story is not readily explained, if he be supposed to have had Mark as a source.

(c) The darkness during the crucifixion (Mark xv. 33). This would surely be peculiarly congenial to a writer whose whole work is pervaded by the symbolism of light and darkness. A contrast between the darkness brooding over the earth and the real and eternal glory of the Cross would appear to be entirely in his vein, and to fit perfectly into his theological scheme.[1] If he knew it from Mark, why should he omit it?

(d) The rending of the veil of the temple (Mark xv. 38). This would seem to yield a perfect climax for the Johannine series of temple-imagery. The cleansing of the temple signifies, on the one hand, the passing of a limited and temporal order of worship and the opening of a new way of worship ἐν πνεύματι, and this as part of the work which Christ has to

---

[1] In ix. 4–5 the departure of Christ from the world is symbolized by nightfall. In xii. 35–6 the 'lifting up' of the Son of Man is the withdrawal of light and the coming of darkness. How natural it would have been, and how much in our author's manner, to symbolize this by darkness over the whole earth!

complete (τελειοῦν) (John ii. 18–19, iv. 23–4, 34); and, on the other hand, it signifies the destruction of Christ's own body and its raising from death (John ii. 21–2). At the point where John reports the death of Christ with the word τετέλεσται on his lips, the natural sequel, in his own order of thought, would seem to be, 'the veil of the temple was rent in twain'. If this stood in the tradition known to this evangelist, would he have omitted it?

(e) The confession of the centurion, οὗτος ὁ ἄνθρωπος υἱὸς θεοῦ ἦν (Mark xv. 39). There is nothing un-Johannine about the expression, for although the evangelist prefers for himself the form (ὁ) υἱὸς τοῦ θεοῦ, yet he allows the anarthrous form in the mouth of strangers (xix. 7). The purpose for which he wrote his gospel was to lead its readers to believe that Jesus is the Son of God (xx. 31). With his insistence upon μαρτυρία he might have been expected to welcome a confession of Jesus as such by a Gentile.

These two 'signs' (as John might have called them) and the accompanying μαρτυρία would seem to be so entirely germane to the general outlook and manner of this evangelist that it would be surprising if he had found them in his source and excluded them. There is of course an element of subjectivity in any attempt to conjecture the mental processes of an author, yet anyone who would maintain that John is here dependent on the Synoptics is bound to suggest some plausible reason for the rejection of these data—and he has a difficult task.[1]

So much for John's 'omissions'. Of his additions, or supplements, to the common contents of the Passion narrative we have already considered

---

[1] It is not difficult to find theological equivalents for the three passages in other parts of the gospel, and it is argued that having already given expression to the ideas our author did not think it necessary to insert their symbols here—as (it may be) he has omitted Gethsemane because it has an equivalent in xii. 27–30, and omitted the sacramental words and acts at the Last Supper because they have an equivalent in vi. 50–1. But this argument is not well founded in our author's actual practice. It is his custom to offer *both* the direct theological expression of a theme *and* its embodiment in a symbol. The fact that he has expounded a theme does not seem to be a reason for dispensing with the corresponding symbolism, but rather a reason for supplying it. Thus 'I am the light of the world', with the development of the idea in viii. 12, is taken up in the story of the healing of the blind in ix. 3–7. The pronouncement, ἔρχεται ὥρα καὶ νῦν ἐστὶν ὅτε οἱ νεκροὶ ἀκούσουσιν τῆς φωνῆς τοῦ υἱοῦ τοῦ θεοῦ καὶ οἱ ἀκούσαντες 3ήσουσιν (v. 25), is taken up in the story of the raising of Lazarus. The presence of passages which are the theological equivalent of the 'signs' of the darkness and the rending of the veil is therefore no valid reason to account for the absence of the 'signs' themselves. It proves that there was at any rate no theological reason for their omission.

the two short dialogues in xix. 21–2 and 26–7. There remains the remarkable passage which may be said to take the place of the 'signs' which follow the death of Jesus in Mark, xix. 31–7. The effective core of the passage is clearly to be sought in the citation of two passages from the Old Testament: (a) ὀστοῦν οὐ συντριβήσεται αὐτοῦ, which, as I have argued elsewhere,[1] is more likely to have been taken from Ps. xxxiii. 21 than from the regulations for Passover in Exod. xii. 46 or Num. ix. 12, and (b) ὄψονται εἰς ὃν ἐξεκέντησαν, from Zech. xii. 10. In view of the importance of *testimonia* for the formation of the Passion tradition, we shall do well to make them the starting point for our investigation of this *pericopé*.

The first quotation, if it be held to come from the regulations for Passover, is designed to assimilate the death of Christ to that of the paschal victim, and so to suggest an interpretation of its significance. If it is from Ps. xxxiii, it presents him in the guise of the Righteous Sufferer who is preserved by divine power in all his afflictions, and finally redeemed from them all. There is evidence that this psalm was held to contain the promise of the resurrection of the body.[2] To the evangelist therefore it would suggest the promise of Christ's resurrection. The 'sign' of such preservation and final deliverance is the *literal* fulfilment of the promise, Κύριος φυλάσσει πάντα τὰ ὀστᾶ αὐτῶν, ἓν ἐξ αὐτῶν οὐ συντριβήσεται. The feature, therefore, which the evangelist finds apposite is a negative one: the bones of the Crucified were *not* broken. But that would have been true of most crucifixions, for we have no evidence that *crurifragium* (a perfectly well-recognized punishment in itself) was a usual or normal accompaniment of this form of execution, though it may well have been used on occasion to hasten death. There was therefore no need for the evangelist to do more, in order to point the fulfilment of the Old Testament, than to call attention to the fact that Jesus died in a way which did *not* involve (as

---

[1] See above, pp. 42–4.

[2] There is a rabbinic interpretation of Ps. xxxiv. 21 (M.T. = xxxiii. 21, LXX), which apparently takes the clause אַחַת מֵהֵנָּה לֹא נִשְׁבָּרָה in the sense 'one of them shall not be broken up' (which is grammatically possible); there is one bone in the body (the coccyx) which will resist the process of corruption, and from this bone the resurrection-body will be reconstructed (see *Polii Synopsis Scripturae Sacrae Interpretum*, Frankfurt, 1712, *ad loc.* and citations in Buxtorf, *Lexicon Chaldaicum Talmudicum et Rabbinicum*, *s.vv.* לוּז, תַּרְוָד). Obviously this interpretation is not presupposed in our text, but it may fairly be taken as evidence that the psalm was, in some quarters at least, taken to mean that God preserves the body of the righteous not from death but through death to the day of resurrection.

for example stoning[1] might involve) the breaking of bones, but preserved the integrity of the frame. It is open to anyone to argue that, wishing to give all possible emphasis to this negative feature, he invented the fiction that in this particular case, for a special reason, the *crurifragium* was employed, but that, contrary to the first intention of the executioners, Jesus was spared it. But surely the simpler hypothesis is that he has followed information received, and that it was the remembered facts that first drew the attention of Christian thinkers to the *testimonium* of Ps. xxxiii. 21 rather than the other way round. The reason given for the exceptional, but perhaps not unparalleled, employment of the *crurifragium* is a valid one, and the reason for its restriction to the other two victims is also entirely plausible.

The second quotation is from Zech. xii. 10, in a version which differs from the LXX and anticipates that of Theodotion. The latter part of Zechariah (ix–xiv), as I have shown elsewhere,[2] belongs to the restricted body of prophetic scriptures which can be shown to have been employed from the earliest period as a source of *testimonia*. Such testimonies are in the gospels (with few exceptions) uniformly employed with the purpose of identifying Christ with the messianic figures of prophecy by 'pin-pointing' particular incidents or traits of his story which lend themselves to description in the language of the Old Testament. Thus we have from Zechariah the picture of the peaceful King entering Jerusalem, and of the stricken Shepherd whose flock is scattered. In exactly the same vein John gives us here the picture of the martyred Leader whose wounded body is a spectacle to his murderers. The present passage, therefore, falls naturally into line, in character and intention, with the primitive use of testimonies. It betrays nothing of the distinctively Johannine theology,[3] but implies a

---

[1] The proper penalty, according to *Sanh.* 43, for the crimes of which Jesus was accused.　　　　　　　　　　　[2] See *According to the Scriptures*, pp. 64–7.

[3] In Rev. i. 7, Zech. xii. 10 is cited after the same version as that of John xix. 37, though not in identical words. But the apocalyptist has a more extended passage before him; the lamentation of the tribes in Zech. xii. 10–14 (which is not represented in John xix. 37) is summarized in the phrase κόψονται ἐπ' αὐτὸν πᾶσαι αἱ φυλαὶ τῆς γῆς, where the words πᾶσαι αἱ φυλαὶ τῆς γῆς echo the well-known testimony of Gen. xii. 3. This prophecy from Zechariah is ingeniously conflated with Dan. vii. 13, and so referred to the final advent of Christ. The apocalyptist has preserved a trait of the original prophecy which does not appear in John, namely the idea that the sight of the martyred Leader's wounded body will bring his murderers to a sense of what they have done and move them to sorrow. But otherwise the use of the passage in Rev. i. 7 has a sophistication which is absent from John xix. 37. The evangelist's use of it belongs to a simpler and (we may suppose) more primitive stage of testimony-research.

Christology of the *gemeinchristlich* type which underlies also the Synoptic Gospels.

It is of course possible that, as Matthew, having before him Zech. ix–xiv as a recognized source of testimonies, exploited Zech. xi. 13 to reveal how much Judas was paid for his treachery, so John has produced the incident of the lance-thrust out of Zech. xii. 10. But in fact the analogy between Matt. xxvii. 3–10 and John xix. 32–7 is remote; there is a sophistication about Matthew's procedure which contrasts with the simplicity of John's, and almost certainly represents a later stage of the use of testimonies. There is nothing against the *prima facie* view that we are here dealing with genuinely traditional material.

I conclude that the incident of the *crurifragium*, and that of the lance-thrust, were probably transmitted, along with the testimonies by which they are accompanied, in the special form of tradition which the Fourth Evangelist had received. How far they are to be accepted as historical fact is a further question. But no one seriously doubts that the prophetic picture of the stricken Shepherd and his scattered flock accurately symbolizes the true situation when the blow fell on Jesus and his followers were dispersed; and only an extreme hypercriticism has ever doubted that Jesus did in fact ride into Jerusalem on a donkey, suggesting the prophetic picture of the peaceful King. There is no inherent reason why the other testimony from Zechariah should not be taken similarly at its face value. The *testimonium* from Ps. xxxiii almost certainly corresponds literally with historical facts, whether or not the particular way in which John has fitted it into the story is to be accepted.

This brings us to a feature of this passage which we have not hitherto noticed: the report of the issue of blood and water from the side of the Crucified. This report is not supported by any quotation from the Old Testament. On the contrary, it is unique in the whole gospel in being declared to rest upon eyewitness: ὁ ἑωρακὼς μεμαρτύρηκεν. It is possible that this means (as has been widely supposed) that the writer himself claims to have been an eyewitness of the incident; possible, but, as it seems to me, unlikely, for it would be an unnatural way of saying it. The natural and straightforward meaning is that someone, not the author, had, to the author's knowledge, witnessed the occurrence,[1] and that it is

---

[1] The assumption frequently made that ὁ ἑωρακὼς was the Beloved Disciple (whether conceived as the author or as his informant) is difficult to reconcile with the statement of xix. 27 that this disciple took the Mother home ἀπ' ἐκείνης τῆς ὥρας, from which it would seem to follow that from that point he was no longer at Golgotha.

here recorded on the testimony of that witness, whoever he may have been. In any case, whether the witness is the evangelist or another, I can see no reasonable way of avoiding the conclusion that the evangelist intends to assure his readers that his account rests, whether directly or indirectly, on the testimony of an eyewitness. Not only so, he formally affirms that the testimony is genuine (ἀληθινή) and that the witness must be believed to be a veracious witness (ὅτι ἀληθῆ λέγει).[1] He could not have expressed himself more emphatically or more unequivocally.

[1] Ὁ ἑωρακὼς μεμαρτύρηκεν: such is the basic statement. Ἀληθινὴ αὐτοῦ ἐστὶν ἡ μαρτυρία: this is the evangelist's own comment upon it, meaning, probably, that he accepts this as (not a guess or an opinion but) a genuine or authentic piece of evidence. Ἐκεῖνος οἶδεν ὅτι ἀληθῆ λέγει: here the question has been much debated, who is meant by ἐκεῖνος? The alternatives seem to be (a) that ἐκεῖνος is Christ (or God) and that the sentence is a solemn asseveration: 'The Lord Himself knows that this is the truth', and (b) that ἐκεῖνος is the witness. The question must be discussed on the basis of Johannine usage. First, ἐκεῖνος is twice used absolutely, i.e. without any strict grammatical connection defining the identity of the person intended (though it may be gathered from the context: xix. 21, ἐκεῖνος εἶπεν, Βασιλεύς εἰμι τῶν Ἰουδαίων)—ἐκεῖνος is Jesus, but the word in the mouths of the priests has a derogatory tone, '*That* fellow claimed to be King of the Jews!'; vii. 11, the Jews at the Feast ask Ποῦ ἐστιν ἐκεῖνος; again ἐκεῖνος is Jesus; there is nothing actually derogatory, but it is, shall we say, a little off-hand. (The same phrase in ix. 12 refers back directly to ὁ ἄνθρωπος ὁ λεγόμενος Ἰησοῦς.) Secondly, it is used in dialogue to indicate a change of speaker, ix. 9, 11, 25, 36, xiii. 25, xviii. 17, 25, xx. 15, 16. Thirdly, it is used pleonastically, in apposition to the true subject of the sentence: i. 18, μονογενὴς υἱὸς ὁ ὢν εἰς τὸν κόλπον τοῦ πατρὸς ἐκεῖνος ἐξηγήσατο, i. 33, ὁ πέμψας με βαπτίζειν ἐν ὕδατι ἐκεῖνός μοι εἶπεν..., and so v. 11, 37, x. 1, xii. 48, xiv. 21, 26, xvi. 13. Fourthly, it resumes one of the terms of the foregoing sentence, or series of sentences: e.g. v. 33–5, ἀπεστάλκατε πρὸς Ἰωάννην...ἐκεῖνος ἦν ὁ λύχνος ὁ καιόμενος, viii. 44, ὑμεῖς ἐκ τοῦ πατρὸς τοῦ διαβόλου ἐστέ...ἐκεῖνος ἀνθρωποκτόνος ἦν ἀπ' ἀρχῆς, and so in various ways iv. 25, v. 19, 35, 38, 46, viii. 42, 44, ix. 12, 37, xi. 29, xiii. 30, xv. 26, xvi. 8, 14. Fifthly, it points to the person who is identified in a relative or participial clause: ix. 37, ὁ λαλῶν μετά σου ἐκεῖνός ἐστιν (*scil.* ὁ υἱὸς τοῦ ἀνθρώπου), xiii. 26, ἐκεῖνός ἐστιν ᾧ ἐγὼ βάψω τὸ ψωμίον καὶ δώσω αὐτῷ. It is clear that the present case could fall, grammatically, only into the first or the fourth group. If ἐκεῖνος is here used absolutely, it could refer to Christ (or God), but such a use would contrast violently with the only two examples of the absolute use that we have noted. Certainly ἐκεῖνος can refer to God the Father (as in vi. 29, viii. 42) or to Christ (as in i. 18, v. 11, or to the Holy Spirit (as in xiv. 26, xv. 26, xvi. 8); but in every such case the pronoun either stands in apposition or resumes one of the terms of a previous sentence. But here the only term in the previous sentence to which it could possibly refer is ὁ ἑωρακώς. Unless, therefore, the passage falls outside the range of known Johannine usage, ἐκεῖνος must be the witness. Not only does the evangelist commit himself to the genuineness or authenticity of the testimony; he affirms that the witness himself spoke with full knowledge of the facts and was conscious of speaking the truth. His identity therefore must have been known to the evangelist, who had

The statement that blood and water issued from the side of the Crucified has for the evangelist profound theological significance. Αἷμα καὶ ὕδωρ: we have been left in no doubt what these symbols stand for. The 'blood' of the Son of Man is ἀληθὴς πόσις, which confers eternal life through union with Christ (vi. 54–6). The 'water' that Christ gives is a perpetual fountain of eternal life (iv. 14); the 'streams of living water' that flow from his κοιλία are no other than the very life-giving Spirit that believers receive (vii. 38–9). It is an easy inference that the statement, ἐξῆλθεν αἷμα καὶ ὕδωρ, is purely symbolical. Nothing could be more plausible—until we are brought up sharply by those uncompromising words, ὁ ἑωρακὼς μεμαρτύρηκεν. You cannot 'see' a theologumenon; you can see only sensible facts.[1] Was our author the kind of person to say, 'an eyewitness has given evidence of this', and to go out of his way to affirm the authenticity and veracity of this evidence, when all he is offering to his readers is a deeply suggestive symbol? That is a question upon which each student of the gospel will form his own judgement; a measure of subjectivity cannot be avoided. For my part, I confess I cannot bring myself to believe that he was that kind of person.

Someone, then, upon whose word our evangelist was prepared to rely, observed what he took in good faith to be an issue of blood and water from the side of the Crucified, and the evangelist eagerly availed himself of the symbolic meanings which this observation suggested. This particular item, therefore, in his narrative he would seem not to have taken from the common tradition: it is a piece of supplementary information which he fits into the story as he has it from tradition. If my argument above is sound, this traditional narrative probably contained the statement that the body of Jesus was pierced by a lance-thrust, and supported this statement by a quotation from the Old Testament.[2] To this our evangelist

complete confidence in his competence (as one who knew the facts) and his good faith. To brush aside this cumulative asseveration is temerarious in any critic.

[1] To understand ὁρᾶν here of spiritual vision is entirely arbitrary.

[2] It is no doubt conceivable that the passage from Zechariah might have been adduced as a testimonium without reference to a lance-thrust, the 'piercing' being that of the nails in the hands (and feet). But for this the obvious testimony would have been Ps. xxi. 17, ὤρυξαν χεῖράς μου καὶ πόδας, with a different verb. Ἐκκεντεῖν is the conventional rendering in the LXX of דָּקָר, and this is constantly used of 'running through' with a weapon; e.g. Judg. ix. 54, 1 Chron. x. 4, Jer. xliv (xxxvii). 10. John has rightly equated it with νύσσειν (xix. 34), which is used from Homer onwards for a spear-thrust (Il. v. 45–6, Τὸν μὲν ἄρ' Ἰδομενεὺς δουρίκλυτος ἔγχεϊ μακρῷ Νύξ' ἵππων ἐπιβησόμενον κατὰ δεξιὸν ὦμον). It is therefore probable that the reference to the lance-thrust is bound up with the citation of Zech. xii. 10.

has added an observation of the immediate effect of the lance-thrust, for which observation he takes personal responsibility on the word of someone whom he could trust.

If we ask further what it was that the witness saw, we are on more speculative ground. But it seems worth while to refer to a recent study of the medical aspect of the death of Christ as described in the gospels: *Circonstances et Cause de la Mort du Christ*, by Raymond Schmittlein (Éditions Art et Science, Bade, 1950). The author, basing his argument upon researches made during the late war into traumatic shock, shows that all the statements of the gospels are consistent with the view that this was the immediate cause of death. It is unnecessary here to follow his careful argument step by step, but for our present purpose the following summarizing passage is relevant:

On sait que toutes les autopsies faites sur les cadavres de soldats ayant succombé au choc ont montré de l'œdème dans les poumons et les parenchymes avec effusion du liquide d'œdème dans les cavités séreuses. Le sang que les assistants voient s'écouler du côté de Jésus (et non du cœur) est simplement le produit de l'hémorragie intérieure causée par la vaso-dilatation, et l'eau n'est autre chose que le liquide d'œdème amassé dans les cavités séreuses, libéré par le coup de lance (*op. cit.* p. 92).

I have no competence to assess the value of the medical evidence adduced, but so far as a layman can judge, it would appear to deserve serious consideration. If it holds, then Schmittlein's interpretation of the gospel data is persuasive.

7. THE REUNION

All four evangelists have in their several ways marked the close of the narrative of the crucifixion of Jesus. Mark and Matthew, having recorded his death, add certain accompanying 'signs', leading up to the pagan centurion's acclamation of the Crucified as υἱὸς θεοῦ. Luke has a corresponding passage, in briefer and less emphatic terms; his version of the centurion's confession, ὁ ἄνθρωπος οὗτος δίκαιος ἦν,[1] lacks the climactic force of the Marcan and Matthaean form, but he has compensated by adding a conclusion in which (as in a Greek tragedy) a chorus of bystanders comments upon the action of the drama: 'All the crowds who had gathered at the place for the spectacle, when they had seen all that happened, went home beating their breasts.'[2] The intention is clear; as in Mark and Matthew, the story of the sufferings and death of Jesus is complete, and the tension is relaxed. With the introduction of the women and then of Joseph of Arimathaea begins the fresh chapter of the story which will culminate in the testimony to his resurrection.

In the Fourth Gospel the same general pattern is to be observed, although almost every detail is different. After recording the death of Jesus, the evangelist, like Mark, adds two 'signs' which accompanied it. They are different from those of the other gospels, but like them serve as pointers to the significance of the Crucifixion—a significance here clarified by references to Scripture. Then, like the others, John embarks on a fresh chapter. He has no need to introduce the women at this point, since they have already appeared at an earlier point in the narrative, and they are not needed (except for Mary Magdalene) as characters in the ensuing scene. It is therefore Joseph of Arimathaea whose entrance opens the action.

(a) The Entombment (xix. 38–42)

Mark, having brought on the scene the women who are to be witnesses both of the burial of Jesus and of the unexpected sequel (xvi. 1 sqq.),

---

[1] In the dramatic situation, this means no more than, 'This man was innocent'; the centurion recognizes that there has been a miscarriage of justice; but the Christian reader will remember that the sufferings of Christ have been assimilated to those of the 'righteous' in the psalms.

[2] This, we may reasonably suspect, is the contribution of the evangelist, with his Greek instinct for literary effect, rather than an original feature of the tradition. In John we return to the more traditional scheme represented by Mark and Matthew, though hardly in dependence on them.

gives a somewhat detailed account of the interview between Joseph and Pilate, and then records the burial of the body of the Crucified, wrapped in a winding sheet, in a rock-hewn tomb closed with a large stone. Matthew and Luke have abridged the interview with Pilate, but otherwise follow Mark fairly closely, though with verbal variations.

The Johannine account runs roughly parallel. There is a concise report of the interview with Pilate, and a more detailed account of the process of burial, introducing features absent from the Synoptics while passing over some details which they contain. In particular, John does not say that the tomb was rock-hewn, or that it was closed with a stone. Yet in the sequel he speaks of the stone being removed (ἠρμένον, xx. 1, where the Synoptics use some form of the verb ἀνα-, ἀποκυλίειν). We may, therefore, probably understand that the source which John is following (whether Synoptic or not) did contain this feature. To that extent he must be supposed to have abbreviated the account which had come down to him. Yet he also adds details which are not in our other sources. He records that the tomb was in a garden, and that the garden was near Golgotha. More importantly, he describes an embalming of the body with a mixture of myrrh and aloes, provided by Nicodemus, who does not appear in the other gospels.

It would be easy enough to regard this as no more than a secondary account based on the Synoptics, if we supposed the introduction of Nicodemus to be due to a special interest of this evangelist in a *dramatis persona* whom he has brought into his story more than once, and if we attributed the account of an embalming to his reluctance to contemplate a dishonoured burial for his Lord. His omissions would scarcely need any special explanation. There are a few points of contact with the language of the Synoptic accounts, though they are not particularly striking. All gospels, naturally, have the name Joseph of Arimathaea, and the phrase τὸ σῶμα τοῦ Ἰησοῦ, without which the story could not be told at all. For the rest, John agrees with Matthew against the others in the term he uses for the tomb, μνημεῖον, where Mark and Luke, according to what appears the best text, have μνῆμα, and in describing Joseph as a μαθητής (Matthew using the verb μαθητεύεσθαι). He agrees with Mark and Luke against Matthew in naming the day, Friday[1] (παρασκευή, which Mark explains as

---

[1] Matthew however has given the term παρασκευή at an earlier point, xxvii. 62, where there is no Synoptic parallel, and where he appears to say that παρασκευή was the *morrow* of the Crucifixion. Possibly he understood παρασκευή to mean, not Friday, but the Eve of Passover (ערב הפסח = παρασκευή τοῦ πάσχα). Fortunately we are not here concerned to unravel Matthew's chronology.

προσάββατον), and, negatively, in saying nothing of Joseph's ownership of the tomb; according to John it was chosen simply because it was near at hand, though of this the others say nothing. He agrees with Matthew and Luke against Mark in using the simple ἔθηκεν for the deposition of the body, where Mark has κατέθηκεν, and in one place he has what might be taken for a conflation of Matthew and Luke: μνημεῖον καινόν (cf. Matthew, ἐν τῷ καινῷ αὐτοῦ μνημείῳ), ἐν ᾧ οὐδέπω οὐδεὶς ἦν τεθειμένος (cf. Luke, ἐν μνήματι...οὗ οὐκ ἦν οὐδεὶς οὔπω κείμενος).[1] Over against these agreements, such as they are, we may note that for Mark's ἠτήσατο τὸ σῶμα John has ἠρώτησεν ἵνα ἄρῃ τὸ σῶμα, and that Pilate's consent is expressed in Mark by ἐδωρήσατο, in Matthew by ἐκέλευσεν ἀποδοθῆναι, in John by ἐπέτρεψεν. Where Mark and Luke have καθελών John has ἦρεν (τὸ σῶμα), though at a later point he agrees with Matthew in using the verb λαβεῖν. Where Mark has ἐνείλησεν τῇ σινδόνι, and Matthew and Luke ἐνετύλιξεν σινδόνι, John has ἔδησαν ὀθονίοις. None of these variations seem to have any significance. They are trivial enough. So indeed are the agreements. It is clear that any theory of dependence of John on the Synoptics here would need to postulate conflation of at least two sources, Matthew and Luke. But the resemblances are insufficient to support any such theory. The simpler hypothesis is that he follows an independent tradition of some kind, though it may well be that he has elaborated it.[2]

---

[1] The situation is somewhat similar to that which we observe on a comparison of Mark i. 32 with the Synoptic parallels. Mark has ὀψίας γενομένης ὅτε ἔδυσεν ὁ ἥλιος. Matthew has ὀψίας γενομένης only, Luke δύνοντος τοῦ ἡλίου only. This has often been adduced as evidence for the dependence of both on Mark. I do not, however, remember that anyone has argued that in our present passage Matthew and Luke are dependent on John, each similarly reproducing one part of his complete phrase!

[2] It seems likely that the somewhat extravagant estimate of the weight of myrrh and aloes provided is a touch introduced by the evangelist, who perhaps is somewhat addicted to numbers, especially large numbers (six ὑδρίαι each holding two or three μετρηταί, 153 fishes—if the appendix is by the same author). The use of myrrh and aloes is not attested in rabbinic sources (according to S.–B.), and does not seem to be καθὼς ἔθος ἐστὶν τοῖς 'Ιουδαίοις ἐνταφιάζειν. We could well allow the copious μῖγμα σμύρνης καὶ ἀλόης to be a part of the evangelist's elaboration. But that does not necessarily carry with it the whole episode of the embalming. It may no doubt have an honorific motive. Yet the Synoptic account is not altogether without difficulties. According to Mark Joseph had time enough on Friday to buy a winding sheet (ἀγοράσας σινδόνα, xv. 46); why did he not also buy other things necessary for the funeral rites? We are insufficiently informed; but it is not axiomatic that the Synoptic account is better based than the Johannine. Nor is it certain that Nicodemus is a less historical character than Joseph. The incidental note that the tomb was in a garden and near to Golgotha has the appearance of resting on information

(b) The Discovery of the Empty Tomb (xx. 1–10)

The common nucleus of the narrative in all gospels is that early on Sunday morning Mary Magdalene (alone or with others) came to the tomb, found the stone which had sealed it removed, and encountered either a young man (Mark), or an angel (Matthew) or two men (Luke) or two angels (John, cf. Luke xxiv. 23). Outside this common nucleus even the Synoptics vary considerably among themselves, and John's account takes a widely different course. John agrees with Mark in placing the visit 'early on Sunday morning' (τῇ μιᾷ τῶν σαββάτων πρωΐ): for πρωΐ Luke has the more recherché phrase ὄρθρου βαθέως, while Matthew has an entirely different form of expression, whose meaning has baffled commentators. Beyond that, only the name Mary Magdalene,[1] the terms μνημεῖον and λίθος, and forms of the verb ἔρχεσθαι, are common to the Fourth Gospel and the Synoptics. Its story in fact is a different one. The Magdalene alone visits the tomb, for what reason we are not told. It could not have been to anoint the body, as Mark and Luke aver, since Joseph and Nicodemus have already performed that office. (But Matthew also knows nothing of the project; the women, he says, simply came θεωρῆσαι τὸν τάφον. Perhaps John took the same view.) The moment she saw that the stone had been removed she ran away, and only on a second visit did she venture to look into the tomb (παρέκυψεν εἰς τὸ μνημεῖον), without entering it (as Mark and Luke say she did); and then it was that she saw the two angels. They, however, play no real part in the Johannine narrative: they give no information (as they do in the other gospels) of the resurrection of Jesus; they do not need to do so, for at this point the story of the discovery of the empty tomb melts into a story of the first appearance of the risen Christ.

Meanwhile, however, there has been a further stage of the discovery, to which the evangelist evidently attaches greater importance. Mary Magdalene having reported the situation, Peter and the Beloved Disciple

received rather than on the story-teller's imagination—especially in an author whose topographical information can sometimes be proved to be good.

[1] Yet even here Matthew does not perhaps follow Mark exactly, if, as is probable, he uses the form Μαριάμ (א Θ etc.) for Mark's Μαρία. The mention of the women in Matt. xxviii. 1 comes between two longish paragraphs, xxvii. 62–6 and xxviii. 2–4, which have no contact with Mark, and if Matthew had before him Mark's perfectly perspicuous indications of time, it is hard to see why he should have reduced them to unintelligible confusion unless he was following also a different tradition. In Luke again, although he appears to follow Mark in outline, there is so much non-Marcan material that his version can hardly be fully accounted for by a mere 'editing' of Mark.

visit the tomb. The story of their experience is told with great dramatic vigour, and in considerable detail. It is they, and not Mary Magdalene or the other women, who enter the tomb (Peter, as afterwards the other, εἰσῆλθεν εἰς τὸ μνημεῖον, echoing Mark's εἰσελθοῦσαι εἰς τὸ μνημεῖον), and there they see, not an angel, or a young man in white, but simply the graveclothes in orderly arrangement. The theological interest is manifest in the climax to which the story works: εἶδεν καὶ ἐπίστευσεν, where πιστεύειν is clearly used absolutely, and the juxtaposition of 'seeing' and 'believing' points to a favourite theme of this evangelist,[1] whose power of dramatic narrative we can also recognize in the whole cast of the story. Yet the statement that others of the followers of Jesus beside the women saw the empty tomb is not peculiar to the Fourth Gospel. In the course of the story of the walk to Emmaus Luke (xxiv. 22–4) makes the two travellers rehearse the main facts of Easter morning: first, certain women visited the tomb at dawn, reported it empty, and claimed to have had a vision of angels who told them that Jesus was alive; secondly, 'some of our associates' (τινὲς τῶν σὺν ἡμῖν) visited the tomb and confirmed the women's report, without, however, seeing the risen Lord. Luke, as I have observed elsewhere,[2] has packed into the Emmaus story a comprehensive summary of the testimony to Christ's resurrection, as it reached him; and just as it included an appearance to Peter, of which his narrative says nothing, so also it included a visit of certain disciples to the tomb. Whether the phrase τινὲς τῶν σὺν ἡμῖν is likely to have been employed if it had been known, or believed, that one of them was the chief of the apostles, is another question. Even if it had been known, the phrase is nevertheless dramatically appropriate in the mouth of Cleopas talking with a total stranger (as he supposed). But we must reckon with the tendency to introduce well-known names into stories originally anonymous.[3] However this may be, it is clear that Luke was acquainted with a tradition that certain disciples were first-hand witnesses to the empty tomb. It may have been the same tradition upon which John worked. That John borrowed from Luke is as

---

[1] See *Interpretation*, pp. 185–6.

[2] *Studies in the Gospels: Essays in Memory of R. H. Lightfoot*, ed. D. E. Nineham (Blackwell), p. 14.

[3] In [Mark] xvi. 12 we have an appearance of the risen Christ δυσὶν ἐξ αὐτῶν, without names. In Luke xxiv. 18 one of them is named, Cleopas. Are we to say that Luke has introduced a 'legendary' trait in naming the originally anonymous? Most critics, I think, have regarded Luke here as primary and pseudo-Mark as secondary. If on the other hand Luke xxiv. 24 has τινὲς ἐξ ἡμῶν while John names one of them, Peter, are we to apply the same reasoning?

unlikely as that Luke borrowed from John; but the story, however it may have been elaborated by our evangelist, is clearly not his invention.

The substantial degree of variation among all gospels in the account of the burial and of the discovery of the empty tomb suggests that for this part of the narrative there were multiple traditions, of which traces appear in Matthew and Luke, in spite of their general adherence to the Marcan pattern, and it is in no way surprising that John shows traces of yet another form of tradition, which at one significant point agrees with the Lucan summary in xxiv. 22–4.

(c) The Appearances of the Risen Christ (xx. 11–xxi. 23)

Down to this point, in spite of substantial variations, we have been able to follow a common line of continuity in the narrative of all four gospels, and there is no difficulty in recognizing a further stage of the Passion narrative. The general manner of narration has been kept up. All through, the evangelists have, in one way or another, marked the passage of time: Thursday evening, Thursday night, Friday morning and various times during the day, Friday evening, Saturday, Sunday morning.[1] From this point, however, it is more difficult to discover any common pattern. Mark (in the authentic text) deserts us. Matthew carries the continuity a stage further by connecting the story of the women at the tomb with an appearance of the risen Christ, but then loses it while he relates how certain false rumours arose, and after that suddenly transports the disciples to Galilee for the final scene. Luke jumps at once from dawn on Sunday to the evening of the same day, alluding to intervening events in a series of 'flash-backs'. Between Matthew and Luke there is nothing in common. John presents a more successful appearance of continuity. Like Matthew he passes on from the discovery of the empty tomb to an appearance of Christ to Mary Magdalene, and then, carrying on the style of narration which has prevailed in the Passion narrative, he proceeds, οὔσης οὖν ὀψίας τῇ ἡμέρᾳ ἐκείνῃ τῇ μιᾷ σαββάτων, and relates an appearance to the disciples. In similar terms the final scene, with Thomas, is introduced by the words, μεθ' ἡμέρας ὀκτώ.

---

[1] The historical value of this chronology has been questioned by some critics, most recently by Mlle A. Jaubert (*La Date de la Cène*). But there is little doubt that all four forms of the Passion narrative are constructed on this scheme, whether or not it is artificial. If my general argument is sound, and the data point to the existence of three independent pre-canonical forms of Passion tradition, the likelihood is increased that the chronological framework corresponds, broadly at least, to the sequence of events.

We are probably safe in assuming that any traditional Passion narrative would follow the primitive formula: (*a*) ἀπέθανεν, (*b*) ἐτάφη, (*c*) ἐγήγερται, (*d*) ὤφθη (1 Cor. xv. 3–5). In other words, the account of (*a*) the Crucifixion would be followed by an account of (*b*) the burial and (*c*) the subsequent discovery of the empty tomb; and thus far we seem able to recognize a common primitive pattern in all gospels. This should be further followed by (*d*) some account of appearances of the Risen Christ; and so it is in all gospels except Mark, who nevertheless indicates that he knew of such appearances. But in the accounts of these appearances we can no longer discern the common primitive pattern of narrative; each evangelist goes his own way, and only in the Fourth Gospel is something apparently preserved of the chronological structure characteristic of other parts of the Passion narrative.

But further, the several narratives of the appearances of the Risen Christ form separable units in a way that the successive episodes of the earlier parts of the Passion narrative do not. I have elsewhere[1] examined them in detail, and shown that these narratives are, in form, closely similar to the *pericopae* which form-critics have separated out in other parts of the gospels as examples of units of oral tradition. Two types are represented, the concise (analogous to the so-called 'paradigms', 'apophthegms', or 'pronouncement-stories') and the circumstantial (analogous to the *Novellen*, or 'tales'). As elsewhere in the gospels, some of our *pericopae* are 'impure' examples of their type. I showed reason for classifying as examples of the 'concise' type the appearances to the women in Matt. xxviii. 8–10, and to the disciples in Matt. xxviii. 16–20, [Mark] xvi. 14–15, John xx. 19–21, with Luke xxiv. 36–49 as an 'impure' example, containing much apologetic expansion; and as examples of the 'circumstantial' type Luke xxiv. 13–35, John xxi. 1–14. All the 'concise' *pericopae* are constructed on a common pattern which can be recognized (with very slight aberrations from the norm) in all gospels. The pattern may be represented as follows:

(A) The situation: Christ's followers bereft of their Lord.

(B) The appearance of Christ.

(C) His greeting.

(D) The recognition (ἀναγνώρισις).

(E) His word of command.

[1] In an essay contributed to *Studies in the Gospels: Essays in Memory of R. H. Lightfoot*, ed. D. E. Nineham, pp. 9–35. Much of what here follows summarizes what I have said in the Lightfoot volume, to which the reader is referred for the arguments by which positions here taken are supported.

Much of this common pattern can be recognized also in the 'circumstantial' *pericopae*. There is a tendency to expand section (E) of the pattern with didactic material, having in general the character of a last charge or 'testament' to the Church, or else to make the story an introduction to a discourse or dialogue having that character. Thus in John xx. 19–21 the appearance of the Lord (which properly ends, as comparison shows, with the word of command, καθὼς ἀπέσταλκέν με ὁ πατὴρ κἀγὼ πέμπω ὑμᾶς) is made to lead up to the gift of the Spirit[1] and the investing of the apostles with authority in the Church;[2] and in xxi the word of command is replaced by the long dialogue with Peter and the Beloved Disciple, 15–23, which is in some sort an equivalent for the commissioning of the apostles in John xx. 21 b, Matt. xxviii. 18–20, [Mark] xvi. 15–18, Luke xxiv. 44–9.

So far, therefore, the phenomena suggest that John is drawing upon a stock of traditional stories about the appearances of the Risen Christ already formed at an early date, and employed independently by all evangelists. In so far as there are resemblances between the Johannine and the Synoptic *pericopae*, they are not such as to require the hypothesis of literary dependence for their explanation. That there is some affinity between the story of the appearance by the Sea of Galilee in John xxi and the story of the draught of fishes in Luke v. 1–11 is clear, but to attempt to account for it as due to borrowing on the part of the one evangelist or the other would darken rather than clarify the problem. In

---

[1] The 'Johannine Pentecost' of xx. 22 has no parallel in the gospels. It is in some sort an alternative version of the story in Acts ii, and in a very broad sense a common tradition of an event remembered in the Church may lie behind both. But that event is conceived in entirely different ways, and there is no manifest contact between John and Acts, or the form of tradition which each represents. The concept of the Spirit here differs markedly from the highly personal concept of the Paraclete which is this evangelist's most distinctive contribution to pneumatology, and from this it might be argued that he is here using a form which had come down to him. But the impersonal concept of spirit, as analogous to breath (as here) or wind (as in iii. 8) or flowing water (as in vii. 38–9), is perhaps no less characteristic of his thought than the idea of the Paraclete; the idea of πνεῦμα as wind or breath (ἀὴρ κινούμενος) goes back to primitive stages of thought, but the combination of the apparently naïve with the refined and sophisticated is a feature stamped deeply on Johannine thought (see further *Interpretation*, pp. 213–27). On the relation of John xx. 22 to Acts ii. 1–4, there is an acute and illuminating discussion in Bishop Cassian (Serge Bésobrasoff), *La Pentecôte Johannique*, though his contention that ἡ ἡμέρα ἐκείνη in John xx. 19 is not the same day as that to which the previous *pericopé* refers but the great Day of the Lord's return (cf. xvi. 26), i.e. of the coming of the Spirit (not Easter but Whitsunday), seems something of a *tour de force* of harmonization.

[2] On the saying in xx. 23, see pp. 347–9.

THE REUNION

John xx. 19–21 and Luke xxiv. 36–43 there is the common feature that the Risen Lord displays his wounds as evidence of his identity; but not only are the terms used different (in Luke, ἴδετε τὰς χεῖράς μου καὶ τοὺς πόδας μου; in John, ἔδειξεν καὶ τὰς χεῖρας καὶ τὴν πλευρὰν αὐτοῖς), but the Lucan account is far more elaborate and more undisguisedly apologetic.[1] If we were to postulate borrowing on the one side or the other, Luke must be the borrower. But there is in fact so little coincidence in verbal expression that there is no sufficient ground for the hypothesis of literary dependence.

There remain two *pericopae* which do not readily conform to either of the types we have recognized.

(i) The story of Doubting Thomas (xx. 26–9) can never have stood as an independent unit, since it would be unintelligible except in the light of the connecting passage, xx. 28–9, which in turn presupposes xx. 19–23. Moreover, a distinctively Johannine theme, that of 'seeing' and 'believing', is not merely introduced as an element in the story, or as a comment on it, as in xx. 8; it dominates the whole. I have suggested elsewhere that we should recognize here a dramatization (in our author's manner) of the traditional motive of the incredulity of some or all of the disciples.[2] In [Mark] xvi. 14 'The Eleven' are taken to task for ἀπιστία. In Luke xxiv. 37 *sqq.* they are confused, uncertain and incredulous (τεταραγμένοι... διαλογισμοὶ ἐν καρδίᾳ...ἀπιστούντων) and after a rebuke their doubts are removed by proof tendered. In Matt. xxviii. 17 they fall into two groups, one of which has doubts (οἱ δὲ ἐδίστασαν) until the Lord speaks. John, it appears, has brought out this contrast of belief and unbelief by making Thomas the spokesman of the incredulous, and representing him as having been absent when Christ appeared to his disciples; although this

---

[1] The phrases καὶ λέγει αὐτοῖς, Εἰρήνη ὑμῖν in Luke xxiv. 36 and καὶ τοῦτο εἰπὼν ἔδειξεν αὐτοῖς τὰς χεῖρας καὶ τοὺς πόδας in xxiv. 40, though they are attested in אBWΘ etc., are in all probability due to assimilation to John. There remains the only parallel, ἔστη ἐν μέσῳ αὐτῶν (Luke), ἔστη εἰς τὸ μέσον (John)—certainly no strong evidence of borrowing. See *Studies in the Gospels*, pp. 16–18.

[2] Some degree of doubt or uncertainty seems to be implied in almost all these *pericopae* even where it is not expressly mentioned (see *op. cit.* p. 12). The 'longer ending' of Mark (the latest treatment of the theme, probably, in the N.T.) is pervaded with the contrast of belief and unbelief; the words πιστεύειν, ἀπιστεῖν, ἀπιστία, occur seven times within these few verses. This may be taken as indicating the way in which narratives of the Christophanies were employed in the early Church for paraenetic purposes; the moral is, ὁ πιστεύσας σωθήσεται, ὁ δὲ ἀπιστήσας κατακριθήσεται ([Mark] xvi. 16). Here we have a *Sitz im Leben* for the formulation of the tradition in several of its forms.

absence seems to be something of an afterthought, for in the *pericopé* which I have taken to be based on a form of the common tradition οἱ μαθηταί (that is, the loyal eleven) are present, without any hint of an absentee.

(ii) The story of Mary Magdalene at the tomb (xx. 11–17) does not conform closely with either of our types of traditional unit. It is indeed not difficult to recognize the five elements which are more or less constant.[1] Although the story is told with great economy of words, it has features which would associate it with the 'circumstantial' rather than the 'concise' type. That the word of command, with which, as is usual, the *pericopé* closes, is couched in strongly Johannine terms, is not exceptional; all evangelists, as we have seen, allow themselves some measure of freedom in treating the final section (E) of the pattern. But the dialogue between Jesus and Mary has no analogue, and it shows a psychological subtlety which is quite exceptional in these stories. We can only say that if a traditional unit underlies this *pericopé*, it has been fairly completely remoulded.

In content, though not in form, the passage has some affinity with Matt. xxviii. 9–10, where certain women are met on their way by the risen Christ. The two verses form a complete *pericopé* of the 'concise' type, except that the first element (A) is wanting, since the passage as we have it is linked with the discovery of the empty tomb. Verse 8, which replaces the usual introduction, may well be an editorial supplement. It deftly turns Mark's abrupt ἐφοβοῦντο γάρ into a suitable transitional passage,[2]

[1] See *op. cit.* p. 18.

[2] The signs of editorial work here are plain. After the non-Marcan insertion, xxviii. 2–4, Matthew is clearly following Mark xvi. 6–8. But in 8b he gives a different turn to the scene. Mark says the women were trembling and beside themselves, and in fact so much afraid that they did not deliver their message (οὐδενὶ οὐδὲν εἶπαν, ἐφοβοῦντο γάρ). Matthew admits that they were afraid, but their fear, he says, was mingled with joy (μετὰ φόβου καὶ χαρᾶς), and instead of simply taking flight (ἔφυγον) they hurried to fulfil their errand (ἔδραμον ἀπαγγεῖλαι τοῖς μαθηταῖς). He does not, however, so far contradict Mark as to say that they did actually deliver their message. Their hurried journey is interrupted by an appearance of the risen Christ, who charges them with a message, not to the disciples but to his ἀδελφοί, and after that the story takes an entirely different line. The statement that it was while the women were on their way (πορευομένων αὐτῶν) that the guard from the tomb made their report, and took a bribe to spread a false rumour, is clearly a piece of artificial composition. There is no essential connection between 9–10 and 11–15, or again between this passage and 16–20, which begins as abruptly as any narrative *pericopé* in the earlier part of the gospels. It is no unreasonable suspicion that 9–10 was originally as independent as either of the two paragraphs which follow. It may well have begun (*exempli gratia*) καὶ ἰδοὺ γυναῖκές τινες ἐπορεύοντο, καὶ 'Ιησοῦς ὑπήντησεν αὐταῖς κ.τ.λ. (cf. the opening of the Emmaus *pericopé* in Luke xxiv. 13).

and leads up to what may have been an originally independent *pericopé*. The name of Mary Magdalene is not present in this *pericopé*; we infer it from xxviii. 1; but in any case hers is the one name which is constant in all lists of the women.

Beyond this there are two features of the Matthaean *pericopé* which have some contact with the Johannine. In Matt. xxviii. 9 the women clasp the feet of Jesus as they do him reverence (ἐκράτησαν αὐτοῦ τοὺς πόδας καὶ προσεκύνησαν αὐτῷ). Something of the kind may be presupposed in the Johannine Μή μου ἅπτου, the present imperative in the negative often having the sense 'stop doing. . .'. But this is not certain.[1] (*b*) In both, a message is sent to the 'brothers' of Jesus. Matthew does not record the delivery of the message, but John says that it was delivered to the *disciples*. Yet in the tradition which both appear to be following it is not clear that the 'brothers' are identical with the disciples. Nowhere, unless in this passage, are the disciples called brothers of Jesus. In John ii. 12 ἀδελφοί and μαθηταί are clearly distinguished. In the early Church the ἀδελφοὶ τοῦ κυρίου as 'Founder's kin' (δεσπόσυνοι) formed a group distinct from the apostles.[2] The leading member of this group was James ὁ ἀδελφὸς τοῦ κυρίου. We know that James was claimed as one of the witnesses to the appearances of the risen Christ, and he had certainly changed his attitude to Jesus between the period represented by Mark iii. 31 and John vii. 3–5 and that represented by Acts i. 14, xii. 17, Gal. i. 19. It is a not unreasonable conjecture that the story of the appearance to Mary Magdalene or to the women belongs to the same strain of tradition as the appearance to James, a tradition associated with the circle of the ἀδελφοί rather than with the circle of the Twelve.

At any rate, it appears that there is some contact here between the tradition represented by Matthew and that represented by the Fourth Gospel.[3] But there is not the slightest ground for supposing that this

---

[1] See *Interpretation*, p. 443.

[2] 1 Cor. ix. 5, Acts i. 14. If we have regard to the *Sitz im Leben* in the early Church, it seems unlikely that the well-defined group called ἀδελφοὶ τοῦ κυρίου should be confused with the quite distinct group of the Twelve; and in any case the gospels give no indication that Jesus would have referred to the disciples as 'my brothers' (Mark iii. 34–5 cannot be so understood); on the contrary they are 'brothers' to one another, but he is their 'rabbi' (Matt. xxiii. 8).

[3] Yet it is not after all the *same* story. In John Mary is still at the tomb when the Lord appears to her; in Matthew the women, including by implication Mary Magdalene, are hurrying away to fulfil their errand. If there is anything in the suggestion made above, that Matt. xxviii. 9–10 is a truncated unit whose introduction has been replaced by a re-writing of Mark xvi. 8b, it is possible that the two stories were

contact was literary. I have discussed the Johannine *pericopé* elsewhere with some particularity, and I may be allowed here to quote the conclusion of the discussion.[1]

This story never came out of any common stock of tradition; it has an arresting individuality. We seem to be shut up to two alternatives. Either we have a free, imaginative composition based upon the bare tradition of an appearance to Mary Magdalene, akin to that represented by Matt. xxviii. 9–10, or else the story came through some highly individual channel, directly from the source, and the narrator stood near enough to catch the nuances of the original experience. It would be hazardous to dogmatize. The power to render psychological traits imaginatively with convincing insight cannot be denied to a writer to whom we owe the masterly character-parts of Pontius Pilate and the Woman of Samaria. Yet I cannot for long rid myself of the feeling (it can be no more than a feeling) that this *pericopé* has something indefinably first-hand about it. It stands in any case alone. There is nothing quite like it in the gospels. Is there anything quite like it in all ancient literature?

If we now review all the Johannine stories of appearances of the Risen Christ, there seems some degree of probability that the semblance of a continuous narration (after the manner of the Passion narrative down to the discovery of the empty tomb) is largely due to the 'editorial' work of the evangelist, and that he had before him a collection of units of tradition analogous to the 'pronouncement-stories' and 'tales' incorporated in the earlier portions of the gospels. That the appearance to the seven disciples at the Sea of Galilee in ch. xxi is entirely discontinuous with what went before is obvious, whether the addition of this appendix to the completed gospel be an afterthought of the evangelist himself or the work of a different author. The episode of Doubting Thomas in xx. 26–9 is linked with the preceding episode in a way which is no less artificial than subtle.[2] In xx. 19–23 there is no single trait which would prepare the reader to expect anything like the Thomas episode; it is entirely complete in itself. The opening of this *pericopé*, οὔσης οὖν ὀψίας τῇ ἡμέρᾳ ἐκείνῃ, looks very precise; yet we have almost exactly the same phrase in Mark iv. 35, where

---

originally distinct, the one telling how Mary Magdalene saw the Lord at the tomb, the other telling how the *other* women, having left the tomb, were met by the Lord. Even so there is contact between the two in that here alone a message is sent to the ἀδελφοί instead of to the μαθηταί.

[1] *Studies in the Gospels*, pp. 18–20.

[2] The literal-minded interpreter might ask himself, Did Thomas, then, alone of the apostles, have no share in the gift of the Spirit, and was he alone not given authority in the Church, since he was absent on the crucial occasion?

most recent critics have regarded the connection with the foregoing chapter of parables as editorial. The phrase is in fact one of the usual vague transitional formulae introducing a fresh *pericopé*, compare Matt. xiii. 1, xxii. 23.[1] Thus the connections of the *pericopé*, before and after, are tenuous, and there is good reason to regard it as an originally independent unit. Moving backwards, we come upon a *pericopé* which is not self-explanatory or complete in itself: the appearance to Mary Magdalene (xx. 11–18), which demands some introduction beyond what is given in xx. 11. In fact, such an introduction is supplied in xx. 1. The episode of the two disciples at the tomb, complete in itself, is interpolated into what is otherwise a straightforward story about Mary Magdalene, verses 2–3 serving as transition.[2] That this episode could be, and was, handed down outside its Johannine context is clear from Luke xxiv. 24. We seem therefore to have come upon one more trace of 'editorial' work on the part of our evangelist. The episode of the two disciples being removed, together with the probably editorial link in xx. 2–3, we are left with a passage which carries the narrative continuously forward from the discovery of the empty tomb to the first appearance of the risen Christ. The continuity may again be editorial, but if, as I am disposed to think, the story of Mary Magdalene represents a good tradition, unknown to Luke, better preserved here than in Matt. xxviii (though the evangelist has written it up in his own manner), then it must from the first have referred to an incident whose setting is necessarily at Jerusalem and early on Easter Day.

Of the other episodes, Matt. xxviii. 16–20 and John xxi. 1–14 are located in Galilee, and must have been so located from the first formation of the tradition. Luke xxiv. 13–32 is specifically located at Emmaus and on the road between that village and Jerusalem. The tradition represented by Luke xxiv. 36–43 and John xx. 19–21 (for the two are pretty clearly variants of the same tradition) has no express temporal or local setting, though Luke has set it in Jerusalem on Easter Day by the connection he has constructed between it and the Emmaus story, and John also conceives it as set in Jerusalem, for that is where the motive of 'fear of the Jews' is operative (xx. 19, cf. vii. 13, ix. 22, xix. 38), and (from the position he has given it) on the evening of Easter Day. But we may say that the tradition

---

[1] It is noteworthy that in Bishop Cassian's acute, if not altogether convincing, analysis, the phrase τῇ ἡμέρᾳ ἐκείνῃ has no reference to the preceding *pericopé*, *op. cit.* pp. 48–9.

[2] The transition in xx. 10–11 is thoroughly 'literary': ἀπῆλθον οὖν...οἱ μαθηταί, Μαρία δὲ εἱστήκει κ.τ.λ. Cf. xix. 24–5, οἱ μὲν οὖν στρατιῶται ταῦτα ἐποίησαν, εἱστήκεσαν δὲ κ.τ.λ.

behind the Fourth Gospel, as distinct from the gospel in its present form, knew, like Matthew, only one appearance of the Risen Christ in Jerusalem, and, again like Matthew, knew also of one appearance in Galilee, though this was not utilized in the gospel as at first conceived. But since both Luke and John have understood the incident which is common to both (independently) as taking place in Jerusalem we may probably be content to follow their guidance, though with the reservation that both may have been influenced in their 'editorial' work by a certain prejudice in favour of Jerusalem. In itself the incident might equally well have happened in Galilee.

To sum up: the evidence of the few passages which suggest *prima facie* literary dependence of the Fourth Gospel upon the others in the Passion narrative is not sufficient to prove such dependence. On the contrary there is cumulative evidence that the Johannine version represents (subject to some measure of 'writing up' by the evangelist) an independent strain of the common oral tradition, differing from the strains of tradition underlying Mark (Matthew) and Luke, though controlled by the same general *schema*.[1] Its apparent contacts with Jewish tradition, and the appreciation it shows of the situation before the great rebellion of A.D. 66, make it probable that this tradition was formulated, substantially, before that date, and in Palestine. Where its data differ from those of the Synoptics (whether by omission, supplement or apparent contradiction) they deserve to be

---

[1] It is the general *schema*, or pattern (outlined in pp. 28–30 above), that is common to all three strains of tradition, and not a residuum left after the elimination of all peculiarities in one gospel and another. It would be an illusion to suppose that by such a process of elimination we could arrive at *the* primitive tradition. The oral tradition lying behind the gospels must be supposed to have been from the first (like other oral traditions) manifold, rich in variety, complex, and not necessarily even wholly consistent in detail. (When did a number of witnesses of strange and rapidly moving events ever give an exactly identical *précis* of the sequence before there was time to collate and unify their stories?) The peculiar elements which we note in one gospel and another are no doubt in part due to development under the influence of detectable motives, but it may be taken as certain that some of the peculiarities are remnants of an original complexity not yet wholly smoothed out, rather than later accretions upon an original uniformity. Cf. some observations upon the transmission of medieval poetry in H. J. Chaytor, *From Script to Print* (Cambridge, 1945), ch. VI, where he speaks, in particular, of the two recensions of the *Chanson de Roland* and of the *Storia di Buove*, and shows that it is idle to inquire which is the more original. The conditions of transmission of the primitive Christian traditions were no doubt widely different, but there is sufficient analogy to throw some light upon our problem. I have quoted from this chapter in my article 'The Beatitudes', in *Mélanges Bibliques rédigés en l'Honneur d'André Robert*, pp. 404–10.

treated with respect, though the decision between our authorities depends on wider considerations than those here taken into account. The extent to which the narrative has been subjected to the influence of the specifically Johannine theology is confined to a few (readily separable) passages,[1] though apologetic motives already recognizable in the Synoptic narratives have sometimes been given greater emphasis.

[1] See above, pp. 75–6, 97–8, 123–4, 135, 145–6; *Interpretation*, pp. 432–8.

B. THE MINISTRY

1. PRELUDE TO THE PASSION

The earlier chapters of the gospel (ii–xii), dealing with the Ministry of Jesus Christ in Jerusalem, Galilee, and elsewhere, do not follow, like the later chapters with which we have dealt, a continuous line of narrative. The argument, indeed, is continuous, and clearly envisaged by the author as a whole, to which each successive stage contributes. It is therefore all the more significant that the narrative is presented, in the main, by way of detached incidents, related often in a manner sufficiently reminiscent of that of the Synoptics to invite comparison. In this section of the book I shall investigate some of the narrative *pericopae*, asking whether traces of the tradition which we have seen reason to infer behind the Passion narrative are to be discerned here also.

We begin with three narrative *pericopae* which have more or less close relations with the Passion narrative, either intrinsically by virtue of their content, or through the place assigned to them in the pattern of the gospels. These are the Triumphal Entry, the Cleansing of the Temple and the Anointing at Bethany.

(a) The Triumphal Entry (xii. 12–16)

Neither in John nor in the Synoptics has the *pericopé* of the Entry the normal form of a unit of narrative, with conventional opening and conclusion. There is therefore no direct evidence that it ever formed such a unit by itself, though it may, of course, have done so.

In Mark the story of the actual entry into Jerusalem is recounted quite briefly in xi. 8–10. But it is impossible to begin with verse 8, which is continuous with verse 7, describing how the disciples brought 'the colt' (τὸν πῶλον). This presupposes some previous account of 'the colt', and this is given in a detailed narrative occupying verses 1–6. It begins with a clause making the topography somewhat more precise than is usual in Mark: 'When they were approaching Jerusalem, and came to Bethphage and Bethany[1] towards the Mount of Olives....' This would certainly be an odd opening for a conventional narrative unit. It is probably to be

---

[1] Both names are probably to be read, though the MSS. are not entirely unanimous; Bethany is omitted in D 700 and a few Old Latin MSS., but this may be assimilation to Matthew, where Bethany is poorly attested and is almost certainly not genuine.

linked closely with the foregoing passages, which relate that Jesus was 'on the road, going up to Jerusalem' (x. 32), and then bring him to Jericho (x. 46), and record how 'as he was leaving Jericho', he healed a blind man, who 'followed him on the way' (x. 52). All this is presupposed in the opening clause of xi. 1, which in this connection becomes fully intelligible. The narrative closes with the acclamations of the crowd, and then we are brought back to the theme of the journey, which now reaches its end: 'He entered Jerusalem and went into the temple'. It appears therefore that Mark intends to present the Entry as an episode—the last episode—in a long journey which he has traced through several stages, whether the account of it reached him in this form, or whether his own art is responsible for the continuity.[1]

In John the story of the Entry is told in four (five) verses, xii. 12–15(16), including two passages from the Old Testament quoted at length. It has at first sight more of the aspect of a conventional *pericopé* than Mark's, having its own introduction and ending with a comment, like so many narrative units in the Synoptics. But the comments and supplements in verses 16–19 are almost certainly the editorial work of the evangelist, whose purpose is clearly discernible in them.[2] There is no real conclusion to the narrative. The opening clause, again, is perhaps no real beginning. As it stands, it links the story with what has immediately preceded by the temporal note, τῇ ἐπαύριον, namely the day following the supper at Bethany. This, however, is a formula of transition used by this evangelist in four other places, in all of which it seems to have a somewhat artificial character.[3] The phrase which follows, 'The great mass of people who had come for the Feast, hearing that Jesus was coming to Jerusalem...',

---

[1] I have elsewhere argued for the likelihood that the 'fragments of an itinerary' which crop up from time to time in Mark may in fact have formed part of an outline designed to serve as introduction to the Passion narrative (see *New Testament Studies*, pp. 1–11; also below, pp. 233–4). [2] See *Interpretation*, pp. 370–1.

[3] Three of these are from ch. i. 29, 35, 43, and seem to serve rather to articulate the stages of the exposition of the theme than to give a day-to-day chronology. The scheme runs thus: first day, John the Baptist points to the 'Coming One' without naming him; second day, John identifies the 'Coming One'; third day, his testimony brings results in the adherence of disciples to Jesus; fourth day, the activity of John is over and Jesus and his disciples occupy the stage (see also pp. 302–3). In vi. 22 also the 'morrow' may be a device to keep the narrative (vi. 1–21) and the subsequent dialogue (vi. 22–59) distinct, while indicating the relation between them. Τῇ ἐπαύριον occurs once only in Mark, xi. 12, where some critics have suspected that it is a feature of Mark's careful editorship, but perhaps without due cause, and once in Matt., xxvii. 62, where it sets a chronological puzzle. It does not occur in Luke, but is frequent in Acts, where it seems to be always realistic.

would no doubt be sufficiently intelligible without further explanation to readers who were acquainted with Jewish customs, but it seems to be intended to refer back to xi. 55, where we were told: 'The Jewish Passover was at hand, and many went up to Jerusalem from the country.' It is therefore not clear that the story of the Entry reached John (any more than it reached Mark) as a complete unit. In both gospels the *pericopé* is clamped into the longer narrative. But it is far from being the *same* narrative. In John, as in Mark, the ride is from Bethany to Jerusalem, but the setting is different. In Mark, so far as the reader is informed, the journey has been continuous from some point beyond Jericho, no halts for the night being mentioned.[1] Apparently the party halts at Bethany only long enough to procure a riding animal, and proceeds at once to Jerusalem, arriving in the temple precinct late in the evening. In John, Jesus has arrived at Bethany the previous day, and having dined and slept there, sets out afresh for Jerusalem. How much of this is editorial it would be hard to say. Certainly the connecting passage, xii. 9–11, which is taken up in the further connecting passage after the *pericopé* of the Entry, xii. 17–19, serves an obvious purpose of the evangelist. But at least we can say this: that we get not the slightest help towards explaining the Johannine setting of the incident from a comparison with Mark, and that there is so far nothing to suggest dependence on him.

In both gospels the irreducible nucleus of the *pericopé* itself is the acclamation, ὡσαννά· εὐλογημένος ὁ ἐρχόμενος ἐν ὀνόματι κυρίου, which both evangelists give in identical terms, being those of the LXX of Ps. cxvii. 25, except that for the LXX σῶσον δή both give the transliterated Hebrew ὡσαννά.[2] Mark adds an acclamation of 'the coming kingdom of our father David', along with the barely intelligible ὡσαννὰ ἐν τοῖς ὑψίστοις. John adds to the sentence from Psalm cxvii a clause identifying 'him who comes' with 'the King of Israel'. Luke also has βασιλεύς here,

---

[1] Luke has provided a night's lodging at Jericho, with the local Inspector of Taxes.

[2] The coincident variation from the LXX would be but a flimsy ground for inferring literary dependence. The acclamation was probably incorporated at an early date in liturgical usage, where a characteristic conservatism tended to preserve Hebrew or Aramaic words and phrases; cf. *Did.* x. 6, ὡσαννὰ τῷ θεῷ Δαυίδ. Ὁ ἐρχόμενος is by itself a fixed title, cf. Matt. xi. 3, Heb. x. 37, elaborated characteristically by the Fourth Evangelist, vi. 14, xi. 27, iii. 31. It does not seem necessary to depart from the construction of the Hebrew, which gives the meaning 'May he who comes be blessed by the use of the name Jahveh', i.e. by the formula, 'The Lord bless thee', the phrase בְּשֵׁם יהוה being instrumental. But to Christian readers it might suggest the meaning 'May the Coming One be praised *as* Κύριος', cf. εἰς ὄνομα in Matt. x. 41–2.

interpolated into the sentence from the psalm, and Matthew may perhaps be said to have come halfway in substituting 'the son of David' for 'the kingdom of our father David'; but there is nothing to suggest a literary dependence of our gospel on either of the others. Βασιλεὺς τοῦ Ἰσραήλ is a title which John alone puts into the mouth of adherents of Jesus (here and in i. 49); Matthew and Mark confine its use to mockery by opponents. It does not however follow that its insertion here is the work of the evangelist, for the title βασιλεύς is already present in the *testimonium* from Zechariah (to which we shall come in a moment), and βασιλεὺς τοῦ Ἰσραήλ smacks of a messianism more Jewish than Christian. It is probable that the Fourth Evangelist, who shows himself more sensitive than the others to the idea of the messianic kingship, has preserved a primitive title.

In addition to the acclamation from Ps. cxvii, John quotes a *testimonium* from Zech. ix. 9, which is also given by Matthew, but in a different translation and at a different point in the story. Mark (followed here by Luke) does not quote Zechariah. That is not to say that the testimony was unknown to the tradition he followed. In one respect his language echoes that of the LXX of Zech. ix. 9 more faithfully than that of Matthew or of John: they (following the Hebrew) describe the animal as an ass (ὄνος, Matthew; ὀνάριον, John). Mark does not; his πῶλος ἐφ᾽ ὃν οὐδεὶς οὔπω ἀνθρώπων κεκάθικεν is a fair equivalent for the πῶλος νέος of the LXX.[1]

Beyond the quotations from the Old Testament, there is very little similarity between John and the Synoptics. They differ, in fact, in every point where it is possible to differ in relating the same incident. In Mark Jesus is acclaimed by 'those who preceded and followed', in John by the crowd who 'came out to meet him': Mark describes an escort, John a reception party. In Mark they lay upon the road cloaks and στιβάδας[2] cut from the fields, in Matthew clothes and κλάδους ἀπὸ τῶν δένδρων, in John they take τὰ βαΐα τῶν φοινίκων,[3] not, apparently, strewing them on the road but holding them in their hands. Not only so; the whole construc-

---

[1] It is altogether unlikely that Mark conceived the πῶλος to be anything other than a young donkey. Horses were scarcely used for riding among the Jews, except by the army. It is only as the warrior Messiah of apocalypse that Christ rides a horse, with the celestial cavalry following, Rev. xix. 11–21.

[2] Στιβάς seems generally to mean a bundle of straw or rushes used as a palliasse; here, perhaps, we are to think of armfuls of such growth gathered from the neighbouring fields.

[3] Many critics have made heavy weather of John's statement that palm-branches were used, on the ground that palms do not grow at Jerusalem. They may not, for all I know; but they must have been readily obtainable. Not only were they available for the Maccabaean processions, but at the Feast of Tabernacles all worshippers were

tion of the narrative is different. Mark (followed by the other Synoptics) begins with an elaborate account of how Jesus sent disciples to fetch the πῶλος and how they brought and caparisoned it, and then how the crowd, apparently inspired by their example, laid cloaks and στιβάδας on the road. It is an unpremeditated outburst of enthusiasm. John begins with the pilgrims assembled at Jerusalem for Passover, and records how, hearing that Jesus was on his way to the city, they (first) took palm-branches and (then) went out to meet him. It is a planned ovation. The palms even suggest a triumphal procession, like that of Judas Maccabaeus (2 Macc. x. 7) and of his brother Simon (1 Macc. xiii. 51). It may no doubt be possible to harmonize the two accounts, but it is exceedingly difficult to see how one could be derived from the other. *Prima facie*, at any rate, Mark's account is the story which would be told by one of those who accompanied Jesus, and John's is the story which would be told by one of those who were at Jerusalem and heard of his approach.[1] They are different stories; which is the more credible, historically, it is not easy to say, but it may not be out of place to observe that if John may have made a triumph out of a spontaneous and almost accidental demonstration, it is equally possible that Mark, writing at Rome, had his reasons for toning down this dangerous picture of the King of Israel acclaimed as he rides in triumph into his capital city.[2] However that may be, anyone who should wish to maintain that the Johannine account is in any sense derived from the Marcan must do so on *a priori* grounds, without any support whatever from the actual texts. It seems clear that there were variant traditions, having no more in common than the acclamation from Ps. cxvii and, in all probability, a reference to the prophecy of Zechariah, and describing the corresponding actions in different terms. If, as is possible but far from proven, both traditions placed the Entry in the setting of a longer narrative of the journey of Jesus to Jerusalem, once again the itineraries seem to be independent.

(b) *The Cleansing of the Temple (ii. 13–22)*

The *pericopé* of the Cleansing runs on generally parallel lines in John and Mark (here followed closely by the other Synoptics). It is essentially a

obliged to provide themselves with palm-fronds (כַּפֹּת תְּמָרִים, κάλλυνθρα φοινίκων, Lev. xxiii. 40). It is to be noted that John does not suggest that the βαΐα τῶν φοινίκων were picked casually by the wayside, like Mark's στιβάδες and Matthew's κλάδοι τῶν δένδρων. They were carried by pilgrims who had planned an ovation beforehand.

[1] For the possible significance of this, see pp. 245–6.
[2] See also pp. 112–15, 213–17.

story of action—the action of clearing the temple court of intrusive traders. In both, the action is accompanied by a saying of Jesus—a different saying in each. In neither is the saying the kind of general maxim, interesting for its own sake, in which 'pronouncement stories' often culminate; it is strictly relative to the particular situation and fully intelligible only in that relation—part of the story, therefore, rather than an article of teaching introduced by the story.

In the account of the action the two versions have in common the words for Jerusalem, temple, sellers, money-changers,[1] tables and pigeons. While the money-changers are 'sitting' (καθήμενοι) in John, the poulterers have 'seats' (καθέδρας) in Mark. The verb ἐκβάλλειν is used in both, together with the similarly sounding κατέστρεψεν in Mark and ἀνέτρεψεν in John. That is to say, the salient features of the scene are described in similar terms, which could hardly be avoided. It is clearly the same scene that is being described,[2] though different points are selected for emphasis. Mark says nothing of the oxen and sheep, which figure largely in John, and perhaps called for the use of the φραγέλλιον,[3] which is also peculiar to John. John, in fact, makes more of the drama of the scene, with the animals rushing through the crowded court, and the floor littered with the small change (κέρματα) from the overturned tables. Mark, on the other

[1] Κολλυβιστής, a non-classical word (said to be of Semitic origin) common in Hellenistic Greek from the third century B.C. But John has also κερματιστής, a word which seems so far not to have been found outside the N.T. and literature influenced by it. But the verb κερματίζειν occurs in a papyrus of the second century A.D. and its compound κατακερματίζειν in a papyrus of A.D. 60 (M.–M.), so that the non-occurrence of the noun is probably accidental. It would be a tenable view that John followed a tradition which used the term κερματιστής, but that he conflated this with Mark; but the evidence is not sufficient.

[2] The suggestion that the temple was twice cleansed is the last resort of a desperate determination to harmonize Mark and John at all costs. The only legitimate question is whether the (single) cleansing is to be placed early or late in the Ministry.

[3] Φραγέλλιον is the Latin *flagellum*, which is used of a whip for driving cattle (as well as of other kinds of whip). Here the τε...καί clause should, in accord with normal usage, be epexegetic of πάντας (cf. Matt. xxii. 10, συνήγαγον πάντας οὕς εὗρον, πονηρούς τε καὶ ἀγαθούς, and so frequently). The masculine can be used where nouns of different genders are comprehended in a collective term. Thus the meaning would be 'he drove them all out, viz. sheep and oxen alike' (but see Field, *Notes on the Translation of the N.T.*, pp. 85–6, who rejects the arguments of 'grammatical purists'). In Luke xxii. 66, τὸ πρεσβυτέριον τοῦ λαοῦ ἀρχιερεῖς τε καὶ γραμματεῖς, the meaning intended (in defiance of normal grammatical usage) would appear to be 'elders, chief priests and doctors of the law', the three 'estates' of the Sanhedrin—unless indeed Luke (not too well informed about Jewish Palestine) took πρεσβυτέριον as a synonym for συνέδριον and named only its two dominant components.

hand, draws attention to the traffic control which Jesus succeeded in establishing in the temple court, of which John says nothing.

Further, so far as there can be variation within so simple a pattern, John and Mark differ significantly. Mark, having brought Jesus into the temple precinct, plunges at once into the action, which he describes almost in one breath. He then adds that Jesus proceeded to teach,[1] and sums up his teaching in a pregnant sentence composed mainly of two quotations from the Old Testament. He is enforcing the moral of the action. In John the story is articulated into three stages. First, he describes the scene that met the eyes of Jesus as he entered the sacred courts: 'He found the sellers of oxen, sheep and pigeons, and the money-changers sitting.' Then follows the action: 'He made a whip of cords and drove them out of the temple, sheep and oxen and all.' Finally, there is a direct address to the pigeon-dealers: 'Take these things away; do not turn my Father's house into a bazaar.' This saying is not a mere comment pointing the moral; it is part of the action: the cattle are driven away, the tables overturned, but you cannot drive caged pigeons, and it would be brutal to overturn their cages; all you can do is to order the dealers off.

The action is now complete, but a note is added, that the disciples were reminded of a passage from the Old Testament: 'My zeal for thy house will destroy me' (ii. 17). The disciples are not said to have remembered the saying of Jesus, or to have understood it for the first time, after his resurrection, as in ii. 22. Dramatically (whether or not in actual fact) they here contemplate with foreboding the reckless action of their Master, in a situation of manifest tension, reflecting that it was written in scripture that the Servant of God would fall a victim to his zeal for the temple.

The significance which each evangelist attached to the incident is to be gathered from the passages of the Old Testament which are quoted or echoed in the respective gospels. In Mark Jesus quotes Isa. lvi. 7 (verbally after the LXX): ὁ οἶκός μου οἶκος προσευχῆς κληθήσεται πᾶσιν τοῖς ἔθνεσιν, combining it with an allusion to Jer. vii. 11: μὴ σπήλαιον λῃστῶν ὁ οἶκός μου οὗ ἐπικέκληται τὸ ὄνομά μου ἐπ᾽ αὐτῷ ἐκεῖ ἐνώπιον ὑμῶν; The former comes from a passage in which the prophet, assured that the great day of deliverance is dawning (ἤγγικεν τὸ σωτήριόν μου παραγίνεσθαι), proclaims the acceptance of aliens (בְּנֵי־הַנֵּכָר, ἀλλογενεῖς) into communion

---

[1] Ἐδίδασκεν καὶ ἔλεγεν αὐτοῖς. The tenses indicate that a sustained process of teaching is meant, the keynote of which, perhaps, is given in the sentence which follows. Αὐτοῖς probably refers rather to the hierarchy or their representatives than to the traders who have already been expelled (cf. ὑμεῖς πεποιήκατε . . .).

with the God of Israel, and declares that the temple shall henceforth be the centre of a universal religion.[1] The quotation from Jeremiah belongs to a context in which the prophet denounces the profanation of the temple by those who believe themselves to be protected by its sanctity from the judgement of God upon their evil lives. The Cleansing of the Temple, therefore, for Mark, signifies the dawning of a day in which this profanation will be ended and all nations will be drawn to the true worship of God.

In John, the passage of which the disciples are said to have been reminded is Ps. lxviii. 10. This psalm is one of those most freely drawn upon for *testimonia*.[2] In this gospel we have already met with an allusion to verse 5, οἱ μισοῦντές με δωρεάν. But there is a further partly concealed allusion to the Old Testament, in the words, Μὴ ποιεῖτε τὸν οἶκον τοῦ πατρός μου οἶκον ἐμπορίου. The allusion is to Zech. xiv. 21. The second half of Zechariah is one of the parts of scripture freely drawn upon for *testimonia*.[3] The last chapter describes the Day of the Lord, when 'the Lord my God will come, and all his holy ones with him' (xiv. 5).[4] On that day, the prophet continues, ἐξελεύσεται ὕδωρ ζῶν ἐξ Ἱερουσαλήμ (xiv. 8)— one of the passages underlying the Johannine symbolism of 'living water', especially in vii. 38.[5] The closing verse of the chapter (and of the book) reads, וְלֹא־יִהְיֶה כְנַעֲנִי עוֹד בְּבֵית־יהוה צְבָאוֹת בַּיּוֹם הַהוּא, which, as recent commentators seem to agree, should be translated, 'On that day there will be no more a *trader* in the house of the Lord', the word כְּנַעֲנִי being used, here as elsewhere, for 'trader',[6] presumably because the Canaanites, or Phoenicians, were the great mercantile people of the ancient Levant. It is a synonym of רוֹכֵל and סוֹחֵר, both of which are rendered by ἔμπορος in the LXX. In Ezek. xvii. 4 we have the parallelism אֶל־אֶרֶץ כְּנַעַן בְּעִיר רֹכְלִים. In Ezek. xxvii. 3 רֹכֶלֶת הָעַמִּים is rendered, τῷ ἐμπορίῳ τῶν λαῶν. It would therefore be legitimate to translate Zech. xiv. 21 οὐκ ἔσται ἔμπορος ἔτι ἐν τῷ οἴκῳ κυρίου παντοκράτορος ἐν τῇ ἡμέρᾳ ἐκείνῃ, and its affinity with the Johannine passage would then become clear, the expression ὁ οἶκος τοῦ πατρός μου being the Christian equivalent for ὁ

---

[1] Matthew and Luke, omitting πᾶσιν τοῖς ἔθνεσιν, have missed the point of the quotation: in Mark the contrast is not between a place of prayer and a place of trade, but between the stronghold of a faction and a home for all mankind.

[2] See *According to the Scriptures*, pp. 58–9, and cf. pp. 38, 74–5 above.

[3] See *According to the Scriptures*, pp. 64–6.

[4] This prophecy is echoed in 1 Thess. iii. 13.

[5] See *Interpretation*, pp. 349–50.

[6] Cf. Zeph. i. 11, where כָּל־עַם כְּנַעַן, in parallelism with כָּל־נְטִילֵי כָסֶף, surely means 'all merchants'.

οἶκος κυρίου παντοκράτορος. The evangelist, it appears, intends to represent the expulsion of traders from the temple as a sign that the Day of the Lord is here.

We therefore have before us another example of a phenomenon that we observed in the Passion narrative: the formative motive of the *pericopé* is indicated by references to the Old Testament, and these references differ in the two gospels, though they are drawn from the common sources of *testimonia*. In Mark, the central interest of the incident resides in the contrast between the prophecy in the Book of Isaiah pronouncing the temple to be a 'house of prayer for all nations', and its actual condition as the stronghold of an impious hierarchy—with the implication that the doom pronounced by Jeremiah is impending (cf. Mark xiii. 2). In John the interest resides, on the one hand, in the solemn purging of the temple as a sign of the Day of the Lord, as predicted by Zechariah, and on the other hand in the thought of the fatal consequences of such zeal as is depicted in Ps. lxviii—a veiled forecast of the Passion. The fact that the two narratives are framed upon a different combination of testimonies argues for independent formation. Both are rooted in the primitive use of scripture to interpret the events of the Gospel story.

In John and Mark alike the *pericopé* of the Cleansing is formally complete in itself, but it will be of some interest to consider the sequel in each of them. In Mark the story ends, formally, with the sentence summing up the teaching of Jesus in terms of prophecy, xi. 17. At that point the unity of time and place which is essential to a narrative unit of tradition is broken. Verses 18–19 are of the nature of a *Sammelbericht*, the main verbs being in the tense of continuous action: ἐζήτουν, ἐφοβοῦντο, ἐξεπλήσσοντο, ἐξεπορεύοντο. The evangelist is describing, not the particular effect of the Cleansing of the Temple, but the situation in Jerusalem during the days immediately preceding the arrest of Jesus: the authorities aggressive but afraid to act, the people in a perpetual state of astonishment, while Jesus 'made a practice of going out of the city' at nightfall. It has been suspected by a number of critics of various schools that Mark's editorial hand has been particularly busy in the composition of this part of his gospel, containing the preliminaries to the Passion narrative, and there certainly seems to have been some dislocation of material here. The true sequel to the *pericopé* of the Cleansing is surely xi. 27–8, where the authorities confront Jesus in the temple with the question, ᾽Εν ποίᾳ ἐξουσίᾳ ταῦτα ποιεῖς; If we ask, to what ταῦτα refers, the only possible answer would seem to be that it refers to the Cleansing of the Temple, the only thing that

Jesus can be said to have 'done' since he arrived in Jerusalem. The authorities formally demand to know what right he claims to perform so high-handed an action. The question is rebutted by a reference to the baptism of John, and Mark utilizes it to introduce a long series of controversial dialogues upon a variety of topics, in which the precise issue arising out of the Cleansing of the Temple is lost sight of.

In John, on the contrary, the authorities there and then confront Jesus with the question, Τί σημεῖον δεικνύεις ἡμῖν ὅτι ταῦτα ποιεῖς; (cf. Mark's ταῦτα ποιεῖς). We might paraphrase, 'In view of the drastic action you have taken, show us your credentials'. The implication is the same as in Mark, but Jesus here replies with the saying about the destruction of the temple which I have already discussed.[1] No doubt the saying was one which 'floated' without context. Mark does not pretend to know on what occasion it was actually uttered; indeed he casts doubt (probably unnecessary doubt) upon its authenticity. John has found for it an appropriate setting.

But should we attribute this setting entirely to the evangelist? The interpretation he has given to the saying must certainly be put to his credit.[2] It presupposes the equivalence of the 'body' of Christ with the Church which is the spiritual 'temple', and we have reason to believe that this double equivalence goes back to Paul. Yet the association of the Cleansing of the Temple with the death and resurrection of Jesus (in some sense) seems to be given in the tradition as known to John; for (i) the testimony from Ps. lxviii. 10 is an oblique pointer to the approaching death of Jesus, implying that his action in the temple sealed his doom— which is what we should gather from Mark; and (ii) the 'three days' interval of the temple-saying belongs essentially to the tradition of the resurrection in all its forms (=τῇ τρίτῃ ἡμέρᾳ). As we so often find, even the boldest flights of Johannine theology have a firm starting point in the tradition. The further development of the dialogue, however, with the misunderstanding on the part of auditors to give an opening for further clarification, is characteristic work of this evangelist.

To sum up: there are sound reasons for the conclusion that in his account of the Cleansing of the Temple John followed an independent strain of tradition, which probably contained both the narrative and a brief controversial dialogue provoked by it, the latter probably ending with the saying, Λύσατε τὸν ναὸν κ.τ.λ. In all probability Mark had a

---

[1] See above, pp. 89–91.   [2] See *Interpretation*, pp. 300–2.

corresponding tradition of action and dialogue, but he has separated them in the course of composition, and his variant form of the saying is incorporated in his Passion narrative. Any dependence of John on Mark here is most improbable, but the conclusion that he was working upon a given tradition is confirmed when we observe that having, for the purposes of his theological exposition, chosen to connect the hostile action of the authorities closely with the raising of Lazarus,[1] and having, again for theological reasons,[2] placed the Cleansing of the Temple near the beginning of the series of scenes from the Ministry, he has yet clearly betrayed a consciousness that the Cleansing was intimately connected with the death of Jesus. The connection, therefore, must have been given in the tradition known to him.

(c) *The Anointing at Bethany* (xii. 1–8)

In John and Mark alike the *pericopé* of the Anointing forms a completely self-contained unit, beginning with an introduction which sets the scene (somewhat fuller in John than in Mark), and ending with a significant saying of Jesus. It is, however, not to be described as a 'pronouncement story', for the concluding saying (whether we follow Mark or John) is no general maxim but has meaning only as an element in the story itself, which is essentially a story of action. The *pericopé* is differently placed: in Mark it is interpolated in the Passion narrative; in John it precedes the Triumphal Entry. But there is another passage of which we have to take account: Luke also has a story about an anointing by a woman, in a totally different context, vii. 36–50. There is only the slightest possible contact between Mark and Luke, but the Johannine *pericopé* shows some similarity to each of them. In all three the fundamental pattern is the same: (i) the scene; (ii) the woman introduced; (iii) the anointing; (iv) a dialogue in which Jesus rebuts objections. The dialogue, however, in Luke follows entirely different lines from those followed in the Marcan and Johannine *pericopae*, and in instituting a comparison between Luke and John we need take account only of the incident itself (see Table 3).

While all three place the scene at table during a meal, Mark and Luke agree against John in giving the host the name of Simon, though for Mark he is a leper, for Luke a Pharisee; that both happen to use the same verb for sitting at table, κατακεῖσθαι, while John uses ἀνακεῖσθαι, is hardly significant. John agrees with Mark against Luke in naming Bethany as the

---

[1] See *Interpretation*, pp. 366–7. [2] See *op. cit.*, pp. 300–3.

place of the entertainment, and observes that it was the home of Lazarus, who was one of the party, though whether as host or as guest is not made clear. His sister Martha waits at table (διηκόνει, as in Luke x. 40). The woman who is the central character is said by John to be Mary, the other sister; in Mark and Luke she is anonymous. All say that she brought perfume (μύρον), John giving the weight, one λίτρα, while the others name the container, a 'vase' (ἀλάβαστρος). About the nature of the μύρον there is some divergence. Luke leaves it at that. In Mark, according to most MSS. and versions, we have the definition, νάρδου πιστικῆς πολυτελοῦς, but for the last word many MSS., including AW and Θ, give πολυτίμου, and Codex Bezae omits the whole phrase. In Matthew the words νάρδου πιστικῆς are absent, as indeed they are also in one minuscule of Mark, supported by one MS. of the Peshitta. In John the MSS. are almost unanimous in reading μύρου νάρδου πιστικῆς πολυτίμου. Codex Bezae omits νάρδου, and in the Bodmer papyrus this word is written in above the line. The omission would seem to be accidental, since μύρου πιστικῆς is a *monstrum*. Yet there is another possibility, that the original text of John, like that of Matthew, omitted νάρδου πιστικῆς, and that the restoration of these words was intended but left imperfect in the archetype of Codex Bezae and the Bodmer papyrus: a bare possibility. On the other hand, the πολυτίμου of some MSS. in Mark (where πολυτελοῦς is certainly original) would seem to be due to assimilation to John, and it is not impossible that the words νάρδου πιστικῆς in Mark are also due to assimilation to John, and were not present in the copy of Mark used by the author of Matthew. In short, it is probable but not certain that John and Mark agreed in using the rare word πιστικῆς, a word of uncertain meaning, which does not occur elsewhere in the New Testament.

Table 3. *Three stories of anointing by a woman*

Fundamental Pattern: (1) The scene; (2) the woman introduced; (3) the anointing; (4) dialogue.

Mark xiv. 3–9	John xii. 1–8	Luke vii. 36–50
(1) Jesus was at Bethany (in the house of Simon the leper), at table (κατακειμένου αὐτοῦ)	Jesus came to Bethany (the home of Lazarus); they made supper for him, Martha serving, Lazarus sitting at table (εἷς ἦν ἐκ τῶν ἀνακειμένων σὺν αὐτῷ)	Jesus was invited to a meal by a Pharisee (named Simon, vii. 40); he entered the house and sat at table (εἰσελθὼν κατεκλίθη ... κατάκειται ἐν τῇ οἰκίᾳ)

Table 3. *Three stories of anointing by a woman (continued)*

Mark xiv. 3–9	John xii. 1–8	Luke vii. 36–50
(2) ἦλθεν γυνὴ ἔχουσα ἀλάβαστρον μύρου νάρδου πιστικῆς[1] πολυτελοῦς[2]	ἡ Μαριὰμ λαβοῦσα λίτραν μύρου νάρδου πιστικῆς πολυτίμου	γυνὴ ἥτις ἦν ἐν τῇ πόλει ἁμαρτωλός...καὶ κομίσασα ἀλάβαστρον μύρου...
(3) συντρίψασα τὴν ἀλάβαστρον κατέχεεν αὐτοῦ τῆς κεφαλῆς	ἤλειψεν τοὺς πόδας τοῦ Ἰησοῦ καὶ ἐξέμαξεν ταῖς θριξὶν αὐτῆς τοὺς πόδας αὐτοῦ	κλαίουσα τοῖς δάκρυσιν ἤρξατο βρέχειν τοὺς πόδας αὐτοῦ καὶ ταῖς θριξὶν τῆς κεφαλῆς αὐτῆς ἐξέμασσεν καὶ κατεφίλει τοὺς πόδας αὐτοῦ καὶ ἤλειφεν τῷ μύρῳ
(4) (*a*) The spectators cavilled:	(*a*) Judas cavilled:	(*a*) The host cavilled (aside): 'If this were a prophet he would know what kind of woman it is'
εἰς τί ἡ ἀπώλεια αὕτη τοῦ μύρου γέγονεν; ἠδύνατο γὰρ τοῦτο τὸ μύρον πραθῆναι ἐπάνω δηναρίων τριακοσίων καὶ δοθῆναι τοῖς πτωχοῖς	διὰ τί τοῦτο τὸ μύρον οὐκ ἐπράθη τριακοσίων δηναρίων καὶ ἐδόθη πτωχοῖς;	(*b*) Jesus replied with a parable, which led to a colloquy with the host
(*b*) Jesus replied: (i) ἄφετε αὐτήν· why worry her? she has done a fine thing to me	(*b*) Jesus replied: (i) ἄφες αὐτήν	(*c*) Jesus addressed the woman: ἀφεῶνταί σου αἱ ἁμαρτίαι (*d*) The spectators asked: 'Who is this who forgives sins?'
(ii) πάντοτε γὰρ τοὺς πτωχοὺς ἔχετε κ.τ.λ. ἐμὲ δὲ οὐ πάντοτε ἔχετε		(*e*) Jesus addressed the woman: ἡ πίστις σου σέσωκέν σε· πορεύου εἰς εἰρήνην
(iii) ὃ ἔσχεν ἐποίησεν, προέλαβεν μυρίσαι τὸ σῶμά μου εἰς τὸν ἐνταφιασμόν	(ii) ἵνα εἰς τὴν ἡμέραν τοῦ ἐνταφιασμοῦ μου τηρήσῃ αὐτό	
(iv) 'wherever the gospel is preached her good deed shall be commemorated'	[(iii) τοὺς πτωχοὺς γὰρ πάντοτε ἔχετε μεθ' ἑαυτῶν ἐμὲ δὲ οὐ πάντοτε ἔχετε.][3]	

[1] Omit. D 248, Syr. pesh (1 MS.).   [2] Omit. D.
[3] Omit. D, Syrsin ἐμὲ...ἔχετε omit. Λ, Syr. pesh.

At this point John and Mark diverge widely. In Mark, the woman breaks the vase and pours the perfume over the head of Jesus. In John she anoints his feet and dries them with her hair. This looks like a shorter version of Luke's description, according to which the woman washed his feet with her tears, drying them with her hair, and then, and not till then, applied the perfume. The terms used by John all reappear in the longer account of Luke: ἀλείφειν, τοὺς πόδας αὐτοῦ, ἐκμάσσειν, ταῖς θριξὶν αὐτῆς. Beyond this point there is nothing in common between Luke and John, who, after a statement which is present in neither of the others, that the whole house was pervaded by the odour, resumes contact with the Marcan narrative. While Mark says that 'certain persons' (τινές) took exception to the woman's act, though only in an 'aside' (πρὸς ἑαυτούς), John says it was Judas Iscariot who expressed disapproval. But the actual comment in John reads like an abbreviation of Mark, all of his words, including the estimate of the value of the perfume at 300 denarii, recurring in Mark's somewhat longer form.

In Mark, Jesus replies to the criticism with four aphorisms: (i) a vindication of the woman's act; (ii) a maxim providing its justification; (iii) an interpretation of the act; (iv) a declaration that wherever the Gospel is proclaimed the woman's act will be commemorated. The last of these does not appear in any form in John; it seems likely that it was not part of the tradition as it reached Mark, but was added by him editorially, perhaps to explain why the story is included in the Passion narrative. The first and third aphorisms appear in John in a telescoped form, but with substantially different wording, which we must consider presently. The second aphorism appears in most MSS. of John at the end of the dialogue.

Mark	John (T.R.)
πάντοτε γὰρ τοὺς πτωχοὺς ἔχετε μεθ᾽ ἑαυτῶν	τοὺς πτωχοὺς γὰρ πάντοτε ἔχετε μεθ᾽ ἑαυτῶν
καὶ ὅταν θέλητε δύνασθε αὐτοῖς εὖ ποιῆσαι	
ἐμὲ δὲ οὐ πάντοτε ἔχετε	ἐμὲ δὲ οὐ πάντοτε ἔχετε

This sentence, however, is absent from Codex Bezae and the Sinaitic Syriac, and the latter part of it, ἐμὲ δὲ...ἔχετε, is absent from the late uncial Λ and the Peshitta. The possibility again suggests itself that assimilation has been at work and that the second aphorism of Mark was no part of the original text of John. In favour of this view we may note (i) that the combination of Codex Bezae and the Sinaitic Syriac has often preserved a very ancient form of text, (ii) that the additional words agree closely with the text of *Matthew*, omitting the Marcan καὶ ὅταν θέλητε δύνασθε αὐτοῖς εὖ ποιῆσαι, which Matthew also omits, (iii) that the plurals, ἔχετε, ἑαυτῶν, fit the Matthaean (and Marcan) plural ἄφετε, but not the Johannine ἄφες, and (iv) that the words are added at the end, with no very clear logical connection, instead of forming an organic step in the argument, as they do in Mark and Matthew. There is nothing conclusive in these arguments, but on the whole, considering how strong is the tendency to assimilation in our MSS., they seem to establish a certain probability that the aphorism about the poor is not part of the original text of John, in which the reply of Jesus consisted of one sentence only, the one about keeping the perfume for the day of burial. The text of John here is not entirely certain, but in any case it reproduces the Marcan ἄφετε αὐτήν (xiv. 6), turned into the singular, as the Johannine context demands, and the single word ἐνταφιασμόν. We shall have to look further at this sentence presently.

Clearly there is a certain *prima facie* case for the dependence of John upon Mark as a documentary source, although it may not be so strong as it appears at first sight, since it is by no means certain that the two gospels agree in the aphorism about the poor and the strange word πιστικῆς. Yet apart from these uncertain agreements there are significant echoes of language, notably in the wording of the objection, and the echo of Mark's ἄφετε αὐτήν and ἐνταφιασμόν, over and above the similarity of pattern, even in detail.

Let us then tentatively adopt the hypothesis that John is here dependent on Mark. How then are we to account for the not inconsiderable differences between them? Some of these indeed scarcely pose a problem: the amount of abbreviation at some points and expansion at others does not exceed the range of what is common in places where literary dependence is taken as certain (for example, as between Matthew and Mark). The attachment of names to anonymous characters is a frequent feature of secondary versions of narratives, though it is noteworthy that if the names of Mary and Judas are here introduced the name of Simon is suppressed. Upon our present hypothesis, the names of Mary and Judas, as well as those of Lazarus and Martha, might be accounted for either as legendary development or as due to superior information—though, it may be observed, if the evangelist had such information at his disposal it is not obvious why he should have chosen to copy the work of a less well-informed writer. But the hypothesis begins to run into real difficulties when we reach the description of the woman's act, which is, after all, the kernel of the whole story. It might be possible to suggest reasons why John should have substituted anointing (ἀλείφειν) of the feet for affusion (καταχεῖν) of perfume over the head, but the strange thing is that he here apparently reproduces the language of Luke at least as closely as he reproduces that of Mark at other points. If the echoes of Marcan language are held to prove literary dependence on Mark, the echoes of Lucan language here should prove literary dependence on Luke. But Luke is speaking of a woman with a disreputable past, and the whole point of his story depends upon the sinfulness of her former life, now forgiven. I find it very difficult to conceive of John, with Luke (*ex hypothesi*) in his hands, deliberately transferring this description to a character of whom he never suggests anything like a shady past, and embodying it in a story, derived from Mark, whose point is something entirely different.

We now come to the dialogue, in which we have noted certain resemblances to Mark, and no resemblance to Luke. The crucial point is the comparison of the two versions of the aphorism about the anointing of the body for burial. Mark reads: προέλαβεν μυρίσαι τὸ σῶμά μου εἰς τὸν ἐνταφιασμόν. The act is a veritable anointing for burial, only it is 'proleptic', antedated. We ask, first, what motive John could have had for altering this at all. It is clear from the use of the term ἐνταφιασμός that he intends to associate the act in some way with the approaching death and burial of Jesus. But according to John the body of Jesus was in fact embalmed before burial, whereas according to Mark the 'proleptic' anointing was the only one. This might perhaps explain why John did not choose to adopt Mark's words. But what did he substitute for them? Our authorities do not agree. The Textus Receptus, with support from such respectable MSS. as Codex Alexandrinus, fam. 1 and fam. 13, reads, ἄφετε αὐτήν· εἰς τὴν ἡμέραν τοῦ ἐνταφιασμοῦ μου τετήρηκεν αὐτό. Against this, B, D, and some other uncials, supported by most of the Old Latin MSS. and some other versions, read, ἄφες αὐτὴν ἵνα εἰς τὴν ἡμέραν τοῦ ἐνταφιασμοῦ μου τηρήσῃ αὐτό.[1] The Textus Receptus gives a plain meaning: 'Let her alone; she has kept it for the day of my burial'. The answer to Judas's question, why the perfume was not sold for the benefit

---

[1] The reading of the Sinaitic Syriac, ܩܒ݂ܪ ܠܗ ܢܛܪ, is rendered by Burkitt (*Evangelion Da-Mepharreshe, ad loc.*) 'Suffer her to keep it', by Merx (*Die Vier Kanonischen Evangelien*, vol. III, *ad loc.*) 'Laß sie [daß] sie es bewahre'; but he points out that it might equally well represent ἄφες αὐτήν, τηρεῖ αὐτό, i.e. 'Let her alone: she is keeping it'. 'Aber', he adds, 'vernünftig ist nur die Lesart τετήρηκε, denn Maria hat die bis dahin aufgehobene Salbe schon verwendet.... Was sie ausgegossen hat, das kann sie nicht bewahren', with which I am disposed to concur.

of the poor, is that Mary had kept it by her to be used in preparation for the burial of Jesus. In using it now, six days before the event, she has, in effect, applied it to its intended purpose. This would fit admirably into the Johannine context, given the kind of irony which this evangelist habitually practises. Symbolically, the day on which Mary anoints the body of Jesus *is* the day of his burial.

Yet if the maxim, *ardua lectio potior*, is to be applied, there is no doubt which way it points. For the alternative reading is so 'arduous' that its meaning is quite uncertain. 'Let her keep it for the day of my burial.' That is the apparent meaning. But Mary has already used the perfume, and cannot therefore keep it for a future occasion. Most commentators assume that what is meant is the *residue* of the perfume. John does not say, as Mark does, that the vase was broken and the perfume poured out; all he says is that it was used to anoint the feet; and this would not necessarily exhaust a *litra* of the perfume. There might remain sufficient to be used on another occasion. The answer, then, to Judas's question is that Mary shall be allowed to keep the *residue* for the day of the burial of Jesus. But the question, in its Johannine form, runs, 'Why *was* this perfume not sold and the proceeds given to the poor?' It was *not* sold, and it is no answer to say 'Let her keep the rest of it for a future occasion'. Moreover, this is not what John says. There is a perfectly good Greek word for 'residue', τὸ περισσεῦον, and this word is not strange to our evangelist, who speaks of the residue of bread after the feeding of the multitude as τὰ περισσεύσαντα κλάσματα. But there is a more serious difficulty still. According to John, on the day of the burial of Jesus Nicodemus provided no less than 100 λίτραι of spices. The meagre remnant of Mary's single *litra* was neither used nor needed. There is therefore an apparent inconsistency between our present passage, as read in what appears to be the best attested text, and John xix. 39–40. I can easily conceive of the evangelist as taking over from some source a statement which, though it needs some adjustment to the implications of his narrative elsewhere, does not flatly contradict it, but I do find it hard to imagine him going out of his way to introduce such a statement by way of a 'correction' of Mark. The only way in which I can understand the passage in a sense strictly congruous with John's apparent intention is to construe τηρήσῃ as if it were τετηρηκυῖα ᾖ: 'Allow her to have kept it.' In other words 'She has kept it for the day of my burial; indulge her so far, and do not complain of her conduct'. But this is a rather violent construction. I cannot, however, help feeling that the scribe or editor who introduced τετήρηκεν had a true appreciation of the evangelist's intention—unless, indeed, the Textus Receptus should for once have preserved the true reading against the 'better' MSS.[1]

The hypothesis, then, that John is here directly dependent on Mark, strongly based though it appeared to be, is not entirely satisfying as an explanation of the facts. In particular, it fails to explain why, in a setting resembling that of Mark, John has described the action in terms resembling those of Luke in a widely different setting. Moreover, it requires us to understand, from the Fourth Evangelist's known tendency and point of view, the substitution of the Johannine form of the reply of Jesus for the Marcan form, and this we have not been able to do.

I shall now propose an alternative hypothesis, but this will call for some preliminary discussion. This is not the only place in the gospels where certain details of a story seem to have wandered from one *pericopé* to another. I would adduce in particular two well-known examples.

(i) Luke x. 25–8, the dialogue with a 'lawyer' which leads to the parable of the Good Samaritan. The latter we may, for our present purpose, neglect. The *pericopé* begins with a question from the lawyer: 'What shall I do to inherit eternal life?' The answer is given (by the lawyer himself in response to a leading question) in terms of the two commandments of love to God and neighbour. The question appears to be a doublet of that asked by the man of great possessions in a Marcan dialogue (Mark x. 17), and the answer a doublet of that given in Mark xii. 29–30 to the 'scribe' who asked a different question, namely 'Which is the first commandment?' How are these phenomena to be accounted for? A mechanical application of the theory of documentary sources represents Luke as copying the question from Mark x. 17 (which however he has duly copied in its proper context) and then copying the answer from Mark xii. 29, transferring it, strangely enough, from Jesus himself to his interlocutor. This I find completely incredible as an account of the actions of a reasonable person.[2] Now let us state the problem afresh. The gospels

---

[1] The BD text might be acceptable if τηρεῖν were understood as meaning 'to keep in mind', like συντηρεῖν (ἐν τῇ καρδίᾳ) in Lk. ii. 19, 51, διατηρεῖν in Gen. xxxvii. 11. Αὐτό might then be the act rather than the ointment. 'Mary should treasure up the memory [of the ointment or of the use she has made of it] for the day when she and others would wish, but would be unable, to anoint the dead body.' So, tentatively, D. Daube, *The N.T. and Rabbinic Judaism*, pp. 317–20, following a suggestion by C. F. D. Moule.

[2] The careful investigation of the Lucan 'great interpolation', undertaken some years ago by the Oxford Seminar under Sanday, reached the conclusion that in the whole of this part of the gospel there is no evidence worth anything to show that

report two questions: A, 'What shall I do to inherit eternal life?', and B, 'Which is the first commandment?' And they report two answers: X, adducing the second table of the decalogue,[1] and Y, combining the two commandments of love to God and neighbour. Mark has two dialogues on these themes. In ch. x he combines A and X, in ch. xii, B and Y. Luke, who simply follows Mark in the former dialogue and omits the latter, gives, in ch. x, a dialogue which combines A and Y. I suggest that this kind of cross-combination is more easily carried out in the course of oral transmission than in composition from literary sources.

(ii) Matt. ix. 27–31, the healing of two blind men. This is in some sort a doublet of Matt. xx. 29–34, which is also a story about the healing of two blind men. In every other respect, however, than the presence of the second patient, this corresponds closely with the Marcan story of the healing of Bartimaeus (x. 46–52), and is firmly fixed into the context of that story. Here literary dependence is hardly in doubt. But a theory that Matthew, while copying this story from Mark at this point (with some slight modification), wrote up the other story of two blind men from the same source, has no probability. The earlier passage, ix. 27–31, is a typical narrative *pericopé* of conventional form, agreeing, in fact, more faithfully with traditional patterns[2] than the Marcan *pericopé* of Bartimaeus. Such patterns are regarded by form-critics as indicative of oral tradition. All probability is on the side of the view that the *pericopé*, Matt. ix. 27–31, was formed independently within that tradition.

The story may be analysed as follows:

(1) Two blind men cried, Ἐλέησον ἡμᾶς υἱὲ Δαυείδ.

(2) Jesus asked, Πιστεύετε ὅτι δύναμαι τοῦτο ποιῆσαι; and they replied, Ναὶ κύριε.

(3) He touched their eyes,

(4) and said, Κατὰ τὴν πίστιν ὑμῶν γενηθήτω ὑμῖν.

(5) Thereupon their eyes were opened.

(6) Jesus ἐνεβριμήθη and said, Ὁρᾶτε μηδεὶς γινωσκέτω.

(7) They spread the news abroad.

Luke depended on Mark at all, and their argument has, in my belief, never been shaken, so far at least as its negative conclusions are concerned (see *Oxford Studies in the Synoptic Problem*, ed. W. Sanday (1911), pp. 29–75). As a matter of fact the theory of Luke's direct dependence on Mark at this point is now, I think, held in its purity by few critics, if any.

[1] This appears to be the intention, though the citation in Mark x. 19 is not complete. Of course, this is not the final answer in Mark—nor, it may be observed, is the citation of the two great commandments final in Luke.

[2] Apart from the exceptional change of scene in the middle of the story.

Of these features, (1) appears in Mark's story of Bartimaeus; (2) has no exact parallel, but the same design to elicit faith is otherwise expressed in other stories, for example, in the Marcan stories of Jairus's daughter (v. 36) and the Epileptic Boy (ix. 23), and in the Johannine story of the son of the βασιλικός (see below, pp. 192–3); (3) is a commonplace of stories of healing, occurring, for example, in the Marcan story of the blind man of Bethsaida (viii. 22), though not in that of blind Bartimaeus, either in Mark or in Matthew; (4) recurs in a slightly different form in Matt. viii. 13 (the centurion), ὡς ἐπίστευσας γενηθήτω σοι, but not in the other gospels, Mark and Luke preferring the form ἡ πίστις σου σέσωκέν σε *vel sim.*; (5) does not recur in precisely this form in other stories of the healing of the blind, but is a natural alternative for ἀναβλέπειν to describe the recovery of sight (compare Matt. xx. 33, John ix. 26); (6) recurs in Mark i. 43–4 (the leper), where the coincidence of language is striking, ἐμβριμησά-μενος αὐτῷ...λέγει αὐτῷ Ὅρα μηδενὶ μηδὲν εἴπῃς; (7) also recurs in Mark i. 45, where again the verb διαφημίζειν is used.

Here we observe the combination of details or features of narrative which elsewhere appear in other combinations. The most striking is the combination of the appeal, ἐλέησον υἱὲ Δαυείδ, which appears in the Marcan story of Bartimaeus, with the ἐμβρίμησις and the abortive prohibition of publicity, which appear in the Marcan story of the leper. One way of explaining these phenomena is to say that Matthew copied ἐλέησον υἱὲ Δαυείδ out of Mark x. 47, and the prohibition, with ἐμβριμᾶσθαι and διαφημίζειν, from Mark i. 43–5—and no doubt the other details from this, that, or the other place in Mark. It is surely a more plausible hypothesis that the varying combination of details took place at the oral stage, before the *pericopé* had reached the relatively final form in which it was written down.

These examples may suffice. I believe we are led to conceive the process of oral tradition and its reduction to writing somewhat as follows. The units of tradition which have been identified and described by form-critics were shaped, as they hold, in response to the needs of various activities of the early Church, such as those of the mission to unbelievers, the instruction of converts, and the worship of the congregation. But the materials out of which they were formed were already in existence, as an unarticulated wealth of recollections and reminiscences of the words and deeds of Jesus—mixed, it may be, with the reflections and interpretations of his followers.[1] It was out of this unformed or fluid tradition that the units of

[1] Especially reflections and interpretations prompted by the study of Old Testament scriptures in their bearing upon the career of Jesus and his Passion in particular.

narrative and teaching crystallized into the forms we know. At the early, unformed, stage we have to think, not of distinct narratives, with their individual features sharply marked, as we have them in the gospels, but of a host of remembered traits and turns of expression, often disjoined and without context, but abounding in characteristic detail. It was remembered, for example (to revert to the instances I have adduced), that Jesus was addressed by suppliants in the striking, and perhaps compromising, terms, ἐλέησον υἱὲ Δαυείδ, that on occasion he 'passionately' (ἐμβριμησάμενος) forbade his patients to make publicity for him, that he was asked such questions as 'Which is the first commandment?' and 'What shall I do to inherit eternal life?', and that he referred inquirers to the commandments of the Decalogue, but laid especial stress on the two commandments of love to God and neighbour. But the precise occasions with which these features of his Ministry were associated were perhaps not always remembered, or were remembered differently by different witnesses; for the association of ideas is a very individual thing, and it often affects our recollection of events.

To return from this long digression to the passage in the Fourth Gospel from which we started, I now offer an alternative hypothesis to account for the phenomena of the three stories of anointing, namely that the variations arose in the course of oral transmission, and that the cross-combinations of different features and details are incidental to the process of shaping individual units of narrative out of the primitive, unformed, tradition. On this hypothesis, each evangelist used independently a separate strand of tradition, and the strands overlapped. In the process of embodying the unit of tradition in a written composition each evangelist has, no doubt, contributed something of his own, but the substance of the pericopé in each of its three forms is traditional.

The case is not entirely clear, but I would submit that this hypothesis explains more of the facts, and leaves fewer difficulties unexplained, than the hypothesis of literary dependence of John on Mark or Luke or both.

The central *motif* is that of an act of homage rendered to Jesus by a woman (whose identity, probably, was unknown to the primitive tradition and has been supplied by our evangelist). In one strand of tradition this act was described as the washing and anointing of the feet, in another as the pouring of perfume over the head. Associated with this is the acceptance of the act by Jesus (against detraction). In one strand of tradition he accepts it as an anticipatory or symbolic preparation of his body for burial, in another simply as the expression of a love kindled by gratitude for many sins forgiven. At this point the strand of tradition followed by Luke connects itself with another *motif*, that of the Pharisee and the sinner—which in other forms appears elsewhere in the gospels and the story is elaborated to bring out this *motif*, the woman's act being set forth in its three stages, the washing, the kiss, the anointing, as enhanced compensation for three courtesies due to an honoured guest which the proud Pharisee has omitted. In John the act is described, essentially as in Luke, but simply and without the pointed elaboration. In Mark the verb for 'anointing' (ἀλείφειν) is not used, but the woman's action is described in terms which seem to hint at the ceremonial anointing of kings and priests; cf. 1 Kms. x. 1 (of Saul), καὶ ἔλαβεν Σαμουὴλ τὸν φακὸν τοῦ ἐλαίου καὶ ἐπέχεεν ἐπὶ τὴν κεφαλὴν αὐτοῦ, and similarly 4 Kms. ix. 6 (of Solomon), Exod. xxix. 7 (of Aaron).[1] If any such suggestion is present, it would seem to have been inherent in this strand of tradition, since Mark shows no consciousness of it, and is not likely to have introduced it. In John there is no shadow of any such suggestion, and the fact tells, so far as it goes, against the theory that John was acquainted with the Marcan form of the story, since the idea of an anointing, as of a king or priest, which is also an embalming of the dead, would be congenial to his conception of the messianic King whose throne is a cross.

[1] The proper term for such anointing is χρίειν, not ἀλείφειν, and Mark is therefore consistent in avoiding the latter term and using καταχεῖν, which is a variant of the ἐπιχεῖν associated with χρίειν in the three passages cited.

2. STORIES OF HEALING

The work of Jesus as healer, which bulks so large in the Synoptic narrative, and has a place also in the traditional summary of his Ministry in the *kerygma* of Acts x. 38, is but feebly represented in the Fourth Gospel. Three miracles of healing, at Cana, at Bethesda and at Siloam, are evidently selected for the use that can be made of them in the exposition of Johannine theology. To these may be added the story of the raising of Lazarus, but this, though it has obvious affinities with the healing miracles in general, demands special treatment. All are presented as σημεῖα,[1] that is, actions significant or symbolical of profound doctrinal truths; but this does not settle the question whether the evangelist composed them with this purpose in view, or drew them from the Synoptic Gospels or from some other traditional source. It is this question that we have now to consider.

(a) The Healing at Bethesda (*John v. 1–9*)

The general pattern or form of the Bethesda story, like that of several *pericopae* in the Synoptic Gospels (see Table 4), is determined by a feature common to them all: that Jesus takes action on his own initiative, without any appeal either from the patient or from his friends. The Johannine *pericopé* does not precisely conform to any one of the others, nor indeed are any two of them exactly alike in all respects, but the general similarity is unmistakable, and invites comparison in detail.

If we leave out of account for the moment the setting of the scene (which is more elaborate in John than in the others), we observe that all begin with an introduction of the patient and some indication of his symptoms or of the circumstances. In John, the nature of the malady is left vague, but its duration is noted: the man had been ill for thirty-eight years, as in Luke xiii. 16 the patient had been crippled for eighteen years, and as, again, in Mark v. 25 the patient had suffered for twelve years. There follows a brief colloquy between Jesus and his patient, preparing the way for the healing word. In the cases of dropsy and withered arm the way is prepared by a question to critics, to which their silence is an implied answer. In the case of the widow's son of Nain Jesus first addresses the

---

[1] The first and third explicitly (iv. 54, ix. 16), and it is obvious that the Bethesda healing has the same intention.

Fundamental pattern: (1) The scene; (2) the patient and his condition; (3) intervention by Jesus, leading up to word and/or act of healing; (4) recovery of patient; (5) the sequel (not necessarily integral to the *pericope*).

	(i) The Crippled Woman (Luke xiii. 10–17)	(ii) The Widow's Son of Nain (Luke vii. 11–17)	(iii) The Healing at Bethesda (John v. 1–8)	(iv) The Withered Hand (Mark iii. 1–6)	(v) The Dropsy (Luke xiv. 1–6)
1.	He was teaching in a synagogue on the Sabbath	He entered Nain, accompanied by disciples and people	There was a feast and Jesus went up to Jerusalem [Topography of Bethesda: concourse of invalids at the Pool]	He went to synagogue	He went to dine with a Pharisee on the Sabbath (They were watching him)
2.	καὶ ἰδοὺ γυνὴ πνεῦμα ἔχουσα ἀσθενείας (ill for 18 years and bent double)	καὶ ἰδοὺ ἐξεκομίζετο τεθνηκώς (the only son of a widow) (a crowd attended)	ἦν δέ τις ἄνθρωπος ἐκεῖ λη΄ ἔτη ἔχων ἐν τῇ ἀσθενείᾳ αὐτοῦ	καὶ ἦν ἐκεῖ ἄνθρωπος ἐξηραμμένην ἔχων τὴν χεῖρα (They watched to see if he would heal on the Sabbath)	καὶ ἰδοὺ ἄνθρωπός τις ἦν ὑδρωπικός
3.	ἰδὼν δὲ αὐτὴν ὁ Ἰησοῦς προσεφώνησεν	ἰδὼν αὐτὴν ὁ Κύριος ἐσπλαγχνίσθη / He said, Μὴ κλαῖε / (and halted the procession by touching the bier)	τοῦτον ἰδὼν ὁ Ἰησοῦς κατακείμενον (discovering that he had been there long) said, Θέλεις ὑγιὴς γενέσθαι; (The man replied evasively)	Jesus said, Ἔγειρε εἰς τὸ μέσον / (Jesus said, "Ἔξεστιν τοῖς σάββασιν ἀγαθὸν ποιῆσαι κ.τ.λ.; The critics were silent) Jesus said, Ἔκτεινον τὴν χεῖρα	(Jesus said, "Ἔξεστιν τῷ σαββάτῳ θεραπεῦσαι; The critics were silent)
4.	Jesus said, Ἀπολέλυσαι τῆς ἀσθενείας σου καὶ ἐπέθηκεν αὐτῇ τὰς χεῖρας / παραχρῆμα ἀνωρθώθη καὶ ἐδόξασεν τὸν θεόν / (The ἀρχισυνάγωγος cavilled: Jesus replied: the people rejoiced)	Jesus said, Νεανίσκε, σοὶ λέγω, ἐγέρθητι / καὶ ἀνεκάθισεν ὁ νεκρὸς καὶ ἤρξατο λαλεῖν κ.τ.λ. / (The people praised God, and the affair was noised abroad)	Jesus said, Ἔγειρε, ἆρον τὸν κράββατόν σου καὶ περιπάτει / καὶ εὐθέως ἐγένετο ὑγιὴς ὁ ἄνθρωπος κ.τ.λ. It was Sabbath that day (The Jews cavilled: a controversy followed)	καὶ ἐξέτεινεν καὶ ἀπεκατεστάθη ἡ χεὶρ αὐτοῦ / (A plot was laid against the life of Jesus)	ἐπιλαβόμενος ἰάσατο αὐτὸν καὶ ἀπέλυσεν / (Jesus added a clinching argument)

mother in words intended not only to comfort but to awaken faith and expectancy, μὴ κλαῖε, and then touches the bier, both bringing the bearers to a standstill and, once again, awakening expectation, before the life-giving word is spoken. Similarly in the case of the withered arm the command, ἔγειρε εἰς τὸ μέσον, is intended not only to call the attention of critics, but also to arouse expectancy in the patient. In our Bethesda *pericopé* the address to the patient is more challenging: θέλεις ὑγιὴς γενέσθαι; 'Do you really want to become a healthy man?' 'Have you the will to health?' The man's reply is a feeble excuse,[1] which shows that his will to health has been weak. In view of this, the further command, 'Rise, pick up your stretcher and walk!' is felt as a further challenge to the man's enfeebled will, and, in fact, as a demand for his co-operation in the cure. This throws light in turn upon the story of the withered arm, where the command, ἔκτεινον τὴν χεῖρα, can now be seen to be a similar demand for the patient's co-operation and a test of his will to health. So also in the Marcan story of the paralytic, where the healing word is a command in terms similar to those of the Johannine *pericopé*: ἔγειρε ἆρον τὸν κράβαττόν σου καὶ ὕπαγε[2] εἰς τὸν οἶκόν σου (Mark ii. 11).

It is often assumed that we have here proof of John's dependence on Mark, but this does not seem to be a necessary inference.[3] In the more or less stereotyped forms in which these stories reached the evangelists, each type of case had its appropriate formula of healing. Thus, for a deaf mute the word is ἐφφαθά,[4] for a leper, a command to report to the priests, with or without the word καθαρίσθητι.[5] In cases of possession the word ἔξελθε is essential.[6] Where the initiative of the patient is emphasized, the

---

[1] There is a note at once of complaint and of self-exculpation, which is in tone not unlike the appeal of the leper in Pap. Egerton 2.

[2] Matthew (ix. 5) and Luke (v. 23) have, at the first occurrence, περιπάτει, as in John, and some MSS. have introduced this in the corresponding place in Mark, by assimilation; all the Synoptics have ὕπαγε at the second occurrence. If John took ἆρον τὸν κράβαττόν σου from Mark, did he take περιπάτει from Matthew or Luke? That he should have altered ὑπάγειν, if that word lay before him, is unlikely, since he uses the verb more frequently than any other evangelist.

[3] That both should use the term κράβαττος means only that the vocabulary of the earliest Greek-speaking Christians was that of the vulgar spoken Koiné. They were not acquainted with the canon of Phrynichus: σκίμπους λέγε ἀλλὰ μὴ κράβαττος. Matthew and Luke, having some modest literary aspirations, tend to substitute κλίνη or κλινίδιον (though Luke has passed κράβαττος in Acts v. 15, ix. 33). In other words, the point calling for explanation is, not why Mark and John agree in using the natural term κράβαττος, but why Luke and Matthew avoid it.

[4] Mark vii. 34.   [5] Mark i. 41, 44, Luke xvii. 14, Pap. Eg. 2.

[6] Mark i. 25, v. 8, ix. 25.

formula ἡ πίστις σου σέσωκέν σε, or the like,[1] is appropriate. On this principle, the obviously appropriate formula for patients bedridden with complete or partial paralysis is that which we find in the Marcan story of the paralytic and the Johannine story of the healing at Bethesda, and we may with some confidence regard it as integral to the tradition, without any need to assume borrowing on either side.

The colloquy between Healer and patient deserves further consideration. Such brief dialogues are frequently introduced in healing stories of various types, in order to bring out certain aspects of the conditions under which, or the means by which, the healing is effected. Questions are raised regarding the power of the Healer and his willingness to heal. Thus, the leper says, ἐὰν θέλῃς δύνασαι (Mark i. 40), the father of the epileptic boy says, εἴ τι δύνῃ βοήθησον (Mark ix. 23), and in each case the course of the narrative leaves the reader in no doubt that both power and will are present. But there is the further question of the patient's own will to be healed. This question is not explicitly raised in the Synoptics, though, as we have seen, the demand for co-operation implied in the commands, ἔκτεινον τὴν χεῖρα, ἆρον τὸν κράβαττον, πορευθέντες ἐπιδείξατε ἑαυτοὺς τοῖς ἱερεῦσιν, amounts to a test of the patient's willingness. The will to health, in fact, is included in what is meant by πίστις.[2] The 'faith' of the woman with the haemorrhage (Mark v. 34), of Bartimaeus (Mark x. 52), of the friends of the paralytic in the Marcan story (Mark ii. 5), and of the Canaanite mother in Matthew (xv. 28), is exhibited in the sheer determination with which they press for a cure, whether for themselves or for those they represent.[3] The question, therefore, 'Have you the will to be healed?' is implicit in such stories. John makes it explicit.

[1] Mark v. 34, x. 52, Luke xvii. 19, Matt. ix. 29, viii. 13.

[2] The extent to which the word πίστις in the Synoptic Gospels carries over something of the meaning of the Hebrew אמונה, of which it is the regular equivalent in the LXX, merits consideration. אמונה is primarily firmness, steadfastness, constancy, and this quality is certainly displayed by the persons here mentioned as examples of πίστις.

[3] The dialogue with the father of the epileptic boy is instructive. He begins by raising the question of the Healer's power to heal. Jesus subtly turns the question back upon the man himself, for πάντα δυνατὰ τῷ πιστεύοντι is intended, and the man understands it, as a challenge to his faith. He replies, πιστεύω, βοήθει μου τῇ ἀπιστίᾳ. The βοήθει is now an appeal, not directly for a manifestation of the Healer's power, but for a strengthening of his own faith. In the Bethesda pericopé what Jesus has done for the man is essentially to awaken his faith, in the sense of his will to be healed. There is no direct contact between the two narratives, but the two evangelists are talking about the same thing, and this thing is intrinsic to the tradition in its varying forms.

The close of the narrative follows the common pattern. The man is cured, and his actions put the reality of the cure beyond doubt. At this point we learn that the incident took place on a sabbath, and this leads to a controversial dialogue which, in the Johannine manner, culminates in a monologue upon a theological theme. The dialogue is connected some-what artificially with the miracle through the question of sabbath observance which it raised.[1] This artificiality is a strong reason for believing that John did not compose the story freely as an introduction to the dialogue; if he had done so, we should have expected something which would more naturally suggest its main theme. It is far more likely that the evangelist has utilized traditional material and made it serve his purpose as best he could.

In three of the other healing stories of this group a work of healing on the sabbath arouses controversy. In the cases of dropsy and of withered arm it takes the form of a brief colloquy[2] embedded in the account of the healing, and corresponding, formally, with the colloquy between Healer and patient in the Bethesda *pericopé*. In the case of the crippled woman the healing is complete and the controversy follows, though in Luke the fact that the day was a sabbath has already been noted, as it has not been in John. There is the further similarity that in the Lucan, as in the Johannine, *pericopé* the controversy is introduced by an address of the Jewish authorities to the patient (in John) or the spectators (in Luke). But the resemblance is superficial. It is possible that we have here an instance of details 'wandering' in the oral tradition (a phenomenon to which I have already drawn attention),[3] but it is also possible (and perhaps likely) that the evangelist has at this point added a detail (itself traditional) to a story which came down to him without it, and thus supplied an artificial link with the theological discussion he had designed to introduce.

The whole story, then, from the introduction of the patient at verse 5 to the establishment of the reality of the cure at verse 9 (with or without the note which follows, ἦν δὲ σάββατον ἐν ἐκείνῃ τῇ ἡμέρᾳ) moves entirely within the ambience of traditional narratives of healing as they are amply known to us from the Synoptic Gospels. Yet it does not simply imitate

---

[1] See *Interpretation*, pp. 319–20.
[2] In intention it is a dialogue; the critics say nothing, but their silence is eloquent— a feature which occurs in other passages of dialogue form: Mark ix. 34, Matt. xxii. 46. The effect is the same when the interlocutors reply, 'We do not know' (Mark xi. 33).
[3] See above, pp. 169–73.

Synoptic forms, but develops them in an individual way.[1] In particular, the dialogue is intimately related to themes intrinsic to the tradition of narratives of healing, and supplements the discussion of such themes in the Synoptics by making explicit a point which they left just beneath the surface.

It remains to consider the first stage of the narrative, in which the scene is set. This is unusually long and elaborate, even when the text has been corrected by the omission of verses 3 b–4 of the Textus Receptus, which are absent from most of our reputable authorities and are almost universally held to be an interpolated gloss. If we read verse 1 followed immediately by verse 5, we have a sufficiently close parallel to the introductions to the stories of the withered arm and the crippled woman as well as several other healing narratives: 'After this there was a Jewish festival and Jesus went up to Jerusalem; and there was a man there who had been ill for thirty-eight years.' Yet something more than that is needed, if the reader is to understand the dialogue between Healer and patient. He should know at least that the scene is placed at the edge of a pool or tank (κολυμβήθρα), into which the patient is expected to plunge, and that there was a sufficient number of invalids seeking a cure to cause competition for places (verse 7).[2] The excuse, 'I have no one to throw me into the pool when the water is troubled, and while I am coming someone else steps down before me', is so essentially related to the main motive of the narrative (faith as the will to health) that it could not have been omitted without spoiling the whole point. It appears, therefore, that something like verses 2–3a must from the first have been integral to the narrative. Even in the Synoptics a *pericopé* is sometimes introduced with some greater fulness of detail than usual, where it is called for by the development of the story. Thus the Marcan story of the paralytic is introduced not only by the statement that Jesus entered Capernaum and that his return was widely noted, but also by a description of the overcrowding of the house where he was staying (Mark ii. 1–2), and this description is necessary to an understanding of the drastic measures adopted by the patient's friends, which in turn give a sharp point to the words, 'Jesus,

---

[1] Similarly Bultmann *ad loc.* 'eine Wundergeschichte, und zwar eine Heilungsgeschichte, die in manchen Zügen an synoptische Heilungsgeschichten erinnert, aber nicht aus der synoptischen Tradition stammt'.

[2] That the pool was fed from an intermittent spring it is perhaps not essentially necessary that he should know, though the glossator thought it was; it could be inferred from the course of the dialogue itself.

seeing their faith, said . . .'. Again, the Lucan story of the ten lepers has an unusually full topographical introduction: 'On his way to Jerusalem, he was passing between Samaria and Galilee, and as he was entering a village he was met by ten lepers' (Luke xvii. 11–12). This information helps the reader to understand how it came about that the group of lepers was partly Jewish, partly Samaritan; on the borders of Samaria such a mixture would be more likely than elsewhere.

It is therefore not without parallel that John has introduced his story with the statement that there was a pool surrounded by invalids waiting their turn to plunge into the healing waters, nor is there any great difficulty in supposing such material to be part of the tradition as it reached him. What *is* unlike the forms of traditional narrative known to us from the Synoptics is the communication of detailed topographical information in a style which is almost that of a guide-book: 'There is in Jerusalem, near the Sheep-gate, a pool called in Hebrew Bethesda,[1] which has five colonnades.' It has been held that the evangelist invented the five στοαί as a symbol of the five books of the Torah. It remains possible that he did intend the στοαί to be symbolical, but there is now evidence which absolves him of the need for inventing them.[2] Recent excavations in Jerusalem have revealed the existence of a pool in the required vicinity, with structural remains which the excavators interpret as the foundations of colonnades running round the edge of the pool and across it in the middle (4+1=5), dividing it into an upper and a lower pool.[3] As it is unlikely that these structures escaped destruction in the sack of the city in A.D. 70, it appears that a knowledge of them must have reached the evangelist by tradition, unless indeed he was one who had been well acquainted with the city before the catastrophe. We must, however, note that this gospel shows elsewhere a special interest in topography, apparently for its own sake. Whether this is a personal idiosyncrasy of the evangelist, which affected his treatment of his material, or whether the strain of tradition upon which he worked was richer in topographical detail than that represented by the Synoptics, must for the present remain an open question.[4]

---

[1] The extensive variations of text in this verse do not here concern us.

[2] See J. Jeremias, *Die Wiederentdeckung von Bethesda*, and for a remarkable corroboration from the Copper Scroll of Qumran, *id.* in *Expository Times*, vol. LXXI (1960), pp. 227 *sqq.*

[3] The latter being the *jemumith* ('little sea') of the Scroll.

[4] See below, pp. 244–5.

(b) The Healing at Siloam (John ix. 1–7)

This narrative again serves to introduce one of the most highly wrought of the Johannine dramatic dialogues, which has no resemblance to anything in the Synoptic Gospels. But the story itself constitutes a *pericopé* with much similarity to a group of Synoptic healing narratives (see Table 5).

The story appears to begin abruptly: καὶ παράγων εἶδεν ἄνθρωπον. . . . It is by no means an unparalleled opening for a traditional unit of narrative; cf. Mark i. 16, καὶ παράγων παρὰ τὴν θάλασσαν τῆς Γαλιλαίας εἶδεν . . ., ii. 14, καὶ παράγων εἶδεν Λευείν . . ., and similarly at the beginning of a healing *pericopé*, Matt. ix. 27, καὶ παράγοντι ἐκεῖθεν τῷ Ἰησοῦ ἠκολούθησαν αὐτῷ δύο τυφλοί. It is, however, possible that the closing words of chapter viii should be connected with what follows: 'He left the temple, and as he passed by. . .'[1] (compare Mark xiii. 1 καὶ ἐκπορευομένου αὐτοῦ ἐκ τοῦ ἱεροῦ λέγει αὐτῷ εἷς τῶν μαθητῶν. . .). We should then have a parallel to the opening of the story of the healing of Simon's mother-in-law: καὶ εὐθὺς ἐκ τῆς συναγωγῆς ἐξελθόντες. . . .

In either case, the encounter is a casual one, as in the narratives of our first group. As at Bethesda and at Nain, Jesus 'saw' the sufferer. But on the present occasion the 'seeing' does not at once lead to active intervention, which waits upon the initiative of a third party: the disciples draw their Master's attention to the blind man. To that extent the present narrative falls into line with the others which I have included in group II (with which it has other contacts also), though the interposition of the disciples here is different in intention from that of the friendly neighbours of the blind man of Bethsaida and of the deaf-mute of Decapolis in Mark, or of those who informed Jesus of the illness of Simon's mother-in-law. It is curious that in other places where the disciples intervene their attitude is unhelpful: according to Matthew (xv. 23) they urged their Master to dismiss the 'Canaanite' mother who was calling after them in the street, and according to Mark (x. 13) they scolded the fathers (αὐτοῖς) who wished to bring their children to him. In the present narrative their attitude is neutral. They use the example of the blind man to raise a

---

[1] It has been observed that if the clause καὶ ἐξῆλθεν ἐκ τοῦ ἱεροῦ is intended to go with the foregoing, Ἰησοῦς δὲ ἐκρύβη, we should have expected the reverse order, viz. he went out of the temple and hid himself. There is force in this, but it is perhaps not conclusive. On the whole I am disposed to agree with Bultmann that the true beginning is καὶ παράγων εἶδεν.

Table 5. Stories of healing, Group II

Fundamental pattern: (1) The setting (not necessarily integral to the *pericope*); (2) the patient and his condition; (3) intervention by third party; (4) the healing act (a) and/or word (b); (5) recovery of the patient; (6) sequel (not necessarily integral to the *pericope*).

	(i) Simon's Mother-in-law (Mark i. 29–31)	(ii) The Dumb Man of Decapolis (Mark vii. 31–7)	(iii) The Blind Man of Bethsaida (Mark viii. 22–6)	(iv) The Blind Man at Siloam (John ix. 1–7)
1.	They left the synagogue and entered the house of Simon and Andrew, with James and John	(He left the territory of Tyre…and passed through Decapolis)	(They came to Bethsaida)	(He left the temple, viii. 59)
2.	Simon's mother-in-law κατέκειτο πυρέσσουσα	φέρουσιν αὐτῷ κωφὸν καὶ μογιλάλον	φέρουσιν αὐτῷ τυφλόν	παράγων εἶδεν ἄνθρωπον τυφλὸν ἐκ γενετῆς
3.	They told him about her	They begged him to lay his hand on him	They begged him to touch him	The disciples asked, Τίς ἥμαρτεν;
4.	Jesus (a) προσελθὼν ἤγειρεν αὐτὴν κρατήσας τῆς χειρός	Jesus (a) touched his ears and tongue, looked to heaven and sighed (b) said Ἐφφαθά	Jesus (a) spat upon his eyes and laid his hands on him (b) said Εἴ τι βλέπεις; (The cure being incomplete, the imposition of hands was repeated)	[The reply, Οὔτε οὗτος οὔτε οἱ γονεῖς, leads to a brief discourse, ending, φῶς εἰμὶ τοῦ κόσμου] Jesus (a) spat upon the ground, made clay, and put it on his eyes (b) said Ὕπαγε νίψαι κ.τ.λ.
5.	The fever left her	Hearing and speech were restored καὶ ἐλάλει ὀρθῶς	διέβλεψεν καὶ ἀπεκατεστάθη καὶ ἐνέβλεπεν τηλαυγῶς ἅπαντα	ἀπῆλθεν καὶ ἐνίψατο καὶ ἦλθεν βλέπων
6.	διηκόνει αὐτοῖς	διεστείλατο αὐτοῖς ἵνα μηδενὶ λέγωσιν (but the matter was noised abroad and aroused favourable comment)	He sent him home saying Μηδὲ εἰς τὴν κώμην εἰσέλθῃς	(Comments of neighbours and observers led to objections to healing on the Sabbath, and to further developments)

question of speculative theology, and this gives rise to a short dialogue, to which I shall return in a moment. In other narratives of this group there is no such dialogue, though, as we have seen, it is a common enough feature of healing narratives.

After the word which concludes the dialogue (ix. 5) the healing proceeds. As in the case of the blind man of Bethsaida and the deaf-mute of Decapolis, spittle is employed in the cure, though not in exactly the same way. But at this point the narratives of Mark and of John diverge significantly. In Mark viii. 23–5, after the application of spittle the blind man is asked whether he can see, and by degrees his sight returns. In the case of the deaf-mute (Mark vii. 32–5) the operation with spittle is accompanied by a healing word, ἐφφαθά, spoken after a pause in which the Healer looks up to heaven and utters a sigh (with which we may compare John xi. 41, where Jesus at the grave of Lazarus lifts his eyes to heaven and prays). Thereupon the patient immediately recovers speech and hearing.[1] In our present passage, on the other hand, after the operation with spittle, the patient is bidden, 'Go and wash in the pool of Siloam'. He goes, carries out his instructions, and emerges with the power of sight. This gives a different aspect to the story: the co-operation of the patient is demanded. His readiness to obey the command of Jesus is an essential element in the cure, and is in fact a measure of his faith, though John does not use the term. The fact that he goes to Siloam unaccompanied (it would appear) by Jesus, supported only by his own faith and determination, makes the contribution of the patient to his own recovery more marked, in contrast to the blind man and the deaf-mute in Mark, who are passive throughout. As we have seen, this demand for co-operation from the patient is not a specifically Johannine trait. Not only the man healed at Bethesda, but the paralytic and the man with a withered arm in Mark, and the lepers in Mark and Luke, are all invited to exercise and prove their faith in co-operative action. The closest parallel, indeed, to our present passage is afforded by Luke xvii. 11–19, where the lepers go to report themselves to the sanitary authorities without any guarantee of their cure beyond the word of Jesus and their own faith.

---

[1] It is sometimes suggested that the στεναγμός of Mark vii. 34 was a forcing of the breath through mouth and nostrils, designed to suggest to the patient that he should imitate the action, and so help to clear the ἀκοαί and to 'loosen the bond of his tongue'. But all this is alien to the character of these traditional narratives. We should think rather of the emotion which accompanies the cure of the leper in Mark. i. 43, and the raising of Lazarus in John. xi. 33–38.

There is, however, no other healing *pericopé* where washing is a part of the process of cure. Are we to say that John has introduced this feature into a narrative which is otherwise a mere *rechauffé* of Mark, in order to exploit the symbolism of the incident: a blind man given sight by washing in water stands for the convert 'enlightened' by baptism? Such a symbolic interpretation is certainly intended. This raises the further question: is the name Siloam introduced for the sake of its (alleged) etymological meaning, ἀπεσταλμένος?[1] The true πηγὴ ὕδατος, the true 'Siloam', is Christ, 'sent' by the Father to enlighten the world. That is certainly the sense in which the evangelist wishes his readers to understand the whole episode—the narrative and the ensuing dialogue[2]—and we must credit him with the lucky bit of etymological learning. But are we then to imagine him as starting with the idea, 'sent', and inventing out of that idea, with the help of etymology, a name which luckily turns out to be that of a real place (not an imaginary place like Nephelokokkygia or Eatanswill), and, still more luckily, a place where it was possible to wash with water? No one, perhaps, can say it is impossible; I cannot think it likely; such lucky coincidences are rare. Of the reverse process we have abundant instances, where genuine names of real places (or people) are supplied with an etymology, real or fictitious (for this purpose the one is as good as the other), which points to a symbolic meaning. It is, for example, one of the favourite devices of Philo, a writer with whom our writer has much in common. Analogy would suggest that he started with the name Siloam as a datum, and gave its popular etymology a dexterous twist which made it serviceable to his purpose. If so, then there is no reason why the washing (which has intrinsic association with the pool of Siloam) should not be an integral part of the story as it reached the evangelist in tradition. As the appropriate form of co-operative action for a paralytic is to pick up his stretcher, and for a leper to report to the priest, so the appropriate action for a blind man is to wash off the mud-pack which the Healer has placed on his eyes. I should not venture to say that the alternative view is excluded, but I believe that the balance of probability inclines heavily to the side I have indicated.

If so, then the entire narrative (excluding for the moment the short dialogue embedded in it, verses 2–5) is cast in a traditional mould. It does

---

[1] The derivation of the name שִׁלֹחַ from the root שלח, 'send', is regarded by philologists as possible but not certain; but as a piece of *Volksetymologie* at least the understanding of שִׁלֹחַ, the name of an underground aqueduct, giving vent to the waters of a spring, which in Latin is *emissarium*, is most natural.

[2] See *Interpretation*, p. 357.

not directly imitate any particular *pericopé* in the Synoptic Gospels, but combines in a distinctive way motives which appear in various *pericopae*, yet combines them within a framework which in every respect follows familiar traditional patterns of healing narrative. It is worth observing that in the course of the long dialogue which follows the evangelist has enriched the story with additional details: that the patient was a comparatively young man (he was of age but his parents were still living (ix. 18–21)), that he was accustomed to sit and beg (presumably, in view of viii. 59b, at the entrance to the temple, like the cripple of Acts iii. 2), and was therefore a familiar figure to the public (ix. 8); but John has not taken the liberty of introducing these traits into the traditional form of narrative, where they would be out of place. The controversial dialogue itself is wholly extraneous to the narrative, and connected with it in a way which, for all its subtlety and verisimilitude, is obviously literary artifice. It is not until verse 14 that we are told that the incident took place on a sabbath. This would appear not to have been a feature of the narrative from which the evangelist started, as the similar statement *may* have been in the story of Bethesda (v. 9).[1]

But we have still to consider the short dialogue which forms part of the narrative itself (ix. 2–5). As we have seen, the incorporation of a dialogue in a healing narrative is in itself not unusual, but there are here some peculiar features. The aphorism with which it concludes, ὅταν ἐν τῷ κόσμῳ ὦ φῶς εἰμὶ τοῦ κόσμου, is a typically Johannine expression of a typically Johannine idea (compare viii. 12). This at least must be a contribution of the evangelist. But there are other traces of Johannine language and ideas: the expressions, ἵνα φανερωθῇ τὰ ἔργα τοῦ θεοῦ, ἡμᾶς δεῖ ἐργάζεσθαι τὰ ἔργα τοῦ πέμψαντός με, are thoroughly Johannine,[2] and the antithesis, ἡμέρα–νύξ, is congenial to our author, even though he more often opposes φῶς and σκότος. This last instance, however, is less cogent than might appear. It is true that in xiii. 30, where the evangelist speaks of Judas Iscariot's departure into the night, the word νύξ is

---

[1] See above, p. 178.

[2] Φανεροῦν nine times in John, once in Mark (and twice in pseudo-Mark), not otherwise in the Gospels. Ἔργον twenty-nine times in John, six times in Matthew, twice each in Mark and Luke; ἔργα τοῦ θεοῦ (τοῦ πατρός, τοῦ πέμψαντος) only in John. Ἡμᾶς δεῖ ἐργάζεσθαι is to be read with אBDW etc. The reading ἐμέ in ACΘ etc. is probably a correction, as is the ἡμᾶς after πέμψαντος in אLW. The latter is clearly impossible in view of Johannine usage. The expression 'He who sent me' is a standing equivalent for 'the Father', and it is not surprising that John should here revert to it after using ἡμᾶς in the first place. Ὁ πέμψας με occurs twenty-six times in John, not elsewhere.

pretty certainly intended to suggest the ideas associated with σκότος—the realm of falsehood, error, and unreality—but it is also dictated by the dramatic situation.[1] The only other place where the actual antithesis, ἡμέρα–νύξ, appears is xi. 9–10.[2] I shall discuss that passage below,[3] and I shall argue that there is no reason against recognizing it as substantially traditional, rather than as the composition of the evangelist. In our present passage the transition from the imagery of day and night in verse 4 to the φῶς εἰμὶ τοῦ κόσμου of verse 5 is violent. In verse 4, 'day' stands for the normal span of human activity on earth, and 'night' for its cessation ('Man goeth forth unto his work and to his labour until the evening'). Jesus is apparently included among those who must work while work on earth is possible, since death waits for all men. In verse 5 he is himself the light in which men must walk and work, and which nears its setting (xii. 35–6) as his own death approaches. It appears, then, that the two verses are not *in pari materia*. Nor, apart from the mere cast of phrase, is there anything specifically Johannine about the sentiment of verse 4, which is of the nature of proverbial wisdom. Rabbi Tarphon (c. A.D. 100) is quoted as saying, 'The day is short and there is much work to be done; the workers are lazy and the reward is great and the Master of the house is urgent', and Rabbi Simeon ben Eleazar (c. 190) as saying, 'Work so long as you can and it is possible for you and it is still within your power' (cited by S.-B. *ad loc.*). Verses 3–4 therefore might well be a re-casting in Johannine language of material for which the evangelist himself is not primarily responsible.

Let us then consider the dialogue (verses 2–4) on this hypothesis. It begins, like the typical Synoptic dialogues (and unlike those which are most characteristic of the Fourth Gospel),[4] with a question addressed to Jesus. The question here posed is that of theodicy—the problem of sin and suffering in a peculiarly baffling instance: 'Who sinned, this man or his parents, that he should have been born blind?' In other healing narratives there are discussions of such questions as the legitimacy of healing on the

[1] See above, pp. 53–4.
[2] With xi. 9, ἐάν τις περιπατῇ ἐν τῇ νυκτί, cf. xii. 35, ὁ περιπατῶν ἐν τῇ σκοτίᾳ. The antithesis ἡμέρα–νύξ is as early as 1 Thess. v. 1–8, a passage closely related both to the primitive catechism and to the tradition of the sayings of Jesus (see my article, 'The Teaching of Jesus and the Primitive Catechism', in *New Testament Studies: Essays in Memory of T. W. Manson*, ed. A. J. B. Higgins, Manchester Univ. Press, 1959). It is primitive-Christian rather than Johannine.
[3] Pp. 373–9.
[4] See below, pp. 316–19.

sabbath,[1] the propriety of extending the benefits of Christ's work to Gentiles,[2] the nature and power of faith,[3] and the forgiveness of sins.[4] But in no other healing *pericopé*, either in the Synoptics or in the Fourth Gospel, is a question of speculative theology raised. Indeed the Fourth Evangelist nowhere else shows any interest in the problem of theodicy— a fact which tells, *pro tanto*, against the view that this little dialogue is his own original composition. In the Synoptics, however, if we extend our survey to dialogues of similar structure outside healing contexts, we find at least one which does deal with the problem of theodicy—the discussion of the tragic fate of the Galilaeans whose blood Pilate mingled with their sacrifices, and of the eighteen men killed by the collapse of the tower at Siloam (Luke xiii. 1–5). There the problem is raised not by the disciples, but by unnamed persons (τινές) who report the massacre of the Galilaeans,[5] and Jesus in replying adduces the parallel case. There, as here, the problem is that of the divine justice in apportioning suffering to men. In both cases the interlocutors tacitly assume the principle that suffering, under the dispensation of a just Providence, must be retribution for sin. The answer of Jesus in both cases repudiates the use of this principle as a basis for moral judgements: οὐχί, λέγω ὑμῖν (Luke), οὔτε οὗτος ἥμαρτεν οὔτε οἱ γονεῖς αὐτοῦ (John). In Luke he says, in effect, 'The question of the special sinfulness of the victims does not concern you; their fate should teach you to take seriously your own moral responsibility'; in John, 'The question of the sinfulness of the blind man does not concern you; his need challenges your faith in the power of God to meet the need, and your willingness to make use of the limited opportunities of doing His work'. We may compare again the discussion embedded in the Marcan story of the paralytic (ii. 1–12). Having regard to contemporary beliefs we are to understand that the sight of a man so afflicted immediately suggested to observers that he was a sinner lying under the judgement of God. Jesus corrects this by asserting his ἐξουσία to forgive sin, and confirming it by an act of healing; and this act is (in Johannine phrase) an ἔργον τοῦ θεοῦ, for the critics ask, Τίς δύναται ἀφιέναι ἁμαρτίας εἰ μὴ εἷς ὁ θεός; Down to the end of verse 3, therefore, there is nothing alien to the tradition as we

---

[1] Mark iii. 1–6, and, in particular, Luke xiii. 10–17, xiv. 1–6.
[2] Mark vii. 27–9; Matt. xv. 24–8.
[3] Mark v. 35–6, ix. 22–4; Matt. viii. 5–10, ix. 28–9; John iv. 46–54.
[4] Mark ii. 5–11.
[5] It is true that the interlocutors do not explicitly ask the question, but we are clearly intended to understand that their report raised it by implication. Jesus certainly takes it in that sense.

know it from the Synoptics, apart from the actual wording, ἵνα φανερωθῇ τὰ ἔργα τοῦ θεοῦ ἐν αὐτῷ. This is certainly Johannine vocabulary through and through. But the idea is in no sense peculiarly Johannine. In Luke the exorcisms which Jesus performed are wrought 'by the finger of God' (Luke xi. 20), in Matthew 'by the Spirit of God' (Matt. xii. 28), and in both they are signs that the kingdom of God has come. This is what John means by the manifestation of τὰ ἔργα τοῦ θεοῦ.

With verse 4 we enter upon more doubtful ground. The sudden introduction of the first person plural, ἡμᾶς δεῖ ἐργάζεσθαι, finds parallels in other places where the evangelist seems to forget for the moment that he is reporting (ostensibly) what Jesus said upon a particular occasion in the past, and speaks in the name of the contemporary Church;[1] though before the end of the sentence he recurs to the more normal first person singular: '*We* must do the works of Him who sent *me*'. Yet here again, as we have seen, we may well have a Johannine reshaping of a gnomic saying which already had a place in the tradition.

I conclude that if we omit the etymological note in verse 7 and the *Ich-Wort* in verse 5, we may with some confidence regard the *pericopé*, ix. 1 (? viii. 59 b)–ix. 7 as a typical unit of narrative shaped in the same mould as the Synoptic narratives, yet having independent traits which make it unlikely that it was copied, or imitated, from Synoptic models, and probable that it reached John independently. If so, we must suppose that in 3 b–4 he has partly rewritten traditional material in his own idiom, as he has done elsewhere. But the contrast should be noted between verses 3–4, where the language is John's but the ideas are in no way peculiar to his way of thinking, and verse 5, which is Johannine through and through, in thought and in expression, and which moreover involves a violent shift of the metaphor of light and darkness.

(c) The Healing at Cana (John iv. 46–54)

The form of this *pericopé* is dictated by the fact that it narrates a case of healing at a distance, so that the colloquy between Jesus and the parent who intercedes for his absent child is an essential element. It falls naturally to be compared with two narratives of healing at a distance in the Synoptic Gospels, namely those of the Centurion's Boy[2] at Capernaum and of the

---

[1] So iii. 11, iv. 22, cf. i. 14, 16.

[2] The part of the narrative common to Matthew and Luke calls the patient only παῖς. Luke, at the beginning and again at the end of the *pericopé*, uses the term δοῦλος. But the dialogue, which is common to both, appears to distinguish the

Table 6. *Stories of healing, Group III*

Fundamental pattern: (1) The scene; (2) approach of suppliant; (3) dialogue beginning with appeal and ending with word of healing; (4) recovery of the patient.

	(i) The Centurion (Matthew viii. 5–13)	(ii) The 'Nobleman' (John iv. 46–54)	(iii) The Syrophoenician Woman (Mark vii. 24–30)
1.	He entered Capernaum	He came again to Cana	He left for the territory of Tyre (and tried unsuccessfully to avoid notice)
2.	A centurion approached with an appeal	A βασιλικός (a) whose son was sick at Capernaum (b) hearing that Jesus had come (c) went to him	A woman (b) hearing of him (a) whose daughter was demon-possessed (c) came and fell at his feet
3.	The appeal: 'My son is gravely ill at home' The response: 'I will come and heal him' The suppliant demurred: 'I am not worthy; speak the word: I know what authority is' Commendation of the suppliant's faith (elaborated), leading up to— —the healing word: Ὕπαγε· ὡς ἐπίστευσας γενηθήτω σοι	The appeal: ἠρώτα ἵνα καταβῇ καὶ ἰάσηται αὐτοῦ τὸν υἱόν (for he was near death) Jesus demurred: 'If you do not see signs and wonders you will not believe' The suppliant insisted: 'Come down ere my son die' The healing word: Πορεύου· ὁ υἱός σου ζῇ	The appeal: ἠρώτα αὐτὸν ἵνα τὸ δαιμόνιον ἐκβάλῃ Jesus demurred: 'It is not right to give the children's food to dogs' The suppliant insisted: 'The dogs may have the crumbs' Implied commendation of the suppliant's attitude, διὰ τὸν λόγον τοῦτον, leading up to— —the healing word: Ὕπαγε· ἐξελήλυθεν τὸ δαιμόνιον
4.	The boy was cured ἐν τῇ ὥρᾳ ἐκείνῃ	(Elaborated) The boy recovered ἐκείνῃ τῇ ὥρᾳ (The sequel: καὶ ἐπίστευσεν αὐτὸς καὶ ἡ οἰκία αὐτοῦ ὅλη)	She went and found the girl in bed and the demon gone

daughter of the Syrophoenician or Canaanite woman in the territory of Tyre (see Table 6). Of each of these we have two versions, of the former in Matt. viii. 5–13 and Luke vii. 2–10, and of the latter in Mark vii. 24–30 and Matt. xv. 21–8. It is instructive to examine the variations between the two versions in each case. While preserving the general pattern, the accounts vary substantially in detail and in language, exhibiting close verbal resemblance only in the dialogue embedded in the narrative.[1]

The Johannine *pericopé* is formally closest to the story of the foreign woman's daughter as it appears in Mark, corresponding with it step by step (as shown in the table) until the final stage. Here Mark says that the mother returned home and found her daughter in bed in a normal condition. Matthew does not even mention the journey home, but simply reports the fact that the girl recovered from the moment (ἀπὸ τῆς ὥρας ἐκείνης) when Jesus spoke the words, γενηθήτω σοι ὡς θέλεις. In John this final stage is expanded into a dramatic scene. The father is on his way home when he is met by his slaves bringing the good news of his son's recovery. He asks them when the boy took a turn for the better (κομψότερον ἔσχεν). They reply, 'Yesterday at 1 p.m. the fever abated'. The father recognizes that it was at that very moment (ἐκείνη τῇ ὥρᾳ, compare Matthew's ἀπὸ τῆς ὥρας ἐκείνης) that Jesus had spoken the words, ὁ υἱός σου ζῇ. The

δοῦλος from the παῖς. The original intention was probably to represent him as the officer's son. Similarly in John the terms παῖς and υἱός are interchangeable.

[1] It is by no means certain that the original text of Matt. xv. 26–7 was as close to Mark as our MSS. represent it. The Sinaitic Syriac reads: ܘܗܘ ܪܘ ܠܚܝ ܘ̣ܠܐܕ ܟ̣ܝ ܠ ܘܐܠܐ ܟ̣ܚ ܠܐܕܡ ܘ̣. A. Merx, *ad loc.*, takes 26 as a question: 'Is it not fitting to take the bread which the children throw to the dogs?', i.e. if the Jews reject the benefits which Christ offers, surely it is permissible for the Gentiles to receive them. The woman replies: 'Yes; even the dogs eat from their masters' table and live'—it is not a case of some occasional or exceptional indulgence: as the house-dogs have a right to enough food from their masters' table to keep them alive, so the Gentiles have a right, along with Israel, to what is necessary to salvation. D. S. Margoliouth (*Expositor*, 8th series, vol. XXII, pp. 1–10) proposed to take verse 26 as a statement: 'Surely you would not stoop to accept the leavings of the Jews', cf. pseudo-Phocylides, 144: μηδ' ἄλλου παρὰ δαιτὸς ἔδου σκυβάλισμα τραπέζης. The woman counters with a sentiment of Homer, τραπεζῆες κύνες ἀνδρῶν γίγνοντ'· ἀγλαΐης δ' ἕνεκεν κομέουσιν ἄνακτες (*Od.* XVII. 309–10).

In view of the strong tendency to assimilation, we must allow for the possibility, or even probability, that the verbal agreement between Matthew and Mark is by no means so close as it appears, and there remains no strong argument in favour of the view that Matthew is here 'editing' Mark. The variations may well have arisen in oral tradition, and the two are reproducing different strains of that tradition.

threefold repetition of these pregnant words seems designed to emphasize the life-giving power of the word of Christ, and so to prepare for the discourse of v. 19 *sqq.* (compare v. 21, ὁ υἱὸς οὓς θέλει ζωοποιεῖ).[1] But it is only the *repetition* that we need attribute to this motive. The expression itself is natural enough where a patient in imminent danger of death is restored; compare Mark v. 23, of Jairus's daughter (who at this point ἐσχάτως ἔχει): ἵνα σωθῇ καὶ ζήσῃ. Similarly in 4 Kms. viii. 9–10, Hazael inquires of Elisha, εἰ ζήσομαι ἐκ τῆς ἀρρωστίας μου ταύτης; and Elisha replies, ζωῇ ζήσῃ. The point so effectively dramatized is the same as that of Matthew's curt conclusion. In other respects the Matthaean version of the *pericope* of the foreign woman's daughter is less close in form to the Johannine narrative than the Marcan.

A similar pattern is followed in the Matthaean version of the *pericope* of the centurion, and again it ends with the statement that the patient recovered 'at that very moment' (ἐν τῇ ὥρᾳ ἐκείνῃ, which agrees more closely with John's ἐκείνῃ τῇ ὥρᾳ than with Matthew's own conclusion of the companion story, ἀπὸ τῆς ὥρας ἐκείνης). The dialogue, however, here takes a different course, and is expanded with material which Luke gives in other contexts. Luke, on the other hand, has expanded the opening part of the narrative in such a way as to alter the whole picture. In his version the centurion never appears in person; his striking utterance about the authority exercised by one who is himself under authority is merely reported by friends who come to intercede, and it is the friends who on returning find the patient restored to health. The centurion himself, presumably, has been at home all the time, to witness the sudden recovery. Luke's story, in fact, is a different story built round the same dialogue, and it has little contact with the Johannine *pericope*.

In John the *pericope* closes with a sentence to which there is no parallel in either of the Synoptic narratives, in either of their forms—a sentence recording the further result of the healing. Synoptic *pericopae* frequently end with the sequel to the miracle, but this is usually in terms of the effect on spectators—ἐθαμβήθησαν, ἐξεπλήσσοντο, ἐφοβήθησαν, ἐξέστησαν, ἐδόξαζον τὸν θεόν,[2] or again, ἐξῆλθεν ἡ ἀκοὴ αὐτοῦ, or the like[3]— unless the reaction is hostile. In only three cases is there any indication of the effect on the patient, beyond his actual recovery.[4] The sequel in our present

---

[1] See *Interpretation*, pp. 318–19.

[2] Mark i. 27, vii. 37, v. 15, v. 42; Matt. xv. 31; Mark ii. 12.

[3] Mark i. 28; Luke vii. 17.

[4] Mark v. 18, the Gerasene demoniac wished to accompany Jesus; Mark x. 52, Bartimaeus ἠκολούθει αὐτῷ ἐν τῇ ὁδῷ (Luke adds, δοξάζων τὸν θεόν), which,

passage is unparalleled in the gospels: ἐπίστευσεν αὐτὸς καὶ ἡ οἰκία αὐτοῦ ὅλη. But I will defer consideration of this for the moment, while we examine the dialogue between Jesus and the suppliant parent according to John.

It is in form closely parallel to the corresponding dialogue in the Marcan *pericopé* of the Syrophoenician: the parent requests the aid of Jesus for the afflicted child; he demurs; the parent insists, and Jesus says, 'Go; your child is recovering'. In content, however, there is a difference. In Mark the dialogue concerns the propriety of extending the benefit of Christ's work to Gentiles. In John, it has to do with faith, like the dialogue in the *pericopé* of the centurion. To the father's plea Jesus replies, ἐὰν μὴ σημεῖα καὶ τέρατα ἴδητε οὐ μὴ πιστεύσητε. It is to be observed (i) that the verb is in the second person plural, and therefore the saying is not, primarily at least, a judgement upon the man, as is often assumed; (ii) that the combination σημεῖα καὶ τέρατα (=אֹתוֹת וּמֹפְתִים), a phrase out of the Old Testament, though it is common in the Acts and not uncommon in the Epistles, occurs in one context only in the Synoptic Gospels (in the Apocalyptic Discourse, of *false* miracles), and only here in the Fourth Gospel, in which the term σημεῖον by itself has a pregnant meaning; (iii) that elsewhere in John faith is assumed to be the normal sequel to 'seeing signs', without any indication that this ought not to be so; compare ii. 23, iii. 2, ix. 16; although such faith is often imperfect, and needs for its perfection a deeper understanding of the meaning of the σημεῖον.[1] It is those who do 'see signs' and yet do not believe who are reproached, xii. 37.

All this suggests that there is an originally non-Johannine element in the dialogue. The statement, 'You (namely the Palestinian public)[2] will not have faith unless you see signs and prodigies', lies well within the circle of ideas represented in the Synoptic tradition,[3] although the Jewish public are also reproached (as in John) because in spite of being witnesses of δυνάμεις they have not repented.[4] It is noteworthy that in the *pericopé* of

---

however, perhaps does not imply that he became a 'follower' in the specific sense; Luke xvii. 15, the cured leper returned δοξάζων τὸν θεόν. But these do not amount to much.

[1] See *Interpretation*, pp. 300–1, 334–5.

[2] There is no suggestion that the βασιλικός is a Gentile, so that the 'you', in the plural, may well be virtually equivalent to 'Israel' in Matt. viii. 10.

[3] Cf. Matt. xvi. 4, γενεὰ πονηρὰ καὶ μοιχαλὶς σημεῖον ἐπιζητεῖ, Mark ix. 19, ὦ γενεὰ ἄπιστος ἕως πότε... ἀνέξομαι ὑμᾶς;

[4] Matt. xi. 20–4.

the centurion, according to both Matthew and Luke, Jesus complains that he has failed to find such faith as he desires anywhere in Israel—which, though by no means the same thing as the reproach in John iv. 48, reflects the same situation.

On hearing the word of Jesus, 'Go; your son lives', the parent, we are told, ἐπίστευσεν τῷ λόγῳ. In the story of the centurion in Matthew and Luke, and in that of the Canaanite woman in Matthew (though not in the parallel story in Mark, except by implication), the faith of the parent is commended, and is regarded as a condition of the cure; but in each of these instances the faith precedes the healing word of Jesus, which is spoken in response to faith. Further, the sense of πιστεύειν in John iv. 50 is not quite the same as that of πίστις in the Synoptic parallels. As if to make it clear that this is only the most elementary stage of what he would call 'faith', the evangelist says only that the parent 'believed what Jesus said' (compare ii. 22). Faith in a more complete sense comes as a result of the healing, as we are told in iv. 53: ἐπίστευσεν αὐτὸς καὶ ἡ οἰκία αὐτοῦ ὅλη. Even there πιστεύειν has not the full sense which it bears in many passages of this gospel.[1] The nearest analogues to John iv. 53 are to be found in Acts xviii. 8, ἐπίστευσεν τῷ κυρίῳ σὺν ὅλῳ τῷ οἴκῳ αὐτοῦ, xvi. 34, πανοικεὶ πεπιστευκὼς τῷ θεῷ. For the absolute use of πιστεύειν in the sense, 'to accept Christianity', compare also Acts viii. 13, xiii. 12 (both as the result of miracles), xiii. 48, xvii. 12. We seem therefore to have a form of expression coined in the environment of the Gentile mission as it is described in Acts, where the adhesion of a whole family to the Christian faith is regarded as a satisfactory result of the apostolic preaching and of the 'signs and prodigies' which accompanied it. When the word πιστεύειν is used of such household conversions, it can hardly bear exactly either the meaning which πίστις conveys in the Synoptic Gospels, or the more profound meaning which is characteristic of the Fourth Gospel.

To sum up: we have found a series of indications that the narrative of the Nobleman's Son was drawn from a tradition cast in the same mould as traditions behind the Synoptic Gospels, with the usual degree of variation to be observed among the Synoptics themselves. It is very commonly held that this *pericopé* refers to the same incident as that which Matthew and Luke describe in the *pericopé* of the Centurion. The differences are obvious, but there are common features which may be stated as follows: A person holding secular rank, resident at Capernaum, approached Jesus on behalf of his sick boy (=son in John, and so probably in Matthew, but

---

[1] See *Interpretation*, pp. 182–6.

not in Luke), the boy being absent. There ensued a dialogue on the theme of faith, in the course of which Jesus deplored the lack of faith among his public. He then spoke a word assuring the father of his child's recovery. The boy in fact recovered, according to Matthew and John (but not Luke) at (or from) that very moment.[1] It may be that all three evangelists are indeed describing one and the same incident, in different forms which the narrative had assumed in the course of oral transmission, though I should have more hesitation than I formerly had in affirming this view.[2] But if so it is surely manifest that John is not using either of the others as a source. If we compare Luke with Matthew, it is clear that in spite of the substantial differences between them the core of the *pericopé*, the dialogue between Jesus and the centurion, must have come from some common source (unless one of the evangelists copied from the other). There is no such common nucleus in the stories of John on the one hand and the Synoptics on the other. The central interest of the Synoptic narrative lies in the remarkable faith of a Gentile, which leads him to affirm that the bare word of Jesus, even at a distance, will suffice to cure the sick boy, and the dialogue elaborates, not the miraculous power of the word, but the remarkable quality of the centurion's faith, which is justified in the result. In John the central interest lies in the life-giving power of the word of Christ. It is not said that the man was a Gentile; he expects Jesus to come to his house, several miles away, to heal his son, never dreaming of the possibility of an instant cure at a distance; his faith, first awakened by the word of Jesus, becomes effective in the fullest sense only after the event has proved the power of the word; the elaboration of the narrative is wholly devoted to emphasizing this power. Thus treated, the narrative obviously lends itself to the purposes of Johannine theology. But the word of Jesus is no less powerful in the Synoptic stories: Ταλιθὰ κούμ, νεανίσκε ἐγέρθητι, are just as effective as ὁ υἱός σου ζῆ. The ideas present in

[1] Matthew describes an instantaneous cure: ἰάθη ὁ παῖς ἐν τῇ ὥρᾳ ἐκείνῃ. John describes a crisis in the disease at which a reduction of the high temperature indicates a turn for the better (κομψότερον ἔσχεν); it is this sudden fall of temperature, and not the complete cure, that took place instantaneously (ἐκείνῃ τῇ ὥρᾳ).

[2] It is matter for reflection that the Johannine *pericopé* of the Nobleman's Son pairs with the Marcan Syrophoenician Woman rather than with the Matthaean or Lucan Centurion's Boy, so far as form is concerned. In all such cases we have a choice of two possibilities: either a single incident (or dialogue, it may be) has developed different forms in different branches of tradition, or originally distinct incidents have become assimilated by the transference of details in the course of transmission (see above, pp. 169–73). I should not care to choose dogmatically between these alternatives in the present instance.

the Johannine *pericopé* lie, as we have seen, well within the traditional circle. There is no reason to suppose that Johannine theology provided the formative motive. There is every probability that we have here an independent formation within the common oral tradition. In view of the use of the expression σημεῖα καὶ τέρατα, and of the type of language used in Acts to describe household conversions in the course of the Gentile mission, we may suspect that the tradition upon which John here worked received its shape in a similar environment, and may represent a strain of development later than the principal strains of Synoptic tradition.[1]

[1] It is significant that the Synoptic Gospels, although they were written at a time when the Gentile mission was well advanced, never import into the Ministry of Jesus this idea of collective conversion of a family; and this is true of Luke no less than the others, although in Acts the same author refers to such conversions as a well-known phenomenon. The Synoptics, in this respect as in others, preserve the outlook of the primitive tradition of the Ministry, while John, here at least, appears to betray a later stage in its development. But this is the only instance where this particular feature occurs.

3. THE FEEDING OF THE MULTITUDE, AND CONTIGUOUS MATTER

The sixth chapter of the Gospel according to John has for centrepiece a long dialogue upon the theme of Bread of Life, to which the evangelist has appended a note that it took place in the synagogue at Capernaum (vi. 25–59). Two shorter dialogues are added, each with brief introductory and explanatory notes (60–5, 66–71). He has provided a setting for the whole, in which we find parallels to two narratives which are contiguous also in Mark—the Feeding of the Multitude (vi. 1–13) and the Walking on the Sea (16–21). We observe further that the second of the short dialogues (66–71) has some similarity to the Marcan *pericopé* of the Confession at Caesarea Philippi (Mark viii. 27–30), and that in the course of the long dialogue there is a passage (vi. 30) which recalls the Marcan *pericopé* about the demand for a 'sign' (Mark viii. 11–12). In this comparatively short part, therefore, of the Fourth Gospel there is an unusual number of points of contact with Mark, and the parallels are all to be found in Mark vi and viii. In Mark vi the Feeding of the Multitude is immediately followed by the Walking on the Sea, and in Mark viii it is immediately followed by the demand for a 'sign', which in turn, after two intervening *pericopae*, is followed by the Confession at Caesarea Philippi. The question arises, whether this is to be accounted for by John's use of Mark, or whether we are to infer an independent strain of tradition which over this section of the gospel ran parallel to an unusual degree with the tradition behind Mark. It may be observed that if we should be led to the former conclusion it would be without prejudice to the theory of a non-Marcan tradition in other parts of the gospel. This is the only extended part of the Fourth Gospel dealing with the northern or Galilaean activity of Jesus, which bulks most largely in Mark, and there would be no inherent improbability in the view that the evangelist, following in the main a tradition which was little interested in Galilee, turned to Mark for information about this phase of the Ministry.

We may start with the two narrative passages, taking first the shorter and simpler of the two.

(a) The Walking on the Sea (John vi. 16–21, Mark vi. 47–53)

The Johannine *pericopé* is the more succinct, occupying only twelve lines (in Nestle) to Mark's sixteen (or twenty if we include verse 45, which really corresponds with John vi. 16). It has, moreover, more nearly the conventional form of a traditional narrative *pericopé*, with its own opening phrase, ὡς δὲ ὀψία ἐγένετο, and its natural conclusion, whereas the Marcan *pericopé* is interlocked with the preceding narrative, and tails off in editorial comments of the evangelist. It is however doubtful if phrases like ὡς δὲ ὀψία ἐγένετο are ever the true opening of an independent *pericopé*. Everywhere they connect the passage with a preceding account of events earlier in the same day, whether this connection is original (as it probably is in the Passion narrative, Mark xiv. 17, xv. 42, but perhaps not John xx. 19) or supplied by the evangelist in the course of composition.[1] So here, the phrase refers back to the preceding narrative and presupposes a knowledge of the course of events during the day now closing.

If we compare the language of the Marcan and Johannine versions of the story we find that both give the words of Jesus, ἐγώ εἰμι, μὴ φοβεῖσθε, identically, but beyond this the only words in common are those for boat, embark, across, sea, wind, and row, with the indispensable περιπατεῖν ἐπὶ τῆς θαλάσσης, and without these it is difficult to see how the story could be told at all.[2]

The form or pattern of the *pericopé* differs markedly in the two gospels, chiefly because in John the story is told consistently from the point of view of the disciples, while in Mark it is told mainly, though not consistently, from the point of view of Jesus. Mark tells how *Jesus*, left alone on shore, *saw his disciples* labouring at the oar, and about the fourth watch *came* towards them, *wishing* to pass them by; but when they shrank in terror he spoke to them and went aboard. John says that the *disciples*

---

[1] Mark i. 32, ὀψίας δὲ γενομένης ὅτε ἔδυσεν ὁ ἥλιος, introduces a sort of *coda* to the series of events conceived as happening on one sabbath; iv. 35, καὶ λέγει αὐτοῖς ἐν ἐκείνῃ τῇ ἡμέρᾳ ὀψίας γενομένης, links (perhaps artificially) the *pericopé* of the Stilling of the Storm with the teaching by the lake-side; xi. 11 and 19 form the close, not the opening, of a *pericopé*, and belong to a part of the gospel where the passage of time is carefully noted; Matt. xiv. 15, ὀψίας δὲ γενομένης, marks a stage in the development of a situation, not its beginning, as does the καὶ ὀψίας γενομένης of Mark vi. 47 (our present passage).

[2] The apparent parallel of ὡς δὲ ὀψία ἐγένετο (John) and ὀψίας γενομένης (Mark) is no real parallel, since evening comes at different points in the story: in John they embark ὡς ὀψία ἐγένετο, in Mark ὀψίας γενομένης they are already half-way across. Similarly, although both use the verb ἐθέλειν of an apparently unfulfilled intention, in Mark it is the intention of *Jesus* to pass by the boat, in John the intention of the *disciples* to take him aboard. These coincidences therefore amount to nothing. The references just given show how natural, and how frequent, are these allusions to the coming of evening in the gospel narratives, and ἐθέλειν is one of the commonest words.

went down to the sea and embarked, and after rowing about 25–30 stades (the rowers being aware of the distance, the Spectator of the lapse of time) *they saw* Jesus approaching and were terrified. He spoke to them, and *they wished* to take him on board, but the boat reached the shore. The voyage of the disciples is thus complete: at evening they embarked, at the darkest hour the storm broke, 25–30 stades from the point of embarkation they saw Jesus approaching, and finally they reached the shore. In Mark the account of the voyage is less clear, and it has in fact no proper ending, for the phrase διαπεράσαντες ἦλθον ἐπὶ τὴν γῆν is a mere link with the following *pericopé*.

Moreover, the controlling motive of the story differs in the two accounts. In Mark it is essentially a miracle-story, and closes, as miracle-stories do, with an expression of amazement: λίαν ἐκ περισσοῦ ἐν ἑαυτοῖς ἐξίσταντο. In John there is no such comment. It has often been noted that in his version the story *need* not be miraculous at all. The crucial phrase, περιπατοῦντα ἐπὶ τῆς θαλάσσης, in most contexts would naturally mean 'walking *by* the sea', that is on the beach, as ἐπὶ τῆς γῆς in verse 21 means, not 'on land', but 'by' or 'at the land'—'off shore', as we say. Similarly in xxi. 1 ἐπὶ τῆς θαλάσσης almost certainly refers to the appearance of the risen Christ *by* the sea, not to the position of the seven disciples *on* the sea.[1] The story therefore *could* be read in the sense that the disciples had rowed the greater part of the distance across the lake when they saw Jesus walking on the beach (which they were now approaching, though in the darkness and confusion they were not aware of it), and prepared to take him on board, but found that by this time the boat had touched land. Not that this is how John intended it to be read (vi. 25); but it seems clear that the element of sheer miracle is not here the main motive. For that we must look elsewhere. It is surely the Ἐγώ εἰμι that stands out. In the theological interpretation which John has given to the whole passage this formula no doubt carries mysterious significance.[2] But the words themselves are no Johannine interpolation. They occur identically in Mark, and we may fairly take them to be essential to the tradition in any form which it may have assumed. It is the recognition of Jesus, unexpectedly present to his disciples in their need, that is the true centre of the story. We cannot

---

[1] Ἐφανέρωσεν ἑαυτὸν τοῖς μαθηταῖς ἐπὶ τῆς θαλάσσης would naturally mean that the disciples saw *him* on the beach (as the author goes on to relate). If the meaning were that the Lord appeared to the disciples when *they* were on the sea, we should expect τοῖς μαθηταῖς οὖσιν ἐπὶ τῆς θαλάσσης.

[2] See *Interpretation*, pp. 344–5.

but be reminded of the post-resurrection narratives, where the ἀναγνώρισις of the Risen Christ, unexpectedly appearing to his bereaved disciples,
is the invariable point of emphasis. This raises the question, whether this
pericopé, as has been suggested, was in the earliest tradition a post-
resurrection narrative.[1] There is much to be said for the suggestion. It is
certainly very close to the general pattern of such narratives. Moreover,
we have in John xxi an account of an appearance of the Risen Christ to his
disciples ἐπὶ τῆς θαλάσσης, which has some points of contact with our
present passage. As here, so there, they are in trouble on the sea. As here,
so there, Christ is at first unrecognized, and the ἀναγνώρισις is the climax
of the story, the exclamation of the beloved disciple, ὁ κύριός ἐστιν,
corresponding with the ἐγώ εἰμι of our present passage. The Marcan
version has little resemblance to the post-resurrection narratives, or to the
Johannine version of the story of the Walking on the Sea. The difference
of pattern is manifest. So far, then, a theory that the Johannine narrative
is based on the Marcan would find singularly little evidence in its
favour.

But it is necessary to take into account the close relation of this pericopé
with that of the Feeding of the Multitude. As I have noted, in Mark vi the
two narratives are interlocked: verse 45, which records the embarkation
of the disciples, is continued in verse 47, and the intervening verse relates
the dispersal of the crowd and the retirement of Jesus to the mountain,
which is properly the conclusion of the narrative of the Feeding of the
Multitude. In John there is an intervening episode to which we must
presently give attention, and then the first narrative is wound up with the
statement that Jesus retired to the mountain, before the embarkation is
recorded and the second narrative begins. Yet, as we have seen, a connection with the preceding narrative is implied in the phrase, ὡς δὲ ὀψία
ἐγένετο. Here the chances would seem about evenly balanced, that John
has smoothed out the sequence in the process of inserting a fresh detail
(in verse 15) or that Mark has interlocked the narratives to restore continuity after leaving something out. To this question we shall have to recur.

(b) The Feeding of the Multitude (John vi. 1–14, Mark vi. 35–44,
viii. 1–8)

Here we have to take into account two passages in Mark (both reproduced
in Matthew, one only in Luke), both of which alike tell how Jesus fed a

[1] See my article, 'The Appearances of the Risen Christ', in Studies in the Gospels:
Essays in Memory of R. H. Lightfoot, ed. D. E. Nineham (Blackwell, 1955), pp. 23–4.

large number of people on a very small allowance of loaves and fishes. The two differ in many details, but there is so much in common that the view is very widely held that there were two independent versions of the tradition at the pre-canonical stage, of which Mark has followed one in ch. vi and the other in ch. viii. His reasons for the duplication, and the significance which he intended to attach to it, are legitimate subjects for speculation, which does not concern us here; but the existence of two separate forms of tradition for the story of the Feeding of the Multitude is hardly in doubt. The question before us is whether there may have been a third strand of tradition, which John has followed.

In none of the three versions does this narrative fall readily within any ordinary classification of forms. It does not seem to be presented primarily as a miracle-story in the usual sense: in neither of the Marcan versions is there any such comment as 'they were astonished', which commonly marks such a story. Instead, Mark tells us that 'they did not understand' (οὐ συνῆκαν ἐπὶ τοῖς ἄρτοις, Mark vi. 52; compare the whole paragraph, Mark viii. 17–21, which elaborates the theme of their non-comprehension). That is to say, it is the story of a mystery, which calls for some penetration beneath the ostensible facts. Similarly in John it is a σημεῖον, a symbolic act which points beyond itself. True, for John other deeds of Jesus are also 'signs' in the same sense, but in the Synoptics this alone is expressly presented as a mystery. We now observe that in Mark viii the central part of the *pericopé* has a form which strongly recalls that of the account of the sacramental words and actions at the Last Supper, as given both in Mark and in Paul.

1 Cor. xi. 23–5	Mark xiv. 22–4	Mark viii. 6–8
ἔλαβεν ἄρτον	λαβὼν ἄρτον	λαβὼν τοὺς ἑπτὰ ἄρτους
καὶ εὐχαριστήσας	εὐλογήσας	εὐχαριστήσας
ἔκλασεν	ἔκλασεν	ἔκλασεν
	καὶ ἔδωκεν αὐτοῖς	καὶ ἐδίδου τοῖς μαθηταῖς αὐτοῦ
(καὶ εἶπεν κ.τ.λ.)		(ἵνα παρατιθῶσιν κ.τ.λ.)
ὡσαύτως τὸ ποτήριον	καὶ λαβὼν ποτήριον	καὶ εἶχαν ἰχθύδια ὀλίγα
μετὰ τὸ δειπνῆσαι		
	εὐχαριστήσας	καὶ εὐλογήσας αὐτά
(λέγων κ.τ.λ.)	ἔδωκεν αὐτοῖς	εἶπεν καὶ ταῦτα παρατιθέναι
	καὶ ἔπιον ἐξ αὐτοῦ πάντες	καὶ ἔφαγον καὶ ἐχορτάσθησαν

It is pertinent to bear in mind that in early Christian art (from the second century) bread and fish, as well as bread and wine, appear frequently in eucharistic symbolism, and that in the veiled language of the second-century epitaph of Avircius Marcellus at Hierapolis the τροφή of Christians is described as fish, bread and wine:

Πίστις πάντη δὲ προῆγε
καὶ παρέθηκε τροφὴν πάντη, ἰχθὺν ἀπὸ πηγῆς
παμμεγεθῆ, καθαρόν, ὃν ἐδράξατο παρθένος ἁγνή,
καὶ τοῦτον ἐπέδωκε φίλοις ἔσθειν διὰ παντός,
οἶνον χρηστὸν ἔχουσα, κέρασμα διδοῦσα μετ᾽ ἄρτου.[1]

In Mark vi the resemblance to the account of the Last Supper is less close than in Mark viii, but the essential liturgical expressions are there: λαβὼν τοὺς ἄρτους, εὐλόγησεν, κατέκλασεν, ἐδίδου. To John's account we shall come in a moment.

In both of the Marcan *pericopae* the sacramental breaking of bread is introduced by a narrative setting the scene, and a dialogue between Jesus and his disciples. In Mark viii this is all done very briefly, and the dialogue is just sufficient to lead up to the pregnant question, Πόθεν τούτους δυνήσεταί τις ὧδε χορτάσαι ἄρτων ἐπ᾽ ἐρημίας;—which, surely not accidentally, recalls the supply of food to Israel in the wilderness; compare Exod. xvi. 32, where Moses is ordered to store the manna, ἵνα ἴδωσιν τὸν ἄρτον ὃν ἐφάγετε ὑμεῖς ἐν τῇ ἐρήμῳ. In Mark vi this introductory matter is given in a greatly extended form, with much added detail, not strictly necessary to the main intention of the passage, but serving to give it force and liveliness. To this extent the classification of this *pericopé* (though not of its doublet in ch. viii) among the *Novellen* or 'tales' is justified. Yet it is a 'tale' embracing what we may fairly call a liturgical recital.

In John vi the form of the *pericopé* stands somewhere between the fulness and elaboration of Mark vi and the relative conciseness of Mark viii (see Table 7). The setting of the scene follows neither Marcan passage closely, but has some resemblance (which we must consider later) to the Matthaean version of the second feeding *pericopé* (Matt. xv. 29–39). But the properly comparable portion of these *pericopae* begins in all cases with the dialogue. In John the dialogue is initiated by Jesus, as in Mark viii, and not by the disciples, as in Mark vi. But as in Mark vi, and not in Mark viii, the disciples (in John, one of the disciples) estimate the cost of feeding the crowd at 200 denarii. The question, what provisions are actually in hand, which occurs in both Mark vi and Mark viii, and is answered by the disciples, is not asked in John, but one of the disciples volunteers the information. As in Mark vi, there are five loaves and two fishes, and not

[1] The text given after C. K. Kaufmann, *Handbuch der altchristlichen Epigraphik*, p. 171.

Table 7. *Feeding of the Multitude*

	Mark viii. 1–8	John vi. 1–14	Mark vi. 31–44
Setting	There was a great crowd with nothing to eat	He crossed the Sea of Galilee; a crowd followed; he went with his disciples εἰς τὸ ὄρος.	They went by boat εἰς ἔρημον τόπον. Many assembled and προῆλθον αὐτούς Jesus ἐσπλαγχνίσθη ἐπ' αὐτούς and taught
Dialogue	Jesus began: σπλαγχ-νίζομαι ἐπὶ τὸν ὄχλον κ.τ.λ.	Jesus began: πόθεν ἀγοράσωμεν ἄρτους ἵνα φάγωσιν οὗτοι;	The disciples began: ἔρημος ὁ τόπος: send them away. Jesus: δότε αὐτοῖς ὑμεῖς φαγεῖν
	Disciples: πόθεν τούτους δυνήσεταί τις ὧδε χορτάσαι; Jesus: πόσους ἔχετε ἄρτους; Disciples: ἑπτά [Matthew + καὶ ὀλίγα ἰχθύδια]	Philip: διακοσίων δηναρίων ἄρτοι οὐκ ἀρκοῦσιν Andrew: a boy has πέντε ἄρτους καὶ δύο ὀψάρια	Disciples: ἀγορά-σωμεν δηναρίων δια-κοσίων ἄρτους κ.τ.λ. Jesus: πόσους ἔχετε ἄρτους; Disciples: πέντε καὶ δύο ἰχθύας [Luke + there were 5000 ἄνδρες]
	Jesus παραγγέλλει ἀναπεσεῖν	Jesus: ποιήσατε τοὺς ἀνθρώπους ἀνα-πεσεῖν They sat down, about 5000 ἄνδρες	Jesus ἐπέταξεν αὐτοῖς ἀνακλιθῆ-ναι κ.τ.λ.
The sacra-mental acts	λαβὼν τοὺς ἑπτὰ ἄρτους [Matthew + καὶ τοὺς ἰχθύας] εὐχαριστήσας ἔκλασεν καὶ ἐδίδου τοῖς μαθηταῖς αὐτοῦ ἵνα παρατιθῶσιν καὶ παρέθηκαν τῷ ὄχλῳ καὶ εἶχαν ἰχθύδια ὀλίγα καὶ εὐλογήσας αὐτὰ εἶπεν καὶ ταῦτα παρατιθέναι καὶ ἔφαγον καὶ ἐχορτάσθησαν	ἔλαβεν οὖν τοὺς ἄρτους καὶ εὐχαριστήσας διέδωκεν τοῖς ἀνακειμένοις ὁμοίως καὶ ἐκ τῶν ὀψαρίων ὅσον ἤθελον [cf. ἐφάγετε ἐκ τῶν ἄρτων καὶ ἐχορ-τάσθητε, vi. 26]	λαβὼν τοὺς πέντε ἄρτους καὶ τοὺς δύο ἰχθύας εὐλόγησεν καὶ κατέ-κλασεν τοὺς ἄρτους καὶ ἐδίδου τοῖς μαθη-ταῖς ἵνα παρατιθῶσιν αὐτοῖς καὶ τοὺς δύο ἰχθύας ἐμέρισεν πᾶσιν καὶ ἔφαγον πάντες καὶ ἐχορτάσθησαν

Table 7. *Feeding of the Multitude (continued)*

The sequel		ὡς ἐνεπλήσθησαν, Jesus said: συναγά-γετε τὰ περισσεύ-σαντα κλάσματα κ.τ.λ.	
	ἦραν περισσεύματα κλασμάτων ἑπτὰ σπυρίδας	They filled 12 κόφινοι with κλάσματα left over from the loaves	ἦραν κλασμάτων δώδεκα κοφίνων πληρώματα καὶ ἀπὸ τῶν ἰχθύων
Appended notes	There were about 4000 ἄνδρες [Matthew + χωρὶς γυναι-κῶν καὶ παιδίων]	(cf. *supra*, ἄνδρες ὡς πεντακισχίλιοι)	There were 5000 ἄνδρες [Matthew + χωρὶς γυναικῶν καὶ παιδίων]
		They said, οὗτός ἐστιν ἀληθῶς ὁ προφήτης ὁ ἐρχόμενος	

seven loaves and 'a few' fishes, as in Mark viii; but while in Mark the fishes are ἰχθύες or ἰχθύδια, in John they are ὀψάρια, and according to him they were provided by a boy (παιδάριον) who is unknown to Mark. John's ποιήσατε τοὺς ἀνθρώπους ἀναπεσεῖν resembles the wording of Mark viii. 6, παραγγέλλει τῷ ὄχλῳ ἀναπεσεῖν, more closely than that of Mark vi. 39, ἐπέταξεν αὐτοῖς ἀνακλιθῆναι, but it is in Mark vi and John alone that we learn that it was a grassy spot (ἦν δὲ χόρτος πολὺς ἐν τῷ τόπῳ, John vi. 10; ἐπὶ τῷ χλωρῷ χόρτῳ, Mark vi. 39). At this point John introduces his estimate of the number of participants, which in both the Marcan *pericopae* is placed at the end, though Luke, in the parallel to Mark vi, brings it in as an explanatory note on the dialogue (Luke ix. 14). John's estimate of five thousand males agrees with that of Mark vi against the four thousand (the masculine numeral) of Mark viii.

We now come to the sacramental acts which in all our accounts form the core of the narrative. Here John uses the terms λαβεῖν, διαδιδόναι (for διδόναι of both Marcan accounts), and εὐχαριστεῖν, which in Mark viii (as in Mark xiv) alternates with εὐλογεῖν, Mark vi having εὐλογεῖν only. Rather surprisingly, John omits the term for 'breaking' the bread, ἔκλασεν in Mark viii. 6, κατέκλασεν in Mark vi. 41. Yet he has κλάσματα, which in both Marcan accounts stands for the broken pieces of bread, and which in the *Didaché* (ix. 3–4) is a technical term for the broken bread of the

Eucharist. In John, as in Mark vi, there is no separate blessing, or thanks-giving, over the fish, as there is in Mark viii. John's expression, ὁμοίως ἐκ τῶν ὀψαρίων ὅσον ἤθελον, corresponds functionally with Mark's καὶ τοὺς δύο ἰχθύας ἐμέρισεν[1] πᾶσιν, without any resemblance in language. The conclusion of the meal, which in both Marcan *pericopae* reads, ἔφαγον καὶ ἐχορτάσθησαν, is missing in John, who has a different conclusion; but that he was acquainted with the Marcan conclusion, or one like it, is proved by the back-reference to the narrative in John vi. 26, where Jesus says to the people, ἐφάγετε ἐκ τῶν ἄρτων καὶ ἐχορτάσθητε.

At this point both of the Marcan *pericopae* add, in continuation of the same sentence, that an astonishingly large quantity of broken pieces was gathered up after the meal: in Mark vi. 43, δώδεκα κόφινοι; in Mark viii. 8, ἑπτὰ σπυρίδες. John here departs from the common pattern of narrative. The satisfaction of the people's hunger is relegated to a subordinate clause, ὡς δὲ ἐνεπλήσθησαν,[2] and the main sentence introduces a command of Jesus: λέγει τοῖς μαθηταῖς αὐτοῦ, Συναγάγετε τὰ περισσεύσαντα κλάσματα ἵνα μή τι ἀπόληται. The collection is made, and yields enough to fill twelve κόφινοι, as in Mark vi. 43, though the expressions, τὰ περισσεύσαντα κλάσματα, δώδεκα κοφίνους κλασμάτων ἃ ἐπερίσσευσαν, resemble that of

---

[1] Cf. Luke xxii. 17, λάβετε τοῦτο καὶ διαμερίσατε εἰς ἑαυτούς (of the ποτήριον).

[2] The verb ἐμπίμπλασθαι is not elsewhere found in the Fourth Gospel. We should therefore be chary of assuming that the variation from the Synoptic χορτάζ-εσθαι is due simply to rewriting by the evangelist. In the LXX χορτάζεσθαι and ἐμπίμπλασθαι are alternative renderings of forms of the root שׂבע. Thus, in Isa. xliv. 16, אָכַל...וְיִשְׂבָּע is rendered ἔφαγεν καὶ ἐνεπλήσθη, while in Ps. lxxx (lxxxi). 17 אַשְׂבִּיעֶךָ...יַאֲכִילֵהוּ becomes ἐψώμισεν...ἐχόρτασεν. The divine promise of future blessings in Ps. xxxvi (xxxvii). 19, בִּימֵי רְעָבוֹן יִשְׂבָּעוּ, is rendered, ἐν ἡμέραις λιμοῦ χορτασθήσονται, in Ps. cxxxi (cxxxii). 15, אֶבְיוֹנֶיהָ אַשְׂבִּיעַ לֶחֶם, τοὺς πτωχοὺς αὐτῆς χορτάσω ἄρτους, but in Joel ii. 26, וַאֲכַלְתֶּם אָכוֹל וְשָׂבוֹעַ, the LXX has φάγεσθε ἐσθίοντες καὶ ἐμπλησθήσεσθε. These promises are echoed in the Beatitudes, where Matthew and Luke give χορτασθήσονται, χορτασθήσεσθε. Accordingly, in the Synoptic accounts of the Feeding of the Multitude, conceived as a piece of prophetic symbolism signifying the fulfilment of such promises, χορ-τασθῆναι is used. But it is noteworthy that in the liturgy of the *Didaché*, where the κλάσμα and ποτήριον are sacramental symbols of the πνευματικὴ τροφή τε καὶ ποτὸς καὶ ζωὴ αἰώνιος given through Christ, we have μετὰ τὸ ἐμπλησθῆναι οὕτως εὐχαριστήσατε (x. 1). There are other points of contact between the prayers of the *Didaché* and the Fourth Gospel (see my article, 'Eucharistic Symbolism in the Fourth Gospel', in *Expositor*, 8th series, vol. II (1911), pp. 530–46). Thus it is probable that this ἅπαξ λεγόμενον in the gospel goes back to a liturgical tradition different from that which lies behind the Synoptics, the different choice of verbs going back originally to variant translations of Old Testament *testimonia*.

Mark viii. 8, περισσεύματα κλασμάτων ἑπτὰ σπυρίδας, more closely than anything in Mark vi.

The significance of this departure from the common pattern at the close of the *pericopé* we must consider later. For the present we may survey again the complex relations of likeness and difference between the Johannine account and the two Marcan *pericopae*. Where the Marcan versions diverge, it resembles Mark vi in the main, but there are curious agreements with Mark viii against Mark vi. The most significant of these is the use of the term εὐχαριστεῖν in place of εὐλογεῖν. In Mark vi. 41 εὐλόγησεν represents the Hebrew בֵּרַךְ, and means 'said the Blessing' (the implied object of the verb being 'God'). In Mark viii. 7 the same word is used, but with ἰχθύδια (represented by αὐτά) as direct object, involving a shift in meaning. But in this context, with reference to the bread, we have εὐχαριστήσας, intransitive, in the sense 'gave thanks'—to God, of course, by implication, but the verb is used absolutely. This is a Hellenistic usage, without biblical background,[1] which early established itself in Christian liturgical language: it is found both in 1 Cor. xi. 24 and repeatedly in *Didaché* ix–x. It is this verb alone which occurs in John, and it is noteworthy that in referring back to the incident he uses the expression, which might almost serve as caption to this *pericopé*, ἔφαγον τὸν ἄρτον εὐχαριστήσαντος τοῦ κυρίου (John vi. 23).[2] The emphatic use of this term makes the link with the liturgical tradition at least as clear as it is in Mark viii, although otherwise sacramental language is less prominent even than in Mark vi, since the verb κλάσαι is absent.

If we are to account for the Johannine version by literary derivation from Mark, it appears that we must assume that *both* Marcan *pericopae* were laid under contribution, either by deliberate conflation or because our evangelist, while following Mark vi in the main, was haunted by memories of Mark viii. But we have still to inquire whether there are any departures from the two Marcan models, by way of omission, addition, or modification, for which it would be natural to infer a source other than Mark.

We have already noted that the absence of the phrase ἔφαγον καὶ ἐχορτάσθησαν, which is present in both Marcan *pericopae*, may be discounted because there is a clear reminiscence of it (whether derived

---

[1] On εὐχαριστεῖν see W. L. Knox, *Some Hellenistic Elements in Primitive Christianity*, pp. 3–5.

[2] The words εὐχαριστήσαντος τοῦ κυρίου are omitted by D, Syrsin and some other authorities, and may possibly be a gloss; if so, an editor is emphasizing a feature already prominent in the original text.

directly from Mark or from a similar source) in the ἐφάγετε ἐκ τῶν ἄρτων καὶ ἐχορτάσθητε of vi. 26. Rather more significant, perhaps, is the absence from the story of any reference to the 'wilderness' (ἔρημος τόπος, Mark vi. 31, 32, 35, ἐρημία, Mark viii. 5). This certainly is strange, since, as we have seen, there is already in Mark a probable oblique reference to the supply of manna ἐν τῇ ἐρήμῳ, and John makes this reference explicit in the discourse which follows the narrative, vi. 31. If the source he was following already indicated that the Feeding of the Multitude took place in the 'wilderness', we should hardly have expected him to leave out such a valuable pointer to the meaning he wished to attach to the incident.

Over against these 'omissions' we may set certain supplementary details. Where Mark speaks of the disciples as a body, John assigns their interposition in the dialogue to individual speakers, Philip and Andrew. This individualizing of actors in a story is often, though not always, a sign of 'legendary' development. The same may be said of the παιδάριον who so opportunely provides loaves and fishes.

Again, the description of the loaves as κρίθινοι (twice over, vi. 9, 13) is peculiar to John. This feature is widely, and probably rightly, regarded as a reminiscence of 4 Kms. iv. 42–4, where we are told how Elisha fed a considerable number of men on a seemingly inadequate supply of bread. The *pericopé* is worth quoting at length.

Καὶ ἀνὴρ διῆλθεν ἐκ Βαιθσαρεισὰ καὶ ἤνεγκεν πρὸς τὸν ἄνθρωπον τοῦ θεοῦ πρωτογενημάτων εἴκοσι ἄρτους κριθίνους καὶ παλάθας· καὶ εἶπεν, Δότε τῷ λαῷ καὶ ἐσθιέτωσαν. καὶ εἶπεν ὁ λειτουργὸς αὐτοῦ, Τί; δῶ τοῦτο ἐνώπιον ἑκατὸν ἀνδρῶν; καὶ εἶπεν, Δὸς τῷ λαῷ καὶ ἐσθιέτωσαν, ὅτι τάδε λέγει Κύριος, Φάγονται καὶ καταλείψουσιν[1] · καὶ ἔφαγον καὶ κατέλιπον[1] κατὰ τὸ ῥῆμα Κυρίου.

If this passage served in any sense as a model for the evangelists, it must be supposed to have been in the minds of all four; or, more probably, to have contributed to the formation of the primitive tradition which in variant strains lies behind the two Marcan *pericopae*. If so, we have to ask whether there is anything in what we know of the Fourth Evangelist's interests and intentions to explain why he alone should have introduced, into a story hypothetically borrowed from Mark, the detail that the loaves were made of barley. The answer, I think, is that there is nothing. It

[1] Καταλείψουσιν = הוֹתַר, κατέλιπον = יוֹתִרוּ. Words from √ יתר are elsewhere rendered by περισσεύειν, περισσός. In the gospels περισσεύειν, περίσσευμα are used of the surplus bread. If the story of Elisha and the barley loaves was in the minds of those who framed the tradition, it was either the Hebrew original or a non-septuagintal Greek version that they followed, and this has penetrated into all four gospels.

seems therefore, so far, more likely that this was a feature in one strain of tradition: that, namely, which was followed by John in distinction from the other three.

Of greater significance is John's departure from the Synoptic pattern at the close of the *pericopé*. The two Marcan *pericopae* bring the story to its natural conclusion with the statement 'they ate and were satisfied and took up (so many) basketfuls of pieces' (as the story in 4 Kingdoms ends with ἔφαγον καὶ κατέλιπον). John, as we have seen, makes a fresh departure with a formal command of Jesus to gather up the surplus pieces, ἵνα μή τι ἀπόληται. The principle that no food should be wasted is frequently enunciated in Rabbinic sources (see S.–B. *ad loc.*); but we have here, it seems, something more. In verse 27 βρῶσις ἀπολλυμένη is contrasted with βρῶσις μένουσα εἰς ζωὴν αἰώνιον, and it is this 'abiding' bread that Christ supplies. It appears, therefore, that the pieces which are to be collected symbolize the bread which 'abides' and is not 'lost'. They do indeed fittingly represent βρῶσις μένουσα, for although the people have been fed and satisfied, the bread remains—more of it than before. It is probable therefore that for John the collection of the large quantity of surplus bread is an *additional* 'sign', and no mere corroboration of the miracle.[1] If so, we may take it that he has rehandled his material in the interest of his own theological ideas, substituting this pregnant conclusion for the ending which, as we have seen, probably stood in his source, whether this source was Mark or an independent tradition.

So far, then, John's departures from Mark might at a pinch be accounted for without postulating any source other than the two Marcan passages,

[1] A more widely held view is that the gathering of the κλάσματα symbolizes the gathering of Christ's people into the unity of the Church, cf. John xvii. 11–12, ἵνα ὦσιν ἕν...οὐδεὶς ἐξ αὐτῶν ἀπώλετο. This may find support from the prayer of the *Didaché* περὶ τοῦ κλάσματος, ix. 4: ὥσπερ ἦν τοῦτο τὸ κλάσμα διεσκορπισμένον ἐπάνω τῶν ὀρέων καὶ συναχθὲν ἐγένετο ἕν, οὕτω συναχθήτω σου ἡ ἐκκλησία ἀπὸ τῶν περάτων τῆς γῆς εἰς τὴν σὴν βασιλείαν. This is attractive, especially in view of the evident contacts between the Fourth Gospel and the liturgy of the *Didaché*. But the idea of unity is not present in John vi. 12–13: the κλάσματα remain distributed over twelve baskets (? one for each apostle)—a singularly infelicitous symbol for the unity of the Church. Further, in the *Didaché* the many grains of corn have been brought together into one κλάσμα, of which the communicants partake in common; in John, *after* the people's communion a vast number of κλάσματα remain as surplus. The symbolism takes a totally different line from that of the *Didaché*. For this reason I prefer the interpretation offered above, in which I follow the guidance of D. Daube, *The New Testament and Rabbinic Judaism*, pp. 36–46 (without necessarily accepting his conclusion 'that John knew the Synoptic version and that his own is a development from it').

the alteration of the conclusion being due to theological motives, the introduction of Philip, Andrew and the παιδάριον to our author's known *penchant* for individual characters in his stories, and the detail of the *barley* loaves to a reminiscence of 4 Kms. iv. 43–4 which may have occurred to him in rewriting the narrative. Yet this latter feature, as we have seen, may carry a different implication, and there are other points which slightly tell in favour of a theory of John's independence of Mark.

But we have not yet taken account of the introduction to the story, which varies considerably in the several versions. In Mark viii there is no introduction; nothing but a setting of the scene in the fewest words possible: ἐν ἐκείναις ταῖς ἡμέραις πάλιν πολλοῦ ὄχλου ὄντος καὶ μὴ ἐχόντων τί φάγωσιν—and with that the dialogue begins, and leads directly to the account of the meal. In Mark vi, on the other hand, we have an unusually long and circumstantial narrative, which explains how it was that Jesus and his disciples were in the 'wilderness' (he had tried to secure privacy by a retreat over the lake), and how nevertheless it came about that he was attended by a vast crowd (they had discovered his destination and forestalled him); which, again, explains the awkward situation of the disciples confronted with a hungry mass of people without resources for supplying them with food: it was because Jesus had been teaching them at great length (διδάσκειν αὐτοὺς πολλά) and the hour grew late. Only then does the *pericopé* proper begin, as in Mark viii, with the dialogue. This circumstantial narrative is reproduced, in somewhat shorter forms, by Matthew and Luke in the parallel contexts; but in Matt. xv, which in the actual story of the meal follows Mark viii closely, we have an entirely different introduction: Jesus went to the shore of the Sea of Galilee (not sailing over it, as in Mark), and thence went up εἰς τὸ ὄρος, and there healed the sick (not teaching the people, as in Mark). Thereupon the *pericopé* of the Feeding begins abruptly with the dialogue between Jesus and his disciples, and from this point Matthew reproduces Mark viii almost *verbatim*.

In John the *pericopé* is introduced by a passage which has some slight points of contact with Mark vi, but resembles Matthew xv much more closely. The relations of the three passages may be set forth as follows.

Matt. xv. 29–31	John vi. 1–5	Mark vi. 32–4
1. ὁ Ἰησοῦς ἦλθεν παρὰ τὴν θάλασσαν τῆς Γαλιλαίας	1. ἀπῆλθεν ὁ Ἰησοῦς πέραν τῆς θαλάσσης τῆς Γαλιλαίας	1. (ἀπῆλθον ἐν τῷ πλοίῳ εἰς ἔρημον τόπον)

3. καὶ προσῆλθον αὐτῷ ὄχλοι πολλοὶ καὶ ἐθεράπευσεν αὐτούς	2. ἠκολούθει δὲ αὐτῷ ὄχλος πολύς, ὅτι ἐθεώρουν τὰ σημεῖα ἃ ἐποίει ἐπὶ τῶν ἀσθενούντων	2. (συνέδραμον ἐκεῖ καὶ προῆλθον αὐτούς)
2. καὶ ἀναβὰς εἰς τὸ ὄρος ἐκάθητο ἐκεῖ	3. ἀνῆλθεν εἰς τὸ ὄρος Ἰησοῦς καὶ ἐκεῖ ἐκάθητο	
	4. θεασάμενος ὅτι πολὺς ὄχλος ἔρχεται πρὸς αὐτόν	4. εἶδεν πολὺν ὄχλον

It is surely clear that if John had any Synoptic model here it was not Mark but Matthew. Apart from one striking verbal agreement, we note that in John and in Matt. xv the scene is laid on τὸ ὄρος (whether this means a particular hill or the hill-country in general), which neither Marcan *pericopé* mentions; and that in John and Matt. xv alike the incident is associated with a ministry of healing, whereas neither says anything of the teaching of the people to which Mark refers. Then should we revise our hypothesis and say that the Johannine account is drawn from the two Matthaean passages rather than from the Marcan? In that case we should still have 200 denarii on our hands, for in neither place does Matthew offer any estimate of the cost of feeding the party. We should therefore have to postulate the use of both Matthew and Mark as sources. This I find incredible as an account of our evangelist's method of composition. It is a more plausible hypothesis that these features of the tradition—the resort to, or over, the Sea of Galilee, the concourse of the crowd, the ascent of τὸ ὄρος, mass-healings—all of them features which crop up throughout the gospels in various connections,[1] were combined in a partly similar way both in a tradition known to Matthew and in a different strand of tradition lying behind John.[2]

We next inquire whether there are in John vi. 1–5 any peculiar features which may be thought to have been derived from such an independent tradition. The first feature to be noted is that John alone states explicitly that the Feeding of the Multitude took place πέραν τῆς θαλάσσης τῆς Γαλιλαίας. It is true that in the context of Mark viii the locality last mentioned is the Decapolis (vii. 31), whose constituent towns were mostly on the east side of the lake, from which a reader might infer (precariously) that the assembly of the four thousand also took place in that region. In

---

[1] Cf. *Interpretation*, p. 333.
[2] For the 'wanderings' of features and details in the tradition, see above, pp. 169–73, 194.

the context of Matt. xv, we are told of a journey from the territory of Tyre and Sidon, παρὰ τὴν θάλασσαν τῆς Γαλιλαίας εἰς τὸ ὄρος, with nothing at all to indicate which shore of the lake is intended. In Mark vi the geography is confused. We are not told what was the starting point (in vi. 32), nor, although the journey to the place where the five thousand assembled was made τῷ πλοίῳ are we told the direction of the voyage. After the meal, the disciples are sent εἰς τὸ πέραν πρὸς Βηθσαιδά—eastward, that is;[1] nevertheless, they arrive in Gennesaret, to the west. It would be an unsafe inference that the Feeding of the Multitude took place on the east side. But in any case I do not believe that our evangelist was the man to make these intricate combinations. The setting πέραν τῆς θαλάσσης is not part of our *pericopé* in any of its Synoptic forms. Nor does it seem likely that the Fourth Evangelist introduced it on his own account. It has no theological significance,[2] nor does it fit in well with any topographical scheme of his own; indeed, it fits so ill that to save his consistency (as they suppose) commentators have felt obliged to make drastic rearrangements.[3] It therefore seems most probable that the tradition known to John contained the topographical datum.

Did it also contain the chronological datum, ἦν δὲ ἐγγὺς τὸ πάσχα (vi. 4)? It is likely enough that John intended to suggest the connection between Passover, 'the feast of the Jews', and the Christian Eucharist, which is typified by the Feeding of the Multitude.[4] Yet he has in no way exploited paschal symbolism in the discourse which follows: the type of the Bread of Life is the manna ἐν τῇ ἐρήμῳ (Passover, unlike Tabernacles, was not a 'wilderness' celebration). This contrasts with the use made of the symbolism of the Feast of Tabernacles in vii–viii.[5] Where reference is made to the Encaenia (Ḥanukka) in x. 22 commentators have failed to find any convincing allusion to the symbolism of the feast in the discourse which follows. As for the other references to Passover, in the Passion narrative it is an original datum of the tradition, while the supposed

[1] There appears to be no solid basis for the view that there was another Bethsaida on the western side, although indeed 'Fisherton' is a name that might conceivably have been duplicated.

[2] It is widely held that the Marcan duplication of the story has a theological motive: the first Feeding is on the western side, in Jewish territory, the second on the eastern side, among Gentiles: 'To the Jew first and also to the Greek.' It may be so (though it might have been more convincing if Mark had made his geography more comprehensible); if so, it is the more remarkable that in John, the most theological of the gospels, there is no possible suggestion of anything of the kind.

[3] See *Interpretation*, p. 340.   [4] See *op. cit.*, p. 333.

[5] See *op. cit.*, pp. 348–51.

'first Passover' of ii. 13, at which the temple was cleansed, is (as I have argued) almost certainly the Passover of the Passion, the position of the *pericopé* of the Cleansing being due to the order in which the evangelist wished to present his great argument.[1] While therefore the introduction of Tabernacles in vii *might* be due entirely to theological considerations,[2] there is no other reference to a feast (unless the present passage be one) of which this can be shown to be true. On the other hand, it is entirely in our author's manner to find in a genuinely traditional datum a hidden symbolic value. I conclude that there is no solid objection to accepting the note of time as well as the note of place as a feature of the independent strain of tradition with which John worked, though it cannot of course be proved that it was such. As for general probability, the season round about Passover is a time when grass is plentiful,[3] as John says it was, and might be 'green' as Mark says it was.

So far we have arrived at the conclusion that, of the two companion narratives with which we are concerned, there is a high degree of probability that the narrative of the Walking on the Sea rests upon a tradition independent of the Synoptics, and a somewhat less strong, but still substantial, probability that the narrative of the Feeding of the Multitude is not a conflation of Matt. xv. 29–31, Mark viii. 1–10, and Mark vi. 34–44 (all of which must have been laid under contribution if John be supposed to have borrowed the narrative from the Synoptics), but again based on independent tradition. We must now raise the further question, whether the *collocation* of the two narratives has a traditional basis, or whether John was dependent on Mark, after all, if not for the whole of his material in the two narratives, at least for their connection; for the third possibility, that the two writers stumbled by sheer accident upon the same sequence, need not be seriously entertained.[4]

[1] See above, pp. 160–2, and cf. *Interpretation*, pp. 384–5, 448.

[2] But see below, pp. 241, 322–4.

[3] 'Towards the end of October heavy rains begin to fall, at intervals, for a day or several days at a time.... Till the end of November the average rainfall is not large, but it increases through December, January and February, begins to abate in March, and is practically over by the middle of April.... In May showers are rare, and from then till October, not only is there no rain, but a cloud seldom passes over the sky' (G. A. Smith, *Historical Geography of the Holy Land*, pp. 64–5). It would appear therefore that March would be the best season for abundant grass, and that green grass would be rarer from the end of April.

[4] Bultmann *ad loc.* regards both narratives as drawn from a source in which they were already associated; the source is not Mark: 'vor allem zeigt sich das eben in der Geschichte des Seewandelns. Diese bekundet in Joh. insofern ein früheres Stadium der Tradition...'.

(c) Relation of the Feeding of the Multitude and the Walking on the Sea

We note first that in each of the Marcan *pericopae* the Feeding of the Multitude is followed by a voyage across the lake. In Mark vi. 45 (as we have seen) the disciples set out for Bethsaida, on the eastern side, but arrive (vi. 53) at Gennesaret, on the western side. The probability is that the name Bethsaida belongs to the *pericopé* of the Feeding,[1] and that the phrase διαπεράσαντες ἐπὶ τὴν γῆν ἦλθον εἰς Γεννησαρέτ, which introduces a typical *Sammelbericht*, owes its position to the editorial work of the evangelist. In Mark viii. 10, again, the reference to a voyage is almost certainly the conclusion of the *pericopé* of the Feeding, and not a part of the 'framework'. The reference to another voyage εἰς τὸ πέραν, almost immediately afterwards, is no doubt the result of editing, and does not help to determine the direction of the voyage of viii. 10. Its destination is concealed in the *vox nihili* δαλμανουθα,[2] and remains for ever unknown, unless we are prepared to accept one or other of the intelligent conjectures which appear in MSS. of Mark viii. 10 and Matt. xv. 39.

It is indeed only in the earlier of the two Marcan narratives that the voyage following the Feeding of the Multitude is associated with the Walking on the Sea; yet it is scarcely doubtful that in each of the underlying forms of tradition the incident ended with a departure from the scene by boat. The hypothesis is by no means unreasonable, that a third form of tradition (such as I have postulated) also contained the same sequence.

We now examine the ways in which the narrative of the voyage is linked to that of the Feeding of the Multitude in Mark and John respectively. In Mark viii. 10 we have the bare notice, 'He dismissed the crowd and forthwith going aboard the boat went to the parts of †Dalmanutha†'. Mark vi is somewhat more informative. Immediately after the meal Jesus

---

[1] In Luke ix. 10 the scene of the Feeding of the Multitude is 'a city called Bethsaida', not an ἔρημος τόπος. This, however, is doubtfully consistent with verse 12, where it is proposed that the crowd shall find 'board and lodging' (ἵνα καταλύσωσιν καὶ εὕρωσιν ἐπισιτισμόν) in the surrounding villages. Yet it may preserve a reminiscence of the eastern setting of the scene.

[2] Of modern conjectures the most attractive is that based upon the fact that in some forms of Aramaic לְמִנְוָתְהָא = εἰς τὰ μέρη. The text therefore might represent לְמִנְוָתְהָא דִּלְמִנְוָתְהָא, where a dittograph has displaced the place-name. But the hypotheses required to account for such a corruption are precarious, and I believe Aramaists do not now favour it.

compelled his disciples (ἠνάγκασεν, as if they were reluctant) to precede him across to Bethsaida, while he dismissed the crowd. He then went up εἰς τὸ ὄρος to pray. The next thing we hear is that he saw them in difficulties from wind and sea, and towards morning (περὶ τετάρτην φυλακὴν τῆς νυκτός) set out to join them. There are several questions we should wish to ask. Why this haste in despatching the disciples, all unwilling, across the lake? Why did Jesus separate himself from them before inducing the crowd to disperse, and after doing so retire to the mountain alone? But questions of this kind are rarely answered in the gospels, which characteristically ignore our modern curiosity about motives and keep to observed facts.

From John, however, we learn a little more. First, the effect of the miracle upon the crowd is noted. As we have seen, Mark gives no indication of the effect, beyond saying that the disciples οὐ συνῆκαν ἐπὶ τοῖς ἄρτοις (vi. 52), and this is clearly no part of the *pericopé* as drawn from tradition. According to John the people now commented, οὗτός ἐστιν ἀληθῶς ὁ προφήτης ὁ ἐρχόμενος εἰς τὸν κόσμον (vi. 14). It appears from Acts iii. 22–3, vii. 37, that there was in primitive Christian thought a strain which found a 'testimony' to the messianic status of Jesus in the promise of a prophet like Moses (Deut. xviii. 15). This is faintly hinted at in the Synoptic Gospels (Mark ix. 7 and parallels). In our present passage it seems clear that the 'coming prophet' is the prophet like Moses, for the people who have hailed Jesus as such are said to have cited the precedent of the gift of manna (vi. 31–2). We are to understand that it was the marvellous supply of food to the hungry multitude that suggested the idea to them. That the advent of a prophet figured in popular expectation at the time we have sufficient, though not copious, evidence. There is therefore no reason why the statement that the crowd hailed Jesus as the coming prophet may not have stood in the primitive tradition. That in face of such public acclamation Jesus should wish to withdraw himself would be entirely consistent with many indications in the Synoptic Gospels. In general, John takes little or no account of the doctrine of the 'messianic secret' which dominates Mark, but here the motive of avoiding public messianic demonstrations crops up in an entirely plausible context, and one, be it observed, where Mark has no reference to it.

According to John, the people who acclaimed Jesus as the coming prophet were prepared to back their opinion with action: they would seize him by force and make him king. There is no hint of anything of the kind in the other gospels. It does, however, offer a plausible answer to the questions which, as we saw, the Marcan narrative leaves in the reader's mind. Why did Jesus take urgent steps to separate his disciples from the crowd? Because there was danger that they might be swept into a movement of popular revolt. Why were they reluctant, so that he had to 'compel' them to embark? Because they were all too ready to be carried away by popular enthusiasm. Why did he, after making sure that the crowd dispersed, retire into the hills? To frustrate any further attempt to force his hand. Whether therefore it is historically veracious or not, John's account has dramatic verisimilitude. Further, it fits perfectly what we know of the situation in Palestine, and the popular mood, about the time. Under the procurator Cuspius Fadus (c. A.D. 43–4) a γόης named Theudas attempted a rising, προφήτης γὰρ ἔλεγεν εἶναι, promising to divide Jordan, no doubt by way of a 'sign' to accredit his divine mission (Joseph. Antiq. xx. 97, compare Acts v. 36). A few years later, under Felix (c. 52–60), a number of impostors τὸν ὄχλον ἔπειθον αὐτοῖς εἰς τὴν ἐρημίαν ἕπεσθαι, δείξειν γὰρ ἔφασαν ἐναργῆ τέρατα καὶ σημεῖα (ibid. xx. 167–8). Among them was an Egyptian ψευδοπροφήτης, who, προφήτης εἶναι λέγων, προφήτου πίστιν ἑαυτῷ ἐπιθείς, led some 30,000 men ἐκ τῆς ἐρημίας to the Mount of Olives for an assault on Jerusalem, promising that its walls should fall down. His aim, we are told, was to overpower the Roman garrison and to rule over the people (id., Bell. Jud. II. 261–2, Antiq. xx. 169–70; compare Acts xxi. 38, ὁ Αἰγύπτιος ὁ πρὸ τούτων τῶν ἡμερῶν ἀναστατώσας καὶ ἐξαγαγὼν εἰς τὴν ἔρημον τοὺς τετρακισχιλίους ἄνδρας τῶν σικαρίων). In all these stories the salient features are the prophet, the 'sign', and the attempted popular rising, all of which recur in the Johannine narrative, though to very different purpose. The incident is not only dramatically convincing in its present setting; it belongs to its period.[1]

It is not recorded that any of these leaders of revolt claimed to be 'Messiah', but the Egyptian is said to have had as his aim, τοῦ δήμου τυραννεῖν. Josephus designedly uses the pejorative term τυραννεῖν, but the meaning is simply that he aspired to be the head of the Jewish state, which is what משיח־ישראל means in the Qumran documents.[2] John similarly does not say that the Galilaean mob recognized Jesus as

[1] Cf. H. Montefiore, 'Revolt in the Desert', in New Testament Studies, vol. VIII, no. 2 (1962), pp. 135–41.
[2] The circumspect phrase of Acts v. 36 (of Theudas), λέγων εἶναί τινα ἑαυτόν, doubtless disguises a similar claim.

'Messiah', but they proposed that he should reign as βασιλεύς. For the evangelist himself, ὁ προφήτης ὁ ἐρχόμενος is not identical with ὁ χριστός (he does not accept the identification implied in Acts iii. 22–3 and elsewhere). Those who acknowledge Jesus as the prophet may have taken a step in the right direction, but they do not, in the Johannine sense, 'believe in' him. Those who do believe in him acknowledge him as Messiah, and therefore as 'King of Israel'. But the present passage does not move on the plane of high Christology; it reflects popular usage of the first century, when it was natural to regard a prophet accredited by 'signs' as a claimant to messiahship. The passages in Josephus show (as Strack–Billerbeck observe *ad loc.*) 'how closely in the thought of the populace in the decades before the destruction of Jerusalem the conceptions of the coming Prophet and of the Deliverer-Messiah belonged together; and the same thing comes out in John vi. 14 *sq.*'

The present passage therefore falls into line with other passages in the Fourth Gospel which bring into relief what we may call the quasi-political aspect of the claims made for Jesus, such as the acclamation of the King of Israel at the entry into Jerusalem, and above all the emphasis on the claim to kingship in the trial before Pilate. In discussing these passages[1] I argued that in the known conditions under which primitive Christians lived in the Roman Empire it would be far easier to account for the toning down of apparently political features if the tradition originally contained such features, than to find reasons why they should be given enhanced importance in the development of a tradition originally innocent of them— or almost innocent, for nothing could eliminate from the record the fact that Jesus was crucified as 'King of the Jews'. If there was a tradition of events belonging to this period of the Ministry which suggested that he was in danger of being made the centre and leader of a movement of popular revolt by the always turbulent and disaffected Galilaeans, we can well understand why in Mark this dangerous feature was glossed over, at the cost of leaving the actions of Jesus and his disciples unexplained. I should find it much more difficult to account for the importation of this suggestion into a narrative, such as that of Mark, which contained no hint of it. I can see no plausible theological motive for such an addition to the narrative.[2] Clearly John wished to use the story of the Feeding of

---

[1] See above, pp. 112–15, 156.
[2] In *Interpretation*, pp. 344–5, I have attempted to deduce the theological significance which the evangelist intended his readers to find symbolized in the sequence of

the Multitude, with its implied sacramental reference, as a 'sign' of the doctrine of Christ as Bread of Life. For that purpose, the simple, quasi-liturgical narrative of Mark viii would surely have been entirely suitable, and sufficient; nothing is gained by introducing at this point the idea of kingship.

I shall venture therefore to propound a theory based upon this and previous discussions. As I have already argued (pp. 171–2 above), while the units of tradition which form-critics have recognized in the *pericopae* of the gospels represent formulations dictated by the varying needs and conditions of the early Church, there is no sufficient reason for assuming that such formulation was a *creatio ex nihilo*. Indeed, that within less than thirty years all that Jesus had said and done had been so largely forgotten that his followers were obliged to think up stories and sayings to meet the new situation I do not find credible. It is, on general grounds of common-sense, more probable that the process by which the tradition received its various forms was one of selection out of a much wider mass of material.[1] In the process of selection much was dropped which was of no immediate utility for the practical purposes of κήρυγμα, διδαχή or liturgical worship. In this way whole classes of material may have vanished, or their remnants may appear as erratic blocks in our gospels. The characteristic features which enable us to distinguish varying strains of tradition lying behind the gospels are due in part to different principles of selection in the varying *milieux* of early Christianity.

Among these varying strains of tradition I believe we have found reason for recognizing one as lying behind portions of the Fourth Gospel. Along with other individual characteristics which mark it out is this repeated reference to the *prima facie* political aspect of the claims made for Jesus. Such references, I should argue, are not late accretions upon the tradition, but surviving fragments of a whole range of facts remembered in the early, unformed tradition about the conflict in which Jesus met his death. These facts belonged to a stage of affairs in Palestine which soon lost interest for the Church in its mission to the world. Not only so, they might easily lend themselves to misconstruction, and so dropped out of the tradition

events, but here as elsewhere I conceive him to have used as symbols data which had reached him by tradition, rather than to have created the facts out of the symbols.

[1] Our evangelist, in fact, is to be taken seriously when he says that he selected out of a large number of unwritten stories about Jesus those which had relevance to his particular aim (xx. 30–1).

in most of its standard forms.[1] On grounds of general probability, in view of the permanent state of disaffection prevailing in Palestine, and particularly in Galilee, all through the period with which we are concerned, we can well believe that the mission of Jesus, in so far as it included a popular appeal to the Galilaean masses, was in danger of becoming involved with such political disturbances. John tells us that it was so, at least at one point in the Ministry, and he goes on to tell us that Jesus avoided such involvement by a hasty retreat to the hills, while his disciples escaped it by a nocturnal flight across the lake in imminent peril of shipwreck. That the evangelist afterwards reassembles the dangerous mob in the synagogue at Capernaum to form an audience for the discourse on the Bread of Life, we may confidently put down to the theological interest which all through this gospel prevails over the purely historical. The other gospels, following a tradition uninterested in the political preoccupations of a bygone age, have recorded the flight but obscured its motive.[2] Even in John the whole crisis is relegated to a subordinate clause: 'When Jesus discovered that they intended to come and seize him to make him king he withdrew to the hills.' At the next stage it would disappear altogether, but the form of tradition which John followed had crystallized at just this stage, and our evangelist has preserved it as it reached him.

[1] We may recall that there is in the gospels no hint that political motives had anything to do with the death of John the Baptist, which is represented as due to the spite of Herodias; but Josephus saw it (probably rightly) as the consequence of a nervous anxiety on the part of Antipas to forestall a possible movement of revolt: πολὺ κρεῖττον ἡγεῖται, πρίν τι νεώτερον ἐξ αὐτοῦ γενέσθαι, προλαβὼν ἀνελεῖν, ἢ μεταβολῆς γενομένης εἰς πράγματα ἐμπεσὼν μετανοεῖν (*Antiq.* XVIII. 118). That Antipas was hostile also to Jesus we learn incidentally from Luke xiii. 31. What were the reasons for his hostility? It is permissible to suspect that at Mark vi. 14 something has dropped out which might have elucidated that point. Herod, we are told, heard about the activities of Jesus; he said, 'John the Baptist has risen from the dead'. But what did he *do* about it? As it stands, the statement is somewhat pointless.

[2] In all the other gospels the quasi-political aspect is but feebly reflected. In Mark, perhaps, the single acclamation as 'Son of David', together with the somewhat muted charge before Pilate, alone hints at it. In Matthew the title 'Son of David' occurs repeatedly, and the political element in the opposition to Jesus is represented in the legend of the hostility of Herod the Great to the infant King of the Jews. Luke allows the crowd at the Triumphal Entry to acclaim the coming King, and he probably understood the charge of διαστρέφειν τὸ ἔθνος, ἀνασείειν τὸν λαόν (xxiii. 2, 5) in a political sense, perhaps wrongly (see above, p. 117). Moreover, some of the expressions in the Magnificat and Benedictus have possible political overtones. These I conceive to be remnants of a part of the original tradition which is almost completely submerged in the Synoptics, but appears a little more clearly in the Fourth Gospel.

(d) The Continuation of the Narrative

If it be thought sufficiently probable that in the Johannine account of the Feeding of the Multitude and its immediate sequel we are in touch with a good and independent tradition, it may be worth while to inquire whether any further traces of such a tradition are to be discovered in the continuation of the narrative.

To begin with, the second Marcan story of the Feeding, followed by a voyage across the lake, leads at once to an extremely brief and enigmatic *pericopé* in which the Pharisees confront Jesus with a demand for a 'sign', which he refuses peremptorily (Mark viii. 11–12). There is no suggestion of this in Mark vi, where the narrative of the Feeding and the voyage is wound up with a typical *Sammelbericht* (vi. 53–6), and this in turn is followed by a controversy with the Pharisees on a quite different topic, that of ceremonial uncleanness. There is therefore no evidence that the demand for a sign was inherently associated in tradition with the Feeding of the Multitude; the collocation is *prima facie* the result of Mark's editing of his material. In Matthew the demand for a sign occurs both in the Marcan context and also in a different context (xii. 38–9, xvi. 1–4). The reply given in both places differs from that given in Mark, and agrees, in the essential non-Marcan clauses, with the version in Luke xi. 29. It is a fairly safe inference that the incident in its non-Marcan form came down by a separate channel of tradition (whether oral or written), and that in xvi. 1–4 Matthew has conflated Mark with his non-Marcan source. The incident itself therefore has a secure place in tradition, but its order in the sequence of events in the Synoptics depends on Mark alone.

In John, however, we have a demand for a sign at much the same point in the narrative as in Mark: viz. after the voyage across the lake which followed upon the Feeding of the Multitude. If John is following Mark, the explanation is simple: after conflating Mark vi. 34–50 and viii. 1–10, he borrows the continuation of the story from Mark viii. 11–12. The actual wording of the demand is not at all close in the two gospels. The Johannine form is closer to what Matthew gives in a totally different context.

Matt. xii. 38	John vi. 29
ἀπεκρίθησαν...λέγοντες Διδάσκαλε,	εἶπον οὖν αὐτῷ
θέλομεν ἀπό σου σημεῖον ἰδεῖν	Τί οὖν ποιεῖς σὺ σημεῖον
	ἵνα ἴδωμεν καὶ πιστεύσωμέν σοι;

In John the questioners go on to cite the precedent of manna in the wilderness, and in the sequel the idea of a 'sign' is no longer in the foreground. Conceivably, as Matt. xii. 38 may represent a second form of the tradition, so John vi. 30 may represent a third form. But it does not fit in well with John vi. 14. There we are told that the Galilaeans *saw* the σημεῖον and hailed Jesus as the coming prophet; here the *same* Galilaeans ask to see a σημεῖον. In the interim Jesus has said 'You seek me, *not* because you saw σημεῖα'. *Prima facie* there is a contradiction, which can be reconciled only through a characteristically Johannine play upon the word σημεῖον. That means that we must allow for a considerable amount of working over by the evangelist. If there was a third form of tradition about the demand for a sign, it has left little recognizable indication of its character. The discourse on the Bread of Life (together with the appended dialogue, vi. 60–5, which is wholly Johannine in ideas and language) is an original composition, into which the occasional allusions to traditional matter are absorbed, being largely transformed in the process.[1]

It is otherwise with the dialogue with which the whole chapter closes, vi. 66–70. The centre of it is Peter's confession, σὺ εἶ ὁ ἅγιος τοῦ θεοῦ. This is very generally regarded as in some sort an equivalent, or counterpart, of the Marcan confession, σὺ εἶ ὁ χριστός, with its Matthaean and Lucan variants. Are we to say that this dialogue is based upon Mark viii. 27–30? If so, how are we to account for the change from the title ὁ χριστός to ὁ ἅγιος τοῦ θεοῦ? John certainly has no kind of disinclination for the title 'Messiah'. Quite the contrary; he dwells upon it, and its implications, more than any of the others. And if for some reason he wished here to avoid that title, why has he chosen ὁ ἅγιος τοῦ θεοῦ, a title which he never uses elsewhere? It will hardly be suggested that he deliberately transferred the acclamation of the demoniac in Mark i. 24 to Peter, even though there is some similarity between the Marcan οἶδά σε τίς εἶ, ὁ ἅγιος τοῦ θεοῦ, and the Johannine ἐγνώκαμεν ὅτι σὺ εἶ ὁ ἅγιος τοῦ θεοῦ. The reason, indeed, which Peter gives for his attachment to his κύριος is thoroughly Johannine:

---

[1] The discourse may be said to have a certain parallel in the dialogue introduced by the saying about leaven in Mark viii. 14–21, which follows upon the *pericopé* about a 'sign'. This is clearly a secondary composition, presupposing the duplication of the story of the Feeding of the Multitude. The main theme of the dialogue is the stupidity of the disciples (οὔπω νοεῖτε οὐδὲ συνίετε; πεπωρωμένην ἔχετε τὴν καρδίαν ὑμῶν; κ.τ.λ.). Its connection with the saying about leaven is artificial and unconvincing. All that the dialogue has in common with the Johannine discourse (apart from its position in the sequence) is the idea that the Feeding of the Multitude is a mystery. There the resemblance ends. In John it is the crowd who fail to 'see signs', not the disciples, who in Mark ὀφθαλμοὺς ἔχοντες οὐ βλέπουσιν.

ρήματα ζωῆς αἰωνίου ἔχεις.[1] The introduction of such language is everywhere to be expected. Beyond this, there does not appear to be anything peculiar to Johannine theology in the whole *pericopé*, though the appended editorial note (vi. 71) is no doubt to be assigned to the evangelist. The rest constitutes a quite normal type of dialogue unit. The occasion is indicated in an introductory sentence (verse 66); Jesus asks a question; Peter replies; Jesus adds a comment. Its form is similar to that of the *pericopé* of the confession at Caesarea in Mark. The content is similar to this extent: that a confession of faith in Christ is followed by a forecast of the Passion—or, more precisely, in John by a forecast of the betrayal which will lead to the Passion. But in nothing is there any echo of Marcan language except in the bare name of Peter, and even here John has 'Simon Peter'.

Let us then examine the *pericopé* more closely. The opening words, ἐκ τούτου, do not differ greatly from such conventional openings as μετὰ ταῦτα, ἐν ἐκείνῳ τῷ καιρῷ, and the like, which serve to link a *pericopé* loosely with what has preceded. As the text now stands, they appear to indicate that the discourse just concluded was the *terminus a quo*, and presumably the reason, for a widespread movement of defection among those who had hitherto followed Jesus. This discourse (whatever traditional elements may have been incorporated in it) is, as I have observed, the composition of the evangelist. But if the *pericopé* we are considering came out of a tradition which did not contain the discourse, the opening words, ἐκ τούτου, might well have referred to the whole episode described earlier in the chapter, especially in verse 15, *possibly* with the demand for a sign which may have followed. However that may be, John reports that from a certain point in the Ministry of Jesus large numbers of former followers deserted him. The expression, ἀπῆλθον εἰς τὰ ὀπίσω, has a Semitic cast, and appears to represent some such Aramaic phrase as אֲזַלוּ לַאֲחוֹרָא, connoting something in the nature of a retreat or withdrawal. It was in this situation, according to John, that Jesus made his

---

[1] These words are by no means essential to the process of thought in the dialogue, for Peter's confession is adequately grounded without them. The whole runs quite naturally: 'From that time many of his disciples withdrew and no longer went with him. So Jesus said to the Twelve, "Do you also mean to go?" Simon Peter answered, "Lord, to whom shall we go? We know that you are the Holy One of God".' The implied situation is that expressed in the question of John the Baptist, Σὺ εἶ ὁ ἐρχόμενος ἢ ἄλλον προσδοκῶμεν; To this question Peter has the answer: he and his companions do not need to await some other to whom they might transfer their allegiance; they *know* that their Master is ὁ ἐρχόμενος.

appeal to the Twelve: μὴ καὶ ὑμεῖς θέλετε ὑπάγειν;[1] And Peter's confession is an affirmation of their unshaken loyalty at a time when others are failing to stay the course. The Twelve, therefore, though John no less than the others regards them as having been deliberately selected by Jesus himself (vi. 70), appear also in the role of a 'faithful remnant' of a much larger body of adherents. Of this the other gospels say nothing, at least explicitly. Yet there are perhaps traces of such a feature of the tradition. In Luke xxii. 28 Jesus says to the Twelve, ὑμεῖς ἐστε οἱ διαμεμενηκότες μετ' ἐμοῦ ἐν τοῖς πειρασμοῖς μου: not, be it observed, 'You have stood by me', but 'You are those who have stood by me'—in contrast, it would seem, with others who had not done so. And if we are prepared to take John's statement seriously, it might illuminate some other passages in the Synoptics. In particular, the recurrent warnings against being 'scandalized' at Jesus, or being ashamed of him, or denying him before men, and of the danger of backsliding,[2] would gain point if there had been numerous actual instances of such conduct—and critics would not have to assume that such sayings are invariably a reading back of the experience of the early Church.[3]

It would appear, therefore, that we have here, as in other places in this gospel, a *pericopé* shaped quite on the traditional pattern, and corresponding in content, in a general way, with a Synoptic *pericopé* of similar pattern, but containing not the faintest indication of literary derivation from any of the Synoptic Gospels; in fact, a *pericopé* for which there are strong grounds for inferring an independent source in tradition.

It is at least a striking coincidence that this dialogue falls into a sequence similar to that which we find in Mark. If we put aside the long discourse, vi. 25–65 (with the link-passage, verses 22–4), as the undoubted composition of the evangelist, the hypothetically traditional sequence is: Feeding of the Multitude, voyage, [demand for a sign], Peter's confession, all of them having parallels within Mark viii. The Johannine version, however, both of the Feeding and of the voyage (which includes the Walking on the Sea), is closer to the duplicate version in Mark vi, while the introduction to the *pericopé* of the Feeding, and the demand for a sign (if this is to be included in the sequence), are closer to Matthew. It is no very rash

---

[1] John thus provides a plausible motive for the question of Jesus which elicits Peter's confession. Mark viii. 27 provides no such motive. The *pericopé* begins abruptly and there is no explanation of the blunt question, Τίνα με λέγουσιν οἱ ἄνθρωποι εἶναι;

[2] Matt. xi. 6, xiii. 21, Mark viii. 38, Matt. x. 33, Luke ix. 62, etc.

[3] I owe this suggestion originally to the late W. L. Knox, who put it forward at a meeting of my seminar at Cambridge.

inference that the sequence of the three (or possibly four) incidents was already established in the primitive tradition. It has been to some extent dislocated in Mark, partly through the duplication of the narrative of the Feeding with the subsequent voyage, and partly through the intrusion of the saying about leaven and the story of the Blind Man of Bethsaida. John also has supplemented the sequence with two additional details of considerable significance: the attempt to seize Jesus and make him king, and the defection of many of his followers. These increase the verisimilitude of the story as a whole, whether or not its verisimilitude derives from its truth to historical fact. If John's account is to be taken seriously, we can see a reason why, at an early stage, this particular part of the Ministry impressed its sequence of events on the memory of the followers of Jesus: it was a crisis and a turning point. The vast assembly, gathered about Jesus on the east side of the Sea of Galilee, somewhere between the shore and the hills, represented a high point in his popularity. But this popularity took a disastrous turn when an attempt was made to force his mission into a political channel. When Jesus firmly resisted the attempt, separating his immediate followers from the crowd and withdrawing to the hills, the result was widespread defection, and the Twelve emerged from the crisis as the faithful remnant with which a fresh start was to be made.

All this largely lost interest as the Church moved out into wider fields and fresh tasks, and for the most part the memories of it which the primitive tradition had preserved survived only in the form of isolated units of teaching and narrative, the former containing warnings against inconstancy and praises and promises to the steadfast, the latter, stories about relations between Jesus and the faithful Twelve as they were *after* the crisis; while the story of the Feeding of the Multitude was retold in forms which, ignoring features of the story liable to misconstruction, insisted on the mystery which lay behind it: οὐ γὰρ συνῆκαν ἐπὶ τοῖς ἄρτοις. In one way, John represents the furthest stage of this development, expounding most fully the mysterious, sacramental, meaning of the incident. Yet he has also reproduced, out of the tradition known to him, some almost forgotten elements in the background of the story which made it at the time so significant for the immediate followers of Jesus.

Such at least is an hypothesis which seems to account for the facts revealed by analysis and comparison of our texts.

4. THE MIRACLE OF THE WINE AND THE RAISING OF LAZARUS

There remain only two major narrative *pericopae* to be discussed: the Miracle of the Wine and the Raising of Lazarus. Neither of these is such as to admit of close comparison with Synoptic *pericopae*, yet each contains elements which show some contact with the tradition as we know it from the Synoptics, and have recognized it in other parts of the Fourth Gospel. Both are pervaded with motives of Johannine theology to a greater extent than the narrative *pericopae* already examined.

(a) The Miracle of the Wine (ii. 1–11)

The intention of this passage I have discussed elsewhere.[1] It is to set forth a 'sign' by which, as the author emphatically says, Christ manifested his glory. The meaning is to be gathered from a study of the imagery employed, in comparison with its use in other writers who show some affinity with the evangelist's way of thinking. In giving ἀντὶ ὕδατος οἶνον Christ is the giver of the knowledge of God which is eternal life; and the water is expressly associated with Jewish rites of purification: ὅτι ὁ νόμος διὰ Μωυσέως ἐδόθη, ἡ χάρις καὶ ἡ ἀλήθεια διὰ Ἰησοῦ Χριστοῦ ἐγένετο. The good wine (which is γνῶσις θεοῦ) has been kept ἕως ἄρτι, namely until the time of the incarnation of the Logos. When Jesus is appealed to he first objects, οὔπω ἥκει ἡ ὥρα μου. Later, when the transformation of water into wine has been effected, we are to understand that the 'hour' has come. The evangelist has exemplified his own maxim, ἔρχεται ὥρα καὶ νῦν ἐστίν. The passage therefore is highly theological in character.

Nevertheless, it has the form of a narrative, broadly similar to that of traditional miracle stories. There is, however, no other narrative *pericopé* at all closely similar except that of the Feeding of the Multitude, especially in its Johannine version. In both stories Jesus is brought into contact with a group of people (the ὄχλος/the wedding guests); a crisis of need supervenes (food/wine); a dialogue ensues between Jesus and his immediate company (the μαθηταί, or Philip and Andrew/his Mother), raising an ἀπορία about the supply of the need; the available resources are mentioned (five loaves/six ὑδρίαι); Jesus gives an order with no apparent immediate bearing upon the supply of the need (ποιήσατε τοὺς ἀνθρώ-

---

[1] See *Interpretation*, pp. 297–300.

πους ἀναπεσεῖν/γεμίσατε τὰς ὑδρίας ὕδατος), and when the order is obeyed the ultimate result is that the need is supplied;[1] but at this point the narratives cease to run even broadly parallel, and the conclusion of the Cana *pericopé* is unlike anything else in the gospels.[2] There is, moreover, one notable difference between the two stories: the sacramental words and acts which are central to the *pericope* of the Feeding are altogether absent from our present passage. That our evangelist intended a eucharistic reference can hardly be doubted,[3] but this has not entered into the *form* of the narrative. For John, and no less for the Synoptics, the main point, and the formative motive, of the narrative of the Feeding of the Multitude is not the sheer miracle as such, but the mystery of the loaves.[4] This motive has had no part in shaping the *pericope* of the marriage at Cana, which *in form* is a miracle story pure and simple, even though it is intended to be understood symbolically.

It is a story about a miraculous supply of wine. This is a popular motive which appears in various local legends here and there in the Greek world. At Andros, on the festal day known as Θεοδοσία, a spring in the temple of Bacchus ran with wine; if, however, the wine was taken out of sight of the temple it tasted like water.[5] At Teos, at stated times a fountain of wine flowed spontaneously in the city—wine, we are told, with a peculiarly fine bouquet.[6] At Elis the priests of Dionysus placed three great empty basins (λέβητας) in a room, sealed them up, and on returning next day found

---

[1] In this story, therefore, Jesus neither acts nor speaks the miracle-working word. The miracle itself takes place off-stage, so to speak. The only complete parallel is the story of the lepers in Luke xvii. 11–19. There are several stories in which obedience to the word of Jesus is a condition of the miracle (see above, pp. 175–6, 183), but in all of them there is either a healing act or a saying which may be understood as the word of power by which the effect is produced. There is nothing of the kind here. It is note-worthy that in Christian art, where the miracle has to be made pictorial, Christ is shown touching the waterpots with his magician's wand. This is a departure from the gospel data.

[2] It may be said that there is a certain parallelism in that the reality of the miracle is verified by the quantity of the food, or the quality of the drink, provided. But this is true only of the Synoptic version of the Feeding of the Multitude. In John the gathering of the twelve basketfuls of fragments is not a verification of the miracle but a further σημεῖον: see above, p. 207.

[3] In early Christian art the six waterpots regularly balance the five, or seven, loaves in symbolic allusions to the Eucharist.

[4] See above, p. 200.

[5] Pliny, *Hist. Nat.* II. 231, XXXI. 16.

[6] Diodorus Siculus, III. 66, Τήϊοι μὲν τεκμήριον φέρουσιν τῆς παρ' αὐτοῖς γενέσεως τοῦ θεοῦ (*scil.* Διονύσου) μέχρι τοῦ νῦν τεταγμένοις χρόνοις ἐν τῇ πόλει πηγὴν αὐτομάτως ἐκ τῆς γῆς οἴνου ῥεῖν εὐωδίᾳ διαφέροντος.

them full of wine.[1] At Haliartus there was a spring in which the infant
Dionysus had been washed; its water was of a clear, sparkling wine-
colour and was very sweet to drink.[2] The daughters of the Delian king
Anius were given by Liber (Bacchus) the power to turn all things into
corn, wine and oil.[3] These stories are usually (perhaps always) associated
with Dionysus.[4] That a Christian evangelist should have consciously
taken over a Dionysiac legend and transferred it, with the implication,
'a greater than Bacchus is here' (as has been suggested), seems contrary to
the whole ethos of the primitive preaching and gospel writing. The time
was not yet when apologists could safely draw parallels between Christ and
the figures of pagan mythology.[5] But folk-tales often forget their origins,
and circulate in disguise, and certainly folk-tale motives, not native to
Christianity, or even Judaism, are to be found in the gospels. The parable
of Dives and Lazarus (Luke xvi. 19–31) appears to be founded upon a tale
about the great man and the poor man in the afterworld which is known
from Egyptian sources.[6] The allusion to a coin found in the mouth of a
fish (Matt. xvii. 27) recalls a whole series of similar tales from the most
varied places.[7] The possibility therefore should not be excluded, that the
transformation of water into wine may have been adapted to Christian
use without any consciousness of its pagan associations.

As we have the story in John ii. 1–11 it bears the sign manual of the

[1] Pausanias, VI. xxvi. 1–2.
[2] Plutarch, *Lysander* XXVIII. 4, οἰνωπὸν ἐπιστίλβει τὸ χρῶμα καὶ διαυγὲς καὶ πιεῖν ἥδιστον.
[3] Ovid, *Metamorphoses* XIII. 650 sqq.
[4] See J. Vürtheim, 'The Miracle of the Wine at Dionysos' Advent', in *Classical Quarterly*, XIV (1920), 92–6, to whom I owe references to the passages cited above. Bauer *ad loc.* adds Euripides, *Bacchae* 706–11, and Horace's Hymn to Bacchus, *Od.* II. 19, which show that this was a standing ingredient of the Dionysiac myth. He also refers to Philostratus, *Vita Apollonii* VI. 20; but it should be noted that Apollonius is not saying that Apollo made Castalia run with wine, but that he *could* have done so had he chosen. This was not Apollo's *métier*. The local legends cited above are more to our purpose.
[5] E.g. Justin, *Apol.* I. 21, 54, II. 11, 69, etc.
[6] See J. Jeremias, *Die Gleichnisse Jesu* (1952), p. 131, and references there.
[7] The earliest known to me is Herodotus's story of the Signet of Polycrates (III. 40–3); the most recent was in the *Evening Standard* for May 25, 1961: 'Toulis Kyriacou, a Cypriot villager from Xylophagou, South Cyprus, lost his gold wedding ring while fishing. Five days later he bought some fish at the market. Inside one of them he found the ring' (the same story, one observes, *minus* Herodotus's moralizing —even to the discovery πέμπτῃ ἢ ἕκτῃ ἡμέρῃ !). The motive is of course utilized in Hans Christian Andersen's 'The Little Tin Soldier'.

evangelist in its language: οὔπω ἥκει ἡ ὥρα μου, καθαρισμὸς τῶν Ἰουδαίων,[1] ἀρχὴ τῶν σημείων, φανεροῦν τὴν δόξαν,[2] πιστεύειν εἰς, are locutions with a Johannine ring. The interest in individual characters (here the Mother and the ἀρχιτρίκλινος, as Philip, Andrew and the παιδάριον in the companion story) is also a Johannine trait (though it is not peculiar to this gospel), and so is the precise measurement both of time (τῇ ἡμέρᾳ τῇ τρίτῃ) and of quantity (ἀνὰ μετρητὰς δύο ἢ τρεῖς). But so much 'Johannism' we should in any case expect; it is seldom that the evangelist fails to put his mark on his material. There are other traits which seem to associate themselves with the earlier tradition. The following should be noted:

(i) The general presupposition of the story is that Jesus was a person likely to contribute to the success of a convivial occasion. This is in harmony with Matt. xi. 19, Luke vii. 34, where he is satirized as ἄνθρωπος φαγὸς καὶ οἰνοπότης.

(ii) The colloquy between Jesus and his Mother has the same suggestion of a certain tension within the family as Mark iii. 32–5, Luke ii. 48–50, John vii. 3–5.

(iii) The idea that with the coming of Christ a new order was inaugurated, which is the overruling theme of the *pericopé* in John, lies behind the whole Synoptic presentation of his Ministry. Not only so, this new order is in Mark ii. 22 compared to οἶνος νέος which bursts the old wine-skins, and in Luke v. 39 those who do not accept the teaching of Jesus are compared to people who, having acquired a taste for old wine, dislike the new, and say, ὁ παλαιὸς χρηστός ἐστιν. Here, on the contrary, the ἀρχιτρίκλινος praises the new wine which Jesus has provided; it is ὁ καλὸς οἶνος, and his only regret is that it was not produced earlier. We are clearly within the same range of imagery.

(iv) The occasion itself, a wedding feast, does not indeed figure in the Synoptic narrative of the Ministry, but it is the background of three parables, that of the Wedding of the King's Son in Matt. xxii. 1–14, that of the Ten Virgins in Matt. xxv. 1–13, and that of the Waiting Servants in Luke xii. 35–6, and it is implied in the parabolic saying about the υἱοὶ τοῦ νυμφῶνος in Mark ii. 19, which in turn has affinity with the saying

[1] The qualification of an institution or usage as being 'of the Jews' is characteristic of this evangelist (cf. ii. 13, v. 1, vi. 4, vii. 2, xi. 55, xix. 42). His interest in Jewish καθαρισμός comes out also in iii. 25.

[2] Φανεροῦν occurs nine times in John, once in Mark, and twice in pseudo-Mark, not in Matthew or Luke, and although the word δόξα is common enough in all gospels, the idea of the δόξα of the incarnate Logos is peculiarly congenial to this evangelist.

about the bridegroom and his friend in John iii. 29. In the Matthaean and Lucan parables the figure of the wedding feast belongs to the eschatological scheme of symbolism. In Mark it carries (as I believe) the idea of a 'realized eschatology'. Similarly in John the 'third day' on which the marriage feast is held is the day of the revelation of the glory of Christ in his incarnation. We are still well within the common tradition.

This leads me to hazard a further suggestion: that the traditional nucleus of this *pericopé* may have been a parable, in which, as in other parables, the setting was a wedding feast. It would not be difficult to imagine a parable beginning, for example, ἄνθρωπός τις ἐποίησε γάμον, and leading up to the pregnant saying, σὺ τετήρηκας τὸν καλὸν οἶνον ἕως ἄρτι, in the sense that the coming of the Kingdom of God with the advent of Christ is the far better thing to which the whole dispensation of law and prophets pointed forward (compare Matt. xiii. 16–17, Luke x. 23–4, Matt. xii. 41–2, Luke xi. 31–2)—an antithesis to Luke's ὁ παλαιὸς χρηστός ἐστιν. Such a parable might, in the development of the tradition, have been turned into an incident in the Ministry of Jesus. In the view of many critics Mark's story of the blasted fig-tree (xi. 12–14, 20–5) has thus passed over from the status of a parable (like Luke's parable of the barren fig-tree, xiii. 6–9, compare his parabolic saying about a συκάμινος, xvii. 6) to that of an actual happening. It may be that in Matt. xvii. 27 we can catch a parabolic saying almost in the act of making the transition. The story ends with the words, 'Go to the sea and cast a hook; pick up the first fish that comes, open its mouth, and you will find a stater; take it and pay the tax for us both'. Matthew does not add (as he might well have done) ἀπελθὼν δὲ εὗρεν καθὼς εἶπεν αὐτῷ. In all probability the saying is a true *Bildwort*. The *pericopé* is not a miracle story, nor a story of action of any kind; it is a 'pronouncement story'. But at the next stage of development it might have been accepted as the record of an incident—as it is probably accepted unthinkingly by many readers.

It is possible that the story of the marriage at Cana had a similar history. This however is conjecture. All that we can say with confidence is that, while John has presented the narrative as a σημεῖον in the service of his theology, and while it is pervaded, to a greater extent than other *pericopae* we have examined, with Johannine motives which have probably transformed it in ways which we cannot define, it nevertheless shows traces of having been formed, at an early pre-canonical stage, in contact with the common tradition. Yet its central feature appears to be of non-Christian origin. The association of the folk-tale motive of the miraculous supply of wine with the *Bildwort* about good wine we may suppose to belong to a relatively late stage in the development of the tradition, but it had probably taken place before the material came into the hands of our evangelist, who exploited it for its symbolic value, thus in a sense restoring it to the status (of an image of the truth) which the (conjectured) original parable possessed.

(b) The Raising of Lazarus (xi. 1–44)

The *pericopé* of the Raising of Lazarus is unique in this gospel for the way in which it combines narrative and discourse in an inseparable whole. Formally, it is a continuous narrative, the longest in the gospel apart from the Passion narrative. As such, it is vivid and dramatic, with much detail which serves to heighten the interest and evoke the reader's imagination. The lively interchange of dialogue, which is characteristic of this writer's manner, runs all through. As elsewhere, individual characters are introduced as interlocutors—Thomas and the sisters Mary and Martha—as well as 'the disciples' collectively; and 'the Jews' appear as a chorus to comment on the action. So far, the passage might be regarded as a peculiarly finished example of the type of *pericopé* which is classified as *Novelle*, or tale. But closer inspection shows that the dialogue is not simply part of the story-teller's technique; it bears the main weight of the author's intention. It is permeated with the distinctive ideas of Johannine theology, as they appear in discourse and dialogue throughout the gospel. Not only so, the structure of the story itself can be seen to be dictated by the Johannine use of symbolism.[1] From another point of view, in fact, the passage might equally well be regarded as a didactic dialogue with elements of symbolic narrative inserted. Our author's more usual practice is to tell a story, and attach to it (whether before or after) a discourse or dialogue indicating the significance he attaches to it. In one case, that of the Healing at Siloam, we noted that a very brief dialogue is inserted in the story itself as a pointer to the meaning (ix. 2–5). But in no other part of the gospel is the unity of the two elements so complete as here.

It seems clear therefore that we are dealing with a highly individual composition, a *Musterstück* of its writer's art. The problem of its possible relation to any pre-Johannine strand of tradition is peculiarly difficult, for anything that may have been taken over has been recast in Johannine idiom of speech and of thought.[2]

---

[1] On the theological significance of the passage, see *Interpretation*, pp. 363–8.

[2] As Johannine traits may be noted the identification of individual characters, the measurement of time and space (two days, four days, fifteen stades), the use of the

The view has met with some favour that this story developed out of a parable. The Lucan parable of Dives and Lazarus ends with the reflection, 'If they will not listen to Moses and the prophets, neither will they listen if someone were to rise from the dead' (xvi. 31). John, it is suggested (or some predecessor), took the hint, and told a story in which a certain Lazarus did rise from the dead, and yet men did not believe. The conjecture has some plausibility, but I cannot think it very firmly based. The Lucan parable is the only one in the gospels in which any character is given a name. Individual names are not usual in miracle stories, but at any rate we have Jairus and Bartimaeus. In other types of narrative we have Simon the leper, Simon the Pharisee, Simon of Cyrene, Joseph of Arimathaea, Zacchaeus, Cleopas, Mary and Martha (not to mention members of the inner circle), all in the Synoptics. None of them *needed* to be named; in similar narratives ἄνθρωπός τις, γυνή τις, proved sufficient. John is even more liberal with proper names. Whether such names are to be regarded as integral to the primitive tradition, or as signs of legendary development, there is nothing exceptional in the occurrence of the name Lazarus here. It is the occurrence of the name in the Lucan *parable* that calls for explanation.[1] Such explanation would be forthcoming, if there existed in pre-Johannine tradition a story about the resurrection of a man called Lazarus, with a general implication that this did not win men to faith in Christ. From that, it would be an easy step to inserting the name in the adapted folk-tale about the rich man and the poor man in Hades.

The theory, then, of development out of a parable or parabolic saying does not seem to bring us much nearer to an identification of the kind of tradition upon which John may have worked. We may make a fresh start from a consideration of the formal structure of the passage.

It begins and closes in ways quite appropriate to a healing-*pericopé*. It begins, ἦν δέ τις ἀσθενῶν (compare Mark i. 23, iii. 1), with some additional details about the patient (compare Mark x. 46). It ends, after the restoration of the patient, with a note of the effect on spectators, and some

---

term οἱ ᾿Ιουδαῖοι. Locutions with a Johannine ring are ὑπέρ τῆς δόξης τοῦ θεοῦ, ἵνα δοξασθῇ ὁ υἱὸς τοῦ θεοῦ, παρρησία, χαίρω δι' ὑμᾶς ἵνα πιστεύσητε, ὅσα ἂν αἰτήσῃ τὸν θεὸν δώσει σοι (cf. xvi. 23), ἐγώ εἰμι, εἰς τὸν αἰῶνα (twelve times in John, twice in Mark, once each in Matthew and Luke), ὁ εἰς τὸν κόσμον ἐρχόμενος, ὄψῃ τὴν δόξαν τοῦ θεοῦ, ἵνα πιστεύσωσιν ὅτι σύ με ἀπέστειλας.

[1] The suggestion that as Lazarus is to run Abraham's errands in Hades he bears the name of Abraham's servant in Gen. xv. 2, Eliezer or Eleazar, is more ingenious than convincing (see J. D. M. Derrett in *New Testament Studies*, VII. 4 (1961), 370–5).

indication of the remoter results (John xi. 45, compare Mark i. 27, ii. 12, v. 42, vii. 37, Luke vii. 16. This immensely long *pericopé*, therefore, has traces of the conventional form of narrative units of tradition.

The attempt, however, by excision of substantial portions of the *pericopé* as it stands, to enucleate a simple story of the raising of the dead, like Luke's account of the Widow's Son of Nain (vii. 11–17), or the Matthaean version of the Raising of Jairus's Daughter (ix. 18–26), meets with little success. The whole passage, narrative and dialogue, is so closely knit together that the disjointing of it leaves only fragments, which can, no doubt, be manipulated into a more or less typical unit, but only by much conjectural rewriting. Nowhere perhaps, in this gospel, have attempts to analyse out a written source, or sources, proved less convincing, and if the evangelist is following a traditional story of fixed pattern, he has covered his tracks.

Nevertheless, if we make allowance for the pervasive presence of Johannine concepts, as well as of Johannine vocabulary and idiom, the passage has more points of contact with Synoptic forms of tradition than are evident at first sight. Our standard of comparison must be, not the concise type of narrative-*pericopé*, such as Dibelius classified as 'paradigms', but the longer, more circumstantial narratives which he called *Novellen*, or 'tales'. In particular, I would draw attention to two such *pericopae*, that of the Epileptic Boy in Mark ix. 14–27, and that of Jairus's Daughter in its Marcan version, v. 21–43. In each of these there are many story-teller's details which are not strictly necessary to carry the main theme of the *pericopé*; yet the length and fulness of the narratives are not entirely due to the introduction of such details.

In the story of the Epileptic Boy, the unusually elaborate description of the symptoms, as well as the heightening of suspense when the cure seems for the moment to be worse than the disease, may no doubt be put down to the interest of the story-teller. But there are other elements of which this is not a sufficient account. The initial failure, showing that neither the father of the boy nor the disciples have the faith which is the condition of healing, provokes from Jesus the outburst, ὦ γενεὰ ἄπιστος, ἕως πότε πρὸς ὑμᾶς ἔσομαι; ἕως πότε ἀνέξομαι ὑμῶν;[1] This is not only dramatically

---

[1] Contrary to the views of some critics, I believe this to be one of the most characteristic and self-authenticating sayings in the gospels. The same sense of strain seems to be reflected in Luke xii. 50, πῶς συνέχομαι ἕως ὅτου τελεσθῇ, and in John viii. 25, τὴν ἀρχὴν ὅτι καὶ λαλῶ ὑμῖν, which I take to mean, 'To think that I am talking with you at all!' (or 'Why am I talking...?'). Cf. Plato, *Gorg.* 478 c: Ἆρ' οὖν οὕτως ἂν περὶ σῶμα εὐδαιμονέστατος ἄνθρωπος εἴη, ἰατρευόμενος,

effective; it introduces the theme of faith, which now becomes the subject of a highly significant dialogue between Jesus and the father of the patient. The dialogue is essential to the progress of the action, but it also makes the whole story manifestly turn upon one of the central evangelical themes, and gives it a significance beyond that of a plain miracle story.

Again, in Mark's version of the story of Jairus's Daughter, the art of the story-teller may be discerned in such traits as the accidental delay, bringing about an interval during which the illness of the child reaches a fatal conclusion, and the picture of the hubbub of professional mourning at the house. Yet the former of these creates the occasion for the enunciation of the great Christian watchword, μὴ φοβοῦ, μόνον πίστευε, and the latter calls forth the pregnant utterance, οὐκ ἀπέθανεν ἀλλὰ καθεύδει. These two sayings, in fact, not only provide the high lights of the narrative, as a dramatic creation, but also give it its special significance as an expression of 'the Gospel of Jesus Christ', which Mark claims to be setting forth.

The description, therefore, of these *pericopae* as *Novellen* is not entirely adequate. It is clear that behind the form which they have taken in the gospels lies a history of the employment of the stories as media for Christian instruction, or, it may be, as illustrations of Christian preaching, and this employment has done much to determine their formal structure.

We now turn to the Johannine narrative. There is much dramatic or picturesque detail. There is, once again, the delay, allowing the illness of the patient to reach a fatal conclusion, and this leads, after much dialogue of a peculiarly Johannine cast, to the theme of death as sleep (xi. 11–14). Then we have, in highly dramatic vein, the journey of Jesus, his arrival four days too late (as it seems), his meeting with the sisters (introducing much characteristic Johannine theology in dialogue form), the scene of mourning, in which Jesus is constrained to join. The outburst of strong emotion which in the Marcan story is provoked by the failure of faith has its parallel here in the statement that when Jesus saw the whole company weeping (compare the mourners in Mark), 'he fumed inwardly and fell into great disquiet' (ἐνεβριμήσατο[1] τῷ πνεύματι καὶ ἐτάραξεν ἑαυτόν— extremely strong expressions). Then the reluctance to open the grave, an

---

ἢ μηδὲ κάμνων ἀρχήν;—Δῆλον ὅτι μηδὲ κάμνων.—Οὐ γὰρ τοῦτ᾽ ἦν εὐδαιμονία, ὡς ἔοικε, κακοῦ ἀπαλλαγή, ἀλλὰ τὴν ἀρχὴν μηδὲ κτῆσις. 'Happiness consists, not in getting rid of a bad thing, but in never having it *at all*.'

[1] The verb ἐμβριμᾶσθαι, expressing violent emotion, must have entered the gospel tradition at an early stage; it occurs not only here (twice) but also (surely independently) in Mark i. 43, xiv. 5, Matt. ix. 30 (see above, pp. 170–1); but nowhere in the N.T. outside the gospels.

indication that faith is lacking, leads up to a dialogue on the theme of faith, elaborated in a distinctively Johannine way, fuller of theological content than the corresponding dialogue in Mark, yet, like it, leading the reader to one of the central conceptions of the Gospel.[1]

Such coincidences are far from proving, or even suggesting a probability, that John borrowed features from Mark. They do suggest that the story of Lazarus, however deeply stamped with the character of Johannine theological ideas and with the language appropriate to them, is not an original allegorical creation. Fundamentally it belongs to the same *genre* as the two Marcan narratives we have studied; it is a recital both dramatic and didactic, and both these qualities have gone to determine its form. There is good reason to believe that, like the Marcan *pericopae*, it has behind it a traditional narrative shaped in the course of Christian teaching and preaching, and then remoulded by our evangelist to convey his own special message. To attempt to reconstruct the story as it may have been handed down in pre-canonical tradition would be idle. John has worked it over too thoroughly. The probability is that this story had never been fully fixed in any conventional pattern, but remained subject to the variations of a fluid and unformed tradition,[2] out of which the evangelist took it, to give it a characteristic literary form dictated by the demands of his particular design.

[1] It may be said that the dialogues in xi. 11–16, 39–40, and in part 7–10, further the action of the story, like those of the Marcan passages, but the longer dialogue in xi. 21–7 is almost pure theological comment.

[2] See above, pp. 169–73, 216–17.

5. TRANSITIONAL PASSAGES AND TOPOGRAPHICAL NOTICES

There remains one further element in the narrative of the Ministry to be examined, namely, the connecting links between one complete section of narrative and the next. In the Synoptic Gospels it has long been observed that throughout the part which precedes the Passion narrative the separate *pericopae* are set in a 'framework' made up of such transitional passages, which provide some measure of continuity and build up a general background of reference. In Matthew and Luke this framework has been much obscured by efforts to secure a smoother flow of narrative, in which the joins in the fabric shall be less conspicuous. In Mark, where there has been less of this smoothing out, the framework material has been shown to consist mainly of the following elements: (*a*) 'Generalizing summaries' (*Sammelberichte*), giving an account of no particular incident, but of the general features of a whole period, long or short, in the course of the Ministry. These *Sammelberichte* are readily identified, in distinction from the *pericopae* which describe particular incidents, by the fact that the verbs are predominantly in the tense of continuous or habitual action (present or imperfect) instead of the aorist of momentary action. (*b*) Topographical data, indicating the field of the Ministry at a given period. These are not always easily distinguished from the indication of place which occasionally opens a *pericopé*, but undoubtedly they occur without connection with the report of any individual incident. These have been described as 'itinerary fragments' (*Bruchstücke eines Itinerars*).[1] I have argued elsewhere that in Mark the generalizing summaries and the itinerary fragments, no less than the *pericopae* which they frame, represent traditional material.[2] The

---

[1] See Karl Ludwig Schmidt, *Rahmen der Geschichte Jesu*.

[2] See 'The Framework of the Gospel Narrative', in *Expository Times*, June 1943, reprinted in *New Testament Studies* (Manchester University Press, 1953). To summarize briefly: I argued that if the transitional passages in Mark (identified by the characteristic marks of the *Sammelbericht* and topographical indications) be written out consecutively, they form, without any manipulation, a continuous outline covering a considerable part of Mark's account of the Ministry. It may be said that this is only natural if Mark, editing material which had come down to him in fragmentary form, wished to provide his readers with a story which could be read continuously. But, as I pointed out, the frame provided (the transitional passages) does not properly fit the pictures to be framed (the separate *pericopae*), and at certain points the outline derived from the transitional passages is not consistent with

question I now raise is whether the transitional passages in the Fourth Gospel show in any degree the characteristics recognizable in those of Mark, and whether there is any reason to suppose that John too drew upon tradition, not only for the Passion narrative and some narrative *pericopae*, but also in some measure for information contained in the transitional passages.

Some of these passages seem to betray the hand of the evangelist in their language and ideas, and to have been introduced to make connections necessary to the development of his doctrinal argument. Among these I should reckon the following:

ii. 23–5, intervening between the story of the Cleansing of the Temple and the dialogue with Nicodemus on regeneration. The expressions, πιστεύειν εἰς τὸ ὄνομα, θεωρεῖν τὰ σημεῖα, and the emphatic use of γινώσκειν and μαρτυρεῖν, have a Johannine ring, and the final statement,

Mark's own arrangement of the *pericopae*. I therefore concluded that the framework material as well as the *pericopae* reached Mark through traditional channels, probably in the form of an outline of the Ministry, but that Mark has partly disrupted this outline in the process of composition, so that it cannot be recovered in its entirety. This view is naturally not congenial to those who believe that early Christians could not possibly have had any interest in the course of events in the earthly life of their Lord. That is something which I do not know. I only submit (*a*) that the outline is there and that it is extremely unlikely that Mark made it up, since it so imperfectly serves his purpose; (*b*) that kerygmatic passages in Acts which I believe to represent early tradition offer the minimal skeleton of an outline, and show at least so much interest in chronological and topographical information, that they record a Galilaean ministry of Jesus which followed the ministry of John the Baptist and preceded a journey to Jerusalem, which journey had for its sequel the passion, death and resurrection of Jesus; and (*c*) that the process of development in gospel writing (in Matthew and Luke as compared with Mark) tends, not to the elaboration of this outline material, but to its elimination in favour either of a more completely topical arrangement (in Matthew) or of an obviously artificial scheme (in Luke, especially in the central portion), from which I should deduce that the nearer we are to primitive tradition, the more recognizable is the underlying outline. My article has been criticized by D. E. Nineham in *Studies in the Gospels, Essays in Memory of R. H. Lightfoot*, pp. 223–39. I have read and carefully considered this essay, without being persuaded to withdraw anything of substance in the view I put forth. Nothing in the way of demonstrative proof is possible in questions of this kind. I am content that my readers should study my article and Professor Nineham's side by side and judge where the greater weight of probability lies. I note that in *J.T.S.* (1958), p. 23, Nineham has a paragraph which appears to admit the possibility (at least *argumenti gratia*) of such an outline as I have reconstructed, observing that it 'would be a medium hitherto overlooked by scholars, through which history, but not the direct testimony of an eyewitness, exercised control over this gospel', which states my own view admirably. For my present purpose it is not essential to assume any conclusions about Mark, though the comparison of Mark with John may be useful.

ἐγίνωσκεν τί ἦν ἐν τῷ ἀνθρώπῳ, prepares for the insight into the mind of Nicodemus which comes out in the succeeding dialogue. The three verses are probably the evangelist's introduction to the *pericopé* of Nicodemus rather than a true transitional passage (compare xi. 55–7).

xii. 17–19, intervening between the Triumphal Entry and the discourse on the meaning of the death of Christ. Once again we have the expressions, μαρτυρεῖν, ποιεῖν σημεῖα, which have a Johannine ring, and on examination it appears that the little paragraph has been skilfully composed so as to bring the Triumphal Entry into the context of the ideas of death and resurrection, and of life through death: the acclamations of the crowd were the result of the 'witness' borne by those who had been present at the Raising of Lazarus. The passage in fact serves to link the death and resurrection of Lazarus with the theme of the death and resurrection of Christ which is now to be expounded.[1] The concluding statement, ὁ κόσμος ὀπίσω αὐτοῦ ἀπῆλθεν, leads up effectively to the appearance of 'Greeks' seeking Jesus, which introduces the succeeding discourse.

But there are other link-passages which deserve more consideration. I adduce the following:

(i) ii. 12, a passage making the transition from the story of the Marriage at Cana to the Cleansing of the Temple.

μετὰ τοῦτο κατέβη εἰς Καφαρναοὺμ αὐτὸς καὶ ἡ μήτηρ αὐτοῦ καὶ οἱ ἀδελφοὶ αὐτοῦ καὶ οἱ μαθηταὶ αὐτοῦ καὶ ἐκεῖ ἔμειναν[2] οὐ πολλὰς ἡμέρας.

This passage is completely out of relation to any other topographical data supplied, and does not in any way contribute to the development either of the narrative or of the thought of the gospel. Capernaum is not mentioned again until iv. 46, and at that point it is not the residence of Jesus (who is at Cana) but of the βασιλικός who seeks help for his son. The next reference is at vi. 17, where it is the destination of a voyage across the lake. Jesus is not said actually to be at Capernaum until vi. 24. Clearly therefore the itinerary datum that Jesus κατέβη εἰς Καφαρναούμ is not the product of any particular interest of the evangelist.

---

[1] See *Interpretation*, pp. 370–1. Observe the way in which the little paragraph is composed. Verse 17 is in substance a summary of the story of the Raising of Lazarus: this is made, *more Johanneo*, the theme of μαρτυρία: it was a σημεῖον in the Johannine sense (18), and as such the true motive of the acclamations of the βασιλεὺς τοῦ 'Ἰσραήλ. The comment of the Pharisees (19) has the characteristic Johannine irony. The whole bears the sign manual of our evangelist.

[2] Ἔμειναν is aorist, but the verb itself is 'linear' and not 'punctiliar' by nature (cf. xi. 54 and p. 243, n. 3).

We now observe that in Matt. iv. 13 there is a similar statement: καταλιπὼν τὴν Ναζαρὰ ἐλθὼν κατῴκησεν εἰς Καφαρναούμ. This is not derived from Mark. Again, Luke iv. 31 has κατῆλθεν εἰς Καφαρναοὺμ πόλιν τῆς Γαλιλαίας. Luke is here, apparently, beginning to follow Mark, but his κατῆλθεν εἰς Καφαρναούμ cannot be regarded as equivalent to Mark's εἰσπορεύονται εἰς Καφαρναούμ, for in the previous *pericopé* of Luke Jesus was at Nazareth, so that his statement here is equivalent to Matthew's in iv. 13, though there is no likelihood that it depends on Matthew. It is always possible that John here followed Matthew, but since we have by this time accumulated a good deal of evidence that he drew independently from tradition, it seems probable that all three evangelists followed a pre-canonical tradition in which it was a datum that during the Galilaean ministry (or part of it) Jesus fixed his headquarters at Capernaum, though John has made no further use of the datum.

(ii) iii. 22–3, a passage making the transition from the dialogue with Nicodemus to a *pericopé* about the relations between Jesus and John the Baptist:

μετὰ ταῦτα ἦλθεν ὁ Ἰησοῦς καὶ οἱ μαθηταὶ αὐτοῦ εἰς τὴν Ἰουδαίαν γῆν καὶ ἐκεῖ διέτριβεν μετ᾽ αὐτῶν καὶ ἐβάπτιζεν. ἦν δὲ καὶ Ἰωάννης βαπτίζων ἐν Αἰνὼν ἐγγὺς τοῦ Σαλείμ, ὅτι ὕδατα πολλὰ ἦν ἐκεῖ, καὶ παρεγίνοντο καὶ ἐβαπτίζοντο.

The passage has strongly marked features which associate it with the Marcan 'framework' passages. The verbs are almost all in the imperfect: διέτριβεν, ἐβάπτιζεν, ἦν βαπτίζων, παρεγίνοντο, ἐβαπτίζοντο. There are topographical indications: ἡ Ἰουδαία γῆ, Αἰνὼν ἐγγὺς τοῦ Σαλείμ, and these, like the 'itinerary fragments' in Mark, relate not to specific incidents but to a whole period of ministry. There is no peculiarly Johannine phraseology. There is, I believe, good ground for thinking that John is here following tradition.

(iii) iv. 1–3. The core of this is an 'itinerary' datum: ἀφῆκεν τὴν Ἰουδαίαν καὶ ἀπῆλθεν πάλιν εἰς τὴν Γαλιλαίαν. To this is added the motive for the move:[1] the Pharisees had heard that Jesus was making and baptizing more disciples than John. This statement, however, is immediately corrected: Jesus did not himself baptize; his disciples did. This seems to

---

[1] In the kind of itinerary material which enters into the Marcan framework it is unusual for any such motive to be assigned. Thus in Mark i. 14, where a similar (possibly the same?) journey to Galilee is reported, we have nothing more than the plain statement, 'After the arrest of John Jesus came to Galilee'. Matthew, however, has altered this into '*When Jesus heard* that John had been arrested he withdrew to Galilee' (iv. 12), which in form is not unlike our present passage: 'When Jesus learnt that. . .he left Judaea and went to Galilee', though the motive is a different one.

be a place where we are driven to postulate more than one hand; no writer, surely, would have produced by his own design so muddled a statement. Since the evangelist has elsewhere recorded, without apparent misgiving, the tradition (if such it be) that Jesus baptized (iii. 22), we must suppose that someone else cut his sentence to pieces. Apart from the awkward parenthesis there are signs of editorial handling. The sentence, iv. 1–3, even after the removal of the parenthesis, is intolerably clumsy, with its three subordinate clauses, one within the other (ὡς ἔγνω...ὅτι ἤκουσαν ...ὅτι ποιεῖ...),[1] and the awkwardness is increased by the juxtaposition of ὁ κύριος in one clause and Ἰησοῦς in the next, referring to the same subject.[2] All this tends, *pro tanto*, to suggest that the evangelist is not composing entirely freely, but making the best of material that had come down to him. When allowance is made for the rehandling, there seems no reason why the itinerary datum should not be accepted as pre-canonical, continuing, perhaps, the summary of this period in the Ministry of Jesus. How much further traditional information may be concealed beneath the author's rewriting it is difficult to say, but it is perhaps not too rash to conclude that it included a statement that the move northward was made at a time when the success of work in Judaea had aroused attention from the authorities. That he went to Galilee because he had become aware of this may also have formed part of the tradition, or it may have been an intelligent inference on the part of the evangelist. In any case, the suggestion that the move to Galilee at this time had something of the character of a withdrawal is not peculiarly Johannine, for Matthew describes it in the terms, ἀνεχώρησεν εἰς τὴν Γαλιλαίαν (iv. 19).[3] On the

[1] The awkwardness may be somewhat relieved if we take the second ὅτι as an instance of ὅτι *recitativum*, virtually equivalent to quotation marks, and conceive the words Ἰησοῦς...Ἰωάννης as *oratio recta*: 'the Pharisees were told, "Jesus is making and baptizing more disciples than John"' (cf. i. 20, 32, iii. 28, iv. 17 *et passim*). But our author can write better Greek than this when he is composing freely.

[2] The use of the title κύριος in narrative belongs to the later strata of the gospels. It is never found in Mark or Matthew, but is common in Luke, alternating with Ἰησοῦς. Similarly it occurs in Eg. Pap. 2, three times, alternating with Ἰησοῦς. In the late Gospel of Peter it is regular. In the Fourth Gospel κύριος in narrative occurs only in vi. 24, xi. 2 (both explanatory notes rather than narrative proper) and in the appendix, xxi. 12.

[3] That Matthew uses ἀναχωρεῖν in the sense of 'withdraw', 'retire', appears from ii. 14 (Joseph with Mary and the Child ἀνεχώρησεν εἰς Αἴγυπτον, before the threats of Herod), ii. 22 (he again ἀνεχώρησεν εἰς τὰ μέρη τῆς Γαλιλαίας for fear of Archelaus), xii. 15 (the Pharisees laid a plot against the life of Jesus, ὁ δὲ Ἰησοῦς γνοὺς [cf. ὡς ἔγνω, John iv. 1] ἀνεχώρησεν ἐκεῖθεν), xiv. 13 (hearing of the execution of John, ἀνεχώρησεν ἐκεῖθεν ἐν πλοίῳ).

whole it seems probable that in Matt. iv. 12, John iv. 1–3 we are in touch, even if indirectly, with a tradition regarding the coming of Jesus to Galilee which is not otherwise represented. It may have been over-shadowed by the emphasis laid in the *kerygma* on the fresh beginning that was made in Galilee.[1]

(iv) iv. 43–5, intervening between the Samaritan episode and the second miracle at Cana:

μετὰ δὲ τὰς δύο ἡμέρας ἐξῆλθεν ἐκεῖθεν εἰς τὴν Γαλιλαίαν. αὐτὸς γὰρ Ἰησοῦς ἐμαρτύρησεν ὅτι προφήτης ἐν τῇ ἰδίᾳ πατρίδι τιμὴν οὐκ ἔχει. ὅτε οὖν ἦλθεν εἰς τὴν Γαλιλαίαν ἐδέξαντο αὐτὸν οἱ Γαλιλαῖοι πάντα ἑωρακότες ὅσα ἐποίησεν ἐν Ἱεροσολύμοις ἐν τῇ ἑορτῇ· καὶ αὐτοὶ γὰρ ἦλθον εἰς τὴν ἑορτήν.

The concluding words (from πάντα ἑωρακότες) seem to be editorial comment, and so probably are the opening words, for this precise measurement of time is characteristic of this gospel. The main purport of the passage is that Jesus left for Galilee, and that he met with a welcome there. The former statement is almost a repetition of iv. 3b, and the overlapping may well be a sign that the Samaritan episode is intruded here into what was originally a single and continuous journey from Judaea to Galilee. The sentence ὅτε οὖν ἦλθεν εἰς τὴν Γαλιλαίαν ἐδέξαντο αὐτὸν οἱ Γαλιλαῖοι is free from distinct marks of Johannine composition; the verb δέχεσθαι does not otherwise occur in this gospel. The Johannine stamp on this passage is in any case not deep. It is perhaps more significant that the statement that Jesus was welcomed by the Galilaeans leads to nothing. It is not required to prepare the way for the healing of the son of the βασιλικός, which does not presuppose any general acceptance of Jesus in Galilee—rather the contrary (iv. 48). The Galilaeans do not appear again until vi. 2, where we are told that Jesus was accompanied by a large crowd because they 'were watching the signs which he was performing', without any suggestion that he had already attracted Galilaean adherents on the strength of a previous ministry in Judaea, as stated in iv. 45. I have

[1] John cannot be said to have a clear or consistent idea about the respective roles of Galilee and Judaea. In ii. 11 Galilee is the scene of the ἀρχὴ σημείων, in agreement with the traditional formula, ἀρξάμενος ἀπὸ τῆς Γαλιλαίας (Luke xxiii. 5, Acts x. 37, implied also in Matthew and Mark); in ch. vi it is the scene of the crucial 'sign' of the Bread, as well as of the abortive attempt 'to make him king', of widespread desertions, and of Peter's confession. Yet we hear nothing of 'making disciples' in Galilee, nor are any Galilaeans said to have 'believed' (with the exception of the family of the βασιλικός at Capernaum), though πιστεύειν is constantly predicated of people in Judaea, in Samaria and in Transjordan. In vii. 1 Galilee is a refuge from the hostility of Judaea, and so, in a sense, in iv. 1–3.

argued above[1] that ch. vi preserves much traditional material, and that the introduction (vi. 1–4), compared with Synoptic parallels, appears to be an integral part of the story of the Feeding of the Multitude and not a mere transitional passage. The present passage betrays at any rate a somewhat different point of view. The one part of it which is undoubtedly traditional is the saying quoted in verse 44, which has parallels in Mark (followed by Matthew) and Luke.

Mark vi. 4	John iv. 44	Luke iv. 24
οὐκ ἔστιν προφήτης ἄτιμος εἰ μὴ ἐν τῇ πατρίδι ἑαυτοῦ[2]	προφήτης ἐν τῇ ἰδίᾳ πατρίδι τιμὴν οὐκ ἔχει	οὐδεὶς προφήτης δεκτός ἐστιν ἐν τῇ πατρίδι ἑαυτοῦ

Here we observe once again a now familiar phenomenon: the Johannine version of a saying does not follow closely any one Synoptic version, but is nearer in some respects to one of the Synoptics and in other respects to another. Here John agrees with Luke in bluntly denying that a prophet is *ever* accepted (honoured) in his πατρίς, without making any statement regarding his status elsewhere, while Matthew and Mark say that the prophet *is* honoured everywhere *except* in his πατρίς. On the other hand, John agrees with Matthew and Mark in speaking of the 'honour' the prophet enjoys everywhere except at home, while Luke speaks of 'acceptance', which is perhaps a shade more modest than honour. The actual difference in meaning is negligible, but as in similar cases it would seem less likely that John combined two other versions (whether by direct copying or through a confused reminiscence of both) than that Mark, Luke and John all drew the saying from variant strains of tradition. We need not therefore assume that the saying reached our evangelist embedded in a context corresponding either to Mark's or to Luke's. In Luke, the πατρίς is, by clear implication, 'Nazareth where he had been brought up', but whether a town where you were brought up, but where you were not born, is properly called your πατρίς is doubtful, and Luke certainly believed Jesus to have been born at Bethlehem. In Mark the πατρίς is not identified by name, but he has placed the incident of the rejection of Jesus

---

[1] See pp. 208–10.

[2] Matt. xiii. 57, according to the best text (BDΘ etc.), has simply ἐν τῇ πατρίδι: other authorities have ἐν τῇ ἰδίᾳ πατρίδι or ἐν τῇ πατρίδι αὐτοῦ. Matthew seldom uses ἴδιος in the sense of the possessive pronoun; John habitually does so; the possessive ἑαυτοῦ does not occur in the Fourth Gospel.

in his πατρίς in a Galilaean context.[1] Where John intends to place the πατρίς is not entirely clear. Jesus, he says, went to Galilee because (γάρ) he knew that in his πατρίς a prophet goes unhonoured. If Galilee is the πατρίς he went there to escape the kind of 'honour' which he did not desire (for example, shall we say, the kind paid him by the Galilaeans in vi. 15 ?). But if so, his expectation was disappointed, for ἐδέξαντο αὐτὸν οἱ Γαλιλαῖοι: he was at least δεκτός there. Then is Judaea the πατρίς? If so, then this is further evidence that the Samaritan episode is intrusive, for as the text stands there is no reference to Judaea nearer than iv. 3, and the implied contrast in iv. 44 would appear to be between Samaria (where the Prophet had received honour) and Galilee—which is most unlikely to be original. Since however there are some other reasons for suspecting that iv. 44 may continue the itinerary of iv. 3 the contrast may originally have been clearly between Judaea and Galilee. Yet even so all is not plain sailing, for if Judaea is the πατρίς[2] the Prophet had received an embarrassing degree of honour, or at least of acceptance, there (iv. 1). It is indeed so difficult to obtain from this passage a clear and consistent impression of the meaning which John attached to the saying that we are almost driven to suppose that he received it from tradition, in general connection with a move from Judaea to Galilee, and inserted it here without completely integrating it into his narrative. The conclusion which I should, very tentatively, suggest is that in iv. 1–3, 43–5 we are in touch with a fragment of 'framework' material which has been largely confused in the process of the composition

---

[1] It is doubtful whether Mark had any real information about this incident. The whole story *could* have been created out of the saying. The datum is that Jesus enjoyed no honour in his πατρίς. Mark has supplemented it by adding καὶ ἐν τοῖς συγγενεῦσιν αὐτοῦ καὶ ἐν τῇ οἰκίᾳ αὐτοῦ. He takes Jesus to his πατρίς, without attempting to identify the place, and brings in the συγγενεῖς by means of a list of the ἀδελφοὶ τοῦ κυρίου (a well-known group in the early Church) and some unnamed sisters. Some critics make great play with 'ideal scenes' supposed to have been created by the evangelists as a setting for traditional sayings. I do not believe there are many such, but this may possibly be one. On the other hand, it appears that the Lucan account of the incident in the synagogue at Nazareth, which could not in any case have been spun out of the saying, is entirely independent of Mark, and if so, we have some additional evidence. What may be taken as certain is that Jesus was known to have uttered this proverbial saying; from which we must needs understand that it reflected his own experience. What particular incident (if any) elicited the comment, to what stage of the Ministry it belonged, or what was the place he called his πατρίς, must remain uncertain.

[2] John may have been aware of the tradition that Jesus was actually born at Bethlehem (but see *Interpretation*, pp. 90–1), or he may have regarded Judaea, or in particular the holy city of Jerusalem, as the true πατρίς of the Messiah.

of this part of the gospel. It contains, be it observed, the only clear recognition in this gospel of a successful ministry in Galilee (except in so far as this is implied in the reference to crowds in the introduction to the story of the Feeding of the Multitude (vi. 2)).

(v) vii. 1–2:

καὶ μετὰ ταῦτα περιεπάτει ὁ Ἰησοῦς ἐν τῇ Γαλιλαίᾳ. οὐ γὰρ ἤθελεν ἐν τῇ Ἰουδαίᾳ περιπατεῖν ὅτι ἐζήτουν αὐτὸν οἱ Ἰουδαῖοι ἀποκτεῖναι.

This has the appearance of a transitional passage, with its verbs in the continuous tense (περιεπάτει, ἤθελεν, ἐζήτουν) and its interest in topography; and it may be such. But it does not in fact make a suitable transition from ch. vi, for Jesus is already in Galilee. Probably the passage is the beginning of the *pericopé*, vii. 2–9, and sets the scene for the dialogue by communicating two pieces of information which are essential if the reader is to understand it: that Jesus was in Galilee and that the Feast of Tabernacles was near.[1]

(vi) x. 40–2:

καὶ ἀπῆλθεν πάλιν πέραν τοῦ Ἰορδάνου εἰς τὸν τόπον ὅπου ἦν Ἰωάννης τὸ πρῶτον βαπτίζων, καὶ ἔμενεν[2] ἐκεῖ. καὶ πολλοὶ ἦλθον πρὸς αὐτὸν καὶ ἔλεγον ὅτι Ἰωάννης μὲν σημεῖον ἐποίησεν οὐδέν, πάντα δὲ ὅσα εἶπεν Ἰωάννης περὶ τούτου ἀληθῆ ἦν. καὶ πολλοὶ ἐπίστευσαν εἰς αὐτὸν ἐκεῖ.

This does form a suitable transition between the scene at the Encaenia in x. 22–39, which ends in the escape of Jesus from an attempt to place him under arrest in the temple, and the story of Lazarus, which presupposes that he is at a distance from Judaea. But it is questionable whether it is more than editorial. The expressions σημεῖα ποιεῖν, πιστεύειν εἰς, are Johannine, and the emphasis on the effect of the testimony of John (though without the word μαρτυρεῖν) is congruous with the evangelist's general attitude. The adjective ἀληθής, again, is a favourite with this evangelist (14 occurrences) and closely associated with his characteristic ideas.[2] The passage however clearly describes a whole period of activity rather than any particular incident, and the verbs ἔμενεν,[3] ἔλεγον are in the continuous tense. The topographical datum, πέραν τοῦ Ἰορδάνου, associates the passage with 'framework' material, and so does the back-reference to the locality of John's early ministry of baptism, meaning, no

[1] Bultmann, *ad loc.*, finds here a *Traditionsstück* which was originally the introduction to a miracle story.

[2] It occurs in one context only in the Synoptics, Mark xii. 14 = Matt. xxii. 16.

[3] So most MSS, but others, including DΘ and 𝔓 45, have ἔμεινεν (see p. 235, n. 2; p. 242, n. 2)

doubt, the 'Bethany-beyond-Jordan' of i. 28.[1] It is possible, or slightly probable, that we have a fragment of 'itinerary' material from tradition, worked over by the evangelist.

(vii) xi. 54:

ὁ οὖν 'Ιησοῦς οὐκέτι παρρησίᾳ περιεπάτει ἐν τοῖς 'Ιουδαίοις ἀλλὰ ἀπῆλθεν ἐκεῖθεν εἰς τὴν χώραν ἐγγὺς τῆς ἐρήμου, εἰς 'Εφραὶμ λεγομένην πόλιν, κἀκεῖ ἔμεινεν μετὰ τῶν μαθητῶν.

The opening words have a Johannine ring; παρρησίᾳ occurs nine times in the Fourth Gospel and once only in the Synoptics, and 'Ιουδαῖοι occurs 69 times in this gospel,[2] while the three Synoptics have it only four times in all, except in the phrase βασιλεὺς τῶν 'Ιουδαίων. They may be an editorial note added in the course of composition. But what follows has the characteristics of 'framework' material. It describes a whole period and not any particular incident,[3] and the topographical interest is marked. The town of Ephraim is not otherwise known to the New Testament.

[1] See below, pp. 249–50.

[2] This writer uses the term οἱ 'Ιουδαῖοι imprecisely. Usually it means either (i) the general body of the Jewish people so far as they are hostile or unfriendly to Christ, or (ii) the Jewish authorities in Jerusalem. Sometimes the two meanings are scarcely distinguished. Occasionally the term appears to be used in a geographical sense, meaning inhabitants of the province of Judaea. ('Judaeans' rather than 'Jews'.) That the adjective 'Ιουδαῖος has a geographical sense is clear from iii. 22, where we have ἡ 'Ιουδαία γῆ. In xi. 7 Jesus proposes to go εἰς τὴν 'Ιουδαίαν. In verse 8 the disciples demur on the ground, ἐζήτουν σε λιθάσαι οἱ 'Ιουδαῖοι, where it would seem natural to understand that they object to entering a territory whose inhabitants (the 'Judaeans') have shown themselves dangerously hostile. In vii. 1 Jesus is unwilling to go about ἐν τῇ 'Ιουδαίᾳ, because οἱ 'Ιουδαῖοι (? the 'Judaeans') are seeking to kill him. Similarly here, xi. 54, Jesus no longer goes about openly ἐν τοῖς 'Ιουδαίοις, which might naturally mean 'among the inhabitants of Judaea', in other words, in Judaea, since he now moves to a different region. But since we do not know exactly where Ephraim was, and therefore whether or not it counted as part of the province of Judaea, it is possible that the stress falls on παρρησίᾳ, the meaning being 'he no longer showed himself *openly* to his adversaries'—as he had previously done. In any case, οἱ 'Ιουδαῖοι seem always to be the enemies (or potential enemies) of Christ, and even if the geographical meaning of the term is present, the other meaning hovers about it. That a Christian writer of the late first century should speak in this way of 'the Jews', especially if he wrote in a gentile environment, is intelligible enough; it would be less easily intelligible in anyone (whether himself of Jewish or gentile origin) writing in a Jewish environment. But it may be that the term was used in a more local sense in the tradition which sometimes shows through.

[3] Most authorities read ἔμεινεν: the tense is aorist, but it is probably rather the 'constative' aorist than the tense of momentary action. In any case the verb μένειν is by nature 'linear' rather than 'punctiliar' in *Aktionsart*. Other authorities, however, including DΘ and the Chester Beatty papyrus 45, read διέτριβεν, but possibly by assimilation to iii. 22.

The uncertainty about its exact situation is in no way unfavourable to the view that John is here reproducing traditional information. It is rather favourable to it, since an author writing at Ephesus late in the first century would scarcely be aware of, or interested in, an obscure Palestinian town, and any mysterious or symbolic meaning of the name is out of the question. From verse 55 the author is laying the scene for the momentous events of the impending Passover, and apparently composing freely. But in 54 there is a reasonable probability that he has preserved traditional material.

I suggest, then, that we have good grounds for accepting the following as traditional data summarizing periods in the Ministry of Jesus, with indications of the places where they were spent:

Jesus went down to Capernaum, and stayed there a short time. After this he went with his disciples to Judaea and stayed there, baptizing. Meanwhile John was baptizing at Aenon-by-Salim, because there was abundant water there, and people kept coming to him and getting baptized....Later, Jesus left Judaea for Galilee, because, as he himself testified, a prophet is not honoured in his own country. So when he arrived in Galilee he was welcomed by the Galilaeans.... Again he went over Jordan, to the place where John had formerly baptized; he stayed there, and many came to him...and from there he went to the region bordering on the Wilderness, to a city called Ephraim, and stayed there with his disciples.

There is little trace here of a coherent outline of the Ministry, such as we may (I believe) reasonably infer to have provided part of the Marcan framework. Yet this exiguous group of passages does afford some ground for concluding that they originally belonged to a single body of tradition, which, like the Marcan 'generalizing summaries' and 'itinerary fragments', recorded in bald outline the main movements of Jesus: where he went and what he did there. Our evangelist has only occasionally made use of such material. In a great part of his work he dispenses with connecting links altogether. The logical development of the thought has completely taken charge. All the more striking is it to find cropping up here and there these small undigested scraps of different material, which I believe we may with some confidence regard as traditional. The names have no particular interest in themselves; there seems to be no discernible reason why they should have been introduced except that they came down as an integral part of an historical tradition, and were preserved as such. The idea that such names as Aenon-by-Salim and Ephraim are introduced for the sake of some recondite symbolic meanings supposed to be attached to them, though once popular, is quite arbitrary, and any attempt to establish such meanings is the merest guesswork. They are less familiar names, but not more laden with mysterious meaning, than the name, for example, of Capernaum, which occurs in similar contexts, and is introduced in exactly the same way.

If then we are justified in holding the topographical data contained in these transitional, or 'framework', passages to be scraps of solid information, then we may extend the argument to place-names occurring in other parts of the work. The names of Bethesda and Siloam are in the same way integral to the narratives in which they occur, and are not introduced simply for the sake of any symbolic meaning, even though a lucky bit of erudition (whether correct or not) enables the evangelist to exploit the etymological meaning of Siloam for symbolic purposes. Nor need we seek any recondite meaning in the names Gabbatha, Sychar or Cana. I am not here raising the question, whether in this or that case the topographical setting of an incident is factually correct; I am arguing that the only reasonable view to take of all this topographical material is that the evangelist worked upon information received; he believed it to be sufficiently trustworthy, and it satisfied an interest in such matters which he shared with other Greek writers of his time, however improper such interest may have been for a Christian evangelist, in the view of some modern writers.

The place-names actually introduced merit some consideration. A certain range of names is common to all gospels, and these we may fairly assume to belong to the basic tradition: the Sea of Galilee, the River Jordan, the Mount of Olives: Judaea, Galilee, Transjordan (πέραν τοῦ 'Ιορδάνου); Capernaum, Bethsaida; Jerusalem, Bethany, Golgotha. In addition to these John has Cana-in-Galilee, Tiberias (and Sea of Tiberias); Samaria (with Luke), Sychar, Aenon, Salim, Bethany-beyond-Jordan, Ephraim; Bethesda, Siloam (with Luke), Kidron, Solomon's Portico, Gabbatha (Lithostroton); also, allusively only, Bethlehem. Of these, Tiberias (Sea of Tiberias) is probably not traditional.[1] Apart from

---

[1] In xxi. 1 the Sea of Galilee is called ἡ θάλασσα τῆς Τιβεριάδος, and τῆς Τιβεριάδος is added to the more familiar name in vi. 1. If ch. xxi is an addition by a different writer (as is possible but by no means certain), he may have been responsible also for the addition in vi. 1. In any case, ἡ θάλασσα τῆς Τιβεριάδος is the form likely to have been familiar to a Hellenistic public. In extant non-biblical literature it appears first in Strabo. The name of Tiberias, built by Antipas as a Greek city, would certainly be more familiar to a Greek public than barbarous names like

this, Cana is the only place in northern Palestine known to John but not to the Synoptics. The large range of northern names which occur in the Synoptics is for the most part absent, including Gennesaret, Chorazin, Decapolis, Caesarea Philippi, Magadan (Magdala), the Country of the Gerasenes (Gadarenes, Gergesenes), the territory of Tyre and Sidon, as well as, in Luke, Nain, Trachonitis, Abilene and Ituraea (though the last three are hardly significant for our purpose). On the other hand, though John has not the Judaean names Bethphage, Gethsemane, and Emmaus (Lucan only), he has nine names of places in Judaea, Samaria or the Jordan valley not known to the Synoptics. The preponderance is marked. Is this accidental? It is true that the evangelist's rigorous selection of incidents may have resulted in the exclusion of 'Galilaean' material known to him, but this is conjectural. In any case his tradition, so far as we know it, was poor in northern material, while it preserved memories of places and events in the south unknown to the tradition followed by the Synoptics.

It would seem natural to infer that the *milieu* in which the tradition behind the Fourth Gospel was transmitted is to be sought in Jerusalem and the south rather than Galilee and the north. Are there any further phenomena in the gospel which would fit a southern *milieu* for the tradition behind it?

I have already drawn attention to the ambiguous and confused references to the sojourn of Jesus in Galilee. The record of his move northwards, which seems to have formed part of the 'itinerary' material, has been dislocated by the editorial work of the evangelist, and no longer gives a clear picture. According to iv. 1–3 Jesus left Judaea because the success of his work there had created an unfavourable impression in Pharisaic circles. According to iv. 43–4 he went to Galilee because a prophet is not honoured in his πατρίς, but we do not know whether the πατρίς is Galilee or Judaea. In neither place does it appear that the evangelist regards the move as a planned beginning of a mission to Galilee, which appears rather as a refuge. This view of the matter is made quite explicit in vii. 1, which I have proposed to treat rather as the introduction of a *pericopé* than as a piece of 'itinerary' material. In any case, the whole suggestion of the passage is that Galilee is a place which offers a safe obscurity, over against Judaea which offers a dangerous though possibly fruitful publicity. Nor does the evangelist show any interest in a Galilaean Ministry as such, apart from the one important incident, or series of incidents, recorded in

Capernaum and Bethsaida. The name is more likely to be due to the evangelist, writing for such a public, than to any tradition.

ch. vi, which, as I have argued, was preserved in more than one line of tradition as a crucial episode in the Ministry. But, in John, it can scarcely be recognized as an episode in a Galilaean Ministry. The Galilaean crowds appear suddenly and without preparation, and they melt away as suddenly. Otherwise, all we are told about Jesus in Galilee is that the Galilaeans welcomed him because they had seen what he did *at Jerusalem*. It is at Jerusalem that the really significant Ministry takes place. Galilee is at best a subordinate field of work.

Here then we have a geographically southern standpoint, associated with a psychologically metropolitan outlook, in contrast to the strongly Galilaean standpoint and outlook revealed in the Synoptic Gospels. I do not find it easy to attribute this to any motives proper to an author writing at Ephesus late in the first century, for at that distance of time and place the petty differences, whether geographical or psychological, between the divisions of a very small country must have faded into insignificance. That there was in the early Church a certain tension between the claims of Galilee and Jerusalem was shown by R. H. Lightfoot in *Locality and Doctrine in the Gospels*. He was mainly concerned with the effects of this tension as reflected in the accounts of the Resurrection of Christ and its sequel, but it may well have extended over a wider area of the tradition. The strain of tradition embodied in the Synoptic Gospels appears to be associated with the Twelve, most of them, if not all, Galilaeans. Was there another group of 'witnesses' to the tradition, connected with Judaea and Jerusalem?

According to the Fourth Gospel there was such a group. I revert to vii. 1–9. The brothers of Jesus say, 'Go to Judaea, in order that *your disciples* may see what you are doing'. The μαθηταί, one naturally supposes, are to be found in Judaea. In iv. 1 Jesus is said to have made many disciples in Judaea, and at least two disciples appear who are apparently domiciled in Judaea, Joseph of Arimathaea (who for Mark is not a μαθητής) and the disciple who was γνωστὸς τῷ ἀρχιερεῖ—for that this person was one of the Twelve is not even remotely hinted.[1] It is to give these and other Judaean disciples the opportunity of seeing the 'works' of Jesus that he is urged, whether sincerely or in sarcasm, to leave the obscurity of the provinces. That such a group may have included, as the Fourth Gospel suggests, former adherents of John the Baptist, whose field of work lay in the south, is entirely credible.

[1] See also pp. 86–8 above.

We find no mention of such a group in the Synoptic Gospels. But few critics at this time of day would be prepared to deny that Jesus had ever visited the capital or won disciples in Judaea before the last week of his life, merely on the grounds that the Marcan scheme does not allow for any such visit. John offers material which we have seen good reason to believe traditional, and which seems to be associated in standpoint and in outlook with Jerusalem and the south; and at the same time he introduces us to a circle capable of becoming the bearers of such a tradition. I think we may reasonably conclude that it was through some such channel that the Fourth Evangelist received, directly or indirectly, the tradition which we have traced in the Passion narrative, in certain *pericopae* of the earlier part of the gospel, and in some transitional passages.

C. JOHN THE BAPTIST AND
THE FIRST DISCIPLES

1. INTRODUCTORY

The treatment in the Fourth Gospel of the ministry of John the Baptist and its relation to the Ministry of Jesus Christ has traits which set it apart from the rest of this gospel as well as from the Synoptic presentation of the same theme. In the work of the Baptist in and for itself the Fourth Evangelist shows little interest[1]—even less, perhaps, than Mark, who has given a sketch of his personal appearance and habits, and a brief characterization, as well as an account of his death.[2] There is nothing here of the prophet of judgement depicted in Matthew and Luke,[3] or of the preacher of righteousness whose down-to-earth morality is exemplified in a passage peculiar to the latter.[4] As might have been expected, the Fourth Evangelist is not concerned to record either the birth and parentage or the death of the Baptist.[5] So far as he may be said to relate any incidents in his life, his report has little contact with that of the other gospels. He is interested in the Baptist solely as the forerunner and herald, or, in his own words, the 'witness', to the Messiah. Upon this aspect of his mission he dwells at greater length than the other evangelists, and makes statements which go beyond anything that they report.

The character in which the Baptist is to be presented is defined in advance by a statement in the Prologue (i. 6–8): the man named John, who was sent from God, (a) was not the Light, but (b) came to bear witness to the Light, (c) in order that through his agency all might become believers. This threefold *schema* controls subsequent sections dealing with the Baptist. The elaborate section headed 'The Testimony of John' is constructed precisely on this pattern: (a) John is *not* the Messiah, *not* Elijah, *not* the Prophet, but only a voice in the wilderness (i. 19–27); (b) he 'bears witness' that Jesus is Lamb of God, Son of God, Baptizer with Holy Spirit (verses 29–34); (c) as a result of this testimony the first

---

[1] With one striking exception, iii. 25, on which see below, pp. 280–1.
[2] Mark i. 4–6.
[3] Matt. iii. 7–10, Luke iii. 7–9, Matt. iii. 12, Luke iii. 17.
[4] Luke iii. 10–14, cf. also Mark vi. 18–20.
[5] Luke i. 5–24, 57–80; Mark vi. 17–29; Matt. xiv. 3–12.

believers are led to Jesus (verses 35–7). In the section iii. 22–30 John repeats, 'I am not the Messiah', and predicts the success of Jesus at his expense. This accounts for points (*a*) and (*b*), point (*c*) being unrepresented here. In the brief summary of x. 41–2 we are told that John (*a*) 'performed no σημεῖον' (such as might have attested a messianic mission), but (*b*) told the truth about Jesus, with the result that (*c*) 'many believed on him'.

It seems clear therefore that the presentation of the mission of the Baptist is governed by a certain schematism. In this it resembles other parts of this gospel, where, however, we have seen grounds for believing that much of the material thus schematized was itself drawn by the evangelist from existing tradition. Sometimes we recognized a tradition represented also in the Synoptic Gospels, though there seemed little reason to suppose that it was drawn directly from them. At other times we seemed to be in contact with a completely non-Synoptic tradition which lay before the evangelist, whether in written or in oral form. We have therefore to ask whether within the dogmatic scheme under which the mission of the Baptist is presented we can discern traces of traditional material.

We may usefully start from a consideration of the topographical data. I have argued that the topographical notes found here and there in the Fourth Gospel are such as cannot reasonably be accounted for except as fragments of historical information which the evangelist has incorporated. The attempt to treat them as symbolical cryptograms breaks down, and there is no ground for supposing that they subserved any special interest either of the evangelist or of his readers.

Among these topographical notes there are three which refer to the work of John the Baptist:

(*a*) i. 28, ταῦτα ἐν Βηθανίᾳ ἐγένετο πέραν τοῦ Ἰορδάνου ὅπου ἦν ὁ Ἰωάννης βαπτίζων. This is taken up in (*b*) x. 40, ἀπῆλθεν πάλιν πέραν τοῦ Ἰορδάνου εἰς τὸν τόπον ὅπου ἦν ὁ Ἰωάννης τὸ πρῶτον βαπτίζων. (*c*) iii. 23, ἦν δὲ καὶ Ἰωάννης βαπτίζων ἐν Αἰνὼν ἐγγὺς τοῦ Σαλείμ, ὅτι ὕδατα πολλὰ ἦν ἐκεῖ. Taking x. 40 to be a mere back-reference to i. 28, we have two distinct statements regarding the scene of the Baptist's activity at two separate periods of his life. There is no interpretation of these statements so probable as that which accepts them at their face value, as undigested scraps of concrete information. It does not follow of necessity that all the incidents associated with these places in the course of the narratives themselves come from the same source, or merit the same degree of credence as historical fact. That question has still to be considered. But we seem to be justified in concluding that the evangelist had at his disposal *some* source of information about John the Baptist which is not otherwise known to us. The question before us therefore may be conceived as an inquiry whether or not other statements that he makes about the Baptist and his work are also derived from this (or some similar) source and are to be accepted as having historical value. In seeking an answer to this question we must analyse three passages dealing with the Baptist: i. 19–42, iii. 22–30, x. 40–2.

2. THE TESTIMONY OF JOHN (i. 19–37)

The general heading, αὕτη ἐστὶν ἡ μαρτυρία τοῦ Ἰωάννου[1] (i. 19), though it is formally connected with the immediately succeeding clauses, in substance covers the whole passage down to i. 34, where the repeated μεμαρτύρηκα fitly rounds it off. This passage, however, falls into two distinct parts (corresponding, as we have seen, to the two clauses of the Prologue, οὐκ ἦν ἐκεῖνος τὸ φῶς, ἀλλ᾽ ἵνα μαρτυρήσῃ περὶ τοῦ φωτός). The first part, 19–27, consists of a dialogue between the Baptist and a deputation from Jewish headquarters at Jerusalem, and has appended to it the note that this dialogue took place at Bethany beyond Jordan. The second part, i. 29–34, consists of two declarations by the Baptist, said to have been delivered on the day following the visit of the deputation. This formally concludes the μαρτυρία, but the repeated proclamation, ἴδε ὁ ἀμνὸς τοῦ θεοῦ, in i. 36 indicates that the narrative contained in i. 35–7 is intended to be closely connected with the foregoing, and to indicate the effect of the 'testimony of John', in accordance with the clause of the Prologue, ἵνα πάντες πιστεύσωσιν δι᾽ αὐτοῦ.

The structure of the passage has a general resemblance to Johannine patterns, but only so far as it consists of a sustained dialogue (19–27) followed by a monologue (29–34), with a short narrative-dialogue (35–9) as an appendix. If neither of the two dialogues nor yet the monologue is very closely similar to typical Johannine compositions in other parts of the gospel, this might be accounted for by difference of subject-matter. Yet it remains true that the Johannine stamp is not so deeply impressed on the material as to drive us to say at once, 'This is the work of the evangelist'. On the other hand the traditional forms known to us chiefly from

---

[1] I am disposed to suggest that this clause is in fact intended as an independent sentence introductory to the whole passage. The 'testimony' itself would thus begin (quite normally) in asyndeton, with a somewhat complicated protasis, ὅτε ἀπέστειλαν...τίς εἶ; the apodosis to which is ὡμολόγησεν καὶ οὐκ ἠρνήσατο. The καί before ὡμολόγησεν might be understood as introducing the apodosis (after the Hebrew idiom), or as emphasizing the verb ('he actually confessed'), or as meaning 'both': 'he both confessed and refused to deny'. In this way the interrogation in its successive stages becomes preliminary to the actual μαρτυρία, which begins with μέσος ὑμῶν στήκει (i. 26), and is continued in the second part. The general heading αὕτη ἐστὶν ἡ μαρτυρία τοῦ Ἰωάννου is taken up in verse 32, καὶ ἐμαρτύρησεν Ἰωάννης, and the whole passage is effectively wound up with the μεμαρτύρηκα of i. 34—'There you have my testimony!'

the Synoptic Gospels are but feebly represented here. In some respects the passage is *sui generis*. But the attempt to analyse its contents may repay the trouble.

(i) *Common ground with the Synoptics*

In the following places the 'Testimony of John' has contact with the Synoptic account of the ministry of John the Baptist.

(*a*) *The citation of the Isaianic* testimonium *about the Voice in the Wilderness* (*i. 23*)

All three Synoptics introduce their account of the Baptist by citing the prophecy of Isaiah xl. 3, in identical form:

φωνὴ βοῶντος ἐν τῇ ἐρήμῳ,
Ἑτοιμάσατε τὴν ὁδὸν κυρίου,
εὐθείας ποιεῖτε τὰς τρίβους αὐτοῦ.

This accords with the text of the LXX, except that the latter has τοῦ θεοῦ ἡμῶν (in parallelism with κυρίου) for αὐτοῦ. The Johannine version is shorter:

φωνὴ βοῶντος ἐν τῇ ἐρήμῳ,
Εὐθύνατε τὴν ὁδὸν κυρίου.

There would be no great difficulty in believing that John drew the quotation from the Synoptics, abbreviating it; but we have found cumulative evidence that in his citation of *testimonia* from the Old Testament he was not dependent on the other gospels for the choice or the wording of the passages adduced,[1] and nothing requires us to believe that he went to them for this quotation.[2]

The other evangelists all introduce the *testimonium* as their own comment upon the facts, using slightly different formulae of quotation. The Fourth Evangelist on the other hand makes the Baptist himself quote Isaiah. He is asked, Σὺ τίς εἶ; and replies, Ἐγὼ φωνὴ βοῶντος κ.τ.λ. Since our author is concerned (as we have seen) to present the Baptist in the character of 'witness', *par excellence*, it may be that he placed the quotation in the mouth of the witness with deliberate intention.[3] Yet in view of a

---

[1] See above, pp. 31–46.

[2] For a discussion of the treatment of this prophecy in the New Testament, see *According to the Scriptures*, pp. 39–40, where I have suggested that reminiscences of the Isaianic context may have coloured the language of John xi. 40 and possibly i. 14.

[3] Similarly, the Descent of the Dove is included in the 'testimony of John', i. 32–4. See pp. 259–61.

passage from the *Manual of Discipline* in the 'Dead Sea Scrolls' it is by no means unlikely that the Baptist should have deliberately set himself to fill the role of the Voice:

When these things come to pass for the community in Israel, by these regulations they shall be separated from the midst of the men of error to go to the wilderness to prepare the way of the Lord, as it is written, 'In the wilderness prepare the way of the Lord, make straight in the desert a highway for our God'. This is the study of the law, as he commanded through Moses.[1]

If the men of Qumran believed themselves to have been called (or believed that they might in future be called, according to the interpretation adopted) to fill the role of the Voice in the Wilderness, so may John the Baptist have believed himself called, though his conception of the role went somewhat beyond 'the study of the law'. If so, the Fourth Evangelist may have followed a good tradition in representing him as citing Isa. xl. 3 to define his own mission, and in this he may be closer to the facts than the Synoptics.

(b) The Prediction of the Coming One and of Baptism with the Spirit (i. 26–7, 33 b)

In the Synoptic Gospels two sayings of the Baptist form the core of the account of his ministry as forerunner and herald of the Messiah. These sayings are variously interwoven in the several gospels.

Mark gives the two sayings in succession:

(a) ἔρχεται ὁ ἰσχυρότερός μου ὀπίσω μου
    οὗ οὐκ εἰμὶ ἱκανὸς κύψας λῦσαι τὸν ἱμάντα τῶν ὑποδημάτων αὐτοῦ.

(b) ἐγὼ ἐβάπτισα ὑμᾶς ὕδατι,
    αὐτὸς δὲ βαπτίσει ὑμᾶς ἐν πνεύματι ἁγίῳ.

The second of the sayings, as Mark gives it, in its crisp antithetic form, is the simplest version of the prediction of spirit-baptism. Something like it appears to underlie also the saying in Acts i. 5, which is again quoted (as a ῥῆμα κυρίου) in Acts xi. 16: 'John baptized with water, but you will be baptized in holy Spirit.'

In Matthew and Luke the two predictions, separate in Mark, are combined, in a chiastic structure, with the result that the two members of the

---

[1] Translation by Millar Burrows, *The Dead Sea Scrolls*, p. 382. See J. A. T. Robinson (now Bishop of Woolwich), 'The Baptism of John and the Qumran Community', in *Harvard Theological Review*, L, 3 (July 1957), pp. 177–9.

prediction of spirit-baptism are disjoined. The simpler form is the Lucan:

ἐγὼ μὲν ὕδατι βαπτίζω ὑμᾶς,
ἔρχεται δὲ ὁ ἰσχυρότερός μου,
οὗ οὐκ εἰμὶ ἱκανὸς λῦσαι τὸν ἱμάντα τῶν ὑποδημάτων αὐτοῦ.
αὐτὸς ὑμᾶς βαπτίσει ἐν πνεύματι ἁγίῳ καὶ πυρί (iii. 16).

Matthew is more elaborate, and his phraseology differs significantly:

ἐγὼ μὲν ὑμᾶς βαπτίζω ἐν ὕδατι εἰς μετάνοιαν,
ὁ δὲ ὀπίσω μου ἐρχόμενος ἰσχυρότερός μου ἐστίν,
οὗ οὐκ εἰμὶ ἱκανὸς τὰ ὑποδήματα βαστάσαι·
αὐτὸς ὑμᾶς βαπτίσει ἐν πνεύματι ἁγίῳ καὶ πυρί (iii. 11).

In the Fourth Gospel the disjunction of the two members of the prediction of spirit-baptism has gone further:

ἐγὼ βαπτίζω ἐν ὕδατι·
μέσος ὑμῶν στήκει ὃν ὑμεῖς οὐκ οἴδατε, ὁ ὀπίσω μου ἐρχόμενος,
οὗ οὐκ εἰμὶ ἐγὼ ἄξιος ἵνα λύσω αὐτοῦ τὸν ἱμάντα τοῦ ὑποδήματος
(i. 26-7)

—and then, after a long interval, in which the most important parts of the 'testimony' have been given—

οὗτός ἐστιν ὁ βαπτίζων ἐν πνεύματι ἁγίῳ (i. 33).

The wide separation of this clause from the clause ἐγὼ βαπτίζω ἐν ὕδατι has brought it into a different syntactical construction, but we can hardly doubt that in the earlier tradition the contrast between water-baptism and spirit-baptism was expressed in a single antithetical sentence. The wide separation of the two members of the antithesis is in all probability the work of the Fourth Evangelist himself. It may be possible to discern a motive for it, if he be supposed to have wished to keep the saying about spirit-baptism in reserve until the presupposition of such baptism had been made clear, namely the descent of the Spirit on Christ himself.

Allowing for this, we may recognize in the Johannine account a general similarity to the Synoptic. It does not however follow any one of the Synoptic versions consistently. As against Mark, who gives the prediction of the Coming One and that of spirit-baptism each as a complete and separate saying, John agrees with Matthew and Luke in fusing the two, and thereby blunting in a measure the point of the antithesis. He further agrees with Matthew and Luke against Mark in giving the present βαπτίζω for the aorist ἐβάπτισα. On the other hand, John shows no knowledge of the additional words καὶ πυρί in Matthew and Luke, but agrees with Mark in the prediction of a baptism ἐν πνεύματι ἁγίῳ simply. As between Matthew and Luke, he agrees with Luke (and Mark) in speaking of untying the shoe-strap instead of carrying the shoes (though John has the singular ὑποδήματος as against the plural in the other three), and he does not give the Matthaean addition εἰς μετάνοιαν. On the other hand, John agrees with Matthew against Luke (and Mark) in making ὁ ὀπίσω μου ἐρχόμενος the subject of the sentence, instead of using the indicative ἔρχεται as predicate.[1] He also gives ἐν ὕδατι with Matthew against Luke and (probably) Mark,[2] who have the simple dative.

John differs from all three Synoptics, not only in divorcing the clause about spirit-baptism from the clause to which it is properly antithetical, and in inserting the significant clause μέσος ὑμῶν στήκει ὃν ὑμεῖς οὐκ οἴδατε (of which more later),[3] but also in omitting all reference to ὁ ἰσχυρότερος and in some verbal details. The substitution of ἵνα λύσω for the infinitive λῦσαι introduces a construction preferred by this writer,[4] and may be assigned to his hand. But the use of ἄξιος in place of ἱκανός[5] is more interesting. Neither adjective occurs elsewhere in the Fourth Gospel. But we have a fourth version of the saying in Acts xiii. 25:

ἔρχεται μετ᾿ ἐμὲ οὗ οὐκ εἰμὶ ἄξιος τὸ ὑπόδημα τῶν ποδῶν λῦσαι.

This should be compared with the version of Luke iii. 16:

ἔρχεται ὁ ἰσχυρότερός μου οὗ οὐκ εἰμὶ ἱκανὸς λῦσαι τὸν ἱμάντα τῶν ὑποδημάτων αὐτοῦ.

The existence of two versions of the same saying, in works presumably by the same author, calls for explanation. The differences may, of course, be the result of mere inadvertence. That would at any rate be more plausible than the view that the author deliberately varied the wording, for no discernible reason. But the occurrence of such 'doublets' has very often proved to be the clue to a duplication of sources. In the present instance the hypothesis that the author of Luke–Acts drew the saying as given in Acts xiii. 25 from a source (oral or written) other than that which he followed in Luke iii. 16 gains probability when we observe that the former agrees with the Johannine version against that of Luke iii. 16 in

---

[1] But in a similar saying peculiar to this gospel he has ὀπίσω μου ἔρχεται ἀνὴρ κ.τ.λ. in one place (i. 30), though in another place he gives it otherwise: ὁ ὀπίσω μου ἐρχόμενος ἔμπροσθέν μου γέγονεν (i. 15). See below, pp. 272–4.

[2] AD and others have ἐν ὕδατι, but this is probably by assimilation to Matthew.

[3] See below, pp. 266–9.

[4] See below, pp. 355–6. John's Greek is here more 'vulgar' than that of the other evangelists.

[5] Ἄξιος is certainly the true reading, though ἱκανός has some feeble support (including however that of the Bodmer papyrus).

three respects: (*a*) in making no mention of ὁ ἰσχυρότερος, (*b*) in using ἄξιος for ἱκανός, and (*c*) in using the singular of ὑπόδημα instead of the plural.

The complicated phenomena of agreement and difference among no fewer than five versions of the Baptist's prediction leave various possibilities open. That the Fourth Evangelist was acquainted with Matthew, Mark, Luke and Acts, and conflated their accounts while introducing fresh matter of his own, could no doubt be believed, with some effort, if on chronological grounds it seemed likely, or even possible. That he based his account upon some one of our documents and happened by accident to hit upon alterations which coincided with the others calls for at least an equal effort of credulity. The simplest, and surely the most probable, hypothesis is that this part of the Baptist's preaching, which was evidently regarded in the early Church as of crucial importance, was preserved in several branches of the tradition, and that variations arose in the process of oral transmission. It is therefore highly probable that John is here following, independently, a special line of tradition. He may no doubt have handled it, after his manner, with some freedom, but it would be unsafe to assume that the significant features peculiar to the Fourth Gospel in this passage are no more than the author's free embellishments of matter drawn at second hand from the Synoptics.

(*c*) *The Baptist's disclaimer of messianic status (i. 20)*

In the dialogue of John i. 19–27 the citation of the Isaianic prophecy of the Voice in the Wilderness is introduced as the Baptist's reply to the question, Σὺ τίς εἶ; He answers first negatively, ἐγὼ οὐκ εἰμὶ ὁ χριστός. When, after similar disclaimers of the titles of Elijah and the Prophet, the question is pressed, Τίς εἶ; he replies, Ἐγὼ φωνὴ βοῶντος κ.τ.λ. Again, the prediction of the Coming One whose shoe-strap the Baptist is not fit to untie is given in reply to the question, 'Why do you baptize, if you are neither the Messiah nor Elijah nor the Prophet?' Thus the fragments of recognizably traditional material which we have already considered have for their background in the Fourth Gospel the question of the status of John the Baptist, and in particular of his possible claim to messianic dignity.

In Matthew and Mark there is no trace of this background, but it appears in two passages of the Lucan writings. In Luke iii. 15 *sq.* we are told that there was widespread speculation among the people about John, μήποτε αὐτὸς εἴη ὁ χριστός, and it was this that led him to foretell the coming of the Stronger One. Again in Acts xiii. 24–5 the historical sketch which forms part of the version of the apostolic *kerygma* attributed to Paul leads up to the statement that John heralded the coming of the Saviour by a baptism of repentance, and then proceeds, ὡς δὲ ἐπλήρου Ἰωάννης τὸν δρόμον ἔλεγεν, Τί ἐμὲ ὑπονοεῖτε εἶναι, οὐκ εἰμὶ ἐγώ· ἀλλ' ἰδοὺ ἔρχεται μετ' ἐμέ κ.τ.λ. The question we have first to consider is whether these statements are likely to rest upon any earlier tradition, or reflect the theological or apologetic interests of the author himself.

In the Third Gospel the prediction of the Coming One (Luke iii. 16) follows Mark pretty closely, and it might be held that the preceding verse (iii. 15) is an editorial introduction which the evangelist himself has added to his derived material, as he has done in other cases. Yet the view is widely held that Luke had a source or sources in addition to Mark for his account of the ministry of the Baptist. Not only does he give John's proclamation of the coming judgement, iii. 7–9, 17, in words which have no parallel in Mark, but are so close to Matthew that a common source is virtually certain, but he adds the ethical preaching of iii. 10–14, which has no parallel in the gospels, though it chimes in with Josephus's description of John as a teacher of morals (*Antiq.* XVIII. 117). It is therefore possible that the editorial introduction in iii. 15 may in substance go back to one of the sources, or lines of tradition, which Luke was following, even if its phrasing be his own.

In Acts xiii. 25 I have already argued that the curious divergence from the version of the same saying given by the same author in Luke iii. 16 suggests the use of a separate source; and indeed the whole cast of the passage about the Baptist in Acts xiii, and its setting in an historical *résumé*, make it doubtful that the author is merely adapting the Synoptic tradition, and point to the probable use of a source of a quite different character from those which are being used in Luke iii. And here the words which specially concern us at present, those in which the Baptist disclaims the messianic dignity, have none of that 'editorial' stamp which we noted in the parallel passage Luke iii. 15, but seem to belong integrally to the context.

There is therefore a reasonable degree of probability that the author of Luke–Acts had some traditional authority for the statement that there was, if not a belief, at least the suggestion of a possibility, that John the Baptist might be the Messiah,[1] and that he expressly repudiated it. Even

---

[1] There may be a hint of some such belief in the statement that some people, including Antipas, imagined John as rising from the dead and working miracles, Mark vi. 14, viii. 28.

if this probability be accepted, it would not necessarily follow that the underlying tradition was either primitive or trustworthy, but it would be of greater antiquity than the period of composition of Luke–Acts.

We now turn to the Fourth Gospel. We have already noted that the form of the prediction of the Coming One shows some similarities to the form given in Acts xiii. 25. Beyond this, there is no such degree of verbal resemblance as would suggest literary dependence of John on either Luke or Acts. The words with which we are more particularly concerned, those regarding the tentative ascription to the Baptist of messianic dignity, and his disclaimer, show no great degree of resemblance in the three documents:

Luke iii. 15–16: διαλογιζομένων πάντων. . . περὶ τοῦ Ἰωάννου μήποτε αὐτὸς εἴη ὁ χριστὸς ἀπεκρίνατο λέγων πᾶσιν ὁ Ἰωάννης, Ἐγὼ μὲν ὕδατι βαπτίζω ὑμᾶς, ἔρχεται δὲ ὁ ἰσχυρότερος κ.τ.λ.

Acts xiii. 25, ὡς δὲ ἐπλήρου Ἰωάννης τὸν δρόμον ἔλεγεν, Τί ἐμὲ ὑπονοεῖτε εἶναι οὐκ εἰμὶ ἐγώ· ἀλλ᾽ ἰδοὺ ἔρχεται κ.τ.λ.

John i. 20 sqq. (They asked) Σὺ τίς εἶ; καὶ ὡμολόγησεν καὶ οὐκ ἠρνήσατο, Ἐγὼ οὐκ εἰμὶ ὁ χριστός. (They questioned him further:) ἀπεκρίθη αὐτοῖς ὁ Ἰωάννης λέγων, Ἐγὼ βαπτίζω ἐν ὕδατι κ.τ.λ.

It would no doubt be possible to compile the Fourth Evangelist's much more lengthy account from the data of Luke–Acts, by picking up a bit here and a bit there. This does not however seem to be the method by which he worked. If on the other hand we were to postulate a kind of generalized memory of the two documents, we should still have to reckon with some chronological difficulty, for it seems that the completion of Luke–Acts cannot be dated much, if any, earlier than the probable date of the Fourth Gospel. The simplest and surely the most probable hypothesis to account for the phenomena is that the Fourth Evangelist was following a tradition which had contact with the tradition we have been led to suspect behind Luke and Acts. It is not part of the common Synoptic tradition.

Against this it may be argued that the theme, 'Not Messiah but witness to the Messiah', is so much a part of the fixed dogmatic scheme under which the Johannine account of the Baptist stands that there is ground for suspecting that we have here rather a theologumenon than a piece of historical tradition. This raises questions which must be more fully considered at a later stage, but we may here observe that there is, so far, no necessary advance in the Fourth Gospel beyond the position of Luke–Acts, and further that, whatever may have been the situation at Ephesus when the gospel was written, any 'messianic' claims that may have been made for John the Baptist at that time and place are likely to have been made more emphatically, and countered more eagerly, when Christianity was a newcomer in a field already occupied by the Baptist and his disciples. There is therefore no difficulty in finding an early *Sitz im Leben* for such a tradition as I have inferred. It is at least as likely that the Fourth Evangelist has provided a dogmatic formula for a long-standing piece of Christian apologetic as that the whole story is the offspring of his fertile brain. Upon the question of the historical credibility of our postulated tradition there will be more to say later.

(d) The Descent of the Dove and the acclamation of Jesus as Son of God (i. 32–4)

This passage corresponds to the *pericopé* of all three Synoptics in which the baptism of Jesus by John is followed immediately by the descent of the Spirit and a voice from heaven declaring him to be Son of God. Verbal agreements however are at a minimum: τὸ πνεῦμα καταβαῖνον ὡς περιστεράν in John, followed by ἔμεινεν ἐπ᾽ αὐτόν, is to be compared with the slightly differing expressions in the other gospels:

Mark i. 10: τὸ πνεῦμα ὡς περιστερὰν καταβαῖνον εἰς αὐτόν.

Matthew iii. 16: πνεῦμα θεοῦ καταβαῖνον ὡσεὶ περιστεράν, ἐρχόμενον ἐπ᾽ αὐτόν.

Luke iii. 22: καταβῆναι τὸ πνεῦμα τὸ ἅγιον σωματικῷ εἴδει ὡς περιστερὰν ἐπ᾽ αὐτόν.

Here we observe once again the agreement of the Fourth Gospel, now with one and now with another of the Synoptics. In the description of the Spirit it agrees with Mark, giving the simple τὸ πνεῦμα without any elaboration. On the other hand, where Mark has the preposition εἰς, John agrees with Matthew and Luke in giving ἐπί, though neither of them uses the verb μένειν. The statement in John that the Spirit descended ἐξ οὐρανοῦ might be regarded as a compendious paraphrase of the Synoptic description of the opening (or rending) of the heavens (or of heaven), the Fourth Gospel agreeing with the Third in using the singular οὐρανός. It is obvious that there is not enough material here to justify the inference either that John does, or that he does not, follow any or all of the Synoptics as a source. The three keywords alone, πνεῦμα, καταβαῖνον, περιστερά, run through all four, and without these the story could hardly be told at all.[1]

---

[1] The choice of words is perhaps not strictly inevitable. In place of περιστερά, which is properly a pigeon, not a dove, but is loosely used for the latter (= Heb. יונה), we might have had τρυγών, which in Philo is a symbol of the Logos; and for καταβαῖνον (a verb which is not elsewhere used of the Spirit) we might have had,

In any case, the points in which the Fourth Gospel diverges from the others are more striking than the resemblances. Apart from the absence of any reference to the baptism of Jesus, the account of the descent of the Dove is introduced in a way entirely peculiar to this gospel. In Luke it is represented as an 'objective' occurrence (ἐγένετο... καταβῆναι τὸ πνεῦμα τὸ ἅγιον σωματικῷ εἴδει); in Matthew and Mark it is said to have been 'seen' by Jesus, and apparently by him alone. In the Fourth Gospel John the Baptist reports it as something which he had himself 'watched' (τεθέαμαι τὸ πνεῦμα καταβαῖνον)—and he alone, as it appears; emphatically he adds, κἀγὼ ἑώρακα.

Again, in the Synoptic Gospels the descent of the Dove is accompanied by a voice from heaven (bath qol) declaring Jesus to be Son of God. In Mark and Luke the voice is addressed directly to Jesus himself (σὺ εἶ ὁ υἱός μου). In Matthew the grammatical third person is substituted for the second (οὗτός ἐστιν ὁ υἱός μου), and the words must be conceived as addressed either to the Baptist, or to the spectators, or to both. In the Fourth Gospel there is no bath qol: John the Baptist himself acclaims Jesus as Son of God: κἀγὼ ἑώρακα καὶ μεμαρτύρηκα ὅτι οὗτός ἐστιν ὁ υἱὸς τοῦ θεοῦ,[2] recalling the Matthaean form of the bath qol at the Baptism, as well as the other bath qol at the Transfiguration, according to all three Synoptics.

The effect of all this is that in place of the account of the inauguration of Jesus as Messiah, which the Synoptics give, the Fourth Gospel gives an account of a prophetic experience of John the Baptist, an experience which qualifies him for the special role which he fills in this gospel, that of the 'witness' to Christ. There is therefore some ground for suspecting

possibly, πῖπτον (cf. Acts viii. 16, x. 44, xi. 15). Yet καταβαίνειν is properly used of the descent of heavenly beings (Rev. x. 1, xx. 1 and in LXX), and there is no reason why Philonic symbolism should be brought in. The intention would seem to be, not to compare the Spirit with a dove (as Luke understood it), but to compare the descent of the Spirit (on this occasion alone) with the flight of a dove.

'As I have seen a snow-white dove   Decline her bosom from above
And down her spotless body fling   Without the motion of a wing,
Till she arrest her seeming fall   Upon some happy pedestal.'

(I owe the suggestion, with the quotation from Charles Cotton, to Canon Adam Fox, who, as I remember, put it forward at a meeting of C. H. Turner's Seminar at Oxford many years ago.) The phrase καταβαῖνον ὡς περιστεράν is an entirely appropriate image of the coming of the Spirit in a way which is unparalleled.

[2] In ℵ, 𝔓 5, some minuscules, some O.L. MSS., and O.S. (Cur.) the reading is ὁ ἐκλεκτός τοῦ θεοῦ, an expression not found elsewhere in the gospels, but cf. Luke ix. 35 (Θ 1) Οὗτός ἐστιν ὁ υἱός μου ὁ ἐκλεκτός (ℵ B etc., ἐκλελεγμένος), xxiii. 35 ὁ χριστός τοῦ θεοῦ ὁ ἐκλεκτός (with some variants). These variations in the MSS. probably have behind them a history in the oral tradition.

that the representation has been influenced by the evangelist's dogmatic presuppositions. It is possible that he started with an account like the Synoptic (whether in direct dependence on one or more of the Synoptic Gospels or on a parallel tradition) and transformed it in accordance with the view he took of the role of the Baptist. On the other hand, if it should seem probable that he possessed some other tradition about the Baptist, independent of the Synoptics, then the possibility should be held open that such tradition may have represented the Baptist, the last of the prophetic succession, as claiming an experience analogous to those of the prophets of the Old Testament: the hearing of the divine word, and the vision confirming it. Unless, however, the hypothesis of such a tradition can be given probability on other grounds, this passage cannot be used to support it.

(ii) *Features peculiar to the Fourth Gospel*

We have now exhausted all the material given under the rubric, 'The Testimony of John', which has anything of substance in common with the Synoptics. For the rest, the most that can be said is that at some few points there are purely formal similarities.

First, the discussion of the identity, or official status, of John the Baptist in i. 21–3 has some resemblance to the discussion of the identity, or official status, of Jesus in Mark viii. 28–9 and parallels. The resemblance may be exhibited as follows:

Synoptic Gospels	Fourth Gospel
Jesus is *not*	John is *not*
John *redivivus*	Messiah
Elijah	Elijah
a prophet	the Prophet
Jesus *is*	John *is*
Messiah	φωνὴ βοῶντος

The resemblance is not close, but it is perhaps closer than the resemblance between Mark viii. 28–9 and any Johannine passage in which the messianic claims of Jesus are discussed (vii. 12, 26–7, 31, 40–1). In any case, this is a sufficiently natural way of leading up to the affirmation which is the main point: that Jesus is Messiah, or that the Baptist fulfils the prophecy of Isaiah. But we might perhaps say that the formal parallel reflects the conception that the mission and function of the two are in some sort analogous although they are also in contrast, and this conception is present elsewhere, and is clearly a feature of the primary tradition.

Secondly, the question to the Baptist, Τί οὖν βαπτίζεις; is somewhat reminiscent of the question put to Jesus in Mark xi. 28 and parallels: Ἐν ποίᾳ ἐξουσίᾳ ταῦτα ποιεῖς; In both cases the challenge is one which grows naturally out of the presumed situation, and the situation itself dictates the form. But it is perhaps worth noting that in the context of Mark xi. 28–33 the analogy between the ministries of Jesus and of John is expressly indicated. The analogy (which lies within limits, like all analogies) is undoubtedly rooted in historical facts.

Thirdly, the account of the descent of the Dove in i. 32 is given in a form which recalls the language of prophetic vision in the Old Testament,[1] and this has a New Testament parallel in Luke x. 18, where Jesus says, ἐθεώρουν τὸν σατανᾶν ὡς ἀστραπὴν ἐκ τοῦ οὐρανοῦ πεσόντα. Similarly here the Baptist says, τεθέαμαι τὸ πνεῦμα καταβαῖνον ὡς περιστερὰν ἐξ οὐρανοῦ. There is no other example of prophetic vision in the Fourth Gospel.[2] The implication is that both Jesus and John are regarded as prophetic figures—not, of course, to the exclusion of the 'more-than-prophetic', even in the case of John (Matt. xi. 9), a fortiori in that of Jesus.

Beyond these three, I can find no place in that part of the Fourth Gospel we are now considering which shows any formal affinity with the Synoptic tradition. We are dealing with exclusively Johannine material. We must now examine some of its salient features, with the question in mind, how far they must be regarded as the creation of the Fourth Evangelist himself, with his known and well-marked tendencies, and how far they may be thought to preserve traits of an older tradition.

(a) The interrogation of the Baptist by a deputation from Jerusalem (i. 19 sqq.)

Such interventions by the Jewish authorities are not unknown to the Synoptic tradition of the Ministry of Jesus,[3] though there is nothing on

---

[1] It is one of the marks of a prophet to have visionary experiences and to be able to make the affirmation, 'I saw'. So Micaiah ben Imlah in 3 Kms. xxii. 17–23, and so Isa. vi. 1, Jer. i. 11–14, Ezek. i. 4 sqq., Amos ix. 1, et passim in vetere testamento. The verb used mostly is ὁρᾶν, ἰδεῖν, but in Daniel (LXX and Theod.) θεωρεῖν is usual.

[2] The vision of God, in a sense which John shares in part with Hellenistic mysticism, is of course something quite different (see Interpretation, pp. 166–8). There are allusions to visions recorded in the Old Testament in i. 51, viii. 56, but this again is a different matter and so is the 'vision' which these two passages offer in prospect. John, like the Synoptics, knows of the hearing of the voice from heaven (bath qol) (xii. 28), which in later Jewish thought is in some sort the equivalent of the word of the Lord to the prophets.

[3] The questioning of John by representatives of various classes in Luke iii. 10–14 is not analogous to our present passage.

this scale. It is of course possible that the evangelist has constructed an 'ideal scene' to introduce the denial of John's claim to messianic status and the assertion of the claim of Jesus. On the other hand, if the author is composing freely, he might have been expected to follow his usual practice in naming the leaders of the Jewish opposition. In viii. 13, ix. 13, xi. 46, xii. 19, these are φαρισαῖοι, in xii. 10, xix. 21, ἀρχιερεῖς. In vii. 32, xviii. 3, ἀρχιερεῖς καὶ φαρισαῖοι send ὑπηρέται to effect an arrest, and in xix. 6, ἀρχιερεῖς καὶ ὑπηρέται act together. Nowhere, apart from our present passage, does the evangelist speak of ἱερεῖς or of Λευεῖται, to say nothing of 'priests and Levites' acting in concert. Nor indeed do the two orders of ministry figure in the other gospels, unless we reckon Luke x. 30–2, where a priest and a Levite are individual characters in the parable.

It has been suggested that the reference to 'priests and Levites' is a literary reminiscence of the Old Testament. If the passage is thought to be the free composition of an Ephesian author towards A.D. 100 that would no doubt be the most plausible explanation, though it would still not adequately explain why the combination occurs here and nowhere else in this gospel. If, however, he was drawing on a tradition going back to the period, before A.D. 70, when the twofold ministry was still functioning conspicuously at Jerusalem, everything falls into place.[1]

In i. 25 the more familiar φαρισαῖοι are introduced. The reading is dubious. The *textus receptus* has καὶ οἱ ἀπεσταλμένοι ἦσαν ἐκ τῶν φαρισαίων, that is 'those who had been sent (namely the priests and Levites of verse

---

[1] The institution of the twofold ministry is given great emphasis in the 'Dead Sea Scrolls'. Not only were 'priests and Levites' the centre of the religious discipline of the community at Qumran, but they are assigned a role of special significance and solemnity in the prospective 'War of the Sons of Light and the Sons of Darkness' (apparently an equivalent for the eschatological 'Armageddon'). The sectarian ministry of 'priests and Levites' at Qumran was held to have prophetic sanction: 'Those who hold fast to it (*scil.* the covenant) are for eternal life, and all the glory of man is theirs; as God established it for them by the prophet Ezekiel, saying, "The priests and the Levites and the sons of Zadok, who kept charge of my sanctuary... they shall offer to me fat and blood" [Ezek. xliv. 15]. The priests are the captivity of Israel who went forth from the land of Judah, and the Levites are those who joined them, and the sons of Zadok are the elect of Israel' ('Damascus Document' = 'Fragments of a Zadokite Work' in Charles, *Apocrypha and Pseudepigrapha*, v–vi. Translation by Millar Burrows, *The Dead Sea Scrolls*, p. 352). The priests and Levites, however, who interrogated John the Baptist belonged to the Jerusalem establishment, which the sectaries seem to have disavowed (Micah Commentary, *ad* i. 6). It would therefore be temerarious to find here any contact between the Fourth Gospel and Qumran. The interest shown by our evangelist in the levitical ministry could be accounted for if the tradition he followed had somewhere in its background an association with priestly circles.

19) belonged to the sect of the Pharisees'. But ℵ A B etc. omit οἱ, and this reading should probably be accepted. The meaning then is, 'Some[1] Pharisees had also been sent'; or 'And some Pharisees had been sent', either, that is, among the deputation mentioned in verse 19 were not only priests and Levites, but some Pharisees, or, in addition to the deputation of priests and Levites there was a second deputation of Pharisees. However the phrase is understood, the use of the term φαρισαῖοι here does not seem to be quite the same as in other parts of the gospel. In vii. 32, 45, xi. 47, xviii. 3 the Pharisees seem to be regarded as a corporate organ of administrative authority, collateral with the hierarchy, with whom on occasion they join to call a meeting of the Sanhedrin. In ch. ix 'the Pharisees' act as an ecclesiastical court, with power to excommunicate (ἐξέβαλον αὐτὸν ἔξω, ix. 34). This does not appear to be historical. The Pharisees formed a sect or party organized in voluntary associations (ḥaburoth), which naturally had disciplinary powers over their own members, while they could no doubt gain such influence in particular synagogues, where members of the ḥaburoth had a majority, as to dictate their proceedings. But although their representatives in the Sanhedrin might at times exercise a preponderant influence there, they were not as a body an organ of constitutional authority. Thus the evangelist seems to have misconceived the situation.[2] In our present passage, however, the Pharisees are either members of a deputation of priests and Levites,[3] or members of a second deputation, in either case commissioned by 'the Jews' (by which the writer means, as often, the Jewish authorities), and not acting on their own account. Moreover, there seems to be a distinction between the questions asked by the priests and Levites and the question asked by the Pharisees. The official deputation, as such, is content with obtaining from the Baptist a disavowal of any dangerous pretensions; its Pharisaic members (or the Pharisaic deputation) wish to probe more deeply into the theoretical basis of his baptism.[4] There is nothing here inconsistent with what we know of

[1] For this use of the partitive genitive with ἐκ, cf. xvi. 17, εἶπαν ἐκ τῶν μαθητῶν αὐτοῦ πρὸς ἀλλήλους.

[2] He may have confused the official γραμματεῖς, who did form an 'estate' of the Sanhedrin, with the voluntary association of Pharisees. Most γραμματεῖς probably did hold Pharisaic views, but certainly not all.

[3] We know that there were Pharisaic priests at the time, and undoubtedly there were Levites who belonged to the party.

[4] Similarly in the Synoptic Gospels the ἀρχιερεῖς καὶ γραμματεῖς καὶ πρεσβύτεροι, i.e. official members of the Sanhedrin, challenge Jesus on the point of authority (Mark xi. 27), while questions of behaviour are propounded by φαρισαῖοι

conditions at the time. At this point the evangelist seems to be following a well-informed tradition.

(b) The Baptist's disclaimer of the status of Elijah (i. 21)

The pattern to which the interrogation of the Baptist conforms we have already considered. To the opening question, Σὺ τίς εἶ; he replies with a disavowal of any pretensions to messianic status. There has been no previous suggestion of any such status. The spontaneous repudiation of the idea no doubt betrays the real interest of the scene for the evangelist: the establishment of the fact that John is not the Messiah but the witness to the Messiah. But the questioners come back with a suggestion of their own: Τί οὖν; σύ 'Ηλείας εἶ; To this John returns a flat denial: Οὐκ εἰμί. In Mark by implication (ix. 13, compare Matt. xvii. 11), and in Matthew explicitly (xi. 14), John is declared to be 'Ηλείας ὁ μέλλων ἔρχεσθαι. Luke stops short of this express identification: John is to go before the face of the Lord ἐν πνεύματι καὶ δυνάμει 'Ηλεία. This would seem to indicate the successor of Elijah rather than Elijah *redivivus*; a successor like Elisha, who received a double portion of his spirit, so that the people said, 'Επανα-πέπαυται τὸ πνεῦμα 'Ηλείου ἐπὶ 'Ελεισαῖε (4 Kms. ii. 9, 15). The Baptist's mission is defined in terms clearly borrowed from Malachi's description of the returning 'Elijah the Tishbite': ἐπιστρέψαι καρδίας πατέρων ἐπὶ τέκνα (Luke i. 17, Mal. iv. 4–5 (iii. 23–4)).[1] In view of these passages the Fourth Evangelist's emphatic denial of the title of Elijah to the Baptist is unexpected.[2]

---

or γραμματεῖς (τῶν φαρισαίων) (Mark ii. 16, vii. 5, etc.), especially in the form, Διὰ τί...; (Mark ii. 18, vii. 5, cf. Τί βαπτίζεις; here).

[1] Perhaps the difference between Elijah *redivivus* and a prophet possessed by the spirit of Elijah and carrying out Elijah's mission was not very clearly conceived.

[2] Strictly speaking it is a denial that the Baptist himself claimed, or accepted, the title, but a tradition which preserved this disclaimer is hardly likely to have affirmed that John nevertheless *was* Elijah the forerunner. The possibility might be considered that the refusal to identify John the Baptist with Elijah is connected with the omission of any reference to the baptism of Jesus, which appears to have been accepted in the early *kerygma* as the 'anointing' of the Messiah (Acts x. 38). This omission has probably some theological significance, but it does not carry with it the rejection of the view that John was Elijah, since in other respects he fills the role. The Synoptic Gospels do not associate the action of John in baptizing Jesus with the character of Elijah; that character is associated with other ideas (the conversion of Israel, Luke i. 17, the ἀποκατάστασις, Mark ix. 12, the breaking-in of the kingdom of heaven, Matt. xi. 12–14), and these are ideas which cannot be said to be inconsistent with Johannine theology, even though the Fourth Gospel uses a different terminology.

It does not seem to be dictated by his dogmatic scheme. For that, it is sufficient that John was not the Messiah; it is not necessary to deny that he was Elijah (whether in the Matthaean or the Lucan sense). Indeed elsewhere in this gospel the Baptist performs functions which properly pertain to Elijah, as the forerunner of the Messiah. It is the purpose of his mission ἵνα φανερωθῇ τῷ 'Ισραήλ (i. 31). Similarly the Jew Trypho in Justin's Dialogue says that the Messiah remains unknown μέχρις ἂν ἐλθὼν 'Ηλίας χρίσῃ αὐτὸν καὶ φανερὸν πᾶσι ποιήσῃ (Dial. c. Tryph. 8). Again, the Baptist is described in John v. 35 as ὁ λύχνος[1] ὁ καιόμενος καὶ φαίνων, words which seem clearly to echo the description of the historical Elijah in Sir. xlviii. 1: ἀνέστη 'Ηλίας προφήτης ὡς πῦρ καὶ ὁ λόγος αὐτοῦ ὡς λαμπὰς ἐκαίετο. It does not appear therefore that the evangelist can have had any theological objection to the current view that John the Baptist was Elijah, which is in fact implied in other parts of his gospel, and the denial of that view in i. 21 can hardly be attributed to the author's known theological tendencies.

The general Synoptic position results from the assimilation of the prophecies of Mal. iii. 1 (ἐξαποστέλλω τὸν ἄγγελον κ.τ.λ.), Mal. iv. 4 (iii. 23) (ἀποστέλλω ὑμῖν 'Ηλείαν τὸν Θεσβίτην κ.τ.λ.), and Isa. xl. 3 (φωνὴ βοῶντος κ.τ.λ.), leading to the fusion of these three figures. There is some doctrinal development behind this. The Fourth Gospel, at this point only, appears to reflect a stage at which this assimilation had not completely taken place, and the Baptist was held to fill the role of the Voice in the Wilderness and of the Messenger (iii. 28) but not that of Elijah the forerunner. Elsewhere the evangelist appears to take what had become the normal view, that the Baptist also filled the role of Elijah (as defined by Sirach, and by the Jewish teachers known to Justin). There is therefore good ground for inferring that in i. 21 the evangelist follows an independent tradition not otherwise known to us.

(c) The unknown Messiah (i. 26)

We now return to the twofold prediction which forms the common nucleus of the Johannine and the Synoptic presentations alike. In so far as the Johannine version runs parallel to the Synoptic we have already considered it. But in one respect the former is unique: the Coming One is

---

[1] 'Ο λύχνος, with the definite article, seems to imply a reference to some well established image, such as that of Sirach, and consequently to the person to whom that image was originally applied.

asserted to be already present *incognito*. The most convenient Synoptic version for comparison is the Matthaean:

Matthew iii. 11	John i. 26–7
ὁ ὀπίσω μου ἐρχόμενος	μέσος ὑμῶν στήκει ὃν ὑμεῖς οὐκ οἴδατε,
ἰσχυρότερός μου ἐστίν,	ὁ ὀπίσω μου ἐρχόμενος,
οὗ οὐκ εἰμὶ ἱκανὸς	οὗ οὐκ εἰμὶ ἄξιος
τὰ ὑποδήματα βαστάσαι.	ἵνα λύω αὐτοῦ τὸν ἱμάντα τοῦ ὑποδήματος.
(In Luke λῦσαι τὸν ἱμάντα	
τῶν ὑποδημάτων αὐτοῦ.)	

Apparently ὁ ὀπίσω μου ἐρχόμενος is here treated, in both gospels, as a fixed title, identifying the person spoken of. In John i. 26 it may be taken either as the direct subject of the verb στήκει, or, perhaps better, as in apposition to the unexpressed subject of that verb, the antecedent to the relative ὅν. In either case, while Matthew asserts that the Coming One is 'stronger' than the Baptist, the Fourth Evangelist asserts that he is already present unknown.[1]

We may first inquire whether this additional clause is likely to have been dictated by motives derived from Johannine theology. That men did not 'know' Christ during his earthly Ministry is an idea which recurs elsewhere in the Fourth Gospel. In vii. 27–8 the Jerusalemites claim that they know all about Jesus, and he admits the claim, on the ordinary work-a-day level, but he adds, 'He who sent me is true, and him you do not know, but I know him'—the implications of which are brought out later in the same series of discourses, viii. 19, where Jesus says, Οὔτε ἐμὲ οἴδατε οὔτε τὸν πατέρα μου· εἰ ἐμὲ ᾔδειτε καὶ τὸν πατέρα μου ἂν ᾔδειτε. It is clear that the 'knowledge' here spoken of is the γνῶσις θεοῦ which is also union with God. Not to 'know' Jesus, in this sense, is the ἄγνοια of the divine Logos, which is darkness and death. In i. 26 the 'knowledge' which the Jews lack is something simpler: they do not recognize for what he is the Messiah who is standing among them. The idea is associated, not with

[1] We have already remarked that there has been some measure of editorial rehandling of this passage, which has impaired the antithesis between water-baptism and spirit-baptism. The antithesis might be restored either in the form, 'I baptize with water; he who stands unknown among you will baptize with Spirit', or in the form, 'I baptize with water; he who comes after me (whose shoe-strap I am not fit to untie) will baptize with Spirit'. Thus there might well have been a conflation of two different versions of the saying. That variant versions of so important a saying should have been handed down in tradition is in no way surprising, and the Fourth Evangelist may have known more than one such version and combined them. But any attempt to restore them must remain conjectural. On ὁ ὀπίσω μου ἐρχόμενος, see below, pp. 272–4.

the distinctive Johannine theology, but with the Jewish belief in the unknown or hidden Messiah. We have already noted the passage in which Justin makes the Jew Trypho say that in his belief Χριστός, εἰ καὶ γεγένηται καὶ ἔστι που, ἄγνωστός ἐστι καὶ οὐδὲ αὐτός πω ἑαυτὸν ἐπίσταται οὐδὲ ἔχει δύναμίν τινα, μέχρις ἂν ἐλθὼν Ἠλίας χρίσῃ αὐτὸν καὶ φανερὸν πᾶσι ποιήσῃ (*Dial. c. Tryph.* 8). Similarly, in another passage of the same dialogue he quotes Jewish διδάσκαλοι as holding that the Messiah has not yet come, εἰ δὲ καὶ ἐληλυθέναι λέγουσιν, οὐ γινώσκεται ὅς ἐστιν, ἀλλ᾽ ὅταν ἐμφανὴς καὶ ἔνδοξος γένηται, τότε γνωσθήσεται ὅς ἐστιν (*op. cit.* 110). It is hard to resist the conclusion that ideas of this kind lie behind John i. 26.[1] According to i. 31 it is the purpose of the Baptist's mission to disclose the identity of the Unknown Messiah. From the moment when his identity is thus disclosed Jesus is no longer (in that sense) the Unknown Messiah. As soon as his Ministry begins he is (in Justin's words) ἐμφανὴς καὶ ἔνδοξος, for ἐφανέρωσεν τὴν δόξαν αὐτοῦ (ii. 11), though in the deeper 'Johannine' sense he remains unknown, even to his disciples (xiv. 9), until his glory is finally revealed in his death and resurrection. There is thus no ground for attributing this additional clause to theological motives characteristic of

---

[1] For various forms of the doctrine of the unknown or hidden Messiah, see S. Mowinckel, *He that Cometh* (Eng. trans. by G. W. Anderson), pp. 304–8; E. Stauffer, 'Agnostos Christos', in *The Background of the N.T. and its Eschatology* (ed. Davies and Daube), pp. 287–91. Stauffer draws attention to Justin's expression, ἔστι που, 'he exists *somewhere*'. There was much speculation about the place where the Messiah might be supposed to be in hiding—at Rome, or in the extreme north, or in the earthly paradise. (The Baptist (according to John i. 26) gave a different answer to the question: the Unknown Messiah is at present in Jewish Palestine, μέσος ὑμῶν.) Justin's dialogue seems to be the earliest datable evidence for this belief. But it is most improbable that such a belief should have been developed in Judaism *after* Christianity had claimed that Jesus, until then unknown, had been anointed to the messianic office by the Baptist, and identified the latter with Elijah (though Stauffer may well be right in deriving the other part of Justin's statement, that the Messiah does not even know himself, from Gnostic sources). The idea occurs in several passages of Talmud and Targum. According to *Midrash Echa* 1.50 the Messiah Menahem son of Hezekiah (cf. p. 100 n. 1) was born on the day of the destruction of the temple, and forthwith swept away by winds and tempests to some unknown place. If, as is supposed, this Menahem is Josephus's Manaimos (in spite of the anachronism involved), the story takes us back to an idea current in the first century, since it is hardly likely that 'messianic' status would be assigned to the rebel leader long after the failure of his enterprise. In any case Stauffer is surely right in holding that Peter's confession of Jesus as Messiah implies that he had shared the belief that the Messiah might well be already on earth in humble and unknown guise. From the time of the confession onwards he and the other disciples are waiting for the moment when their Master will become ἐμφανὴς καὶ ἔνδοξος (... ἐν τῇ δόξῃ σου, Mark x. 37).

the Fourth Evangelist. There is a good case for its derivation from an earlier tradition. It is to be observed that the saying, μέσος ὑμῶν στήκει ὃν ὑμεῖς οὐκ οἴδατε, does not imply the identification of the Coming One with any specific individual; it only affirms the Baptist's conviction that the Messiah awaits the moment of revelation, not in Rome, not in the far north, not in the earthly paradise, still less in heaven, but in Palestine, moving about unknown among the multitudes.

(d) The Lamb of God (i. 29, 36)

The second part of the 'Testimony of John', i. 29 *sqq.*, goes beyond the first part in expressly identifying Jesus with the august figure to whom the Baptist has referred allusively as ὁ ὀπίσω μου ἐρχόμενος. In part, as we have seen, the identification is made in terms common to the Fourth Gospel and the Synoptics. Jesus is the Son of God, who, having been himself invested with the Holy Spirit, administers the spirit-baptism prefigured by John's water-baptism. But in i. 29 a new title is introduced for which there is no Synoptic parallel: ὁ ἀμνὸς τοῦ θεοῦ. The title is as strange to the Fourth Gospel (apart from the present passage) as it is to the others. There is therefore no *prima facie* probability that we are dealing with a pure piece of Johannine theology. Expositors are by no means agreed about the sense in which ἀμνός is to be understood. It has been taken as an allusion to the Paschal lamb, or to the lamb of the sin-offering, or to the ἀμνός to which the Suffering Servant is compared in the LXX of Isa. liii. 7, or indeed as a mistranslation of an original Aramaic טליא intended to mean 'servant', or, finally, as an allusion to the horned lamb of Jewish and Christian apocalypse, the symbol of the messianic leader of God's people.[1] The very fact of this wide divergence proves that the connection of the title with known Johannine Christological categories is by no means clear or simple. The author, no doubt, saw the title in organic relation with his whole theological scheme, but we have perhaps lost the clue to that relation. All we can say with certainty is that he regarded it as a messianic title, since Andrew, having heard the Baptist say, Ἴδε ὁ ἀμνὸς τοῦ θεοῦ, reports to his brother, Εὑρήκαμεν τὸν μεσσίαν. Each of his interpreters will believe that this or that understanding of the meaning of ἀμνός gives the best lead into the author's Christology. That is to say, given the term ἀμνός, we may think we can see how it served the author's theological purpose; but it is difficult indeed to see how it could have been *derived* from Johannine conceptions. We must, it seems, conclude

[1] See *Interpretation*, pp. 230–8.

that the evangelist did not himself invent the title, but drew it from some source in earlier tradition. I have elsewhere[1] observed that in the proem to his gospel the author intended to set forth the traditional messianic titles, as a foundation of acknowledged belief upon which to build his theological edifice, and it seems clear that ὁ ἀμνὸς τοῦ θεοῦ must be included among them, even though direct evidence for its earlier use is lacking. It may be observed that if a reference to Isa. liii. 7 is taken as the clue the title must have arisen in a Hellenistic (Jewish-Hellenistic) *milieu*, where the Old Testament was read in Greek, since ἀμνός is not a true rendering of the Hebrew רחל, 'ewe'. Any of the other four suggested interpretations which I have mentioned would be possible in a non-Hellenized Jewish setting, and indeed in an authentic saying of John the Baptist. In any case it seems clear that we have here pre-Johannine material.

The appended clause, ὁ αἴρων τὴν ἁμαρτίαν τοῦ κόσμου, may be a doctrinal gloss by the evangelist on the traditional title, ὁ ἀμνὸς τοῦ θεοῦ. Yet it does not readily derive from the general theology of the Fourth Gospel, which offers no parallel. The phrase αἴρειν ἁμαρτίας occurs in 1 John iii. 5, but it is not certain that the epistle is to be accepted as evidence for the theology of the evangelist.[2] In itself the expression is biblical in character. If ἀμνός was intended to suggest the lamb of the sin-offering (or the Suffering Servant as himself a sin-offering), then αἴρων ἁμαρτίαν would mean 'removing guilt' (compare 1 Kms. xv. 25, ἆρον δὴ τὸ ἁμάρτημά μου, 1 Kms. xxv. 28, ἆρον δὴ τὸ ἀνόμημα τῆς δούλης σου), an idea otherwise expressed in the ἱλασμός of 1 John ii. 2, iv. 10. If (as I have argued elsewhere) ἀμνός refers to the horned lamb as a messianic symbol, then αἴρων ἁμαρτίαν would mean 'abolishing sin' (as αἴρειν τὰ νόμιμα, 1 Macc. iii. 29, αἴρειν ὄνειδος, Ps. cli. 7), a function of the Messiah in Jewish apocalypse.[3] Neither of these ideas is in any way characteristic of the Fourth Gospel; the idea of expiation is conspicuously absent, and the work of Christ is represented by preference in more positive ways than the abolition of sin (the giving of life and light, etc.). There seems no real

---

[1] *Interpretation*, p. 228.

[2] See my commentary on the Johannine Epistles, pp. xlvii–lvi. It is to be observed that αἴρειν ἁμαρτίας is not the same thing as αἴρειν ἁμαρτίαν. The former refers to sinful acts (including words, thoughts, etc.), the latter to a sinful condition. If, as I suppose, the author of the epistle was a disciple of the evangelist, it is not certain that he has here understood the expression ὁ αἴρων τὴν ἁμαρτίαν τοῦ κόσμου as his teacher meant it.

[3] See *Interpretation*, pp. 237–8.

reason why the whole expression, ὁ ἀμνὸς τοῦ θεοῦ ὁ αἴρων τὴν ἁμαρτίαν τοῦ κόσμου, should not have been used by John the Baptist, or in a traditional account of his preaching.

(e) Οὗτος ἦν ὃν εἶπον (i. 15, 30)

The title ὁ ἀμνὸς τοῦ θεοῦ has been introduced in i. 29 without preparation, and without any indication that it refers to any previous utterance of the Baptist. In the following verse he explains that he is in fact referring to a person of whom he has already spoken: οὗτός ἐστιν ὑπὲρ οὗ ἐγὼ εἶπον, Ὀπίσω μου ἔρχεται ἀνὴρ ὃς ἔμπροσθέν μου γέγονεν, ὅτι πρῶτός μου ἦν. If, however, we turn back to discover when or where the Baptist is supposed to have made this pronouncement, we seek in vain. In the Prologue the same saying (in slightly different wording) is quoted as having been previously uttered: οὗτος ἦν ὃν εἶπον, Ὁ ὀπίσω μου ἐρχόμενος ἔμπροσθέν μου γέγονεν, ὅτι πρῶτός μου ἦν. Since the Prologue is an anticipation of what the gospel is about to say, we may perhaps take it that i. 15 anticipates what is to be recorded in its chronological sequence in i. 30. But that still leaves us without a direct record of the Baptist's utterance of the saying in question. We have only his self-quotation, given in two slightly different forms.

It will be well at this point to consider a further example of self-quotation. In iii. 28 the Baptist again reminds his auditors of what he had previously said. There are here two statements, and as each is introduced with ὅτι we must regard them as separate pronouncements: (a) οὐκ εἰμὶ ἐγὼ ὁ χριστός, (b) ἀπεσταλμένος εἰμὶ ἔμπροσθεν ἐκείνου. The former of these may well be a back-reference to i. 20, where in answer to the question, Σὺ τίς εἶ; the Baptist says, Ἐγὼ οὐκ εἰμὶ ὁ χριστός. But the second statement is nowhere recorded directly.

We have before us therefore two statements which, according to the evangelist, the Baptist said he had made, of which one only is directly recorded in this gospel. The *prima facie* suggestion is that these statements were found in some document, or tradition, referring to the Baptist, which was known to the evangelist or his readers or both. The second of these statements, ἀπεσταλμένος εἰμὶ ἔμπροσθεν ἐκείνου (namely τοῦ χριστοῦ), echoes the prophecy of Mal. iii. 1, especially as it is quoted in Matt. xi. 10, Luke vii. 27: ἰδοὺ ἀποστέλλω τὸν ἄγγελόν μου πρὸ προσώπου σου, ὃς κατασκευάσει τὴν ὁδόν σου ἔμπροσθέν σου.[1] We have sufficient

[1] The prophecy reads in the LXX, closely following the Hebrew, ἰδοὺ ἐξαποστέλλω τὸν ἄγγελόν μου, καὶ ἐπιβλέψεται ὁδὸν πρὸ προσώπου μου. As

evidence that this prophecy, together with that of Isa. xl. 3, belonged to the primitive stock of *testimonia*. In Mark i. 2–3 they are combined. According to John i. 23 the Baptist himself claimed to fulfil the prophecy of the Voice in the Wilderness, and I have tried to show that there is a reasonable probability that this was already present in a pre-Johannine tradition. John iii. 28 seems to imply that the companion prophecy about the Messenger was similarly reported to have been applied by the Baptist to his own mission. Is it not likely that we have here a further reminiscence of the same tradition? In any case it may fairly be said that the formula of self-quotation in iii. 28 covers two propositions, one of which, since it agrees with Luke iii. 15–16, Acts xiii. 25, has good claim to recognition as traditional matter, and the other, alluding to a well-known *testimonium*, is at any rate in that sense traditional. This lends support to the *prima facie* suggestion that in i. 15, 30, the saying quoted is traditional.

If, however, the expression, πρῶτός μου ἦν, is rightly understood as meaning, 'he existed before me' (compare xv. 18, ἐμὲ πρῶτον ὑμῶν μεμίσηκεν, 'they hated me before they hated you'), then the allusion to the Johannine doctrine of the pre-existent Logos (compare viii. 58, πρὶν Ἀβραὰμ γενέσθαι ἐγὼ εἰμί) makes it unlikely that this clause at any rate came out of a tradition of sayings of John the Baptist, though it would still be possible to hold that the evangelist added it, as a theological interpretation, to such a traditional saying.

Leaving aside therefore for the moment the concluding clause, we may examine the rest of the quoted saying. It evidently turns upon the antithesis, ὀπίσω/ἔμπροσθεν. These are natural correlatives, meaning 'behind', 'in front of'. They develop a secondary temporal sense: 'after', 'before'. But there is no instance of these temporal meanings in the New

---

quoted in Mark i. 2 the phrase πρὸ προσώπου has changed its place, so as to qualify ἀποστέλλω, and the pronoun has changed from the first person to the second. As quoted in Matt. xi. 10 the qualifying phrase retains its place at the end of the first clause, but an alternative rendering of the Hebrew לְפָנֶיךָ, with change of person, ἔμπροσθέν σου, is restored to its proper place at the end of the second clause. John gives the gist of the prophecy, without reproducing the parallelism: ἀπεσταλμένος εἰμὶ ἔμπροσθεν ἐκείνου (just as in citing Isa. xl. 3 in i. 23 he has eliminated the repetition). But it is noteworthy that he has adopted the Matthaean ἔμπροσθεν (in place of the LXX πρὸ προσώπου), but made it (by implication) qualify ἀποστέλλω. It would not be surprising if a non-septuagintal translation was current in Christian circles, and Matthew had in a measure conflated this with the LXX form. Similarly in xii. 40 John cites Isa. vi. 9–10 in a non-septuagintal version apparently known also to Paul (see *According to the Scriptures*, pp. 37–9).

Testament[1] unless it be in the two passages of the Fourth Gospel which we are considering, with the allied passages in the other gospels, Mark i. 7, Matt. iii. 11. In the prophecy of Mal. iii. 1, as quoted in Matt. xi. 10, Luke vii. 27 ἔμπροσθέν σου represents (with a change of person) the Hebrew לְפָנֶיׁ (LXX πρὸ προσώπου μου), and is probably intended to mean 'ahead of me', 'in advance of me', as a herald or courier goes ahead of a person of importance; and so also in John iii. 28, which alludes to the same prophecy: ἀπεσταλμένος εἰμὶ ἔμπροσθεν ἐκείνου='I have been sent ahead of him' (not, in a temporal sense, 'as his predecessor'); just as, in John x. 4, the shepherd walks ahead of his flock: ἔμπροσθεν αὐτῶν πορεύεται καὶ τὰ πρόβατα αὐτῷ ἀκολουθεῖ. This simple local sense, however, will not fit John i. 15, 30. Here a somewhat different meaning is required, which, however, is easily derivable from the local sense: 'ranking before'. This does not occur in the New Testament, but is not uncommon in profane Greek;[2] and compare Gen. xlviii. 20, ἔθηκεν τὸν Ἐφραΐμ ἔμπροσθεν τοῦ Μανασσῆ. The meaning is that Ephraim is given precedence over Manasseh, although he was the younger. Thus i. 15, ὁ ὀπίσω μου ἐρχόμενος ἔμπροσθέν μου γέγονεν, would mean, 'he who comes after me has taken precedence of me'—which is perhaps only another way of expressing the idea more picturesquely represented in the words, 'he who comes after me, whose shoe-strap I am not fit to untie' (i. 27).

But this leaves open the question, in what sense is Jesus 'after' John the Baptist? After in time, it is usually assumed, that is, appearing on the stage of history later than John, and in the Synoptic forms of the Baptist's saying this seems natural. But if so, we have here an imperfect antithesis: ὀπίσω, 'after' in time, ἔμπροσθεν, 'before' in rank. There may no doubt be a play on words; but it is a fact not to be taken lightly that of 35 occurrences of ὀπίσω in the New Testament there is not one (apart from the saying of the Baptist which we are considering, in its various forms) in which it has a temporal sense. Ὀπίσω with the genitive is constantly used with reference to the followers or adherents of the person named in the genitive.[3] In particular, ἔρχεσθαι ὀπίσω τινός (the phrase we have here)

[1] In Phil. iii. 13, τὰ ὀπίσω means the past and τὰ ἔμπροσθεν the future, but the spacial metaphor is clearly alive: the runner has the course already traversed at his back, and looks in front of him to the remainder of the track. When the terms are used in a truly temporal sense, it is with a meaning the reverse of that which they bear in Phil. iii. 13: ὀπίσω means later in time, ἔμπροσθεν earlier.

[2] Examples from Plato and Demosthenes in Arndt–Gingrich, *Greek–English Lexicon of the New Testament*.

[3] Acts v. 37, ἀπέστησεν λαὸν ὀπίσω αὐτοῦ (Judas of Galilee), xx. 30, ἀποσπᾶν τοὺς μαθητὰς ὀπίσω ἑαυτῶν (heretical teachers), Luke xxi. 8, μὴ πορευθῆτε ὀπίσω

is the standing expression for adhering to the cause of a person, mostly of the disciples 'following' Jesus.[1] The expression in John i. 30, ὀπίσω μου ἔρχεται ἀνήρ, would in any other context almost certainly be understood as meaning, 'there is a man following me', that is, among my disciples or adherents. It is true that this would be somewhat less natural where the expression ὁ ὀπίσω μου ἐρχόμενος is used (John i. 15, Matt. iii. 11), though even there the meaning 'a follower of mine' would be possible, since the article with the participle is not necessarily the equivalent of our definite article. If we ask, whether the version in i. 15 or in i. 30 is more likely to be traditional, it may at least be said that i. 30 comes naturally in a piece of narrative, while i. 15 is embedded in a formal theological statement.

If the evangelist may be supposed to have received such a saying by tradition, he may well have given it the desired theological direction by adding a clause to the effect that this precedence in rank or status was the fitting, and indeed the inevitable, result of the pre-existence of Christ. Yet it is possible that the words, πρῶτός μου ἦν, whatever metaphysical meaning the evangelist may have found in them, had originally a simpler meaning. Πρῶτος often has the meaning, 'first in rank', 'superior'; thus πρῶτός μου might well mean 'my superior', and ἦν might be, not the verb of existence, but the simple copula. The past tense could be understood as an instance of the well-established idiom in which it expresses 'a fact which is and always has been the same' (L. and S., 1927, p. 489 a), as, in particular, in the Aristotelian formula, τὸ τί ἦν εἶναι, used to express the essential nature of a thing; or, 'a fact which is just recognized as such by the speaker or writer, having previously been denied, overlooked, or not understood' (Goodwin, *Moods and Tenses of the Greek Verb*, 1889, p. 13). The Baptist has now realized (we may suppose) that there is a man among his followers (ὀπίσω μου ἔρχεται ἀνήρ) who is and always has been essentially his superior, and so acknowledges that he must yield him precedence. We may therefore translate, 'There is a man in my following who has taken precedence of me, because he is and always has been essentially my superior'.

αὐτῶν (false messiahs), 1 Tim. v. 15, ἐξετράπησαν ὀπίσω τοῦ σατανᾶ. Mark viii. 33, ὕπαγε ὀπίσω μου Σατανᾶ, is eccentric; see my article in *J.T.S.* v. 2 (Oct. 1934), 246–7.

[1] So δεῦτε ὀπίσω μου, Matt. iv. 19, Mark i. 17, ἀπῆλθον ὀπίσω αὐτοῦ, Mark i. 20, ὀπίσω μου ἐλθεῖν, Matt. xvi. 24, Mark viii. 34, Lk. ix. 23, εἴ τις θέλει ὀπίσω μου ἔρχεσθαι, xiv. 27, ὅστις οὐ βαστάζει τὸν σταυρὸν αὐτοῦ καὶ ἔρχεται ὀπίσω μου, John xii. 19, ὁ κόσμος ὀπίσω αὐτοῦ ἀπῆλθεν. Elsewhere in John we have the expression εἰς τὰ ὀπίσω (vi. 66, xviii. 6), which is obviously local in meaning.

I should not care to urge this interpretation of the phrase πρῶτός μου ἦν as more than a distinct possibility, but I should seriously argue that in the words ὀπίσω μου ἔρχεται ἀνήρ we are reaching back to a stage of tradition scarcely represented elsewhere in the gospels, and that our evangelist has reproduced a feature of that early tradition, not directly, but indirectly by means of the device of self-quotation, namely that Jesus was at one time regarded as a follower or adherent of John the Baptist. If, as the Synoptic Gospels report, he accepted baptism at his hands, how else should he be regarded? That the fact should be obscured in the development of the tradition of the Church was to be expected.

The remaining portion of the 'Testimony of John' (i. 31–4) we have already reviewed. We have seen that it reproduces certain traits of the Synoptic account of the baptism of Jesus, whether in dependence on the Synoptics or, more probably, in dependence on some parallel strain of tradition, but that it departs significantly from that account, especially in omitting all reference to the baptism itself, in representing the descent of the Dove as a visionary experience of the Baptist, narrated in a form comparable to that of prophetic visions in the Old Testament and of the vision of Jesus in Luke x. 18, and finally in attributing the acclamation of Jesus as Son of God to the Baptist instead of to a voice from heaven. All this is congruous with the evangelist's insistence that the Baptist appeared on the stage of history as the witness *par excellence* to the messianic dignity of Jesus—as that and nothing else. Accordingly, while he appears to define the function of the Baptist in terms of the Jewish doctrine of Elijah the Forerunner, as attested by Justin, he allows him to discharge only one part of Elijah's task, that of identifying the Messiah (ἵνα φανερωθῇ τῷ 'Ισραήλ), and not that of anointing him. In i. 21 the Baptist was represented as repudiating the role of Elijah, which is assigned to him here, as elsewhere in the New Testament. So far therefore our present passage stands nearer to what was apparently normal early Christian belief than the tradition represented in i. 21; but on the other hand it differs from the kerygmatic passage, Acts x. 38, which, probably reflecting normal belief, accepts the baptism of Jesus as his 'anointing' for the messianic office. We may probably see here the hand of the evangelist himself at work, modifying the special tradition which had come down to him, but not conforming it to the position represented by the Synoptic Gospels.

Yet there is after all little in the 'Testimony of John' which is either exclusively or distinctively Johannine in a doctrinal sense. It is particularly striking that although the evangelist has indicated in the Prologue that the 'man sent from God' is to bear witness to the Light, the 'Testimony of John' contains no reference to Christ as Light, no reference to his 'glory', and no reference to his power to exercise the divine prerogatives of κρίσις and ζωοποίησις, and if there is any reference to the saving efficacy of his death (in i. 29) it is not in Johannine terms.[1] On the other hand it is possible to recognize certain apologetic or controversial motives, such as may well have affected the tradition before it reached our evangelist.

This analysis of the Testimony of John has shown that in the first part, verses 19–27—the part associated with the traditional datum that John baptized at Bethany beyond Jordan (verse 28)—there is little or nothing which seems to derive from the special views of the evangelist. Everything in it can be related to Jewish beliefs or practices of the first century, unless it be the suggestion that John was taken to be a possible candidate for messiahship, and this can be traced to early Christian tradition outside the Fourth Gospel. In one point at least it appears to contradict the position represented elsewhere in this gospel, namely the repudiation of John's identity with Elijah. In the second part, verses 29–34, there is evidence of traditional material lying behind the Johannine presentation, but evidence also of some pragmatic rehandling of the material in the interests of Johannine doctrine. It is perhaps not without significance that the difference in this respect between the two parts coincides with the change from dialogue to monologue.

(iii) *The effect of the Testimony of John (i. 35–7, x. 40–2)*

The verses which follow upon the 'Testimony of John', i. 35–7, make a transition to a further series of 'testimonies' which occupies the remainder of the chapter. If they are regarded as a plain narrative of an actual occurrence, there are certain questions that arise. Why, for example, was it necessary for the Baptist to repeat his testimony 'on the following day'? To what audience, then, was the impressive pronouncement of i. 29 addressed? Were none of his disciples then present? Or, being present, did they remain unimpressed? The raising of such questions lays bare the artificiality of the composition. But if these verses be regarded as designed

---

[1] Since the Spirit is ζωοποιοῦν (vi. 63) and regenerates (iii. 5), and is also the Agent of judgement (xvi. 8–11), we can easily see how the concept of spirit-baptism might lead into both these distinctively Johannine doctrines, but the concept itself, and the phrase βαπτίζειν ἐν πνεύματι ἁγίῳ, are common to John and the Synoptics and are certainly primitive.

to carry forward the presentation of the mission of the Baptist, in the terms of i. 6–8, then everything falls into place. After showing how John came 'to bear witness to the Light', the evangelist goes on to show how the purpose of his testimony, 'that all might become believers through his agency', began to be fulfilled. For this purpose he sets the stage afresh, noting that two of John's disciples were present to hear him bear his testimony (i. 35). He then repeats the solemn announcement, Ἴδε ὁ ἀμνὸς τοῦ θεοῦ, adding again, for emphasis, that the two disciples heard it—and that, as a direct result, ἠκολούθησαν τῷ Ἰησοῦ. This last phrase, although in the dramatic situation it has the perfectly simple and appropriate meaning that they accompanied Jesus to his lodging, can hardly have been used without at least an oblique reference to the pregnant sense which that expression bore in the language of the primitive Church: they became adherents of Jesus. The clause is the appropriate climax to a passage which tells of the winning of disciples (cf. Mark i. 18, ii. 14, and similarly ἀπῆλθον ὀπίσω αὐτοῦ, Mark i. 20), and the *pericopé* should properly end here. The evangelist has illustrated his theme that the testimony of John led men to believe in Christ. The *pericopé* however is expanded in i. 38–9 with dramatic detail which leads into a fresh narrative. After i. 37 the account of the Baptist's mission fades away, and we hear about the adhesion of various disciples to Jesus. This passage must be examined subsequently.[1] At this point we note that the editorial hand of the evangelist is so evident in the composition of the *pericopé* i. 35–7 that we can no longer trace any traditional form behind it—though that is not necessarily to deny the possibility that the evangelist had access to some kind of information on the strength of which he may have composed the passage.

To complete, however, the theme of the testimony of John and its results we must here refer to a later passage (already briefly discussed, pp. 241–2) in which the evangelist alludes to its continuing effects in the region where the Baptist had first worked, x. 40–2. The opening verse, καὶ ἀπῆλθεν πέραν τοῦ Ἰορδάνου εἰς τὸν τόπον ὅπου ἦν Ἰωάννης τὸ πρῶτον βαπτίζων καὶ ἔμενεν ἐκεῖ, has some of the marks of the 'framework' material to which elsewhere I have proposed to attach some value as preserving early tradition: it purports to give part of an itinerary of Jesus, and to summarize a period of his activity (the verb ἔμενεν being, appropriately, in the continuous tense). The allusion to 'the place where John

[1] See below, pp. 302–12.

administered baptism at first' appears to refer back to i. 28, Βηθανία πέραν τοῦ 'Ιορδάνου ὅπου ἦν ὁ 'Ιωάννης βαπτίζων. In that case it is editorial, though the place-name is traditional. In verses 41–2 there are several traits which suggest the hand of the evangelist (see above, p. 249). Moreover, as I have observed, the whole passage fits very closely into the dogmatic scheme propounded in i. 6–8. Whatever authority the evangelist may have had for the statements he makes, he has so rehandled his material in 41–2 as to leave no tangible evidence of any traditional source. At most, then, we may with some degree of probability assign to pre-canonical tradition the statement that at one period of his Ministry Jesus worked in the district of Transjordan which had been the scene of the Baptist's earlier activity. That he built upon the foundations which his predecessor had laid is probable in the nature of the case, but the statement that his success here was due to the testimony of John may either be derived from trustworthy information or may be simply the evangelist's intelligent inference.

3. JOHN AT AENON-BY-SALIM (iii. 22–30)

The whole passage, iii. 22–36 (as I have argued elsewhere),[1] is best regarded as an explanatory appendix to the dialogue with Nicodemus and the discourse which grows out of it. Verses 31–6 are in large measure a recapitulation of ideas found in iii. 1–21, with some additional points. Verses 22–30 seem to stand apart, and indeed to interrupt the line of thought, so much so that many critics have proposed some rearrangement. But I have tried to show that the confronting of John with Jesus, of John's baptism with baptism by Christ (that is, in the evangelist's intention, the Church's sacrament of baptism), provides an essential link in the argument. The observation, however, remains valid that verses 22–30 form a unit, by itself, contrasting in form, manner and language with what precedes and follows. *Prima facie*, there is here as strong a case as anywhere in the gospel for considering the view that the evangelist is composing out of pre-existing materials.

When, however, we scrutinize verses 22–30, it appears that this short passage is itself not altogether homogeneous. There seem to be traces of the evangelist's editorial work within it as well as in the linking of it with its context. An analysis, verse by verse, may be useful.

iii. 22. This appears to belong to the class of 'itinerary fragments', similar to those which in Mark serve as part of the framework of the narrative (see above, pp. 233–42). Some of them, at least, appear to have good claim to be derived from pre-canonical tradition, and this may well be one.[2] It records laconically a period of activity: both verbs, διέτριβεν and ἐβάπτιζεν, are in the tense of continuous or repeated action. During this period, the evangelist states, Jesus was at work in Judaea.

iii. 23. This is one of the topographical notes which appear from time to time in this gospel, and which (I have argued) can most reasonably be accounted for as fragments of traditional material. It fixes the locality of the Baptist's activity during one whole period of his ministry.[3] John, we must presume, at some point left Bethany-beyond-Jordan, and began working at Aenon-by-Salim.

iii. 24 is an editorial note indicating that the period referred to was prior to the arrest of the Baptist by Antipas, as recorded in Mark vi. 17–18 and

---

[1] *Interpretation*, pp. 308–11.   [2] See above, p. 236.   [3] *Ibid.*

(perhaps independently) Luke iii. 19–20, as well as in Josephus, *Antiq.* XVIII. 119. That he was at liberty during the period indicated is sufficiently obvious, but the evangelist evidently has in mind possible readers who might find a difficulty because they were acquainted with an account of the Ministry of Jesus beginning after the imprisonment of John. Such an account we have in Mark (i. 14). It may be, then, that the evangelist is 'correcting' Mark. But it was not Mark alone who represented the Ministry of Jesus as coming μετὰ τὸ βάπτισμα ὃ ἐκήρυξεν 'Ιωάννης, and as 'beginning from Galilee' (Acts x. 37). Our author may be correcting a view which was widely current, on the basis of what he believed to be better information. In any case the note seems to be inserted to justify the conjunction of the two statements, that Jesus was working in Judaea and that John was similarly working at Aenon-by-Salim, as if they were contemporaneous.

iii. 25. An entirely detached statement about a controversy between 'some of John's disciples'[1] and 'Jews', or, 'a Jew'.[2] The subject of the debate is 'purification'. For the purposes of the author's theology it is probable that this reference to καθαρισμός (cf. ii. 6) served as a hint that John's baptism was of a kind comparable with the ceremonial ordinances of Judaism, in contrast to the regenerating baptism of the Church. But it is most unlikely that he invented it deliberately with this intention. The curious thing is that it leads to nothing. On analogy with other passages in the gospels we should expect this reference to a discussion to lead up to a dialogue dealing with the theme propounded for discussion. But here the dialogue which follows turns upon an entirely different point. It looks as if iii. 25 were the remnant of an introduction to a dialogue which has

---

[1] The grammatical construction is not too clear. It would be possible to construe ἐγένετο ἐκ τῶν μαθητῶν 'Ιωάννου with ἐκ denoting origin: 'a dispute was raised by the disciples of John'; but in view of our author's use of the partitive ἐκ elsewhere, it is perhaps best to understand it as = ζήτησις μαθητῶν τινων, 'a disputation of some of John's disciples with Jews' (or 'a Jew').

[2] The text is uncertain. The plural 'Ιουδαίων, read by ℵ, Θ, fam. 13, Latin versions, and the Curetonian Syriac, is now supported by the Bodmer papyrus (𝔓 66), which, dated by palaeographical experts to about A.D. 200, or to the early third century, is now our earliest MS. of any substantial portion of the Fourth Gospel. The singular 'Ιουδαίου is read by ABW and other uncials, as well as by one corrector of ℵ. Weight of authority appears to favour the plural. Yet the singular would be so unusual, and 'Jews', quite vaguely, are so frequently mentioned as interlocutors, that its 'correction' by scribes would be readily explicable. That we should expect τινός with the singular, and perhaps the article with the plural, is an objection which might cut both ways. The proposed emendation, τῶν 'Ιησοῦ for 'Ιουδαίου, though ingenious, is arbitrary and uncalled for.

not been preserved. It appears to have no bearing upon the relation of the ministry of John the Baptist to the Christian movement to which it was the prelude, but only upon its relation to Jewish practices of the time. This is strangely out of tune with the general tendency of this evangelist, whose interest in the Baptist, generally speaking, is confined to his function as a 'witness'. Indeed this brief note has every appearance of being a surviving example, almost unique in the New Testament, of a tradition interested in the work of John the Baptist as a movement of reform within Judaism, and not merely as ancillary to Christianity.[1] As such, I should be disposed to claim for it a high degree of historical value, so far as it goes. If the contentious 'Jews' (or 'Jew') of iii. 25 might be supposed to have some connection with sectaries like those of the Qumran community, with its intense interest in lustrations, a discussion with the followers of one who practised a different form of καθαρισμός would be entirely appropriate to the place and time to which the incident is assigned.

iii. 26–30. This passage forms a complete *pericopé* having many of the marks which distinguish 'pronouncement stories' in the other gospels. A question is raised (not expressly but by clear implication) (verse 26). To this the Baptist replies with an aphorism (verse 27) and a parable (verse 29), to which is appended a further aphorism (verse 30) applying the parable and answering the implied question. But there are signs of editorial handling.

To begin with, in verse 28 the evangelist would seem, as I have suggested above (pp. 271–2), to have taken from tradition a saying attributed to the Baptist and a *testimonium* from the Old Testament, and inserted them here through the device of self-quotation with the intention of making the purport of John's reply more explicit. The editorial hand is manifest, yet the material seems to be traditional.

In verse 27 we have an aphorism in language of a strongly Johannine cast, and in the cryptic and oracular manner characteristic of this author. The meaning is not entirely clear. Is the Baptist supposed to confess that he has his own modest gift from God and cannot expect to succeed beyond its appointed limits? Or is he saying that the growing success of Jesus should not excite envy, because it is not the result of any sort of self-

---

[1] Another fragment of such a tradition may be preserved in Luke iii. 10–14. The sayings given in Matt. iii. 7–10, Luke iii. 7–9, were no doubt originally directed towards a situation within Judaism, but they have been preserved in Christian tradition because they were interpreted with reference to the crisis provoked by the appearance of Jesus and its sequel.

aggrandizement on his part, but the sign of the acceptance by him of what God has appointed? In any case the thought and language point to composition by the evangelist himself, rather than to any traditional source.

The parable (verse 29) is much nearer to traditional forms familiar from the Synoptic Gospels. Only the last clause of iii. 29, which is by way of pointing the moral, and not necessarily an original part of the parable, has the clear stamp of Johannine authorship: αὕτη οὖν ἡ χαρὰ ἡ ἐμὴ πεπλή-ρωται.[1] Even so, it echoes the expression χαρᾷ χαίρει in the preceding sentence, and this is not Johannine idiom.[2] The evangelist has a certain predilection for the use of the term φωνή[3] of human speech, and especially for the expression φωνῆς (φωνήν) ἀκούειν.[4] This predilection may be thought to be reflected in the language of the parable, though the actual phrase is not used. It is not quite obvious why the bridesman's friend should take special pleasure in *hearing* the bridegroom speak; it is perhaps easier to see why John the Baptist (in the application of the parable) should take pleasure in hearing Jesus speak. But these Johannine traits (if such they be) may be no more than the effect of some such small measure of rewriting as we have noted elsewhere, and the parable may well be traditional.

Most of the parables handed down in tradition are attributed to Jesus. This, though it is similar in character, is attributed to John the Baptist. In the Synoptic Gospels the Baptist utters parabolic sayings, though not parables in the narrower sense. He portrays the Coming One as a harvester who appears with his winnowing fan in his hand, and separates wheat from chaff, storing the former and burning the latter (Matt. iii. 12, Luke iii. 17). This is a genuine picture from real life and demands no allegorization; we are not required to say what the fan stands for, or what realities are symbolized by the ἀποθήκη and the πῦρ ἄσβεστον.[5] A subsidiary picture is that of the owner of an orchard or oliveyard (for such we must suppose him) who sets out to clear away the trees that do not bear, and is

[1] Cf. John xv. 11, xvi. 24, xvii. 13, imitated perhaps in 1 John i. 4, 2 John 12.

[2] The 'cognate dative', intensifying the verb (as in Luke xxii. 15, Acts v. 28, Jas. v. 17, and in quotations from the O.T.), is not elsewhere found in the Fourth Gospel. Θανάτῳ ἀποθνήσκειν in xviii. 32 is not an example. The actual phrase χαρᾷ χαίρειν is not found in the N.T. unless we reckon 1 Thess. iii. 9, and compare 1 Pet. i. 8.

[3] This predilection is shared, to a lesser degree, by Luke, but the word is rare in the other gospels, except in such phrases as φωνῇ μεγάλῃ.

[4] Nine times in John, never in the Synoptics, except in quotations from the O.T.

[5] A fire kept perpetually burning is a perfectly proper feature of such agricultural operations. Any gardener feels proud when his bonfire proves ἄσβεστον!

already applying his axe to their roots (Matt. iii. 10, Luke iii. 9). There is no reason why such sayings should not be accepted as authentic utterances of the Baptist, and they are not essentially different either from parabolic sayings attributed to Jesus, or from the parable we are considering. Nor does there seem to be any reason why the tradition which contained the parabolic sayings of Matt. iii and Luke iii should not have included also the parable of the Bridegroom and the Bridegroom's friend. The possibility indeed cannot be ruled out that it was so included originally as a parable of Jesus, since we have evidence of an interchange of sayings between Jesus and John in our authorities;[1] but at least by the time the aphorism in verse 30 came to be attached to it the attribution to John was fixed, and we have no other guidance to follow.

To proceed, verse 30 is the type of aphorism which in the Synoptics not infrequently enforces the application of a parable or parabolic saying.[2] Similarly, too, the introductory verse, 26, in which the question is raised (by implication), is sufficiently akin in form to such introductions in the Synoptic Gospels. Only the clause, ᾧ σὺ μεμαρτύρηκας, harping, in our author's manner, on the theme of μαρτυρία, and serving as a back-reference to i. 29–34, may be regarded as a feature of composition. From verse 31 on we have, to all appearance, undiluted Johannine theology, and the contrast in form and manner to verses 22–30 is marked.

This analysis confirms the impression which the passage makes *prima facie*, of being a composition out of materials, in part at any rate, pre-existing. Without pretending to draw the line too exactly, we seem reasonably safe in regarding as substantially traditional the following: (*a*) the itinerary fragment, verse 22, (*b*) the topographical note, verse 23, (*c*) the disputation with Jews (or a Jew), verse 25, (*d*) the parable, verse 29, with something by way of introduction and of application. It is, of course, possible that the parable came down, as apparently did some of the

---

[1] See p. 331.

[2] E.g. Mark ii. 17b, οὐκ ἦλθον καλέσαι δικαίους ἀλλὰ ἁμαρτωλούς, Matt. xxii. 14, πολλοί εἰσιν κλητοὶ ὀλίγοι δὲ ἐκλεκτοί, Matt. vi. 24, οὐ δύνασθε θεῷ δουλεύειν καὶ μαμωνᾷ, Luke xvi. 8, οἱ υἱοὶ τοῦ αἰῶνος κ.τ.λ., xvi. 10, ὁ πιστὸς ἐν ἐλαχίστῳ καὶ ἐν πολλῷ κ.τ.λ. In this last example it is by no means clear that the aphorism, though employed to point the moral of the parable, really arises out of it. In the next following examples the aphorism occurs also in non-parabolic contexts, and may well have had no original connection with the parable in question: Matt. xx. 15 (cf. xix. 30), Matt. xxv. 29 = Luke xix. 26 (cf. Mark iv. 25 and parallels). And so here the parable and the aphorism may well have come down separately, in the earliest tradition.

Synoptic parables, as an independent saying without either introduction or application, but the whole *pericopé*, verses 26–30, is so reminiscent of a familiar Synoptic form, in which a parable is provided with a setting (and so unlike this evangelist's usual manner), that it invites serious consideration as a piece of tradition, rehandled more or less in the process of composition. Let us, by way of experiment, take, as the probable nucleus of the whole, something on the following lines:

People came to him (John) and said, 'Rabbi, ἴδε οὗτος βαπτίζει'. John answered, 'The man who is getting married is the bridegroom; the bridegroom's friend, who stands by and listens to him, is delighted to hear the bridegroom's voice'.

This is a typical parabolic *pericopé*, as may be seen by comparison with the other gospels, as, for instance, with Mark ii. 18, where, as it happens, there is also some similarity in the imagery employed:

People came and said to him (Jesus), 'Why is it that while the disciples of John and those of the Pharisees are fasting, yours are not?' Jesus replied, 'Can the groomsmen fast while the bridegroom is with them?'

How much of what follows in Mark by way of application is an original part of the *pericopé* is a point on which critics and expositors are uncertain, and there is a similar uncertainty about the Johannine context. But reflection on the proposed nucleus will show at once that it could not have stood alone, just as it is. The reader must know who is meant by οὗτος, and something is needed to indicate the bearing of the remark, ἴδε οὗτος βαπτίζει. Something, therefore, conveying the information given in verses 22–3 seems indispensable to an understanding of the dialogue, and something of the kind must have been handed down along with it.

Again, if we have regard to analogy with parabolic *pericopae* in the Synoptic Gospels, the parable may or may not have been provided with a 'moral', or 'application'. As it stands, we seem to be given a choice of two (as in Luke xvi. 8–12 we are offered a choice of four): (*a*) the Baptist is delighted to hear of the success of Jesus even though it puts his work in the shade, as the 'best man' at a wedding is delighted to attend upon the bridegroom; (*b*) Christ must (in the providential ordering of things) advance while the Baptist declines. The former of these seems to arise more naturally out of the parable itself, but, as we have seen, it is couched in suspiciously 'Johannine' language. The latter is not Johannine in vocabulary, and so far as form and language go it might well be traditional.[1]

[1] The verbs αὐξάνειν and ἐλαττοῦν are not found elsewhere in the Fourth Gospel. The former is common in most parts of the N.T. The latter is found only in

If we take the parable by itself, it might have been spoken without direct reference to Jesus. The figures of bridegroom and bridegroom's friend might form a pair like those of the master and the menial slave too humble even to remove his shoes, with reference, not to the historical relations between Jesus and John the Baptist, but to the ideal relation of the Messiah to his forerunner. The aphorism, however, ἐκεῖνον δεῖ αὐξάνειν ἐμὲ δὲ ἐλαττοῦσθαι, seems necessarily to point to a definite person set in contrast to the Baptist himself, but if the aphorism was originally handed down out of connection with the parable (after some Synoptic analogies) it would not carry the necessary implication that Jesus was Messiah. If we are asking, not immediately what the Baptist may be supposed actually to have said, but, as the first stage, what was handed down in the tradition as it reached the evangelist, the probability seems strong that the parable, with the aphorism, ἐκεῖνον δεῖ κ.τ.λ., was already incorporated in an account of a period in the ministries of Jesus and of the Baptist when they were at work contemporaneously and in places not far distant from one another.

If so, then this account included the statement that during this period Jesus, like John, was accustomed to administer baptism. This is a statement for which nothing else in the New Testament prepares us. It seems indeed to have caused some difficulty to the writer of iv. 2, whoever he may have been; for after a statement that the Pharisees had heard ὅτι Ἰησοῦς πλείονας μαθητὰς ποιεῖ καὶ βαπτίζει ἢ Ἰωάννης, he has added a parenthesis explaining that this was an inaccurate report. The disciples of Jesus did baptize, but their Master did not—unless in the sense, *qui facit per alium facit per se.* If the parenthetic clause is the work of the evangelist himself, then we could infer with confidence that the statement in iii. 22, 26 was drawn by him from some earlier source. But it is difficult to believe that any writer would have made a statement and contradicted it in the same breath, to the hopeless ruin of his sentence. It seems that here at least we must allow for the work of a subsequent editor, who took exception to the idea that Jesus was (as it were) a second Baptist. In that case, the evangelist takes full responsibility for this somewhat surprising

a quotation from the O.T. (Heb. ii. 7, 9). Both are good biblical words. Their use in Jewish-Hellenistic contexts, and the use of the corresponding terms in rabbinic Hebrew in antithesis, just as here, are amply illustrated by Schlatter, *Der Evangelist Johannes*, p. 109. It is unnecessary to assume (with Bauer *ad loc.*) that the language of the present passage depends on the Hellenistic use of the words for the waxing and waning of the light of the heavenly bodies, though it is likely enough that the evangelist was aware of this additional (and entirely appropriate) shade of meaning.

statement. It would no doubt be congenial with his general attitude to represent Jesus, not as receiving baptism from John, but as himself administering it, in so far as the incarnate Logos must be thought of as always active and never merely passive. Moreover, I have elsewhere suggested that in the development of the great argument the passage iii. 22–36 is intended (among other things) to explicate the meaning of regeneration ἐξ ὕδατος καὶ πνεύματος in relation to the work of Christ, and in particular to link the ideas of ὕδωρ and πνεῦμα through the idea of baptism—the Church's baptism, that is to say, in contrast to that of John, which was ἐξ ὕδατος alone. The Agent in such baptism is Christ himself. The reader already knows that Christ is ὁ βαπτίζων ἐν πνεύματι ἁγίῳ. That his baptism (the Church's baptism) is also ἐν ὕδατι is dramatically exhibited in the picture of Jesus himself administering the rite alongside of, and in contrast to, the Baptism of John. This I believe to be a probable explanation of the evangelist's intention in placing the *pericopé* iii. 26–30, with the introductory matter of verses 22–4, at this particular point, where it has often been thought to interrupt the connection between what precedes it and what follows. It might be argued that if there is this strong theological interest in the idea that Jesus administered baptism, that idea may have a theological and not an historical basis. But if there is anything in the argument I have advanced in favour of the dependence of this passage upon pre-canonical tradition, then the statement, thrice repeated, that Jesus baptized must, it seems, be accepted as an integral part of that tradition.[1] The evangelist, I conceive, here as elsewhere, took up an element in the tradition as it reached him, and exploited it theologically. If it ran counter to some beliefs or prejudices in the Church (as iv. 2 would seem to imply), that is perhaps so far in favour of an historical basis rather than otherwise.

To the question of the historical value of the account of the work of John the Baptist in the Fourth Gospel, taken as a whole, I shall turn in a moment. Our investigation of the passage about John at Aenon-by-Salim has yielded the following results: the passage has few traits which appear to associate it with the characteristic Johannine theology, and comparatively few traces of this evangelist's language or style. The form of the passage as a whole is strikingly unlike the forms which prevail in the Fourth Gospel, and on the other hand it shows, when allowance is

---

[1] It would be possible to suppose that in iv. 2 the words καὶ βαπτίζει were inserted, and that in iii. 22 ἐβάπτιζεν was substituted for ἐδίδασκεν or the like, but in iii. 26 οὗτος βαπτίζει is indispensable.

made for some measure of editorial handling in the process of composition, an unusually close affinity with traditional forms known from the Synoptics: on the one hand with the *Sammelberichte*, and 'itinerary' material, which in Mark help to make up the framework of the narrative, and on the other hand with *pericopae* having the character of 'pronouncement-stories'. On these grounds it is highly probable that we are here in touch with pre-canonical tradition.

4. THE BAPTIST IN THE FOURTH GOSPEL AND IN THE SYNOPTICS

The foregoing investigation has led to the probable conclusion that in giving his account of the ministry of John the Baptist and its relation to the Ministry of Jesus Christ the Fourth Evangelist has drawn largely upon material which reached him in traditional form. Some of it overlaps with material known to us in the Synoptic Gospels, but there is no sufficient reason to suppose that they served as sources to our author. The tradition which he followed doubtless transmitted more information than he has chosen to include. We have noted at least one slight pointer to the kind of thing which he has excluded: the curious note about a controversy with Jews περὶ καθαρισμοῦ (iii. 25).[1] It seems that in another passage, viii. 39–41, we have reminiscences of teaching attributed to the Baptist in Matt. iii. 9, Luke iii. 8, though the teaching has here been incorporated in a discourse of Jesus.[2] Both these scraps would seem to have belonged originally to a body of material which referred to the work of John as a reformer within Judaism.[3] In that side of his work our evangelist is not interested. What he has given is the result of a process of severe selection, governed by his avowed purpose, to exhibit the Baptist as the great witness to Christ. In pursuance of this purpose he has (as we have seen reason to believe) rehandled his material to an extent difficult to define with precision, but not sufficient to obscure altogether its traditional character. There is singularly little in the relevant passages which bears any clear mark of the highly distinctive Johannine theology, and perhaps nothing at all which recalls the Hellenistic strain in it. On the other hand, we have noted several apparent points of contact with Jewish conditions, practices, or modes of thought and language belonging to the first century.[4] We are therefore encouraged to believe that we have before us something more than an imaginative construction serving dogmatic ends; that in fact this section of the gospel should be approached as a rendering—a

---

[1] Pp. 280–1.

[2] See my article, 'À l'arrière-plan d'un dialogue johannique', in *Revue d'Histoire et de Philosophie religieuses* (1957), no. 1 (pp. 330–2).

[3] These are the only places where it is at all plausible to suggest that our evangelist was dependent upon a tradition formed within a 'Baptist' community.

[4] See pp. 253, 265–9.

somewhat free rendering it may be—of a tradition with a genuinely historical content.

The picture as the evangelist has given it is on the whole perspicuous and coherent. As compared with the Synoptic picture it has certain basic elements in common, but it comes out very differently.

It is common to all our gospels that John the Baptist appeared in a role best described through the Isaianic prophecy of the Voice in the Wilderness (Isa. xl. 3), which all of them cite. According to the Fourth Gospel the Baptist expressly claimed this role for himself. This may or may not be so, but it is in itself entirely credible in view of the significance which we now know to have been attached to that prophecy in sectarian Judaism of the period. This implies that he came forward as the herald of an approaching divine interposition in human affairs. Another way of describing his mission, common to all gospels, is based on Malachi's prophecy of the Messenger (Mal. iii. 1–4). This prophetic figure was in early Christian thought identified with the figure of 'Elijah the Tishbite' in the same book (Mal. iv. 4 (iii. 23)). The identification appears not to have been attributed to the Baptist himself in the tradition behind the Fourth Gospel, for in the *locus classicus* he emphatically repudiates the role of Elijah (i. 21). There can be traced in the other gospels also a certain hesitancy or ambiguity in the doctrine of Elijah the forerunner, although it appears to have become well established before the time when the Fourth Gospel was written. It is probable that we should accept John i. 21 as a surviving scrap of an earlier and credible tradition according to which John the Baptist rejected the role, though it was afterwards fixed upon him in Christian thought.

It is again common ground that in the course of his forecasts of the approaching divine interposition the Baptist spoke of One who was to come. In both branches of the tradition he is said to have expressed his sense of the overwhelming superiority of this august Figure by saying, in a homely metaphor, that he was himself not fit to be his lackey. His own baptism with water was at once the sign, preparation and foil to a baptism with the Holy Spirit which the Coming One would administer. In view of ideas about baptism and about the Spirit attested in the 'Dead Sea Scrolls',[1] we need no longer entertain serious doubts about the historicity of this cardinal point in the Baptist's predictions.

So far we are on reasonably firm ground. We now come to the first substantial difference between the Fourth Gospel and the Synoptics.

---

[1] E.g. *Manual of Discipline, ap.* Millar Burrows, *op. cit.* pp. 373, 376.

According to the former, the Baptist not only foretold the coming of the One who should baptize with Holy Spirit; he declared that he was already present unknown. That the idea of the Unknown Messiah was in various forms current in the first century we have sufficient evidence. That the Baptist himself held it is necessarily presupposed by the question he is said to have asked in Matt. xi. 2, Luke vii. 19, for he could hardly have entertained the idea that Jesus was the Coming One unless he took for granted that *some* person moving on the contemporary scene was the Messiah *incognito*. The homely metaphor he employs to emphasize the superiority of the Coming One almost demands that he conceived himself as standing in this relation of unquestionable subordination to some contemporary whom he expected to meet face to face, and who therefore must have been at the time not far away, ready to be discovered. That he believed his own mission to be designed (in the divine purpose) to bring about that discovery in due time, and that meanwhile he himself remained in ignorance (i. 31), is entirely credible in the situation.

We may therefore accept from the Fourth Gospel that John the Baptist not only proclaimed the approaching advent of the Messiah, but also declared that he was at that moment present unknown, and might any day be identified. If this was his message, and not simply one more repetition of the age-long promise that the Messiah would appear in the future, even in the near future, it would go far to account for the immense stir which his preaching evidently caused.

The Fourth Gospel however goes on to say that the day came when John did actually identify the Coming One, and declared that Jesus was he: οὗτος ἦν ὃν εἶπον. It is at this point that he comes nearest to giving the Coming One the title of Messiah (which both here and in the Synoptics he seems to avoid). Ὁ ἀμνὸς τοῦ θεοῦ is a title entirely strange to the Johannine theology proper, which the evangelist equates with Μεσσίας (i. 36, 41). This express identification of Jesus as Messiah has no parallel in the Synoptic Gospels and is difficult to reconcile with their data. It is, however, underlined by our evangelist in the statement that it was the words, Ἴδε ὁ ἀμνὸς τοῦ θεοῦ, that brought to Jesus his first disciples. The problem raised I shall discuss presently, but meanwhile it will be well to give some consideration to a further point in which the Fourth Gospel appears to differ from the Synoptics.

It states that there was a period during which Jesus and John the Baptist were at work simultaneously. The Synoptics, *prima facie*, do not seem to leave room for such a period of parallel ministry. It appears, however, that they imply something of the kind in the parable of the Children in the Market-place and the saying which applies it to the existing situation (Matt. xi. 16–19, Luke vii. 31–5). The Jewish public is represented as observing and commenting upon the contrasting behaviour of Jesus and of John the Baptist. The clauses referring to the two are strictly parallel:

ἦλθεν Ἰωάννης...   καὶ λέγουσιν...
ἦλθεν ὁ υἱὸς τοῦ ἀνθρώπου...   καὶ λέγουσιν...[1]

The implication is that the people have before them two persons engaged in comparable activities, and comment adversely on both, though for different reasons. It would not, I think, have occurred to any reader to understand the passage as referring to anything other than the contemporaneous activities of the two, if it had not appeared in a context which seems to indicate the contrary. But most critics are now agreed that the discourse in which it is incorporated, whether in its longer Matthaean or its shorter Lucan version, is a compilation of originally separate *pericopae*. There is therefore no reason why we should not take the parable, with its application,[2] at face value, as evidence that the tradition behind the Synoptic Gospels, no less than that behind the Fourth Gospel, knew of a period when both Jesus and John were at work.[3]

At what stage in the Ministry of Jesus these comments and comparisons are supposed to be made, or where he is supposed to be at the time, the passage in question does not inform us. Matthew and Luke have placed it in the context of the Galilaean Ministry, after the arrest of John, but that

---

[1] So Matthew; Luke gives the verb in the perfect, ἐλήλυθεν, without difference of meaning. Matthew's aorist must be taken as referring to events in the immediate and not in the 'historical' past; the English equivalent is the perfect with 'have': cf. Matt. x. 34, Mark ii. 17, Luke xii. 49, xix. 10. For λέγουσιν Luke gives λέγετε, giving the saying an even greater immediacy of application.

[2] This seems a clear instance where the 'application' is an integral element in the tradition by which the parable came down; see *Parables of the Kingdom* (Nisbet, 1961), pp. 14–16, 88 (Collins, 1961), pp. 24–5, 86.

[3] In Mark ii. 18 it is not clear whether the 'disciples of John' are adherents in attendance on a master still in active work, or a group which, having lost its leader by imprisonment or death, still follows the rule of life which he had laid down. But in one way the passage is analogous to that which we are studying: unnamed people bear tales between the two leaders or their entourage without their coming into personal contact. It is of course true that in other passages Jesus refers to the ministry of the Baptist as something complete and bygone: Mark xi. 29–30, Matt. xi. 12, and perhaps 7–11. No one doubts that Jesus continued to work for some time after John was removed from the scene.

seems clearly wrong. There is nothing intrinsic to the *pericopé* which points to Galilee rather than Judaea. It is true that the occasion on which Jesus is expressly recorded to have consorted with 'publicans and sinners', Mark ii. 13–17, is most naturally placed in Galilee, but it is not to be thought that the practice was confined to one region or period.[1] There is therefore no real difficulty in accepting the data of the Fourth Gospel: that before the imprisonment of John the Baptist, while he was at work at Aenon-by-Salim, Jesus was also at work in Judaea, and that his work there ended with a journey to Galilee. Whether the reason for the move was, as the Fourth Gospel has it, the unwelcome attention of the 'Pharisees' to his growing success, or, as we might gather from the Synoptics, the arrest of the Baptist, we are perhaps not entitled to say. Both reasons may well have been operative: both the hostility of Antipas to John and the hostility of the 'Pharisees' to Jesus. And perhaps there were other reasons. More often than not there is more than one reason for a far-reaching change of plans.

During the period in question, our author says, Jesus, like John, administered baptism. I have suggested reasons for believing that this was an element in the tradition as it reached him, and not a reflection of his own theology. It is a surprising statement, and a statement which an early editor of the gospel felt obliged to qualify. The conventional summaries of the activity of Jesus speak of his teaching and healing, or, in the Fourth Gospel, teaching and 'working signs'. Here alone we read of his baptizing. To the mind of the early Church, so far as we are able to read it behind our documents, the suggestion that Jesus at any time put himself on the same level with John—even on the same apparent level—would be unwelcome. All the more probable is it that we are here dealing with an undigested scrap of genuine information. It would fit all our data if we supposed that in early days, when he might be regarded as a follower of the Baptist (possibly even by John himself, if my suggested rendering of John i. 30 be thought acceptable), Jesus was engaged in a mission essentially similar to that of the Baptist. It was a provisional and pre-paratory stage. In recent discussions of the question whether or not Jesus claimed to be Messiah, it is often suggested that during his earthly life he was no more than 'Messiah-designate', and acted as his own fore-runner. This theory seems to me to do too much violence to the data of the gospels. But I believe that this is precisely what Jesus was doing in the period to which John iii. 22–30 refers: he was acting as his own fore-

[1] Luke knows of one instance at least in Judaea (xix. 1–10).

runner. His time (as our evangelist might have put it) was not yet come. When, however, the Jewish authorities began to take hostile note of his proceedings, and when (immediately afterwards, possibly) the work of the forerunner was forcibly cut short, the hour struck. Then it was that Jesus came into Galilee, announcing, says Mark, πεπλήρωται ὁ καιρὸς καὶ ἤγγικεν ἡ βασιλεία τοῦ θεοῦ. This would give an intelligible sequence, and it would explain why in the *kerygma* the *motif*, 'beginning from Galilee', is so constant. It was evidently known also to the Fourth Evangelist, who records that it was in Galilee that the ἀρχὴ σημείων first manifested the glory of Christ. Whatever preparatory work had gone on, it was when Jesus moved northwards into Galilee that the train of events began in which the early believers, taught by Jesus himself, recognized the coming of the Kingdom of God, the days of the Messiah.

We must now return to John the Baptist. When he became aware that Jesus was duplicating his own ministry, and doing it with a success that promised to put his own work in the shade, what was his response? According to John iii. 22–30 he accepted the situation as being of divine appointment (δεῖ), and rejoiced that Jesus was advancing while his own cause declined, using a parable about the bridegroom and the bridegroom's friend. The evangelist no doubt understood this in the sense that John believed Jesus to be the Messiah. He has indicated this in two places where there is reason to suspect some addition to the traditional material: (*a*) the clause ᾧ σὺ μεμαρτύρηκας (iii. 26), which refers the reader back to the 'testimony of John' in i. 29–34; and (*b*) the double quotation of what the Baptist had formerly said in iii. 28. We may fairly take this self-quotation to be a device for introducing something which the evangelist wishes his readers to have in mind in reading the verses that follow. He is saying, in effect, 'I would have you bear in mind, first, that John the Baptist, as I have told you, expressly denied that he was the Messiah (i. 21), and secondly, that his ministry, as all Christians agree, was the fulfilment of the prophecy of Malachi about the Messenger sent ahead to prepare the way of the Lord'. The reader who is thus prepared will inevitably understand the Bridegroom of the parable as a cryptogram for the Messiah, and the ἐκεῖνον δεῖ αὐξάνειν of the following aphorism as a prophetic affirmation that the Messiah must go forward to victory. But without the hint in iii. 28 neither the parable nor the aphorism *necessarily* amounts to an express declaration of the Messiahship of Jesus (see above, pp. 284–5).

Both could be understood in the sense that the Baptist recognized in Jesus another, and more effective, herald of the approaching divine intervention. Why may he not, for example, at this time have cast Jesus for the role of Elijah, which he had rejected for himself?

At this point we may recall a Synoptic *pericopé*, Matt. xi. 2–6, Luke vii. 18–23, which postulates a situation similar in some respects to that of John iii. 22–30. Jesus and John are not in direct contact, but the latter is in a position to receive accounts of what Jesus is doing (περὶ πάντων τούτων, says Luke, τὰ ἔργα τοῦ χριστοῦ, says Matthew), and messengers pass between them. The accounts he has received prompt John to ask the question, whether Jesus is perhaps the Coming One of whom he had himself spoken. It would be easy enough to understand this as the next stage to that represented in John iii. 29–30. According to Matthew, John was at this time in prison, but the words ἐν τῷ δεσμωτηρίῳ have no parallel in Luke, and probably do not belong to the common source they are following; they may be no more than Matthew's intelligent inference from the statement which he has reproduced after Mark (Matt. iv. 12–17, Mark i. 14), that Jesus began his Ministry in Galilee after John's arrest. It is therefore *possible* that John was in fact still at liberty at the time when he sent his message, and we should be in a situation similar to that contemplated in John iii. 22–30.[1] But if so, then the reconstruction by which I have just proposed to combine the data of the Fourth Gospel and of the Synoptics will not hold; for it is essential to the *pericopé* we are considering that the miracles which portend the messianic age are already in process. It therefore belongs to a period after the 'beginning of signs' in Galilee, after the proclamation of the Kingdom of God, and cannot, without departing too far from our evidence, be placed in the preparatory or provisional stage of the Ministry of Jesus. John was now in prison, and Jesus had moved to Galilee.

Yet the suggestion that the question, σὺ εἶ ὁ ἐρχόμενος; represents the next stage of development in the Baptist's views after that represented by John iii. 22–30 remains open. On that view, Matt. xi. 2–6 would not be inconsistent with John iii. 22–30, but it would contradict the explicit statements of John i. 29–34, where the Baptist, before the Ministry of Jesus had even begun, immediately after the occasion which we must needs

---

[1] Would John, it may be asked, imprisoned in the fortress of Machaerus because Antipas thought his influence politically dangerous (Josephus, *Antiq.* XVIII. 118), have been permitted free intercourse with his adherents, and allowed to send messages to potential accomplices outside?

identify with his baptism as recorded in the Synoptics, expressly identifies Jesus as 'him of whom I spoke', as the Baptizer with holy Spirit, as the Son of God, as the Lamb of God—in other words, as the Messiah. The difficulty of accepting that statement, and at the same time giving the Synoptic Gospels the degree of credence which in general they seem to merit, lies not simply in their silence about any such 'testimony of John'. It is a difficulty that goes deeper. According to Matt. xi. 11 John the Baptist, though a prophet and more than a prophet, though as great a man as any born of woman, is yet not 'in the Kingdom of God'. To be in the kingdom, to receive it, to receive Christ, to confess him, are, if not identical concepts, at least so closely bound together that no one who confesses Christ could be said to be outside the Kingdom of God. Yet John is outside. Either he had never confessed Christ, or having once confessed he fell away from his faith. The latter hypothesis has sometimes been advanced to reconcile the discrepancy in our traditions. John, it is suggested, may have wavered, either through the disappointment of his hopes of drastic action by the Messiah, or simply through the natural depression of a frustrated and imprisoned man. This might find support in the saying with which the reply to his question ends in Matt. xi. 6, Luke vii. 23: μακάριός ἐστιν ὃς ἐὰν μὴ σκανδαλισθῇ ἐν ἐμοί. The verb σκανδαλί-ζεσθαι is often used with the implied sense of a falling away from faith or loyalty. The saying might therefore imply either that the Baptist has fallen away, or that he is in grave danger of doing so. If the former, then he might properly be said to be outside the Kingdom of God; if the latter, perhaps not so properly.

This is a not impossible reading between the lines. But it is strange that there is in no other passage of the Synoptics any hint that John had ever confessed Christ, though without knowing this a reader could hardly be expected to divine the meaning now proposed for Matt. xi. 6, Luke vii. 23. There is indeed one passage which might be taken to imply that John privately believed Jesus to be Messiah from the first. In the Matthaean account John is already aware, before baptizing Jesus, that he is at least his own spiritual superior, and after the baptism the voice from heaven proclaims, Οὗτός ἐστιν ὁ υἱός μου ὁ ἀγαπητός. It is therefore addressed, not to Jesus, but, apparently, to the Baptist, who may therefore be presumed to know the truth from this time on. But there is no suggestion that he communicated what he knew to anyone else. Matthew's account still differs widely from that of the Fourth Gospel, where John sees the vision of the descent of the Dove (and, if we choose to read between the lines, hears the voice), and proceeds to tell of the vision and to repeat the terms of the *bath qol*: Οὗτός ἐστιν ὁ υἱὸς τοῦ θεοῦ.

It may be suggested that it was only to a few intimates that he made this disclosure, and that they (for whatever reason) kept it dark. We are indeed told directly only of two disciples who heard John speak, and the implication of iii. 26, x. 41, that his testimony was more widely divulged, and of v. 33–5, that it was known to 'the Jews', might be discounted as editorial generalization. Yet it is doubtful whether a communication to a select few would be what this evangelist means by μαρτυρία. If we are to take him at his word, one of the two who heard John speak was Andrew, and he immediately told the secret to his brother Simon Peter. There is certainly no suggestion in the Synoptics that these two brothers knew that Jesus was Messiah when they left their nets and followed him. Nor, when the disciples asked in perplexity after the storm at sea, Τίς ἄρα οὗτός ἐστιν; (Mark iv. 41),[1] does it appear that Simon and Andrew were less perplexed than the rest. And the scene at Caesarea Philippi (Mark viii. 27–30) would lose much of its dramatic force if Peter had known all along that Jesus was the Messiah.[2] Least of all could Matthew's addition to that scene be justified: σὰρξ καὶ αἷμα οὐκ ἀπεκάλυψέν σοι (Matt. xvi. 17), if in fact it was Peter's own brother who had made the revelation on the strength of something that John the Baptist had said.

No; I can see no reasonable way of removing the discrepancy among our sources. We must choose between the Fourth Gospel and the Synoptics. If we ask how far it is possible that the several accounts have been affected by doctrinal tendencies, it might be urged that the Marcan doctrine of the 'messianic secret' has weighed unduly with the Synoptics. But it may be urged with much greater plausibility that the Fourth Evangelist is deeply committed to the view that the 'testimony of John' has a significant place in Christian apologetic, and that he may therefore be expected to make the most of anything in his tradition which would support that view.

[1] At a pinch it might be argued that Matthew (viii. 27) has altered this to Ποταπός ἐστιν οὗτος; on the assumption that Peter (and others) already knew that Jesus was (or was to be) Messiah, in some sense, but felt that their recent experience opened up fresh vistas of the nature and origin of the Messiah, going beyond anything they had dreamed of. But such subtlety is out of place.

[2] I should not, however, lay too great stress on this. The really new and important truth communicated in this *pericopé* is not that Jesus is Messiah, but that the Messiah must suffer, and the scene would still retain significance if Peter had cherished the belief that Jesus was Messiah, in the popular sense. Jesus makes him confess this in order to disabuse him. So Mark, but not so Matthew.

The *locus classicus* for the Johannine doctrine of μαρτυρία is the second part of the great discourse which follows upon the two 'signs' displaying the power of the life-giving Word (v. 31–47). In the first part of the discourse Jesus has seemed to put forward the kind of evidence which is inadmissible in a court of law because it is a man's testimony on his own behalf. He goes on to say that he has independent corroborative evidence. In the first instance there is the testimony of John, the 'burning and shining lamp', in whose light for a time the Jews rejoiced. But, the discourse proceeds, this is merely human testimony after all; the ultimate testimony is that of God himself. It is written, on the one hand, in the scriptures, and, on the other hand, in the actual 'works' of Christ. The Jews do not believe because, not having the word of God in their hearts, they cannot understand His word in the scriptures, and, not being willing to 'come to' Christ, they do not see the true significance of that which he does.

We can hardly be wrong in seeing here a reflection of the experience of Christian missionaries. They based their apologetic partly upon the self-evidencing work of Christ, and partly upon the Old Testament scriptures newly interpreted. On both sides they often encountered obdurate disbelief, but they found that those who had God's word in their heart ('the scattered children of God', of John xi. 52), and who would 'come to' Christ, laying themselves open to his impact upon them, received the truth. It need hardly be pointed out how the gospels, Johannine and Synoptic alike, carry out this scheme. They set forth the ἔργα τοῦ χριστοῦ (which include his sufferings), and they relate them to the prophetic heritage of Israel by their use of *testimonia*. But the third element in the μαρτυρία as conceived by the Fourth Evangelist is employed in the Synoptic Gospels only to a limited extent. The Baptist, they report, announced the approaching advent of the Messiah. As the Voice in the Wilderness, as the Messenger, as Elijah the forerunner, he prepared the scene into which Jesus entered proclaiming the Kingdom of God; and he was the agent (though perhaps the unconscious agent) through whom Jesus was inaugurated into the messianic office. Finally, by asking the question, σὺ εἶ ὁ ἐρχόμενος; he opened the way for the true interpretation of the ἔργα τοῦ χριστοῦ. In this sense John was a witness to the messiahship of Jesus.[1] So much is common ground. The Fourth Evangelist will go beyond this: the Baptist must not only, like another Merlin, prepare

---

[1] The way in which the 'testimony of John' was employed in Christian apologetic is well illustrated by Acts xiii. 24–5.

the Siege Perilous for the Galahad who is to come; he must also point out beyond mistake its fated Occupant.

We seem to detect something of the way in which the case is built up. In the passage headed 'The Testimony of John' there is, down to i. 27, nothing that is not, essentially, in harmony with the Synoptics. In i. 29–34 the evangelist has taken certain elements out of tradition and given them a turn which makes them into direct affirmations of the messiahship of Jesus (which perhaps they were not originally). The operative clause is, Οὗτός ἐστιν ὑπὲρ οὗ ἐγὼ εἶπον, which in effect applies to the Person now before him all that John had said about the coming Messiah, or the unknown Messiah already present. Again, the description of the descent of the Dove, with the solemn affirmation that Jesus is the Son of God, deeply rooted in both sides of the tradition, is put into the mouth of the Baptist and so becomes a part of his testimony. Only the declaration, Ἴδε ὁ ἀμνὸς τοῦ θεοῦ, is without parallel. That the title itself derives from a pre-Johannine tradition is almost certain. It is, however, possible that, like some other appellations (ὁ ἰσχυρότερός μου, ὁ ὀπίσω μου ἐρχόμενος οὗ οὐκ εἰμὶ ἄξιος κ.τ.λ., and the Synoptic images of the woodman with his axe and the winnower with his fan), it was there applied to an ideal figure of the future, and that the form in which it now appears is in effect governed by the rubric, οὗτός ἐστιν ὃν εἶπον.

In what *Sitz im Leben* are we to suppose this development to have taken place? The answer to that question will partly depend on the weight assigned to the alleged evidence for a community of followers of John the Baptist functioning as a powerful rival to the Christian Church in its mission to the Hellenistic world about the close of the first century. If such a community be postulated, then we have our *Sitz im Leben*. There were of course many communities and sects of various kinds which practised lustrations and baptisms (the newly discovered Qumran community is one of them). But so far as I can see, there is no sufficient evidence either that they seriously challenged the Christian mission or that they looked to John the Baptist as their founder, or claimed for him the dignities which in the New Testament are assigned to Jesus Christ.[1] We must, I think, look in a somewhat different direction.

There is something strange about the way in which, in v. 32–6, the evangelist qualifies his respect for the testimony of John. It is introduced

[1] To base a theory upon the evidence of the late and heretical Clementine romance is to build a house upon sand.

as an argument *ad hominem*, addressed to those who had sent to inquire of John and had received his answer. In i. 19–27 these are the official representatives of Judaism (sufficiently denominated in v. 16 οἱ Ἰουδαῖοι). In terms of the evangelist's actual public they may stand for any orthodox Jews. For them the testimony of John ought to carry weight. Yet the influence of John upon Judaism had in fact been only temporary (πρὸς ὥραν). Moreover, Christ does not ask for human testimony (v. 34); he has testimony μείζω τοῦ Ἰωάννου (v. 36). What does this mean but that, by the time the evangelist wrote, the appeal to the testimony of John no longer carried weight? It had availed only temporarily and *vis-à-vis* a particular public. In view of this it is doubtful if we ought to lay upon the evangelist the whole, or perhaps even the main, responsibility for the re-orientation of the tradition. As we have seen, the passages concerned with the Baptist are full of apparently traditional elements; distinctively 'Johannine' elements, identifiable as such, are few. It looks as if the process of development was already afoot before the tradition reached the evangelist, though he has brought it to a new and conclusive stage.

If we ask, again, what is his main motive, the key is perhaps given by i. 20: ὡμολόγησεν καὶ οὐκ ἠρνήσατο, to which is added: ὡμολόγησεν ὅτι Ἐγὼ οὐκ εἰμὶ ὁ χριστός. That is a very peculiar way of expressing his meaning. The words οὐκ εἰμί are a form of speech which in Greek is properly called ἄρνησις, denial or negation. A Greek writer would naturally have said, ἠρνήσατο λέγων Οὐκ εἰμί. And in fact that is the form of phrase which our evangelist himself uses in recording Peter's 'denial' of his Lord: ἠρνήσατο καὶ εἶπεν Οὐκ εἰμί (xviii. 25). In view of the deep significance which the terms ὁμολογεῖν and ἀρνεῖσθαι have in the vocabulary of the New Testament,[1] the expression in John i. 20 would inevitably mean, for any Christian reader of the period, 'He confessed Christ and did not deny him'. In other words, the evangelist is claiming the Baptist as the first Christian 'confessor', in contrast to the view represented in the Synoptic Gospels that he was not 'in the Kingdom of God'. It is the Johannine view that has prevailed, and affected the liturgy and the calendar of the Church.

The Baptist therefore is not treated as a rival who must be subpoenaed to give evidence in favour of Christ. He is claimed as one of Christ's own

[1] E.g. Matt. x. 32–3 = Luke xii. 8–9 (the fundamental passage), 1 John ii. 22–3 (and see my note *ad loc.* in the Moffatt Commentary), cf. 2 Tim. ii. 12–13; ὁμολογεῖν in John ix. 22 is confessing Christ, ἀρνεῖσθαι in xviii. 25–7 is denying him. The words become almost technical: ὁμολογεῖν, Rom. x. 9–10, 1 Tim. vi. 12, Heb. iv. 14; ἀρνεῖσθαι, Acts iii. 13–14, 1 Tim. v. 8, Rev. ii. 13, iii. 8, Jude 4, 2 Pet. ii. 1.

people. The *Sitz im Leben* which we should infer is one in which it was desired that persons who had followed the Baptist should be regarded as adoptive members of the Church. Such a situation seems to be indicated, and for Ephesus, the home of this gospel, in Acts xviii. 24–xix. 7. It is an enigmatic passage, which has been made to bear a large edifice of conjectural constructions. But on the face of it Apollos and the twelve μαθηταί are not treated as converts from a rival sect. As followers of the Baptist they are already, in some sense, Christians (for μαθηταί, used absolutely, never means anything else in the New Testament), though their Christianity is in some way incomplete. With such persons it might be effective to hold up their old teacher as an example: he confessed Christ and did not deny him, ὡμολόγησεν καὶ οὐκ ἠρνήσατο, and they should do the same. If the passage in Acts has any significance as a pointer to what happened to the surviving followers of the Baptist, it suggests, not that they perpetuated a community carrying on a vigorous mission in rivalry with the Church, but that (so far as they did not remain within the Jewish fold) they were absorbed into the Christian Church; and this is in all probability the truth. Apollos and the twelve μαθηταί had been personal followers of the Baptist. Paul's encounter with them must be dated about A.D. 55–7. After that time the supply of such persons must have rapidly declined. I suggest that this gives a rough limit for the period to which we may assign the main development of the tradition here followed by the Fourth Evangelist. There can, I think, be no reasonable doubt that this tradition included very primitive material, but before it reached our evangelist it had undergone development in the environment indicated.

What measure of historical truth, then, if any, can we assign to the statement of the Fourth Gospel that John the Baptist bore witness to Christ? The following points appear to be historical:

(i) His preaching, taking up ideas which were very much in the air at the time, and bringing them to a sharp point, aroused a widespread conviction that a divine interposition was impending, and his use of the rite of baptism gave concrete expression to the conviction.

(ii) He placed the ideal figure of the Messiah fully in the centre of the picture of the crisis now impending.[1] He thus diffused an atmosphere in which the appearance of a messianic personality was actively expected.

---

[1] In distinction from some other ways of thought, such as those of Qumran, with which in some respects he had some affinity.

(iii) He went further and declared that the Messiah was already μέσος ὑμῶν, though incognito, thus intensifying the expectancy.

(iv) Jesus, known to have been baptized by John, and regarded as one of his followers, soon began a mission of his own, parallel to that of John, but quickly becoming more effective.

(v) John, hearing of this, recognized that Jesus was his superior, welcomed his success, foretold that his own work must now be over-shadowed by that of Jesus, and eventually suggested that Jesus might indeed be the Coming One, the Messiah, without, apparently, arriving at a firm conviction that this was so.

(vi) Some, probably many, of those who had received baptism from John and were in some sense his disciples, became adherents of Jesus. They did not feel that they were thereby deserting their former teacher, but that they were pursuing the natural course pointed out to them both by his own attitude and by the logic of events, especially when John was imprisoned and shortly afterwards executed.

(vii) These disciples, first of John and afterwards of Jesus, came before long to the conviction that Jesus was indeed the Messiah of whom John had spoken, and came to it as the logical conclusion of the process which John had set on foot.

The whole process might not unjustly be characterized in the words of the Prologue: Οὗτος ἦλθεν εἰς μαρτυρίαν ἵνα μαρτυρήσῃ περὶ τοῦ φωτός, ἵνα πάντες πιστεύσωσιν δι' αὐτοῦ. For John the Baptist did make certain great affirmations regarding God's revelation of Himself to men, and the Person through whom the revelation should be made, which did prepare people to recognize Jesus for what he was, and did in the end lead them to believe in him. The story that John expressly and explicitly hailed Jesus as Messiah (ἴδε ὁ ἀμνὸς τοῦ θεοῦ), and that one of his disciples, hearing these words, told others, εὑρήκαμεν τὸν μεσσίαν, we may take as a dramatic and symbolic picture of the total process.

5. THE FIRST DISCIPLES (i. 35–51)

We have seen that this passage sets out, in verses 35–7, to illustrate the theme that it was through the 'testimony' of the Baptist that men came to believe in Jesus. The direct treatment, however, of this theme is exhausted by the end of verse 37, where the words, ἠκολούθησαν τῷ Ἰησοῦ, form the appropriate close to a *pericopé* of this kind, though the effects of the testimony are perpetuated in a kind of chain-reaction: Andrew is brought to Christ by John, Philip by Andrew (?) and Nathaniel by Philip. But in fact the interest has by this time shifted to a different theme. The main purpose of the passage, from verse 40 onwards, is to deploy a series of 'testimonies' supplementary to that of John, and these are so arranged that the several persons summoned as witnesses assign to Jesus, one after another, various titles of dignity: Andrew names him Messiah, Philip describes him as the Fulfiller of law and prophets, Nathaniel acclaims him as Son of God and King of Israel. The passage works up to a climax in which Jesus himself takes up the theme and in mysterious terms speaks of the angels ascending and descending upon the Son of Man, thus completing the series of messianic titles by the addition of the one which in all the gospels alike is used by him alone. This pronouncement, as I have shown elsewhere,[1] is related at a profound level to the whole Johannine theology. We have, therefore, evidence of the hand of the evangelist in the composition of the passage.

Yet it is not clear that all the material is homogeneous. The theme of 'testimony' is interwoven with another: that of the adhesion of certain persons to Jesus as disciples. From this point of view the passage is in some sort the equivalent of the *pericopae* in the Synoptic Gospels which record the 'call' of disciples—yet with a difference. In the Synoptic Gospels Jesus spontaneously chooses his disciples, and appoints them to specified tasks. The fishermen are called from their nets to follow him and to become fishers of men; the publican is called to leave his douane.[2] The

---

[1] *Interpretation*, pp. 244–9.

[2] Mark i. 16–20, ii. 14, with parallels in Matthew and Luke. In Mark x. 21–2 the call ἀκολούθει μοι meets with no response; in Luke ix. 59 the response is doubtful. In Matt. viii. 19, Luke ix. 57 we have the only instance in the Synoptics (unless we reckon the demoniac of Gadara, Mark v. 18) of a man spontaneously offering himself for discipleship (in the restricted sense), and here the response of Jesus is not encouraging.

initiative lies entirely with Jesus; the men respond. We cannot suppose that the Fourth Evangelist intended to dissent from this view of the situation. Indeed, he says, more emphatically than any of the others, Οὐχ ὑμεῖς με ἐξελέξασθε ἀλλ' ἐγὼ ἐξελεξάμην ὑμᾶς καὶ ἔθηκα ὑμᾶς (xv. 16, compare vi. 70). We should have expected that any account he might give of the adhesion of disciples would be so disposed as to emphasize the free initiative of Jesus. But the stories in i. 35–51 do nothing of the kind. One only of the five persons mentioned is 'called', in the familiar words, Ἀκολούθει μοι. Of the others, two seek Jesus as a result of the 'testimony of John', and two are introduced by friends.[1] The initiative is taken by the disciples themselves or their sponsors. Although therefore there is good ground for finding a doctrinal motive for the deploying of these 'testimonies', and although the Johannine theology clearly emerges, there are other elements in the stories which are not so easily derived from Johannine motives, and we are justified in asking whether these elements may be traceable to pre-canonical tradition.

First, some general considerations. The Fourth Gospel, like the others, knows that Jesus had a body of disciples, among whom there were twelve who formed an inner group. It gives no list of names, as do the others, though their lists do not tally in all respects.[2] Of the names known from other lists, the Fourth Gospel has Simon Peter, Andrew, Philip, Thomas, Judas Iscariot, in common with Matthew and Mark, and another Judas in common with Luke. The appendix also mentions the sons of Zebedee, who appear in the other lists (but not here) as James and John. In addition this gospel gives the name of Nathaniel, who (according to the appendix at least) appears to be reckoned among the Twelve, but is unknown to the Synoptics. The *prima facie* suggestion is that this evangelist followed a list which differed from other traditional lists to much the same degree as the three lists in the Synoptic Gospels (and the fourth in Acts) differ among themselves.

Apart from the formal lists, Mark and Matthew record the occasions on which five named disciples adhered to Jesus. The names given do not precisely coincide. Both give Peter, Andrew,[3] James and John; in addition one gives Levi, the other Matthew, both being described as publicans.

[1] If, in i. 43, the verbs ἠθέλησεν, εὑρίσκει, have Andrew for subject (as is probable), Philip too is introduced in the first place by a friend, before he is 'called' by Jesus.

[2] The list of the Eleven in Acts i. 13 is identical, except in order, with the list of the Twelve in Luke vi. 14–16, without Judas Iscariot.

[3] Luke omits Andrew (see v. 1–11), thus reducing the group to four.

Similarly, the Fourth Gospel records the adhesion of five individuals, of whom four are named, Andrew, Peter, Philip and Nathaniel. The fifth remains anonymous.[1] This recurrence of a group of five may be fortuitous; that it should be derived from the Synoptics is most improbable. It might possibly preserve a reminiscence of some common tradition that Jesus started with five disciples. As it happens, there seems to be a trace of some such tradition in a Jewish source. A *baraita* in *Bab. Sanh.* 44 reads, 'Our rabbis taught: Jesus had five disciples, Mattai, Naqai, Netser, Buni, and Toda'.[2] Of these names, it seems reasonable to identify מתאי with the Ματθαῖος of the gospels, and תודה with the Θαδδαῖος of Mark,[3] who is probably unknown to the other gospels, though in Matt. x. 3 some MSS. have this name, others Λεββαῖος (?=Mark's Λευΐ), and others conflate the two as Λεββαῖος ὁ ἐπικληθεὶς Θαδδαῖος. This curious piece of Jewish tradition makes it less likely that the occurrence of a group of five in John and in the Synoptics is mere coincidence. It is in fact a somewhat probable inference that just as the dominant tradition affirmed the existence of the group of twelve, without being entirely agreed about their names, so other branches of tradition spoke of an earlier group of five, without, again, being able to provide an agreed list of names.

Of the five names, two are common to John and the Synoptics, Andrew and Simon Peter, but the order of precedence differs. In all Synoptic lists of the Twelve, Simon Peter stands first. In Mark and Luke Andrew comes second, but in Matthew and in the list of Acts i. 13 he has fallen to fourth place, James and John having moved up to the second and third, with James taking precedence in Mark and John in Acts. In John i. 40–1 Andrew takes precedence of his brother. There is one other list of

[1] The assumption that the anonymous is John son of Zebedee is entirely gratuitous, nor is there any sound reason for identifying him either with the unnamed disciple of xviii. 15, who was γνωστὸς τῷ ἀρχιερεῖ, or with the disciple, also unnamed, ὃν ἠγάπα ὁ ᾿Ιησοῦς. The argument that anonymous characters in the story may be identified with one another and with the author is a very odd one.

[2] This *baraita* follows immediately upon the one which records that Jesus was hanged on the eve of Passover (see p. 100). It is followed by a fanciful account of the condemnation of the five to death, but this is said to be marked as of later (Amoraic) derivation by Aramaic language and punning witticisms (according to Klausner, *Jesus of Nazareth*, pp. 28–9).

[3] Attempts to identify the other three names are temerarious. There is a *baraita* (*Taanith* 20a) which says that Buni was the real name of the person called Naqdimon ben Gorion. But to identify the Buni of *Sanh.* 44 with Naqdimon ben Gorion, to infer that he is mentioned in the Fourth Gospel as Nicodemus, and so to find a place for him among the disciples, is too speculative. There is nothing to connect the Jerusalem millionaire Naqdimon ben Gorion with the rabbi of John iii. 1.

disciples where he similarly stands at the head, namely that of Papias, who, in an oft-quoted passage preserved by Eusebius (*H.E.* III. 39. 4), enumerates those 'disciples of the Lord' whose sayings he took every opportunity of learning from oral tradition: τί Ἀνδρέας ἢ τί Πέτρος εἶπεν, ἢ τί Φίλιππος, ἢ τί Θωμᾶς ἢ Ἰάκωβος, ἢ τί Ἰωάννης ἢ Ματθαῖος, ἢ τις ἕτερος τῶν κυρίου μαθητῶν. Here then we have a list of seven, with Andrew firmly in the first place. Papias of Hierapolis speaks for the Church in Asia, including, no doubt, the Church of Ephesus, the presumed home of the Fourth Gospel. We may find here a hint that at Ephesus Andrew did enjoy a certain priority of esteem. This is reflected in the passage before us, where he is the first to be named among the first five disciples.

Starting, then, with Andrew, we come to Peter, and then to Philip; and here again the order is that of Papias, though in the Synoptics this disciple is not among the first five to adhere to Jesus, and his name comes no higher than fifth in the list of twelve. That Philip enjoyed high esteem in the Church in Asia we know from Polycrates, bishop of Ephesus in the reign of Commodus, who is quoted by Eusebius (*H.E.* v. 24. 2) as enumerating the μεγάλα στοιχεῖα who died in that province, and first among them Φίλιππον τῶν δώδεκα ἀποστόλων, ὃς κεκοίμηται ἐν Ἱεραπόλει.[1] It certainly looks as if we were in touch with a tradition proper to Ephesus, in which the view taken of relations among the Twelve was not exactly that which became dominant elsewhere. It may be for this reason that our evangelist has given a certain prominence to Andrew and Philip at two other points, vi. 5–8, xii. 20–2, though in the latter place it is natural enough that the two disciples bearing Greek names should introduce the Greek inquirers.

At any rate, there is enough here to suggest that the Fourth Evangelist worked upon a tradition about the first followers of Jesus independent of the Synoptics, and that elements of that tradition have been incorporated in the 'chapter of witness', although that chapter in its resultant form bears clear marks of artificial composition. I now proceed to more detailed examination of the passage.

The passage before us consists (after the verses which link it with the foregoing passage) of three separate *pericopae*, which the evangelist, by

---

[1] It has been doubted whether there may not have been some confusion between Philip the apostle and Philip the deacon. Did they both have remarkable daughters? Or is it possible that the same Philip has by some means got into both lists—the seven and the twelve?

deft editorial work, has woven into a continuous narrative. Each *pericopé*, however, has its own special interest and a form corresponding.

(i) *The Naming of Peter, i. 40–2*

The main interest of this little *pericopé* clearly lies in verse 42, where Jesus gives Simon the name Cephas=Peter. The meeting between the two is contrived by Andrew, who, informing his brother that he has found the Messiah, brings him to be introduced. The opening verse 40 links the passage with what has preceded by identifying Andrew as one of the two disciples of John formerly mentioned anonymously. It might conceivably be an editorial addition made in the process of composition. We turn at once, therefore, to the saying of Jesus which is the core of the *pericopé*: Σὺ εἶ Σίμων ὁ υἱὸς ’Ιωάννου· σὺ κληθήσῃ Κηφᾶς.

That a leading figure of the early Church, whose proper name was Simon, was also known as Kephas (כֵּיפָא) in Aramaic, or Πέτρος in Greek, is one of the most securely attested facts in the New Testament. Paul, who knew him well, calls him Κηφᾶς eight times, Πέτρος twice. In the Acts of the Apostles he is generally Πέτρος, sometimes Σίμων or Σίμων Πέτρος (Σ. ὁ ἐπικαλούμενος Π.), once Συμεών,[1] never Κηφᾶς. In the Synoptic Gospels he is usually Πέτρος, sometimes Σίμων, rarely Σίμων Πέτρος (Σ. ὁ λεγόμενος Π.), never Κηφᾶς. John has Σίμων Πέτρος seventeen times, Πέτρος *simpliciter* fifteen times. In the present context alone, apart from a passage in the appendix (xxi. 15–17), he has Σίμων, and in both these contexts a patronymic is added. Moreover, in the present passage alone he has Κηφᾶς, which otherwise does not occur outside the Pauline epistles, but is certainly primitive. Clearly our passage stands in contrast to normal Johannine usage, and invites the question, whether the evangelist may not be reproducing without change an element in the tradition which had come down to him, whether orally or in writing.

We are here told how, when Andrew introduced his brother Simon (called by anticipation Σίμων Πέτρος), Jesus, addressing him formally by name and patronymic as ‘Simon son of John’, adds, Σὺ κληθήσῃ Κηφᾶς. For the benefit of monoglot Greek readers the evangelist appends the note, ὃ ἑρμηνεύεται Πέτρος. The implication is that the familiar name, Cephas or Peter,[2] was given to Simon by Jesus.

---

[1] Συμεὼν Πέτρος in 2 Pet. i. 1 may be a deliberate archaism. The first epistle uses the simple Πέτρος which was usual among Greek-speaking Christians.

[2] It is not properly a name, either in Aramaic or in Greek, but a descriptive nickname (see O. Cullmann, *Peter, Disciple, Apostle, Martyr*, Eng. trans., pp. 18–20).

There is a partial parallel in Matt. xvi. 17–18: Μακάριος εἶ, Σίμων Βαριωνᾶ... κἀγὼ δέ σοι λέγω ὅτι Σὺ εἶ Πέτρος. The implication here as in John (though less clearly than in John) is that Jesus gave Simon the name by which he came to be known. That he did in fact do so is stated in explicit terms by Mark (iii. 16), and, after him, by Luke (vi. 14), though neither of these reports a scene which might be regarded as the actual giving of the name. As against them, Matthew and John agree in describing such a scene. The setting in the two gospels is entirely different, but they have in common (*a*) the address by name and patronymic, unique in the canonical gospels, except for John xxi. 15–17; and (*b*) the giving of the descriptive nickname. In both points, however, there are characteristic differences.

(*a*) Matthew gives the patronymic as Βαριωνᾶ, John as υἱὸς ᾽Ιωάννου.[1] According to the Gospel MS. 366, in a marginal note on Matt. xvi. 17, Τὸ ᾽Ιουδαϊκόν (generally taken to be the Gospel according to the Hebrews) had υἱὲ ᾽Ιωάννο (*sic* for ᾽Ιωάννου), in the corresponding context. Similarly, according to the Latin translation of [Origen], *In Matt.*, ad xix. 16 *sqq.*, the Gospel according to the Hebrews had a peculiar version of the dialogue with the rich man reported in that *pericopé* of Matthew, ending with the words, 'et conversus dixit Simoni discipulo suo sedenti apud se, "Simon fili Joanne,[2] facilius est camelum intrare per foramen acus quam divitem in regnum caelorum"'. It appears therefore that in a context entirely apart from the one we are considering the patronymic 'Son of John' is independently attested. We cannot therefore plausibly attribute the form given in John i. 42 to the evangelist's own revision of the Matthaean text; it is more probable that there was a separate line of tradition upon which both the Fourth Gospel and the Gospel according to the Hebrews drew, according to which the father of Simon Peter was not Jonah but John.[3]

---

[1] So אB*LW 33 etc. AB³ΓΔ have ᾽Ιωνᾶ, perhaps by assimilation to Matthew.

[2] 'Son of Joanna', apparently (cf. Luke viii. 3); but the use of a metronymic is extremely rare (ὁ υἱὸς τῆς Μαρίας in Mark vi. 3, if this is the true reading, is an obvious exception). Since 366 seems to guarantee υἱὸς ᾽Ιωάννου for the Gospel according to the Hebrews, it is probable that here too the Greek had υἱὲ ᾽Ιωάννου. Or should we conjecture a hybrid form Joannas, ᾽Ιωαννᾶς?

[3] It is not important for our present purpose to answer the question, whether ᾽Ιωνᾶς was a possible alternative way of Graecizing the Hebrew יְהוֹחָנָן. S.–B. *ad* Matt. xvi. 17 seem to go too far in denying (on the authority of Dalman) that there is evidence for Βαριωνᾶ as an 'abbreviation' of בַּר־יוֹחָנָן. In 1 Chron. xxvi. 3 the Hebrew has יְהוֹחָנָן, and cod. B of the LXX gives ᾽Ιωνᾶς (A ᾽Ιωνᾶ). Again, in

(b) It is remarkable that John gives the Aramaic form of the name, Κηφᾶς=כֵּיפָא, which occurs nowhere else in the Gospels. That it was the name by which the apostle was known by Aramaic-speaking Christians in the earliest days does not admit of doubt, in view of the evidence of the Pauline epistles. That John should have taken over the saying from Matthew, and having translated his Πέτρος into Κηφᾶς, retranslated it for his Greek readers, is incredible. Only an alternative tradition of one kind or another can reasonably account for the Johannine version. And it must have been a tradition either in Aramaic or very closely related to the Aramaic tradition of the Church's earliest days.

The conclusion may be drawn, with the greatest degree of probability that such matters admit, that Matthew and John represent divergent and independent traditions regarding the naming of Peter. That the two traditions were nearly related appears from the striking similarity of form (σὺ εἶ, the use of the patronymic, the name, or appellative, Κηφᾶς=Πέτρος) underlying the differences. Whether Matthew or John is closer to the primitive form is a question which can be answered only conjecturally, but it would be difficult to maintain that Matthew is *clearly* more primitive than John.

The question now arises, whether not only the saying of Jesus, but also the other statements here made, have any traditional basis, namely that Peter was introduced to Jesus by his brother Andrew, and that Andrew, not Peter, was the first disciple to confess Jesus as Messiah. Both these statements in effect claim for Andrew the first place among the Twelve, which is normally assigned to Peter, not only in the Synoptic Gospels but also in the Fourth Gospel. In John no less than in the others Peter acts as spokesman for the rest, notably in the passage which corresponds to the *pericopé* of Caesarea Philippi in the Synoptics. If in some passages the primacy of Peter seems to be diminished by being shared with a second person, it is not Andrew but the Beloved Disciple who shares the honour.[1] There is therefore no obvious motive which might have led the evangelist to transfer the credit of the first messianic confession from Peter to his brother, without something in his sources to authorize the

---

Ezra x. 6 the Hebrew has לְשֶׁבַת יְהוֹחָנָן for which B (1 Esdr. ix. 1) gives τὸ παστοφόριον Ἰωνᾶ (A Ἰωανάν). The form Ἰωνάν, which occurs not infrequently in MSS. of the LXX for יוֹחָנָן or יְהוֹחָנָי, may perhaps be regarded as a kind of transitional form.

[1] See O. Cullmann, *op. cit.* pp. 27–30.

transfer. We have seen that there was a tendency in the Church in Asia to bring Andrew forward. Moreover, Papias speaks of his interest in learning 'what Andrew said' from oral tradition. Papias may have been, as Eusebius says, πάνυ σμικρὸς τῇ διανοίᾳ, and we can see for ourselves that his Greek is both slipshod and obscure, but there is no reason to impugn his honesty. There was therefore current in Asia during the second century an oral tradition which at any rate purported to go back to Andrew. It may well be that we here encounter the influence of some such tradition, whether or not we judge it credible.

(ii) The Call of Philip (i. 43–4)

This little pericopé is similar in form to the stories of the calling of disciples in the Synoptic Gospels (compare especially Mark ii. 14). It might well either have been modelled on those stories or cast independently in the same mould. The one feature which rather favours the hypothesis of an independent tradition is the note appended: ἦν δὲ ὁ Φίλιππος ἀπὸ Βηθσαιδὰ ἐκ τῆς πόλεως ᾿Ανδρέου καὶ Πέτρου. ('Andrew and Peter' again, we note, not 'Peter and Andrew', as the Synoptics would have said.) It is difficult to suggest any motive which might have led the evangelist to invent such a statement, or indeed any motive for including it at all except an interest in what he believed to be a fact.[1] Nor could the statement have been derived from the Synoptics, which have given most readers the impression that the home of Peter and Andrew was Capernaum. At any rate they lived in a house there, with Peter's mother-in-law, while Jesus was at work in that city, according to Mark i. 29–31. And although the Synoptics several times mention Bethsaida, especially as the scene of various δυνάμεις (Matt. xi. 21, Mark viii. 22, Luke ix. 10), there is no hint that any of the disciples were natives of the place. Once again, as with other topographical data in this gospel, it seems only reasonable to take the statement at face value, as a piece of information which had reached

---

[1] The statement that Philip was a fellow-townsman of Andrew and Peter would seem to be intended to explain why he comes next on the scene. This would be more natural if the subject of the verbs ἠθέλησεν and εὑρίσκει is taken to be not Jesus but Andrew, and this would tend to support the reading πρῶτον in i. 41. The first thing Andrew did was to find his brother; the next thing, before leaving for Galilee, his native place, was to find his fellow-townsman Philip. We should then understand that having found him, he brought him to Jesus, as he had brought Peter. There is therefore a sufficient motive for the words, ἐκ τῆς πόλεως ᾿Α. καὶ Π., but no particular reason why the name Bethsaida should be introduced, unless the evangelist believed it was actually the πόλις in question, and presumably had reason so to believe.

the evangelist from a source which he considered trustworthy.[1] It is again perhaps relevant to recall that Philip held a special place in the regard of the Church in Asia, and that Papias provides evidence that an oral tradition purporting to derive from him was current in the second century. It is therefore possible that we are once more on the line of transmission which ultimately reached Papias. If however the line of transmission was Asian, the tradition was hardly formed there, since it shows interest in Palestinian topography.

(iii) *Dialogue with Nathaniel (i. 45–51)*

The core of this *pericopé* is to be found in Nathaniel's confession, 'Ραββεί, σὺ εἶ ὁ υἱὸς τοῦ θεοῦ, σὺ βασιλεὺς εἶ τοῦ 'Ισραήλ, with the reply of Jesus bringing the series of messianic titles to its close and climax with the 'Son of Man' (49–51). This is preceded by a dialogue of unusual form, in which Jesus makes an observation not to, but about, Nathaniel (περὶ αὐτοῦ), and Nathaniel, apparently overhearing, asks, Πόθεν με γινώσκεις; To this Jesus makes the enigmatic reply, 'Before Philip accosted you I saw you under the fig-tree'.[2] It is this evidence of Jesus's knowledge of him, it seems, that evokes Nathaniel's confession. But we have still not worked back to a likely opening for the *pericopé*, for the words εἶδεν ὁ 'Ιησοῦς ἐρχόμενον πρὸς αὐτόν leave the reader still asking questions. The introductory verse 45 explains the situation, and at the same time gives an opportunity for one more expression of the messianic idea: Jesus is the

[1] Philip's provenance from Bethsaida is again referred to in xii. 21, and there it is definitely stated, as it is perhaps implied in i. 44, that Bethsaida belonged to Galilee. The Bethsaida which the tetrarch Philip rebuilt and named Julias was in Gaulanitis to the east of Jordan and the Sea of Galilee (Joseph. *Antiq.* XVIII. 28, *B.J.* II. 168). This may, however, have been administratively part of Galilee; at any rate there seems to have been some looseness about nomenclature in these parts: Judas of Gamala (*Antiq.* XVIII. 4) is called indifferently Γαυλανίτης (*ibid.*) and Γαλιλαῖος (*ibid.* 23). There is no sufficient evidence for a town of that name on the west side. That the old name persisted among the local inhabitants after the refounding is intelligible enough. Did a British farmer of the fourth century who brought his produce to Londinium speak of going to Augusta? I doubt it. But a later writer detached from tradition would probably have written 'Ιουλιάς, as Josephus mostly does.

[2] Of the various attempts which have been made to explain the purport of 'seeing under the fig-tree', the most persuasive, to my mind, is that offered by C. F. D. Moule in *J.T.S.*, n.s., V, 2 (1954), pp. 210–11. He refers to Susanna, verses 51–9, where Daniel tests the two witnesses by asking them, separately, 'Υπὸ τί δένδρον εἶδες αὐτούς; The diversity of their answers exposes the falsity of their allegations. That the question 'Under what tree?' had some currency with reference to the examination of evidence is shown by passages from tractate *Sanhedrin* which Moule cites after D. Daube.

one ὃν ἔγραψεν Μωυσῆς ἐν τῷ νόμῳ καὶ οἱ προφῆται. This verse, however, falls outside the regular form of such *pericopae*, in that it involves a breach of the unity of time and place which is characteristic of them, for clearly the place where Philip 'finds' Nathaniel is not the place where Jesus meets him. Moreover, this transition is so contrived as to carry on the 'chain-reaction' set up by the 'testimony of John', and is therefore under some suspicion of being editorial work on the part of the evangelist. The *pericopé* is thus in any case exceptional in structure, and does not readily associate itself with traditional patterns. If any traditional material lies behind it, it has been thoroughly remodelled. As it lies before us, it has fairly obvious traits of Christian apologetic. When the Christian preacher declares Christ to be the fulfilment of law and prophets, he is met with the retort that a man from Nazareth (or indeed from anywhere in Galilee, vii. 52) is disqualified for any such role.[1] The reply is an invitation to 'come and see', which is in effect an invitation to the reader to contemplate the picture of the ἔργα τοῦ χριστοῦ which the evangelist has presented. In them he may see that union of heaven and earth which is prefigured in the vision of Jacob's ladder. Whether or not Nathaniel is an historical character,[2] he appears in this dialogue as a representative of the 'true Israelite with nothing crafty in him'. Such an 'Israelite', being ἐκ τῆς ἀληθείας, is one of the destined subjects of the kingdom of Christ (xviii. 37), and in that sense confesses him as βασιλεὺς τοῦ 'Ισραήλ.

If there is anything in this, we must further ask, to what audience is such apologetic addressed? It is clear that it moves entirely within the field of Jewish ideas. Jesus is presented as the King of Israel, as the fulfilment of law and prophets. The destined convert is ἀληθῶς 'Ισραηλίτης. The subsidiary motives—the prejudice against Galilaeans, and the pro-

---

[1] The description, 'Ιησοῦν υἱὸν τοῦ 'Ιωσήφ, τὸν ἀπὸ Ναζαρέτ ('Jesus ben-Joseph, who comes from Nazareth'), is in a form which makes it extremely unlikely that there is a reference to the 'Messiah from Joseph' as the fulfiller of prophecy, as some have suggested. The date at which the idea of this Messiah appears, and its origin, are obscure (see Mowinckel, *He that Cometh*, pp. 289, 291), but it seems clear that Nathaniel has no idea that he is being told of a 'ben-Joseph' in that sense; he is clearly thinking of an individual known, as was usual, by name and patronymic, and the fact that he comes from Nazareth makes it unlikely that he can amount to much. A derogatory reference to Jesus's Galilaean home is surely more likely to belong to an early Palestinian tradition than to be a late development.

[2] The name Nathaniel may, for all we know, be taken out of tradition, but in this context he is a symbolical *dramatis persona*. There is no reason why he should not be provided with the patronymic Βαρθολομαῖος and identified with the person bearing that patronymic who appears in lists of the Twelve; but again there is no particular reason why he should.

verbial ὑπὸ τὴν συκῆν—belong to a Jewish environment, and would be barely intelligible to a Hellenistic public. Even the high doctrine in which it culminates, though this may well be an addition by the evangelist, is in terms of rabbinic interpretations of Gen. xxviii. 12, which would not be valid for a reader of the LXX.[1] We seem therefore driven to the conclusion that the original *Sitz im Leben* for the formation of this dialogue (which has been fitted editorially into its present context) is the Christian mission in controversy with Jewish opposition. It may well give us a clue to the kind of Jewish-Christian thought which the evangelist took as a starting point for his theological adventure. But its claim to embody any historical tradition is slender.

[1] See *Interpretation*, pp. 245–6.

PART II

THE SAYINGS

1. DISCOURSE AND DIALOGUE IN THE FOURTH GOSPEL

It is a trite observation that the presentation of the teaching of Jesus in the Fourth Gospel is widely different in form and manner from that in the Synoptic Gospels. The teaching is given mainly in a series of long and elaborate discourses, partly dialogue, partly monologue, with a tendency to make a dialogue lead up to a monologue in which its theme is more fully explored, or expounded in greater detail.[1] In the Synoptic Gospels there are indeed a few monologues of some length, but critical analysis makes it almost certain that these are in general the result of an editorial process in which originally detached *pericopae* have been combined, either by simply stitching them together or by supplying a framework which imposes a certain unity upon them.[2] The longest monologues which are complete units in themselves are probably the more elaborate parables, such as the Prodigal Son and the Talents, and the Judgement-scene miscalled the parable of the Sheep and Goats. But any comparison of these with the Johannine discourses serves only to bring out the fundamental diversity. Nor does the composition of the latter show any considerable similarity to the editorial processes which have produced such passages as the Sermon on the Mount or the Eschatological Discourse of Mark xiii and parallels. There are, it is true, a few apparent examples of sequences of sayings such as lie behind the Synoptic report of the teaching (as we shall see presently),[3] but rarely, if ever, do the Johannine discourses lend themselves to analysis into separate *pericopae* like those of the Synoptics. We must conclude that the Fourth Evangelist worked on a radically different principle of composition.

A comparison of dialogue forms may bring us somewhat nearer to a

---

[1] See *Interpretation*, p. 400.

[2] Mark ix. 33–50 is a passage where originally separate sayings are connected by nothing more than recurrent *Stichworte*. In Matt. vii. 6–27, x. 32–42 the connection is hardly more organic. In Matt. v. 17–48 sayings which comparison with other gospels shows to have had an independent existence in tradition are brought into a certain unity by being subsumed under a single motive: the contrast of the old law and the new; and in Mark xiii. 14–27 sayings some of which occur elsewhere in different settings are fitted into a pattern derived from apocalyptic. I need not adduce further examples.

[3] See below, pp. 388–405.

definition of the Johannine method of presenting the teaching.[1] In the Synoptic Gospels dialogues abound; indeed the dialogue is one of their most characteristic forms. Martin Albertz, in his book *Die Synoptischen Streitgespräche*, published some years ago (1921) but still the most useful study of the subject, collected seventeen 'controversial dialogues', and examined them with respect to the form in which they are framed. His observations are broadly applicable also to those dialogues which may be described as didactic rather than controversial. He observes that these dialogues occur as small rounded units, extremely concise in style, with lines sharply drawn. There is no picturesque description, seldom any attempt at characterization, any indication of motive, or any psychological or emotional colouring beyond the very simplest. The normal pattern consists of (*a*) a brief indication of the occasion, (*b*) an interchange of speech and reply, each as a rule no longer than a sentence or two, with never more than three speeches for each interlocutor, and often fewer than this, and (*c*) sometimes, but not always, a summary statement of the effect produced. Nearly always the dialogue is initiated by a question or objection addressed to Jesus, which elicits his pronouncement on the matter in hand. Exceptionally he takes the initiative himself. In any case the dialogue is so framed that his pronouncement stands out with the utmost distinctness, so that it may remain clear-cut in the memory of hearer or reader. The pattern of dialogue so described Albertz compares with examples of dialogues from Jewish sources, and he shows that the form is similar to that in which the pronouncements of contemporary rabbis were handed down.

We now turn to the Fourth Gospel, where the use of dialogue is even more ubiquitous and on a far more elaborate scale. Dialogue is employed, as in the Synoptics, to exhibit the teaching of Jesus, to bring out its meaning, and to illustrate it by way of contrast with other views. As the Synoptic dialogues often lead up to a series of further sayings of Jesus developing the same or kindred themes, so in John a dialogue constantly introduces a discourse delivered by way of monologue. So far, there is a broad similarity. Beyond this, however, there is a marked contrast in form.

We miss, in the main, the brevity and conciseness upon which the form-critics lay stress. Those traits whose *absence* is regarded by Albertz and

[1] I have discussed 'The Dialogue Form in the Gospels' in an article under that title in the *Bulletin of the John Rylands Library*, XXXVII, 1 (September 1954). Portions of that article are here reprinted, by permission of the Librarian. The parts, however, dealing with the Synoptic dialogues are only summarized here.

others as characterizing the Synoptic dialogue form are often *present* in the Fourth Gospel. Particulars of time and place are frequent: a dialogue takes place at Jerusalem, in the temple, in the treasury, in Solomon's cloister; or in the synagogue at Capernaum; or at a city of Samaria called Sychar, near the property which Jacob gave to his son Joseph, where Jacob's well was. One dialogue takes place in the middle of the Feast of Tabernacles, another on the last day of the same festival, another at the Encaenia in winter. Individual characterization, again, which is slight in the Synoptics, sometimes emerges strikingly in John: the Samaritan Woman at the well, and Pontius Pilate, are full-length character studies like nothing that the Synoptics offer, and even characters more lightly sketched, such as those of Caiaphas the High Priest (xi. 49–50), the blind beggar badgered by the court (ix. 24–34), the apostle Thomas, with his odd but entirely convincing combination of pessimism and impulsiveness (xi. 16, xx. 24–5, 28), and others, go beyond almost anything in the Synoptic dialogues except, perhaps, the Lucan picture (x. 38–42) of Martha and Mary (whose characters emerge also in the Fourth Gospel).

Coming more directly to matters of form, we observe that whereas in the Synoptics it is the exception for a dialogue to be initiated by Jesus,[1] and the rule is for it to be initiated by an interlocutor, the reverse is true in the Fourth Gospel.[2] A dialogue commonly opens with an oracular

---

[1] In the Synoptic Gospels, in the following places dialogues (including a few so brief that they might better be classified as 'apophthegms') are initiated by persons who approach Jesus with questions or objections: Mark ii. 16, 18, 24, Matt. xii. 10 (but in the similar *pericopae* in Mark iii. 1–6, Luke vi. 9, xiv. 1–5 the question is raised by Jesus), Mark iii. 22, vii. 1, 5, viii. 11, Matt. xvii. 24, Mark ix. 38, Luke x. 25, 40, xiii. 1, 14, 23, 31, xvi. 14, xvii. 20, Mark x. 2, 17, 35, xi. 28, xii. 14, 18–19, 28. In the following passages the initiative is taken by Jesus: Luke iv. 21 (but in the similar passage, Mark vi. 1–6, it is the comment of the audience that opens the conversation; in both gospels, however, this is obviously a special case), Mark viii. 15, 27, ix. 33, Luke xiv. 3 (cf. Mark iii. 4), Mark xii. 35. In Mark x. 14 his initiative is only apparent, for the disciples' rebuke to those who brought children really opens the conversation.

[2] In John dialogue is often so continuous that it is not easy to define when a particular dialogue properly begins, but in the following passages it is clear that an utterance of Jesus either starts the colloquy or sets it on a fresh course: iii. 3 (for Nicodemus's conventional compliment leads to nothing), iv. 7, 10, v. 17 (or 19), vi. 26 (for again the banal question, πότε ὧδε γέγονας; leads to nothing), vii. 16, 37, viii. 12, 21, 31, ix. 39, xiii. 31, xiv. 1–3, xvi. 16. These cover the typical Johannine dialogues. The only Synoptic dialogue which in any degree approaches the Johannine type is Mark viii. 15 *sqq.*, which begins with an enigmatic word of Jesus about leaven. Its similarity, however, to the Johannine pattern is limited. It is generally held to be a late formation (see below, p. 330). There are places where the initiative is taken by others: iii. 26, iv. 31, vii. 3, ix. 2, x. 24, xiii. 6 (which, however, is clearly a

utterance by Jesus. The interlocutor makes a response which indicates either blank incomprehension or else a crude misunderstanding. Jesus sometimes retorts with a reproach, but always the failure to understand provides him with an occasion to explicate the enigmatic saying or to carry the thought further. The part played by the interlocutor seldom goes beyond this. He is there to misunderstand and so to give opportunity for the development of the theme. Rarely can he be said to make any positive contribution, except indeed by way of the typical Johannine irony, as when 'the Jews' urge in controversy the orthodox doctrines that the Messiah must be of unknown origin and that he must 'abide for ever', thinking that they have scored effective points against the claims of Jesus, whereas, for the evangelist, they have corroborated cardinal truths about the nature and destiny of Christ (viii. 27–9, xii. 34–6). In the Synoptic dialogues the interlocutor is constantly induced to make a contribution to the discussion: the Pharisees and Herodians produce a denarius, and confirm the fact that it bears Caesar's image and superscription (Mark xii. 16); the man of great possessions lays himself open to the final pronouncement of Jesus by claiming to have kept all the commandments (which every instructed Jew knew to provide the way to the life of the Age to Come) (Mark x. 20); Peter is able to answer the factual question, whether the Roman Empire exacts tribute from its own citizens or from foreigners, and this enables Jesus to lay down the general principle, ἄραγε ἐλεύθεροί εἰσιν οἱ υἱοί (Matt. xvii. 24–7). In general, the answers which Jesus gives to his questioners, in the Synoptic dialogues, are such as to encourage or provoke them to answer their own questions. This is not so in the Fourth Gospel. It is true that the entire gospel challenges its reader, often by irony, paradox, or riddling speech, to dig more deeply, but the *dramatis personae* do not set him an example. In the main, at any rate, their role is passive and they serve as foils.

The differences in form which we have noted cannot be adequately accounted for by saying that whereas the Synoptics preserve many traits of oral tradition the Fourth Gospel is a highly literary composition. That is true,[1] but the typical Johannine dialogues could not have been derived by any amount of merely literary manipulation from the Synoptic model.

special case), xii. 21–2 (more apparent than real). Of these, iii. 26, iv. 31, vii. 3, ix. 2, x. 24 approximate in some degree to the Synoptic pattern, and justify the raising of the question whether we have here a survival of pre-Johannine forms (see pp. 91, 185–8, 281–3, 322–6).

[1] Though, as we shall see, the oral tradition is by no means entirely obliterated in John.

We must therefore look elsewhere for parallels which may possibly throw some light on the origin and affinities of the Johannine form.

In the Hellenistic world there was a long tradition of the use of dialogue as a vehicle for philosophical or religious teaching. The great exemplar was Plato, whose Socratic dialogues were classical. Other writers followed his initiative. Aristotle's 'exoteric' works are understood to have been in dialogue form. For a time the dialogue seems to have been in partial eclipse, and its place was taken by the *diatribé*, which itself has dialogue features. But it is doubtful if philosophical dialogues ever completely ceased to be composed. In any case, there seems to have been a revival of interest in this form shortly before and after the beginning of the Christian era. Cicero's Latin dialogues were inspired by Greek models (chiefly, however, Plato himself, it appears). Plutarch, whose period of activity covers that of the Fourth Evangelist, has left some dialogues. A little later come the sparkling satirical dialogues of Lucian of Samosata. Somewhere between Plutarch and Lucian, it appears, are the earliest extant Hermetic dialogues, which were probably not the first of their kind. The Hermetists, whose philosophy owed much to Plato, were no doubt inspired by his example to put forward their teaching in dialogue form. Their works are indeed not comparable with the earliest Socratic dialogues; they lack their vivacity, their dramatic characterization, and the lifelike interplay of mind with mind. But these qualities are not always to be found in Plato himself. In some of his later dialogues the colloquy becomes little more than a device for introducing long monologues. In the *Timaeus*, for example, it introduces a lengthy discourse of Timaeus the Locrian on cosmology; and the *Timaeus* was 'the Bible of the later Platonism', and seems to have had more influence on Hermetism than any other Platonic dialogue.

Now the Hermetic dialogues show certain features which we have noted in those of the Fourth Gospel in contrast with the Synoptics. In one respect, indeed, they are not comparable: they have none of the lively characterization which, as we have seen, distinguishes John from the Synoptics; Asklepios and Tat, the usual recipients of Hermetic revelation, are no more than lay figures. In contrast, if John cannot rival Plato at his best in this respect, his work will stand comparison with any other dialogues of similar date. Nor do the Hermetists provide those notes of time and place by which John conveys a sense of reality. But the general pattern is often strikingly similar. Here too we find the oracular utterance of the teacher, met by the pupil with incomprehension or misunderstanding, and as in John, this sometimes provokes a reprimand, but invariably leads to a further explication of the theme. The interlocutor plays an essentially passive part; his interpellations do no more than provide the teacher with an occasion to elaborate his thought. In John and the *Hermetica* alike the pupil (or opponent) sometimes appears almost unnaturally dense.

To cite a few examples, taken almost at random: in the dialogue 'On Universal Mind' (Περὶ Νοῦ Κοινοῦ) Hermes is instructing Tat:

No dead thing [he says] ever was or is or shall be in the world.... Deadness is corruption, and corruption is destruction, and how can any part of an incorruptible thing be destroyed?—But, father [Tat rejoins], do not living beings in the world die, being parts of it?—Hush, my child [εὐφήμησον, ὦ τέκνον]. You are being deceived by the mere word by which the phenomenon is denoted. Living beings, my child, do not die, but as composite bodies they are dissolved; and dissolution is not death, but the separation of a mixture into its components (*C.H.* xii. 15 *sqq.*).[1]

Again, in the Dialogue called 'The Bowl' (Κρατήρ), Hermes has discoursed upon the way to the knowledge (γνῶσις) which is perfection. Tat has expressed the desire to be initiated into γνῶσις. Hermes replies:

My child, unless you first hate your body you cannot love yourself, but if you love yourself you will possess reason, and having reason you will partake of knowledge.—What do you mean by that, father?—My child, it is impossible to be concerned about mortal and about immortal things at once. Existing things are of two kinds, corporeal and incorporeal, the mortal and the immortal, and the choice of one or the other is open to him who will choose... (*C.H.* iv. 6).[2]

---

[1] Tat is confused by the ambiguity of the terms νεκρότης, φθορά, and needs to be taught that ἀπολέσθαι is not synonymous with ἀποθνήσκειν, which, on the contrary, means no more than διαλύεσθαι. Similarly in John xi. 23 Martha fails to understand what Jesus means by ἀναστήσεται, and her misunderstanding leads to the very precise definition which follows. In John xiv. 21–2 the verb ἐμφανίζειν needs to be reinterpreted, and Judas's bewilderment over it gives the opportunity. In viii. 22, xiii. 33, xiv. 2 the verbs ὑπάγειν, πορεύεσθαι, are similarly misunderstood, both by the Jews of Jerusalem and later by the disciples, and in each case the misunderstanding leads to more precise and pregnant definition of the idea.

[2] The expressions σῶμα μισεῖν, σεαυτὸν φιλεῖν, leave Tat bewildered: the idea that you could love yourself while hating your body seems to the naïve intelligence self-contradictory. His bewilderment gives Hermes the opportunity to expound in detail his doctrine of the immateriality, and indeed the divinity, of the real self of man. Somewhat similarly, in John vi. 41 Jesus says ἐγώ εἰμι ὁ ἄρτος ὁ καταβὰς ἐκ τοῦ οὐρανοῦ, and as Tat asks, Πῶς ταῦτα λέγεις; so the Jews ask, Πῶς νῦν λέγει ὅτι 'Εκ τοῦ οὐρανοῦ καταβέβηκα; Again in viii. 32 Jesus says, ἡ ἀλήθεια ἐλευθερώσει ὑμᾶς. The Jews object: οὐδενὶ δεδουλεύκαμεν πώποτε· πῶς σὺ λέγεις ὅτι 'Ελεύθεροι γενήσεσθε; In each case the question leads to an important development of the thought.

Once again, in 'The Key of Hermes' ('Ερμοῦ Τρισμεγίστου Κλείς), Hermes has described to Asklepios the nature of the beatific vision; he adds:

It is impossible, my child, for a soul to be deified while it is still in a human body—Deified, father [exclaims Asklepios], what do you mean?—Every separated soul, my child, undergoes changes.—Separated? Again, what do you mean?—Did you not hear me say [Hermes replies] in my General Discourses (ἐν τοῖς Γενικοῖς), that all our souls are derived from one Soul?... [There follows a long exposition of this theme.] (*C.H.* x. 6–7).[1]

To take one more example, the important dialogue 'De Regeneratione' (Περὶ Παλιγγενεσίας), which has, by the way, notable points of contact with the thought of the Fourth Gospel, begins with Tat reminding Hermes that in his General Discourses he had enunciated the maxim, μηδένα δύνασθαι σωθῆναι πρὸ τῆς παλιγγενεσίας, and asks for an elucidation. Hermes then embarks on a detailed exposition of the doctrine of rebirth, which leads up to the initiation (or rebirth) of Tat (*C.H.* xiii. 1).[2]

It is clear, then, that the same formative principle is at work in the Fourth Gospel and in the Hermetic dialogues, however different the content may be. The evangelist, it seems, has moulded his material in forms based upon current Hellenistic models of philosophical and religious teaching,[3] instead of following the forms, of Jewish origin, represented in the Synoptic Gospels. The typical Johannine dialogue must be accepted as an original literary creation owing, so far as form is concerned, little or nothing to the primitive Christian tradition. This does not prejudge the question of the source of the material which was moulded into this literary form. To this question we must presently return. But first it will be well to consider the few examples of dialogue in forms

---

[1] Asklepios is puzzled about the meaning of the terms ἀποθεωθῆναι, διαιρετῆς: Τὸ ἀποθεωθῆναι πῶς λέγεις, ὦ πάτερ; Πῶς πάλιν διαιρετῆς; Similarly in John xvi. 16 the disciples are puzzled by the statement, μικρὸν καὶ οὐκέτι θεωρεῖτέ με καὶ πάλιν μικρὸν καὶ ὄψεσθέ με κ.τ.λ. Τοῦτο τί ἐστιν ὃ λέγει, τὸ μικρόν; they ask.

[2] In somewhat similar terms Jesus says to Nicodemus, ἐὰν μή τις γεννηθῇ ἄνωθεν, οὐ δύναται ἰδεῖν τὴν βασιλείαν τοῦ θεοῦ, iii. 3. Nicodemus professes to take this in a crudely literal sense: μὴ δύναται εἰς τὴν κοιλίαν τῆς μητρὸς αὐτοῦ δεύτερον εἰσελθεῖν καὶ γεννηθῆναι; Similarly Tat: ἀγνοῶ, ὦ τρισμέγιστε, ἐξ οἵας μήτρας ἄνθρωπος ἐγεννήθη, σπορᾶς δὲ ποίας. (If, as is thought possible, there is Christian influence in this late dialogue, it still illustrates the easy interchange of pattern between the two schools of thought.) This crude literalism is found several times in Johannine dialogues: iv. 11, 15, 33, vi. 34, 52, ix. 39–40. The interlocutors are constantly represented as thinking on the material level.

[3] Is there any evidence to suggest that John could have learnt this method of presenting religious teaching at Qumran? I know of none.

approximating more or less closely to those common in the Synoptics. Such examples are all the more significant because they contrast with this evangelist's individual manner.

There are five dialogues which here come chiefly under consideration. Of these the first (A), iii. 25–30, has John the Baptist and not Jesus as principal speaker; it has already been considered.[1] The second (B), vi. 67–70, is in some sort a parallel to the *pericopé* of Peter's confession at Caesarea Philippi in the Synoptics, and has been dealt with in connection with the narrative;[2] and so has (C), the little dialogue embedded in the story of the healing at Siloam, ix. 2–5.[3] I turn to the remaining two.

John vii. 3 sqq. Dialogue of Jesus with his 'brothers' (D)

This is a passage thoroughly characteristic of the Fourth Evangelist, in language, style and ideas. Yet the general pattern of the dialogue is similar to that of Luke xiii. 31 *sqq.*, the Pharisees' Warning. The parallelism may be exhibited thus:

	John	Luke
Approach to Jesus	εἶπον πρὸς αὐτὸν οἱ ἀδελφοὶ αὐτοῦ	προσῆλθάν τινες τῶν φαρισαίων λέγοντες αὐτῷ
Advice offered	μεταβῆθι ἐντεῦθεν καὶ ὕπαγε εἰς τὴν ᾽Ιουδαίαν	ἔξελθε καὶ πορεύου ἐντεῦθεν
Reason given	οὐδεὶς γάρ τι ἐν κρυπτῷ ποιεῖ κ.τ.λ.	ὅτι ῾Ηρῴδης θέλει σε ἀποκτεῖναι
Advice rejected	λέγει αὐτοῖς ὁ ᾽Ιησοῦς ἐγώ οὐκ ἀναβαίνω εἰς τὴν ἑορτὴν ταύτην...	καὶ εἶπεν αὐτοῖς, ἰδοὺ ἐκβάλλω δαιμόνια κ.τ.λ.
Reason given	ὅτι ὁ ἐμὸς καιρὸς οὔπω πεπλήρωται	ὅτι οὐκ ἐνδέχεται προφήτην ἀπολέσθαι ἔξω ᾽Ιερουσαλήμ

Not only is the outline similar. The purport is also similar in some respects. In both passages Jesus rejects an attempt to dictate his course of action by reference to prudential considerations. In both he affirms, not without some asperity, his independence and sovereign freedom to choose his course, subject to a providence which ordains the time (ὁ ἐμὸς καιρός), or the place (οὐκ ἔξω ᾽Ιερουσαλήμ), of the great encounter. In both there is a hint of the approaching climax (πεπλήρωται—τελειοῦμαι).[4] Moreover, in

---

[1] See above, pp. 280–7.   [2] See above, pp. 219–21.
[3] See above, pp. 185–8.
[4] If there were any reason for suggesting the possibility of dependence of John upon Luke in this passage, it might be urged against it that τελειοῦν, which occurs

both there is some ambiguity about the motives of the interlocutors. 'Brothers' and Pharisees ostensibly offer friendly advice or warning, but the reply leaves the genuineness of their friendship in some doubt (John expressly says that the 'brothers' were unbelieving). Finally, both passages are in some way associated with the move from Galilee[1] to Jerusalem (or Judaea).

Where similarity of fundamental form is combined with the apparent play of similar motives, it is difficult not to believe that John is reaching back to the common tradition. It is to be observed that the move from Galilee to Jerusalem seems to have had from the earliest stages a peculiar significance in the gospel story.[2] And yet the reason for the move, and its purpose, are left largely in uncertainty. Various incidents appear to be associated with it. Mark, by his arrangement of *pericopae* in ch. vii, has suggested that it was as the result of a clash with the Pharisees that Jesus left Galilee (ἐκεῖθεν δὲ ἀναστὰς ἀπῆλθεν εἰς τὰ ὅρια Τύρου, vii. 24). Once again, the arrangement in ch. viii suggests that a hasty passage across the Lake (from some place whose name is concealed by the *vox nihili* Δαλμανουθα) was the result of another clash when the demand for a 'sign' was bluntly refused (viii. 11–13, 22). After that point Mark never brings Jesus to Galilee except incognito (ix. 30), and at the point where he finally leaves for the south no reason or motive is alleged (καὶ ἐκεῖθεν ἀναστὰς ἔρχεται εἰς τὰ ὅρια τῆς 'Ιουδαίας καὶ πέραν τοῦ 'Ιορδάνου, x. 1). We are left to infer the motive from the proximity of various fore-casts of rejection, sufferings and death which are in store at Jerusalem (the name only in x. 33, but it is implied in the reference to the constituent 'estates' of the Sanhedrin in viii. 31, compare also ix. 30–1, x. 39, 45). Luke (ix. 31) makes explicit what is implied in Mark. All this is apparently 'editorial' work on the part of the evangelists, how far resting upon existing information we can only surmise. What we do seem justified in

in Luke here and in one other place, is one of John's great theological terms (iv. 34, v. 36, xvii. 4, 23; once only in the sense of the 'fulfilment' of scripture, xix. 28); he would therefore have no motive for changing it to πληροῦν, a verb which he uses eight times for the 'fulfilment' of a prophetic word, once for the 'filling' of a space, and four times with reference to χαρά or λύπη, but never either for the completion of a period of time or in a pregnant theological sense.

[1] In John the introduction (vii. 1) makes it clear that the place is intended to be Galilee. In Luke the topography is vague, but from internal evidence we gather that the scene is somewhere in the dominions of Antipas, i.e. either Galilee or Trans-jordan. The proposed destination is indicated expressly in John, more cryptically in Luke.

[2] See *Interpretation*, pp. 384–5.

saying is that tradition preserved the memory of a crisis and a turning point, the seriousness of which was reflected in a wealth of anecdotes shaped by motives in one way or another related to the abandonment of Galilee as a field of work (whether by way of retirement, flight, or planned tactics), or to a march on Jerusalem (whether or not connected directly with the abandonment of Galilee). Some of these anecdotes seem un-related to what we may describe as the main presuppositions of the narrative. Such is the story of the Pharisees' warning, which has various unexpected features. The difficulty which critics and expositors have found in fitting it into any smooth and coherent narrative of the Ministry is by no means adverse to its acceptance as a scrap of authentic reminis-cence; indeed it is rather in its favour. I suggest that we might say the same of John's story about the 'brothers'. The ἀδελφοὶ τοῦ κυρίου, who were well recognized in the early Church as a compact body of 'Founder's kin', make only enigmatic appearances in the gospels. Their intervention in Mark iii. 31–5 is as ambiguous[1] as in John vii. But the detachment of Jesus from his immediate relations implied in Mark iii. 34–5 must be accepted as an integral part of the tradition.[2] On the other hand, it is certain that the ἀδελφοί were among the believers in the earliest days of the Church. It is also certain that James ὁ ἀδελφὸς τοῦ κυρίου was among those who were cited in the earliest known form of *kerygma* as witnesses to the resurrection (1 Cor. xv. 7, compare Gal. i. 19). According to Matt. xxviii. 10, John xx. 17[3] a special message announcing the resurrec-tion was sent to the ἀδελφοί of Jesus, and this may be not unrelated to the appearance to James, for I see no reason why the ἀδελφοί in those places should be other than the persons to whom that term is normally applied. In short, the ἀδελφοί of Jesus are established figures in the early tradition, even though their status in the gospel story is ill-defined. It is probable that this *pericopé* of John, having so many points of contact with other elements in the tradition which we have reason to believe primitive, was

[1] The construction we are to put upon it depends largely upon the answers to two questions: (*a*) is Mark iii. 21 so closely connected with verses 31–5 that we may identify οἱ παρ' αὐτοῦ with ἡ μήτηρ καὶ οἱ ἀδελφοί? and (*b*) what is the subject of ἔλεγον?

[2] See *History and the Gospel*, pp. 95–6.

[3] It is to be noted that in John this message is in the terms, ἀναβαίνω πρὸς τὸν πατέρα. This clearly answers to the οὐκ ἀναβαίνω of vii. 8, and establishes the identity (in the evangelist's intention) of the ἀδελφοί in the two passages. See my essay in *Studies in the Gospels, Essays in Memory of R. H. Lightfoot*, ed. D. E. Nineham, p. 19.

drawn from the common reservoir, though he has written it up in his own style to serve the purpose of introduction to one of his most elaborate compositions, the sequence of controversial dialogues in chs. vii–viii.[1]

John iv. 31–4. Dialogue between Jesus and his disciples on the subject of food (E)

This short dialogue seems to be complete in itself, with some resemblance to the Synoptic pattern.[2] It has no intrinsic connection either with the foregoing dialogue with the Samaritan woman or with the sequence of sayings which follows.[3] The dramatic verisimilitude is due to the skill with which the author employs a favourite technique.[4] In weaving the little dialogue into the main texture of the 'Book of Signs' at this point, he has prepared a transition from the theme of 'living water' to that of the βρῶσις μένουσα εἰς ζωὴν αἰώνιον in vi. 27 *sqq.* But in ch. vi Christ is the giver of the true βρῶσις, as in iv. 10 he is the giver of ὕδωρ ζῶν, whereas here he is himself nourished upon the βρῶσις ἣν ὑμεῖς οὐκ οἴδατε, which is not at all the same thing. We are therefore justified in treating iv. 31–4 as a separate *pericopé*.

As such, it resembles the Synoptic pattern in so far as it opens with an address of the disciples to their Master, and closes, after an interchange of one sentence only on each side of the colloquy, with a pregnant saying of Jesus. On the other hand, it has some of the essential characteristics of the Johannine form of dialogue, in that Jesus first utters an oracular saying, ἐγὼ βρῶσιν ἔχω φαγεῖν ἣν ὑμεῖς οὐκ οἴδατε, which his interlocutors misunderstand (μή τις ἤνεγκεν αὐτῷ φαγεῖν;), and then explains his meaning. The language, moreover, ἵνα...τελειώσω αὐτοῦ τὸ ἔργον, has the Johannine stamp.

To turn now from form to content, the motive of the dialogue is simple: Jesus is confronted with a reminder of his bodily needs, or, to put it more generally, with the exigencies of his human condition. He replies in terms of 'sublimation': there is other 'food' than that which meets the eye. This

---

[1] See *Interpretation*, pp. 351–2.

[2] If we regard the words ἐν τῷ μεταξύ as an editorial link, the opening, ἠρώτων αὐτὸν οἱ μαθηταί, is hardly more abrupt than ἠρώτα δέ τις αὐτὸν τῶν φαρισαίων (Luke vii. 36), καὶ ἐπηρώτων αὐτὸν λέγοντες (Mark ix. 11, where the question has no intrinsic relation to what has preceded), ἔφη αὐτῷ ὁ Ἰωάννης (Mark ix. 38), τότε προσελθὼν ὁ Πέτρος εἶπεν αὐτῷ (Matt. xviii. 21), εἶπεν δέ τις ἐκ τοῦ ὄχλου αὐτῷ (Luke xii. 13), or even παρῆσαν δέ τινες ἐν αὐτῷ τῷ καιρῷ ἀπαγγέλλοντες αὐτῷ (Luke xiii. 1, for the phrase ἐν αὐτῷ τῷ καιρῷ is evidently editorial, and unilluminating).

[3] See pp. 391–400.   [4] See *Interpretation*, pp. 315, 357–8.

motive appears elsewhere. In Mark iii. 31–5, a *pericopé* which has some superficial formal similarity with John iv. 31–4, Jesus is confronted with the demands of family ties—another case of the exigencies of the human condition. He responds with the question, Τίς ἐστιν ἡ μήτηρ μου καὶ οἱ ἀδελφοί μου; Without waiting for the reply of his interlocutors, he proceeds to 'sublimate' the idea of family relationships, as in John iv. 34 he 'sublimates' the idea of food. And it is to be noted that in both cases the 'sublimation' is in terms of doing the will of God (ὃς ἂν ποιήσῃ τὸ θέλημα τοῦ θεοῦ, οὗτος ἀδελφός μου καὶ ἀδελφὴ καὶ μήτηρ ἐστίν, cf. ἐμὸν βρῶμά ἐστιν ἵνα ποιῶ τὸ θέλημα τοῦ πέμψαντός με).

But there is another Synoptic *pericopé*, entirely different in form, the purport of which is even nearer to that of the Johannine passage we are considering, namely the Temptation narrative in Matt. iv. 1–4, Luke iv. 1–4. There we are told that Jesus was hungry, as he was (it is implied) when the disciples offered him bread.[1] He is invited to satisfy his hunger by supernatural power, as in John he is invited to satisfy it with the bread they have bought. The reply is given in words borrowed from the Old Testament: οὐκ ἐπ᾽ ἄρτῳ μόνῳ ζήσεται ὁ ἄνθρωπος, ἀλλ᾽ ἐπὶ παντὶ ῥήματι ἐκπορευομένῳ διὰ στόματος θεοῦ. The meaning doubtless intended (whatever may have been the intention of the Hebrew of Deut. viii. 3) is that man's true life is sustained by obeying the commandments of God; for the temptations are essentially a test of obedience. In other words, it is sustained by doing the will of God, as John has it. There is exactly the same 'sublimation' of the idea of food. Anything like direct dependence is not to be thought of, but a *pericopé* expressing a thought so close to that of the Synoptics, and showing analogies with Synoptic forms,[2] has

[1] The suggestion that the Johannine dialogue is intended to convey the meaning that Christ, as a heavenly Being moving on earth, does not require bodily food, is unwarranted. His request for a drink in iv. 7 is no more a piece of play-acting than the weariness that led him to sit down by the well, nor are his tears at the grave of Lazarus or his thirst on the cross conceived in docetic terms. It is the essential Johannine paradox that he, who in his human condition (σάρξ) was tired out with walking and thirsty from the heat, was also the renewer of life, the giver of living water. The mood of the spirit in which devotion to the divine will puts hunger into the background is a truly human mood, both here and in the Temptation narrative.

[2] There is a less significant analogy in Mark viii. 14 *sqq.* which, as we have seen, is perhaps the only Synoptic dialogue which approximates in any significant degree to the Johannine form. Here it is the absence of bread, not the offer of it, that gives occasion for an oracular saying which the interlocutors misunderstand. Bread suggests leaven, and leaven is taken as a symbol for an evil influence. But the relation of the oracular saying to its occasion, and the explanation offered, are laboured and unconvincing. The passage is widely regarded as secondary and composite.

surely strong claims to be accepted as derived from a common tradition, although John has put his stamp upon it.

Two further passages may be added where there are features which recall those of Synoptic dialogues, though the resultant form is not significantly similar.

John ix. 38-41. Dialogue with the Pharisees on blindness (F)

Here we have a short dialogue with something of the epigrammatic conciseness of many Synoptic dialogues. In the structure of this part of the gospel it has an important function as a link[1] between the trial scene of ix. 13–34 and the παροιμία of the Shepherd and the Robber[2] which follows; but it appears to be complete in itself, and might well have been handed down apart from its present context as a separate *pericopé*. Its pattern is more Johannine than Synoptic. It begins with an oracular utterance of Jesus: εἰς κρίμα ἐγὼ εἰς τὸν κόσμον τοῦτον ἦλθον, ἵνα οἱ μὴ βλέποντες βλέπωσιν καὶ οἱ βλέποντες τυφλοὶ γένωνται. To this his interlocutors respond with what is ostensibly the usual request for clarification, but is really intended as a protest: μὴ καὶ ἡμεῖς τυφλοί ἐσμεν; Jesus replies in terms which have something of a Johannine ring, but are certainly not peculiarly Johannine in purport: εἰ τυφλοὶ ἦτε οὐκ ἂν εἴχετε ἁμαρτίαν· νῦν δὲ λέγετε ὅτι Βλέπομεν· ἡ ἁμαρτία ὑμῶν μένει. The expression ἁμαρτίαν ἔχειν is peculiar to the Fourth Gospel and 1 John among New Testament writings (John xv. 24, 1 John i. 7), and μένειν is a word to which our evangelist is excessively addicted.[3]

In spite of all this, there are certain traits which seem to associate this *pericopé* with the tradition behind the Synoptics. The opening pronouncement is very much in the same vein as, for example, Luke xii. 49, πῦρ ἦλθον βαλεῖν ἐπὶ τὴν γῆν, which is explicated by the prediction of divisions in families. Such divisions have the character of κρίσις in its Johannine sense, which always has some suggestion of 'discrimination'.[4] The protest of the Pharisees, with its suggestion of self-exculpation, may be compared with the protest of the νομικοί in Luke xi. 45: διδάσκαλε, ταῦτα λέγων καὶ ἡμᾶς ὑβρίζεις, or even with the question asked by the νομικός who wished δικαιῶσαι ἑαυτόν in Luke x. 29. Again, the 'blindness' of the Pharisees is arraigned, not only frequently in Matthew (xv. 14, xxiii. 16,

---

[1] See *Interpretation*, pp. 358–9.   [2] See below, pp. 382–5.

[3] Μένειν occurs about forty times, and frequently in a pregnant sense, as here, against a dozen times in the whole of the Synoptic Gospels.

[4] See *Interpretation*, pp. 208–9.

17, 19, 24, 26) but notably in the parabolic saying about the Blind leading the Blind, which belongs to the most primitive stratum of the Synoptic Gospels (Matt. xv. 14, Luke vi. 39). The parable of the Mote and the Beam (Matt. vii. 3–5, Luke vi. 41–2), again drawn from the very primitive tradition underlying Matthew and Luke, stigmatizes the 'hypocrite' who, like the Pharisees of our passage, claims acuteness of vision but misses the obvious, because he *will* not see it. The setting of this parable, both in Matthew and in Luke, brings such wilful blindness under the threat of judgement (μὴ κρίνετε ἵνα μὴ κριθῆτε). That the coming of Christ brings judicial blindness on the obdurate is forcibly stated in Mark iv. 12, ἐκείνοις δὲ τοῖς ἔξω ἐν παραβολαῖς πάντα γίνεται ἵνα βλέποντες βλέπωσιν καὶ μὴ ἴδωσιν. John agrees with Mark in the use of ἵνα (where Matthew softens the pronouncement down to ὅτι βλέποντες οὐ βλέπουσιν). This apparent echo of Marcan language is not to be put down to borrowing. John goes back to a non-septuagintal version of Isa. vi. 9–10 which is quoted directly in xii. 40.[1] It appears, then, that although the dialogue as we have it bears the Johannine stamp, it reaches back into a common tradition which emerges in other ways in the Synoptic Gospels.

John iii. 1–3. Dialogue with Nicodemus (G)

The opening words only of this dialogue show a certain resemblance to the opening of the dialogue on the payment of tribute in Mark xii. 14, and a closer parallel to the version of that dialogue in Egerton Papyrus 2.

John	Pap. Eg. 2	Mark
ῥαββεί	διδάσκαλε ᾿Ιησοῦ	διδάσκαλε
οἴδαμεν ὅτι ἀπὸ θεοῦ	οἴδαμεν ὅτι ἀπὸ θεοῦ	οἴδαμεν ὅτι ἀληθὴς εἶ
ἐλήλυθας διδάσκαλος	ἐλήλυθας	καὶ οὐ μέλει σοι
		περὶ οὐδενός
οὐδεὶς γὰρ δύναται	ἃ γὰρ σὺ ποιεῖς	ἀλλ᾿ ἐπ᾿ ἀληθείας τὴν
ταῦτα τὰ σημεῖα ποιεῖν		ὁδὸν τοῦ θεοῦ διδάσκεις
ἃ σὺ ποιεῖς	μαρτυρεῖ	
ἐὰν μὴ ᾖ ὁ θεὸς	ὑπὲρ τοὺς προφήτας	
μετ᾿ αὐτοῦ	πάντας	

Beyond this point the three passages diverge completely.[2] In John the complimentary opening does not lead (as we have been led to expect) to

[1] See *According to the Scriptures*, pp. 36–9.
[2] For the relation of the three passages to one another see the discussion in my book *New Testament Studies*, pp. 36–40. I am however less sure than I then was that the passage in Pap. Eg. 2 is a direct borrowing from the Fourth Gospel, in view of the striking departure from the Johannine form, and the reference to the superiority

a question. Instead, Jesus (*more Johanneo*) abruptly throws out an oracular saying, which forms the theme of a dialogue of entirely non-Synoptic character.

It is tempting to suggest that we have here the meagre remnant of a dialogue of Synoptic form which the Fourth Evangelist may have taken over to serve as exordium to a discussion which he wished to introduce. The theme of the missing question, and of the lost dialogue to which it may have led up, would offer a wide field for inconclusive and unprofitable conjecture. It is more probable that the complimentary approach,[1] and its repudiation (or at least its non-acknowledgement) by Jesus, was a standing feature of the dialogue tradition in the oral stage, quite likely representing an historical trait, and that it could appear independently in various settings. If so, then we should recognize here one more slight piece of evidence that the Fourth Evangelist was in touch with the common oral tradition in one of its branches.

Of the seven passages here adduced, four (B, C, D, E) point directly to contact with early forms of tradition, two (F, G) somewhat more remotely, but with strong probability. The remaining one (A), in spite of some problematical features, has also, in all probability, traditional roots. In all these cases the formal resemblance to Synoptic dialogues made it antecedently likely that some common basis in tradition might be discovered. We must now return to those Johannine dialogues which have no such formal resemblance to those of the Synoptics, and inquire whether any trace of traditional material can be discovered underlying the entirely non-traditional forms. It is theoretically possible either that John was acquainted with dialogues of the Synoptic type, and deliberately remoulded them, or that he had at his disposal a tradition still partly fluid, not yet fully crystallized into fixed forms, which he could deal with as he chose. There are some indications in favour of the latter alternative. We meet with themes which are treated in the Synoptic Gospels in forms characteristic of those works, and which appear in the Fourth Gospel in widely

---

of Jesus to the prophets, which recalls rather the Gospel according to the Hebrews. Although I believe that in the first fragment of Pap. Eg. 2 there is a direct quotation from the Fourth Gospel, I now think it more probable that fragment 2 is a divergent rendering of a common tradition all through (as it pretty clearly is in its main substance).

[1] The *captatio benevolentiae* is a recognized element in classical rhetoric, well exemplified in Acts xxiv. 2–3, xxvi. 2–3. The διδάσκαλε ἀγαθέ of Mark x. 17 is similar in intention, and is similarly repudiated by Jesus.

different forms, and yet in ways which suggest that some common tradition lies behind both.

For example, in Mark viii. 11–21 there is a dialogue beginning with the request for a sign and its refusal, and leading up, through an enigmatic saying about leaven, to a reference to the multiplication of the loaves, so framed as to suggest that there is a mystery about it; the dialogue ends with the reproach, οὔπω συνίετε; Matthew has the demand for a sign and its refusal, not only in a passage parallel with Mark (xvi. 1–4), but also in a different context (xii. 38–9). Here it has no connection with the mystery of the loaves, but leads up to a cryptic allusion to the 'three days' between the death and resurrection of the Son of Man. Now John also has the demand for a sign in two different contexts. In vi. 30 it is associated with the narrative of the Feeding of the Multitude,[1] and with the mystery of bread, in a dialogue which also alludes to the death of Christ and his ὕψωσις (vi. 51, 62). In ii. 18 it is associated with the Cleansing of the Temple, and leads up to the saying, λύσατε τὸν ναὸν τοῦτον καὶ ἐν τρισὶν ἡμέραις ἐγερῶ αὐτόν (the 'three days' once again), and this saying, John says, referred to the death and resurrection of Christ. I cannot bring myself to believe that John had before him these passages in Matthew and Mark, and deliberately unpicked them in order to weave the material into a different fabric. Yet it is clear that he was working with material which the other evangelists also had. The most probable explanation, it seems, is that all three evangelists (or, if you will, their immediate sources) had before them a fluid and unformed tradition in which reminiscence and reflection were already mingled, and that each formulated the material after his own fashion.

Again, the long discourse in viii. 31–58 may fairly be described as a *locus classicus* of Johannine theology.[2] It appears to reflect controversies between Gentile and Jewish Christians in the Church, and it argues, at certain points, from premises which recall the maxims of Stoic philosophy.[3] But it is all held together by repeated references to Abraham (who does

---

[1] See above, pp. 218–19.

[2] For a fuller discussion of this passage see my article, 'À l'arrière-plan d'un dialogue johannique', in *Revue d'Histoire et de Philosophie Religieuses*, 1957, no. 1, pp. 5–17.

[3] Γνώσεσθε τὴν ἀλήθειαν καὶ ἡ ἀλήθεια ἐλευθερώσει ὑμᾶς = μόνος ὁ σοφὸς ἐλεύθερος. Πᾶς ὁ ποιῶν τὴν ἁμαρτίαν δοῦλός ἐστιν = οὐδεὶς ἁμαρτάνων ἐλεύθερός ἐστιν. For Stoic testimonies to these maxims see Wetstein and Bauer *ad loc.* That such maxims were adopted by Jewish rabbis (in the sense that freedom comes through knowledge of Torah) was to be expected (see S.–B. *ad loc.*).

not otherwise appear in this gospel), and we can trace, at one point certainly, and perhaps elsewhere, reminiscences of Jewish arguments and speculations about the patriarch.[1] In one place we suddenly encounter expressions which recall passages in the Synoptic Gospels. The Jews with whom Jesus is in controversy repudiate his offer of the truth that liberates on the ground that, being σπέρμα ᾽Αβραάμ, they possess inalienable liberty: ὁ πατὴρ ἡμῶν ᾽Αβραάμ ἐστιν, they repeat. Jesus retorts, εἰ τέκνα τοῦ ᾽Αβραάμ ἐστε, τὰ ἔργα τοῦ ᾽Αβραάμ ποιεῖτε, where ποιεῖτε is probably imperative: 'If you are children of Abraham, do as Abraham did.' We are reminded of the saying of John the Baptist, ποιήσατε καρπὸν ἄξιον τῆς μετανοίας, καὶ μὴ δόξητε λέγειν ἐν ἑαυτοῖς, Πατέρα ἔχομεν τὸν ᾽Αβραάμ (Matt. iii. 8–9, and, with insignificant differences, Luke iii. 8). That words assigned to John the Baptist in one gospel are assigned to Jesus in another is a phenomenon to be observed within the Synoptic Gospels themselves, and there is nothing surprising here if our evangelist has given to Jesus words which in Matthew and Luke are given to the Baptist. The earliest Christian tradition contained sayings of John and of Jesus, and did not always distinguish clearly between them.[2] It would be very strange if John viii. 39 had no relation to the closely similar passage Matt. iii. 8–9. It would be no less strange if our author, with Matthew before him, deliberately took the words from the Baptist and assigned them to Jesus. It is more reasonable to suppose that Matthew and John alike drew from primitive tradition.

Further, the next step in the argument is the claim of the Jews to be, not only children of Abraham, but children of God: ἕνα πατέρα ἔχομεν τὸν θεόν (the turn of phrase is like that of Matt. iii. 9, πατέρα ἔχομεν τὸν ᾽Αβραάμ). In Matt. xxiii. 9 we read, πατέρα μὴ καλέσητε ὑμῶν ἐπὶ τῆς γῆς· εἷς γάρ ἐστιν ὑμῶν ὁ πατὴρ ὁ οὐράνιος. This comes in rather oddly in its Matthaean context. In verse 8 the disciples are forbidden to be called 'Rabbi', since Christ alone is their διδάσκαλος. In verse 10 they are forbidden to be called καθηγητής, since Christ alone is their καθηγητής. These seem to be doublets, in which the Jewish title Rabbi alternates with the Greek title καθηγητής. But verse 9 does not forbid the disciples *to be called* 'Father'. That would have been sufficiently in accord with verses 8

---

[1] Certainly in viii. 36, and see S.–B.'s notes on the passage.

[2] Μετανοεῖτε, ἤγγικεν γὰρ ἡ βασιλεία κ.τ.λ.: John in Matt. iii. 2, Jesus in Mark i. 1. Γεννήματα ἐχιδνῶν: John in Matt. iii. 7, Jesus in Matt. xxiii. 33. Bultmann perhaps goes too far in saying (*Geschichte der synoptischen Tradition*, p. 123) that the attribution of sayings to John rather than to Jesus is 'bloßer Zufall', but the distinction is certainly not absolute in the early tradition.

and 10; apparently Jewish teachers were sometimes called 'Abba'. But it forbids them *to call* anyone else 'father'. Who is the earthly father to whom they must not give that name? There is a *baraita*[1] which says, 'One calls "father" none but the three' (namely Abraham, Isaac and Jacob). It is perhaps not too wild a conjecture that the saying in Matt. xxiii. 9 was intended to mean 'Call no earthly being "father"—*not even Abraham*—since you all have one Father in heaven'. This would move on the same plane of thought as Matt. iii. 8–9. If so, then John viii. 39–42 may well hark back to the same tradition. The Jews have begun by claiming that Abraham is their father. Then they shift their ground, and, in the sense of Matt. xxiii. 9 (as originally intended), call no earthly being their father, since they have one Father, God. This claim is rebutted on the same ground as before: like father, like child; Abraham's children do the works of Abraham; God's children do the works of God. At any rate, it seems that the mind of our evangelist is here moving among ideas which were represented in the most primitive tradition, and, if there is anything in the conjecture which I have hazarded, he would appear to have received that tradition in a sense, and in a setting, more original than that which Matthew has given it.

To take another example, of a rather different kind: in John vii. 23–4 Jesus defends himself on a charge of violating the Sabbath by healing: 'If a man receives circumcision on the Sabbath in order that the Law of Moses may not be broken, are you angry with me because I made an *entire* man well (ὅλον ἄνθρωπον ὑγιῆ ἐποίησα) on the Sabbath?' Why ὅλον ἄνθρωπον? The clue is to be found in several passages in the rabbinic writings, cited by Strack–Billerbeck *ad loc.* and *ad* Matt. xii. 10. The most noteworthy, perhaps, is the passage of *Mechilta*, 109b, on Exod. xxxi. 13, which reports a colloquy of certain rabbis, including Eliezer ben Azariah and Aqiba—a colloquy which therefore cannot be dated long after A.D. 100. The question is raised: From what passage of scripture can it be shown that the saving of human life (פִּקּוּחַ נֶפֶשׁ) repels the Sabbath? Various opinions are cited. The reply of Rabbi Eliezer was: 'If circumcision, which affects only one of a man's bodily members, repels the Sabbath, how much more does that apply to *his entire body*.' Clearly, an argument of that kind is indicated in John vii. 23. But further, the same question is propounded in Mark iii. 4: 'Is it lawful on the Sabbath to save life (ψυχὴν σῶσαι)?' and in Matt. xii. 10: 'Is it lawful on the Sabbath to heal

---

[1] *Berachoth*, 16b, cited by S.–B. *ad loc.*

(θεραπεῦσαι);' (ψυχὴν σῶσαι and θεραπεῦσαι serving as diverse equivalents for נֶפֶשׁ פִּקּוּחַ). Again, in the same passage of *Mechilta* R. Jose the Galilaean (*c.* A.D. 110) is cited as saying, 'The Sabbath is given to you and not you to the Sabbath'. The saying in Mark ii. 27, τὸ σάββατον διὰ τὸν ἄνθρωπον ἐγένετο καὶ οὐχ ὁ ἄνθρωπος διὰ τὸ σάββατον, is evidently moulded on the same pattern as the maxim of R. Jose, which in some form was probably already current before his time. It seems a legitimate inference that there was a Christian *halacha* upon the Sabbath, based upon discussions parallel to those which are attested for the rabbinical schools.[1] And the significant thing (for our present purpose) is that elements of this *halacha* appear both in various passages of Mark and Matthew and also in John. There is no question of John borrowing from either of the others; it is difficult to resist the conclusion that a common tradition lies behind the three. The *Sitz im Leben* of such a tradition must have been within a Jewish environment such as that of the primitive Church, and in all probability it belongs to an early period. Once the Church, by that time mainly Gentile, had ceased to have relations with the synagogue, such discussions would no longer be kept alive, and only isolated traces of them remain, embedded in the gospels. In John vii. 23 the remaining trace is an argument which is barely intelligible outside its Jewish context.

Finally, there are places where the Fourth Gospel appears to echo the language of the Lord's Prayer:

Matt. vi. 9–13	John
Πάτερ...ἁγιασθήτω τὸ ὄνομά σου	xvii. 11 Πάτερ ἅγιε τήρησον αὐτοὺς ἐν τῷ ὀνόματί σου
τὸν ἄρτον ἡμῶν τὸν ἐπιούσιον δὸς ἡμῖν σήμερον	vi. 33 ὁ πατήρ μου δίδωσιν ὑμῖν τὸν ἄρτον ἐκ τοῦ οὐρανοῦ τὸν ἀληθινόν
ῥῦσαι ἡμᾶς ἀπὸ τοῦ πονηροῦ	xvii. 15 ἵνα τηρήσῃς αὐτοὺς ἐκ τοῦ πονηροῦ

Such passages seem to presuppose a homiletical treatment of the several petitions of the prayer: in the sanctity of the name of the Father is the strong protection of believers; the Father in heaven to whom they pray for ἄρτος ἐπιούσιος answers the prayer by the gift of ἄρτος ἀληθινός, and while they are by his appointment still in the world, with all its perils and trials, he answers the prayer for deliverance from the evil that is in the

---

[1] I see no reasonable ground for denying that such *halacha* goes back to Jesus himself, but I am not here discussing that question.

world. That these coincidences are purely fortuitous it is difficult to believe. It will not, I think, be argued that John needed to learn his Paternoster out of the Gospel according to Matthew. The prayer must have belonged to the liturgical tradition of the Church from the earliest period, and it is from that source that both Matthew and John (as well as Luke) have drawn.

In view of all this, there would seem to be a strong presumption that even where John is to all appearance composing most freely, there is, sometimes at least, an older tradition behind him. With this presumption in mind we shall now proceed to a review of some passages where it seems possible to infer the use of such tradition.

2. SAYINGS COMMON TO JOHN
AND THE SYNOPTICS

We may start with some sayings which are common to John and the Synoptics, that is, passages which in form and content alike are identical, or closely similar, while differing verbally. We shall always have in mind the question whether these verbal differences are such as to suggest a rephrasing by John of material borrowed by him from the other gospels, or such as could better be accounted for by the hypothesis of variation within a common oral tradition. The sayings here in question are in the main those which have the succinct, aphoristic form which makes each of them a complete unit in itself.

Two such sayings have already been noted in association with narrative *pericopae*: John ii. 19, λύσατε τὸν ναὸν κ.τ.λ.,[1] and iv. 44, the prophet in his πατρίς.[2] Of the former it seemed possible to conclude, with the highest degree of probability attainable in these matters, that it was drawn independently from a separate branch of the common tradition; in regard to the second the same conclusion seemed justified, if with somewhat less cogency. I proceed to further examples, where the sayings are embedded in discourse or dialogue.[3]

(i) John xiii. 16:

> Οὐκ ἔστιν δοῦλος μείζων τοῦ κυρίου αὐτοῦ,
> οὐδὲ ἀπόστολος μείζων τοῦ πέμψαντος αὐτόν.

To this saying there are partial parallels in the Synoptics. The closest is Matt. x. 24–5, as read in the majority of MSS.:

> Οὐκ ἔστιν μαθητὴς ὑπὲρ τὸν διδάσκαλον
> οὐδὲ δοῦλος ὑπὲρ τὸν κύριον αὐτοῦ.
> ἀρκετὸν τῷ μαθητῇ ἵνα γένηται ὡς ὁ διδάσκαλος αὐτοῦ
> καὶ ὁ δοῦλος ὡς ὁ κύριος αὐτοῦ.

The Old Latin MS. *k*, however, and the Sinaitic Syriac (a formidable combination) omit the words οὐδὲ δοῦλος ... κύριον αὐτοῦ,[4] thus reducing

---

[1] See above, pp. 88–91.   [2] See above, pp. 239–40.

[3] The following pages (335–49) are in large measure reproduced from an article in *New Testament Studies*, vol. II, no. 2 (November 1955).

[4] I do not discuss the question, which reading represents the original text of Matthew. If the shorter is original, the words οὐδὲ δοῦλος ... κύριον αὐτοῦ might have been introduced to complete the balance of clauses, either because it is implied

the first couplet to a single clause, and the quatrain to a triplet. In Luke we have a single couplet which combines one member from each of the two couplets of the longer text of Matthew:

οὐκ ἔστιν μαθητὴς ὑπὲρ τὸν διδάσκαλον,
κατηρτισμένος δὲ πᾶς ἔσται ὡς ὁ διδάσκαλος αὐτοῦ.

The position may be stated as follows: there are four different formations before us: (*a*) a couplet which says simply, in effect, 'A disciple is not superior to his teacher; at best he may be like him' (Luke); (*b*) a triplet, in which the first line is identical with the first line of (*a*), and a couplet follows, in which the second clause of (*a*), about disciple and teacher, is paralleled by a clause about slave and master (Matthew, *k* Syriac); (*c*) a quatrain, in which the second couplet is as in (*b*), and the first couplet is also in parallelism, adding the relation of slave and master to that of disciple and teacher (Matthew, T.R.); and (*d*) a couplet in which the first line is equivalent to the second line of (*c*), and the second line, instead of speaking of disciple and teacher, speaks of apostle and sender (John).

Since the Johannine form has nothing directly in common with (*a*) or (*b*), it is only the longer text of Matthew that can be considered as a possible source for John. If it is to be regarded as such, we have to account for three changes: (i) the omission of the second couplet; (ii) the substitution of ἀπόστολος for μαθητής and of ὁ πέμψας for ὁ διδάσκαλος, with a reversal of order; and (iii) the substitution of ὑπέρ with the accusative for μείζων with the genitive. The last of these is of no great significance. The LXX employs alternatively the comparative of the adjective or ὑπέρ with the accusative to render Hebrew expressions like רב מן ,גדול מן. The differences, therefore, between John and Matthew in this grammatical detail might well go back to different translations of an Aramaic original; or, since John never uses ὑπέρ with the accusative, while he is rather addicted to locutions with μείζων, he might himself have been responsible for the change.

As for (i), the omission of the second couplet, all we can say is that the idea that the slave should be like his master, and content to be so without expecting to be in any way superior to him, does not appear uncongenial to an evangelist who has placed this saying immediately after the Twelve have been assured that they do well to call Jesus κύριος, since that is what he is, and at the same time are exhorted to follow his example (xiii. 13–15),

in the second clause of the second couplet, or by assimilation to John. But the longer text may well be original, and if John had a Synoptic model at all, it must have been the longer text of Matthew.

and who at a later point (xv. 20) cites the present saying as a warning to the disciples that they cannot expect to have a fairer lot than their Master's.

Then what about (ii), the change from μαθητής to ἀπόστολος, with the correlative substitution of ὁ πέμψας for ὁ διδάσκαλος? It might be urged that since διδάσκαλος and κύριος (in that order) are the titles which the evangelist has just given as those acceptable to Jesus from his followers, we should conclude that he was acquainted with the Matthacan couplet, which has the same titles in the same order. But if so, it is certainly no easier to understand why he has eliminated the relation of disciple and teacher from the Matthaean couplet, and substituted the relation of apostle and sender. Are we to say that he wished at this point to emphasize the new character of the Twelve as responsible envoys of Christ rather than simple pupils? But all through these chapters they continue to be called μαθηταί (except once, when they are οἱ δώδεκα, xx. 24). Indeed, ἀπόστολος is not a Johannine word at all; this is the only place in the Fourth Gospel where it is used. Μαθητής, on the other hand, occurs 78 times in the course of the gospel. It seems therefore improbable that the evangelist, finding in his source a saying in which his favourite word μαθητής was used, should have deliberately altered it into a word which he never uses elsewhere. In the context of xiii. 12–20, where Christ is emphatically both διδάσκαλος and κύριος, the longer Matthaean form of the saying would seem eminently appropriate. Yet John discarded it, if he knew it.

I conclude that there is no convincing reason to be discovered in the known tendencies of this author for the alterations he must have made if John xiii. 16 depends on Matt. x. 24–5, except possibly for the small grammatical 'correction' of ὑπέρ with the accusative into μεῖζων with the genitive. On the other hand, not only the differences between Matthew and John, but also the likenesses and differences between Matthew and Luke, and perhaps even the variant readings in Matthew, might be accounted for if we assumed that this saying circulated orally in variant forms, and that the parallelism of slave/master, apostle/sender on the one hand, and of disciple/teacher, slave/master on the other, was established at a primitive stage of tradition,[1] while a third and simpler form of the

---

[1] Cf. Matt. vii. 9–10, Luke xi. 11–12, where the shorter text should be read in Luke, with B, 440, some O.L. MSS. and Syrsin. Here, as in the saying under discussion, there are three contrasted pairs, (a) bread and stone, (b) fish and snake, (c) egg and scorpion, of which Matthew has (a) and (b), Luke (b) and (c). The attempt to account for these phenomena on a theory of literary dependence, whether of Luke on Matthew or of both on 'Q', meets with little success. The most probable explanation is that the oral tradition transmitted a couplet with antithetical parallelism, and

oral tradition, to the effect, 'A disciple is not superior to his teacher; at best he may be like his teacher', was taken up by Luke, and may possibly have influenced the shorter text of Matthew.

(ii) John xii. 25:

Ὁ φιλῶν τὴν ψυχὴν αὐτοῦ
ἀπολλύει αὐτήν,
καὶ ὁ μισῶν τὴν ψυχὴν αὐτοῦ
ἐν τῷ κόσμῳ τούτῳ
εἰς ζωὴν αἰώνιον
φυλάξει αὐτήν.

Sayings equivalent to this are to be found in five passages of the Synoptic Gospels. These may be reduced to three typical forms.

A.   Ὃς γὰρ ἐὰν θέλῃ τὴν ψυχὴν αὐτοῦ σῶσαι
ἀπολέσει αὐτήν,
ὃς δ' ἂν ἀπολέσῃ τὴν ψυχὴν αὐτοῦ
ἕνεκεν . . .
σώσει αὐτήν.

This form is common to Mark viii. 35 and Luke ix. 24, with slight variations. After ἕνεκεν Luke has ἐμοῦ. Mark, according to a formidable combination of authorities (including the Chester-Beatty papyrus, Codex Bezae and the Sinaitic Syriac), has τοῦ εὐαγγελίου, or, according to the majority of authorities, ἕνεκεν ἐμοῦ καὶ τοῦ εὐαγγελίου, which is possibly a conflate reading. Apart from this, the only difference between Mark and Luke is that the latter has οὗτος σώσει αὐτήν in the last clause.

B.   Ὁ εὑρὼν τὴν ψυχὴν αὐτοῦ
ἀπολέσει αὐτήν,
καὶ ὁ ἀπολέσας τὴν ψυχὴν αὐτοῦ
ἕνεκεν ἐμοῦ
εὑρήσει αὐτήν.

This form is found in Matt. x. 39. The words ἕνεκεν ἐμοῦ, and εὑρήσει in the last clause (but not εὑρών in the first), appear also in Matt. xvi. 25, which otherwise conforms to Mark viii. 35, and which must probably be regarded as a conflation. B is the characteristically Matthaean form.

C.   Ὃς ἐὰν ζητήσῃ τὴν ψυχὴν αὐτοῦ περιποιήσασθαι
ἀπολέσει αὐτήν,
καὶ ὃς ἐὰν ἀπολέσει
ζωογονήσει αὐτήν.

different branches of that tradition gave different pairs. (The Chester-Beatty text, which gives fish and snake, bread and scorpion, is probably a mere blunder.)

This form is found in Luke xvii. 33. It is the characteristically Lucan form, though it has left no trace in the other occurrence of the saying in Luke, which, as we have seen, follows Mark closely. It is to be noted that where Luke is writing independently of Mark he has no ἕνεκεν-clause.

If we now compare the three Synoptic forms of the saying, we observe that the common nucleus of all is a simple example of antithetical parallelism with balanced members, each having protasis and apodosis. In form C this antithetical structure is undisturbed by any additional material. In forms A and B (as well as in the Johannine form) there is an explanatory or qualifying clause, which impairs the balance of the whole. These qualifying clauses we may for the moment neglect, in order to consider more closely the common nucleus of the saying. In the several Synoptic forms the terms of the antithesis are as follows:

A.   σώζειν–ἀπολλύναι in both members,
B.   εὑρεῖν–ἀπολλύναι in both members,
C.   περιποιεῖσθαι–ἀπολλύναι in the first member,
           ζωογονεῖν–ἀπολλύναι in the second member.

The common term throughout is ἀπολλύναι, a verb which has the two meanings (a) 'to lose' (to the detriment primarily of the subject or agent), and (b) 'to destroy', 'spoil', 'kill' (to the detriment primarily of the object). In sense (a) it has εὑρίσκειν as a natural antithesis (cf. Luke xv. 24). Yet if we ask in what sense we are to understand the expression, 'to find the ψυχή', in the protasis of the first member, it is not very easy to give a clear answer, though in the apodosis of the second member it is easier. But ἀπολλύναι in sense (a) may also have as its contrary a word meaning 'to keep', 'preserve', and this sense may be expressed by the verb σώζειν. But again, σώζειν is also used in the LXX as one rendering of the Hiphil of חיה; and so here the Syriac versions render σώζειν by the Aphel of ܚܝܐ. We might therefore understand σώζειν as the antithesis of ἀπολλύναι in sense (b): 'to make alive', in contrast to 'to destroy', 'kill'. It would seem that form A uses the terms with a certain fluidity or ambiguity of meaning, appropriate to an oracular utterance. In form C it would appear that the intention is to give the sense 'to make alive' quite unambiguously, at any rate in the apodosis of the second member, by using the verb ζωογονεῖν, while in the protasis of the first member we have the more colourless περιποιεῖσθαι, which includes the meanings, 'to claim for oneself', 'to keep or preserve for oneself' (and in the latter sense is a synonym for σώζειν). The terms περιποιεῖσθαι, ζωογονεῖν, have a literary flavour[1] which is unlike the generally simple vocabulary of the earliest tradition of the Sayings (so far as it can be recognized in the common element in the gospels). They may well represent a rewriting of form A in which these more literary expressions are substituted for the simpler σῶσαι. If, however, we attribute this rewriting to the third evangelist, and suppose him to have followed either Mark or Matthew, we should have to explain why he omitted the qualifying clause which both these gospels insert in the second member, though in slightly different terms. Where we can do no more than conjecture, it seems rather more probable that the tradition behind form C, as we have it in Luke (but no doubt with σῶσαι or some similar verb rather than Luke's more choice expressions), gave the simple antithetical parallelism with its rhythm unbroken, and that forms A and B represent exegetical additions—ἕνεκεν τοῦ εὐαγγελίου in A and ἕνεκεν ἐμοῦ in B—designed to bring out the implied presupposition that the voluntary loss of the ψυχή has for its motive devotion to the cause of Christ (or of the Gospel), and not (shall we say?) mere recklessness without a moral basis. In short, while it would be *possible* to account for the variant forms by a theory of literary dependence, the evidence for such dependence is by no means compelling, and the phenomena are rather more easily understood if we suppose that the oral tradition lying behind the Synoptic Gospels had already developed variations before anything was fixed in writing.

We now turn to the Fourth Gospel. Here we observe, first, that the qualifying clause which appears in the Synoptic forms A and B is missing in John; and next, that a different qualifying clause is introduced—or rather two explanatory phrases, the one explaining the protasis of the second member and the other its apodosis: the voluntary loss of the ψυχή is a loss 'in this world', and the corresponding promise is 'for eternal life'. This is, even more clearly than the qualifying clause in forms A and B, an exegetical addition. Its language is characteristically Johannine: not only is the word κόσμος about four times as common in the Fourth Gospel as in all the others together, but the phrase ὁ κόσμος οὗτος is peculiar to the Fourth Gospel, in which it occurs eleven times, while ζωὴ αἰώνιος is more than twice as common in this gospel as in the three Synoptics. *Prima facie*, this looks like editorial work on the part of our evangelist, as the ἕνεκεν-clauses in Matthew and Mark may be editorial explanations on their part.

If we disregard these qualifying clauses, we are left with a pure antithetical parallelism, in shape almost identical with that which lies behind

[1] Both are confined (in the N.T.) to the Lucan writings and the Pastoral Epistles.

340

form C, or with forms A and B without the ἕνεκεν-clauses. It is in fact very close indeed to form B: in both, the simpler expressions, ὁ φιλῶν... ὁ μισῶν, ὁ εὑρών...ὁ ἀπολέσας, have a certain neatness, as compared with the cumbrous compound expressions in the others. In sense, ὁ φιλῶν τὴν ψυχήν is certainly less obscure than ὁ εὑρὼν τὴν ψυχήν. It is a more succinct way of saying what Mark says—ὃς ἐὰν θέλῃ τὴν ψυχὴν αὐτοῦ σῶσαι—and what Luke says—ὃς ἐὰν ζητήσῃ τὴν ψυχὴν αὐτοῦ περιποιήσασθαι. Similarly ὁ μισῶν τὴν ψυχὴν αὐτοῦ gives in the fewest possible words the meaning intended by the phrase ὃς ἂν ἀπολέσῃ (ὁ ἀπολέσας) τὴν ψυχὴν αὐτοῦ, which does not make it clear (apart from the ἕνεκεν-clause) that the 'loss', or 'spoiling', contemplated is voluntary and intentional. It is a 'loss' implying a detachment from the self which may aptly be described hyperbolically as 'hatred'. In short, the Johannine version of the saying is closer in shape to Matthew, closer in sense to Mark and Luke, but superior to them all in the combination of elegance with clarity. If we work with the hypothesis that John was using the Synoptics as sources, it would be difficult to say which of them was his starting point. Did he start from Mark or Luke, and arrive at this neat paraphrase, and in doing so produce accidentally a pattern identical with Matthew's? Or did he start from Matthew, and make the not very easy transition from εὑρεῖν/ἀπολλύναι to φιλεῖν/μισεῖν? (The omission of the ἕνεκεν-clause we could understand; John does not use this preposition, nor does he use εὐαγγέλιον.) Or are we to suppose that he studied and compared the two, or all three, and rephrased the whole saying in his own way?

How far is the actual language so 'Johannine' as to suggest such a far-reaching process of rephrasing? The verb ἀπολλύναι, which is constant in all Synoptic forms of the saying, recurs here in the apodosis of the first member, but John uses the present ἀπολλύει, where all other versions have the future ἀπολέσει.[1] This would no doubt be consonant with the Johannine emphasis on judgement and eternal life as realized here and now, but the present is probably gnomic rather than temporal, since its correlative in the apodosis of the second member is future, φυλάξει. The verb φυλάσσειν, an equivalent here for σώζειν, περιποιεῖσθαι, in the sense 'preserve', occurs three times in John, once in Matthew, twice in Mark,

---

[1] It is perhaps worth observing that if the saying was first handed down in Aramaic (which was certainly the language of the most primitive tradition) the difference of tense may not have been discernible; in the Syriac versions ἀπολέσει and ἀπολλύει are alike rendered ܢܘܒܕܝܗ.

and six times in Luke. It is therefore in no sense a 'Johannine' word. The terms φιλεῖν, μισεῖν, are 'Johannine' in the sense that both are more common in John than in any of the others,[1] and that the antithesis, φιλεῖν/ μισεῖν, which occurs in John xv. 18–19 as well as in this passage, is not found in the Synoptic Gospels, in which the antithesis is ἀγαπᾶν/μισεῖν (Matt. v. 43, vi. 24, Luke xvi. 13).

Further, the antithesis φιλεῖν/μισεῖν occurs in a passage in the *Hermetica* which (allowing for the difference of approach) has a certain affinity with the saying we are considering: ἐὰν μὴ πρῶτον τὸ σῶμά σου μισήσῃς, σεαυτὸν φιλῆσαι οὐ δύνασαι (*C.H.* IV. 6, cited above, p. 320).[2] Shall we say, then, that John has rephrased the saying under the influence of Hellenistic ways of speech? It may be so; but on the other hand the antithesis, 'love/hate', is in itself natural, simple and universal; and in particular it is biblical, even though in the LXX, as in the Synoptics, ἀγαπᾶν is preferred to φιλεῖν.[3] It is moreover characteristic of the language of the Old Testament to use ἀγαπᾶν/μισεῖν with reference to moral choice,[4] and also to use μισεῖν hyperbolically.[5] This hyperbolical use is reflected in

[1] Φιλεῖν, five times in Matthew, once in Mark, twice in Luke, thirteen times in John; μισεῖν, five times in Matthew, once in Mark, seven times in Luke, twelve times in John. But φιλεῖν is not 'Johannine' in the sense that it is his preferred term for 'love'; on the contrary he has ἀγαπᾶν thirty-five times—nearly three times as often as φιλεῖν.

[2] Cf. *C.H.* VII. 2, where the body is denounced as 'the robber within your house, who hates you through the things it loves, and envies you through the things it hates' (τὸν δι' ὧν φιλεῖ μισοῦντα καὶ δι' ὧν μισεῖ φθονοῦντα). The meaning seems to be that the body loves worldly pleasure and the like, and so is hostile to the real self, while it hates what is eternal and so grudges the true self the possession of that which is really valuable.

[3] I have noted over twenty places in the LXX where ἀγαπᾶν and μισεῖν stand in antithesis, against only two which have φιλεῖν: Gen. xxxvii. 4, Eccles. iii. 8. But in the former passage ἀγαπᾶν has immediately preceded (Gen. xxxvii. 3) without difference of meaning, and as a translation of the same Hebrew verb (אהב). Perhaps we might add Prov. viii. 13 with 17, where again φιλεῖν and ἀγαπᾶν appear (both = אהב) as against μισεῖν.

[4] E.g. Ps. xliv. 8, ἠγάπησας δικαιοσύνην καὶ ἐμίσησας ἀνομίαν; Amos v. 15, μεμισήκαμεν τὰ πονηρά, καὶ ἠγαπήκαμεν τὰ καλά; Zech. viii. 17, ὅρκον ψευδῆ μὴ ἀγαπᾶτε, διότι ταῦτα πάντα ἐμίσησα, λέγει Κύριος. In association with this 'ethical' use of ἀγαπᾶν and μισεῖν we find expressions like 'to love (hate) oneself (one's soul)'; e.g. Ps. x. 5, ὁ ἀγαπῶν ἀδικίαν μισεῖ τὴν ἑαυτοῦ ψυχήν, Prov. xvi. 3, ὁ τηρῶν ἐλέγχους ἀγαπᾷ ψυχὴν αὐτοῦ, xix. 5, ὁ κτώμενος φρόνησιν ἀγαπᾷ ἑαυτόν. The meaning of such expressions is not quite the same as in John xii. 25, but the passages illustrate the way in which such expressions could be coined.

[5] E.g. when one of two wives is said to be 'loved' and the other 'hated', the meaning may be no more than that the husband prefers the one to the other. Thus in Deut. xxi. 15–17 we have legal provisions regarding ἡ ἠγαπημένη and ἡ μισουμένη

the New Testament. In Luke xiv. 26 anyone who wishes to be a disciple of Jesus is enjoined to 'hate' his father, mother, wife and children. The sense intended is no doubt conveyed with a more prosaic directness in the Matthaean parallel, x. 37, where the follower of Jesus must not love father, mother, son or daughter *more* than he loves his Master;[1] but the Lucan form, with its challenging hyperbole, is surely the more original or, in other words, nearer to the primary tradition. Now in this same passage of Luke the disciple is required to 'hate' his own ψυχή. The expression μισεῖν τὴν ἑαυτοῦ ψυχήν is used here in exactly the same sense as in John. That John owes anything to Luke xiv. 26 is not to be supposed. It follows that in this essential part of the saying we are considering John is moving entirely within the ideas and language of the primary tradition. That he has substituted the less biblical, and apparently less traditional, φιλεῖν for an original ἀγαπᾶν is possible, though there seems little reason why he should have done so, since in general he prefers ἀγαπᾶν. There is nothing against the view that the couplet, simple, rhythmical, and genuinely biblical as it is in language, was handed down by tradition substantially in the terms preserved in John xii. 25 (without the qualifying clauses).

I submit, then, that the least difficult hypothesis to account for the likenesses and differences, not only between John and the Synoptics, but also among the Synoptics themselves, is that this very fundamental saying had a place in many separate branches of oral tradition, and that the variations belong to its pre-literary history, originating, it may be, in varying attempts to translate the Aramaic in which it was first handed down.

(iii) John xiii. 20:

> Ὁ λαμβάνων ἄν τινα πέμψω
> ἐμὲ λαμβάνει,
> ὁ δὲ ἐμὲ λαμβάνων
> λαμβάνει τὸν πέμψαντά με.

respectively; in Gen. xxix. 30–3 we have a specific case: Rachel is the 'beloved' wife and Leah is 'hated' (μισεῖται), but this is paraphrased, ἠγάπησεν Ῥαχὴλ μᾶλλον ἢ Λείαν. Similarly in Matt. vi. 24, Luke xvi. 13, it is not true that the slave of two masters would necessarily 'hate' one of them (in our sense of the word 'hate'); τὸν ἕνα μισήσει καὶ τὸν ἕτερον ἀγαπήσει only means that he is sure to like one better than the other.

[1] The difference between Luke's εἴ τις οὐ μισεῖ τὸν πατέρα and Matthew's ὁ φιλῶν πατέρα ὑπὲρ ἐμέ is precisely that between Gen. xxix. 31, μισεῖται Λεία, and 30, ἠγάπησεν Ῥαχὴλ μᾶλλον ἢ Λείαν. It is a difference in words, and perhaps in emotional tone, but not in substance.

This has an unmistakable parallel in Matt. x. 40:

'Ο δεχόμενος ὑμᾶς
ἐμὲ δέχεται,
καὶ ὁ ἐμὲ δεχόμενος
δέχεται τὸν ἀποστείλαντά με.

Although the vocabulary differs, the sense is the same, and the structure of the two passages is closely similar. In each we have two members in parallelism, each with protasis and apodosis. The Johannine form is rhetorically more elegant, with the two short intermediate clauses enclosed by longer first and last clauses, each of which contains the same verb. The balance of clauses is perfect, and the way in which words are echoed is most effective.

But rhetorical effectiveness does not carry any necessary inference regarding the relative originality of the two forms. If we are to suppose that John is here dependent on Matthew, we shall have to account for three alterations: (a) the substitution of the verb λαμβάνειν for δέχεσθαι, and (b) of πέμπειν for ἀποστέλλειν, and (c) the substitution of the indefinite phrase ἄν τινα πέμψω for the specific ὑμᾶς. Let us take these in turn.

(a) It is true that John has a predilection for the verb λαμβάνειν, which occurs 44 times in his gospel against a single occurrence of δέχεσθαι, though it is only here and in v. 43, and perhaps i. 12, that λαμβάνειν is used for the 'reception' of Christ or his emissaries by the public to whom their mission is addressed. On the other hand δέχεσθαι is used exactly so at its single occurrence in iv. 45, so that the evangelist would not appear to have had any insuperable objection to the word, such as would lead him to alter his supposed Matthaean source.

(b) John uses πέμπειν 32 times (in present, aorist, and future), and ἀποστέλλειν 28 times (in aorist and perfect only). In the *locus classicus* upon the mission of the Twelve both verbs are used: καθὼς ἀπέσταλκέν με ὁ πατὴρ κἀγὼ πέμπω ὑμᾶς (xx. 21). There is thus no discernible reason why he should have altered Matthew's verb here, unless indeed it was for simple euphony.

(c) A change from the specific to the general (from ὑμᾶς to ἄν τινα) would be contrary to the main tendency of the Farewell Discourses, in which we repeatedly find sayings which in the earlier part of the gospel had a general or indefinite form now applied specifically to the disciples.[1]

---

[1] See *Interpretation*, pp. 396–8. And note that in the context of our present saying the address to the disciples as such is particularly pointed. The whole discourse begins with, ὑμεῖς φωνεῖτέ με 'Ο διδάσκαλος, καὶ 'Ο κύριος, and the relation thus

But in order to get this question into its right focus we must take account of a wider range of facts. In the first place, the three aphorisms on 'receiving' which in Matthew follow upon the saying we are at present considering are all in general or indefinite terms: ὁ δεχόμενος προφήτην, ὁ δεχόμενος δίκαιον, ὃς ἐὰν ποτίζῃ ἕνα τῶν μικρῶν τούτων. All these, especially the last, are (so far) nearer in type to John xiii. 20 than to Matt. x. 40.

Further, in Mark and Luke the second member of the parallelism as we have it in John and Matthew occurs attached to a different first member.

Mark ix. 37	Luke ix. 48
Ὃς ἂν ἓν τῶν παιδίων τούτων δέξηται	Ὃς ἐὰν δέξηται τοῦτο τὸ παιδίον
ἐπὶ τῷ ὀνόματί μου	ἐπὶ τῷ ὀνόματί μου
ἐμὲ δέχεται,	ἐμὲ δέχεται,
καὶ ὃς ἂν ἐμὲ δέχηται	καὶ ὃς ἂν ἐμὲ δέχηται
οὐκ ἐμὲ δέχεται	
ἀλλὰ τὸν ἀποστείλαντά με.	δέχεται τὸν ἀποστείλαντά με.

Here the Marcan form has the same degree of generality as Matt. x. 42, while the Lucan is apparently specific, but is surely intended to mean, as Matthew has it in this context, ἓν παιδίον τοιοῦτο (Matt. xviii. 5, where the second member of the couplet is missing). The relation between the saying given in Mark and Luke and that given in Matthew and John is enigmatic, but it does not appear that any simple theory of dependence of Matthew on Mark (or of Mark on Matthew) is entirely convincing. It seems more probable that the elements of these sayings were preserved by oral tradition in varying combinations,[1] and if so, it may be to the oral tradition that we must attribute the variations between Matthew and John as well as among the Synoptics.

To complete our survey of relevant passages we must take note of a saying which in Luke occupies a position corresponding to Matt. x. 40-2, i.e. the close of the Charge to Missionaries (Luke x. 16):

Ὁ ἀκούων ὑμῶν
ἐμοῦ ἀκούει,
καὶ ὁ ἀθετῶν ὑμᾶς
ἐμὲ ἀθετεῖ,
ὁ δὲ ἐμὲ ἀθετῶν
ἀθετεῖ τὸν ἀποστείλαντά με.

established conditions all that follows. Yet the two propositions, οὐκ ἔστιν δοῦλος μείζων κ.τ.λ., and ὁ λαμβάνων ἂν τινα πέμψω κ.τ.λ., stand out as general statements, presupposing, as I shall argue, a traditional form.

[1] I have illustrated above the extent to which, in narrative *pericopae* also, the varying combination of traditional elements may account for differences which have often been put down to an 'editor' dealing with a literary source (see pp. 169–72).

Here, as in the shorter text of Matt. x. 24–5, we have a triplet. The first clause corresponds closely (in form though not in vocabulary) with the first member of the couplet in Matt. x. 40, but the second member is missing. What next follows in Luke is in form exactly parallel to Matt. x. 40, in both members, but in sense it is the negative statement correlative to the positive statement in Matthew and John. Further, the last clause is similar (in form and sense though not in vocabulary) to John xv. 23:

'Ὁ ἐμὲ μισῶν
καὶ τὸν πατέρα μου μισεῖ.

In view of all this it would appear to be idle to set on foot an inquiry into the reasons or motives which might have led Luke, in copying Matthew (or 'Q'), to alter δεχόμενος to ἀκούων, to omit the second member of Matthew's couplet, and to compensate by adding (? out of his own head) the converse of Matthew's saying as a whole; and equally idle to inquire why John (presumed to be copying Luke) altered ἀθετεῖ to μισεῖ, and omitted the first member of the parallelism. It is surely on all grounds more probable that the oral tradition underlying all our written documents contained a number of sayings upon the important theme of the mission of the apostles in the world, and that as such sayings came down through a considerable number of different channels (for no branch of the tradition would neglect them) the possibilities of variation were numerous, especially if we posit a common Aramaic stock, which would put forth divergent branches as soon as attempts were made to turn it into Greek.

It may be that we have still further traces of this multiform tradition of the mission of the apostles. It is to be observed that the sayings ὁ δεχόμενος ὑμᾶς ἐμὲ δέχεται, ὁ ἀκούων ὑμῶν ἐμοῦ ἀκούει, are placed at the end of a sequence of sayings which begins, Ἰδοὺ (ἐγὼ) ἀποστέλλω ὑμᾶς (Matt. x. 16, Luke x. 3). It is the fact that the apostles are 'sent' by Christ himself that justifies the specific statement, 'He who receives (hears) you receives (hears) me', in place of an indefinite ἄν τινα πέμψω. But in order to justify the further statement that the receiving of the apostles amounts in the end to receiving God himself, and that their rejection amounts to a rejection of God, something further is presupposed, and this is given expression in John xx. 21:

καθὼς ἀπέσταλκέν με ὁ πατήρ
κἀγὼ πέμπω ὑμᾶς.

We might indeed put together all these various sayings in a single comprehensive statement, which would run as follows:

(a) As the Father sent me	I send you
(b) He who receives (hears) you (whom I send)	receives (hears) me
(c) He who receives (hears) me	receives him who sent me
(d) He who rejects (hates) you	rejects (hates) me
(e) He who rejects (hates) me	rejects (hates) the Father (who sent me)

I do not pretend to know that any tradition, oral or written, actually contained all this together, but the various sayings imply or presuppose one another and form a complete whole which might be thus set out. Of the various articles of this statement, (a) is in John (the apodosis alone in Matthew and Luke); (b) is in Matthew, Luke and John; (c) is in Matthew, Mark, Luke and John; (d) is in Luke only;[1] (e) is in Luke and John. Any attempt, I submit, to account for these phenomena by a theory of literary dependence must be fruitless. The hypothesis that the evangelists drew upon different branches of a common oral tradition, and that the language they employ, within a form or pattern which remains largely constant, was in large measure determined by variations in that tradition, appears to me the hypothesis which best explains the facts. To return, then, to our question, whether John copied from the Synoptics, or whether there lies behind the Fourth Gospel a special branch of the common tradition, it now appears that, here at least, the saying as given by John (a) has special features of form and language for which the 'editing' of a literary source is not a necessary, or the best, explanation, and (b) in substance and meaning belongs to the same body of teaching on the subject as we find in the Synoptics, and it is highly probable that the Johannine and Synoptic versions were drawn from the same reservoir of tradition through independent channels.

(iv) John xx. 23:

Ἄν τινων ἀφῆτε τὰς ἁμαρτίας,
ἀφέωνται αὐτοῖς·
ἄν τινων κρατῆτε,
κεκράτηνται.

This saying occurs in the Fourth Gospel as a pendant to the solemn commissioning of the apostles, καθὼς ἀπέσταλκέν με ὁ πατὴρ κἀγὼ πέμπω ὑμᾶς. It corresponds in some sort to the saying which forms part of the 'Church order' in Matt. xviii. 18:

Ὅσα ἐὰν δήσητε ἐπὶ τῆς γῆς
ἔσται δεδεμένα ἐν οὐρανῷ,

[1] It is hinted at in John xv. 18 sqq. where the saying οὐκ ἔστιν δοῦλος μείζων τοῦ κυρίου αὐτοῦ is cited in support.

347

καὶ ὅσα ἐὰν λύσητε ἐπὶ τῆς γῆς
ἔσται λελυμένα ἐν οὐρανῷ.

Almost the same words, but with the substitution of singular for plural, occur in the saying addressed to Peter in Matt. xvi. 19. It has been very commonly held that John has given an adaptation of the Matthaean text for gentile readers to whom the expressions 'binding' and 'loosing' would be obscure. It appears that the Johannine form would be a legitimate rendering of the Matthaean, in one aspect at least. The terms δεῖν, λύειν undoubtedly represent the Aramaic אֲסַר and שְׁרָא, Hebrew אָסַר and הִתִּיר (as in Josephus, *B.J.* I. 111 they are represented by λύειν καὶ δεσμεῖν).[1] In the rabbinic literature these terms appear to cover two distinct forms of the exercise of discipline in the synagogue. Their most usual meaning is 'forbid' and 'permit', respectively; but they can also be used with reference to the imposition and the removal of the ban, meaning 'excommunicate', and 'restore to communion', respectively. The Johannine saying appears to contemplate the case of a person who, being in a state of sin, is at the moment outside the fellowship of the Church.[2] To 'remit' his sin is equivalent to admitting him to communion—which might be expressed by λύειν, שְׁרָא, הִתִּיר. To 'retain' his sin is to continue his exclusion, and while this is not quite what is meant by δεῖν, אָסַר, אֲסַר, it is not very remote in meaning. It does therefore seem possible that ἁμαρτίας ἀφιέναι, κρατεῖν might have been employed as a paraphrase for Aramaic expressions which would be entirely unintelligible to Greek ears, and not much more intelligible if they were translated into λύειν and δεῖν. If, however, this paraphrase be attributed to the Fourth Evangelist, supposed to have Matthew before him, and to be 'editing' it freely, we are faced with the difficulty that the expressions ἀφιέναι ἁμαρτίας and κρατεῖν are never found in the Fourth Gospel, apart from this one place. The possibility may be suggested, that since the 'Church order' of

---

[1] See S.–B. *ad* Matt. xvi. 19.

[2] The question may be left open, whether such a person is conceived as a pagan professing conversion and applying for admission to the Church, or a Christian who has offended against the Christian law and is applying for restoration. The latter seems to us the more natural interpretation, but some patristic authorities interpreted the 'power of the keys' in Matt. xvi. 19 with reference to the admission or rejection of candidates for initiation, and in that case the authority to 'bind' and 'loose' should mean authority to refuse and admit. In any case, the moment at which the precept of John xx. 23 comes into force is not the moment when the excommunication of an offender is in contemplation (cf. 1 Cor. v. 3–5), but the moment when a person is outside communion and the question of his admission (or re-admission) is under consideration.

Matt. xviii. 15–20 begins with precepts for the excommunication (ἔστω σοι ὥσπερ ὁ ἐθνικὸς καὶ ὁ τελώνης) and restoration (ἐκέρδησας τὸν ἀδελφόν) of an offending member of the ἐκκλησία, and leads up to the question of ἄφεσις ἁμαρτιῶν (xviii. 21), an attentive reader may have concluded that 'binding' and 'loosing' are to be interpreted in terms of forgiveness, and may have borrowed the term ἀφιέναι ἁμαρτίας from the context. This, however, seems somewhat far-fetched, and in any case it does not account for the use of κρατεῖν, which (as Strack–Billerbeck show) would not properly correspond with δεῖν, but might possibly represent such expressions as שָׁמַר עֲוֹנוֹת Ps. cxxx. 3 (LXX παρατηρεῖν ἀνομίας). In short, the attempt to derive John xx. 23 from Matt. xviii. 18 breaks down. That it is a free invention of the Fourth Evangelist is improbable, since it contains two words which are for him ἅπαξ λεγόμενα. We seem driven to postulate an alternative form of tradition regarding the authority committed to the apostles by the Lord, akin to, though not identical with, the tradition followed by Matthew, an alternative form which the Fourth Evangelist has independently followed.

In these four instances, then, which deserve to rank as *instantiae praerogativae*, the conclusion may be drawn, with the highest degree of probability attainable in such matters, that John is not dependent on the Synoptic Gospels, but is transmitting independently a special form of the common oral tradition. I shall now review a number of further sayings where again both form and content are so closely similar in John and in the Synoptics as to point to derivation from a common tradition, but where the evidence of independent use of such tradition is perhaps less strong than in the first four.

(v) John xvi. 23–4, xiv. 13–14. Sayings on prayer and its answer.

Both these passages contain sayings in aphoristic form:

A. xvi. 23–4: (1) ἄν τι αἰτήσητε τὸν πατέρα δώσει ὑμῖν ἐν τῷ ὀνόματί μου.
　　　　　　　(2) αἰτεῖτε καὶ λήμψεσθε.
B. xiv. 13–14: (1) ὅτι ἂν αἰτήσητε ἐν τῷ ὀνόματί μου τοῦτο ποιήσω.
　　　　　　　(2) ἐάν τι αἰτήσητέ με ἐν τῷ ὀνόματί μου ἐγὼ ποιήσω.

There is a variant of A (1) in xv. 16, where it appears in the form of a final clause: (ἔθηκα ὑμᾶς) ἵνα ὅτι ἂν αἰτήσητε τὸν πατέρα ἐν τῷ ὀνόματί μου δῷ ὑμῖν.[1]

---

[1] We have here a neat example, in a perfectly simple instance, of the way in which sayings which tradition handed down as self-contained aphorisms are woven by this evangelist into the fabric of his composition. When once a categorical proposition

These are all embedded in the structure of the Farewell Discourses, while retaining the aphoristic form. Parallel aphorisms occur in the Synoptic Gospels in widely different contexts. Parallel with the simplest of the Johannine sayings (A (2)) is Matt. vii. 7 (Luke xi. 9): αἰτεῖτε καὶ δοθήσεται ὑμῖν. They are alike both in form and in content, the only difference being that where the Synoptics use the impersonal passive of διδόναι John uses the middle of λαμβάνειν. These are true equivalents, the verbs διδόναι and λαμβάνειν being correlatives.¹ In Matthew and Luke the saying occurs as one member of a triplet ('Ask...seek... knock'), of which there is no trace in John. It is not necessary to suppose that he deliberately disintegrated the Synoptic passage as it lay before him, in order to utilize the single aphorism for his own purpose. The saying may well have circulated separately, as well as, perhaps, in different combinations,² in various strains of tradition.

More significant are some other parallels. With A (1) compare Matt. xxi. 22, πάντα ὅσα ἂν αἰτήσητε ἐν τῇ προσευχῇ πιστεύοντες λήμψεσθε (Mark xi. 25, πάντα ὅσα προσεύχεσθε καὶ αἰτεῖσθε πιστεύετε ὅτι ἐλάβετε καὶ ἔσται ὑμῖν).³ In form the sentences are closely similar. In sense they are funda-

has been turned into a dependent final clause, the process has begun which is carried through on the grand scale in the composition of the Johannine discourses.

¹ It may well be that we are dealing with variant translations of an Aramaic original. In Aramaic the idea of the passive is often expressed by the use of the active verb in the impersonal third person plural. This can be rendered into Greek either (a) literally but misleadingly, by the third person plural, as in Luke vi. 38: μέτρον καλόν...δώσουσιν εἰς τὸν κόλπον ὑμῶν means simply 'good measure will be poured into your lap'; the real Agent contemplated is God; cf. Luke xii. 20, ταύτῃ τῇ νυκτὶ τὴν ψυχήν σου ἀπαιτοῦσιν ἀπό σου. God alone can demand a man's soul of him; or (b) by the use of the passive, as here, δοθήσεται, but that is a little awkward in Greek where no subject is expressed; or (c) by the use of the active of the correlative verb, as here λήμψεσθε, which is the most idiomatic way of rendering it in Greek. Further, since the imperative in the protasis of a conditional sentence is a well-established idiom both in Greek and in Hebrew and Aramaic, αἰτεῖτε καὶ δοθήσεται ὑμῖν might well represent the same original as ἐὰν αἰτήσητε δώσει ὑμῖν (cf. p. 90).

² A parallel to the second member of the Synoptic triplet is found in a different combination in Oxyrhynchus Papyri 654 (= Gospel of Thomas, ed. Guillamont and others, logion 2): μὴ παυσάσθω ὁ ζητῶν ἕως ἂν εὕρῃ.

³ Πιστεύετε...καὶ ἔσται ὑμῖν is probably to be taken as a conditional sentence with the imperative in the protasis (cf. n. 1, above): 'if you believe...it shall be yours'. But Mark gives the bold paradox, 'believe that your have got it, and it shall be yours'. The paradox is absent both from Matthew and from John, but it reappears in 1 John v. 15: ἐὰν οἴδαμεν ὅτι ἀκούει ἡμῶν ὃ ἐὰν αἰτώμεθα, οἴδαμεν ὅτι ἔχομεν τὰ αἰτήματα. This, by implication, is made dependent on faith, and it is faith εἰς τὸ ὄνομα τοῦ υἱοῦ τοῦ θεοῦ.

mentally identical. In language they differ: John here uses διδόναι and Matthew λαμβάνειν, reversing the difference in John xiv. 14, Matt. vii. 7. Clearly the choice of one verb rather than the other is not characteristic of either evangelist, but is a matter of indifference. Λήμψεσθε is rather more natural Greek than the impersonal δοθήσεται ὑμῖν, but where a subject is to hand (ὁ πατήρ, supplied from τὸν πατέρα in the protasis) the active δώσει ὑμῖν is at least equally natural. The supply in John of a personal object to the verb αἰτεῖν—the same object as is understood in Matthew—is a minor divergence. More important is the addition of a different limiting phrase: in Matthew, prayer is promised an answer provided it is offered in faith (πιστεύοντες); in John xvi. 23 the answer is to be given 'in the name' of Christ, and in three other Johannine passages (xiv. 13, 14, xv. 16) the prayer is to be offered 'in the name' of Christ. This looks, *prima facie*, like a peculiarly Johannine development; but it is not clear that John is going altogether outside the range of ideas within which the Synoptics move. In Matt. xviii. 19 we have again a promise of answer to prayer, which has a certain limited resemblance in form and in language to the sayings we are considering: ἐὰν δύο συμφωνήσωσιν... περὶ παντὸς πράγματος οὗ ἐὰν αἰτήσωνται, γενήσεται αὐτοῖς παρὰ τοῦ πατρός μου. Here the condition on which the promise is given is agreement in the object sought, and not either faith (as in Matt. xxi. 22) or asking in the name of Christ (as in John). But the passage proceeds (Matt. xviii. 19), οὗ γάρ εἰσιν δύο ἢ τρεῖς συνηγμένοι εἰς τὸ ἐμὸν ὄνομα ἐκεῖ εἰμὶ ἐν μέσῳ αὐτῶν. The conjunction γάρ indicates that this sentence provides the *Begründung* of the preceding: agreement in prayer assures an answer, *because* Christ is with those who are together 'in his name'— from which it is no long step to the idea that their prayer is itself 'in the name' of Christ. Where John really does depart from the standpoint represented by the Synoptics is in passages where he speaks of prayer as addressed to Christ rather than to the Father (B (2)), and of Christ himself, and not the Father, as giving what is requested (B (1), (2)). Here, it seems, we have passed from the traditional ground where our evangelist starts to his individual theological contribution.

It is clear that these passages in the Fourth Gospel have behind them a tradition which is common also to the Synoptics. The phenomena could, it seems, be explained on the hypothesis that John had Matthew before him, but the evidence does not compel this conclusion. The free variation between the verbs διδόναι and λαμβάνειν, and the way in which language and ideas present in two different places of Matthew come together in John, weigh in favour of an independent use of traditional material.

(vi) John i. 43, xxi. 22, xii. 26. Sayings about following Christ.

The call to 'follow' Christ is so fundamental to the whole gospel picture of his Ministry that we might count on its appearance in any form of the tradition, and it is natural enough that the words ἀκολούθει μοι should occur in John as in the Synoptics, though it is curious that the persons to whom it is addressed in the Fourth Gospel—Philip (i. 43) and Peter (xxi. 22)—are not those to whom it is addressed in the other gospels—the publican (Mark ii. 14 and parallels), and two unnamed persons who fail to respond (Mark x. 21 and parallels, Matt. viii. 21–2=Luke ix. 59). This would be slightly more natural if the traditions of the calling of disciples came to John through a different channel.

Of rather more significance is the recurrence of the verb ἀκολουθεῖν in a saying conceived as a rule for the Christian life:

John xii. 26,   ἐὰν ἐμοί τις διακονῇ ἐμοὶ ἀκολουθείτω.
Matt. xvi. 24,   εἴ τις θέλει ὀπίσω μου ἐλθεῖν . . . ἀκολουθείτω μοι.

(and so with slight modifications in Mark and Luke).

Both in John and in the Synoptics the saying is an element in a larger whole, but its essential structure is the same in them all. The purport is that any discipleship worth the name must involve the 'following' of Christ in a pregnant sense. The sense intended is defined in the Synoptics both by the context in which the saying occurs and by the clause (which I have omitted above), ἀπαρνησάσθω ἑαυτὸν καὶ ἀράτω τὸν σταυρὸν αὐτοῦ. In John it is defined, again, by the context, which speaks first of the 'glorifying' of Christ (his death on the cross), then of the 'death' of the sown grain, and passes on to the equivalent of the prayer of Jesus in Gethsemane (see above, pp. 69–71). Similarly, in xiii. 36–7 the 'following' of Christ is related to his death. The meaning, therefore, is the same in both: ἀκολουθείτω μοι (ἐμοὶ ἀκολουθείτω) means 'do as I do and take the risks I take'. In both versions these words are the apodosis of a sentence, the protasis of which differs. In the Synoptic Gospels the intended meaning seems to be, 'If anyone wishes to accompany me on my travels (? on my last journey to Jerusalem), he must "follow" me'. In John it is, 'If anyone wishes to do me service the only way in which he can do so is to "follow" me'. The verb διακονεῖν is not found in the Fourth Gospel outside this verse, except in its literal sense of waiting at table (xii. 2, compare ii. 5, where the διάκονοι are waiters).[1] It is therefore not very likely that John should have himself introduced it in rephrasing a saying borrowed from the Synoptics. It is more probable that this very fundamental saying came down by more than one channel. In both forms it is no doubt addressed to the Church called to suffer for Christ in the world, but in both it reaches back to his historic Ministry. If any difference is to be detected, it is that διακονεῖν is more readily transferred to the situation of the Christian in the world than ὀπίσω μου ἐλθεῖν, and if so, then the form of tradition behind the Fourth Gospel perhaps betrays a *Sitz im Leben* somewhat farther removed from the original historical situation in the life of Jesus.

(vii) (*a*) John xiii. 17:

> Εἰ ταῦτα οἴδατε, μακάριοί ἐστε ἐὰν
> ποιῆτε αὐτά.

Compare Luke xi. 28:

> Μακάριοι οἱ ἀκούοντες τὸν λόγον
> τοῦ θεοῦ καὶ φυλάσσοντες.

Makarisms, or beatitudes, are numerous in Matthew and Luke, though Mark has none. In John there are only two, of which this is one. That the makarism was one of the characteristic forms in which the teaching of Jesus was handed down, and almost certainly in more than one stream of tradition, we may safely affirm. In purport, this Johannine makarism is very close to the Lucan one here quoted. A similar makarism, in parabolic form, occurs in Matt. xxiv. 46 (Luke xii. 43):

> Μακάριος ὁ δοῦλος ἐκεῖνος ὃν ἐλθὼν ὁ κύριος αὐτοῦ
> εὑρήσει οὕτως ποιοῦντα (namely as instructed by the κύριος).

For the sense, we may compare also Matt. vii. 24 (Luke vi. 47), where the person ὅστις ἀκούει μου τοὺς λόγους καὶ ποιεῖ αὐτούς is represented as a wise builder whose house withstood the storm (and who, in that respect, might be regarded as μακάριος). His opposite, the hearer who does not obey, is otherwise described in Luke xii. 47: ὁ γνοὺς τὸ θέλημα τοῦ κυρίου αὐτοῦ καὶ μὴ . . . ποιήσας. Thus the significant vocabulary of the Johannine form of the saying, εἰδέναι (or γνῶναι), ποιεῖν, μακάριος, is to be found in sayings of similar purport in the Synoptics, though these terms are not all found in any one saying. We are clearly dealing with an idea fundamental to the tradition of the teaching of Jesus, which found various forms of

---

[1] Whereas the Synoptics have it also in the sublimated sense (Mark x. 45 and parallels).

expression.[1] Whether John's makarism derives from reminiscences of the other gospels, or from an independent stream of tradition, the data do not enable us to say with certainty, but at least there is no clear evidence of literary dependence, and it is significant that there are contacts between the Johannine passage and *several* distinct Synoptic passages.

(*b*) John xx. 29:

Μακάριοι οἱ μὴ ἰδόντες καὶ πιστεύσαντες.

I here adduce the other Johannine makarism. It has no Synoptic parallel, and indeed is so characteristic of the doctrine of this gospel[2] that it would be reasonable to regard it as a coinage of the evangelist. Yet if it has no proper Synoptic parallel, there is a saying to which its thought seems to be intimately related:

Matt. xiii. 16:   Ὑμῶν δὲ μακάριοι οἱ ὀφθαλμοὶ ὅτι βλέπουσιν.

Luke x. 23:   Μακάριοι οἱ ὀφθαλμοὶ οἱ βλέποντες ἃ βλέπετε.

Here we have a makarism pronounced upon those who see; John seems to say, 'No: blessed are those who do not see—but have faith!' The *Sitz im Leben*, therefore, of the Johannine saying is the situation of the Church after the resurrection (compare 1 Pet. i. 8 ὃν οὐκ ἰδόντες ἀγαπᾶτε), whereas the Synoptic form makes sense only in the setting of the historic Ministry of Jesus.

We might easily believe that the evangelist had before him the saying reported in Matthew and Luke, whether or not he found it in those writings. But there is perhaps something more to be said. The makarism in John is almost immediately preceded by the saying,

John xx. 27:   Μὴ γίνου ἄπιστος ἀλλὰ πιστός.

Neither of these adjectives is found elsewhere in the Fourth Gospel. In Matthew and Luke, on the other hand, there is a parable which turns upon the difference between the πιστός and the ἄπιστος (Matt. xxiv. 45–51, Luke xii. 42–6: Luke alone actually has the adjective ἄπιστος, but the contrast with the πιστός is implicit in Matthew). A saying such as that of John xx. 27 might well have occurred as the 'moral' of such a parable, just as (in the immediate context, Matt. xxiv. 44, Luke xii. 40) the maxim,

[1] Akin to this is the maxim in John xiv. 23, ἐάν τις ἀγαπᾷ με τὸν λόγον μου τηρήσει, where the language (ἀγαπᾶν of the relation of disciple to Master, and λόγον τηρεῖν) is thoroughly Johannine, but the sentiment is similar to that expressed (negatively) in Luke vi. 46, τί με καλεῖτε Κύριε Κύριε καὶ οὐ ποιεῖτε ἃ λέγω;
[2] See *Interpretation*, pp. 185–6.

καὶ ὑμεῖς γίνεσθε ἕτοιμοι, is the 'moral' of the parable of the unready householder whose house was burgled. Further, there are passages in the Synoptics where Jesus reproaches his disciples for lack of faith: Mark iv. 40: τί δειλοί ἐστε οὕτως; πῶς οὐκ ἔχετε πίστιν; Matt. xiv. 31: ὀλιγόπιστε εἰς τί ἐδίστασας; Here again, the Johannine saying would have been the simplest and most concise way of expressing the idea.

The conclusion would appear to be that in xx. 27 John has reported a saying which, in one form or another, but nowhere in so concise a form as here, is deeply embedded in the gospel record, and that in xx. 29 he has given to it a twist in the direction of his distinctive theology, and coined a makarism after traditional models. Whether the saying in xx. 27 was derived from reminiscences of Synoptic passages or from independent tradition, we have no means of saying.

(viii) John xii. 47:

οὐκ ἦλθον ἵνα κρίνω τὸν κόσμον
ἀλλ' ἵνα σώσω τὸν κόσμον.

Compare Luke ix. 56 (some MSS. and versions):[1]

ὁ γὰρ υἱὸς τοῦ ἀνθρώπου οὐκ ἦλθεν ψυχὰς ἀνθρώπων ἀπολέσαι
ἀλλὰ σῶσαι.

There is a striking agreement between these passages in form and, broadly, in purport, in spite of verbal differences. The alternation between 'Son of Man' and the first person singular is too common in the gospels to need illustration. The form of pronouncement, ἦλθον with the infinitive of purpose or an equivalent ἵνα-clause, is one of the most widely established forms in which the sayings of Jesus are transmitted. It will be worth while to exhibit examples, from the Synoptic Gospels, the Fourth Gospel, and apocryphal Gospels (the Gospel according to the Egyptians, the Ebionite Gospel, and the 'unknown gospel' of Egerton Papyrus 2).

Luke xix. 10: ἦλθεν ὁ υἱὸς τοῦ ἀνθρώπου ζητῆσαι καὶ σῶσαι τὸ ἀπολωλός.[2]
Luke xii. 49: πῦρ ἦλθον βαλεῖν ἐπὶ τὴν γῆν.

[1] So (with slight variants) K, M, Π, Θ, 1, 13 etc., several MSS. of Old Latin and Vulgate, Syriac (cur. pesh. hcl.), Cyprian. The question whether the passage is 'genuine', in the sense of forming part of the text of Luke as it left the author's hand, is for our present purpose not relevant. In all probability it entered the text (at whatever stage) from floating oral tradition, and is authentic evidence for the form and contents of the latter. Other 'interpolations' no doubt had a similar source, such as the Bezan insertion at Luke vi. 5, about the man who worked on the sabbath, not to speak of the *pericopé adulterae* in MSS. of John and Luke.

[2] This is similar in purport to Luke ix. 56, but widely different in form. There is not the least reason to suppose that ix. 56 was derived from xix. 10.

Matt. x. 35:　ἦλθον διχάσαι ἄνθρωπον κατὰ τοῦ πατρὸς αὐτοῦ.

John x. 10:　ἐγὼ ἦλθον ἵνα ζωὴν ἔχωσιν.[1]

John xii. 46:　φῶς εἰς τὸν κόσμον ἐλήλυθα ἵνα πᾶς ὁ πιστεύων εἰς ἐμὲ ἐν τῇ σκοτίᾳ μὴ μείνῃ.

Ev. Ebion.　ἦλθον καταλῦσαι τὰς θυσίας.

Ev. Aegypt.　ἦλθον καταλῦσαι τὰ ἔργα τῆς θηλείας.

Matt. v. 17:　μὴ νομίσητε ὅτι ἦλθον καταλῦσαι τὸν νόμον ἢ τοὺς προφήτας.

Matt. x. 34a:　μὴ νομίσητε ὅτι ἦλθον βαλεῖν εἰρήνην ἐπὶ τὴν γῆν.[2]

Pap. Eg. 2:　μὴ δοκεῖτε ὅτι ἦλθον κατηγορῆσαι ὑμῶν πρὸς τὸν πατέρα μου.[3]

Mark ii. 17:　οὐκ ἦλθον καλέσαι δικαίους ἀλλὰ ἁμαρτωλούς (and parallels).

Mark x. 45:　ὁ υἱὸς τοῦ ἀνθρώπου οὐκ ἦλθεν διακονηθῆναι ἀλλὰ διακονῆσαι (and parallels).

Matt. x. 34b:　οὐκ ἦλθον βαλεῖν εἰρήνην ἀλλὰ μάχαιραν.

John xii. 47:　οὐ γὰρ ἦλθον ἵνα κρίνω τὸν κόσμον ἀλλὰ ἵνα σώσω τὸν κόσμον.

Luke ix. 56:　ὁ γὰρ υἱὸς τοῦ ἀνθρώπου οὐκ ἦλθεν ψυχὰς ἀνθρώπων ἀπολέσαι ἀλλὰ σῶσαι.

The last five of these passages, four drawn from the Synoptics and one from the Fourth Gospel, agree in the form οὐκ ἦλθον...ἀλλά, which was evidently well established in various branches of the tradition. John seems here to have rewritten a traditional saying in his own terms—κρίνειν and κόσμος being among his favourite words. It is more thoroughly rewritten in iii. 17, οὐ γὰρ ἀπέστειλεν ὁ θεὸς τὸν υἱὸν εἰς τὸν κόσμον ἵνα κρίνῃ τὸν κόσμον, ἀλλ' ἵνα σωθῇ ὁ κόσμος δι' αὐτοῦ. In that context it appears as an integral part of an elaborate exposition of the distinctive Johannine theology, but in view of John xii. 47 and the Lucan parallel we seem justified in recognizing here an element in the traditional basis for

[1] John prefers the ἵνα-construction, but he likes to strengthen it by the addition of εἰς τοῦτο or the like: xviii. 37, εἰς τοῦτο ἐλήλυθα εἰς τὸν κόσμον ἵνα μαρτυρήσω τῇ ἀληθείᾳ, ix. 39, εἰς κρίμα ἐγὼ εἰς τὸν κόσμον τοῦτον ἦλθον ἵνα οἱ μὴ βλέποντες βλέπωσιν κ.τ.λ. Similarly of John the Baptist, i. 7: ἦλθεν εἰς μαρτυρίαν ἵνα μαρτυρήσῃ περὶ τοῦ φωτός. The construction ἔρχεσθαι cum inf. he uses only once, iv. 7, ἔρχεται γυνὴ ἐκ τῆς Σαμαρίας ἀντλῆσαι ὕδωρ. In this preference for the construction with ἵνα at the expense of the infinitive, as in some other traits of language, John is well on the line of development towards Modern Greek, and farther advanced on that line than some other N.T. writers (see Geldart, *The Modern Greek Language*, appendix I, on the Greek of the Gospels of St John and St Luke, pp. 179–88).

[2] For this, Luke xii. 51 has δοκεῖτε ὅτι εἰρήνην παρεγενόμην δοῦναι ἐν τῇ γῇ;

[3] This appears to be a modification of John v. 45, μὴ δοκεῖτε ὅτι ἐγὼ κατηγορήσω ὑμῶν πρὸς τὸν πατέρα. The apocryphal form is certainly secondary, for ἦλθον would imply 'I came into this world', but the accusation of the unbelieving Jews before the judgement seat of God would not naturally be conceived as in 'this world'. But note how readily the writer slips into the usual form, ἔρχεσθαι cum inf.

that theology. That it came to John out of the written Gospel according to Luke is less likely than that he took it from oral tradition. In any case we have once again an instructive example of the way in which our evangelist weaves a traditional saying into the fabric of his composition.

(ix) John iii. 18:

> Ὁ πιστεύων εἰς αὐτὸν οὐ κρίνεται·
> ὁ μὴ πιστεύων ἤδη κέκριται.

Compare [Mark] xvi. 16:

> Ὁ πιστεύσας (καὶ βαπτισθεὶς) σωθήσεται,
> ὁ δὲ ἀπιστήσας κατακριθήσεται.

I have elsewhere[1] argued that the 'Longer Ending' of Mark is in part derived from Matthew and Luke, and in part based upon unwritten tradition, but that it shows no clear evidence of derivation from John, though such derivation could not be categorically denied. That the passages here quoted are variants of the same saying seems clear, whatever their relation to one another may be. In purport they are virtually identical, and they are moulded in the same form. In language John iii. 18 shows definitely Johannine traits. The verb κρίνειν is frequent in the Fourth Gospel, and stands for one of its most characteristic ideas—an idea compendiously expressed here: that the 'eschatological' judgement of the world is made present in the Ministry of Jesus Christ (ἤδη κέκριται), and effected through the varying response of men to that Ministry (κέκριται ὅτι μὴ πεπίστευκεν κ.τ.λ.).[2] In John κρίνειν can bear the meaning of κατακρίνειν, which never occurs in the genuine text of Mark, but is here used by pseudo-Mark. The saying therefore falls into line with several others that we have examined, where similarity, or identity, of form and purport goes with characteristic differences of language. That John borrowed directly from pseudo-Mark is unlikely; that pseudo-Mark borrowed from John is possible. If so, then we should have a clear case where the Johannine doctrine of an historical judgement of mankind has been altered into a prediction of coming judgement. But it seems probable rather that both writers are following a current tradition, the more so since the saying we are considering is in pseudo-Mark closely connected with what may be described as a standard account of the appearance of

---

[1] See my essay, 'The Appearances of the Risen Christ', in *Studies in the Gospels, Essays in Memory of R. H. Lightfoot*, ed. D. E. Nineham, pp. 31–2.

[2] See *Interpretation*, pp. 208–12.

the Risen Christ, leading to a charge to his apostles.[1] It is perhaps not too speculative to find further traces of this tradition in the context of John iii. 18. The 'standard' account of the appearance in John is in xx. 19–23, where I have already noted contacts with various elements in the Synoptic tradition.[2] There the charge to apostles takes the form, καθὼς ἀπέσταλκέν με ὁ πατὴρ κἀγὼ πέμπω ὑμᾶς. The mission of the apostles is a counterpart of the sending of Christ. In [Mark] xvi. 16, the mission of the apostles to the world is the prelude to the 'eschatological' judgement upon men. In John iii. 18, the sending of Christ into the world is the occasion of the 'historical' judgement upon men. There is a real parallel between [Mark] xvi. 15–16: πορευθέντες εἰς τὸν κόσμον ἅπαντα κηρύξατε...ὁ πιστεύσας σωθήσεται, ὁ δὲ ἀπιστήσας κατακριθήσεται, and John iii. 17–18: ἀπέστειλεν ὁ θεὸς τὸν υἱὸν εἰς τὸν κόσμον...ἵνα σωθῇ ὁ κόσμος...ὁ πιστεύων εἰς αὐτὸν οὐ κρίνεται, ὁ μὴ πιστεύων ἤδη κέκριται. That John should have placed a saying normally associated with the post-resurrection appearance of Christ in the context of his Ministry would be consistent with his outlook.[3]

(x) John iii. 3:

Ἀμὴν ἀμὴν λέγω σοι, ἐὰν μή τις γεννηθῇ ἄνωθεν οὐ δύναται ἰδεῖν τὴν βασιλείαν τοῦ θεοῦ.

iii. 5:

Ἀμὴν ἀμὴν λέγω σοι, ἐὰν μή τις γεννηθῇ ἐξ ὕδατος καὶ πνεύματος οὐ δύναται εἰσελθεῖν εἰς τὴν βασιλείαν τοῦ θεοῦ.

Compare Matt. xviii. 3:

Ἀμὴν λέγω ὑμῖν, ἐὰν μὴ στραφῆτε καὶ γένησθε ὡς τὰ παιδία οὐ μὴ εἰσέλθητε εἰς τὴν βασιλείαν τῶν οὐρανῶν.

This is a passage which contains one of the most characteristic Johannine doctrines, a doctrine which is not represented in the Synoptic Gospels, nor elsewhere in the New Testament except in 1 Pet. i. 3, 23 and perhaps Jas. i. 18. It has no roots in the Old Testament, nor any very convincing analogy in Jewish thought of the period.[4] On the other hand its affinities with Hellenistic thought are clear.[5] And yet in form the saying is singularly close to Matt. xviii. 3, even down to the introductory formula, ἀμὴν (ἀμὴν) λέγω σοι (ὑμῖν). Moreover this is the only passage in which John

---

[1] See *Studies in the Gospels*, pp. 11–13.   [2] See above, pp. 143–5.

[3] See *Interpretation*, pp. 397–8.

[4] See S.–B., *ad loc.*

[5] See *Interpretation*, pp. 303–5; also my commentary on the Johannine Epistles, pp. 67–9, 74–7.

uses the expression, ἡ βασιλεία τοῦ θεοῦ, which is so frequent in the Synoptics. The explanation that lies to hand is that John has taken over the aphorism from Matthew and adapted it to his own purposes; and this might be the true explanation in this instance. Yet there are some features which may give us pause. In the first place, Matt. xviii. 3 has the expression ἡ βασιλεία τῶν οὐρανῶν, which occurs at least 33 times in the First Gospel, while ἡ βασιλεία τοῦ θεοῦ occurs at most four times.[1] In Mark and Luke the latter expression is found everywhere. Yet John must have followed Matthew if he followed any of the Synoptics, for the partial parallels to this saying in Mark and Luke[2] are quite unlike both Matthew and John. Further, while the expression, εἰσελθεῖν εἰς τὴν βασιλείαν, occurs six times in Matthew, he never uses the expression, ἰδεῖν τὴν βασιλείαν,[3] which occurs here as an alternative. Once again, therefore, as in some other instances, it turns out that if John borrowed at all he must have had two or more gospels before him. Since we have seen good reason to suppose that he had access to an alternative body of tradition, this saying also may have reached him in a form very similar to, but not identical with, that which reached Matthew. But in this instance the evidence does not justify a firm conclusion. In any case John is building upon earlier tradition, whether it reached him orally or through the other gospels. But it is unlikely that his doctrine of rebirth was developed directly out of this saying.[4]

(xi) John x. 15:

> γινώσκει με ὁ πατὴρ κἀγὼ γινώσκω τὸν πατέρα.

This saying, which in its context belongs to the central core of Johannine theology,[5] is nevertheless similar both in form and in content to a saying

---

[1] In Matt. xix. 24 there are variant readings, and sporadically elsewhere.

[2] Mark x. 15, Luke xviii. 17.

[3] This use of ἰδεῖν is probably a Semitism, representing the Hebrew רָאָה with the wide meaning 'experience'; similarly John iii. 36 has ὄψεται ζωήν, and Luke ii. 26 ἰδεῖν θάνατον, and ii. 30 εἶδον τὸ σωτήριον (echoing Isa. xl. 5, quoted Luke iii. 6). Mark (ix. i) has ἕως ἂν ἴδωσιν τὴν βασιλείαν τοῦ θεοῦ ἐληλυθυῖαν ἐν δυνάμει, but the additional participial clause means a certain shift of meaning in the verb.

[4] Except in the sense that the allusion to παιδία, understood as ἀρτιγέννητα βρέφη (1 Pet. ii. 2, with a side reference, perhaps, to the rabbinic saying, 'The proselyte is like a new-born child'), offered a point of attachment for the doctrine of new birth. But the true background of that doctrine, both in primitive Christian thought and in the wider environment, is different, see *Interpretation*, *loc. cit.*

[5] For the place of the idea of 'knowledge' of God in Johannine theology, see *Interpretation*, pp. 151–69. For its Hellenistic affinities see the classical discussion in

which appears in Matthew and in Luke, in slightly different versions, which, according to what most critics regard as the best attested text, read as follows:

Matt. xi. 27	Luke x. 22
οὐδεὶς ἐπιγινώσκει τὸν υἱόν	οὐδεὶς γινώσκει τίς ἐστιν ὁ υἱός
εἰ μὴ ὁ πατήρ,	εἰ μὴ ὁ πατήρ,
οὐδὲ τὸν πατέρα τις ἐπιγινώσκει	καὶ τίς ἐστιν ὁ πατήρ
εἰ μὴ ὁ υἱός	εἰ μὴ ὁ υἱός

In both gospels the MSS. show variant readings, with some amount of assimilation between the two. Further, the saying is often quoted by early writers in terms which agree exactly with the MS. text of neither gospel.[1] This is not the place to discuss the complicated textual problems that arise. But it is on all accounts probable that the variants are not always due to simple manuscript corruption, but afford evidence that the aphorism, like other important and fundamental sayings, was handed down through several different channels of tradition, and that verbal variations arose in the course of oral transmission, without destroying the form or distorting the general purport. If that is so, it is not necessary to attempt to account for the similarities and differences between John and the Synoptics by any theory of literary dependence. John certainly has supplied the aphorism with a context which gives it a special theological colouring. But even in its Synoptic version it has been felt to be curiously 'Johannine'—'a meteorite out of the Johannine heaven', as it has been called—much as in no. x the single occurrence of the expression 'the Kingdom of God' has seemed almost an erratic block of 'Synoptic' material in the Fourth Gospel. The two taken together may aptly illustrate the theme which has been emerging ever more clearly in this investigation—that behind both John and the Synoptics lies a solid body of common tradition, variously exploited by different evangelists. In any

Norden, *Agnostos Theos*. I may observe in passing that the idea of 'knowledge' in the Qumran literature, which is claimed as the direct antecedent of the Johannine doctrine, belongs to a widely different climate of thought (see W. D. Davies, 'Knowledge in the Dead Sea Scrolls and Matthew xi. 25–30', *Harvard Theological Review*, XLVI, 3, July 1953, reprinted in *Christian Origins and Judaism* (Darton, Longman and Todd, 1962)).

[1] The most striking differences are the use of ἔγνω for (ἐπι)γινώσκει and the transposition of clauses. Most commentators have discussed the textual problem (a useful summary in McNeile *ad* Matt. xi. 27, and valuable material in Merx's discussion *ad loc.*; see also Norden, *op. cit.* pp. 277–308), generally in the sense of determining the original text of the canonical gospels. For our present purpose the textual variation is important rather as evidence for varieties of tradition.

case the saying we are now considering belongs to the earliest strain of tradition to which we can hope to penetrate, since it can be traced to the period before the formation of the common source (whether oral or written) of Matthew and Luke (Q), and the evidence suggests that before any written record of it appeared it had developed variant forms, three of which appear independently in Matthew, Luke and John, while others appear in ancient versions and patristic citations. As with other sayings we have examined, John has once again deftly woven traditional material into the fabric of his discourse, but without transforming it beyond recognition.[1]

I now subjoin two sayings in which the aphoristic form is absent or disguised in one or other of the gospels, but which nevertheless show such striking affinity that a common traditional basis seems probable.

(xii) John xvii. 2:

Ἔδωκας αὐτῷ [namely τῷ υἱῷ] ἐξουσίαν πάσης σαρκός.

Compare Matt. xxviii. 18:

Ἐδόθη μοι πᾶσα ἐξουσία ἐν οὐρανῷ καὶ ἐπὶ τῆς γῆς.

In the Fourth Gospel this saying forms part of a passage in which Johannine idiosyncrasies of thought and language are particularly strongly marked.[2] The expression, καθὼς ἔδωκας αὐτῷ ἐξουσίαν πάσης σαρκός, is reminiscent of the close of the hymn in *Poimandres* (*C.H.* I. 32): καθὼς παρέδωκας αὐτῷ (namely τῷ Ἀνθρώπῳ) τὴν πᾶσαν ἐξουσίαν. The *prima facie* suggestion is that we have here a piece of Johannine composition. Yet its affinities with the Matthaean passage are manifest.[3] Then shall we say that John has rewritten the phrase from Matthew in the idiom which

---

[1] On the general background of this saying see W. L. Knox's remarks, *Sources of the Synoptic Gospels*, II, 140–1, with which I heartily agree.

[2] In xvii. 1–5 we have ἐλήλυθεν ἡ ὥρα, δοξάζειν (four times), ζωὴ αἰώνιος, γινώσκειν θεόν, ἀληθινός, ἔργον τελειοῦν, as well as ὃ δέδωκας αὐτῷ, an expression which in varying forms occurs in several contexts, with an ambiguity which is perhaps deliberate; cf. vi. 37, 39, x. 29, xvii. 11, 12, 24. All these have a strongly Johannine flavour.

[3] The form indeed is not identical, since the passive verb has been replaced by the second person of the active, as the context demands, but the difference is not vital, and in meaning the two passages are closely similar. The view that the Johannine ἔδωκας αὐτῷ ἐξουσίαν πάσης σαρκός is the equivalent of the Synoptic πάντα μοι παρεδόθη ὑπὸ τοῦ πατρός μου (Matt. xi. 27, Luke x. 22) cannot be maintained; the παράδοσις of the Synoptic saying is a matter of the revelation of truth, not of delegated authority.

he shares with Hellenistic authors? Perhaps so; yet there are certain considerations that should give us pause. The use of σάρξ as a collective noun meaning 'mankind'[1] is not found elsewhere either in the Fourth Gospel itself[2] or in Hellenistic writings with which it has affinity. It is in fact exclusively biblical,[3] and the expression πᾶσα σάρξ is very frequent in the LXX as a rendering of כָּל־בָּשָׂר. Of eight occurrences in the New Testament five are quotations from the Old Testament. It is therefore a sufficiently uncommon locution in any New Testament writer to draw attention to itself,[4] and especially in an author like John. The expression ἐξουσία πάσης σαρκός does not occur in the Old Testament. The nearest approximation to it is in the part of Daniel for which no Hebrew original is extant, Bel and the Dragon, 5 (LXX and Theodotion): τὸν (ζῶντα) θεὸν τὸν κτίσαντα τὸν οὐρανὸν καὶ τὴν γῆν καὶ ἔχοντα πάσης σαρκὸς κυρείαν. The word κυρεία (also κυριεία and κυρία) is a synonym for ἐξουσία. In Dan. xi. 3, 4 (5) it renders מָשַׁל; outside the Book of Daniel מֶמְשָׁלָה is frequently rendered ἐξουσία.[5] The difference therefore between ἐξουσία and κυρεία is not substantial. The actual phrase ἐδόθη ἐξουσία occurs in the LXX version of Dan. vii. 14, where the investiture of the Son of Man is described: ἐδόθη αὐτῷ ἐξουσία (שָׁלְטָן) καὶ τιμὴ βασιλική, καὶ πάντα τὰ ἔθνη τῆς γῆς κατὰ γένη καὶ πᾶσα δόξα αὐτῷ λατρεύουσα· καὶ ἡ ἐξουσία αὐτοῦ ἐξουσία αἰώνιος. The version of Theodotion runs, αὐτῷ ἐδόθη ἡ ἀρχὴ καὶ ἡ τιμὴ καὶ ἡ βασιλεία, καὶ πάντες οἱ λαοὶ φυλαὶ καὶ γλῶσσαι δουλεύσουσιν αὐτῷ· ἡ ἐξουσία αὐτοῦ ἐξουσία αἰώνιος. It has been widely recognized that behind this scene of the enthronement of the Man over the Beasts lies a good deal of traditional creation-imagery, and that the sovereignty conferred upon the Man is a fulfilment of the grant of lordship over created beings which is a part of the creation story in Gen. i. 28 (compare Ps. viii. 7–8), and which is repeated in the covenant with Noah after the Deluge (Gen. ix. 1–17) (a passage in which the expression πᾶσα σάρξ, in its widest sense, recurs like a refrain). These passages

---

[1] Sometimes it includes also the animal creation, e.g. Gen. vii. 15–16, viii. 17.

[2] When John means 'mankind', he says κόσμος (iii. 16, iv. 42, viii. 26, etc.), though in other passages the same term has to bear a sinister meaning.

[3] I.e. it is found only in translations of Hebrew (or Aramaic) documents or in writings influenced by them.

[4] Only in Mark xiii. 20 (Matt. xxiv. 22) and 1 Cor. i. 29, apart from our present passage, is it used by N.T. writers independently of the O.T., and both of these are fairly obvious imitations of O.T. language.

[5] Outside Daniel, and 2 Macc. viii. 35, the only occurrence of κυρεία in the LXX is Isa. xl. 10, where זְרֹעוֹ מֹשְׁלָה לּוֹ is paraphrased, ὁ βραχίων μετὰ κυρίας.

in Genesis are among the sources of the myth of the heavenly Ἄνθρωπος as it appears in *Poimandres*.[1]

With this background in mind, we may make a fresh approach to John xvii. 2. The sentence, ἔδωκας αὐτῷ ἐξουσίαν πάσης σαρκός, may fairly be said to be an epitome, entirely in biblical language, of the vision of the enthronement of the Son of Man in Dan. vii.[2] The influence which this passage has exerted on the New Testament is generally recognized. Its language is deeply impressed upon the gospel tradition,[3] including the fundamental text, Mark xiv. 62. John is therefore here in close contact with the most central and primitive elements in the tradition. The Matthaean form of the saying is affiliated to the same tradition, without any necessary direct link with John. His use of 'heaven and earth', where John has πᾶσα σάρξ, may look back to Matt. xi. 25, Κύριε τοῦ οὐρανοῦ καὶ τῆς γῆς.[4]

(xiii) John v. 30:

> οὐ ζητῶ τὸ θέλημα τὸ ἐμόν,
> ἀλλὰ τὸ θέλημα τοῦ πέμψαντός με.

vi. 38:

> (καταβέβηκα ἀπὸ τοῦ οὐρανοῦ)
> οὐχ ἵνα ποιῶ τὸ θέλημα τὸ ἐμόν,
> ἀλλὰ τὸ θέλημα τοῦ πέμψαντός με.

compare Luke xxii. 42:

> μὴ τὸ θέλημά μου ἀλλὰ τὸ σὸν γινέσθω.

In the other Synoptic Gospels the form is different. Mark xiv. 36 has, οὐ τί ἐγὼ θέλω ἀλλὰ τί σύ. Matt. xxvi. 39 has, similarly, οὐχ ὡς ἐγὼ θέλω ἀλλ' ὡς σύ, but he follows it up (verse 42) with γενηθήτω τὸ θέλημά σου, which may be an echo of his version of the Lord's prayer. It is clear that the Johannine version is nearer to the Lucan than the latter is to the other Synoptic versions, and the affinity of the two is unmistakable, even though

---

[1] For the relation between Genesis and *Poimandres* see my book, *The Bible and the Greeks*, pp. 145–69.

[2] Πᾶσα σάρξ is a perfect equivalent in brief for πάντες οἱ λαοὶ φυλαὶ καὶ γλῶσσαι.

[3] See my book, *According to the Scriptures*, pp. 67–70.

[4] As John is generally held to 'heighten the Christology' of the gospels, it is perhaps not irrelevant to observe that here, while Matthew attributes to Christ sovereignty in heaven as well as on earth, John speaks only of sovereignty over the human race. There was of course no idea in the author's mind of limiting the sovereignty—which makes it all the more certain that he could not have had the Matthaean form before him.

what is a prayer in Luke is a pronouncement in John. That either of these is derived from the other is possible but unlikely. Nor would it be easy to decide whether the pronouncement or the petition is more original. But that we have here an element in the central core of tradition cannot be reasonably doubted.[1] Comparison with no. xii illustrates the way in which identical material could pass from one form to another in the course of transmission. Here it is John who gives the saying in the form of pronouncement;[2] no. xii, on the contrary, is a pronouncement in the Synoptics and part of a prayer in John. And this may serve as a warning that, although we must give great weight to identity of form as a guide to the traditional basis of reported sayings, there may well be many places where this guidance is not available, but where nevertheless a common traditional basis is probable.

Finally, I will add a saying, unique in the Fourth Gospel, which in form has only a somewhat remote Synoptic parallel, with analogy rather than identity of meaning, but which is not without significance for our purpose.

(xiv) John iii. 8:

τὸ πνεῦμα ὅπου θέλει πνεῖ,
καὶ τὴν φωνὴν αὐτοῦ ἀκούεις,
ἀλλ᾽ οὐκ οἶδας
πόθεν ἔρχεται καὶ ποῦ ὑπάγει.

With this compare Mark iv. 27:

ὁ σπόρος βλαστᾷ καὶ μηκύνεται
ὡς οὐκ οἶδεν αὐτός·
αὐτομάτη ἡ γῆ καρποφορεῖ.

The underlying similarity of pattern would come out even more clearly if we took the liberty of transposing two clauses of Mark:

Mark	John
αὐτομάτη ἡ γῆ καρποφορεῖ	τὸ πνεῦμα ὅπου θέλει πνεῖ,
ὡς οὐκ οἶδεν αὐτός	ἀλλ᾽ οὐκ οἶδας . . . .

[1] It is instructive to observe how the same fundamental conception appears in other parts of the New Testament in widely different forms. Thus in Heb. x. 5–9 it is enforced by the citation of a *testimonium* from Ps. xxxix. 7–9, in Rom. xv. 3 by a citation from Ps. lxviii. 10 (where the very fact that the *testimonium* is somewhat far-fetched shows that the idea itself was not derived from scripture, but from a tradition which sought confirmation in scripture). Cf. what I have said about the *Pedilavium*, above, pp. 60–3. Where a trait is so deeply, so widely and so variously imprinted upon the New Testament writings, we have strong ground for believing it to be in the full sense historical.

[2] And note that in vi. 38 the pronouncement is moulded into a pattern analogous to the traditional ἦλθον-ἵνα type, though the verb καταβέβηκα is purely Johannine.

The Marcan passage is part of a parable; the Johannine may properly be described as a parabolic saying (*Bildwort*). The sentiment of both is identical: a wondering recognition of the spontaneity of natural processes,[1] and their inscrutability by the human mind. Any sort of dependence of one on the other is excluded, but are they not so deeply akin that we could believe them to have come, not only from the same common deposit of tradition, but originally from the same mind? John, *more suo*, has employed the aphorism in the service of one of his most characteristic doctrines, as, in the same context, he has employed a saying about entrance into the Kingdom of God.

---

[1] Πνεῦμα in this clause must be taken in its primary Greek sense = ἀὴρ κινού-μενος, i.e. the wind. But where a term ranges, as πνεῦμα does, by a process of continuous variation, through a wide field of meaning, two meanings which for us lie far apart may both be present to the mind of a writer, and John was certainly not so conscious as we are of the abrupt transition from the meaning 'wind' to the meaning 'spirit' (see *Interpretation*, pp. 213–16).

3. PARABOLIC FORMS

The parable, which in its various forms is so prominent, and so characteristic of the teaching of Jesus, in the Synoptic Gospels, is but feebly represented in the Fourth Gospel. The use of standing symbols for certain abstract ideas—light, water, bread, and the like—belongs to a different way of thinking from the realistic observation of nature and human life which supplies the material of the Synoptic parables.[1] We have noted one true example of a parabolic saying (*Bildwort*) which is comparable with those of the Synoptics—τὸ πνεῦμα ὅπου θέλει πνεῖ κ.τ.λ. (iii. 8). It would not, however, be true to say that parables do not occur, unless the term be restricted to instances where the material offered for illustration or analogy is presented in a continuous narrative, with the use of historic tenses (like the Sower, the Great Feast and the Prodigal Son). This may perhaps be regarded as the classical type of gospel parable. But there is no good reason for restricting the term so narrowly. It is equally applicable where the illustration or analogy is suggested by the description of a single scene, with the use of primary tenses (like the Children in the Market Place), or where a typical or recurrent incident in human experience is brought to mind by means of a compound sentence with ὅταν or ἐπάν in the protasis (like the Returning Demon, or the Marcan form of the Mustard Seed), or by means of a conditional sentence with εἰ, ἐάν in the protasis (like the Matthaean form of the Lost Sheep).[2] These are essentially parabolic just as much as the narrative form, and parables of this type are not altogether lacking in the Fourth Gospel.

(i) John xii. 24. The Grain of Wheat:

> Ἐὰν μὴ ὁ κόκκος τοῦ σίτου
> πεσὼν εἰς τὴν γῆν ἀποθάνῃ,
> αὐτὸς μόνος μένει·
> ἐὰν δὲ ἀποθάνῃ,
> πολὺν καρπὸν φέρει.

Here we have a description of a certain natural phenomenon, a phenomenon so constantly recurrent that it can be stated in the form of an 'observed invariable sequence' (which is what is popularly called a 'law of nature'): 'If A occurs, then B occurs.' The hypothetical form of

[1] See *Interpretation*, pp. 133–44.
[2] See *Parables of the Kingdom* (Nisbet, 1961), pp. 5–7, 15–18 ((Collins, 1961), pp. 16–18).

statement for describing such phenomena is not uncommon in the Synoptics, for example

Matt. v. 13:[1]   ἐὰν τὸ ἅλας μωρανθῇ...
               εἰς οὐδὲν ἰσχύει.

Mark iii. 24:   ἐὰν βασιλεία ἐφ' ἑαυτὴν μερισθῇ,
               οὐ δύναται σταθῆναι ἡ βασιλεία ἐκείνη.

In the latter place a second hypothetical sentence follows, but it does no more than repeat the same 'law', in terms of a household instead of a kingdom.

In the Matthaean form of the parable of the Lost Sheep (xviii. 12–13) we have repeated hypothetical clauses which carry the matter forward by stages to a conclusion:

Ἐὰν γένηταί τινι ἀνθρώπῳ ἑκατὸν πρόβατα καὶ πλανηθῇ ἓν ἐξ αὐτῶν,
οὐχὶ πορευθεὶς ζητεῖ τὸ πλανώμενον;
καὶ ἐὰν γένηται εὑρεῖν αὐτό,
ἀμὴν λέγω ὑμῖν ὅτι χαίρει ἐπ' αὐτῷ κ.τ.λ.[2]

In other cases the repeated hypothetical clauses may bring out a contrast instead of carrying forward a single process.[3] Thus, Matt. vi. 22–3:

Ἐὰν ᾖ ὁ ὀφθαλμός σου ἁπλοῦς,
ὅλον τὸ σῶμά σου φωτεινὸν ἔσται·
ἐὰν δὲ ὁ ὀφθαλμός σου πονηρὸς ᾖ,
ὅλον τὸ σῶμά σου σκοτεινὸν ἔσται.[4]

Formally, this is very close to John xii. 24. Nor does the imagery here employed lie outside the Synoptic range. If John speaks of a κόκκος σίτου,

---

[1] It seems that the Matthaean version (and in a less clear way the Lucan) gives the true apodosis, though the intervening phrase, ἐν τίνι ἁλισθήσεται; (= Mark ix. 59 ἐν τίνι αὐτὸ ἀρτύσετε;), is an apodosis of another kind.

[2] The Lucan form of this parable substitutes participles (ἔχων, ἀπολέσας, εὑρών) for the ἐάν-clauses, thus producing something more like a continuous narrative, which, however, being told in primary, not historic, tenses, emerges as a picture of something that happens repeatedly or customarily, and not a story of something that once happened. But the distinction is obviously one without a real difference.

[3] In the parable of the Faithful and Unfaithful Servants (Matt. xxiv. 45–51, Luke xii. 42–6) the first member of the antithesis has lost its conditional form, but the second member returns to the norm: ἐὰν δὲ εἴπῃ ὁ δοῦλος ἐκεῖνος κ.τ.λ.

[4] The truly parabolic character of this passage is somewhat obscured by those commentators who take as a clue to the meaning the use of the phrase ὀφθαλμὸς πονηρός (= עַיִן רַע) in the sense of 'envy'. No doubt ἐὰν ὁ ὀφθαλμός σου πονηρὸς ᾖ might mean 'if you are envious' (cf. Matt. xx. 15), but, to this, 'your *body* will be all dark' is no proper apodosis; envy darkens the *mind*, not the body. Nor does there seem to be any authority for giving to ἐὰν ὁ ὀφθαλμός σου ἁπλοῦς ᾖ the sense 'if you are generous' (even if, in certain places, the *context* may give to ἁπλοῦς a suggestion of generosity). It seems that the passage is a true parable: 'If your vision is single (e.g. not astigmatic) your whole body will be illumined, but if your vision

THE SAYINGS

the Synoptics speak of a κόκκος σινάπεως, and the Johannine πεσὼν εἰς τὴν γῆν may be regarded as only one more way of describing the phenomenon of sowing for which Mark has ὅταν σπαρῇ ἐπὶ τῆς γῆς, Matthew, λαβὼν ἔσπειρεν ἐν τῷ ἀγρῷ αὐτοῦ, and Luke, λαβὼν ἔβαλεν εἰς κῆπον ἑαυτοῦ.[1] The only phrase which seems to have a distinctively Johannine ring is the weighty αὐτὸς μόνος μένει (compare the pregnant use of μόνος in John viii. 16, 29, xvi. 32).

In the four parables here adduced as partial parallels from the Synoptics, it is instructive to note the different ways in which the application is suggested. In Matt. v. 13 the clue to the parable of Salt is given in the introductory words ὑμεῖς ἐστε τὸ ἅλας τῆς γῆς. In Mark iii. 26 the parables of the divided kingdom and the divided household are given an explicit application in a third parallel sentence: εἰ ὁ Σατανᾶς ἀνέστη ἐφ᾿ ἑαυτὸν, ἐμερίσθη καὶ οὐ δύναται στῆναι. In Matt. xviii. 14 the parable of the Lost Sheep is provided with a moral, 'Thus it is not the will of your Father in heaven that one of these little ones should perish'. Luke (xv. 7) supplies an entirely different 'moral'—strong evidence, this, that neither 'moral' is strictly inseparable from the parable in the history of its transmission. In Matt. vi. 23 the parable of the Eye has a kind of 'appendix' which is apparently intended to hint at its application, but does not in fact pass beyond the bodily imagery of the parable itself; nor does the slightly different 'appendix' in Luke xi. 35, which is elaborated in the following verse.

The Johannine parable of the Grain of Wheat is not provided, explicitly, with any 'moral'. In this it resembles a whole group of Synoptic parables.[2] It is, however, immediately followed by the saying, ὁ φιλῶν τὴν ψυχὴν αὐτοῦ ἀπολλύει αὐτήν κ.τ.λ., and it is clearly the intention of the evangelist that the parable shall be understood in this sense. The juxtaposition of a directly relevant non-parabolic saying as a clue to the application of a parable is a device found also in the Synoptics. As examples, we may take Mark iv. 22, following on the short parable of the Lamp (which in Matt. v. 15–16 is provided with an explicit application, while in Luke xi. 33–5 its

is diseased, your whole body will be dark.' The observation that defect of vision affects the whole of a man's normal bodily activities is a true one (though the Hebraic way of treating parts of the body as exercising individually, and even independently, the functions we associate with them, has determined the terms in which the picture is presented: the eye, through which we become aware of light, is regarded as itself the source of light). It is a 'law of nature', which the hearer is challenged to apply in the field of ethical experience.

[1] Note that in usage πεσεῖν is the passive of βαλεῖν.
[2] See *Parables of the Kingdom* (Nisbet, 1961), pp. 14–19 ((Collins, 1961), pp. 23–7).

juxtaposition with the parable of the Eye may be intended to suggest a clue to both);[1] Luke xi. 5–10, where the saying 'Ask and receive . . .' is appended, without comment, to the parable of the Friend at Midnight; perhaps Luke xii. 47–8, where a general maxim, παντὶ ᾧ ἐδόθη πολύ, πολὺ ӡητηθήσεται παρ' αὐτοῦ κ.τ.λ., is appended to a parabolic saying about slaves. The saying which in the Johannine passage we are examining is appended to the parable of the Grain of Wheat is one which occurs also in the Synoptics.[2]

It appears, therefore, that we have here a *pericopé* which in form, in the character of its imagery, and in the whole manner in which it is presented (apart from the suspiciously Johannine words μόνος μένει), associates itself closely with the tradition of parabolic teaching as we know it from the Synoptics. It would not be plausible to suggest that it was derived from any of the Synoptic parables, but it might well have been drawn from the same reservoir of tradition. That it fits the Johannine theology is undeniable; that it goes beyond what we find, explicitly, in the Synoptics is also true. Yet its association with the saying about 'loving' and 'hating' the ψυχή, which is Synoptic as well as Johannine, is entirely natural and convincing. The passage therefore raises in a pointed way the question which must always be at the back of our minds in this investigation: is it an over-ruling maxim that wherever we find teaching in the Fourth Gospel which goes beyond the Synoptics, it must *necessarily* be credited to the evangelist and denied to the earlier tradition? And if this assumption seems to be a begging of the question, is there, apart from it, any reason at all why such a passage as this, which by every formal test should belong to the common tradition, and associates itself quite naturally with parts of that tradition as known from the Synoptics, should not be accepted as representing an element in the tradition as primitive and authentic as anything which they contain, although for one reason or another they have not taken it up?

(ii) John xvi. 21. The Pains of Childbirth:

> Ἡ γυνὴ ὅταν τίκτῃ
> λύπην ἔχει,
> ὅτι ἦλθεν ἡ ὥρα αὐτῆς·
> ὅταν δὲ γεννήσῃ τὸ παιδίον
> οὐκέτι μνημονεύει τῆς θλίψεως διὰ τὴν χαράν,
> ὅτι ἐγεννήθη ἄνθρωπος εἰς τὸν κόσμον.

---

[1] The three evangelists would appear to have understood this parable in three different ways.

[2] See also above, pp. 338–43.

Here we have a formally balanced composition with two members, each consisting of a protasis and an apodosis, with an appended causal clause, of the form, 'When A occurs, B occurs, because C has occurred'. The structure is analogous to that of the parable of the Grain of Wheat. Like it, the present parable describes a recurrent situation in human experience; but whereas John xii. 24 deals with the kind of observed invariable sequence which we call a 'law' of nature, and the two members present contrasting possibilities of antecedent and consequent in the form of conditional sentences with ἐάν, John xvi. 21 presents two successive stages of a given situation, and the protases are temporal clauses with ὅταν.

There is a fairly close formal parallel in the Lucan parable of the Strong Man armed (Luke xi. 21–2).[1]

Ὅταν ὁ ἰσχυρὸς[2] καθωπλισμένος φυλάσσῃ τὴν ἑαυτοῦ αὐλήν,
ἐν εἰρήνῃ ἐστὶν τὰ ὑπάρχοντα αὐτοῦ·
ἐπὰν δὲ ἰσχυρότερος αὐτοῦ ἐπελθὼν νικήσῃ αὐτόν,
τὴν πανοπλίαν αὐτοῦ αἴρει...καὶ τὰ σκῦλα αὐτοῦ διαδίδωσιν.[3]

There is a partial parallel in the Marcan parable of the Seed growing secretly (iv. 26–9). The construction here is mixed, and the temporal clause, which might well have run, 'When a man has sown seed', has been absorbed into the formula 'The Kingdom of God is like...', to the hopeless detriment of the grammar. But in what should have been the second member the regular form returns:

ὅταν δὲ παραδοῖ ὁ καρπός
εὐθὺς ἀποστέλλει τὸ δρέπανον,
ὅτι παρέστηκεν ὁ θερισμός.

The Marcan *pericopé*, in fact, may be regarded as the wreckage of a regular structure of which the Johannine parable before us is a complete example.

It is clear, then, that in form this parable falls easily within a series well represented in the Synoptics. In language we recognize several apparently Johannine traits.

(a) Λύπη is a word which occurs only once in the Synoptics, and four times in John, but as all four are in this context (if we allow xvi. 6 to be part of the context) we cannot say with confidence whether the evangelist or his tradition is responsible for it.

---

[1] The corresponding parable in Mark iii. 27 is *formally* quite different.

[2] Note ὁ ἰσχυρός, like ἡ γυνή, of the typical figure.

[3] Luke has given a similar form to the parable of the Eye as Light of the Body, using ὅταν...ἐπὰν δέ, where Matthew, with superior logical propriety, has ἐάν... ἐὰν δέ.

(*b*) The phrase ἦλθεν (ἐληλύθει, ἥκει, ἔρχεται) ἡ ὥρα has a strongly Johannine ring (ii. 4, v. 25, 28, vii. 30, viii. 20, xii. 23, xiii. 1, xvi. 2, 4, 21, 25, 32, xvii. 1). In the Synoptics ἥκει (ἤγγικεν) ἡ ὥρα is found in one passage only, Mark xiv. 41, Matt. xxvi. 45. Especially characteristic of this gospel is the expression ἡ ὥρα μου, αὐτοῦ, denoting the predestined 'hour' when Christ is 'lifted up' or 'glorified' and His work 'finished'. The expression ἡ ὥρα αὐτῆς in xvi. 21 inevitably (and surely by design) recalls to the reader's mind the references to that fateful 'hour' which run through the gospel like a refrain. If ἡ ὥρα αὐτῆς were a current Greek expression for the crucial moment in childbirth (as a corresponding phrase is in English), then it might be possible to suppose that the theological use was derived from it, but I have found no evidence that it was so.[1] Indeed the Johannine use of ὥρα with a personal genitive of possession is sufficiently unusual for its frequent employment by this writer to constitute a stylistic idiosyncrasy.[2]

(*c*) The phrase εἰς τὸν κόσμον occurs 14 times in the Fourth Gospel. In the Synoptics this precise phrase does not occur, but in Mark xiv. 9 we have εἰς ὅλον τὸν κόσμον, and in [Mark] xvi. 15, εἰς τὸν κόσμον ἅπαντα.[3]

---

[1] In secular Greek a woman's ὥρα is the bloom of her youth, e.g. Aesch. *Supp* 996–7, ὑμᾶς δ᾽ ἐπαινῶ...ὥραν ἐχούσας τήνδ᾽ ἐπίστρεπτον βροτοῖς, and so also Philo, *De Spec. Leg.* I. 103 (γυναῖκας) πεπρακυίας τὴν ἰδίαν ὥραν.

[2] There is only one example in the N.T. outside the Fourth Gospel, Luke xxii. 53, αὕτη ἐστὶν ὑμῶν ἡ ὥρα. I have found no example in the LXX or in Philo (though τὴν ἰδίαν ὥραν in *De Spec. Leg.*, *loc. cit.*, might be held to imply a genitive), nor do L. and S. give any example. (In Plato, *Critias*, 113 D, εἰς ἀνδρὸς ὥραν ἡκούσης τῆς κόρης, the genitive is only an apparent exception, ἀνδρὸς ὥρα being equivalent to the very common γάμου ὥρα.) The genitive is almost invariably a *genitivus rei*, as in the N.T. ὥρα πειρασμοῦ (Rev. iii. 10), κρίσεως (Rev. xviii. 10—where it would also be possible to take ὥρα-κρίσεως as a unitary expression, with the personal genitive, = 'his hour-of-judgement'). Cf. Eg. Pap. 2, οὔπω ἐληλύθει αὐτοῦ ἡ ὥρα τῆς παραδόσεως.

[3] In the Marcan and pseudo-Marcan passages the expression is used with reference to world-wide missionary activity. A somewhat similar use is found in John viii. 26, ἃ ἤκουσα παρ᾽ αὐτοῦ ταῦτα λαλῶ εἰς τὸν κόσμον, and a more closely similar use in 1 John iv. 1, 2 John 7. Elsewhere in the Fourth Gospel the phrase is used of entrance on the human scene; in xviii. 37 ἐλήλυθα εἰς τὸν κόσμον is in parallelism with γεγέννημαι, and the use in the present passage, ἐγεννήθη εἰς τὸν κόσμον, is in line with this. It corresponds to the use of the equivalent Hebrew expression in rabbinic writings (באה העולם). For the sake of completeness I add that in the rest of the N.T. the expression occurs only in 1 John iv. 9 (of the 'sending' of Christ, as John iii. 17, xvii. 18), 1 Tim. i. 15, Heb. x. 5 (of the entry of Christ into the human scene), 1 Tim. vi. 7 (of birth), and Rom. v. 12 (of the appearance of sin among men). The expression is therefore strongly Johannine, though not exclusively so.

Linguistically, therefore, the passage has a marked Johannine colouring.

Like many parables in the Synoptic Gospels the parable of the Pains of Childbirth is provided with a conclusion applying it to the situation of the hearers:

> καὶ ὑμεῖς οὖν νῦν μὲν λύπην ἔχετε,
> πάλιν δὲ ὄψομαι ὑμᾶς καὶ χαρήσεται ὑμῶν ἡ καρδία,
> καὶ τὴν χαρὰν ὑμῶν οὐδεὶς αἴρει ἀφ' ὑμῶν.

There is in the Synoptics no standard form for the application of parables, but the method here adopted has parallels: namely the repetition of the central idea of the parable (it may be, as here, in the same or similar words), transferred from the personages of the story to the auditors, sometimes, as here, with the use of the emphatic pronoun. Here we have

> λύπην ἔχει, answered by λύπην ἔχετε
> διὰ τὴν χαράν, answered by χαρήσεται ὑμῶν ἡ καρδία.

With this compare Mark xiii. 34–5,

> ἐνετείλατο ἵνα γρηγορῇ / γρηγορεῖτε οὖν.

Matt. xxiv. 43–4,

> εἰ ᾔδει ὁ οἰκοδεσπότης, ἐγρηγόρησεν ἄν / διὰ τοῦτο καὶ ὑμεῖς . . . .

Luke xiv. 31–3,

> τίς βασιλεύς . . . οὐχὶ καθίσας πρῶτον βουλεύσεται εἰ δυνατός ἐστιν;
> οὕτως οὖν πᾶς ἐξ ὑμῶν . . . οὐ δύναται εἶναί μου μαθητής.

Luke xvii. 9–10,

> μὴ ἔχει χάριν τῷ δούλῳ; / οὕτως καὶ ὑμεῖς λέγετε ὅτι Δοῦλοι ἀχρεῖοί ἐσμεν.

It is unnecessary to multiply examples. It is clear that the application in this passage does not differ essentially from Synoptic practice. The form is indeed here expanded beyond the compass of some of our typical cases, but so are some of the Synoptic examples in different ways.

So much for the form; what of the content? We observe, first, that there is a veiled allusion to a passage in the Old Testament, which offers a clue to the general context within which the parable is to be understood: Isa. lxvi. 7–17. Here Jerusalem is a mother in travail (ὠδίνουσα) who bears a son (verse 7); there follows a cry of joy, εὐφράνθητι 'Ιερουσαλήμ... χάρητε ἅμα αὐτῇ χαρᾷ πάντες οἱ ἀγαπῶντες αὐτήν...ὄψεσθε καὶ χαρήσεται ἡ καρδία ὑμῶν (verse 14). Similarly, in the parable of the Seed Growing Secretly in Mark iv. 29 there is an allusion to Joel iii. 13, in that of the Mustard Seed in Mark iv. 32 to Ezek. xvii. 23, and in the same parable in Matt. xiii. 32 to Dan. iv. 9 *sqq.* (Theodotion), not to speak of the plain echo of Isa. v. 1–2 in Mark xii. 1, introducing the parable of the Wicked Husbandmen. In the light of this allusion to Isa. lxvi, our present parable is to be understood within the general context of the idea of the tribulation of God's people, and the joy which their salvation brings, and the καὶ ὑμεῖς brings the disciples themselves into this picture. Beyond this there is no attempt to interpret details of the parable, for example to identify the mother or the child. In the Synoptics, the term ὠδῖνες is applied to the eschatological tribulation preceding the advent of the Son of Man (Mark xiii. 8=חֶבְלוֹ שֶׁל־מָשִׁיחַ). If this parable had appeared, for example, in Matthew the joy 'because a Man is born into the world' might well have been understood of the joy of believers at the second advent of the Lord. It would be entirely in accord with the general position taken by the Fourth Evangelist that the messianic woes and the joy attending the final salvation of the people of God should be understood in terms of the passion and resurrection of Christ.[1] To this extent we must recognize the hand of the evangelist, who has woven the parable, with its application, into a passage in which its keywords—λύπη, χαρά, ὄψεσθαι—recur again and again. Yet he seems to be working upon material which belongs to the common tradition, both by its pattern and by its Old Testament basis, reinterpreting it, and to some extent rewriting it, in accord with his own theological tendency. Whether in fact this tendency is to be attributed entirely to the evangelist himself, or whether the line of tradition he follows gave him a starting point, is a question which should not be decided out of hand.[2]

(iii) John xi. 9–10. The Benighted Traveller:

> Οὐχὶ δώδεκα ὧραί εἰσιν τῆς ἡμέρας;
> ἐάν τις περιπατῇ ἐν τῇ ἡμέρᾳ, οὐ προσκόπτει,
> ὅτι τὸ φῶς τοῦ κόσμου τούτου βλέπει·
> ἐὰν δέ τις περιπατῇ ἐν τῇ νυκτί, προσκόπτει,
> ὅτι τὸ φῶς οὐκ ἔστιν ἐν αὐτῷ.

This saying, embedded in the dialogue introductory to the Raising of Lazarus, has a certain parabolic character. It consists of two elements: (*a*) a rhetorical question, and (*b*) an antithetic structure of two balanced conditional sentences.

(*a*) The rhetorical question is a constant feature of the tradition of the sayings of Jesus. Parables or parabolic sayings are frequently introduced

---

[1] See *Interpretation*, pp. 395–6.   [2] See further below, pp. 430–1.

with a question, or even framed in the form of a question.¹ Most germane
to the passage we are considering are instances of the rhetorical question
as a more forcible way of putting an affirmation or negation, as the case
may be. Thus, in the parable of the Strong Man Bound, Matthew gives
πῶς δύναταί τις εἰσελθεῖν...; that is, of course no one can, as Mark has
it, οὐ δύναται οὐδείς. In the parable of the Lamp under the Bushel,
Mark has the rhetorical question, μήτι ἔρχεται ὁ λύχνος; where the other
two have the categorical negative. In the parabolic saying about the Sons
of the Bridechamber (Mark ii. 19 and parallels) all three have the rhetorical
question with μή. On the other side, the rhetorical question with οὐ is
used as a strong affirmation. In the parable of the Lost Sheep Matthew
gives οὐχὶ ἀφεὶς τὰ ἐνενήκοντα ἐννέα... ӡητεῖ τὸ πλανώμενον; that is, of
course he does so. In the Lucan saying about watering animals on the
Sabbath (not properly parabolic but analogical) we have ἕκαστος ὑμῶν τῷ
σαββάτῳ οὐ λύει τὸν βοῦν; It is this type of rhetorical question that we find
in John xi. 9. It is a device for drawing attention to an elementary and
undeniable fact, which the auditors are invited to consider. In subject-
matter the aphorism is akin to the saying in John ix. 4: ἡμᾶς δεῖ ἐργάӡεσθαι
τὰ ἔργα τοῦ πέμψαντός με ἕως ἡμέρα ἐστιν · ἔρχεται νὺξ ὅτε οὐδεὶς δύναται
ἐργάӡεσθαι. There, however, the terms ἡμέρα and νύξ are pointedly
symbolical; here, the saying is genuinely parabolic, describing in plain
terms an observed phenomenon and leaving the application to the
auditors. As such, it conforms to the style of the Synoptic tradition,
whereas John ix. 4 shows the quasi-allegorical manner characteristic of
the Fourth Evangelist.

(b) The second part of the saying is in form closely similar on the one
hand to the parable of the Grain of Wheat (John xii. 24), where we have, as
here, balanced conditional clauses with ἐάν in antithesis, and on the other
hand to the parable of the Pains of Childbirth (John xvi. 21), where the
antithetic clauses are introduced with ὅταν, and an explanatory clause with
ὅτι is appended to each member. The form may be illustrated by parallels
from the Synoptic Gospels adduced in the discussion of those passages
(pp. 366–73, above).

The saying appears to be in substance a true parable, describing in plain
terms a matter of general experience: he who walks by day walks securely;
the benighted traveller stumbles over unseen obstacles. It is only in the

¹ See Matt. xviii. 12 (τί ὑμῖν δοκεῖ;), xxi. 28–31; Mark xii. 9; Luke x. 36;
Matt. vii. 9–11 (|| Luke xi. 11–13); xxiv. 45 (|| Luke xii. 42); Luke xvii. 7–9,
xiv. 28, 31, xv. 4, 8; Matt. vii. 3 (|| Luke vi. 41); Luke xii. 57; etc.

appended ὅτι-clauses that a possible hint of allegory intrudes. The quali-fication of daylight as φῶς τοῦ κόσμου τούτου might suggest that the parable is to be interpreted with reference to the φῶς ἀληθινόν which is *not* 'of this world'. Ὁ κόσμος οὗτος is a Johannine expression, recurring viii. 23, ix. 39, xii. 25, 31, xiii. 1, xvi. 11, xviii. 36. It does not occur in the Synoptics. The light which the night walker does not have ἐν αὐτῷ[1] might perhaps be more readily understood of the 'inner light' than of the φῶς τοῦ κόσμου τούτου which figures in the parable. John does not, however, elsewhere speak of a man having the divine light 'in' him. In xii. 35, τὸ φῶς ἐν ὑμῖν ἐστίν, the preposition means 'among', and the reference is to the incarnate Word moving upon the human scene, as in i. 14, ἐσκήνωσεν ἐν ἡμῖν. On the other hand, Matthew (vi. 23) and Luke (xi. 35) have τὸ φῶς τὸ ἐν σοί. In that passage the body has been compared with a room lighted by a lamp. If the lamp burns brightly, the room is flooded with light. If the lamp is smoky, such light as there is in the room is little better than darkness. So with the body, and the eye which is its lamp. The expression τὸ φῶς τὸ ἐν σοί may arise out of the comparison. But for a naïve physio-logy the comparison is perhaps something more than a mere analogy; the body is conceived as illumined through the eye, and there is light 'in' the body in a literal sense. There is no reason why the expression τὸ φῶς οὐκ ἔστιν ἐν αὐτῷ in our present passage should not be understood in a similar way, quite literally.

The expressions περιπατεῖν ἐν τῇ ἡμέρᾳ, ἐν τῇ νυκτί, seem to echo viii. 12, xii. 35, περιπατεῖν ἐν τῇ σκοτίᾳ. The corresponding expression περιπατεῖν ἐν τῷ φωτί does not occur in the Fourth Gospel, but it is used in 1 John i. 7 in antithesis to περιπατεῖν ἐν τῷ σκότει. In these charac-teristically Johannine passages φῶς and σκότος (σκοτία) are unmistakably symbolic, and περιπατεῖν has its derived sense, 'to conduct oneself' (representing the Hebrew הלך), as in Paul *passim* and once only in the Synoptic Gospels (Mark vii. 5). In our present passage it may well have its natural sense, 'to walk about', as everywhere else in the Fourth Gospel except viii. 12, xii. 35, as well as in the Synoptics. Moreover, while 'to walk in the light' carries an immediate suggestion of a 'spiritual' meaning, in view of the constant use of φῶς as a religious symbol, 'to walk by day' is a perfectly natural expression, with no *necessary* reference beyond common experience.

---

[1] Dd and some Sahidic MSS. read ἐν αὐτῇ (namely ἐν τῇ νυκτί), which would avoid a non-Johannine locution.

Finally, the verb προσκόπτειν is not found in the Fourth Gospel outside the present context, while it occurs in Matt. vii. 27, as well as in a quotation from the Old Testament in Matt. iv. 6 (Luke iv. 11).

It appears, then, that the Johannine colouring does not go very deep, and there is little reason for regarding this saying as a composition of the evangelist himself. Both the introductory question and the short parable are of standard form, and are in substance genuinely parabolic (and not allegorical). It remains to consider the context and setting of the *pericopé*.

In the dramatic situation the saying is a response to a protest of the disciples against the expressed intention of Jesus to put his head into the lion's mouth by returning to Judaea where his life was recently in danger: Ῥαββεί, νῦν ἐζήτουν σε λιθάσαι οἱ Ἰουδαῖοι, καὶ πάλιν ὑπάγεις ἐκεῖ; [1] In reply to this Jesus reminds them that there are twelve hours in the day. This might imply, 'only twelve hours', or 'fully twelve hours'. The implication intended may perhaps be gathered from a comparison of Luke xiii. 14, where the ἀρχισυνάγωγος protests against healing on the Sabbath in the terms, ἓξ ἡμέραι εἰσὶν ἐν αἷς δεῖ ἐργάζεσθαι: there are six days in a working week, ample time for consulting a healer without encroaching on the Sabbath. So perhaps here: there are twelve hours in a working day (hours in which δεῖ ἐργάζεσθαι, according to John ix. 4), ample time for doing what must be done, without encroaching on the hours of night (when οὐδεὶς δύναται ἐργάζεσθαι). Jesus has his allotted working day—his earthly lifetime—and he can face the dangers of Judaea with no risk of immediately fatal consequences, since the twelfth hour has not yet struck (his ὥρα has not yet come). This is good Johannine doctrine, and so far the saying fits the dramatic situation. That it may also fit an historical situation in the life of Jesus is suggested by comparison with a passage in Luke (xiii. 31–3), where Jesus is warned of threats against his life—not in Judaea, as here, but in Herod's dominions, Galilee or Transjordan—and he replies, in effect, that he proposes to carry on his work according to plan without regard to such threats, since he bears a charmed life until his work reaches its completion, in Jerusalem—τῇ τρίτῃ τελειοῦμαι. This passage is certainly not the source of John xi. 9; it is framed from a

---

[1] The situation is in some sort analogous to that of Matt. xvi. 22–3, where Jesus has declared his intention of going to Jerusalem and has forecast his death there, and Peter replies, Ἵλεώς σοι, κύριε· οὐ μὴ ἔσται σοι τοῦτο. For the significance of the passage in the development of the theological theme of the gospel, see *Interpretation*, pp. 366–7.

different point of view; but it affords independent evidence for a stage in the Ministry essentially similar to that contemplated in the Johannine *pericopé*.[1]

When, however, we pass from the introductory saying to the little parable which follows, the connection of thought is not so clear. It would appear that it is Jesus himself who 'walks by day', as contrasted with the Jews (presumably) who 'walk by night', or, in terms of viii. 12, 'walk in the dark'. But in viii. 12 Jesus is himself the light. It is a harsh transference of imagery to represent him as also 'walking in the light'. It is true that Johannine usage allows some latitude in such expressions. Thus, while in viii. 12 Christ is himself the light, in i. 4 (according to the most probable construction of the passage) the light is 'in' the Word. In 1 John i. 5–7 we read, first, that God *is* light, then that there is no darkness 'in' him, and then that he is 'in' the light: but the language of the epistle is in general looser than that of the gospel. It is not impossible, in terms of Johannine usage, to apply the parable in the sense which the context seems to make inevitable, according to which Jesus is the walker by day who does not stumble. Προσκόπτειν must then be taken, not in the sense of moral failure (for this writer would hardly suggest such an idea, even in order to deny it), but in the sense of physical injury, as in the Temptation narrative (Matt. iv. 6, Luke iv. 11). But it is difficult to believe that the parable was originally coined with this sense in view. The connection may be artificial, and the saying may have had currency independently of this context.

It is probable that the evangelist, while incorporating the little *pericopé* into his narrative of the closing stages of the Ministry of Jesus, intended also a wider application to Christians who, like their Master, might be in danger through persecution. It is made more probable by comparison with ix. 4: ἡμᾶς δεῖ ἐργάζεσθαι τὰ ἔργα τοῦ πέμψαντός με ἕως ἡμέρα ἐστίν. Ostensibly, it is Jesus who must 'manifest the works of God' by healing the blind, but the tell-tale first person plural shows that the evangelist is also thinking of the duty of Christians in the world to 'work the works of God'. So here, it is Christ's followers who are assured that so long as they 'walk by day', or 'walk in the light'—or, in the language of John xv. 6–10, so long as they 'abide in' Christ and 'keep his commandments'—they are immortal until their work is done. Only if they are untrue to him, if they 'walk in the dark', or 'walk by night', is their working day over; they will blunder ineffectively through the rest of their earthly life ('Never

[1] See also above, pp. 322–5.

377

glad, confident morning again'). In this connection the verb προσκόπτειν might have a special force. According to 1 Pet. ii. 8, unbelievers (=those who walk in darkness, or by night, in Johannine terms) προσκόπτουσιν τῷ λόγῳ. As this rests on the *testimonium* from Isa. viii. 14 (compare Rom. ix. 32–3), we may safely take it to be *Gemeingut*, and not peculiar to 'Peter'. In Rom. xiv. 21 προσκόπτειν is used of the moral failure of a Christian. Moreover, in the LXX προσκόπτειν is a synonym of σκανδαλί-ζεσθαι, and πρόσκομμα of σκάνδαλον.[1] Thus the present passage, understood with reference to Christians in fear of persecution, would go well with warnings against being 'scandalized' when affliction or persecution arises διὰ τὸν λόγον (Mark iv. 17, compare Matt. xxiv. 9–10, Mark xiv. 27, Matt. xxvi. 31, John xvi. 1). The outstanding instance of a follower of Christ who was (in this sense) 'scandalized' is for this evangelist Judas Iscariot; and he, we are told, went into the night (xiii. 30).

If therefore the saying is understood with reference to Christians in the world, it is possible without violence to do justice to all the terms of the parable, in a transferred sense; giving to the terms περιπατεῖν and προσκόπτειν a quasi-technical meaning, treating 'day' and 'night' as symbols for spiritual 'light' and 'darkness', and interpreting the 'twelve hours' as the day of opportunity for the service of Christ in this world. So understood, the saying might find a *Sitz im Leben* in the situation in which the Christian mission is being carried on in the face of persecution. It was no doubt in relation to that situation that the saying of Matt. x. 23 found its place in the tradition: ὅταν διώκωσιν ὑμᾶς ἐν τῇ πόλει ταύτῃ φεύγετε εἰς τὴν ἑτέραν· ἀμὴν γὰρ λέγω ὑμῖν, οὐ μὴ τελέσητε τὰς πόλεις τοῦ Ἰσραὴλ ἕως ἔλθῃ ὁ υἱὸς τοῦ ἀνθρώπου. Whatever may have been the original intention of this saying, the early Christian missionary must have understood it as meaning, 'Take persecution as a sign that you are to move to a fresh centre; there is at any rate not too much time to cover the whole field'.[2] John xi. 9, on the other hand, could be understood, with reference

---

[1] Προσκόπτειν and σκανδαλίζεσθαι are both used to translate נִכְשַׁל, πρόσ-κομμα and σκάνδαλον to render מִכְשׁ. In the early Christian version of Isa. viii. 14 (which differs from the LXX and is closer to the Hebrew) πρόσκομμα and σκάνδαλον are used in parallelism (σκάνδαλον representing מִכְשׁוֹל and πρόσ-κομμα נֶגֶף). See *According to the Scriptures*, pp. 41–3.

[2] Paul certainly worked on this principle, at any rate until the time of his Ephesian ministry. According to the narrative of Acts, he retired in face of persecution and started in a fresh centre, and he seems to have felt this movement from place to place as subject to the necessity of covering as much ground as possible (e.g. Rom. xv. 22–4, 2 Cor. x. 16), since ὁ καιρὸς συνεσταλμένος ἐστίν.

to the same situation, as saying, 'There is time enough; the only thing you have to fear is disloyalty to Christ ("walking by night", like Judas); stand and face persecution'.

Yet it may be doubted whether this could have been the original intention of this parable, since, taken in and for itself, it gives no hint of any reference to persecution; it is only the Johannine setting that introduces such a reference. It is probable that any application to the Christian missionary under persecution is secondary. We shall do best to recognize the parable as being, like so many of the Synoptic parables, an appeal to common experience and common sense, which was intended to shock the hearers into a realization of their own situation. As frequently in parables, the sting is in the tail. It is the plight of the benighted traveller that the hearers are to recognize as their own plight, or at least that with which they are threatened. When the hours of daylight are long enough for man's requirements, how foolish to wander abroad at night and risk an accident! The range of imagery is akin to that of the parables of the Eye as Lamp and of the Blind leading the Blind. There is no Synoptic passage which could conceivably have served as source, but there seems no reason why the parable should not have been drawn from the common reservoir of tradition; and it is more likely to have been so derived than to have been composed by the evangelist, since it is not entirely apt to the use which he makes of it.

(iv) John viii. 35. Slave and Son:

'Ο δοῦλος οὐ μένει ἐν τῇ οἰκίᾳ εἰς τὸν αἰῶνα·
ὁ υἱὸς μένει εἰς τὸν αἰῶνα.

This couplet occurs in the course of an elaborate discussion in the form of a dialogue between Jesus and certain Jews who are said to have 'believed him' (viii. 31).[1] Their attitude in the discussion is hardly that of 'believers' in the sense usual in this gospel. It would appear that the evangelist had in mind Christians of Jewish extraction who continued to insist on their privileges as 'birthright members' of the messianic community, over against gentile proselytes. The discussion in fact turns upon such issues as those which are canvassed in Paul's debate with 'Judaizing' Christians, especially in the Epistle to the Galatians: freedom and slavery; sons of Abraham and sons of God. Such Christians are aptly represented by the

[1] On this dialogue see above, pp. 330–2, and my article 'À l'arrière-plan d'un dialogue johannique' in *Revue d'Histoire et de Philosophie Religieuses*, 1957, no. 1, pp. 5–17.

Ἰουδαῖοι οἱ πεπιστευκότες αὐτῷ of our passage. They are 'believers', yet claim that they are inviolably free by virtue of their descent from Abraham, and that, as Israelites, they have God for their Father. The answer to their claim is that no sinner is a free man (verse 34); only the Son who 'takes away sin' (John i. 29) can set him free, whether gentile or Jew (verse 36). As for descent from Abraham, that means nothing apart from ethical likeness to Abraham. The cavillers show by their conduct that their paternity is far less creditable (verses 41, 44). The *Sitz im Leben* for such discussions is to be sought not so much in the situation in Palestine during the Ministry of Jesus as in the controversies which, best known to us from the epistles of Paul, continued for some time to agitate the Church in the Graeco-Roman world. This is confirmed by the strongly Hellenistic colouring of the language and ideas. The propositions, 'The truth will set you free', and 'He who commits sin is a slave',[1] are Stoic maxims.[2]

The aphorism in verse 35, however, does not fit very aptly into this discussion. In verse 36, ὁ υἱός is clearly Christ, who teaches the truth which sets men free (verses 31–2) and whose word does not run (οὐ χωρεῖ) among those natural descendants of Abraham (σπέρμα Ἀβραάμ) who deny their paternity by their actions. But it is only by a rather awkward twist that this is made to carry on the thought of verse 35. If the proposition, ὁ υἱὸς μένει εἰς τὸν αἰῶνα, is to be taken as a Christological statement, as the evangelist probably intended (compare xii. 34), it gives neither a forcible antithesis to the statement, ὁ δοῦλος οὐ μένει ἐν τῇ οἰκίᾳ εἰς τὸν αἰῶνα, nor a plausible premiss for the argument which follows, ἐὰν οὖν ὁ υἱὸς ὑμᾶς ἐλευθερώσῃ ὄντως ἐλεύθεροι ἔσεσθε. We may therefore reasonably raise the question whether the couplet was originally independent of its present context.

It is entirely in the manner of the Synoptic parables that typical figures from real life should be introduced as ὁ δοῦλος, ὁ υἱός. Similarly we have ὁ οἰκοδεσπότης (Luke xii. 39; Matt. xxiv. 43; Luke xiii. 25), ὁ ἰσχυρός (Mark iii. 27), ὁ σπείρων (Mark iv. 3); compare τὸ πνεῦμα τὸ ἀκάθαρτον (Matt. xii. 43, Luke xi. 24), ὁ λύχνος (Mark iv. 21), ἡ συκῆ (Mark xiii. 28). In such cases an English speaker would more naturally use the indefinite article. Thus our present passage should be translated, 'A slave is not a

---

[1] Πᾶς ὁ ποιῶν τὴν ἁμαρτίαν δοῦλός ἐστιν: so read, probably, with Db Syrsin, Clem. Alex. Cf. Epictetus II. i. 23, οὐδεὶς ἁμαρτάνων ἐλεύθερός ἐστιν. The addition of the words τῆς ἁμαρτίας may be due to a reminiscence of Rom. vi. 17, 20.

[2] See above, p. 330, n. 3.

permanent member of the household: a son is a permanent member'.[1]
Many parables turn upon the contrast of two such typical figures: two
builders (Matt. vii. 24–7, Luke vi. 47–9), two sons (Matt. xxi. 28 31), two
debtors (Luke vii. 41–2), two slaves (Matt. xviii. 23–34), Pharisee and
publican (Luke xviii. 9–14), rich man and beggar (Luke xvi. 19–31),
instructed slave and ignorant slave (Luke xii. 47–8), etc. The contrast may
be worked out at greater or less length; in no Synoptic parable is it
presented so concisely as here; but the substance of such a parable is
clearly contained in the two brief clauses. As is usual, the two figures are
contrasted in respect of one single characteristic: here, the son is by
natural right a permanent member of the οἰκία, while the slave holds his
position provisionally, at the master's pleasure. The expression εἰς τὸν
αἰῶνα is much used by this evangelist, though it is not peculiar to him; it
lends itself to the theological (allegorical) interpretation of the parable,
but in itself it need not mean more than 'perpetually', 'permanently'.[2]
Thus we have a true parable, drawing attention to a familiar feature of the
social scene.[3] If we ask how it was intended to be applied, there are two
passages in the gospels which may afford some guidance. In Luke xv. 31
the father in the parable says to the son who has not wandered from home,
Τέκνον, σὺ πάντοτε μετ' ἐμοῦ εἶ. In Matt. xvii. 25–6 we have a short
dialogue occasioned by a demand presented to Jesus through Peter for
payment of the temple-tax. Jesus asks, 'From whom do earthly kings
take tax and toll? ἀπὸ τῶν υἱῶν αὐτῶν ἢ ἀπὸ τῶν ἀλλοτρίων;' Peter
replies, Ἀπὸ τῶν ἀλλοτρίων. From this Jesus draws the inference,
Ἄρα γε ἐλεύθεροί εἰσιν οἱ υἱοί. The 'moral' seems to be that Jesus and his
disciples, being sons of the heavenly king[4] (compare Matt. v. 9, 45,
Luke vi. 35, xx. 36), possess in principle the freedom of the temple which

---

[1] Where a parable has the form of a more or less elaborately developed narrative,
we usually find such expressions as ἄνθρωπός τις, but in the more concise form, the
Gleichnis, approaching more or less closely to the Bildwort, the generic definite
article is usual.

[2] Moulton and Milligan cite examples: ὅπως πλουτήσῃς εἰς αἰῶνα (second-
century papyrus), εὐεργέτην γεγονότα τοῦ δήμου πρὸς τὸν αἰῶνα (inscription,
first century B.C.). With a negative it means simply 'never', e.g. 1 Cor. viii. 13, οὐ
μὴ φάγω κρέα εἰς τὸν αἰῶνα; Mark xi. 14, μηκέτι εἰς τὸν αἰῶνα ἐκ σοῦ μηδεὶς
καρπὸν φάγοι.

[3] Similarly Bultmann ad loc. 'V. 35 scheint ursprünglich ein Bildwort gewesen
zu sein'.

[4] It is true that God is not expressly designated 'king' in the gospels; of course
not: the expression מלכותא דישמיא was invented in order to avoid the
direct form of description. But the 'king of flesh and blood' is a stock character in
rabbinic parables designed to illustrate the dealings of God with men.

is His οἶκος (Matt. xii. 4, xxi. 13), and should not be taxed for its support—in principle, but in practice Jesus proceeds to give instructions for payment of the tax on behalf of Peter and himself. Neither of these passages affords any direct clue to the original intention of the parable we are considering, but they suggest that if we apply the figure of the son who has his inalienable place in the οἰκία to the relation established between men and their God we shall move within the range of ideas associated with Synoptic parables. Much more frequent in the latter is the figure of the δοῦλος and his κύριος,[1] presented in a large variety of concrete relationships such as are observable in actual life. In several parables we have a slave who for one reason or another οὐ μένει ἐν τῇ οἰκίᾳ: the slave who is to be sold for payment of a debt (Matt. xviii. 25), the 'unprofitable servant' who is turned summarily out of doors (Matt. xxv. 30), the slave (an οἰκονόμος according to Luke) who misbehaved himself in his master's absence and was 'cut off'[2] (Matt. xxiv. 50-1; Luke xii. 46), and perhaps that other οἰκονόμος who was dismissed for wasting his master's property and, being incapable of agricultural labour and too proud to beg, proceeded to live by his wits (Luke xvi. 1-8). No exact 'allegorical' equivalent is to be sought in each case, but the idea is never far away that Israel, or the rulers of Israel, if they are false to their trust, forfeit their place as servants of God.

Thus the parable of Slave and Son, though it does not exactly correspond with anything in the Synoptics, and certainly could not have been derived thence, is intelligible within the range of ideas associated with Synoptic parables, without any necessary reference to specifically Johannine ideas. It seems probable that the evangelist took it from the common reservoir of tradition and turned it to his own use, not without some awkwardness.

(v) John x. 1-5. The Shepherd, the Thief, and the Doorkeeper

This passage is expressly described as a παροιμία (x. 6). That term is equivalent to the Synoptic παραβολή. They are alternative renderings of

[1] On the tension between the ideas of Israel as 'servant' (slave) and as 'son' to Jehovah see D. Daube, *The New Testament and Rabbinic Judaism*, pp. 272-8.

[2] Διχοτομήσει αὐτὸν καὶ τὸ μέρος αὐτοῦ μετὰ τῶν ἀπίστων θήσει (Luke). After a man has been 'dichotomized' there is not much point in allotting his portion with the faithless (Matthew's 'hypocrites' may be a trace of allegorization). Possibly διχοτομήσει represents an Aramaic equivalent to the Hebrew כרת, used in the sense frequent in the Pentateuch, e.g. Lev. xvii. 10 sqq. Other suggestions have been made (see Torrey, *Our Translated Gospels*, p. 155; Jeremias, *Die Gleichnisse Jesu*, pp. 44-5). In any case the disgraced slave cannot be said μένειν ἐν τῇ οἰκίᾳ.

Hebrew מָשָׁל, Aramaic מְתַלָה,[1] and we have here, not a distinction of *genres*, but one more indication that John sometimes reaches back to the primitive Aramaic tradition by way of a different Greek translation.[2] We may fairly say, therefore, that John x. 1–5 is the one *pericopé* in this gospel which is offered explicitly as a parable. But is it a parable in anything like the Synoptic sense, or is it an allegory? If the entire passage, x. 1–18, be read as a unit, it is without doubt allegorical, and we commonly read the opening verses in the light of the subsequent elaboration (as the evangelist no doubt intended us to read them). But it has been pointed out that allegorization begins only after verse 6, and that there is nothing in the παροιμία itself, namely in verses 1–5, which necessarily has the character of allegory. I refer here to an article by J. A. T. Robinson (now Bishop of Woolwich), 'The Parable of John x. 1–5', in *Zeitschrift für neutestamentliche Wissenschaft*, XLVI (1955), 233–40, which the reader should consult.[3] His conclusions seem to me to be, broadly, acceptable, and I shall follow the main lines of his treatment, without necessarily agreeing in detail.

The key to the right understanding of the passage he finds in the recognition that we have in verses 1–5 the wreckage of two parables fused into one, the fusion having partly destroyed the original form of both. The first (A) ends with the words, τούτῳ ὁ θυρωρὸς ἀνοίγει (verse 3a). The rest, verses 3b–5, forms a second parable (B), which may have lost its opening.

In B we have a pair of contrasted characters, the Shepherd and the ἀλλότριος. We may compare, in Synoptic parables, the Pharisee and the Publican (Luke xviii. 9–14), the Faithful and the Unfaithful Servant (Matt. xxiv. 45–51; Luke xii. 42–6) or the Two Builders (Matt. vii. 24–7; Luke vi. 47–9). In A the contrasted characters are the Shepherd and the Thief, but here there is a third character, whose behaviour towards the others sets off the contrast. We may compare the father and his two sons in the parables of the Two Sons (Matt. xxi. 28–31) and the Prodigal Son (Luke xv. 11–32). Although, therefore, no exact formal parallel can be cited among Synoptic parables, it is clear that the broad elements of structure are similar. Further, the principal characters of the Johannine παροιμία appear also in Synoptic parables.

---

[1] The 'proverbs' of Solomon, מִשְׁלֵי שְׁלֹמֹה, are παροιμίαι Σολομῶντος in Prov. i. 1, but in 3 Kms. iv. 28 they are παραβολαί.

[2] See above, pp. 58–9, 121 n. 1, 350 n. 1.

[3] Now reprinted in *Twelve New Testament Studies* (S.C.M. Press, 1962).

The Shepherd with his flock appears in the compressed parable inserted into the Matthaean picture of the Last Judgement (xxv. 32),[1] and in the comparison of the Galilaeans to a forsaken flock in Matt. ix. 36,[2] as well as (without being named) in the parable of the Lost Sheep (Matt. xviii. 12–13; Luke xv. 4–7).[3] In all these passages, the Johannine no less than the Synoptic, the relation of shepherd and flock is depicted realistically: in John the shepherd controls the movements of the flock, as in Matthew he ranges the sheep and goats in their proper places. As in John he knows his sheep individually (κατ' ὄνομα),[4] so in the Synoptics he cares for them individually, and will not lose sight of a single one out of a flock of a hundred. In John, the foil to the shepherd's care is the helpless terror of the flock in the presence of a stranger; in Matt. ix. 36 it is the woeful state of sheep with no shepherd at all. All belong to the same realistic scene of pastoral life in Palestine.

In A, the shepherd stands in contrast with the thief. The doorkeeper gives entrance to the former but (it is implied) excludes the latter, who accordingly climbs over the wall. The θυρωρός appears also in the Marcan parable of the Waiting Servants (xiii. 34). Here his business is to stay awake until the master arrives, at some unknown hour during the night, in order (it is implied) to let him in. In the corresponding Lucan parable this is explicit: the servants in a body must wait up for the master ἵνα ἐλθόντος καὶ κρούσαντος εὐθέως ἀνοίξωσιν αὐτῷ (xii. 36). The relations of the θυρωρός to the master in the one case and to the shepherd in the other are closely analogous. The κλέπτης is a character in the little parable which in Matt. xxiv. 43–4, Luke xii. 39–40 is a companion to another parable

---

[1] The whole passage, xxv. 31–46, is often mistakenly styled the 'Parable of the Sheep and Goats', but the only properly parabolic element in it is the one clause in verse 32.

[2] The use of parabolic language where the evangelist is writing in his own person is so unusual that it is legitimate to conjecture that the expression, ἦσαν ἐσκυλμένοι καὶ ἐριμμένοι ὡσεὶ πρόβατα μὴ ἔχοντα ποιμένα, may have come down in tradition as part of a *Herrnwort*. It is in any case noteworthy that it echoes Ezek. xxxiv. 5, and that this chapter of Ezekiel underlies much of the allegorical exposition of the parable of the Shepherd in John x. 7–18 (see *Interpretation*, pp. 358–61).

[3] It is not altogether due to a confusion of ideas that in the tradition of Christian art from the beginning the *Pastor Bonus* is identified with the Figure carrying a lamb on his shoulder, who comes out of the parable of the Lost Sheep.

[4] The expression κατ' ὄνομα means 'individually' or 'one by one'; see my commentary on the Johannine Epistles, *ad* 3 John 15, and examples cited there. There is therefore no necessary implication that the shepherd has given proper names to all the sheep in his flock.

about servants waiting for their master. Here the point is that the thief comes unexpectedly; the householder is to blame because he was not prepared. In John there is no suggestion that the θυρωρός has failed in his duty. The contrast is simply between the shepherd who has a right to enter and the thief who enters illegitimately. The whole emphasis rests upon the point that the θυρωρός admits the rightful entrant (τούτῳ ἀνοίγει).[1]

In both parables, as in those of the Synoptics, the *dramatis personae* act in character. At no point does any unnatural feature suggest that allegorical motives have coloured the picture. There is good reason to believe that the material was drawn from the same reservoir of tradition as the Synoptic parables. In what follows, x. 7–18, the evangelist has exploited it for his own purposes.

(vi) John iii. 29. Bridegroom and Bridegroom's Friend:

Ὁ ἔχων τὴν νύμφην νυμφίος ἐστίν· ὁ δὲ φίλος τοῦ νυμφίου ὁ ἑστηκὼς καὶ ἀκούων αὐτοῦ χαρᾷ χαίρει διὰ τὴν φωνὴν τοῦ νυμφίου.

[1] The Bishop of Woolwich (*op. cit.* p. 237) has suggested an 'application' of the parable which is new so far as my knowledge goes: 'While he is still with them the authorities have a last chance to fulfil their role as the watchmen of the house of Israel... to recognize and admit the master of the house of Israel.' This I believe to be in substance right. Upon the principle that the primary reference of the parables was, historically, contemporary (see my *Parables of the Kingdom*, ch. IV–VI), the relation of shepherd and doorkeeper should find its analogue in the conditions of the Ministry of Jesus, like, for example, the relation of the wicked husbandmen to the landlord and his heir, or of the servants entrusted with money to their absent and returning master. Those parables set forth a relation which has gone wrong: the tenants who ought to have paid their rent in kind to the landlord have murdered his heir; the servant who ought to have invested the money on his master's behalf has buried it. They imply a condemnation of the Jewish authorities who have betrayed their trust. The parables of waiting servants set forth a similar relation, without deciding whether or not the master will be suitably received; they leave the question open, whether or not the authorities will rise to the occasion. The Johannine parable expresses the relation positively, as a challenge to the authorities to act as they clearly ought. We might easily put it in a form common to several Synoptic parables: [Τί ὑμῖν δοκεῖ; ἐὰν ἔλθῃ ὁ ποιμήν, οὐχὶ] τούτῳ ὁ θυρωρὸς ἀνοίγει; The answer clearly is, If he is fit for his post, of course he will do so. Then—what should *you* do? This gives a sharp point to the parable, and brings it into line with the main body of parables in the Synoptics. With the Bishop's application of the κλέπτης I am not so happy. His tracing of the figure through 1 Thessalonians, the Synoptic Gospels and the Apocalypse is indeed acute and illuminating. But in all these, the main point is that the thief comes unexpectedly, unpredictably. There is no slightest suggestion of this in John x. 1. Indeed, the figure of the κλέπτης here is little more than a foil to the ποιμήν, whose admission by the θυρωρός is the central theme, though the κλέπτης-theme is of course exploited by the evangelist in the allegory.

This parable has already been discussed in its context (pp. 282–5 above). It is here adduced as a further example of parabolic forms in the Fourth Gospel, though it is given as a saying of the Baptist and not of Jesus. While it does not exactly conform to the pattern of any Synoptic parable, it appears to belong to the same *genre*. It is a picture from real life, not necessarily demanding any allegorical interpretation.[1] The φίλος τοῦ νυμφίου is presumably the functionary called שׁוֹשְׁבִּין. Compare *Sanh.* iii. 5: 'A friend or an enemy (is disqualified as judge or witness). Who is counted as a friend? One's groomsman (שׁוֹשְׁבִּין).' The meaning intended seems to be that the leading figure at a wedding is not the 'best man' but the bridegroom himself; the best man finds his pleasure in attending to the bridegroom. The picture is realistic, and we do not need to press details, for example to ask who is the bride. So far as language goes, there is little that might betray the hand of the evangelist, and the parable, set as it is in a passage which appears to contain many traditional elements, seems to bear a genuinely traditional stamp.

To sum up: while the usual method of employing imagery in the Fourth Gospel is characteristic of the author, and strikingly different from that of the Synoptic Gospels, we have found six passages[2] which stand out from the rest by their unlikeness to the usual Johannine type, and their similarity to passages in the Synoptics. They are genuinely parabolic, and not allegorical; in form, content, and purport, often even in vocabulary, in spite of such degree of rewriting as we must always expect from our evangelist, they find their natural place in the family to which the Synoptic parables belong. Yet in no case is there the remotest likelihood of deriva-

---

[1] So Bultmann *ad loc.*: 'ein echtes Bildwort liegt vor, keine Allegorie'.

[2] Or rather, seven. Since this chapter was written, I have observed another Johannine parable, which I had missed. In John v. 19–20a (down to . . . αὐτὸς ποιεῖ) we have a perfectly realistic description of a son apprenticed to his father's trade. He does not act on his own initiative; he watches his father at work, and performs each operation as his father performs it. The affectionate father shows the boy all the secrets of his craft. So far there is no single expression which is not appropriate in describing a situation in real life. The passage is a true parable. In the verses which follow (20b–30) it is interpreted and applied in allegorical fashion, in a classical exposition of basic Johannine Christology: the *métier* of the heavenly Father is κρίνειν καὶ ζῳοποιεῖν, and the incarnate Son dutifully carries out the work of the Father. The phenomena are closely analogous to those which we have noted in x. 1–18 (see above, pp. 382–5). I have discussed the passage fully in an article, 'Une parabole cachée dans le quatrième Évangile', in *Revue d'Histoire et de Philosophie Religieuses*, 1962, nos. 2–3, pp. 107–15.

tion from Synoptic sources. It appears therefore in the highest degree probable that at any rate for parts of the teaching of Jesus John drew independently upon the common and primitive tradition, and that he has preserved valuable elements in that tradition which the Synoptic evangelists have neglected.

4. SEQUENCES OF SAYINGS

We have already noted that the Johannine discourses in general are constructed on a characteristic pattern which has no parallel in the Synoptic Gospels. It is all the more significant that there are a few sequences of sayings which approximate to the Synoptic pattern, and stand out in contrast to the Johannine type. Such are the sequences in iv. 31–8, xii. 20–6, xiii. 1–20. But before examining these it will be well to look at some Synoptic sequences. As typical examples we may take the following.

Mark ix. 33–50. The passage begins with a situation briefly described, as the setting for a dialogue with the disciples which ends with a pregnant saying of Jesus (verses 33–7); to this are appended, first, another brief dialogue (verses 38–40), and then three separate sayings, with only the slightest connection with the foregoing dialogues or with one another (verses 41, 42, 43–8); and the sequence tails off with some disjointed sentences.

Luke xi. 14–28. The passage begins with a situation briefly described, here a miracle of exorcism with its effect on observers. There follow a controversial dialogue (verses 15–20), a parable (verses 21–2), a detached saying (verse 23), another parable (verses 24–6), and a short dialogue (or rather 'apophthegm'), which brings the sequence to a close with a pronouncement in the form of a makarism (27–8).

Luke xii. 13–34. The passage begins with an approach to Jesus by a stranger, and his reply. Then follows a pronouncement (15); next a parable (16–21); then a longer utterance in quasi-poetical form (22–31); and the sequence ends with two detached sayings (32, 33–4).

The arrangement of such sequences is no doubt in part the work of the several evangelists, but comparison suggests that something of the kind existed at the pre-canonical stage, and that in Mark and Luke we are nearer to the first sketch, while in Matthew we have a more sophisticated effort to secure logical or rhetorical propriety.[1] There seems good reason

---

[1] W. L. Knox, in his posthumous work, *The Sources of the Synoptic Gospels*, argues persuasively that there is evidence for the existence of such sequences of sayings in the pre-canonical tradition, and that Luke (while modifying them editorially) has preserved their general character better than Matthew. He conceives these sequences as existing in written form, as 'tracts' for the use of Christian teachers and

to suppose that the common tradition contained not only detached units—aphorisms, parables, dialogues and the rest—but also rudimentary sequences, which in some instances have come through (albeit with modifications) into the written gospels. If this be granted, it will be worth while to compare the three sequences I have noted in the Fourth Gospel.

(i) I begin with John xii. 20–6. The sequence opens (like Luke xii. 13–34) with the approach of strangers—Greeks who seek an interview with Jesus through the good offices of Philip and Andrew—and a saying of Jesus elicited in reply (verses 20–3). The saying, ἐλήλυθεν ἡ ὥρα ἵνα δοξασθῇ ὁ υἱὸς τοῦ ἀνθρώπου, bears the Johannine stamp very clearly. A parable follows, the Grain of Wheat (verse 24); next the aphorism, ὁ φιλῶν τὴν ψυχήν κ.τ.λ. (verse 25); and then a second aphorism, ἐὰν ἐμοί τις διακονῇ ἐμοὶ ἀκολουθείτω (verse 26a). Whether verse 26b, ὅπου εἰμὶ ἐγὼ ἐκεῖ καὶ ὁ διάκονος ὁ ἐμὸς ἔσται, is to be regarded as a supplement to verse 26a, or as a separate saying, is doubtful; the idea is similar to that of xiv. 3, and may be of Johannine coinage, but on the other hand the occurrence in xii. 26 may be traditional (especially as it includes the non-Johannine word διάκονος) and the repetition in xiv. 3 the work of the evangelist. In any case 26c, ἐὰν τις ἐμοὶ διακονῇ τιμήσει αὐτὸν ὁ πατήρ, looks like an independent aphorism, with the non-Johannine term διακονεῖν,[1] very much in the spirit of Matt. x. 32, πᾶς ὅστις ὁμολογήσει ἐν ἐμοὶ ἔμπροσθεν τῶν ἀνθρώπων, ὁμολογήσω κἀγὼ ἐν αὐτῷ ἔμπροσθεν τοῦ πατρός μου τοῦ ἐν οὐρανοῖς. After verse 26 the sequence loses touch with the Synoptic pattern, though the content of verses 27–8, an equivalent for the Synoptic prayer of Jesus in Gethsemane, has certainly a traditional basis.[2] But down to the end of verse 26 the analogy with Synoptic sequences is clear. The parable and the two sayings which follow I have already discussed,[3] and I have shown reason to believe that they were drawn from tradition, as was possibly also 26c. Was the sequence also traditional?

---

evangelists, before they were handled by the evangelists (see especially *op. cit.* vol. II, pp. 45–83). Whether this was so or not, we may probably assume that such written 'tracts' would represent earlier practice in oral teaching.

[1] For διάκονος, διακονεῖν, see above, pp. 352–3.

[2] See above, pp. 69–71. Bultmann *ad loc.* points out that the presence of the ὄχλος in verse 29 is inconsistent with the situation implied in verses 20–2, where Jesus is so much apart that applicants for an interview have to use the good offices of two of the Twelve. There is a closely similar case in Mark viii. 34, where the ὄχλος suddenly appears in a scene where *ex hypothesi* Jesus and his disciples are alone (verse 27).

[3] See above, pp. 366–9.

In Mark viii. 34–ix. 1 we have a short sequence which includes parallels (or partial parallels) to the sayings in John xii. 25, 26a, but in reverse order, and also a saying which looks like one member of a couplet preserved in Matt. x. 32–3, and this latter, we have noted, shares a common ethos with John xii. 26c. If it is unlikely (as I have argued above) that the separate sayings were borrowed by John from the Synoptics, it is also unlikely that the sequence as a whole was drawn from them; yet it has a manifest affinity with Mark viii. 34–ix. 1. The most probable conclusion is that John is following (and editing) a traditional sequence.

(ii) Next, xiii. 1–20. This passage begins with a narrative which is evidently elaborated in the interests of Johannine theology, but which, I have argued, has deep roots in tradition.[1] It leads (cf. Mark ix. 33–7) to a dialogue with disciples, leading up to a pregnant saying (verse 15). Three aphorisms follow, the third in the form of a makarism (compare Luke xi. 28) (verses 16–17). The two following verses have features which suggest composition by the evangelist, but the core of them is a *testimonium* from Ps. xl. 10, which must be traditional.[2] The sequence closes with the saying, ὁ λαμβάνων ἄν τινα πέμψω κ.τ.λ. (verse 20). Once again, the analogy with Synoptic sequences is clear. Once again also, two of the sayings have parallels in the other gospels, and are (as I have argued) drawn from tradition.[3] Was the sequence also traditional?

There is in this case no possibility that it was borrowed directly from the other gospels; there is no sequence in the Synoptics as closely related to this as Mark viii. 34–ix. 1 is to John xii. 24–6. The saying οὐκ ἔστιν δοῦλος μείζων κ.τ.λ. has its parallel in one of the sequences which Matthew has appended to the 'Mission Discourse' (itself a compilation) (Matt. x. 24), and the saying ὁ λαμβάνων ἄν τινα πέμψω κ.τ.λ. has a parallel in what appears to be (originally) a quite independent little sequence appended at the end of that discourse (x. 40). The Lucan parallel to ὁ λαμβάνων κ.τ.λ. occurs also in an appendix to the 'Mission Discourse', but in quite different company; and the Lucan parallel to οὐκ ἔστιν δοῦλος μείζων κ.τ.λ. occurs in the Great Sermon (vi. 40). It is no doubt possible to take the view that our evangelist, knowing the Synoptic Gospels, deliberately imitated the arrangement of sayings[4] which he found in them, and picked out a saying here and there to incorporate in a sequence of his own, with all the informality, all the looseness of connection, that we have noted in

---

[1] See above, pp. 59–63.   [2] See above, pp. 36–7.   [3] See above, pp. 335–8, 343–7.
[4] I say 'imitated' because this is not in any case his own individual method of presenting the teaching of Jesus.

the other gospels. But is it not more likely that the sayings came to him already roughly grouped, and that he reproduced the grouping with much the same amount of editing as we observe in similar instances in the Synoptics?

(iii) The third sequence, iv. 31–8, requires, and deserves, more thorough examination. Here we have, first (as in Mark ix. 33–7), a brief description of a situation, leading to a dialogue with disciples, and this culminates in a pregnant saying of Jesus, ἐμὸν βρῶμά ἐστιν ἵνα ποιῶ τὸ θέλημα τοῦ πέμψαντός με καὶ τελειώσω τὸ ἔργον αὐτοῦ (verse 34).[1] There follow three sayings, which we may at this point denominate by catch-phrases: (a) the fields ripe for reaping, (b) the reaper takes his pay, (c) one sows, another reaps. The connection is loose (as in Synoptic sequences), but all are linked together by the general theme of harvest. The connection between the introductory dialogue and the sayings about harvest is far from clear. At most we might discover a connection if we supposed that in verse 37 ὁ σπείρων is Jesus, who by speaking to the Samaritan woman has sown the crop which the disciples are now sent to reap, and that this is the ἔργον he has to finish. Some such train of thought may have been in the mind of the evangelist, but it is hardly intrinsic to the material. The short dialogue on βρῶμα is itself not very clearly related to the foregoing discussion with the Samaritan woman, though the symbolism of drinking in the one case and eating in the other provides a not unnatural association of ideas. But even on that level the transition to the following series of sayings is not easy, for the association of the ideas of eating on the one hand and of sowing and reaping on the other is somewhat remote. In short, the *prima facie* suggestion is that we have here a compact little sequence, similar to those of the Synoptic Gospels, originally unconnected with the main discourse, but attached to it by the evangelist himself.

In certain respects the passage is more akin to Synoptic material than to the rest of the Fourth Gospel. The agricultural imagery which runs through it is as infrequent in the Fourth Gospel as it is frequent in the Synoptics, and it is treated more nearly in the manner of their parabolic sayings than is usual in John. The keywords are nearly all terms which appear in the other gospels: σπείρειν, θερίζειν and θερισμός, χώρα in the sense of 'field', συνάγειν as an agricultural term, κόπος and κοπιᾶν, μισθός, ὀφθαλμοὺς ἐπαίρειν. Of these, only the last is found elsewhere in the Fourth Gospel.

---

[1] On iv. 31–4 see above, pp. 325–7, where I have argued that the little dialogue has a traditional basis.

Of other significant terms, ἀληθινός is almost exclusively Johannine, occurring only once in the Synoptic Gospels, as against ten times in John; εἰς ζωὴν αἰώνιον, though it occurs once in Matthew, is distinctively Johannine; θεᾶσθαι is a word preferred by John, though it is not uncommon in the Synoptics.[1] That ὁμοῦ happens not to occur in the Synoptics (though it does occur in Acts), while John has it three times, is hardly significant, any more than it is significant on the other side that ἰδού, which recurs with such tedious frequency in the Synoptics, is found in the Fourth Gospel only three times outside this context, one of the three being a quotation from the Old Testament.[2]

The extent therefore to which the language of our passage has a distinctively Johannine colouring is slight, and lends little support to a theory that we have here anything like a free composition of the evangelist. It would be a reasonable hypothesis that he is drawing upon material which had come down to him in one way or another, and slightly rewriting it in the process of incorporating it in his work.

In view of the Synoptic affinities of the imagery and vocabulary, it is natural to ask in the first place whether in fact the source upon which the evangelist is drawing is to be found in the Synoptic Gospels themselves. The general theme, that of the relation between sowing and harvest, is certainly present in various Synoptic passages, notably in the parables of the Sower, of the Seed Growing Secretly, and of the Tares. The theme of labour and reward is present in the parable of the Labourers in the Vineyard and in the Lucan parable of Master and Slave as well as in the *Bildwort* ἄξιος ὁ ἐργάτης τοῦ μισθοῦ αὐτοῦ (Luke x. 7).[3] But in none of these cases, in spite of the similarity of theme, and, in part, of vocabulary, is there any such significant resemblance as to suggest literary dependence.

---

[1] Six times in John, four times in Matthew, three times in Luke, and twice in the spurious ending of Mark.

[2] Pilate's ἰδοὺ ὁ ἄνθρωπος is very different from the conventional use of ἰδού in the Synoptics, which is represented by only one place in John (apart from the quotation from Zechariah in xii. 15), viz. xvi. 32. Ἰδοὺ λέγω ὑμῖν is not found in the Synoptics, though ἰδοὺ προείρηκα is in Matt. xxiv. 25 (and, as *v.l.*, Mark xiii. 23), and ἰδοὺ εἶπον in Matt. xxviii. 7.

[3] But it seems likely that the Matthaean version, with τῆς τροφῆς for τοῦ μισθοῦ, better represents the original sense of the saying. At any rate Paul must have so understood it, when he paraphrases it as an injunction that missionaries should ἐκ τοῦ εὐαγγελίου ζῆν. And in the Synoptic context it is 'board and lodging', not payment, that is in view. It remains, however, that Luke was probably acquainted with a form of the tradition which spoke of 'wages', since μισθός is not a Lucan word, occurring (apart from the present passage) only in vi. 23 (Matt. v. 12), 35, whereas Matthew has it ten times.

In Luke x. 1–3 (compare Matt. ix. 37–x. 5) the ideas of the harvest ready for reaping and of the mission of the disciples are associated as they are here:

Luke	John
ὁ μὲν θερισμὸς πολύς	θεάσασθε τὰς χώρας ὅτι λευκαί εἰσιν
οἱ δὲ ἐργάται ὀλίγοι	πρὸς θερισμόν
ἰδοὺ ἀποστέλλω ὑμᾶς	ἐγὼ ἀπέστειλα ὑμᾶς θερίζειν.

The confronting, however, of the two quasi-parallel passages serves to show how little genuine resemblance there is in the formation of the respective sayings, in spite of the unavoidable recurrence of certain terms in passages which deal with the same or closely similar themes. That the Fourth Evangelist has reflected upon the whole body of sayings and parables dealing with the harvest-theme, as he found them in the earlier gospels, and has reproduced their substance in a form which gives them a twist in the direction of his own theological standpoint, is a theory which could not be disproved. Such a theory, however, would be more plausible if the resemblance had been either greater or less than it is. For what we have is neither a characteristic piece of Johannine composition nor an obvious imitation of Synoptic models, but something different from either: sayings of a highly individual character cast in a mould which can be shown to have analogies in the Synoptic tradition; sayings which so far as their form and content go might conceivably have occurred in any of the other gospels, but which in fact have no close parallel there.

The passage we are considering, iv. 35–48, may be taken as consisting primarily of three sayings:

(a) 'Lift up your eyes and survey the fields, and you will see that they are white and ready for reaping.'

(b) 'Already the reaper is taking his pay and gathering a harvest [for eternal life], so that sower and reaper may rejoice together.'

(c) 'I have sent you to reap where you did not labour; other men laboured, and you have entered into their labour.'

It is possible to read these sayings continuously, as carrying on a single theme; but upon closer examination it is not clear that they stand strictly on the same footing. In (a) the disciples are invited to observe that the crop is ready for reaping, but reaping has not yet begun. In (b) the harvest is in full swing; if indeed it is not coming to an end, since the reapers are being paid off. In (c) the disciples are no longer simply invited to take note of the situation; they are themselves the harvesters; they have already been sent to reap, and have already taken part in the work (ἀπέστειλα, εἰσεληλύθατε). The three sayings therefore do not, after

393

all, present a single perspicuous picture, and the suspicion arises that here, as often in the Synoptics, we have a collection of originally independent sayings, connected rather by association of ideas than by a logical development of thought. We may begin by examining each of them individually.

Sayings (*a*) and (*c*) are introduced in a peculiar way. Each is represented as the response to a quoted statement (ὑμεῖς λέγετε, ὁ λόγος ἐστὶν ἀληθινός). In verse 37 it is clear that the λόγος ἀληθινός, 'One sows, another reaps', is a proverbial saying.[1] It is a saying which seems to be echoed also (and surely independently) in Matt. xxv. 24, σκληρὸς εἶ ἄνθρωπος θερίζων ὅπου οὐκ ἔσπειρας (similarly Luke xix. 21). Commentators cite parallels from biblical and profane sources; the proverb is indeed a widespread commonplace. The point of the quotation here is to bring out with vivid force the truth that in this particular case (ἐν τούτῳ) the proverb is fulfilled in a special way: not in the sense that an enemy seizes the crop for which the farmer toiled (as in some Old Testament passages), or in the sense that a hard-fisted capitalist rakes in the profit of other men's industry (as in Matt. xxv. 24), but in the sense that the disciples, setting out on their mission, find that success has been assured through much preparatory work already accomplished by their predecessors.

In verse 35 it is not so clear what the expression, ὑμεῖς λέγετε, implies. If the second person plural is taken strictly, Jesus is commenting upon an observation which the disciples have volunteered. That it is to be understood as a banal remark upon the time of year (as many commentators have assumed, in their anxiety to discover data for a calendar of the Ministry of Jesus) I find entirely incredible; such remarks did not find a place in the gospel tradition. More plausible is the view that the disciples are represented as commenting, in figurative terms, upon the deferment of their hopes. If we ask what, in that case, suggested the figure of harvest, the answer might be that the disciples had in mind the common stock of eschatological imagery. But it seems probable that we have here, as in verse 37, a current saying, the second person being general and not specific.[2] It is true that it does not seem possible to trace such a proverb directly in other sources, nor is it quite clear what interval is supposed to be measured in the τετράμηνος. It is tempting to write the sentence as a (somewhat rough) iambic trimeter, with the initial foot resolved into a tribrach:[3]

$$\breve{\cup}\breve{\cup}\;\;\text{τε}|\text{τράμη}|\text{νος}\;\breve{\cup}\text{χ}\tilde{\omega}\;|\;\text{θερισ}|\text{μὸς}\;\text{ἔρ}|\text{χεται}.$$

[1] So also Bultmann *ad loc.*   [2] So also Bultmann *ad loc.*

[3] Omitting the unnecessary ἐστιν. A similar verse would be obtained by simply omitting the initial ἔτι, but this word seems to be necessary to the sense.

Such a verse might have been current in a Hellenistic setting, as a popular proverb. But in what sense? Apparently the traditional Greek reckoning of the interval between sowing and reaping was six months, not four (from the setting of the Pleiades to their rising). The old suggestion in Wetstein is attractive: that the proverb is applicable when the first green has appeared and the farmer begins to reckon his coming crop, but reminds himself (or is reminded) that much may happen in four months—as much as to say 'Don't count your chickens before they are hatched'. Wetstein cites many passages for the sentiment in general, but none mentioning the period of four months.

If, however, the prosody of the sentence gives a not impossible Greek verse, its syntax is properly Semitic rather than Greek. It is true that Moulton (*Grammar of N.T. Greek*, vol. I, Prolegomena, pp. 69–70) argues that such a construction was not impossible in vulgar Κοινή. But I have not noted any further examples (though there may well be such). In any case, however, the construction is quite common in the LXX,[1] rendering literally a form of sentence which is entirely natural and proper in Hebrew. The saying therefore may be Hebraic in origin, and the quasi-verse fortuitous.[2] In that case its meaning might be quite straightforward: 'Four months from sowing to harvest', for this would correspond well enough with the rabbinic ruling that seedtime ends in the middle of Kisleu and harvest begins in the middle of Nisan.[3] It is conceivable that this ruling was embodied in some such popular saying as we have here, though no parallel can be cited.

[1] E.g. Josh. i. 11, ἔτι τρεῖς ἡμέραι καὶ ὑμεῖς διαβαίνετε, Gen. xl. 13, ἔτι τρεῖς ἡμέραι καὶ μνησθήσεται Φαραὼ τῆς ἀρχῆς σου, Jonah iii. 4, ἔτι τρεῖς (*v.l.* τεσσαράκοντα) ἡμέραι καὶ Νινευὴ καταστραφήσεται, and similarly Exod. xvii. 4, Ps. xxxvi. 10, Hos. i. 4, Isa. x. 25, xxi. 16, and Jer. xxviii. 33, which is in content not unlike our present passage, ἔτι μικρὸν καὶ ἥξει ὁ ἀμητὸς αὐτῆς. John uses this construction again in xiv. 19, ἔτι μικρὸν καὶ ὁ κόσμος με οὐκέτι θεωρεῖ, and without the ἔτι in xvi. 16–17. It is one of his numerous Semitisms. It does not occur elsewhere in the N.T. apart from Heb. x. 37, which is a muddled conflation of two O.T. passages whose syntax is hardly compatible, resulting in a travesty of the Hebrew idiom by one who clearly did not understand it. Linguistically therefore there is no reason why the evangelist should not himself have coined this phrase, but there is also no reason why it should not have been contained in an originally Aramaic tradition.

[2] As are, doubtless, the rough iambic trimeters in Mark iv. 24 (‖ Matt. vii. 2), ἐν ᾧ μέτρῳ μετρεῖτε μετρηθήσεται, Acts xxiii. 5, ἄρχοντα τοῦ λαοῦ σου οὐκ ἐρεῖς κακῶς, Heb. xii. 14, οὗ χωρὶς οὐδεὶς ὄψεται τὸν κύριον, the hexameter in Heb. xii. 13 (T.R.), καὶ τροχιὰς ὀρθὰς ποιήσατε τοῖς ποσὶν ὑμῶν, and probably others.

[3] For the relevant passages see S.–B. *ad loc.*

In the Synoptic Gospels we have two instances at least where the quotation of a popular maxim, expressly given as such, forms part of a saying of Jesus. In Luke iv. 23 Jesus says to the congregation in the synagogue at Nazareth, Πάντως ἐρεῖτέ μοι τὴν παραβολὴν ταύτην, 'Ιατρὲ θεράπευσον σεαυτόν. This introduces a short discourse the purport of which is that (in contradiction to the popular maxim) the divinely commissioned physician is, as often as not, sent to heal strangers, as Elijah was sent to Zarephath and Elisha to Naaman the Syrian. The παραβολή is clearly thought of as a current saying, and it is put into the mouths of the auditors of Jesus. If the ὑμεῖς λέγετε of John iv. 35 puts a popular saying into the mouths of the disciples, in order that Jesus may correct it, then the formal parallel to Luke iv. 23 is close.

The other instance is the *pericopé* about signs of the weather, which occurs in varying forms in Matt. xvi. 2–3, DWΘ etc. (not in אB), and in Luke xii. 54–6. In both forms we have current sayings quoted under the caption λέγετε. In this case Jesus accepts the correctness of the popular saying on its own level, but expresses wonder that such experts in weather forecasting should be so blind to the deeper portents. For comparison we may confront the Johannine passage with the shorter, Matthaean, version of the *pericopé*.

Matthew	John
ὀψίας γενομένης	
λέγετε	οὐχ ὑμεῖς λέγετε
Εὐδία,	῎Ετι τετράμηνός ἐστιν
πυρράζει γὰρ ὁ οὐρανός	καὶ ὁ θερισμὸς ἔρχεται;
τὸ μὲν πρόσωπον τοῦ οὐρανοῦ	ἐπάρατε τοὺς ὀφθαλμοὺς ὑμῶν
γινώσκετε διακρίνειν	καὶ θεάσασθε τὰς χώρας
τὰ δὲ σημεῖα τῶν καιρῶν	ὅτι λευκαί εἰσιν πρὸς θερισμόν.
οὐ δύνασθε	

Formally, the passages are alike in quoting a current saying,[1] in order that it may be corrected, or replaced by a more significant judgement. In substance, they are alike in that in both cases the saying which is quoted refers to natural phenomena (the weather, the growth of crops), and the saying which is substituted for it is analogical (the winning of converts, the 'signs of the times'). There is no closer relationship, and obviously no possibility of derivation, yet the Johannine and the Synoptic passages are cast in the same mould.

It should be observed that, while in these passages of Luke and of John this form of statement is employed to place two points of view in com-

---

[1] Or, less probably, an opinion held by the auditors.

parison and contrast, the same purpose is more frequently served by the use of the dialogue form, where an interlocutor is brought in to give utterance to the one point of view, and Jesus responds with a saying which expresses the other point of view. Thus in Luke xiv. 15 an auditor exclaims (in what might well be quasi-proverbial terms), Μακάριος ὅστις φάγεται ἄρτον ἐν τῇ βασιλείᾳ τοῦ θεοῦ, and Jesus replies with a parable setting the eschatological 'feast' in a somewhat different light. This might obviously have been equally well set forth in a form more like that of John iv. 35, 'Do you not say, "Blessed is he who shall eat bread in the kingdom of God"? But I say unto you....' Or the Johannine saying might have been given in the form, 'The disciples said, Ἔτι τετράμηνος κ.τ.λ. and Jesus answering said, Ἐπάρατε τοὺς ὀφθαλμούς κ.τ.λ.' The two forms are alternative means of attaining the same end,[1] and perhaps equally indigenous to the tradition.

It would be more difficult to find anything like a formal parallel to the other saying, in verse 37. The expression ὁ λόγος ἐστὶν ἀληθινός is unlike anything else in the gospels. It recalls πιστὸς ὁ λόγος and ἀνθρώπινος ὁ λόγος[2] in the Pastoral Epistles. Wetstein cites numerous parallels from profane authors, Greek and Latin. We may with some confidence ascribe the formula introducing the quotation to the evangelist rather than to tradition. It would not be easy to find another instance where Jesus expressly cites a current saying and approves it as true upon its own level, in order to reinterpret it directly upon a deeper level; yet the assumption that men do in fact act upon maxims which are valid on their own level, and that such maxims may be applied with striking effect in the spiritual or ethical sphere, is the presupposition of many parables.[3] It is expressed in the question, Τί ἀφ' ἑαυτῶν οὐ κρίνετε τὸ δίκαιον; which in Luke xii. 57 introduces the parable of the defendant who comes to terms with his adversary betimes. It is implied wherever Jesus tells a parabolic story and asks, Τί δοκεῖ σοι; or the like; or where this question is raised by implication though unexpressed. From one point of view the maxim, ἄλλος ἐστὶν ὁ σπείρων καὶ ἄλλος ὁ θερίζων, might be regarded as a condensed, or implicit, parable, as are many of the *Bildwörter* of the Synoptic Gospels.[4] It is not difficult to imagine the kind of story in which the maxim might

[1] Similarly, the method of the *diatribé*, in which the speaker puts words into the mouth of an imaginary interlocutor (εἴποι ἄν τις or the like), may be compared with that of the philosophical dialogue, where the interlocutors appear in person.
[2] So D and some Latins in 1 Tim. iii. 1, probably rightly.
[3] See *Parables of the Kingdom* (Nisbet, 1961), pp. 9–11 (Collins, 1961), pp. 19–21.
[4] See *op. cit.* (Nisbet, 1961), pp. 5–6 (Collins, 1961), pp. 16–17.

have been dramatized, if we think of such parables as those of the Tares and the Labourers in the Vineyard. Verse 38 would then appear as the 'application' of the parable, analogous to such sayings as those of Luke xvii. 9, xvi. 8, Mark xiii. 35–6, Matt. xxiv. 44, xxv. 13. Regarded in this light, the saying, 'I have sent you to reap a crop for which you did not labour; others laboured, and you have entered into their labour', agrees with what is probably the most primitive form of the application of the gospel parables, in that it is not a universal proposition but one which refers to particular persons in their special situation.[1]

The form of this proposition, however, needs further consideration. The form-critics recognize a class of 'I-sayings'.[2] Inasmuch as the verb ἀπέστειλα is in the first person singular, the saying qualifies for admission to that class, being similar to Matt. x. 16a (Luke x. 3), Mark i. 17, Luke x. 19–20. Like these, it speaks of a relation between Jesus and his disciples, and is therefore just as much a 'you-saying' as an 'I-saying', and if we are to adopt this principle of classification verse 38b is a 'you-saying' simply. Sayings of similar form referring to the situation, mission or destiny of the disciples (though they are more numerous in the Fourth Gospel) are by no means uncommon in the Synoptics, and are characterized by just that intermingling of figurative and direct expressions which we find here, θερίζειν being wholly figurative, but κοπιᾶν, κόπος, being equally appropriate to the picture of agricultural work and to the work of evangelization (compare Gal. iv. 11, Phil. ii. 16 *et passim ap.* Paul). We may compare the following:[3]

Luke x. 3 (Matt. x. 16), ἀποστέλλω ὑμᾶς ὡς ἄρνας ἐν μέσῳ λύκων.

Mark i. 17, ποιήσω ὑμᾶς γενέσθαι ἁλιεῖς ἀνθρώπων.

(Luke v. 10, ἀπὸ τοῦ νῦν ἀνθρώπους ἔσῃ ζωγρῶν.)

Luke x. 23 *sq.* (Matt. xiii. 16 *sq.*), μακάριοι οἱ ὀφθαλμοὶ οἱ βλέποντες ἃ βλέπετε κ.τ.λ.

Luke xxii. 28, ὑμεῖς ἐστε οἱ διαμεμενηκότες μετ' ἐμοῦ ἐν τοῖς πειρασμοῖς μου.

Matt. v. 13, ὑμεῖς ἐστε τὸ ἅλας τῆς γῆς.

Matt. v. 14, ὑμεῖς ἐστε τὸ φῶς τοῦ κόσμου.

Luke xxii. 31, ἰδοὺ ὁ σατανᾶς ἐξῃτήσατο ὑμᾶς τοῦ σινιάσαι ὑμᾶς ὡς τὸν σῖτον·

---

[1] On parables and their application, see *op. cit.* (Nisbet, 1961), pp. 14–19, 85 *sqq.* (Collins, 1961), pp. 23–7, 84 *sqq.*

[2] See R. Bultmann, *Geschichte der synoptischen Tradition*, pp. 161–76. Bultmann's judgements upon the *Ich-worte* are largely subjective and arbitrary.

[3] I have included here only affirmations regarding the disciples in their historical situation, omitting both eschatological predictions about their future destiny, which are on a different footing, and the large body of precepts for their conduct.

None of these sayings shows a form exactly like that of John iv. 38; none of them could have served as a model for it; yet they suffice to show that 'you-sayings' are firmly embedded in the tradition, and have a certain common outlook and ethos marking them as a recognizable class, to which the Johannine saying properly belongs, though its content and purport are not identical with anything in the Synoptic Gospels.

It appears therefore that this third saying of our sequence, though it has no close formal parallel in the other gospels, such as can be produced for the first of the series, nevertheless has subtle associations with Synoptic forms such as make it credible that it had a traditional origin.

Of saying (b) it is more difficult to speak with confidence. As it stands, the Johannine phrase, εἰς ζωὴν αἰώνιον, removes it from the category of truly parabolic utterances, and the expression, ἵνα ὁμοῦ χαίρῃ (in which ὁμοῦ is peculiar to John among the gospels, though that may be accidental), associates itself readily with references to the joy of the disciples in xiv. 28, xvi. 22, xx. 20 (the verb), xv. 11, xvi. 20–7, xvii. 13 (the noun χαρά). The whole sentence might be regarded as a further comment of the evangelist on the saying in verse 35. Yet the situation presupposed, as I have remarked, is not precisely the same: in verse 35 the fields are ready for reaping, in verse 36 the harvest is in full swing (or, perhaps, over). As a comment, therefore, on verse 35 the sentence is not particularly apt. On the other hand, if we leave out of account the phrase εἰς ζωὴν αἰώνιον (as an exegetical comment, compare xii. 25), verse 36 might be taken by itself as a description of a typical situation in real life, quite in the spirit of the Synoptic parables: the farmer has engaged temporary paid labour for the harvest; the men, having completed their task, are drawing their pay, and all the farm labourers, whether or not they have actually been employed in the harvest, will share in the general rejoicings. The ethos of such a saying would be that of Ps. cxxv. 5, οἱ σπείροντες ἐν δάκρυσιν ἐν ἀγαλλιάσει θεριοῦσιν, the only difference being that here the trouble of sowing and the satisfaction of reaping, which in the psalm are experienced by the same persons, are distributed between sower and reaper as distinct characters. The idea of 'the joy of harvest' is at any rate sufficiently natural, and also sufficiently biblical, to stand here without support from the distinctively Johannine conception of the joy of the disciples at reunion with their Lord.

On this view the saying in verse 36 would originally have been, not the sequel to verse 35, as it appears in John, but a parallel description of essentially the same situation from a slightly different standpoint. The expressions, λευκαί εἰσιν (αἱ χῶραι) πρὸς θερισμόν, and ἤδη ὁ θερίζων λαμβάνει τὸν μισθόν, would correspond with the Marcan εὐθὺς ἀποστέλλει τὸ δρέπανον ὅτι παρέστηκεν ὁ θερισμός (Mark iv. 29), and, in a different range of imagery, the Lucan ἤδη ἔτοιμά ἐστιν (Luke xiv. 17). Such a saying might well have been preserved in the primitive tradition; as with the Synoptic parables, we are dispensed from asking what is signified by the various items in the description—who is the sower, who the reaper, and what his μισθός.

The outcome of this long discussion is, I submit, a substantial probability that this sequence of sayings, forming a compact *pericopé* inserted into a long episode of different character, was drawn from a traditional source not identical with the tradition lying behind the Synoptic Gospels, yet having subtle but real affinities with that tradition. If we take this hypothesis, it will be worth while to inquire into the possible *Sitz im Leben* of such a tradition. In its present position in the Fourth Gospel the setting is doubtless that of the missionary church occupied with the work of evangelization in the wide world (symbolized in the main dialogue by the alien population of Samaria). It has often been suggested that the story of a Ministry of Jesus in Samaria, here adopted and elaborated by the Fourth Evangelist, first took shape in connection with the mission to that district recorded in Acts viii. It may be so; but there is in any case no necessary connection between the *pericopé* we are considering and the Samaritan episode, nor does Acts viii provide a plausible setting for the sayings. Each of these sayings might stand by itself, each with a setting of its own.

(*a*) The saying, 'Look at the fields: they are ripe for harvest', is in purport identical with the Synoptic saying, 'The harvest truly is plentiful', though there is no plausibility in the suggestion that the one was derived from the other. When however verse 35 is taken as a whole, it differs from Matt. ix. 37 (Luke x. 2) in that it explicitly sets the affirmation that the harvest is ready over against a prevalent belief that it is still far from ready, but to be expected within a limited (and possibly calculable) period. There is a similarly polemical treatment of the theme in Luke xvii. 20. The Pharisees there ask for a forecast of the time at which the Kingdom of God may be expected to come. Jesus replies (to paraphrase): 'The coming of the Kingdom of God is not an event which you can watch for (as astronomers watch for the appearance of the heavenly bodies in their seasons); you will never be in a position to say "Look! Here it is!" or "There it is!" For the Kingdom of God is ἐντὸς ὑμῶν.' Whatever be the right interpretation of that enigmatic expression,[1] it certainly carries the implication that the Kingdom of God is in some sense a present reality, as opposed to the belief that its coming is a future event whose date might conceivably be predicted. Different as the Johannine saying is in all its details, the essential purport and ethos of both sayings are the same.

What then is the situation in which it was necessary to state this conviction in contradistinction from prevalent beliefs? Was it the situation contemplated, for example, in 2 Pet. iii. 4, when people were asking, wistfully or mockingly, 'Where is the promise of his coming?'? Possibly; the answer here given, widely different as it is from pseudo-Peter's, would be apposite enough: neither in 'a thousand years' nor yet after 'one day', but *now* is the time when the Lord's harvest is being reaped. Or again, it may have been a much earlier situation, when the primitive Church was waiting for the ingathering of the elect at Christ's second coming, soon to occur, as they supposed, and needed to be encouraged to undertake the task of evangelization without tarrying for any. It may be that in such a situation, while some quoted the saying 'You will not have gone through the cities of Israel before the Son of Man comes', or, in more general terms, reminded themselves ὁ καιρὸς συνεσταλμένος ἐστίν, others adduced the saying which underlies our present text.

Yet there are many sayings in the Synoptic Gospels which appear to point to an even more appropriate setting within the Ministry of Jesus himself; sayings which declare, in varying terms and under many different kinds of imagery, that the long expected crisis has at length arrived: πεπλήρωται ὁ καιρός. There are too many of them, and their character is too various,[2] to make the suggestion plausible that they were all coined by

---

[1] See my comment on that passage in *Parables of the Kingdom* (Nisbet, 1961), pp. 62–3 (Collins, 1961), pp. 64–5. I now favour the interpretation put forward by C. H. Roberts in *Harvard Theological Review*, XLI (Jan. 1948), 1–8. He agrees that the rendering 'among you' lacks any substantial support, but refers to passages which suggest that the meaning of ἐντὸς ὑμῶν may be 'within your reach', or 'within your grasp'. This would give an excellent sense. So far from the coming of the Kingdom of God being a remote event, it is a reality here and now available. We have not to 'look out' for it (παρατηρεῖν) but to 'receive' it (δέξασθαι τὴν βασιλείαν τοῦ θεοῦ ὡς παιδίον). In any case ἐντὸς ὑμῶν ἐστιν is a statement in the present tense, and to make it mean 'the Kingdom of God will very soon be among you', as is the fashion at present, is to do violence to language.

[2] See *Parables of the Kingdom* (Nisbet, 1961), pp. 28–35 (Collins, 1961), pp. 35–41.

the early Church at a period when it was necessary to affirm that the advent of the Lord could not long be delayed. On the contrary, there is good reason to believe that many sayings and parables which originally implied the immediacy of the eschatological crisis have been watered down into a promise, or menace, of its near approach.[1] The announcement that the coming of the Kingdom of God was actually in process in the Ministry of Jesus, that the messianic banquet was spread (Luke xiv. 17), that the harvest of the world awaited the reapers (Matt. ix. 37), was startling enough and must certainly have encountered scepticism or doubt on the part both of opponents and of friends. That it should have been stated on occasion in explicit contrast to current belief is in itself probable, even if no Synoptic saying except Luke xvii. 20 attests it. John alone, it appears, has preserved a saying which brings into strong relief what is implicit in many passages of the other gospels, and there is strong reason for supposing that the saying does indeed belong to a situation in the historic Ministry of Jesus.

(b) The second saying, as understood in its present setting by contemporary readers, would carry a pertinent meaning for those who were too anxiously awaiting a future crisis. The evangelist points them to the success of the gentile mission, and assures them, 'This is the harvest of the world: the Lord sowed the seed, we his followers are reaping the harvest, and our "reward" is not only "in heaven"; here and now we may enter into the joy of our Lord'.

Yet we have seen some reason to believe that we have here a genuine parable, only slightly rewritten in the interest of an 'allegorical' interpretation. On general principles of parabolic interpretation we should not be required to ask what is signified by ὁ σπείρων, ὁ θερίζων, and μισθός. All these details go to build up a single picture: it is that of the moment when the year's labour has reached its consummation, and all who have been concerned in it—even in those stages of it which at the time seemed unremunerative—share the joyful sense of effort rewarded, as endeavour and wavering hope pass into realization. In this sense the saying would fit aptly into the period of the Ministry of Jesus when he associated his disciples in his work. According to Matthew and Luke he had regretted the paucity of labourers to deal with an unexpectedly abundant harvest. He then sent out his disciples, who returned flushed with the success of their mission—ὑπέστρεψαν μετὰ χαρᾶς (Luke x. 17). To this situation such

[1] See op. cit. (Nisbet, 1961), pp. 122–36 (Collins, 1961), pp. 115–28.

a saying as that of John iv. 36 would be eminently appropriate: 'Yes, we may all rejoice; the harvest is in full swing.'

(c) In the third saying the distinction of sower and reaper, which in verse 36, I have suggested, is merely incidental to the general picture, is the vital centre. It would apply aptly enough to the situation of the Church in the evangelist's own time. The success of Christian missionaries in the gentile world was an outstanding illustration of the maxim, 'One sows, another reaps'. The preparatory work had been done, not only by Paul and other pioneers, with the work of Christ himself and his immediate disciples behind them, but also through the synagogues of the Dispersion. And this evangelist, who held that there were 'children of God scattered abroad' all over the world, and that Christ had 'other sheep', not of the Jewish fold, to be brought in, would also have in mind the truth that the eternal Word had been sown in the hearts of men before ever they heard the Gospel preached. The sowing had been done; the Christian missionary reaped the harvest. He must be reminded that any success he may have won is due only in small part to his own efforts; others have laboured, he has garnered the fruit of their labours. Read in this way the aorist ἀπέστειλα would refer to an act in the past—the original commission to the Church (represented in this gospel by xx. 21)—and the perfect εἰσεληλύθατε to an activity in the past which continues into the present (the 'punctilinear' *Aktionsart*).

Yet we may ask whether there may not have been a suitable *Sitz im Leben* for such a saying at an earlier date. I have argued that although there is no obvious or precise parallel in the Synoptic Gospels, this saying shows upon examination an unforced correspondence with traditional forms. In the Synoptics, parables, and parabolic sayings, have not infrequently been given a twist which has adapted them to a situation in the history of the early Church, and yet can be shown, upon examination, to belong originally to a situation within the Ministry of Jesus.[1] Can we find such a situation for our present saying? It must be a situation in which Jesus has already associated his disciples in his work, for the aorist ἀπέστειλα is necessarily retrospective (in contrast with the ἀποστέλλω of John xx. 21), while the perfect εἰσεληλύθατε implies that the work continues. It must be taken as one of the assured elements in the primary tradition that at one point in his Ministry Jesus sent his disciples on tour,

---

[1] See *Parables of the Kingdom*, chs. IV and V, and, for a thorough discussion, J. Jeremias, *Die Gleichnisse Jesu*, 2nd ed. (1952), especially pp. 16–81.

or, alternatively, that during one period such missions were a part of his strategy. The saying we are considering would so far be in place at any time after the first sending. But the question we have to answer is, If the disciples are the reapers, who are the sowers? As predecessors in the work, it seems, only the prophets could come into consideration—οἱ προφῆται οἱ πρὸ ὑμῶν, as Matt. v. 12 (Luke vi. 23) has it.[1] In that passage the prophets are exemplars of the persecution which the disciples will suffer for their loyalty to Christ. In Matt. xiii. 17 (Luke x. 24) the prophets are men who desired to see that which the disciples now see. And in our present passage the disciples, who are in the prophetic succession of suffering for the good cause, who possess in realization that which for the prophets existed only as aspiration, are also successors to the prophets in their work; and here also, while the prophets knew only the hope (the sowing), the disciples experience the fulfilment (the harvest). John completes a triad.

The tradition of the mission of the disciples attracted to itself a number of sayings which the Church recalled and preserved because they were felt to be acutely relevant to its own missionary work in the world. The Synoptic 'Mission Discourse', alike in its Matthaean and its Lucan form (substantially as these differ), is clearly a compilation of sayings which may have been uttered on a variety of occasions. If the Johannine sayings in iv. 35–8 had happened to be incorporated along with those which the Synoptics have collected, they could have been read as part of the discourse without any sense of incongruity. Try the experiment.

Do you not say, 'Four months yet to harvest'? I tell you, look around and survey the fields: they are ripe for harvest. The harvest indeed is abundant, but labourers are scarce. Pray the lord of the harvest to send labourers into his harvest. Go, I send you like lambs among wolves.... They returned with joy, saying, 'Lord, even the devils are subject to us in your name'. He replied, 'Already the reaper is drawing his pay, so that sower and reaper may rejoice together. But do not rejoice that the spirits are subject to you; rejoice that your names are enrolled in heaven. One sows, another reaps; I sent you to reap a crop at which you did not labour. Others have laboured, and you have entered into their labour.'

We may conclude with some confidence that these sayings are drawn from the same reservoir of tradition as the kindred sayings in the Synoptics, though by a different channel, and that they belong broadly to the same

[1] Perhaps we should say 'the prophets until John' (cf. Luke xvi. 16).

situation in the Ministry of Jesus. John shows no awareness of the mission of the disciples as an historical incident, or at any rate no interest in it; for him there is one 'sending'—the final commission of xx. 21. But he has nevertheless taken from the common tradition sayings which presuppose the mission, and so incidentally provides independent confirmation of the Synoptic report that Jesus did associate his disciples with his own work by sending them out to carry his message to the public at large.

5. PREDICTIONS

The Synoptic Gospels contain a considerable body of sayings cast into the form of prediction of future events, after the manner of Old Testament prophecy or of Jewish apocalypse. As we have them, some of these appear to refer to events immediately impending at the assumed time of their utterance, such as the fate of Jesus himself, his betrayal by Judas, his denial by Peter and his desertion by the Twelve, his sufferings and death. Others seem to have a more extended perspective, though still within a limited historical frame, such as the siege and capture of Jerusalem and the destruction of the temple, the mission of the Church to Israel and to the Gentiles, and the growing intensity of persecution. Others, to all appearance, defy any attempt to place them in an intelligible historical series, and borrow the fantastic colouring of apocalyptic, such as the final and unprecedented tribulation, the collapse of the astral universe, and the coming of the Son of Man on the clouds. It is admittedly not easy in every case to determine into which of these three classes of prediction a given saying should be placed: whether, for example, the restoration of the temple is to be thought of as the historical sequel to its destruction by the armies of Rome, or as a feature of the grand ἀποκατάστασις πάντων, or in some other way,[1] and whether the prediction of the session of the Son of Man at God's right hand, and his coming with the clouds, is to be taken as referring to trans-historical realities, or to an event of the comparatively remote future, or (as would seem to be implied in Matthew's ἀπ᾽ ἄρτι and Luke's ἀπὸ τοῦ νῦν) as referring in cryptic symbolism to contemporary or impending happenings on the historical plane.[2]

For our present purpose it is not necessary to determine these questions, but it is well to have them in mind in considering predictive sayings in the Fourth Gospel. The latter are far fewer in number. Forecasts of public

[1] See *Parables of the Kingdom* (Nisbet, 1961), pp. 42–5, 53–5 (Collins, 1961), pp. 47–50, 56–8.

[2] I have discussed this question in *Parables of the Kingdom* (Nisbet, 1961), pp. 68–84 (Collins, 1961), pp. 69–83. I now state more positively the view which I suggested in the first edition of that book, viz. that as in Daniel the victory of the Son of Man is a visionary symbol of a strictly historical event believed to be immediately impending—the victory of the Jews over the Seleucid empire—so in Mark xiv. 62 the same symbol stands for a directly impending event—the death and resurrection of Jesus, conceived as his vindication (see also J. A. T. Robinson, *Jesus and His Coming*, 1957).

disasters and cosmic catastrophes are absent. The only coming event depicted in anything like apocalyptic colours is the general resurrection of the dead, which is foretold in terms close to Jewish tradition—except that the summons to rise comes from Christ himself[1] (v. 28–9). This doctrine is nowhere explicitly enunciated in the Synoptic Gospels, though it is presupposed in the Judgement Scene of Matt. xxv. 31–46, and perhaps in some few other sayings. The Johannine predictions, apart from those which clearly refer to immediately impending events—the betrayal by Judas, the desertion of the disciples, and Peter's denial, as well as the crucifixion of Jesus himself—fall chiefly under two heads: (i) predictions of Christ's return after death (corresponding broadly with the Synoptic predictions of his resurrection and coming in glory), and (ii) forecasts of the future destiny of his followers. I shall take the latter first.

(i) *The Disciples and their Future*

In the Synoptic Gospels there is a large and elaborate body of prediction dealing with the prospects of the followers of Jesus after his death and resurrection. It is collected chiefly in the 'Mission Discourse' of Matt. x and in the 'Eschatological Discourse' of Mark xiii and parallels. Briefly, they are to expect to be brought to trial, first in Jewish ecclesiastical courts and then in secular courts. This will in some cases result in the death penalty. But the trials will give them the opportunity of effective 'witness', in which they will have the help of the Spirit (or of Christ himself). Meanwhile the propagation of the Gospel will go forward, until it has been proclaimed all over the world. Then persecution will grow in intensity, there will be apostasies and inner treachery, and the breaking of family ties will lead into the general anarchy of the final tribulation, which, however, will be survived by those who endure to the end. From this point the predictions pass beyond the bounds of imaginable history and are absorbed into the fantasies of apocalyptic. All this is worked out in

---

[1] There are two passages which at first sight may seem to have a certain apocalyptic colouring, and have been thought to refer to future events after the death of Christ: i. 51, which speaks of heaven opened and angels ascending and descending, and vi. 62, which speaks of the vision of Christ ascending. But closer inspection shows that the former, with its reference to Gen. xxviii. 12, has nothing to do with apocalyptic visions of the future; it is to be interpreted with reference to the ministry of the incarnate Logos (see *Interpretation*, pp. 228, 245–6); and the ἀνάβασις of vi. 62 is the whole process which begins with the passion and death of Christ, and is consummated in his resurrection and the gift of the Spirit—the process otherwise described by the verbs ὑψωθῆναι, δοξασθῆναι (see *Interpretation*, pp. 244–7, 441–3).

considerable detail. The suspicion is not unjustified that some of the detail is *ex eventu*.

The corresponding predictions of the Fourth Gospel are contained in the Farewell Discourses. They are of modest bulk in comparison. Among them are some which refer so plainly to the interior life of the Christian that it is impossible to associate them with any definite overt event:[1] after Christ's departure the disciples will learn to pray in his name (xvi. 26), they will have the 'knowledge' which is union with God (xiv. 20), and will therefore 'live' in the pregnant sense, and finally Christ will take them to be with himself (xiv. 3), and he will raise them to life on the Last Day (vi. 39). All this is alien to the Synoptic outlook, and it is so much of a piece with the whole Johannine theology that it may with probability be assigned to the evangelist, whatever nucleus of older tradition, no longer recognizable, may lie within it. At one point only the Johannine picture of the Christian life as lived after Christ's departure and return (that is of the interior life of the Church) has contact with the Synoptic predictions: in the promise of the help of the Holy Spirit. But this will be best dealt with when we have considered the few Johannine predictions which appear to point to concrete features of the historical scene.

First, the disciples will be the objects of hatred and persecution. The terminology here is of the most general character: μισεῖν, διώκειν, θλῖψις, ἀποκτείνειν, διὰ τὸ ὄνομα. All these are common to John and the Synoptics, as the following table will show.

(*a*) John xv. 18: ὁ κόσμος ὑμᾶς μισεῖ   Mark xiii. 13: ἔσεσθε μισούμενοι ὑπὸ πάντων
Luke vi. 22: μακάριοί ἐστε ὅταν μισήσωσιν ὑμᾶς οἱ ἄνθρωποι.

The present tense in John is clearly intended to refer to a period which in the dramatic situation is future, although for the evangelist and his readers it is present. In the Johannine context the simple statement is elaborated theologically: the disciples are hated by the world because they are not ἐκ τοῦ κόσμου, but are elected by Christ out of the world. The prototype of such hatred is the hatred directed towards Christ himself. This last point has a certain contact with a trait of the Synoptic predictions: Matt. x. 25, εἰ τὸν οἰκοδεσπότην Βεεζεβοὺλ ἐπεκάλεσαν, πόσῳ μᾶλλον τοὺς οἰκιακοὺς αὐτοῦ. This is illustrated by the proverbial saying, 'The slave is not greater than his master', which duly reappears in John xv. 20.

[1] On the significance of such sayings see C. F. D. Moule, *The Birth of the New Testament* (Black, 1962), p. 98.

PREDICTIONS

(*b*) John xv. 20: ὑμᾶς διώξουσιν   Luke xxi. 12: ἐπιβαλοῦσιν ἐφ' ὑμᾶς τὰς
χεῖρας αὐτῶν καὶ διώξουσιν
Matt. v. 11: μακάριοί ἐστε ὅταν
ὀνειδίσωσιν ὑμᾶς καὶ διώξωσιν.

In John this is another example of the maxim, 'Like master like slave': εἰ
ἐμὲ ἐδίωξαν καὶ ὑμᾶς διώξουσιν, and this is followed by yet another example:
εἰ τὸν λόγον μου ἐτήρησαν [*per impossibile!*] καὶ τὸν ὑμέτερον τηρήσουσιν,
which leads out beyond the Synoptic setting.

(*c*) John xvi. 33: ἐν τῷ κόσμῳ   Matt. xxiv. 9: παραδώσουσιν ὑμᾶς
θλῖψιν ἔχετε   εἰς θλῖψιν.
(present in future sense, as above)

Compare Matt. xiii. 21, γενομένης θλίψεως ἢ διωγμοῦ διὰ τὸν λόγον.
Elsewhere in the Synoptics θλῖψις is the final tribulation preceding the end
of all.

(*d*) John xvi. 2: ἔρχεται ὥρα ἵνα   Matt. xxiv. 9: παραδώσουσιν ὑμᾶς εἰς
πᾶς ὁ ἀποκτείνας ὑμᾶς δόξῃ   θλῖψιν καὶ ἀποκτενοῦσιν ὑμᾶς, καὶ
λατρείαν προσφέρειν τῷ θεῷ   ἔσεσθε μισούμενοι
(combining the three terms, διώκειν,
θλῖψις, ἀποκτείνειν).

The perception that the persecutors ply their odious trade as a work of
piety may probably reflect the experience of the early Church, but the
forecast of martyrdom seems to be firmly rooted in the tradition. Compare Luke xxi. 16, θανατώσουσιν ἐξ ὑμῶν καὶ ἔσεσθε μισούμενοι ὑπὸ
πάντων, and the saying common (with insignificant variation) to Matthew
and Luke, μὴ φοβεῖσθε ἀπὸ τῶν ἀποκτεννόντων τὸ σῶμα (Matt. x. 28,
Lk. xii. 4).

(*e*) John xv. 21: ταῦτα πάντα (name-   Mark xiii. 13 (and parallels in
ly all that is involved in hatred   Matt. and Luke): ἔσεσθε μισούμενοι
and persecution) ποιήσουσιν εἰς   ὑπὸ πάντων διὰ τὸ ὄνομά μου.
ὑμᾶς διὰ τὸ ὄνομά μου

The way in which these five terms recur in various permutations and
combinations would be consistent with the view that the Fourth Evangelist
was working upon recollections of the Synoptic Gospels, but it would
more naturally suggest that they belong to a nucleus of tradition common
to all, worked up by each according to his particular tendency—in the
Synoptics by way of elaboration in the light of the experience of the
persecuted Church, and in John in accordance with his theological interest.

Beyond these quite general predictions of hatred, persecution and
martyrdom for the Name, John has one distinctive feature—exclusion

from the synagogue: xvi. 2 ἀποσυναγώγους ποιήσουσιν ὑμᾶς. The word ἀποσυνάγωγος is not found in the other gospels, being in fact peculiar to John among New Testament writers. But the same meaning is probably intended in Luke vi. 22, μακάριοί ἐστε ὅταν μισήσωσιν ὑμᾶς οἱ ἄνθρωποι καὶ ὅταν ἀφορίσωσιν ὑμᾶς. Any dependence of John on Luke is excluded, but it appears that, in the traditions followed by both, the prospect of excommunication from the synagogue was held before the disciples. Elsewhere in the Synoptics the followers of Christ are to be brought before synagogues (Luke xxi. 12) or Jewish courts (συνέδρια, Mark xiii. 9, Matt. x. 17), and are to be flogged in synagogues (εἰς συναγωγὰς δαρή-σεσθε, Mark xiii. 9; ἐν ταῖς συναγωγαῖς αὐτῶν μαστιγώσουσιν ὑμᾶς, Matt. x. 17). Of such procedure we have examples in the early Church (Acts iv. 5 *sqq.*, v. 21 *sqq.*, 40; 2 Cor. xi. 24), but it does not appear, so far as we can gather from the texts, that either the Twelve or Paul or other Jewish Christians regarded themselves as excluded from the Jewish community or from synagogue worship. We must, however, conclude, it seems, that the prospect of such exclusion was before Christians of Jewish origin early enough, at least, to have entered into the common tradition behind both Luke and John. The latter, indeed, believed that the threat of excommunication was present, and that it was actually enforced, even during the historical Ministry of Jesus (John ix. 22, 34, xii. 42). Whether or not this is a throwing back of later conditions we have perhaps not sufficient evidence to decide, but xvi. 2 seems rather to imply that this threat was not before the followers of Christ during his Ministry but would become a matter of experience in the persecutions which would follow his death.

We now pass to a further point. In the Synoptic forecasts of persecution the arrest and trial of Christians are regarded as opportunities for 'witness', and in giving such witness they are promised the help of Christ himself or of the Holy Spirit. The expressions used vary considerably, as the following table will show.

A. Matt. x. 17–19	B. Mark xiii. 9–11
(Christians will be brought to trial)	(Christians will be brought to trial)
εἰς μαρτύριον αὐτοῖς καὶ τοῖς ἔθνεσιν.	εἰς μαρτύριον αὐτοῖς...καὶ ὅταν
ὅταν δὲ παραδῶσιν ὑμᾶς μὴ μερι-μνήσητε πῶς ἢ τί λαλήσητε· οὐ γὰρ ὑμεῖς ἐστε οἱ λαλοῦντες ἀλλὰ τὸ πνεῦμα τοῦ πατρὸς ὑμῶν τὸ λαλοῦν ἐν ὑμῖν.	ἄγωσιν ὑμᾶς παραδιδόντες μὴ προ-μεριμνᾶτε τί λαλήσητε, ἀλλ' ὃ ἐὰν δοθῇ ὑμῖν ἐν ἐκείνη τῇ ὥρᾳ τοῦτο λαλεῖτε· οὐ γάρ ἐστε ὑμεῖς οἱ λαλοῦντες ἀλλὰ τὸ πνεῦμα τὸ ἅγιον.

C. Luke xii. 11–12

(No reference to μαρτύριον) ὅταν δὲ εἰσφέρωσιν ὑμᾶς ἐπὶ τὰς συναγωγὰς καὶ τὰς ἀρχὰς καὶ τὰς ἐξουσίας μὴ μεριμνήσητε πῶς ἢ τί ἀπολογήσησθε ἢ τί εἴπητε· τὸ γὰρ ἅγιον πνεῦμα διδάξει ὑμᾶς ἐν αὐτῇ τῇ ὥρᾳ ἃ δεῖ εἰπεῖν.

D. Luke xxi. 13–15

ἀποβήσεται ὑμῖν εἰς μαρτύριον. θέτε οὖν ἐν ταῖς καρδίαις ὑμῶν μὴ προμελετᾶν ἀπολογηθῆναι· ἐγὼ γὰρ δώσω ὑμῖν στόμα καὶ σοφίαν ᾗ οὐ δυνήσονται ἀντιστῆναι ἢ ἀντειπεῖν ἅπαντες οἱ ἀντικείμενοι ὑμῖν.

The very fact that Luke produces two strikingly different versions of what is in substance the same saying proves that we are here dealing with variant pre-canonical forms of tradition. Moreover there is good reason for believing that in x. 17–42, or at least in parts of this section, Matthew is following a tradition independent of Mark xiii. We are justified in concluding that the call to Christians to 'witness' to Christ before courts of justice, and the promise that they should receive help in doing so, was so deeply rooted in the oral tradition that it appeared in several branches of that tradition, taking slightly different forms.

We now observe that in John there are traces of the same sequence of ideas. In xv. 18 sqq., after a long passage about hatred and persecution (εἰ ὁ κόσμος ὑμᾶς μισεῖ, γινώσκετε ὅτι ἐμὲ πρῶτον ὑμῶν μεμίσηκεν...εἰ ἐμὲ ἐδίωξαν καὶ ὑμᾶς διώξουσιν...μεμισήκασιν καὶ ἐμὲ καὶ τὸν πατέρα μου...), we have a passage which echoes the terms we have noted in the four Synoptic passages: τὸ πνεῦμα...μαρτυρήσει καὶ ὑμεῖς μαρτυρεῖτε. This form of statement might be said to combine the ideas of A and B on the one hand, that the Spirit will speak for the disciples, and of C on the other hand, that the Spirit will teach them what to say;[1] in either case, the persecution to which they are subjected gives the opportunity of 'witness'. The Johannine discourse then proceeds to the themes of excommunication and martyrdom, which, as we have seen, have close traditional connections with the themes of witness and of the Spirit. It is true, of course, that all these themes are here worked out in a fashion which is distinctively Johannine, and, in particular, the Spirit is given the title παράκλητος, which is in all probability an original contribution of this evangelist. But it is a title which exactly describes the function of the Spirit in the Synoptic passages, that of counsel for the defence, and this is elaborated in the strongly Johannine passage which follows (xvi. 8–11).

[1] The standpoint represented in D has a somewhat remote parallel in the apparent equation of the coming of the Paraclete with Christ's own return, John xiv. 16–18.

Here the Spirit plays the part of 'advocate': he cross-examines the oppos-ing party and exposes the falsity of its claims (ἐλέγξει τὸν κόσμον). Only it now appears that the Church has gone over to the offensive, and the Spirit is counsel for the prosecution. The trials of Christians before Jewish and secular courts have turned into a judgement scene in which the parties are the world on the one hand and on the other hand the Church with its Advocate the Holy Spirit. In all this we have one of the most impressive examples of this evangelist's exposition of theological ideas, but it has as its centre a sequence of themes related at point after point to similar sequences in the Synoptics, though never with such close resemblance as to make literary dependence the most probable hypothesis. As we have seen, there are strong grounds for believing that within the Synoptics themselves variant forms of oral tradition covering these themes have been laid under contribution. It becomes a highly probable inference that John was acquainted with another such variant form of tradition.

On that hypothesis we may ask whether there are any signs which might point to the *Sitz im Leben* in which such sayings may have received the form in which they have come down. In the Synoptics it is fairly clear that (whatever original sayings may lie behind them) the predictions are formed with events and conditions in view which belong to the period between the death of Jesus and the Jewish War: in particular the vigorous prosecution of the gentile mission and the trials of Christian confessors and martyrs before Roman as well as Jewish tribunals. In the Fourth Gospel the followers of Christ are threatened with excommunication from the synagogue—a menace which would have no terrors for any but Jewish Christians. They may have to face martyrdom, but it is clearly at the hands of their fellow-Jews, since the persecutors believe themselves to be rendering service to God. There is no reference to persecution by the secular authorities. There is indeed a large-scale controversy between the Church and 'the world', but in this the Church is on the offensive. It is only in this sense that there can be said to be any reference here to the gentile mission, such as we find in the Synoptic predictions. This is certainly not because our evangelist had no interest in the world-wide appeal of the Gospel: he believed that there were sheep of Christ's flock to be brought in, who were not of the Jewish fold, and that one effect of the death of Christ would be to gather in these scattered children of God and to draw all mankind to him. Moreover, he shows special interest in the evangelization of Samaritans, as surrogates for the gentile world. If the tradition he followed had contained such predictions as those of

Mark xiii. 10, Matt. xxiv. 14, Luke xxiv. 47 (combined with the theme of 'witness' (verse 48)), or such injunctions as those of Matt. xxviii. 19, there seems no reason why he should have omitted them. Arguments *e silentio* are notoriously precarious, but it is fair to say that there is nothing to suggest that the tradition which the Fourth Evangelist followed for predictions of the future of the disciples was formed in any environment but that of a Jewish-Christian community, absorbed in the task of witness before their fellow-Jews, and dreading, next to martyrdom, exclusion from the commonwealth of Israel. Such would seem to be its *Sitz im Leben*.

(ii) *The Death of Christ and its Sequel*

The Fourth Gospel, like the others, contains forecasts of the death of Jesus and its sequel, but they are cast in a different mould. They are contained in the Farewell Discourses. The first part of the discourses, the great dialogue which runs from xiii. 31 to xiv. 31, is pervaded and dominated by the theme of departure and return. This theme is set forth in characteristically Johannine language and style and interwoven with distinctively Johannine ideas. Nowhere, perhaps, is it more difficult to establish any direct relation between John and the Synoptics. Nowhere, certainly, is there less ground to infer anything like literary dependence. It may, however, be worth while to essay a comparison. This will necessitate a preliminary examination of the Synoptic predictions.

These fall into two groups. The one group is couched in terms of death and resurrection on the third day, or after three days; the other in apocalyptic terms of the coming of the Son of Man at the End. Thus, in Mark viii. 31 and parallels we have the sequence: sufferings, death, resurrection; but in Mark viii. 38 we read of the Coming of the Son of Man (ὅταν ἔλθῃ ἐν τῇ δόξῃ: Matt. xvi. 27 is more explicit, μέλλει ὁ υἱὸς τοῦ ἀνθρώπου ἔρχεσθαι ἐν τῇ δόξῃ). Again, in Mark x. 34 and parallels we have the same sequence: sufferings, death, resurrection; but in Mark x. 37 the sons of Zebedee ask for places of honour ἐν τῇ δόξῃ σου (for which Matt. xx. 21 gives ἐν τῇ βασιλείᾳ σου); nothing in the foregoing passage has prepared the reader for the firm but unexplained assumption that Christ will be enthroned in glory. We have only been told that he will rise again. This is the more striking because in the immediate context of verse 37 there is a veiled but unmistakable allusion to the death of Jesus (his 'cup' and 'baptism', verse 39), and yet no allusion to his resurrection from death. In none of the passages which forecast resurrection is there any reference to *parusia*, and similarly in the forecasts of the coming of the Son of Man there is no reference to resurrection (see, in addition to the passages already adduced, Mark xiii. 26, 35, Matt. xxv. 31, etc.). This is particularly striking in Mark xiv. 62 (and the parallel in Matthew), where Jesus in immediate prospect of death speaks, not of resurrection, but of coming with the clouds.

There is thus no place where the Synoptic predictions give the sequence: sufferings, death, resurrection, *parusia*. The phenomena would so far be consistent with the view that Jesus spoke in broad, general terms, suggestive rather than precise, with the use of varying imagery, of a renewal of life and activity upon an enhanced level after death, and that these terms were understood, sometimes as referring to a return from the grave to his followers, and restored fellowship with them on earth, and sometimes as referring to a final consummation beyond history; that in fact resurrection and *parusia* are, in these predictions, different aspects of the same reality.[1]

This view might find support in the observation that certain terms, and symbols, seem to be used, now in resurrection-passages, and now in *parusia*-passages. Thus, Christ is to be 'seen' alive after death. In Mark xvi. 6–7 this is associated with resurrection: ἠγέρθη... προάγει ὑμᾶς εἰς τὴν Γαλιλαίαν· ἐκεῖ αὐτὸν ὄψεσθε. In Mark xiv. 62, xiii. 26 it is associated with *parusia*: ὄψεσθε τὸν υἱὸν τοῦ ἀνθρώπου... ἐρχόμενον μετὰ τῶν νεφελῶν τοῦ οὐρανοῦ· ὄψονται τὸν υἱὸν τοῦ ἀνθρώπου ἐρχόμενον ἐν νεφέλαις μετὰ δυνάμεως πολλῆς καὶ δόξης.

Again, the disciples are to 'eat and drink' with Christ after his death. In Luke xxii. 28–30, διατίθεμαι ὑμῖν... ἵνα ἔσθητε καὶ πίνητε ἐπὶ τῆς τραπέζης μου ἐν τῇ βασιλείᾳ μου, this is associated with *parusia* (implied in the term βασιλεία). Matthew (who does not, however, speak here of eating and drinking at Christ's table) places the scene explicitly ἐν τῇ παλιγγενεσίᾳ (xix. 28). On the other hand, in Acts x. 41 Peter says, συνεφάγομεν καὶ συνεπίομεν αὐτῷ μετὰ τὸ ἀναστῆναι αὐτὸν ἐκ νεκρῶν. There is some sort of equivalence between ἐν τῇ βασιλείᾳ and μετὰ τὸ ἀναστῆναι. In Matt. xxvi. 29, in giving the cup to his disciples Jesus speaks of the day ὅταν αὐτὸ πίνω μεθ᾽ ὑμῶν καινὸν ἐν τῇ βασιλείᾳ τοῦ πατρός μου, namely, a day beyond history. But in Rev. iii. 20 the glorified Christ says, ἔστηκα ἐπὶ τὴν θύραν... ἐάν τις... ἀνοίξῃ τὴν θύραν... δειπνήσω μετ᾽ αὐτοῦ, καὶ αὐτὸς μετ᾽ ἐμοῦ. That is, the table-fellowship between Christ and his followers is not placed either during the limited period following

[1] See *Parables of the Kingdom* (Nisbet, 1961), pp. 74–7 (Collins, 1961), pp. 74–6.

the resurrection or at the παλιγγενεσία, or 'day of the Son of Man', but belongs to the continuing experience of the Church on earth. And this is the more striking because this book is apocalyptic through and through, and moreover the expression 'at the door' is in Mark xiii. 29 an expression for the nearness of the *parusia*

Once again, in Mark xiii. 27 a feature of the Coming of the Son of Man is the gathering of the elect: ἐπισυνάξει τοὺς ἐκλεκτούς. Similarly in 2 Thess. ii. 1 the ἐπισυναγωγή of Christians is an accompaniment of the παρουσία τοῦ κυρίου. But in Matt. xviii. 20 the Church is constituted on earth οὖ εἰσιν δύο ἢ τρεῖς συνηγμένοι εἰς τὸ ἐμὸν ὄνομα, for there they will find the presence of the Lord, who is with them (μεθ' ὑμῶν), not at the End, but during the whole period ἕως τῆς συντελείας τοῦ αἰῶνος. Accordingly, the term ἐπισυναγωγή is used to denote both the final gathering of the elect and the regular church-meetings of a local congregation (Heb. x. 25) assembled 'in the name of the Lord Jesus' (1 Cor. v. 4).[1]

Finally, even the investiture of Christ with universal sovereignty, which is usually associated with his coming at the End (for example, Matt. xxv. 31, xiii. 41), may also be associated with his resurrection. Thus in Matt. xxviii the announcement (verse 7), ἠγέρθη ἀπὸ τῶν νεκρῶν καὶ ἰδοὺ προάγει ὑμᾶς εἰς τὴν Γαλιλαίαν· ἐκεῖ αὐτὸν ὄψεσθε, repeated as from the mouth of Jesus himself (verse 10), ἵνα ἀπέλθωσιν εἰς τὴν Γαλιλαίαν κἀκεῖ με ὄψονται, leads up to a scene in which he is invested with all authority in heaven and on earth (verses 16–18). It is, in fact, a *parusia*-scene, but presented in terms of resurrection, with none of the 'properties' of apocalyptic: cosmic catastrophes, supernatural light (δόξα), clouds, angels, and the like.

The passages here cited are drawn partly from the gospels and partly from other early writings; both are equally valuable as showing that the mind of the Church oscillated between, or employed indifferently, two ways of conceiving, or at any rate of presenting, the truth of Christ's victory over death. On the one hand it was thought of as the restoration of fellowship between Christ and his followers under earthly conditions, on the other hand in terms of the συντέλεια τοῦ αἰῶνος. These two modes of thought are reflected in the varying forms of prediction in the Synoptic

---

[1] In John xi. 52 the gathering of God's children (ἵνα καὶ τὰ τέκνα τοῦ θεοῦ τὰ διεσκορπισμένα συναγάγῃ εἰς ἕν) is connected directly with the death of Jesus. A similar connection might be inferred from x. 15–17, though it is not made quite explicit.

Gospels. It is a reasonable hypothesis that the differences between the two forms may have been exaggerated in the course of transmission by making each more explicit and precise, and that the original utterances of Jesus which were the starting point of the tradition were comparatively imprecise and undifferentiated.

We now turn to the Fourth Gospel, and observe at once that the language of the Synoptic predictions is not echoed here. The keywords of resurrection-passages—παθεῖν, ἀποκτείνειν, (σταυροῦν,) ἀναστῆναι, ἐγερθῆναι—are missing. So, equally, is παρουσία, and although the term ἔρχεσθαι is freely used, it is dissociated from the apocalyptic imagery which accompanies it in the Synoptic Gospels: there is nothing about clouds, or angels, or a throne; and δόξα, which no longer stands for a visible, quasi-physical radiance, but for a profoundly theological idea,[1] is no matter of prediction: Christ is already glorified. There is even a certain polemic against the idea of the *parusia* as a cosmic event: Christ is *not* to be manifested to the world, but to his own (xiv. 22); once he has left the world to go to the Father the world sees no more of him (xiv. 19)—in contrast to Mark xiii. 26, τότε ὄψονται τὸν υἱὸν τοῦ ἀνθρώπου ἐρχόμενον.[2] The evangelist appears to have designed to offer a thoroughgoing re-interpretation of eschatological ideas current in the Church of his time,

[1] See *Interpretation*, pp. 206–8.

[2] In the apostrophe to Jerusalem, Matt. xxiii. 37–9, Luke xiii. 34–5, Jesus declares, οὐ μὴ ἴδητέ με ἀπ᾽ ἄρτι ἕως ἂν εἴπητε· Εὐλογημένος ὁ ἐρχόμενος ἐν ὀνόματι κυρίου. In its Lucan setting this might be taken as a forecast of the acclamations at the Triumphal Entry into Jerusalem, but in the Matthaean setting the Entry is already past, and we seem driven to an interpretation of the saying (in this evangelist's intention) as an apocalyptic prediction of a second coming to Jerusalem. In that case it offers a partial parallel to John xiv. 19, ἔτι μικρὸν καὶ ὁ κόσμος με οὐκέτι θεωρεῖ, and might conceivably have a common traditional background. But whereas the Matthaean passage predicts (if this is indeed the meaning intended) a temporary disappearance of Christ from the sight of non-believers, to be followed (it is implied in the ἕως ἄν. . . clause) by his reappearance, John seems to deny that non-believers will ever see him again; for while the declaration to the disciples, μικρὸν καὶ οὐκέτι θεωρεῖτέ με, is balanced by the promise, πάλιν μικρὸν καὶ ὄψεσθέ με, the similar declaration to non-believers has no such sequel (cf. the declaration, ὅπου ἐγὼ ὑπάγω ὑμεῖς οὐ δύνασθε ἐλθεῖν, addressed without qualification to 'the Jews', vii. 34, viii. 21, xiii. 33, but qualified when addressed to the disciples by the promise, ἀκολουθήσεις δὲ ὕστερον (xiii. 36)). It is in harmony with the same tendency that the prophecy of Zech. xii. 10, which in Rev. i. 7 is applied to the *parusia*, is in John xix. 37 said to be fulfilled at the crucifixion. No doubt Christ is to be 'seen' in some sense at the Last Day, when he summons the dead, both good and wicked, out of their graves (v. 28), but the evangelist seems unwilling to allow the vision of Christ to 'the world', so far as it remains unbelieving, in any conceivable future. This is distinct from the view of the Synoptic Gospels.

and known to us partly from the Synoptic Gospels. Thus the whole body of prediction is recast in terms of Johannine theology. The regulative concept is that of Christ's departure and return. He is 'journeying to the Father' (πρὸς τὸν πατέρα πορεύομαι, xiv. 12), and will 'come again' (πάλιν ἔρχομαι, xiv. 3). The 'coming', however, is not that of traditional eschatology: it is a return to the temporarily 'orphaned' disciples: οὐκ ἀφήσω ὑμᾶς ὀρφανούς, ἔρχομαι πρὸς ὑμᾶς (xiv. 18). The whole transaction is thus contemplated from the point of view of the disciples (and of Christ himself), and not from the point of view of world-history.

The theme, however, of journey-and-return is not entirely unknown to the Synoptics, though it does not there provide the framework for direct predictions of Christ's death and its sequel. There are parables which speak of a master who goes away, leaving his servants behind, and subsequently returns. The terms used, in Mark xiii. 34–5, are ἀπόδημος/ ἔρχεται, in Matt. xxv. 14–19, ἀποδημῶν/ἔρχεται, in Luke xix. 12–15, ἐπορεύθη/ἐπανελθών. (In John, the correlatives are πορεύομαι (ὑπάγω)/ ἔρχομαι.) Whatever may have been the original reference of these parables, their present form has clearly been moulded by the intention to identify the journeying and returning master with Christ himself. Stages in the process of this identification can be traced. Thus, in Mark xiii. 35 the question is, πότε ὁ κύριος τῆς οἰκίας ἔρχεται; but in the brief reminiscence of this parable in Matt. xxiv. 42 the question is, ποίᾳ ἡμέρᾳ ὁ κύριος ὑμῶν ἔρχεται; Again, in Matt. xxv. 14 *sqq.* the parable of the Money in Trust is told as a straightforward story, with no explicit indication of the application intended, though the evangelist's view is sufficiently disclosed by the fact that he has placed it in a group of parables and sayings illustrating the nature of the future *parusia*, and attached it directly to the warning, 'Keep awake, because *you* do not know the day or the hour' (xxv. 13). Inferentially, the servants in the parable are Christ's disciples, and he is the master who leaves them and goes on a journey from which he returns. Luke has indicated the same intention in a different way. The parable, he says, was told because people thought that the Kingdom of God was about to appear immediately (xix. 11); and he has expanded the simple ἄνθρωπος ἀποδημῶν into the statement, ἄνθρωπός τις εὐγενὴς ἐπορεύθη εἰς χώραν μακρὰν λαβεῖν ἑαυτῷ βασιλείαν καὶ ὑποστρέψαι. The allegorical intention lies on the surface: the Kingdom of God will *not* appear immediately; on the contrary, Jesus must journey far to receive his kingdom; then he will return as King (ἐπανελθεῖν λαβόντα τὴν βασιλείαν). Starting from parables which in their nature are suggestive rather than precise, and

417

admit of more than one interpretation, the Synoptic evangelists have produced scarcely veiled predictions of the *parusia*. The simple idea which lies at the root of it all is that of journey-and-return. This idea we find also in John, treated here, not as a symbolic prediction of *parusia*, but as the nearest possible approach to the essential truth about the death of Jesus: it is a temporary separation from his disciples, to be followed by reunion. So indeed it is in the Synoptics; but the ethos of the situation as conceived by John is widely different. In the other gospels the servants (the disciples, or, more properly, the Church) await the Master's return with some apprehension (φοβερά τις ἐκδοχὴ κρίσεως as Heb. x. 27 has it). In John the departure of the Lord is a deep grief to his disciples, and his return brings pure joy. The elaboration of the theme we may safely put down to the evangelist, as the elaboration of the same theme in the Synoptics may also be put down to those evangelists—or, perhaps, to the general thought of the circle within which their material took shape. But the common theme lies behind both. We have no right to say, either that it 'originally' referred to the *parusia* and was reinterpreted by John, or that it 'originally' referred to the resurrection, and was transferred to the *parusia* in Synoptic circles. The starting point would appear to be some oracular utterance of Jesus conveying, perhaps in figurative terms, the assurance that his death meant a separation which was only temporary and would be succeeded by restored relations with his followers, to their abiding satisfaction. Some found the fulfilment of this in his resurrection, others awaited the fulfilment at the συντέλεια τοῦ αἰῶνος, and the traditional sayings were moulded in tradition accordingly. It may be added that although John clearly regards the resurrection of Christ as his promised return, there is almost nothing in the actual language he uses which ties the idea of return down unmistakably to the resurrection, excluding every other interpretation.[1] Much of it is still suggestive rather than precise, and in that closer, perhaps, than might be supposed to the general character of the earliest tradition, in spite of all rewriting.

The theme of departure and return, which has dominated the dialogue, xiii. 31–xiv. 31, is out of sight all through ch. xv and down to xvi. 4. Indeed this long monologue, which is concerned with the life of Christians after the resurrection of the Lord, and includes the predictions of persecution for them which we have already considered, barely alludes obliquely to the death of Christ (xv. 13). In xvi. 5 the earlier theme returns, with

[1] See *Interpretation*, pp. 394–6.

the words, νῦν ὑπάγω πρὸς τὸν πέμψαντά με, and verbs of 'going' (ἀπελθεῖν, πορευθῆναι) come up again (xvi. 7), indicating that the reader is being brought back to the thought of the death of Christ, though with the notable difference that we hear no longer of his return, its place being taken by the coming of the Paraclete. In xvi. 10 the idea of Christ's departure is associated with that of his *disappearance* from human sight: πρὸς τὸν πατέρα ὑπάγω καὶ οὐκέτι θεωρεῖτέ με. And in xvi. 16 the dialogue is briefly resumed, after the long monologue, with a characteristic oracular saying: μικρὸν καὶ οὐκέτι θεωρεῖτέ με καὶ πάλιν μικρὸν καὶ ὄψεσθέ με. Verbs of 'seeing' prevail through the next few verses.

We have already noted that the Synoptic Gospels also contain predictions that Christ will be 'seen' after his death. In Mark xvi. 7 this 'seeing' is associated with the resurrection, in Mark xiii. 26, Matt. xvi. 28, with the *parusia*. In John the language employed might in itself be appropriate to either. The reference to the pains of childbirth in the parable of xvi. 21 would be susceptible of interpretation with reference to the ὠδῖνες, or חֶבְלוֹ שֶׁל־מָשִׁיחַ, which figure in the Eschatological Discourse (Mark xiii. 3). But the joy of the mother at the birth of her child is clearly intended by our evangelist to suggest the joy of the disciples at the return of their risen Lord (cf. xx. 20).[1] And this is confirmed by xiv. 21–2, where Christ will 'manifest' himself (ἐμφανίσω ἐμαυτόν) to his followers, and this is explained in terms of his continuing presence with the believer (xiv. 23).

It is noteworthy that in xvi. 17 the two propositions, μικρὸν καὶ οὐ θεωρεῖτέ με κ.τ.λ., and ὑπάγω πρὸς τὸν πατέρα[2] (which we may perhaps consider as implying its correlative πάλιν ἔρχομαι), are coupled together as cryptic or oracular utterances needing explanation. This would be very natural if the evangelist were acquainted with a tradition which transmitted these ambiguous utterances, and was aware that they were variously understood. His intention clearly is to fix their meaning as predictions of the death and resurrection of Christ, and not of an apocalyptic appearance at the end of the age. I have argued above that certain phenomena in the Synoptic Gospels might reasonably be explained on the hypothesis that the earliest tradition of all contained predictions in broad, general terms

---

[1] See above, pp. 369–73; *Interpretation*, p. 396.

[2] The words, ὅτι ὑπάγω πρὸς τὸν πατέρα, are read in AΘ and T.R. after ὄψεσθέ με in verse 16, but they are not present in אBDW and other better texts. They seem to have been inserted by scribes who supposed that verse 17 is simply repeating verse 16, not perceiving that the evangelist's intention is to resume in a single statement the two ways of regarding the death of Christ, as disappearance in xvi. 16 and as departure in xiii. 31–xiv. 31.

of the death of Jesus and of renewed life and activity after death, and that these were made more explicit in the course of the development of the tradition, bifurcating in the direction of predictions of resurrection and of *parusia* respectively. It now appears that the Fourth Gospel contains oracular sayings of just such an ambiguous character: 'I am going away and shall return', and 'You will lose sight of me but will see me again'. The two metaphors employed—departure and return, disappearance and reappearance—are the simplest possible, and being suggestive rather than explicit they invite the attempts to give them a more specific meaning which may lie behind the various forms of prediction found in the Synoptic Gospels. If tradition transmitted such a saying as ὑπάγω καὶ πάλιν ἔρχομαι, it would be easy to understand why parables which spoke of a journey and return, even though this was not their dominant feature, were early taken to refer to Christ's return after death; and if it transmitted such a saying as μικρὸν καὶ οὐκέτι θεωρεῖτέ με καὶ πάλιν μικρὸν καὶ ὄψεσθέ με, it was natural that the question should be raised, in what sense did Jesus encourage his disciples to expect to see him again, and equally natural that different answers to the question should be given in the light of subsequent experience and reflection, and should enter into different branches of the tradition. In a word, I suggest that John is here reaching back to a very early form of tradition indeed, and making it the point of departure for his profound theological reinterpretation; and further, that the oracular sayings which he reports have good claim to represent authentically, in substance if not verbally, what Jesus actually said to his disciples—a better claim than the more elaborate and detailed predictions which the Synoptics offer.

SUMMARY AND CONCLUSION

SUMMARY AND CONCLUSION

The above argument has led to the conclusion that behind the Fourth Gospel lies an ancient tradition independent of the other gospels, and meriting serious consideration as a contribution to our knowledge of the historical facts concerning Jesus Christ. For this conclusion I should claim a high degree of probability—certainty in such matters is seldom to be attained. In assessing the evidence at various points I have tried to estimate varying degrees of probability. But it should be observed that the argument is cumulative, and interlocking. No accumulation of bare possibilities, of course, could amount to more than a possibility in the end, and an accumulation of marginal probabilities is not worth much more. But where in one place phenomena pointing to a comparatively modest degree of probability can be shown to be closely related, or significantly analogous, to phenomena in other places where the degree of probability is high, the resultant level of probability is raised; and within such an interlocking structure even mere possibilities may (sometimes) come to wear a different aspect. I have aimed at building up such a structure, sustained at some crucial points by evidence which seems to me to yield conclusions of the highest degree of probability attainable in this field, and bonded together by cross-correspondences. No doubt the argument may be weakened at this point or that, but I believe the total structure to constitute a formidable case for the conclusion I have put forward.

The case could be assailed if one or other of the following hypotheses were adopted: (i) That our evangelist had before him Matthew, Mark, Luke and perhaps Acts,[1] and made a mosaic out of them all. This is too improbable an hypothesis to be seriously entertained, though some writers who speak vaguely of the dependence of John on the Synoptics might seem to imply something of the kind. (ii) That he had made himself so familiar with the earlier gospels (and perhaps Acts) that reminiscences of all came unbidden into his mind as he composed his own work. I see no way of disproving such an hypothesis, but there are some considerations which tell against it. The present tendency of criticism is to reduce the interval between the date of composition of Matthew and Luke and that of the composition of the Fourth Gospel. The former tends to be pushed nearer to the end of the first

---

[1] See above, pp. 79, 83–5, 91–2, 209, 254–8, 259, 343–7, etc.

century—say 85 for Luke, 90 for Acts, hardly earlier for Matthew—while the discovery of Rylands Papyrus Gk. 457 and Egerton Papyrus 2 has persuaded most critics that a date later than 120 for the Fourth Gospel is virtually impossible, and that a date not far from 100, rather before than after, is reasonable. Thus although it might have been possible, at a pinch, for our evangelist to have copies of the other gospels before him when he wrote, it seems unlikely that there was any one Christian centre where, in the short time since their publication, all three Synoptic Gospels had attained, together, such a position that it would be natural for a writer to use all three as equipollent sources, and still more unlikely that they had held this position long enough for him to have soaked himself in them so thoroughly as this hypothesis requires.

All through I have assumed that the tradition we are trying to track down was oral. That any authentic information about Jesus must at first have been transmitted orally does not admit of doubt, and all recent work has tended to emphasize both the importance and the persistence of oral tradition. That some parts of it may have been written down by way of *aide-mémoire* is always possible, and such written sources may have intervened between the strictly oral tradition and our Fourth Gospel. If so, I am not concerned with them; I am trying to discover where, if at all, the finished work still betrays the existence and character of the oral tradition upon which, whether directly or through the medium of written memoranda, it depends.

Assuming, then, that such pre-canonical tradition does lie behind this gospel, what may we say about its character?

(i) It shows contact with an original Aramaic tradition such as must necessarily be postulated for anything which claims to go back to the beginnings of Christianity, since there is no reasonable doubt that Jesus used that language, and that his personal disciples must have used it in transmitting his sayings and telling stories about him. Here the argument must be stated circumspectly. The evangelist himself was probably a speaker of Aramaic; at any rate traces of Aramaic idiom are to be detected almost everywhere. The mere presence, therefore, of 'Semitisms' is in itself no indication of an underlying tradition. But where passages in John are clearly parallel, or very closely related, to passages in the Synoptics, and John introduces Aramaic terms not present in the others, the fact is significant. Thus, where the others speak of Χριστός and Πέτρος, John alone has Μεσσίας and Κηφᾶς. Again, he employs different

Greek words to translate Aramaic terms which must have been common to him and the others, for example παροιμία for מָתְלָא where they have παραβολή,[1] σάρξ for בִּשְׂרָא where they have σῶμα.[2] He employs the Semitism ἐντεῦθεν καὶ ἐντεῦθεν for 'on either side', where the others, in a passage strictly parallel, have the good Greek idiom, ἐκ δεξιῶν...ἐξ ἀριστερῶν.[3] Again, the differences between the Johannine and the Synoptic versions of what is obviously the same saying may sometimes go back to variant translations of the same original. Thus, ἐὰν αἰτήσητε λήμψεσθε, ἄν τι αἰτήτητε δώσει ὑμῖν and αἰτεῖτε καὶ δοθήσεται ὑμῖν, might well be alternative renderings of an identical expression.[4]

(ii) There are some features in the pre-canonical Johannine tradition which appear to point to a Jewish (Jewish-Christian) setting.

(a) There are allusions to well attested Jewish beliefs, in particular to the belief that the Messiah would remain unknown until Elijah identified him[5] and the belief in the High Priest's *jure dignitatis* gift of prophecy;[6] and there are expressions which seem to have point only in a Jewish environment, for example, the curious ὑπὸ τὴν συκῆν εἶδόν σε.[7]

(b) There are points of contact with Jewish tradition. The date of the crucifixion, παρασκευὴ τοῦ πάσχα = עֶרֶב הַפֶּסַח, differs from the Synoptic dating, but agrees with that of the tractate *Sanhedrin*.[8] The charges alleged against Jesus in that tractate seem to be those presupposed in the account of the examination before the High Priest.[9] The statement that at the time (c. A.D. 30) the Sanhedrin had lost the power of inflicting the death sentence—a statement whose meaning and validity have been the subject of much dispute—is in any case contained both in the Fourth Gospel and in the tractate *Sanhedrin*.[10] Again, the Jewish tradition that Jesus had five disciples has a curious parallel (hardly accidental) in the Johannine account of the adhesion of *five* disciples and no more (though the existence of a body of twelve is of course assumed).[11]

The discussion of the Sabbath in John vii. 22–4, taken along with similar discussions in the Synoptics, appears to point to an early Christian *halakha* on the subject, analogous to rabbinic *halakha*,[12] such as can hardly be supposed to have originated in any but a Jewish-Christian environ-

---

[1] See p. 383.   [2] See p. 59.

[3] See p. 121.   [4] See p. 350, cf. 348.   [5] See p. 266.

[6] Although the *pericopé* about the prophecy of Caiaphas may not be part of the general body of tradition, it betrays the *milieu* in which John sought information (see p. 24).

[7] See p. 310.   [8] See pp. 109–10.   [9] See p. 95.

[10] See p. 106.   [11] See pp. 303–4.   [12] See pp. 332–3.

ment. The forecasts of persecution for the disciples hold up exclusion from the synagogue as the fate most to be dreaded (next to death itself), and this cannot have held any terrors for any but a Jewish-Christian community.[1] Such a community must therefore be postulated as the bearer of at any rate this part of the tradition.

(iii) There are indications which point to a certain geographical and chronological setting for the tradition. It gave native (Hebrew or Aramaic) names of places,[2] for which the evangelist has occasionally supplied a Greek equivalent (Gabbatha, λιθόστρωτον, Golgotha, κρανίου τόπος) as a concession to his Greek readers. It appears to have been well informed about the topography of Jerusalem and southern Palestine, less well informed, perhaps, about the north.[3] This apparent interest in the capital and the south is accompanied by a certain metropolitan outlook, even prejudice, which is more likely to have been intrinsic to this particular branch of the tradition than to have been imported by an evangelist writing outside Palestine at a later date.[4] We must almost certainly attribute also to the tradition itself the remarkable awareness of the political situation which existed in Judaea in the half-century preceding the outbreak of the great rebellion, and which had entirely passed away at any date to which the composition of the Fourth Gospel may be reasonably assigned.[5]

The basic tradition, therefore, on which the evangelist is working was shaped (it appears) in a Jewish-Christian environment still in touch with the synagogue, in Palestine, at a relatively early date, at any rate before the rebellion of A.D. 66. Most of the material we have investigated would fit into such an environment. Yet there are in places signs of development either at a later date or outside Palestine, or both. Here it is difficult to speak with confidence, because we have to allow for the evangelist's rehandling of his traditional material, and on any showing this is considerable. But two points at least have emerged where the development would seem to have taken place before this rehandling. (1) In the story of the healing at Cana the reference to household conversion seems to reflect the experience of the Gentile mission as recorded in Acts;[6] and (2) the 'Testimony of John', while it is well grounded in first-century Jewish belief and practice,

[1] See p. 412.
[2] The name Tiberias occurs in vi. 1, 23, xxi. 1, but is almost certainly not integral to the traditional material.
[3] See pp. 244–5.   [4] See pp. 245–6.   [5] See p. 120.
[6] See p. 193.

426

and has only the slightest marks of the distinctively Johannine theology—
and these readily separable—appears to reflect a situation such as that
portrayed in Acts xviii. 24–xix. 7 for Ephesus, the probable home of this
gospel.[1] When, however, these have been noted, it is the more remarkable
how comparatively little the traditional narratives have been affected by
late, non-Palestinian influences, and how much has come through, even
in the report of the teaching, in which we can recognize the authentic
atmosphere of early Palestinian Christianity.

(iv) The relation between our inferred pre-Johannine tradition and that
behind the Synoptics has been constantly under consideration throughout
this book. It seems worth while here to put together some points that
have emerged.

(a) The forms of oral tradition, both in narrative and in teaching,
which form-criticism recognizes in the Synoptics, reappear in John. One
of the most primitive forms, it seems, is that which may be roughly
indicated by the scheme, action–dialogue–pronouncement. There is at
least one clear case where John has preserved this primitive sequence and
Mark has disintegrated it in the course of composition: namely the
Cleansing of the Temple with the controversy and sayings following.[2]
There may be other cases.

(b) If presumably traditional units of narrative or teaching be arranged
in series according to form and content, there are Johannine units which
fit neatly into the Synoptic series, and often provide a supplement, or
complement, to the latter. Thus the Synoptic parables can be arranged, on
the basis of form, in a series showing continuous variation within a
general pattern, and three Johannine parables at least—the Grain of Wheat,
the Benighted Traveller, and the Pains of Childbirth—find a natural place
within the series, no one of them showing precise formal identity with any
one Synoptic model, but each furnishing one more example of the range
of variation within the common pattern.[3] Again, the sayings on harvest
in John iv. 34–8 fall perfectly within the fairly extensive series of sayings
associated with the mission of the disciples in the Synoptic Gospels, and
probably throw further light upon that episode in the Ministry.[4] Once
again (and here the affinity is one of content rather than of form), the
relation of the disciples to their predecessors the prophets is illustrated in
Synoptic sayings which speak of the sufferings which are the lot of both,
and of the fulfilment of prophetic aspirations in the experience of the

[1] See pp. 298–300.   [2] See pp. 160–2.   [3] See pp. 366–79.
[4] See above, p. 404.

427

disciples; the Johannine saying, ἄλλοι κεκοπιάκασιν καὶ ὑμεῖς εἰς τὸν κόπον αὐτῶν εἰσεληλύθατε, if I have understood it aright, completes the triad.[1]

Similarly with narrative units; the three healing narratives, as I have shown, find a perfectly natural place, formally, within the Synoptic series, each conforming to the pattern of one particular group, not by way of exact identity, but as another example of continuous variation within the general pattern.[2] Not only so; to look beyond the mere form, in the healing at Bethesda the question Θέλεις ὑγιὴς γενέσθαι; recalls the ἐὰν θέλῃς δύνασαι of Mark i. 40, and that recalls in turn the εἴ τι δύνῃ of Mark ix. 23, with the reply; in fact, John aptly fills a gap left by the Synoptics in the underlying discussion of the factors involved in miracles of healing: the power of the Healer, the will of the Healer, the will of the patient.[3]

(c) There are places where the Johannine tradition appears to supplement the Synoptic in the sense of clarifying points left obscure. For example, the Marcan story of Peter's confession begins with the abrupt question, Τίνα με λέγουσιν οἱ ἄνθρωποι εἶναι; No motive, or special occasion, for such a question is indicated. In the Johannine account of the confession widespread desertions lead naturally to the question, Μὴ καὶ ὑμεῖς θέλετε ὑπάγειν; To which Peter's profession of loyalty is an equally natural reply. And further, this report of the defection of disciples would explain the scattered references in the Synoptics to the danger of falling away, without the necessity of bringing in the later experience of the Church under persecution.[4] Again, Mark's account of the Feeding of the Multitude and the sequel leaves the reader asking questions to which he supplies no clue. The Johannine report of an attempted *émeute* makes everything clear.[5] There are other instances where the Johannine account appears more perspicuous than the Synoptic, and is at least plausible, but it is always possible that this is to be put to the account of our highly intelligent author. In the two cases just cited, however, at least, there are good grounds for believing that he is following a fuller tradition.

(v) In any attempt to determine the actual contents and scope of our inferred tradition it needs always to be borne in mind (a) that there may well be genuinely traditional material so completely absorbed into Johannine composition that it cannot be identified by the methods here employed, and (b) that the evangelist must not be supposed to have reproduced the whole of the tradition known to him. Indeed he has given

---

[1] See above, p. 404. [2] See Tables 6–7, pp. 175, 182, 189. [3] See above, p. 177.
[4] See p. 219. [5] See pp. 213–15.

a pretty broad hint that he made a selection from a large body of material at his disposal, and that this material was primarily in the nature of narrative (it was concerned with σημεῖα witnessed by the disciples, xx. 30). Any tentative description, therefore, of the contents of the pre-Johannine tradition must be understood in the sense, 'this at least', not 'this and no more'.

With this proviso, I offer the following summary account of what the tradition we are seeking probably contained, mentioning only salient points.

(a) It contained a much fuller account than we have elsewhere of the ministry of John the Baptist, including his work as a reformer within Judaism, though this has left only slight, but valuable, traces in our gospel. The relation of John's ministry to first-century Jewish beliefs is indicated convincingly (within the limits of the author's interest), and we are given to understand, more clearly than we could from the Synoptics alone, why John's ministry was so important in preparing the way for that of Jesus.

(b) The tradition also contained explicit testimonies on the part of the Baptist to the messianic status of Jesus, but these, I have suggested, may have developed in a somewhat later environment, though still earlier than the date of composition of the gospel.

(c) It transmitted a credible account of an early ministry of Jesus in southern Palestine, a ministry parallel to that of John and including, like his, the administration of the rite of baptism. It also gave some account of the relations between Jesus and the Baptist during this period of ministry, and of the circumstances in which it closed, but this has become somewhat obscured in the composition of the gospel. Its statement, however, that disciples of the Baptist came over to Jesus has probability on its side.

(d) It contained, like the Synoptics, some account of the work of Jesus as healer, but very little of this has been utilized by our author in composing his gospel; enough, however, to make it clear that this work was not confined either to Galilee or to the south.

(e) It preserved a considerable body of topographical information, indicating at least certain steps in the itinerary of Jesus and some of the scenes of his work; in particular, in southern Palestine and Transjordan, virtually ignored by the Synoptics.

(f) It probably had more to say about the Galilaean Ministry than our author has allowed us to see, though it was almost certainly less interested than the Synoptics in Galilee. In any case it preserved a full and striking account of the events in which the Galilaean Ministry appears to have ended, including an attempted messianic rising which created a dangerous situation, followed by widespread desertion of followers, and a pledge of loyalty on the part of the Twelve, who thus appear in the guise of a 'faithful remnant'.

(g) The pre-Johannine tradition had a full and detailed account of the Passion and the events immediately preceding it. The Passion narrative proper is constructed on the primitive scheme common to all gospels, and represents a third development of it, along with the forms behind Mark (Matthew) and Luke. In many points it supplements the Synoptics, or deviates from them in significant ways. In particular, it lays much emphasis (in contrast to the other versions of the tradition) on the political aspect of the conflict in which Jesus met his death.

(h) In respect of the sayings of Jesus, the content of the tradition is more difficult to define, because so much of the teaching in the Fourth Gospel is embodied in literary forms which are an original creation of the evangelist. But it is clear that he had at his disposal a body of traditional sayings, parables, and dialogues, handed down separately or in formal sequences, which were drawn from the same general reservoir as those in the Synoptic Gospels, dealing with the same, or kindred, themes. In regard to one group of sayings at least, the predictions of the return of Christ, the tradition followed by our evangelist appears to reach back to a stage distinctly more primitive than that represented in the other gospels. If we ask further, how much of the teaching of Jesus in the Fourth Gospel, where it cannot be controlled by comparison with the Synoptics, may be supposed to have a traditional source or basis, the question is not easily answered. But a few points have emerged which bear upon it.

(1) We have found material, closely related to the Synoptic tradition, so deeply embedded in some of the Johannine discourses and dialogues as to be apparently inseparable from the argument of which they form part. It is impossible to say whether other traditional elements, not identifiable by comparison with the Synoptics, may be similarly embedded. In particular, in examining parallels to Synoptic sayings we found ourselves several times brought directly to the heart of Johannine theology. Perhaps the most striking example, though by no means the only one, is the saying about the reciprocal 'knowledge' of Father and Son. The idea is central to the theology of the Fourth Gospel, but the saying was transmitted in one of the most primitive strata of tradition, that, namely,

which lies behind Matthew and Luke.[1] If those evangelists had not happened to include this one isolated saying, we should never have suspected that we had before us anything but a purely Johannine theologumenon.

(2) Passages which we should have no hesitation in recognizing as Johannine in doctrine, with no Synoptic parallel, are sometimes framed in purely traditional forms. There seems no reason to doubt that in such cases John did find in tradition a direct starting point for the development of his distinctive theology. Such, for example, are the parable of the Grain of Wheat[2] and the parabolic saying about the wind.[3] There may well be other cases where the original form has been disguised beyond recognition, and where nevertheless there was a traditional basis.

Such examples allow of no positive inference, but they may rightly serve as warning against a hasty assumption that nothing in the Fourth Gospel which cannot be corroborated from the Synoptics has any claim to be regarded as part of the early tradition of the sayings of Jesus. That tradition was probably more manifold than we are apt to suppose, and the fact that a substantial element in the Johannine report of the teaching can be traced with great probability to traditional sources suggests that he was more dependent on information received than might appear, although he has developed it in new and original ways. But I do not at present see any way of identifying further traditional material in the Fourth Gospel, where comparison with the other gospels fails us, without giving undue weight to subjective impressions.

Not that such impressions are altogether without relevance to the problem. On the contrary, in the ultimate assessment and interpretation of the evidence I believe that subjective impressions, where they are the outcome of long, patient, and sympathetic brooding over the material, may have a valuable and perhaps indispensable part to play. But in this book I have attempted a critical and historical investigation as objective as the nature of the material allows. What then has in fact been gained, if the conclusions here set forth are accepted? If it be granted that the first step towards a knowledge of the facts concerning Jesus is to recover the tradition about him passed on by his followers, as nearly as may be in its pristine state, allowing for its rich and sometimes perplexing diversity, then the comparison of different strains of tradition is of the utmost value.

---

[1] See pp. 359–61, and, for other examples, pp. 354–5, 361–3, 417–19.
[2] See pp. 369–73.　　　　　　　　　[3] See pp. 364–5.

It enables us to take, as it were, a stereoscopic view of the facts, from more than one angle. The strain of tradition recovered from the Fourth Gospel (if the above conclusions be accepted) is capable of being compared with other strains, corroborating or supplementing them, correcting them or being corrected by them, and of being in the end, perhaps, integrated into a consistent picture of the facts as they were handed down by the first witnesses.

This is of course not the end of the task. To reach some measure of objective historical judgement (relatively objective, as all such judgements must be), the tradition, envisaged as clearly as may be, must be set firmly in its total historical environment, by the use of all available evidence. Our knowledge of this environment—of outward conditions and of what was in the minds of men—is in our time receiving welcome increment, both from freshly discovered material and from the intensive study of the period from many points of view. The enterprise of working towards a clear and well-based conception of the historical facts upon which our religion is founded is a promising one, and the mood of defeatism which for some time prevailed is rightly beginning to give way to a more hopeful resumption of the 'quest of the historical Jesus'. These larger tasks I have not essayed in this book, which is designed to clarify one particular source of evidence, so that it may, as I hope, be available for use towards the great end of our studies.

INDEX LOCORVM

I. IN SCRIPTVRIS VETERIS TESTAMENTI ET APOCRYPHIS

[References are to the LXX, ed. Swete (Cambridge). The books
are listed in the LXX order.]

Genesis	PAGE	3 Kingdoms = 1 Kings	PAGE
i. 28	362	iv. 28	383
vii. 15–16	362	xxii. 17–23	262
viii. 17	362		
ix. 1–17	362	4 Kingdoms = 2 Kings	
xii. 3	132	ii. 9, 15	265
xv. 2	229	iv. 42–4	206
xxviii. 12	312	viii. 9–10	191
xxix. 30–3	343	ix. 6	173
xxxvii. 3–4	342		
xl. 13	395	1 Chronicles	
xlviii. 20	273	x. 4	135
		xxvi. 3	307
Leviticus			
iv. 3	94	1 Esdras	
xvii. 10 sqq.	382	v. 43 (44)	90
xxiii. 40	156	ix. 1 (= Ezra x. 6)	308
Numbers		2 Esdras	
ix. 12	43, 131	xv. 10	87
xxii. 24	121	(= Nehemiah v. 10)	
Deuteronomy		Psalms	
xiii. 6–7	95	viii. 7–8	362
xviii. 15	213	x. 5	342
xxi. 15–17	342	xxi. 2	32, 34, 42, 48
		xxi. 7	38, 48
Joshua		xxi. 8–9	32, 33, 34, 48, 74
i. 11	395	xxi. 13	48
viii. 22	121	xxi. 17	48, 135
xxii. 13	94	xxi. 19	32, 33, 34, 40–1, 47, 122
		xxi. 21–2	48
Judges		xxi. 25	71
ix. 54	135	xxvi. 5–6	77
		xxvi. 12	31, 34, 77
1 Kingdoms = 1 Samuel		xxx. 6	33, 34
x. 1	173	xxx. 14	23
xv. 25	270	xxxiii. 9, 11, 13–17b, 19	44
xxv. 28	270	xxxiii. 21	33, 34, 43–4, 131
		xxxiv. 4	76
2 Kingdoms = 2 Samuel		xxxiv. 11	31, 34, 38, 76
ii. 13	121		

II. IN SCRIPTVRIS NOVI TESTAMENTI

INDEX LOCORVM

III. IN LIBRIS VETERVM CHRISTIANORVM

IV. IN LIBRIS IVDAICIS

INDEX LOCORVM
V. IN LIBRIS ETHNICIS

INDEX NOMINVM

ST. MARY'S COLLEGE OF MARYLAND
ST. MARY'S CITY, MARYLAND

47524